Patterns for College Writing

A RHETORICAL READER AND GUIDE

TWELFTH EDITION

Patterns for College Writing

A RHETORICAL READER AND GUIDE

Laurie G. Kirszner
University of the Sciences

Stephen R. Mandell
Drexel University

BEDFORD/ST. MARTIN'S
Boston • New York

For Bedford/St. Martin's

Executive Editor: John Sullivan
Production Editor: Jessica Skrocki Gould
Senior Production Supervisor: Jennifer Peterson
Senior Marketing Manager: Molly Parke
Editorial Assistant: Alyssa Demirjian
Copy Editor: Diana P. George
Indexer: Leoni Z. McVey
Photo Researcher: Lynn Tews
Permissions Manager: Kalina K. Ingham
Art Director: Lucy Krikorian
Text Design: Brian Salisbury
Cover Design: Marine Miller
Cover Art: André Derain, *Mountains at Collioure,* 1905, John Hay Whitney Collection,
    Image courtesy of the National Gallery of Art, Washington, oil on canvas © 2011
    Artists Rights Society (ARS), New York/ADAGP, Paris
Composition: Achorn International, Inc.
Printing and Binding: RR Donnelley and Sons

President: Joan E. Feinberg
Editorial Director: Denise B. Wydra
Editor in Chief: Karen S. Henry
Director of Marketing: Karen R. Soeltz
Director of Production: Susan W. Brown
Associate Director, Editorial Production: Elise S. Kaiser
Managing Editor: Shuli Traub

Library of Congress Control Number: 2011931599

For information, write: Bedford/St. Martin's, 75 Arlington Street, Boston, MA 02116
    (617-399-4000)

ISBN: 978-0-312-67684-1 (paperback)
ISBN: 978-0-312-62307-4 (High School edition)

Acknowledgments

*Acknowledgments and copyrights appear at the back of the book on pages 769–773, which
constitute an extension of the copyright page. It is a violation of the law to reproduce these
selections by any means whatsoever without the written permission of the copyright holder.*

For Peter Phelps (1936–1990), with thanks

PREFACE

Since it was first published, *Patterns for College Writing* has been used by millions of students at colleges and universities across the United States. We have been delighted by the overwhelmingly positive response to the first eleven editions of *Patterns,* and we continue to be gratified by positive feedback from the many instructors who find *Patterns* to be the most accessible and the most pedagogically sound rhetoric-reader they have ever used. In preparing this twelfth edition, we have worked hard to fine-tune the features that have made *Patterns* the most popular composition reader available today and to develop new features to enhance the book's usefulness for both instructors and students.

What Instructors and Students Like about *Patterns for College Writing*

An Emphasis on Critical Reading

The Introduction, "How to Use This Book," and Chapter 1, "Reading to Write: Becoming a Critical Reader," prepare students to become analytical readers and writers by showing them how to apply critical reading strategies to a typical selection and by providing sample responses to the various kinds of writing prompts in the book. Not only does this material introduce students to the book's features, but it also prepares them to tackle reading and writing assignments in their other courses.

Extensive Coverage of the Writing Process

The remaining chapters in Part One, "The Writing Process" (Chapters 2 through 5), comprise a "mini-rhetoric," offering advice on drafting, writing, revising, and editing as they introduce students to activities such as freewriting, brainstorming, clustering, and journal writing. These chapters also include numerous writing exercises to give students opportunities for immediate practice.

Detailed Coverage of the Patterns of Development

In Part Two, "Readings for Writers," Chapters 6 through 14 explain and illustrate the patterns of development that students typically use in their college writing assignments: narration, description, exemplification, process, cause and effect, comparison and contrast, classification and division, definition, and argumentation. Each chapter begins with a comprehensive introduction that presents a definition and a paragraph-length example of the pattern to be discussed and then explains the particular writing strategies and applications associated with it. Next, each chapter analyzes one or two annotated student essays to show how the pattern can be used in particular college writing situations. Chapter 15, "Combining the Patterns," illustrates how the various patterns of development discussed in Chapters 6 through 14 can work together in an essay.

A Diverse and Popular Selection of Readings

Varied in subject, style, and cultural perspective, the sixty-nine professional selections engage students while providing them with outstanding models for writing. We have tried to achieve a balance between classic authors (George Orwell, Jessica Mitford, E. B. White, Martin Luther King Jr.) and newer voices (Sherman Alexie, Amy Chua, Amanda Brown) so that instructors have a broad range of readings to choose from.

More Student Essays Than Any Comparable Text

To provide students with realistic models for improving their own writing, we include sixteen sample student essays (one new to this edition). These essays are available as transparency masters so that instructors can use them more effectively in the classroom. They can also be downloaded from the *Patterns for College Writing* companion Web site, **bedfordstmartins .com/patterns**.

Helpful Coverage of Grammar Issues

Grammar in Context boxes in chapter introductions offer specific advice on how to identify and correct the grammar, mechanics, and punctuation problems that students are likely to encounter when they work with particular patterns of development. Practice exercises for mastering these grammar skills are available on *Re:Writing*, a comprehensive online exercise collection accessible at the *Patterns* companion Web site.

Apparatus Designed to Help Students Learn

Each professional essay in the text is followed by four types of questions. These questions are designed to help students assess their understanding of the essay's content and of the writer's purpose and audience; to recognize the stylistic and structural techniques used to shape the essay; and to become sensitive to the nuances of language. Each essay is also accompanied by a Journal Entry prompt, Writing Workshop topics (suggestions for full-length writing assignments), and Thematic Connections that identify related readings in the text. Also following each essay is a Combining the Patterns feature that focuses on different patterns of development used in the essay and possible alternatives to these patterns. Each chapter ends with a list of Writing Assignments and a Collaborative Activity. Many of these assignments and activities have been updated to reflect the most current topics as well as the most up-to-date trends and sites available on the Web.

Extensive Cultural and Historical Background for All Readings

In addition to a biographical headnote, each reading is preceded by a headnote containing essential background information to help students make connections between the reading and the historical, social, and economic forces that shaped it.

An Introduction to Visual Texts

Every rhetorical chapter includes a visual text — such as a photograph, a piece of fine art, or panels from a graphic novel — that provides an accessible introduction to each rhetorical pattern. Apparatus that helps students discuss the pattern in its visual form follows each image.

Thorough Coverage of Working with Sources

"Part Three: Working with Sources" takes students through the process of writing a research paper and includes a model student paper in MLA style. (The Appendix addresses APA style and includes a model APA paper.)

What's New in This Edition

Engaging New Readings

The twenty-seven new professional essays treat topics of current interest. Deborah L. Rhode discusses "Why Looks Are the Last Bastion of Discrimination," Paul H. Rubin makes a surprising case for "Environmentalism as Religion," and Maria Hinojosa, in "A Supreme Sotomayor: How My Country Has Caught Up to Me," shows how one judicial appointment has ramifications for all Latinas. In all cases, readings have been carefully selected for their high-interest subject matter as well as for their effectiveness as teachable models for student writing.

Argumentation Chapter Updated

The argumentation chapter now includes two new debates ("Are Internships Fair to Students?" and "Should American Citizenship Be a Birthright?") and two new casebooks ("How Can We Address the Shortage of Organ Donors?" and "Should Government Tax Sugary Drinks?").

More Support for Critical Reading

A new introductory chapter, "Reading to Write: Becoming a Critical Reader," explains and illustrates the process of previewing, annotating, and summarizing and includes examples and exercises for active learning.

More Help with Research

Coverage of research has been expanded, with three full chapters in the new Part Three devoted to finding, evaluating, and integrating sources; avoiding plagiarism; and documenting sources in MLA style. Part Three includes exercises to help students practice their research skills as they learn. An Appendix, "Documenting Sources: APA," explains APA style and includes a model student paper.

You Get More Digital Choices for *Patterns for College Writing*

Patterns for College Writing doesn't stop with the book. Online, you'll find both free and affordable premium resources to help students get even more out of the book and your course. You'll also find convenient instructor resources, such as downloadable sample syllabi, classroom activities, and even a nationwide community of teachers. To learn more about or order any of the products below, contact your Bedford/St. Martin's sales representative, email sales support (**sales_support@bfwpub.com**), or visit the Web site at **bedfordstmartins.com**.

Companion Web Site for *Patterns for College Writing* bedfordstmartins.com/patterns

Our companion Web site enables you to send students to free and open resources, choose flexible premium resources to supplement your print text, or upgrade to an expanding collection of innovative digital content.

Free and open resources for *Patterns for College Writing* provide students with easy-to-access reference materials, visual tutorials, and support for working with sources.

- Reading comprehension quizzes
- Debate topics
- Chapter-specific exercises
- Downloadable PDF files of the peer editing worksheets
- *Research and Documentation Online* by Diana Hacker, which offers research sources for more than thirty disciplines and documentation guidelines, models, and sample papers in MLA, APA, *Chicago,* and CSE styles

- *Bedford Bibliographer:* a tool for collecting source information and making a bibliography in MLA, APA, and *Chicago* styles

VideoCentral is a growing collection of videos for the writing class that captures real-world, academic, and student writers talking about how and why they write. *VideoCentral* can be packaged for free with *Patterns for College Writing.* An activation code is required. To order *VideoCentral* packaged with the print book, use ISBN 978-0-312-53975-7.

Re:Writing Plus gathers all of Bedford/St. Martin's premium digital content for composition into one online collection. It includes hundreds of model documents, the first ever peer review game, and *VideoCentral.* *Re:Writing Plus* can be purchased separately or packaged with the print book at a significant discount. An activation code is required. To order *Re:Writing Plus* packaged with the print book, use ISBN 978-0-312-53982-5.

A Variety of E-Book Options

An electronic edition of *Patterns for College Writing* is available in a variety of e-book formats that can be downloaded to a computer, tablet, or e-reader. Your students get the content you want in a convenient format — for about half the cost of a print book. We give you two options: our Bedford/St. Martin's e-book is optimized for reading and studying online, available from **bedfordstmartins.com/patterns**. Our CourseSmart e-book can be downloaded or used online, whichever is more convenient for your students. See **bedfordstmartins.com/ebooks** for details.

Instructor Resources

You have a lot to do in your course. Bedford/St. Martin's wants to make it easy for you to find the support you need — and to access it quickly.

Resources for Instructors Using Patterns for College Writing is available in PDF format that can be downloaded from the companion Web site at **bedfordstmartins.com/patterns**. In addition to chapter overviews and teaching tips, the Instructor's Manual includes sample syllabi and suggestions for classroom activities.

TeachingCentral (**bedfordstmartins.com/teachingcentral**) offers the entire list of Bedford/St. Martin's print and online professional resources in one place. You'll find landmark reference works, sourcebooks on pedagogical issues, award-winning collections, and practical advice for the classroom — all free for instructors.

Bits (**bedfordbits.com**) collects creative ideas for teaching a range of composition topics in an easily searchable blog. A community of teachers — leading scholars, authors, and editors — discuss revision, research, grammar and style, technology, peer review, and much more. Take, use, adapt, and pass the ideas around. Then, come back to the site to comment or share your own suggestion.

Content cartridges for the most common course management systems — Blackboard, WebCT, Angel, and Desire2Learn — allow you to easily download digital content for your course. To find the cartridges available with *Patterns for College Writing,* visit **bedfordstmartins.com/patterns /catalog**.

Acknowledgments

As always, friends, colleagues, students, and family all helped this project along. Of particular value were the responses to questionnaires sent to users of the eleventh edition, and we thank each of the instructors who responded so frankly and helpfully: Emily Berg, Reedley College; Deanie Carlton, Polk State College; Angela Chilton, Tarrant County College; Holly DeGrow, Mt. Hood Community College; Dr. George Edwards Jr., Tarrant County College; Sallyanne H. Fitzgerald, Polk State College; Jim Frank, St. Clair County Community College; Melissa Freitas, Massasoit Community College; Holly French-Hart, Bossier Parish Community College; Larry Gilbert, Ivy Tech Community College; John R. Hart, Motlow State Community College; Charles Hill, Gadsden State Community College; Anneliese Homan, State Fair Community College; Patricia D. Jackson, Norfolk State University; Nancy Kerr, North Lake College; Madelaine Kingsbury, Overbrook High School; Michael Kleeberg, Ivy Tech Community College; Patricia M. Leonard, Carl Sandburg High School; Amelia L. Lopez, Harold Washington College; John S. Lusk, St. Clair County Community College; Susan McKinnis, Allen Community College; Eric Norment, Bridgewater State University; Carol Pearson, West Georgia Technical College; Rosie Soy, Hudson County Community College; Wes Spratlin, Motlow State Community College; Elizabeth H. Stringer, East Mississippi Community College; Charrolee Thompson, Massasoit Community College; Gina Thompson, East Mississippi Community College; Usha Wadhwani, New Jersey City University; Jane Williams, Arizona Western College; Natasha Molet Worthington, Wayne Community College; Rose N. Yesu, Massasoit Community College.

We are also grateful to those instructors who responded to an in-depth review letter: Heidi Ajrami, Victoria College; Jacqueline Allen Trimble, Huntingdon College; Rhonda Armstrong, Paris Junior College; Jose M. Blanco, Miami Dade College; Robert E. Cummings, University of Mississippi; Rita B. Dandridge, Virginia State University; Chip Dunkin, University of Mississippi; Michael Allan Earle, St. Petersburg College; George Edwards Jr., Tarrant County College; Holly French-Hart, Bossier Parish Community College; David S. Hainline, Lee College; Catherine F. Heath, Victoria College; Beverly Holmes, Northwest Florida State College; Linda LaPointe, St. Petersburg College; Bryan Moore, Arkansas State University; Ann H. Moser, Virginia Western Community College; Jeffrey Rubinstein, Hillsborough Community College; Elizabeth Starr, Ivy Tech Community College; Robert A. Taylor, Florida Institute of Technology; Gina Thompson, East

Mississippi Community College; Cheli J. Turner, Greenville Technical College; Janet M. Willman, Hillsborough Community College.

Special thanks go to Jeff Ousborne for his help with some of the apparatus and for revising the headnotes and the *Resources for Instructors*.

Through twelve editions of *Patterns for College Writing*, we have enjoyed a wonderful working relationship with Bedford/St. Martin's. We have always found the editorial and production staff to be efficient, cooperative, and generous with their time and advice. As always, we appreciate the encouragement and advice of our longtime friend, Nancy Perry. In addition, we thank Joan Feinberg, president of Bedford/St. Martin's, for her support for this project and for her trust in us. During our work on this edition, we have benefited from our productive relationship with John Sullivan, our editor, who helped us make this edition of *Patterns* the best it could be. We are also grateful to Jessica Gould, project editor, and Shuli Traub, managing editor, for their work overseeing the production of this edition; Lucy Krikorian and Brian Salisbury for the new interior design; Donna Dennison for the attractive new cover; Shannon Walsh, associate editor, for her help throughout the project; and editorial assistant Alyssa Demirjian, for her invaluable help with tasks large and small.

We are fortunate to have enjoyed our long and fulfilling collaboration; we know how rare a successful partnership like ours is. We also know how lucky we are to have our families help keep us in touch with the things that really matter.

Laurie G. Kirszner
Stephen R. Mandell

CONTENTS

7 Description   151

"It is a dish that has become an extension of himself, that he has perfected, and to which he has earned the copyright. A dish that will die with him when he dies."

"There was a horrifying rush of cheddar taste, followed immediately by the dull tang of soybean flour — the main ingredient in Gaines-burgers."

"Like me, perhaps, the people around me had in mind images from television and newspaper pictures: the collapsing buildings, the running office workers, the black plume of smoke against a bright blue sky. Like me, they were probably trying to superimpose those terrible images onto the industrious emptiness right in front of them."

8 Exemplification   211

9 Process   263

"My first view in the mirror blotted out the hurting. I'd seen some pretty conks, but when it's the first time, on your *own* head, the transformation, after the lifetime of kinks, is staggering."

"You will face a coordination problem if you are a general deploying troops, tanks, helicopters, food, tents, and medical supplies, or if you are the CEO of a large company juggling the demands of design, personnel, inventory, and production.

And these days, you will face a coordination problem if you want to get a cup of coffee."

10   Cause and Effect   321

"When Ulysses S. Grant and Robert E. Lee met in the parlor of a modest house at Appomattox Court House, Virginia, on April 9, 1865, to work out the terms for the surrender of Lee's Army of Northern Virginia, a great chapter in American life came to a close, and a great new chapter began."

14   Argumentation   525

PART THREE: Working with Sources   703

THEMATIC GUIDE TO THE CONTENTS

Business and Work

Sports

Race and Culture

Gender

Nature and the Environment

Media and Society

History and Politics

Ethics

Citizenship

Introduction: How to Use This Book

This is a book of readings, but it is also a book about writing. Every reading selection here is followed by questions and exercises designed to help you become a thoughtful and proficient writer. The study questions that accompany the essays in this text encourage you to think critically about writers' ideas. Although some of the questions (particularly those listed under **Comprehension**) call for fairly straightforward, factual responses, other questions (particularly the **Journal Entry** assignments) invite more complex responses that reflect your individual reaction to the selections.

On the following page, "'What's in a Name?'" by Henry Louis Gates Jr., is typical of the essays in this text. It is preceded by a **headnote** that gives readers information about the author's life and career. This headnote includes a **background** section that provides a social, historical, and cultural context for the essay.

HENRY LOUIS GATES JR.

"What's in a Name?"

Henry Louis Gates Jr. was born in 1950 in Keyser, West Virginia, and grew up in the small town of Piedmont. Currently W. E. B. Du Bois Professor of Humanities and director of the W. E. B. Du Bois Institute for African-American Research at Harvard, he has edited many collections of works by African-American writers and published several volumes of literary criticism. However, he is probably best known as a social critic whose books and articles for a general audience explore a wide variety of issues and themes, often focusing on race and culture. In the following essay, which originally appeared in the journal *Dissent,* Gates recalls a childhood experience that occurred during the mid-1950s.

Background on the civil rights movement In the mid-1950s, the first stirrings of the civil rights movement were under way, and in 1954 and 1955 the U.S. Supreme Court handed down decisions declaring racial segregation unconstitutional in public schools. Still, much of the country — particularly the South — remained largely segregated until Congress passed the Civil Rights Act of 1964, which prohibited discrimination based on race, color, religion, or national origin in businesses (including restaurants and theaters) covered by interstate commerce laws, as well as in employment. This was followed by the Voting Rights Act of 1965, which guaranteed equal access to the polls, and the Civil Rights Act of 1968, which prohibited discrimination in housing and real estate. At the time of the experience Gates recalls here — before these laws were enacted — prejudice and discrimination against African Americans were the norm in many communities, including those outside the South.

The question of color takes up much space in these pages, but the question of color, especially in this country, operates to hide the graver questions of the self.

— JAMES BALDWIN, 1961

. . . blood, darky, Tar Baby, Kaffir, shine . . . moor, blackamoor, Jim Crow, spook . . . quadroon, meriney, red bone, high yellow . . . Mammy, porch monkey, home, homeboy, George . . . spearchucker, schwarze, Leroy, Smokey . . . mouli, buck. Ethiopian, brother, sistah.

— TREY ELLIS, 1989

I had forgotten the incident completely, until I read Trey Ellis's essay 1 "Remember My Name" in a recent issue of the *Village Voice* (June 13, 1989). But there, in the middle of an extended italicized list of the bynames of "the race" ("the race" or "our people" being the terms my parents used in polite or reverential discourse, "jigaboo" or "nigger" more commonly used in anger, jest, or pure disgust), it was: "George." Now the events of that very brief exchange return to mind so vividly that I wonder why I had forgotten it.

❦

My father and I were walking home at dusk from his second job. He 2
"moonlighted" as a janitor in the evenings for the telephone company. Every day but Saturday, he would come home at 3:30 from his regular job at the paper mill, wash up, eat supper, then at 4:30 head downtown to his second job. He used to make jokes frequently about a union official who moonlighted. I never got the joke, but he and his friends thought it was hilarious. All I knew was that my family always ate well, that my brother and I had new clothes to wear, and that all of the white people in Piedmont, West Virginia, treated my parents with an odd mixture of resentment and respect that even we understood at the time had something directly to do with a small but certain measure of financial security.

He had left a little early that evening because I was with him and I had 3
to be in bed early. I could not have been more than five or six, and we had stopped off at the Cut-Rate Drug Store (where no black person in town but my father could sit down to eat, and eat off real plates with real silverware) so that I could buy some caramel ice cream, two scoops in a wafer cone, please, which I was busy licking when Mr. Wilson walked by.

Mr. Wilson was a very quiet man, whose stony, brooding, silent manner 4
seemed designed to scare off any overtures of friendship, even from white people. He was Irish, as was one-third of our village (another third being Italian), the more affluent among whom sent their children to "Catholic School" across the bridge in Maryland. He had white straight hair, like my Uncle Joe, whom he uncannily resembled, and he carried a black worn metal lunch pail, the kind that Riley* carried on the television show. My father always spoke to him, and for reasons that we never did understand, he always spoke to my father.

"Hello, Mr. Wilson," I heard my father say.   5

"Hello, George."   6

I stopped licking my ice cream cone, and asked my Dad in a loud voice 7
why Mr. Wilson had called him "George."

"Doesn't he know your name, Daddy? Why don't you tell him your 8
name? Your name isn't George."

For a moment I tried to think of who Mr. Wilson was mixing Pop up 9
with. But we didn't have any Georges among the colored people in Piedmont; nor were there colored Georges living in the neighboring towns and working at the mill.

"Tell him your name, Daddy."   10

"He knows my name, boy," my father said after a long pause. "He calls 11
all colored people George."

A long silence ensued. It was "one of those things," as my Mom would 12
put it. Even then, that early, I knew when I was in the presence of "one of those things," one of those things that provided a glimpse, through a

---

* Eds. note — The lead character in the 1950s television program *The Life of Riley*, about a white working-class family and their neighbors.

rent curtain, at another world that we could not affect but that affected us. There would be a painful moment of silence, and you would wait for it to give way to a discussion of a black superstar such as Sugar Ray or Jackie Robinson.

"Nobody hits better in a clutch than Jackie Robinson."   13

"That's right. Nobody."   14

I never again looked Mr. Wilson in the eye.   15

• • •

Responding to an Essay

The study questions that follow each essay in this text will help you to **think critically** about what you are reading — that is, to ask questions and draw conclusions. (Critical thinking and reading are discussed in Chapter 1 of this book.) Five types of questions follow each essay:

- *Comprehension* questions help you to measure your understanding of what the writer is saying.
- *Purpose and Audience* questions ask you to consider why, and for whom, each selection was written and to examine the implications of the writer's choices in view of a particular purpose or intended audience.
- *Style and Structure* questions encourage you to examine the decisions the writer has made about elements such as arrangement of ideas, paragraphing, sentence structure, word choice, and imagery.
- *Vocabulary Projects* ask you to define certain words, to consider the connotations of others, and to examine the writer's reasons for selecting particular words or patterns of language.
- *Journal Entry* assignments ask you to write a short, informal response to what you read and to speculate freely about related ideas — perhaps exploring ethical issues raised by the selection or offering your opinions about the writer's statements. Briefer, less polished, and less structured than full-length essays, journal entries may suggest ideas for more formal kinds of writing.

Following these sets of questions are three additional features:

- *Writing Workshop* assignments ask you to write essays structured according to the pattern of development explained and illustrated in the chapter.
- *Combining the Patterns* questions focus on the various patterns of development — other than the essay's dominant pattern — that the writer uses. These questions ask why a writer uses particular patterns (narration, description, exemplification, process, cause and effect, comparison and contrast, classification and division, definition), what each pattern contributes to the essay, and what other choices the writer might have had.

• *Thematic Connections* identify other readings in this book that explore similar themes. Reading these related works will enhance your understanding and appreciation of the original work and perhaps give you material to write about.

Following are some examples of study questions and possible responses, as well as a **Writing Workshop** assignment and **Thematic Connections**, for "'What's in a Name?'" (page 2). The numbers in parentheses after quotations refer to the paragraphs in which the quotations appear.

Comprehension

1. *In paragraph 1, Gates wonders why he forgot about the exchange between his father and Mr. Wilson. Why do you think he forgot about it?*

    Gates may have forgotten about the incident simply because it was something that happened a long time ago or because such incidents were commonplace when he was a child. Alternatively, he may *not* have forgotten the exchange between his father and Mr. Wilson but pushed it out of his mind because he found it so painful. (After all, he says he never again looked Mr. Wilson in the eye.)

2. *How is the social status of Gates's family different from that of other African-American families in Piedmont, West Virginia? How does Gates account for this difference?*

    Gates's family is different from other African-American families in town in that they are treated with "an odd mixture of resentment and respect" (2) by whites. Although other blacks are not permitted to eat at the drugstore, Mr. Gates is. Gates attributes this social status to his family's "small but certain measure of financial security" (2). Even so, when Mr. Wilson insults Mr. Gates, the privileged status of the Gates family is revealed as a sham.

3. *What does Gates mean when he says, "It was 'one of those things,' as my Mom would put it" (12)?*

    Gates's comment indicates that the family learned to see such mistreatment as routine. In context, the word *things* in paragraph 12 refers to the kind of incident that gives Gates and his family a glimpse of the way the white world operates.

4. *Why does Gates's family turn to a discussion of a "black superstar" after a "painful moment of silence" (12) such as the one he describes?*

    Although Gates does not explain the family's behavior, we can infer that they speak of African-American heroes like prizefighter Sugar Ray Robinson and baseball player Jackie Robinson to make themselves feel better. Such discussions are a way of balancing the negative images of African Americans created by incidents such as the one Gates describes and of bolstering the low self-esteem the family felt as a result. These heroes seem to have won the respect denied to the Gates family; to mention them is to participate vicariously in their glory.

5. *Why do you think Gates "never again looked Mr. Wilson in the eye" (15)?*

    Gates may have felt that Mr. Wilson was somehow the enemy, not to be trusted, because he had insulted Gates's father. Or, he may have been ashamed to look him in the eye because he believed his father should have insisted on being addressed properly.

Purpose and Audience

1. *Why do you think Gates introduces his narrative with the two quotations he selects? How do you suppose he expects his audience to react to them? How do you react?*

    Gates begins with two quotations, both by African-American writers, written nearly thirty years apart. Baldwin's words seem to suggest that, in the United States, "the question of color" is a barrier to understanding "the graver questions of the self." That is, the labels *black* and *white* may mask more fundamental characteristics or issues. Ellis's list of names (many pejorative) for African Americans illustrates the fact that epithets can dehumanize people — they can, in effect, rob a person of his or her "self." This issue of the discrepancy between a name and what lies behind it is central to Gates's essay. In one sense, then, Gates begins with these two quotations because they are relevant to the issues he will discuss. More specifically, he is using the two quotations — particularly Ellis's shocking string of unpleasant names — to arouse interest in his topic and provide an intellectual and emotional context for his story. He may also be intending to make his white readers uncomfortable and his black readers angry. How you react depends on your attitudes about race (and perhaps about language).

2. *What is the point of Gates's narrative? That is, why does he recount the incident?*

    Certainly Gates wishes to make readers aware of the awkward, and potentially dangerous, position of his father (and, by extension, of other African Americans) in a small southern town in the 1950s. He also shows us how names help to shape people's perceptions and actions: as long as Mr. Wilson can call all black men "George," he can continue to see them as insignificant and treat them as inferiors. The title of the piece suggests that the way names shape perceptions is the writer's main point.

3. *The title of this selection, which Gates places in quotation marks, is an allusion to act 2, scene 2, of Shakespeare's* Romeo and Juliet, *in which Juliet says, "What's in a name? That which we call a rose / By any other name would smell as sweet." Why do you think Gates chose this title? Does he expect his audience to recognize the quotation?*

    Because his work was originally published in a journal read by a well-educated audience, Gates would have expected readers to recognize the **allusion** (and also to know a good deal about 1950s race relations). Although Gates could not have been certain that all members of this audience would recognize the reference to *Romeo and Juliet,* he could have been reasonably sure that if they did, it would enhance their understanding of the selection. In Shakespeare's play, the two lovers are kept apart essentially because of their names: she is a Capulet and he is a Montague, and the two families are involved in a bitter feud. In the speech from which Gates takes the title quotation, Juliet questions the logic of such a situation. In her view, what a person is called should not determine how he or she is regarded — and this, of course, is Gates's point as well. Even if readers do not recognize the allusion, the title still foreshadows the selection's focus on names.

Style and Structure

1. *Does paragraph 1 add something vital to the narrative, or would Gates's story make sense without the introduction? Could another kind of introduction work as well?*

   Gates's first paragraph supplies the context in which the incident is to be read — that is, it makes clear that Mr. Wilson's calling Mr. Gates "George" was not an isolated incident but part of a pattern of behavior that allowed those in positions of power to mistreat those they considered inferior. For this reason, it is an effective introduction. Although the narrative would make sense without paragraph 1, the story's full impact would probably not be as great. Still, Gates could have begun differently. For example, he could have started with the incident itself (paragraph 2) and interjected his comments about the significance of names later in the piece. He also could have begun with the exchange of dialogue in paragraphs 5 through 11 and then introduced the current paragraph 1 to supply the incident's context.

2. *What does the use of dialogue contribute to the narrative? Would the selection have a different impact without dialogue? Explain.*

   Gates was five or six years old when the incident occurred, and the dialogue helps to establish the child's innocence as well as his father's quiet acceptance of the situation. In short, the dialogue is a valuable addition to the piece because it creates two characters, one innocent and one resigned to injustice, both of whom contrast with the voice of the adult narrator: wise, worldly, but also angry and perhaps ashamed, the voice of a man who has benefited from the sacrifices of men like Gates's father.

3. *Why do you think Gates supplies the specific details he chooses in paragraphs 2 and 3? In paragraph 4? Is all this information necessary?*

   The details Gates provides in paragraphs 2 and 3 help to establish the status of his family in Piedmont; because readers have this information, the fact that the family was ultimately disregarded and discounted by some whites emerges as deeply ironic. The information in paragraph 4 also contributes to this **irony**. Here we learn that Mr. Wilson was not liked by many whites, that he looked like Gates's Uncle Joe, and that he carried a lunch box — in other words, that he had no special status in the town apart from that conferred by race.

Vocabulary Projects

1. *Define each of the following words as it is used in this selection:*

   bynames (1) — nicknames
   measure (2) — extent or degree
   uncannily (4) — strangely
   ensued (12) — followed
   rent (12) — torn

2. *Consider the connotations of the words* colored *and* black, *both used by Gates to refer to African Americans. What different associations does each word have? Why does Gates use both — for example,* colored *in paragraph 9 and* black *in paragraph 12? What is your response to the father's use of the term* boy *in paragraph 11?*

   In the 1950s, when the incident Gates describes took place, the term *colored* was still widely used, along with *Negro*, to designate Americans of

African descent. In the 1960s, the terms *Afro-American* and *black* replaced the earlier names, with *black* emerging as the preferred term and remaining dominant through the 1980s. Today, although *black* is preferred by some, *African American* is used more and more often. Because the term *colored* is the oldest designation, it may seem old-fashioned and even racist today; *black*, which connoted a certain degree of militancy in the 1960s, is probably now considered a neutral term by most people. Gates uses both words because he is speaking from two time periods. In paragraph 9, re-creating the thoughts and words of a child in a 1950s southern town, he uses the term *colored*; in paragraph 12, the adult Gates, commenting in 1989 on the incident, uses *black*. The substitution of *African American* for the older terms might give the narrative a more contemporary flavor, but it might also seem awkward or forced — and, in paragraph 9, inappropriately formal. As far as the term *boy* is concerned, different readers are apt to have different responses. Although the father's use of the term can be seen as affectionate, it can also be seen as derisive in this context since it echoes the bigot's use of *boy* for all black males, regardless of age or accomplishments.

Journal Entry

Do you think Gates's parents should have used experiences like the one in "'What's in a Name?'" to educate him about the family's social status in the community? Why do you think they chose instead to dismiss such incidents as "one of those things" (12)?

Your responses to these questions will reflect your own opinions, based on your background and experiences as well as on your interpretation of the reading selection.

Writing Workshop

Write about a time when you, like Gates's father, could have spoken out in protest but chose not to. Would you make the same decision today?

By the time you approach the Writing Workshop assignments, you will have read an essay, responded to study questions about it, discussed it in class, and perhaps considered its relationship to other essays in the text. Often, your next step will be to write an essay in response to one of the Writing Workshop questions. (Chapters 2–4 follow Laura Bobnak, a first-year composition student, through the process of writing an essay in response to this Writing Workshop assignment.)

Combining the Patterns

Although **narration** *is the pattern of development that dominates "'What's in a Name?'" and gives it its structure, Gates also uses* **exemplification,** *presenting an extended example to support his thesis. What is this example? What does it illustrate? Would several brief examples have been more convincing?*

The extended example is the story of the encounter between Gates's father and Mr. Wilson, which compellingly illustrates the kind of behavior African Americans were often forced to adopt in the 1950s. Because

Gates's introduction focuses on "the incident" (1), one extended example is enough (although he alludes to other incidents in paragraph 12).

Thematic Connections

- " 'Girl' " (page 258)
- "The 'Black Table' Is Still There" (page 349)

As you read and think about the selections in this text, you should begin to see thematic links among them. Such parallels can add to your interest and understanding as well as give you ideas for class discussion and writing.

For example, Jamaica Kincaid's short story "Girl," also by an African-American writer, has some parallels with Gates's autobiographical essay. Like Gates, Kincaid's protagonist seems to occupy a subservient position in a society whose rules she must obey. The lessons in life skills that are enumerated in the story are also similar to the lesson Gates learns from his father.

Another related work is Lawrence Otis Graham's "The 'Black Table' Is Still There." The writer, an African-American man, returns in 1991 to his junior high school, where he sees the lunch tables as segregated as they were when he was a student there. Unlike Gates's essay, which discusses a specific incident that took place in the South in the 1950s, Graham's examines an ongoing situation that may apply to schools all over the United States. Thus, it provides a more contemporary — and, perhaps, wider — context for discussing issues of race and class.

In the process of thinking about Gates's narrative, discussing it in class, or preparing to write an essay on a related topic (such as the one listed under Writing Workshop on page 8), you might find it useful to read Kincaid's story and Graham's essay.

Responding to Other Texts

The first selection in Chapters 6 through 14 of this book is a visual text. It is followed by **Reading Images** questions, a **Journal Entry**, and a short list of **Thematic Connections** that will help you understand the image and shape your response to it.

The final selection in each chapter, a story or poem, is followed by **Reading Literature** questions, a **Journal Entry**, and **Thematic Connections**.

NOTE: At the end of each chapter, **Writing Assignments** offer additional practice in writing essays structured according to a particular pattern of development, and a **Collaborative Activity** suggests an idea for a group project.

PART ONE

The Writing Process

Every reading selection in this book is the result of a struggle between a writer and his or her material. If a writer's struggle is successful, the finished work is welded together without a visible seam, and readers have no sense of the frustration the writer experienced while rearranging ideas or hunting for the right word. Writing is no easy business, even for a professional writer. Still, although there is no simple formula for good writing, some approaches are easier and more productive than others.

At this point you may be asking yourself, "So what? What has this got to do with me? I'm not a professional writer." True enough, but during the next few years you will be doing a good deal of writing. Throughout your college career, you will write midterms, final exams, lab reports, essays, and research papers. In your professional life, you may write progress reports, proposals, business correspondence, and memos. As diverse as these tasks are, they have something in common: they can be made easier if you are familiar with the stages of the **writing process** — a process experienced writers follow when they write.

THE WRITING PROCESS

- **Invention** (also called **prewriting**) During invention, you decide what to write about and gather information to support or explain what you want to say.
- **Arrangement** During arrangement, you decide how you are going to organize your ideas.
- **Drafting and revising** During drafting and revising, you write several drafts as you reconsider your ideas and refine your style and structure.
- **Editing and proofreading** During editing, you focus on grammar and punctuation as well as on sentence style and word choice. During proofreading, you correct spelling, mechanical errors, and typos and check your essay's format.

Although the writing process is usually presented as a series of neatly defined steps, that model does not reflect the way people actually write. Ideas do not always flow easily, and the central point you set out to develop does not always wind up in the essay you ultimately write. In addition, writing often progresses in fits and starts, with ideas occurring sporadically or not at all. Surprisingly, much good writing occurs when a writer gets stuck or confused but continues to work until ideas begin to take shape.

Because the writing process is so erratic, its stages overlap. Most writers engage in invention, arrangement, drafting and revision, and editing simultaneously — finding ideas, considering possible methods of organization, looking for the right words, and correcting grammar and punctuation all at the same time. In fact, writing is such an idiosyncratic process that no two writers approach the writing process in exactly the same way. Some people outline; others do not. Some take elaborate notes during the invention stage; others keep track of everything in their heads.

The writing process discussed throughout this book reflects the many choices writers make at various stages of composition. But regardless of writers' different approaches, one thing is certain: the more you write, the better acquainted you will become with your personal writing process and the better you will learn how to modify it to suit various writing tasks. The four chapters that follow, which treat individual stages of the writing process, will help you define your needs as a writer and understand your options as you approach writing assignments in college and beyond.

Reading to Write: Becoming a Critical Reader

On a purely practical level, you will read the selections in this text to answer study questions and prepare for class discussions (and, often, for writing). More significantly, however, you will also read to evaluate the ideas of others, to form judgments, and to develop original viewpoints. In other words, you will engage in **critical reading**.

By introducing you to new ideas and new ways of thinking about familiar concepts, reading prepares you to respond critically to the ideas of others and to develop ideas of your own. When you read critically, you can form opinions, exchange insights with others in conversation, ask and answer questions, and develop ideas that can be further explored in writing. For all of these reasons, critical reading is a vital part of your education.

Understanding Critical Reading

Reading is a two-way street. Readers are presented with a writer's ideas, but they also bring their own ideas to what they read. After all, readers have different national, ethnic, cultural, and geographic backgrounds and different kinds of knowledge and experiences, so they may react differently to a particular essay or story. For example, readers from an economically and ethnically homogeneous suburban neighborhood may have difficulty understanding a story about class conflict, but they may also be more objective than readers who are struggling with such conflict in their own lives.

These differences in readers' responses do not mean that every interpretation is acceptable, that an essay or story or poem may mean whatever a reader wants it to mean. Readers must make sure they are not distorting a writer's words, overlooking (or ignoring) significant details, or seeing things in an essay or story that do not exist. It is not important for all readers to agree on a particular interpretation of a work. It *is* important, however, for each reader to develop an interpretation that the work itself supports.

When you read an essay in this text, or any reading selection that you expect to discuss in class, you should read it carefully, ideally more than once. If a selection is accompanied by a headnote or other background material, as the selections in this book are, you should read this material as well because it will help you to understand the selection. Keep in mind that some of the selections you read may eventually be used as sources for writing. In these cases, it is especially important that you understand what you are reading and can formulate a thoughtful response to the writer's ideas. (For information on how to evaluate the sources you read, see Chapter 16.)

⬛ TECH TIP: Naming Your Files

If you take notes about your sources on your computer, it's important to give each file an accurate and descriptive title so you can find it when you need it. Your file name should identify the class for which you're writing and the due date.

Comp-Plagiarism essay-9.25

Once you develop a system that works for you, you should use it consistently — for example, always listing elements (class, assignment, date) in the same order for each project. You can also create a separate folder for each class and then use subfolders for each assignment, gathering together all your notes and drafts for an assignment.

To get the most out of your reading, you should use **active reading** strategies. In practical terms, this means actively participating in the reading process: approaching an assigned reading with a clear understanding of your purpose and marking the text to help you understand what you are reading.

Determining Your Purpose

Even before you start reading, you should ask yourself some questions about your **purpose** — why you are reading. The answers to these questions will help you understand what kind of information you hope to get out of your reading and how you will use this information.

✔CHECKLIST   Questions about Your Purpose

- Will you be expected to discuss what you are reading? If so, will you discuss it in class? In a conference with your instructor?
- Will you have to write about what you are reading? If so, will you be expected to write an informal response (for example, a journal entry) or a more formal one (for example, an essay)?
- Will you be tested on the material?

Previewing

When you **preview**, you try to get a sense of the writer's main idea, key supporting points, and general emphasis. You can begin by focusing on the title, the first paragraph (which often contains a purpose statement or overview), and the last paragraph (which may contain a summary of the writer's main idea). You should also look for clues to the writer's message in the passage's **visual signals** and **verbal signals**.

Using Visual Signals

- Look at the title.
- Look at the opening and closing paragraphs.
- Look at each paragraph's first sentence.
- Look for headings.
- Look for *italicized* and **boldfaced** words.
- Look for numbered lists.
- Look for bulleted lists (like this one).
- Look at any visuals (graphs, charts, tables, photographs, and so on).
- Look at any information that is boxed.
- Look at any information that is in color.

Using Verbal Signals

- Look for phrases that signal emphasis ("The *primary* reason"; "The *most important* idea").
- Look for repeated words and phrases.
- Look for words that signal addition (*also, in addition, furthermore*).
- Look for words that signal time sequence (*first, after, then, next, finally*).
- Look for words that identify causes and effects (*because, as a result, for this reason*).
- Look for words that introduce examples (*for example, for instance*).
- Look for words that signal comparison (*likewise, similarly*).
- Look for words that signal contrast (*unlike, although, in contrast*).
- Look for words that signal contradiction (*however, on the contrary*).
- Look for words that signal a narrowing of the writer's focus (*in fact, specifically, in other words*).
- Look for words that signal summaries or conclusions (*to sum up, in conclusion*).

When you have finished previewing the passage, you should have a general sense of what the writer wants to communicate.

As you read and reread, you will record your reactions in writing. These notations will help you to understand the writer's ideas and your own thoughts about those ideas. Every reader develops a different system of recording responses, but many readers learn to use a combination of *highlighting* and *annotating*.

Keep in mind that the process of highlighting and annotating that will be explained and illustrated in the pages that follow is not an end in itself but a step toward fully understanding what you have read. Annotations suggest questions; in your search for answers, you may ask your instructor for clarification, or you may raise particularly puzzling or provocative points during class discussion or in a study group meeting. After your questions have been answered, you will be able to discuss and write about what you have read with greater accuracy, confidence, and authority.

Highlighting

When you **highlight**, you mark the text. You might, for example, underline (or double underline) important concepts, box key terms, number a series of related points, circle an unfamiliar word (or place a question mark beside it), draw a vertical line in the margin beside a particularly interesting passage, draw arrows to connect related points, or star discussions of the work's central issues or main idea.

The following pages reprint a column by journalist Brent Staples that focuses on the issue of plagiarism among college students. The column, "Cutting and Pasting: A Senior Thesis by (Insert Name)," and the accompanying headnote and background material, have been highlighted by a student.

BRENT STAPLES

Cutting and Pasting: A Senior Thesis by (Insert Name)

Born in 1951 in Chester, Pennsylvania, Brent Staples is a writer and member of the editorial board of the *New York Times*. He often writes about culture, politics, race, and education. Staples has a B.A. in behavioral science from Widener University and a Ph.D. in psychology from the University of Chicago. Before joining the *New York Times*, he wrote for the *Chicago Sun-Times, Chicago Reader, Chicago Magazine*, and the jazz magazine *Down Beat*. His work has also appeared in publications such as *Ms.* and *Harper's*. Staples is the author of a memoir, *Parallel Time: Growing Up in Black and White* (1994).

Background on prevalence of cheating and plagiarism in high school and college Recent studies suggest that high school and college students are increasingly likely to cheat or plagiarize. For example, one Duke University study conducted from 2002 to 2005 showed that 70 percent of the 50,000 undergraduate students surveyed admitted to cheating on occasion. A 2008 survey of high school students by the Center for Youth Ethics at the Josephson Institute showed that 82 percent had copied from another student's work, while 36 percent said that they had used the Internet to plagiarize an assignment. Moreover, students tend to view such academic dishonesty with indifference: according to surveys by the Center for Academic Integrity, only 29 percent of undergraduates believe unattributed copying from the Web rises to the level of "serious cheating."

Observers have proposed various reasons for the prevalence of plagiarism. Some point to new technologies that allow instant access to an apparently ① "common" store of unlimited information, as sites like Wikipedia challenge traditional notions of singular authorship, originality, and intellectual property. Others see the problem as the result of declining personal morality and of a ② culture that rewards shady behavior. And many view plagiarism as the unavoidable consequence of the pressures many students feel. ③

Academic institutions have responded to the problem in a number of ways. Most colleges now use the Internet-based detection service Turnitin.com, which scans students' essays for plagiarism. But a recent study by the National Bureau of Economic Research concluded that simply showing a Web tutorial on the issue could reduce instances of plagiarism by two-thirds. Schools such as Duke University and Bowdoin College now require incoming students to complete this online instruction before they enroll. Additionally, the research of Rutgers professor Ronald McCabe, who founded the Center for Academic Integrity, indicates that honor codes — already in place at many colleges and universities — help create a campus culture of academic integrity.

A friend who teaches at a well-known eastern uni- 1
versity told me recently that plagiarism was turning
him into a cop. He begins the semester collecting evidence, in the form of an in-class essay that gives him a
sense of how well students think and write. He looks
back at the samples later when students turn in papers
that feature their own, less-than-perfect prose alongside expertly written passages lifted verbatim from the
Web.

"I have to assume that in every class, someone will 2
do it," he said. "It doesn't stop them if you say, 'This is
plagiarism. I won't accept it.' I have to tell them that it
is a failing offense and could lead me to file a complaint
with the university, which could lead to them being put
on probation or being asked to leave."

Not everyone who gets caught knows enough 3
about what they did to be remorseful. Recently, for example, a student who plagiarized a sizable chunk of a
paper essentially told my friend to keep his shirt on,
that what he'd done was no big deal. Beyond that, the
student said, he would be ashamed to go home to the
family with an F.

As my friend sees it: "This represents a shift away 4
from the view of education as the process of intellectual
engagement through which we learn to think critically
and toward the view of education as mere training. In
training, you are trying to find the right answer at any
cost, not trying to improve your mind."

Like many other professors, he no longer sees tra- 5
ditional term papers as a valid index of student competence. To get an accurate, Internet-free reading of how
much students have learned, he gives them written assignments in class — where they can be watched.

These kinds of precautions are no longer unusual 6
in the college world. As Trip Gabriel pointed out in the
Times recently, more than half the colleges in the country have retained services that check student papers for
material lifted from the Internet and elsewhere. Many
schools now require incoming students to take online
tutorials that explain what plagiarism is and how to
avoid it.

Nationally, discussions about plagiarism tend to 7
focus on questions of ethics. But as David Pritchard,
a physics professor at the Massachusetts Institute of
Technology, told me recently: "The big sleeping dog

here is not the moral issue. The problem is that kids don't learn if they don't do the work."

Prof. Pritchard and his colleagues illustrated the 8 point in a study of cheating behavior by M.I.T. students who used an online system to complete homework. The students who were found to have copied the most answers from others started out with the same math and physics skills as their harder-working classmates. But by skipping the actual work in homework, they fell behind in understanding and became significantly more likely to fail.

* *   The Pritchard axiom — that repetitive cheating 9 undermines learning — has ominous implications for a world in which even junior high school students cut and paste from the Internet instead of producing their own writing.

If we look closely at plagiarism as practiced by 10 youngsters, we can see that they have a different relationship to the printed word than did the generations before them. When many young people think of writing, they don't think of fashioning original sentences into a sustained thought. They think of making something like a collage of found passages and ideas from the Internet.

✓   They become like rap musicians who construct 11 what they describe as new works by "sampling" (which is to say, cutting and pasting) beats and refrains from the works of others.

This habit of mind is already pervasive in the cul- 12 ture and will be difficult to roll back. But parents, teachers, and policy makers need to understand that this is not just a matter of personal style or generational expression. It's a question of whether we can preserve the methods through which education at its best teaches people to think critically and originally.

⋅   ⋅   ⋅

The student who highlighted Staples's column and its accompanying material was preparing for a class discussion of a group of related articles on the problem of academic cheating. To prepare for class, she began by using a variety of symbols, including underlining and asterisks, to identify the writer's key ideas and mark points she might want to think further about. This highlighting laid the groundwork for the careful annotations she would make when she reread the article.

Exercise 1

Preview the following article. Then, highlight it to identify the writer's main idea and key supporting points. (Previewing and highlighting the article's headnote and background material will help you to understand the article's ideas.) You might circle unfamiliar words, underline key terms or concepts, or draw lines or arrows to connect related ideas.

MARIA HINOJOSA

A Supreme Sotomayor: How My Country Has Caught Up to Me

Broadcast journalist Maria Hinojosa currently hosts the newsmagazine show "Maria Hinojosa: One-on-One" and serves as senior correspondent for "NOW" — both on PBS. She was born in Mexico City in 1961 and earned an undergraduate degree from Barnard College in New York City. A winner of the Robert F. Kennedy Journalism Award, Hinojosa has also worked for CBS, CNN, and other broadcast outlets. She is the author of *Crews: Gang Members Talk to Maria Hinojosa* (1995) and *Raising Paul: Adventures Raising Myself and My Son* (2000).

Background on Female Supreme Court Justices Although Justice Sonia Sotomayor is the first Latin American to sit on the U.S. Supreme Court, she is not the first woman on the Court. In 1981, President Ronald Reagan nominated Sandra Day O'Connor as the first female associate justice; generally viewed as a moderate "swing vote" on many controversial issues, including abortion, she served until her retirement in 2006. Sotomayor is also not the *only* female justice on the Supreme Court. Ruth Bader Ginsburg, nominated in 1993 by President Bill Clinton, and Elena Kagan, nominated in 2010 by Barack Obama, both now serve on the Court. As these appointments have broken the long tradition of males on the Supreme Court, many observers have begun to discuss the role that race, gender, religion, class, and ethnicity may play in future Supreme Court decisions.

The phone call came just minutes after Sonia Sotomayor was nomi- 1 nated by President Barack Obama to the Supreme Court. Rose Arce, my former producer at CNN and a Peruvian-American, told me the news. I let out an excited shout: *What!?!?*

Though Sonia Sotomayor had all of the qualifications, I was truly 2 not expecting to hear the news and could scarcely believe it. Do we really have a Puerto Rican woman from the South Bronx nominated to serve on SCOTUS? Like they say on "Saturday Night Live" — really? No! *Really?*

My friends — accomplished lawyers, a newspaper publisher, reporters 3 of the highest caliber — were all asking, "Are we dreaming?" We all needed reassurance. My high-powered Latina friends are not just Puerto Rican. They are Mexican, Colombian, Cuban, Dominican, and more. And now a woman just like us is being nominated for the highest court of the land. I ask again: Really?

I cannot begin to imagine all the tears shed by Latinas across this coun- 4 try on Tuesday. This nomination, like nothing before it, has made it finally clear that we exist as intellectual arbiters in our America. We exist as powerbrokers. It is a dynamic we are working hard to grasp and own and make real. Sotomayor has made it real for all of us.

All this unity notwithstanding, this nomination has the deepest and 5 most profound meaning for my Puerto Rican sisters. Stereotypes of Puerto Rican women from NYC run so deep in our popular culture. I can still hear Mick Jagger singing, "We're gonna come around at 12 with some Puerto Rican girls that are just dyin' to meet you. We're gonna bring a case of wine. Hey, let's go mess and fool around. You know, like we used to."

My Puerto Rican hermanas know that on some level they have always 6 been fighting against a pervasive image. They are brilliant and accomplished but oftentimes minimized to a mere stereotype that is disconnected from reality.

What President Obama has done for men of color, Sonia Sotomayor 7 will do for Puerto Rican women. She will forever and profoundly change the image of what a "Puerto Rican girl" really is.

I myself was used to being the "first" — the first Latina hired at NPR in 8 Washington, D.C.; the first Latina correspondent for CNN; the first Latina anchor and correspondent for PBS. The new paradigm is that we are now going beyond "firsts." Just look at Sotomayor — she's got that wavy-hair-with-the-big-earrings thing. She wears bright colors. She smiles broadly and she means it! She could be me! My 11-year-old daughter sees her on TV and remarks that Sotomayor looks "a lot like Mami's friends."

I want my daughter to avoid this image popular culture has main- 9 tained about Puerto Rican women and Latinas in general. This is why I take my daughter to maligned and misunderstood barrios, and why she hangs out with me and my high-powered Latina sisters. She can see what is real and what is not; she is living it.

Sotomayor's stomping ground of the South Bronx — no stranger to 10 vicious stereotyping — also produced MacArthur Genius Award–winning environmentalist Majora Carter and Emmy-nominated musician Bobby Sanabria (only the beginning of a long list of erudite South Bronxers). In the true South Bronx, the sounds of conga playing in the middle of the night are welcomed as a sign of joy and passion, not bothersome noise. The true South Bronx is populated by bustling families and kids on their way to work and school who for decades bravely endured and pushed through the drug dealers and users who flooded the neighborhood.

That is the essence of who Sonia Sotomayor is. She pushed through. 11 She stayed focused. She worked hard. She never closed the doors on herself, like so many strong women of color sometimes do. . . .

Sotomayor will also hopefully break down stereotypes Mexicanos and 12 other Latinos have about Puerto Ricans. Those groups listen to the Rolling Stones too.

This Friday night I will go to a Cuban playwright's brownstone in Span- 13 ish Harlem, where we will listen to El Gran Combo and toast a Latina who has "made it." My daughter will be with me. And while I remain stunned by the shocking reality of my country so quickly changing to reflect me and my reality, I am sure my daughter won't have it. My America was always, at best, a place of hopeful change. In her America, a black man can and does become president; a Latina can and does end up on the Supreme Court.

And so this is how it feels to be living in a time of change — feeling the 14 bumps of transformation like sudden conga beats in the night, beats that surprise at first, but ones I ultimately welcome with joy and hope.

. . .

Annotating

When you **annotate**, you carry on a conversation with the text. In marginal notes, you can ask questions, suggest possible parallels with other reading selections or with your own experiences, argue with the writer's points, comment on the writer's style or word choice, or define unfamiliar terms and concepts.

TECH TIP: Taking Notes

If you use your computer when you take notes instead of writing annotations on the page, be sure to label each note so you remember where it came from. (You will need this information for your paper's parenthetical references and works-cited page.) Include the author's name and the title of the reading selection as well as the page on which the information you are citing appears. Also note the page and paragraph number where you found the information so you will be able to find it again.

The questions below can guide you as you read and help you make useful annotations.

CHECKLIST   Questions for Critical Reading

- What is the writer's general subject?
- What is the writer's main point?
- What are the writer's key supporting points?
- Does the writer seem to have a particular purpose in mind?
- What kind of audience is the writer addressing?
- What are the writer's assumptions about audience? About subject?
- Are the writer's ideas consistent with your own?
- Does the writer reveal any biases?
- Do you have any knowledge that challenges the writer's ideas?
- Is any information missing?
- Are any sequential or logical links missing?
- Can you identify themes or ideas that also appear in other works you have read?
- Can you identify parallels with your own experience?

The following pages reproduce the student's highlighting of "Cutting and Pasting: A Senior Thesis by (Insert Name)" from page 18 and also include her annotations. (She annotated the headnote and background material as well, but these annotations are not shown here.)

Teachers as cops

A friend who teaches at a well-known eastern university told me recently that plagiarism was turning him into a cop. He begins the semester collecting evidence, in the form of an in-class essay that gives him a sense of how well students think and write. He looks back at the samples later when students turn in papers that feature their own, less-than-perfect prose alongside expertly written passages lifted verbatim from the Web. 1

Teachers resigned to situation

"I have to assume that in every class, someone will do it," he said. "It doesn't stop them if you say, 'This is plagiarism. I won't accept it.' I have to tell them that it is a failing offense and could lead me to file a complaint with the university, which could lead to them being put on probation or being asked to leave." 2

Not everyone who gets caught knows enough about what they did to be remorseful. Recently, for example, a student who plagiarized a sizable chunk of a paper essentially told my friend to keep his shirt on, that what he'd done was no big deal. Beyond that, the student said, he would be ashamed to go home to the family with an F. 3

Key problem—Move from "intellectual engagement" and critical thinking to "mere training"

✳

As my friend sees it: "This represents a shift away from the view of education as the process of intellectual engagement through which we learn to think critically and toward the view of education as mere training. In training, you are trying to find the right answer at any cost, not trying to improve your mind." 4

Like many other professors, he no longer sees traditional term papers as a valid index of student competence. To get an accurate, Internet-free reading of how much students have learned, he gives them written assignments in class — where they can be watched. 5

Colleges as police states!

These kinds of precautions are no longer unusual in the college world. As Trip Gabriel pointed out in the *Times* recently, more than half the colleges in the country have retained services that check student papers for material lifted from the Internet and elsewhere. Many schools now require incoming students to take online tutorials that explain what plagiarism is and how to avoid it. 6

Problem isn't
just ethics

Nationally, discussions about plagiarism tend to 7
focus on questions of ethics. But as David Pritchard,
a physics professor at the Massachusetts Institute of
Technology, told me recently: "The big sleeping dog
here is not the moral issue. The problem is that kids
don't learn if they don't do the work."

Prof. Pritchard and his colleagues illustrated the 8
point in a study of cheating behavior by M.I.T. students
who used an online system to complete homework. The
students who were found to have copied the most answers from others started out with the same math and
physics skills as their harder-working classmates. But
by skipping the actual work in homework, they fell behind in understanding and became significantly more
likely to fail.

The Pritchard axiom — that repetitive cheating 9
undermines learning — has ominous implications for
a world in which even junior high school students cut
and paste from the Internet instead of producing their
own writing.

True

If we look closely at plagiarism as practiced by 10
youngsters, we can see that they have a different relationship to the printed word than did the generations
before them. When many young people think of writing, they don't think of fashioning original sentences
into a sustained thought. They think of making something like a collage of found passages and ideas from
the Internet.

"Cutting and
pasting"="sampling"

They become like rap musicians who construct 11
what they describe as new works by "sampling" (which
is to say, cutting and pasting) beats and refrains from
the works of others.

What's the answer to
this question? (What
can schools do? Who
is responsible for
solving problem?)

This habit of mind is already pervasive in the cul- 12
ture and will be difficult to roll back. But parents, teachers, and policy makers need to understand that this is
not just a matter of personal style or generational expression. It's a question of whether we can preserve the
methods through which education at its best teaches
people to think critically and originally.

· · ·

As illustrated above, the student who annotated Staples's column on
cheating supplemented her highlighting with brief marginal summaries to
help her understand key points. She also wrote down questions that she
thought would help her focus her responses.

SUMMARIZING KEY IDEAS

One strategy that can help you understand what you are reading is **summarizing** a writer's key ideas, as the student writer does in her marginal annotations of the Staples column on pages 24–25. Putting a writer's ideas into your own words can make an unfamiliar or complex concept more accessible and useful to you. For more on summarizing, see page 712.

Exercise 2

Now, add annotations to the Hinojosa article and related material that you highlighted for Exercise 1. This time, focus on summarizing the writer's key points and on asking questions that will prepare you for discussing (and perhaps writing about) this article.

Reading Visual Texts

The process you use when you react to a **visual text** — a photograph; an advertisement; a diagram, graph, or chart; or a work of fine art, for example — is much the same as the one you use when you respond to a written text. Here too, your goal is to understand the text, and highlighting and annotating a visual text can help you interpret it.

With visual texts, however, instead of identifying elements like particular words and ideas, you identify visual elements. These might include the use of color; the arrangement of shapes; the contrast between large and small or light and dark; and, of course, the particular images the visual includes.

As you approach a visual, you might ask questions like those on the following checklist.

✓ CHECKLIST   Reading Visual Texts

- Why was the visual created?
- What kind of audience is it aimed at?
- How would you characterize the visual? For example, is it fine art? An advertisement? A technical diagram? A chart or graph?
- What is the visual's most important or most striking image? What makes this image dominate the page?
- How is blank space used to emphasize (or de-emphasize) individual images?
- How does contrast between light and dark (or use of color) work to emphasize (or de-emphasize) individual images?
- What objects are depicted in the visual?
- Does the visual include any images of people? If so, how do the people depicted interact with one another? What is their relationship to various objects depicted in the visual?
- Does the visual include any words? If so, what is their function? What is the relationship between the visual's words and its images?

The following photograph, one of four included in "Four Tattoos" (page 226), illustrates a student's highlighting and annotating of a visual text. (See page 227 for study questions about these images.)

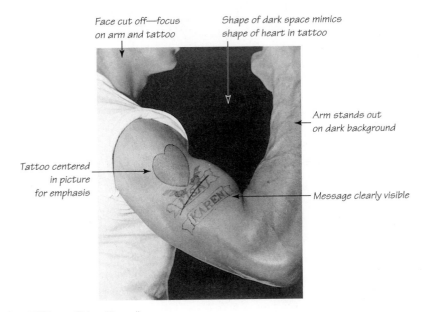

Face cut off—focus on arm and tattoo

Shape of dark space mimics shape of heart in tattoo

Arm stands out on dark background

Tattoo centered in picture for emphasis

Message clearly visible

Alex Williams, "~~Lisa~~, Karen"

Exercise 3

In this text, visuals are included in Chapters 6–14, where they are the first reading selection in each chapter. Choose one of these visuals, and highlight and annotate it. When you have finished, write a sentence that sums up what you think the visual is trying to communicate and how successful it is at accomplishing its goals.

2

Invention

Invention, or **prewriting**, is an important (and, frequently, the most neglected) part of the writing process. At this stage, you discover what interests you about your subject and consider what ideas to develop in your essay.

When you are given a writing assignment, you may be tempted to start writing a first draft immediately. Before writing, however, you should be sure you understand your assignment and its limits, and you should think about what you want to say. Time spent on these issues now will pay off later when you draft your essay.

Understanding Your Assignment

Almost everything you write in college begins as an *assignment*. Some assignments will be direct and easy to understand:

Write about an experience that changed your life.

Discuss the procedure you used to synthesize ammonia.

Others will be difficult and complex:

Using Jonathan Kozol's essay "The Human Cost of an Illiterate Society" as source material, write an essay using as your thesis the following statement by James Madison: "A people who mean to be their own governors must arm themselves with the power knowledge gives."

Before beginning to write, you need to understand what your assignment is asking you to do. If the assignment is written as a question, read it carefully several times, and underline its key words. If the assignment is read aloud by your instructor, be sure to copy it accurately. (A mistaken word — *analyze* for *compare*, for example — can make quite a difference.) If you are confused about anything, ask your instructor for clarification. Remember that no matter how well written an essay is, it will fall short if it does not address the assignment.

Setting Limits

Once you understand the assignment, you should consider its *length, purpose, audience,* and *occasion* and your own *knowledge* of the subject. Each of these factors helps you determine what you will say about your subject.

Length

Often, your instructor will specify the **length** of a paper, and this word or page limit has a direct bearing on your paper's focus. For example, you would need a narrower topic for a two-page essay than for a ten-page one. Similarly, you could not discuss a question as thoroughly during an hour-long exam as you might in a paper written over several days.

If your instructor sets no page limit, consider how the nature of the assignment suggests a paper's length. A *summary* of a chapter or an article, for instance, should be much shorter than the original, whereas an *analysis* of a poem will most likely be longer than the poem itself. If you are uncertain about the appropriate length for your paper, consult your instructor.

Purpose

Your **purpose** also limits what you say and how you say it. For example, if you were writing a job application letter, you would not emphasize the same elements of college life as you would in an email to a friend. In the first case, you would want to persuade the reader to hire you, so you might include your grade-point average, a list of the relevant courses you took, and perhaps the work you did for a service-learning course. In the second case, you would want to inform and perhaps entertain, so you might share anecdotes about dorm life or describe one of your favorite instructors. In each case, your purpose would help you determine what information to include to evoke a particular response in a specific audience.

In general, you can classify your purposes for writing according to your relationship to the audience.

- In **expressive writing**, you convey personal feelings or impressions to readers. Expressive writing is used in diaries, personal emails and journals, and often in narrative and descriptive essays as well.
- In **informative writing**, you inform readers about something. Informative writing is used in essay exams, lab reports, and expository essays as well as in some research papers and personal Web pages.
- In **persuasive writing**, you try to convince readers to act or think in a certain way. Persuasive writing is used in editorials, argumentative essays, proposals, research papers, and many types of electronic documents such as blogs and Web pages.

In addition to these general purposes, you might have a more specific purpose — to analyze, entertain, hypothesize, assess, summarize, question, report, recommend, suggest, evaluate, describe, recount, request, instruct, and so on. For example, suppose you wrote a report on homelessness in your community. Your general purpose might be to *inform* readers of the situation, but you might also want to *assess* the problem and *instruct* readers how to help those in need.

Audience

To be effective, your essay should be written with a particular **audience** in mind. An audience can be an *individual* (your instructor, for example), or it can be a *group* (like your classmates or coworkers). Your essay can address a *specialized* audience (such as a group of medical doctors or economists) or a *general* or *universal* audience whose members have little in common (such as the readers of a newspaper or magazine).

In college, your audience is usually your instructor, and your purpose in most cases is to demonstrate your mastery of the subject matter, your reasoning ability, and your competence as a writer. Other audiences may include classmates, professional colleagues, or members of your community. Considering the age and gender of your audience, its political and religious values, its social and educational level, and its interest in your subject may help you define it.

Often, you will find that your audience is just too diverse to be categorized. In such cases, many writers imagine a general (or universal) audience and make points that they think will appeal to a variety of readers. At other times, writers identify a common denominator, a role that characterizes the entire audience. For instance, when a report on the dangers of smoking asserts, "Now is the time for health-conscious individuals to demand that cigarettes be removed from the market," it automatically casts its audience in the role of health-conscious individuals.

After you define your audience, you have to determine how much (or how little) its members know about your subject. This consideration helps you decide how much information your readers will need in order to understand the discussion. Are they highly informed? If so, you can present your points without much explanation. Are they relatively uninformed? If this is the case, you will have to include definitions of key terms, background information, and summaries of basic research.

Keep in mind that experts in one field will need background information in other fields. If, for example, you were writing an analysis of Joseph Conrad's *Heart of Darkness,* you could assume that the literature instructor who assigned the novel would not need a plot summary. However, if you wrote an essay for your history instructor that used *Heart of Darkness* to illustrate the evils of European colonialism in nineteenth-century Africa, you would probably include a short plot summary. (Even though your history instructor would know a lot about colonialism in Africa, she might not be familiar with Conrad's work.)

Occasion

In general, **occasion** refers to the situation (or situations) that leads someone to write about a topic. Obviously, in an academic writing situation, the occasion is almost always a specific assignment. The occasion suggests a specific audience — for example, a history instructor — as well as a specific purpose — for example, to discuss the causes of World War I. In fact, even the format of a paper — whether you use (or do not use) headings or whether you present your response to an assignment as an essay, as a technical report, or as a PowerPoint presentation — is determined by the occasion for your writing. For this reason, a paper suitable for a psychology or sociology class might not be suitable for a composition class.

Like college writing assignments, each writing task you do outside of school requires an approach that suits the occasion. An email to coworkers, for instance, may be less formal than a report to a manager. In addition, the occasion suggests how much (or how little) information the piece of writing includes. Finally, your occasion suggests your purpose. For example, an email to members of an online discussion group might be strictly informational, whereas an email to a state senator about preserving a local landmark would be persuasive as well as informative.

Knowledge

What you know (and do not know) about a subject determines what you can say about it. Before writing about any subject, ask yourself what you know about the subject and what you need to find out.

Different writing situations require different kinds of knowledge. A personal essay will draw on your own experiences and observations; a term paper will require you to gain new knowledge through research. In many cases, your page limit and the amount of time you are given to do the assignment will help you decide how much information you need to gather before you can begin.

✔CHECKLIST Setting Limits

Length
- Has your instructor specified a length?
- Does the nature of your assignment suggest a length?

Purpose
- Is your general purpose to express personal feelings? To inform? To persuade?
- In addition to your general purpose, do you have any more specific purposes?
- Does your assignment provide any guidelines about purpose?

Audience
- Is your audience a group or an individual?
- Are you going to address a specialized or a general audience?

- Should you take into consideration the audience's age, gender, education, biases, or political or social values?
- Should you cast your audience in a particular role?
- How much can you assume your audience knows about your subject?

Occasion
- Are you writing in class or at home?
- Are you addressing a situation outside the academic setting?
- What special approaches does your occasion for writing require?

Knowledge
- What do you know about your subject?
- What do you need to find out?

Exercise 1

Decide whether or not each of the following topics is appropriate for the stated limits, and then write a few sentences to explain why each topic is or is not acceptable.

1. *A two-to-three-page paper*   A history of animal testing in medical research labs
2. *A two-hour final exam*   The effectiveness of bilingual education programs
3. *A one-hour in-class essay*   An interpretation of one of Andy Warhol's paintings of Campbell's soup cans
4. *An email to your college newspaper*   A discussion of your school's policy on plagiarism

Exercise 2

Make a list of the different audiences to whom you speak or write in your daily life. (Consider all the different people you see regularly, such as family members, your roommate, instructors, your boss, your friends, and so on.) Then, record your answers to the following questions:

1. Do you speak or write to each person in the same way and about the same things? If not, how do your approaches to these people differ?
2. List some subjects that would interest some of these people but not others. How do you account for these differences?
3. Choose one of the following subjects, and describe how you would speak or write to different audiences about it.
   - A change that improved your life
   - Censoring Internet content
   - Taking a year off before college
   - Reality TV shows

Moving from Subject to Topic

Although many essays begin as specific assignments, some begin as broad areas of interest or concern. These **general subjects** always need to be narrowed to **specific topics** that can be discussed within the limits of the assignment. For example, a subject like stem-cell research could be interesting, but it is too complicated to write about for any college assignment except in a general way. You need to limit such a subject to a topic that can be covered within the time and space available.

GENERAL SUBJECT	SPECIFIC TOPIC
Stem-cell research	Using stem-cell research to cure multiple sclerosis
Herman Melville's *Billy Budd*	Billy Budd as a Christ figure
Constitutional law	One unforeseen result of the *Miranda* ruling
The Internet	The uses of chat rooms in composition classes

Two strategies can help you narrow a general subject to a specific topic: *questions for probing* and *freewriting*.

Questions for Probing

One way to move from a general subject to a specific topic is to examine your subject by asking a series of questions about it. These **questions for probing** are useful because they reflect how your mind operates — for instance, finding similarities and differences, or dividing a whole into its parts. By asking the questions on the following checklist, you can explore your subject systematically. Not all questions will work for every subject, but any single question may elicit many different answers, and each answer is a possible topic for your essay.

✔ **CHECKLIST**   Questions for Probing

What happened?
When did it happen?
Where did it happen?
Who did it?
What does it look like?
What are its characteristics?
What impressions does it make?
What are some typical cases or examples of it?
How did it happen?
What makes it work?
How is it made?

Why did it happen?
What caused it?
What does it cause?
What are its effects?
How is it like other things?
How is it different from other things?
What are its parts or types?
How can its parts or types be separated or grouped?
Do its parts or types fit into a logical order?
Into what categories can its parts or types be arranged?
On what basis can it be categorized?
How can it be defined?
How does it resemble other members of its class?
How does it differ from other members of its class?

When applied to a subject, some of these questions can yield many workable topics, including some you might never have considered had you not asked the questions. For example, by applying this approach to the general subject "the Brooklyn Bridge," you can generate more ideas and topics than you need:

What happened? A short history of the Brooklyn Bridge

What does it look like? A description of the Brooklyn Bridge

How is it made? The construction of the Brooklyn Bridge

What are its effects? The impact of the Brooklyn Bridge on American writers

How does it differ from other members of its class? Innovations in the design of the Brooklyn Bridge

At this point in the writing process, you want to come up with possible topics, and the more ideas you have, the wider your choice. Begin by jotting down all the topics you think of. (You can repeat the process of probing several times to limit topics further.) Once you have a list of topics, eliminate those that do not interest you or are too complex or too simple to fit your assignment. When you have discarded these less promising topics, you should still have several left. You can then select the topic that best suits your paper's length, purpose, audience, and occasion, as well as your interests and your knowledge of the subject.

▛ TECH TIP: Questions for Probing

You can store the questions for probing listed on pages 34–35 in a file that you can open whenever you have a new subject. Make sure you keep a record of your answers. If the topic you have chosen is too difficult or too narrow, you can return to the questions-for-probing file and probe your subject again.

Exercise 3

Indicate whether each of the following is a general subject or a specific topic that is narrow enough for a short essay.

1. An argument against fast-food ads that are aimed at young children
2. Home schooling
3. Cell phones and driving
4. Changes in U.S. immigration laws
5. Requiring college students to study a foreign language
6. The advantages of funding health care for children of undocumented workers
7. A comparison of small-town and big-city living
8. Student loans
9. The advantages of service-learning courses
10. The need for totally electric cars

Exercise 4

In preparation for writing a 750-word essay, choose two of the following general subjects, and generate three or four specific topics from each by using as many of the questions for probing as you can.

1. Credit-card fraud
2. Job interviews
3. Identity theft
4. Gasoline prices
5. Substance abuse
6. Climate change
7. The minimum wage
8. Age discrimination
9. Cyberbullying
10. The need for recycling
11. The person you admire most
12. Rising college tuition
13. Online courses
14. Sensational trials
15. The widespread use of surveillance cameras

Freewriting

Another strategy for moving from subject to topic is **freewriting**. You can use freewriting at any stage of the writing process — for example, to generate supporting information or to find a thesis. However, freewriting is a particularly useful way to narrow a general subject or assignment.

When you freewrite, you write for a fixed period, perhaps five or ten minutes, without stopping and without paying attention to spelling, grammar, or punctuation. Your goal is to get your ideas down on paper so that you can react to them and shape them. If you have nothing to say, write down anything until ideas begin to emerge — and in time they will. The secret is to *keep writing*. Try to focus on your subject, but don't worry if you wander off in other directions. The object of freewriting is to let your ideas flow. Often, your best ideas will come from the unexpected connections you make as you write.

After completing your freewriting, read what you have written and look for ideas you can write about. Some writers underline ideas they think they might explore in their essays. Any of these ideas could become essay topics, or they could become subjects for other freewriting exercises. You might want to freewrite again, using a new idea as your focus. This process of writing more and more specific freewriting exercises — called **focused freewriting** or **looping** — can often yield a great deal of useful information and help you decide on a workable topic.

▉ TECH TIP: Freewriting

If you freewrite on a computer, you may find that staring at your own words causes you to go blank. One possible solution is to turn down the brightness until the screen becomes dark and then to freewrite. This technique allows you to block out distracting elements and concentrate on just your ideas. Once you finish freewriting, turn up the brightness, and see what you have.

A STUDENT WRITER: Freewriting

After reading, highlighting, and annotating Henry Louis Gates Jr.'s "'What's in a Name?'" (page 17), Laura Bobnak, a student in a composition class, decided to write an essay in response to this Writing Workshop question.

> Write about a time when you, like Gates's father, could have spoken out in protest but chose not to. Would you make the same decision today?

In an attempt to narrow this assignment to a workable topic, Laura did the following freewriting exercise.

> Write for ten minutes . . . ten minutes . . . at 9 o'clock in the morning — Just what I want to do in the morning — If you can't think of something to say, just write about anything. Right! Time to get this over with — An experience — should have talked — I can think of plenty of times I should have kept quiet! I should have brought a bottle of water to class. I

wonder what the people next to me are writing about. That reminds me. Next to me. Jeff Servin in chemistry. The time I saw him cheating. I was mad but I didn't do anything. I studied so hard and all he did was cheat. I was so mad. Nobody else seemed to care. What's the difference between now and then? It's only a year and a half. . . . Honor code? Maturity? A lot of people cheated in high school. I bet I could write about this — Before and after, etc. My attitude then and now.

After some initial floundering, Laura discovered an idea that could be the basis for her essay. Although her discussion of the incident still had to be developed, Laura's freewriting helped her discover a possible topic for her essay: a time she saw someone cheating and did not speak out.

Exercise 5

Do a five-minute freewriting exercise on one of the topics you generated in Exercise 4 (page 36).

Exercise 6

Read what you have just written, underline the most interesting ideas, and choose one idea as a topic you could write about in a short essay. Freewrite about this topic for another five minutes to narrow it further and to generate ideas for your essay. Underline the ideas that seem most useful.

Finding Something to Say

Once you have narrowed your subject to a workable topic, you need to find something to say about it. *Brainstorming* and *journal writing* are useful tools for generating ideas, and both can be helpful at this stage of the writing process (and whenever you need to find additional material).

Brainstorming

Brainstorming is a way of discovering ideas about your topic. You can brainstorm in a group, exchanging ideas with several students in your composition class and noting the most useful ideas. You can also brainstorm on your own, quickly recording every fact, idea, or detail you can think of that relates to your topic. Your notes might include words, phrases, statements, questions, or even drawings or diagrams. Jot them down in the order in which you think of them. Some of the items may be inspired by your class notes; others may be ideas you got from reading or from talking with friends; and still other items may be ideas you have begun to wonder about, points you thought of while moving from subject to topic, or thoughts that occurred to you as you brainstormed.

A STUDENT WRITER: Brainstorming

To narrow her topic further and find something to say about it, Laura Bobnak made the brainstorming notes shown on page 40. After reading these notes several times, Laura decided to concentrate on the differences between her current and earlier attitudes toward cheating. She knew that she could write a lot about this idea and relate it to the assignment, and she felt confident that her topic would be interesting both to her instructor and to the other students in the class.

TECH TIP: Brainstorming

Your word-processing program makes it easy to create bulleted or numbered lists and gives you the flexibility to experiment with different ways of arranging and grouping items from your brainstorming notes. You can even use the drawing tools to make diagrams.

Journal Writing

Journal writing can be a useful source of ideas at any stage of the writing process. Many writers routinely keep a journal, jotting down experiences or exploring ideas they may want to use when they write. They write journal entries even when they have no particular writing project in mind. Often, these journal entries are the kernels from which longer pieces of writing develop. Your instructor may ask you to keep a writing journal, or you may decide to do so on your own. In either case, you will find your journal entries are likely to be more narrowly focused than freewriting or brainstorming, perhaps examining a small part of a reading selection or even one particular statement. Sometimes you will write in your journal in response to specific questions, such as the Journal Entry assignments that appear throughout this book. Assignments like these can help you start thinking about a reading selection that you may later discuss in class or write about.

A STUDENT WRITER: Journal Writing

In the following journal entry, Laura Bobnak explores one idea from her brainstorming notes — her thoughts about her college's honor code.

At orientation, the dean of students talked about the college's honor code. She talked about how we were a community of scholars who were here for a common purpose — to take part in an intellectual conversation. According to her, the purpose of the honor code is to make sure this conversation continues uninterrupted. This idea sounded dumb at orientation, but now it makes sense. If I saw someone cheating, I'd tell the instructor. First, though, I'd ask the *student* to go to the instructor. I don't see this as "telling" or "squealing." We're

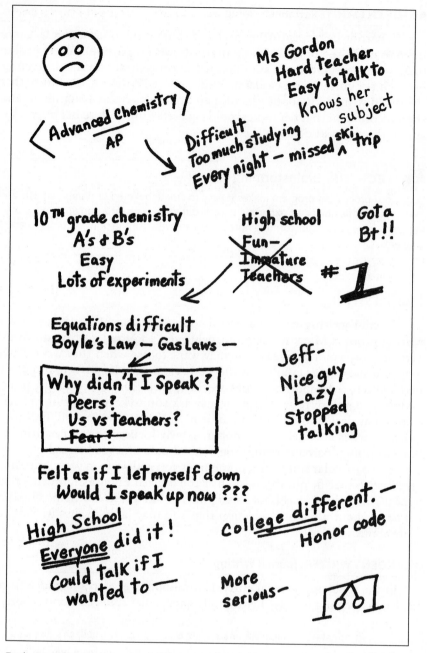

Brainstorming notes

all here to get an education, and we should be able to assume everyone is being honest and fair. Besides, why should I go to all the trouble of studying while someone else does nothing and gets the same grade?

Even though Laura eventually included only a small part of this entry in her paper, writing in her journal helped her focus her ideas about her topic.

TECH TIP: Keeping a Journal

Keeping your journal in a computer file has some obvious advantages. Not only can you maintain a neat record of your ideas, but you can also easily move entries from your journal into an essay without retyping them. Make sure, however, that you clearly distinguish between your ideas and those of your sources. If you paste material from your sources directly into your journal and then paste that material into your paper without documenting it, you are committing plagiarism. (For information on avoiding plagiarism, see Chapter 17.)

Grouping Ideas

Once you have generated material for your essay, you will want to group ideas that belong together. *Clustering* and *outlining* can help you do this.

Clustering

Clustering is a way of visually arranging ideas so that you can tell at a glance where ideas belong and whether or not you need more information. Although you can use clustering at an earlier stage of the writing process, it is especially useful now for seeing how your ideas fit together. (Clustering can also help you narrow your paper's topic even further. If you find that your cluster diagram is too detailed, you can write about just one branch of the cluster.)

Begin clustering by writing your topic in the center of a sheet of paper. After circling the topic, surround it with the words and phrases that identify the major points you intend to discuss. (You can get ideas from your brainstorming notes, from your journal, and from your freewriting.) Circle these words and phrases, and connect them to the topic in the center. Next, construct other clusters of ideas relating to each major point, and draw lines connecting them to the appropriate point. By dividing and subdividing your points, you get more specific as you move outward from the center. In the process, you identify the facts, details, examples, and opinions that illustrate and expand your main points.

A STUDENT WRITER: Clustering

Because Laura Bobnak was not very visually oriented, she chose not to use this method of grouping her ideas. If she had, however, her cluster diagram might have looked like this.

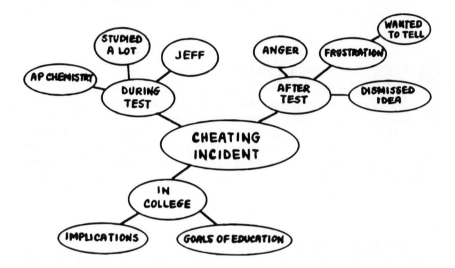

Making an Informal Outline

As an alternative or follow-up to clustering, you can organize your notes from brainstorming or other invention techniques into an **informal outline**. Informal outlines do not include all the major divisions and subdivisions of your paper the way formal outlines do; they simply suggest the shape of your emerging essay. Quite often an informal outline is just a list of your major points presented in a tentative order. Sometimes, however, an informal outline will include supporting details or suggest a pattern of development.

🔲 **TECH TIP:** Making an Informal Outline

You can easily arrange the notes you generated in your invention activities into an informal outline. You can construct an informal outline by typing words or phrases from your notes and rearranging them until the order makes sense. Later, you can use the categories from this informal outline to construct a formal outline (see page 62).

A STUDENT WRITER: Making an Informal Outline

The following informal outline shows how Laura Bobnak grouped her ideas.

During test
    Found test hard
    Saw Jeff cheating
After test
    Got angry
    Wanted to tell
    Dismissed idea
In college
    Understand implications of cheating
    Understand goals of education

Exercise 7

Continue your work on the topic you selected in Exercise 6 (page 38). Brainstorm about your topic; then, select the ideas you plan to explore in your essay, and use either clustering or an informal outline to help you group related ideas together.

Understanding Thesis and Support

Once you have grouped your ideas, you need to consider your essay's thesis. A **thesis** is the main idea of your essay, its central point. The concept

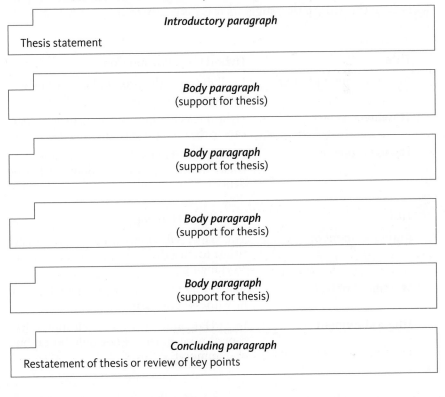

Introductory paragraph
Thesis statement

Body paragraph
(support for thesis)

Body paragraph
(support for thesis)

Body paragraph
(support for thesis)

Body paragraph
(support for thesis)

Concluding paragraph
Restatement of thesis or review of key points

of *thesis and support* — stating your thesis and developing ideas that explain and expand it — is central to college writing.

The essays you write will consist of several paragraphs: an **introduction** that presents your thesis statement, several **body paragraphs** that develop and support your thesis, and a **conclusion** that reinforces your thesis and provides closure. Your thesis holds this structure together; it is the center that the rest of your essay develops around.

Developing a Thesis

Defining the Thesis Statement

A **thesis statement** is more than a *title*, an *announcement of your intent*, or a *statement of fact*. Although a descriptive title orients your readers, it is not detailed enough to reveal your essay's purpose or direction. An announcement of your intent can reveal more, but it is stylistically distracting. Finally, a statement of fact — such as a historical fact or a statistic — is a dead end and therefore cannot be developed into an essay. For example, a statement like "Alaska became a state in 1959" or "Tuberculosis is highly contagious" or "The population of Greece is about ten million" provides your essay with no direction. However, a judgment or opinion *can* be an effective thesis — for instance, "The continuing threat of tuberculosis, particularly in the inner cities, suggests it is necessary to frequently test high-risk populations."

Title	Hybrid Cars: Pro and Con
Announcement of intent	I will examine the pros and cons of hybrid cars that use both gasoline and electricity.
Statement of fact	Hybrid cars are more energy efficient than cars with standard gasoline engines.
Thesis statement	Hybrid cars that use both gasoline and electricity would decrease our country's dependence on foreign oil.
Title	Orwell's "A Hanging"
Announcement of intent	This paper will discuss George Orwell's attitude toward the death penalty in his essay "A Hanging."
Statement of fact	In his essay, Orwell describes a hanging that he witnessed in Burma.
Thesis statement	In "A Hanging," George Orwell shows that capital punishment is not only brutal but also immoral.

Title	Speaking Out
Announcement of intent	This essay will discuss a time when I could have spoken out but did not.
Statement of fact	Once I saw someone cheating and did not speak out.
Thesis statement	As I look back at the cheating I witnessed, I wonder why I kept silent and what would have happened if I had acted.

WHAT A GOOD THESIS DOES

For writers

It helps writers plan an essay.
It helps writers organize ideas in an essay.
It helps writers unify all the ideas in an essay.

For readers

It identifies the main idea of an essay.
It guides readers through an essay.
It clarifies the subject and the focus of an essay.

Deciding on a Thesis

No rules determine when you formulate your thesis; the decision depends on the scope of your assignment, your knowledge of the subject, and your method of writing. When you know a lot about a subject, you may come up with a thesis before doing any invention activities (freewriting or brainstorming, for example). At other times, you may have to review your notes and then think of a single statement that communicates your position on the topic. Occasionally, your assignment may specify a thesis by telling you to take a particular position on a topic. In any case, you should decide on a thesis statement before you begin to write your first draft.

As you write, you will continue to discover new ideas, and you will probably move in directions that you did not anticipate. For this reason, the thesis statement you develop at this stage of the writing process is only **tentative**. Still, because a tentative thesis helps you to focus your ideas, it is essential at the initial stages of writing. As you draft your essay, review your thesis statement in light of the points you make, and revise it accordingly.

Stating Your Thesis

It is a good idea to include a one-sentence statement of your thesis early in your essay. An effective thesis statement has three characteristics:

1. **An effective thesis statement clearly expresses your essay's main idea.** It does more than state your topic; it indicates what you will say about your topic, and it signals how you will approach your material. The following thesis statement, from the essay "Grant and Lee: A Study in Contrasts" by Bruce Catton (page 393), clearly communicates the writer's main idea.

> They [Grant and Lee] were two strong men, these oddly different generals, and they represented the strengths of two conflicting currents that, through them, had come into final collision.

This statement says that the essay will compare and contrast Grant and Lee. Specifically, it indicates that Catton will present the two Civil War generals as symbols of two opposing historical currents. If the statement had been less fully developed — for example, had Catton written, "Grant and Lee were quite different from each other" — it would have just echoed the essay's title.

2. **An effective thesis statement communicates your essay's purpose.** Whether your purpose is to evaluate or analyze or simply to describe or inform, your thesis statement should communicate that purpose to your readers. In general terms, your thesis can be **expressive**, conveying a mood or impression; it can be **informative**, perhaps listing the major points you will discuss or presenting an objective overview of the essay; or it can be **persuasive**, taking a strong stand or outlining the position you will argue.

Each of the following thesis statements communicates a different purpose.

To express feelings   The city's homeless families live in heartbreaking surroundings.

To inform   The plight of the homeless has become so serious that it is a major priority for many city governments.

To persuade   The best way to address the problems of the homeless is to renovate abandoned city buildings to create suitable housing for homeless families.

3. **An effective thesis statement is clearly worded.** To communicate your essay's main idea, an effective thesis statement should be clearly worded. (It should also speak for itself. It is not necessary to write, "My thesis is that . . ." or "The thesis of this paper is. . . .") The thesis statement should give a straightforward and accurate indication of what follows, and it should not mislead readers about the essay's direction, emphasis, scope, content, or viewpoint. Vague language, confusing abstractions, irrelevant details, and unnecessarily complex terminology have no place in a thesis statement. Keep in mind, too, that your thesis statement should not make promises that your essay is not going to keep. For example, if you are going to discuss just the *effects* of new immigration laws, your thesis statement should not emphasize the events that resulted in their passage.

Your thesis statement cannot, of course, include every point you will discuss in your essay. Still, it should be specific enough to indicate your direction and scope. The sentence "New immigration laws have failed to stem the tide of illegal immigrants" is not an effective thesis statement because it does not give your essay much focus. Which immigration laws will you be examining? Which illegal immigrants? The following sentence, however, *is* an effective thesis statement. It clearly indicates what the writer is going to discuss, and it establishes a specific direction for the essay.

> Because they do not take into account the economic causes of immigration, current immigration laws do little to decrease the number of illegal immigrants coming from Mexico into the United States.

Implying a Thesis

Like an explicitly stated thesis, an **implied thesis** conveys an essay's purpose, but it does not do so explicitly. Instead, the selection and arrangement of the essay's ideas suggest the purpose. Professional writers sometimes prefer this option because an implied thesis is subtler than a stated thesis. (An implied thesis is especially useful in narratives, descriptions, and some arguments, where an explicit thesis would seem heavy-handed or arbitrary.) In most college writing, however, you should state your thesis to avoid any risk of being misunderstood or of wandering away from your topic.

A STUDENT WRITER: Developing a Thesis

After experimenting with different ways of arranging her ideas for her essay, Laura Bobnak summed them up in a tentative thesis statement.

> As I look back at the cheating I witnessed, I wonder why I kept silent and what would have happened if I had acted.

✔ CHECKLIST   Stating Your Thesis

- Do you state your thesis in one complete, concise sentence?
- Does your thesis indicate your purpose?
- Is your thesis suited to the assignment?
- Does your thesis clearly convey the main idea you intend to support in your essay?
- Does your thesis suggest how you will organize your essay?

Exercise 8

Assess the strengths and weaknesses of the following as thesis statements.

1. My instructor has an attendance policy.
2. My instructor should change her attendance policy because it is bad.
3. My instructor should change her attendance policy because it is unreasonable, inflexible, and unfair.

4. For many people, a community college makes more sense than a four-year college or university.

5. Some children show violent behavior.

6. Violence is a problem in our society.

7. Conflict-resolution courses should be taught to help prevent violence in America's schools.

8. Social networking sites such as Facebook can cause problems.

9. Facebook attracts many college students.

10. College students should be careful of what material they put on their Facebook pages because prospective employers routinely check them.

Exercise 9

Rewrite the following factual statements to make them effective thesis statements. Make sure each thesis statement is a clearly and specifically worded sentence.

1. Many hospitals will not admit patients without health insurance because they are afraid that such patients will not be able to pay their bills.

2. Several Supreme Court decisions have said that art containing explicit sexual images is not necessarily pornographic.

3. Many women earn less money than men do, in part because they drop out of the workforce during their child-rearing years.

4. People who watch more than five hours of television a day tend to think the world is more violent than do people who watch less than two hours of television daily.

5. In recent years, the suicide rate among teenagers — especially middle- and upper-middle-class teenagers — has risen dramatically.

Exercise 10

Read the following sentences from "The Argument Culture" by Deborah Tannen. Then, formulate a one-sentence thesis statement that summarizes the key points Tannen makes about the nature of argument in our culture.

- "More and more, our public interactions have become like arguing with a spouse."
- "Nearly everything is framed as a battle or game in which winning or losing is the main concern."
- "The argument culture pervades every aspect of our lives today."
- "Issues from global warming to abortion are depicted as two-sided arguments, when in fact most Americans' views lie somewhere in the middle."
- "What's wrong with the argument culture is the ubiquity, the knee-jerk nature of approaching any issue, problem, or public person in an adversarial way."

- "If you fight to win, the temptation is great to deny facts that support your opponent's views and say only what supports your side."
- "We must expand the notion of 'debate' to include more dialogue."
- "Perhaps it is time to re-examine the assumption that audiences always prefer a fight."
- "Instead of insisting on hearing 'both sides,' let's insist on hearing 'all sides.'"

Exercise 11

Go through as many steps as you need to formulate an effective thesis statement for the essay you have been working on.

3

Arrangement

Each of the tasks discussed in Chapter 2 represents choices you have to make about your topic and your material. Now, before you actually begin to write, you have another choice to make — how to arrange your material into an essay.

Recognizing a Pattern

Sometimes arranging your ideas will be easy because your assignment specifies a particular pattern of development. This may be the case in a composition class, where the instructor may assign a descriptive or a narrative essay. Also, certain assignments or exam questions suggest how your material should be structured. For example, an instructor might ask you to tell about how something works, or an exam question might ask you to trace the circumstances leading up to an event. If you are perceptive, you will realize that your instructor is asking for a process essay and that the exam question is asking for either a narrative or a cause-and-effect response. The important thing is to recognize the clues such assignments give (or those you find in your topic or thesis statement) and to structure your essay accordingly.

One clue to structuring your essay can be found in the questions that proved most helpful when you probed your subject (see pages 34–35). For example, if questions like "What happened?" and "When did it happen?" yielded the most useful information about your topic, you should consider structuring your paper as a narrative. The chart on page 52 links various questions to the patterns of development they suggest. Notice that the terms in the right-hand column — narration, description, and so on — identify patterns of development that can help order your ideas. Chapters 6 through 13 explain and illustrate each of these patterns.

✔**CHECKLIST**   **Recognizing a Pattern**

What happened?
When did it happen?   } Narration
Where did it happen?
Who did it?

What does it look like?
What are its characteristics?   } Description
What impressions does it make?

What are some typical cases
   or examples of it?   } Exemplification

How did it happen?
What makes it work?   } Process
How is it made?

Why did it happen?
What caused it?
What does it cause?   } Cause and effect
What are its effects?

How is it like other things?
How is it different from other   } Comparison and contrast
   things?

What are its parts or types?
How can its parts or types be
   separated or grouped?
Do its parts or types fit into a
   logical order?   } Classification and division
Into what categories can its
   parts or types be arranged?
On what basis can it be
   categorized?

How can it be defined?
How does it resemble other
   members of its class?   } Definition
How does it differ from other
   members of its class?

Understanding the Parts of the Essay

No matter what pattern of development you use, your essay should have a beginning, a middle, and an end — that is, an *introduction*, a *body*, and a *conclusion*.

The Introduction

The **introduction** of your essay, usually one paragraph and rarely more than two, introduces your subject, creates interest, and often states your thesis.

You can use a variety of strategies to introduce an essay and engage your readers' interest. Here are several options for beginning an essay (in each paragraph, the thesis statement is underlined).

1. You can begin with *background information*. This approach works well when you know the audience is already interested in your topic and you can come directly to the point. This strategy is especially useful for exams, where there is no need (or time) for subtlety.

> With inflation low, many companies have understandably lowered prices, and the oil industry should be no exception. Consequently, homeowners have begun wondering whether the high price of home heating oil is justified given the economic climate. It makes sense, therefore, for us to start examining the pricing policies of the major American oil companies.   (economics essay)

2. You can introduce an essay with your own original *definition* of a relevant term or concept. This technique is especially useful for research papers or exams, where the meaning of a specific term is crucial.

> Democracy is a form of government in which power is given to and exercised by the people. This may be true in theory, but some recent elections have raised concerns about the future of democracy. Extensive voting-machine irregularities and "ghost voting" have jeopardized people's faith in the democratic process.   (political science exam)

3. You can begin your essay with an *anecdote* or *story* that leads readers to your thesis.

> Three years ago, I went with my grandparents to my first auction. They live in a small town outside of Lancaster, Pennsylvania, where it is common for people to auction off the contents of a home when someone moves or dies. As I walked through the crowd, I smelled the funnel cakes frying in the food trucks, heard the hypnotic chanting of the auctioneer, and sensed the excitement of the crowd. Two hours later, I walked off with an old trunk that I had bought for thirty dollars and a passion for auctions that I still have today.   (composition essay)

4. You can begin with a *question*.

> What was it like to live through the Holocaust? Elie Wiesel, in *One Generation After*, answers this question by presenting a series of accounts about ordinary people who found themselves imprisoned in Nazi death camps. As he does so, he challenges some of the assumptions we have about the Holocaust and those who survived.   (sociology book report)

5. You can begin with a *quotation*. If it arouses interest, it can encourage your audience to read further.

"The rich are different," F. Scott Fitzgerald said more than seventy years ago. Apparently, they still are. As an examination of the tax code shows, the wealthy receive many more benefits than the middle class or the poor do. (accounting paper)

6. You can begin with a *surprising statement*. An unexpected statement catches readers' attention and makes them want to read more.

Believe it or not, most people who live in the suburbs are not white and rich. My family, for example, fits into neither of these categories. Ten years ago, my family and I came to the United States from Pakistan. My parents were poor then, and by some standards, they are still poor even though they both work two jobs. Still, they eventually saved enough to buy a small house in the suburbs of Chicago. Throughout the country, there are many suburban families like mine who are working hard to make ends meet so that their children can get a good education and go to college. (composition essay)

7. You can begin with a *contradiction*. You can open your essay with an idea that most people believe is true and then get readers' attention by showing that it is inaccurate or ill advised.

Many people think that after the Declaration of Independence was signed in 1776, the colonists defeated the British army in battle after battle. This commonly held belief is incorrect. The truth is that the colonial army lost most of its battles. The British were defeated not because the colonial army was stronger, but because George Washington refused to be lured into a costly winner-take-all battle and because the British government lost interest in pursuing an expensive war three thousand miles from home. (history take-home exam)

8. You can begin with a *fact* or *statistic*.

According to a recent government study, recipients of Medicare will spend billions of dollars on drugs over the next ten years. This is a very large amount of money, and it illustrates why lawmakers must do more to help older Americans with the cost of medications. Although the current legislation is an important first step, more must be done to help the elderly afford the drugs they need. (public policy essay)

No matter which strategy you select, your introduction should be consistent in tone with the rest of your essay. If it is not, it can misrepresent your intentions and even damage your credibility. (For this reason, it is a good idea not to write your introduction until after you have finished your rough draft.) A technical report, for instance, should have an introduction that reflects the formality and objectivity the occasion requires. The introduction to an autobiographical essay, however, should have a more informal, subjective tone.

> ✔ **CHECKLIST**   What Not to Do in an Introduction
>
> - **Don't apologize.** Never use phrases such as "in my opinion" or "I may not be an expert, but. . . ." By doing so, you suggest that you don't really know your subject.
> - **Don't begin with a dictionary definition.** Avoid beginning an essay with phrases like "According to Webster's Dictionary. . . ." This type of introduction is overused and trite. If you want to use a definition, develop your own.
> - **Don't announce what you intend to do.** Don't begin with phrases such as "In this paper I will . . ." or "The purpose of this essay is to. . . ." Use your introduction to create interest in your topic, and let readers discover your intention when they get to your thesis statement.
> - **Don't wander.** Your introduction should draw readers into your essay as soon as possible. Avoid irrelevant comments or annoying digressions that will distract readers and make them want to stop reading.

Exercise 1

Look through magazine articles or the essays in this book, and find one example of each kind of introduction. Why do you think each introductory strategy was chosen? What other strategies might have worked?

The Body Paragraphs

The middle section, or **body**, of your essay develops your thesis. The body paragraphs present the support that convinces your audience your thesis is reasonable. To do so, each body paragraph should be *unified, coherent,* and *well developed.* It should also follow a particular pattern of development and should clearly support your thesis.

• *Each body paragraph should be unified.*   A paragraph is **unified** when each sentence relates directly to the main idea of the paragraph. Frequently, the main idea of a paragraph is stated in a **topic sentence**. Like a thesis statement, a topic sentence acts as a guidepost, making it easy for readers to follow the paragraph's discussion. Although the placement of a topic sentence depends on a writer's purpose and subject, beginning writers often make it the first sentence of a paragraph.

Sometimes the main idea of a paragraph is not stated but **implied** by the sentences in the paragraph. Professional writers often use this technique because they believe that in some situations — especially narratives and descriptions — a topic sentence can seem forced or awkward. As a beginning writer, however, you will find it helpful to use topic sentences to keep your paragraphs focused.

Whether or not you include a topic sentence, remember that each sentence in a paragraph should develop the paragraph's main idea. If the sentences in a paragraph do not support the main idea, the paragraph will lack unity.

In the following excerpt from a student essay, notice how the topic sentence (underlined) unifies the paragraph by summarizing its main idea:

Another problem with fast food is that it contains additives. Fast-food companies know that to keep their customers happy, they have to give them food that tastes good, and this is where the trouble starts. For example, to give fries flavor, McDonald's used to fry their potatoes in beef fat. Shockingly, their fries actually had more saturated fat than their hamburgers did. When the public found out how unhealthy their fries were, the company switched to vegetable oil. What most people don't know, however, is that McDonald's adds a chemical derived from animals to the vegetable oil to give it the taste of beef tallow.

The topic sentence, placed at the beginning of the paragraph, enables readers to grasp the writer's point immediately. The examples that follow all relate to that point, making the paragraph unified.

• *Each body paragraph should be coherent.*   A paragraph is **coherent** if its sentences are smoothly and logically connected to one another. Coherence can be strengthened in three ways. First, you can repeat **key words** to carry concepts from one sentence to another and to echo important terms. Second, you can use **pronouns** to refer to key nouns in previous sentences. Finally, you can use **transitions**, words or expressions that show chronological sequence, cause and effect, and so on (see the list of transitions on page 57). These three strategies for connecting sentences — which you can also use to connect paragraphs within an essay — indicate for your readers the exact relationships among your ideas.

The following paragraph, from George Orwell's "Shooting an Elephant" (page 133), uses repeated key words, pronouns, and transitions to achieve coherence.

I got up. The Burmans were already racing past me across the mud. It was obvious that the elephant would never rise again, but he was not dead. He was breathing very rhythmically with long rattling gasps, his great mound of a side painfully rising and falling. His mouth was wide open — I could see far down into the caverns of pale pink throat. I waited a long time for him to die, but his breathing did not weaken. Finally, I fired my two remaining shots into the spot where I thought his heart must be. The thick blood welled out of him like red velvet, but still he did not die. His body did not even jerk when the shots hit him, the tortured breathing continued without a pause. He was dying, very slowly and in great agony, but in some world remote from me where not even a bullet could damage him further. I felt that I had got to put an end to that dreadful noise. It seemed dreadful to see the great beast lying there, powerless to move and yet powerless to die, and not even to be able to finish him. I sent back for my small rifle and poured shot after shot into his heart and down his throat. They seemed to make no impression. The tortured gasps continued as steadily as the ticking of a clock.

TRANSITIONS

SEQUENCE OR ADDITION

again	first, ... second, ... third	next
also	furthermore	one ... another
and	in addition	still
besides	last	too
finally	moreover	

TIME

afterward	finally	simultaneously
as soon as	immediately	since
at first	in the meantime	soon
at the same time	later	subsequently
before	meanwhile	then
earlier	next	until
eventually	now	

COMPARISON

also	likewise
in comparison	similarly
in the same way	

CONTRAST

although	in contrast	on the one hand ...
but	instead	on the other hand ...
conversely	nevertheless	still
despite	nonetheless	whereas
even though	on the contrary	yet
however		

EXAMPLES

for example	specifically
for instance	that is
in fact	thus
namely	

CONCLUSIONS OR SUMMARIES

as a result	in summary
in conclusion	therefore
in short	thus

CAUSES OR EFFECTS

as a result	so
because	then
consequently	therefore
since	

Orwell keeps his narrative coherent by using transitional expressions (*already, finally, when the shots hit him*) to signal the passing of time. He uses pronouns (*he, his*) in nearly every sentence to refer back to the elephant, the topic of his paragraph. Finally, he repeats key words like *shots* and *die* (and its variants *dead* and *dying*) to link the whole paragraph's sentences together.

    • *Each body paragraph should be well developed.*   A paragraph is **well developed** if it contains the **support** — examples, reasons, and so on — readers need to understand its main idea. If a paragraph is not adequately developed, readers will feel they have been given only a partial picture of the subject.

    If you decide you need more information in a paragraph, you can look back at your brainstorming notes. If this doesn't help, you can freewrite or brainstorm again, talk with friends and instructors, read more about your topic, or (with your instructor's permission) do some research. Your assignment and your topic will determine the kind and amount of information you need.

TYPES OF SUPPORT

- **Examples** Specific illustrations of a general idea or concept
- **Reasons** Underlying causes or explanations
- **Facts** Pieces of information that can be verified or proved
- **Statistics** Numerical data (for example, results of studies by reputable authorities or organizations)
- **Details** Parts or portions of a whole (for example, steps in a process)
- **Expert opinions** Statements by recognized authorities in a particular field
- **Personal experiences** Events that you lived through
- **Visuals** Diagrams, charts, graphs, or photographs

✔CHECKLIST   Effective Support

- **Support should be relevant.** Body paragraphs should clearly relate to your essay's thesis. Irrelevant material — material that does not pertain to the thesis — should be deleted.
- **Support should be specific.** Body paragraphs should contain support that is specific, not general or vague. Specific examples, clear reasons, and precise explanations engage readers and communicate your ideas to them.
- **Support should be adequate.** Body paragraphs should contain enough facts, reasons, and examples to support your thesis. How much support you need depends on your audience, your purpose, and the scope of your thesis.

- **Support should be representative.** Body paragraphs should present support that is typical, not atypical. For example, suppose you write a paper claiming that flu shots do not work. Your support for this claim is that your grandmother got the flu even though she was vaccinated. This example is not representative because studies show that most people who get vaccinated do not get the flu.
- **Support should be documented.** Support that comes from research (print sources and the Internet, for example) should be documented. (For more information on proper documentation, see the Appendix). **Plagiarism** — failure to document the ideas and words of others — is not only unfair but also dishonest. Always use proper documentation to acknowledge your debt to your sources — and keep in mind that words and ideas you borrow from the essays in this book must also be documented. (For more information on avoiding plagiarism, see Chapter 17.)

The following student paragraph uses two examples to support its topic sentence.

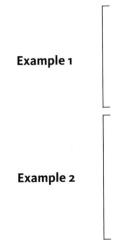

Example 1

Just look at how males have been taught that extravagance is a positive characteristic. Scrooge, the main character of Dickens's *A Christmas Carol*, is portrayed as an evil man until he gives up his miserly ways and freely distributes gifts and money on Christmas day. This behavior, of course, is rewarded when people change their opinions about him and decide that he isn't such a bad person

Example 2

after all. Diamond Jim Brady is another interesting example. This individual was a nineteenth-century financier who was known for his extravagant taste in women and food. On any given night, he would eat enough food to feed at least ten of the numerous poor who roamed the streets of New York at that time. Yet, despite his selfishness and infantile self-gratification, Diamond Jim Brady's name has become associated with the good life.

- *Each body paragraph should follow a particular pattern of development.* In addition to making sure your body paragraphs are unified, coherent, and well developed, you need to organize each paragraph according to a specific pattern of development. (Chapters 6 through 13 each begin with a paragraph-length example of the pattern discussed in the chapter.)
- *Each body paragraph should clearly support the thesis statement.* No matter how many body paragraphs your essay has — three, four, five, or even more — each paragraph should introduce and develop an idea that supports the essay's thesis. Each paragraph's topic sentence should express one of these supporting points. The diagram on page 60 illustrates this thesis- and-support structure.

Introductory paragraph

> *Thesis statement:* Despite the emphasis by journalists on objective reporting, there are <u>three reasons</u> why television news is anything but objective.

Body paragraph

> *Topic sentence:* Television news is not objective because the people who gather and report the news are biased.

Body paragraph

> *Topic sentence:* In addition, television news is not objective because networks face pressure from sponsors.

Body paragraph

> *Topic sentence:* Finally, television news is not objective because networks focus on ratings rather than content.

Concluding paragraph

> *Restatement of thesis:* Even though television journalists claim to strive for objectivity, the truth is that this ideal has been impossible to achieve.

Exercise 2

Choose a body paragraph from one of the essays in this book. Using the criteria discussed on pages 55–60, decide whether the paragraph is unified, coherent, and well developed.

Exercise 3

Choose one essay in this book, and underline its thesis statement. Then, determine how its body paragraphs support that thesis statement. (Note that in a long essay, several body paragraphs may develop a single supporting point, and some paragraphs may serve as transitions from one point to another.)

The Conclusion

Since readers remember best what they read last, your **conclusion** is very important. Always end your essay in a way that reinforces your thesis and your purpose.

Like your introduction, your conclusion is rarely longer than a paragraph. Regardless of its length, however, your conclusion should be consistent with the rest of your essay—that is, it should not introduce points you have not discussed earlier. Frequently, a conclusion will restate your essay's main idea or review your key points.

Here are several strategies you can use to conclude an essay:

1. You can conclude your essay by *reviewing your key points* or *restating your thesis.*

> Rotation of crops provided several benefits. It enriched soil by giving it a rest; it enabled farmers to vary their production; and it ended the cycle of "boom or bust" that had characterized the prewar South's economy when cotton was the primary crop. Of course, this innovation did not solve all the economic problems of the postwar South, but it did lay the groundwork for the healthy economy this region enjoys today.
>
> (history exam)

2. You can end a discussion of a problem with a *recommendation of a course of action.*

> Well-qualified teachers are becoming harder and harder to find. For this reason, school boards should reassess their ideas about what qualifies someone to teach. At the present time, people who have spent their lives working in a particular field are denied certification because they have not taken education courses. This policy deprives school systems of talented teachers. In order to ensure that students have the best possible teachers, school boards should consider applicants' real-world experience when evaluating their qualifications.　　　　(education essay)

3. You can conclude with a *prediction*. Be sure, however, that your prediction follows logically from the points you have made in the essay. Your conclusion is no place to make new points or to change direction.

> Campaign advertisements should help people understand a political candidate's qualifications and where he or she stands on critical issues. They should not appeal to people's fears or greed. Above all, they should not personally attack other candidates or oversimplify complex issues. If campaign advertisements continue to do these things, the American people will disregard them and reject the candidates they promote.
>
> (political science essay)

4. You can end with a relevant *quotation*.

> In *Walden*, Henry David Thoreau says, "The mass of men lead lives of quiet desperation." This sentiment is reinforced by a drive through the Hill District of our city. Perhaps the work of the men and women who run the clinic on Jefferson Street cannot totally change this situation, but it can give us hope to know that some people, at least, are working for the betterment of us all.　　　　(public health essay)

> ☑**CHECKLIST**   What Not to Do in a Conclusion
> - **Don't end by repeating the exact words of your thesis and listing your main points.** Avoid boring endings that tell readers what they already know.
> - **Don't end with an empty phrase.** Avoid ending with a cliché like "This just goes to prove that you can never be too careful."
> - **Don't introduce new points or go off in new directions.** Your conclusion should not introduce new points for discussion. It should reinforce the points you have already made in your essay.
> - **Don't end with an unnecessary announcement.** Don't end by saying that you are ending — for example, "In conclusion, let me say. . . ." The tone of your conclusion should signal that the essay is drawing to a close.

Exercise 4

Look through magazine articles or the essays in this book, and find one example of each kind of conclusion. Why do you think each concluding strategy was chosen? What other strategies might have worked?

Constructing a Formal Outline

Before you begin to write, you may decide to construct a **formal outline** to guide you. Whereas informal outlines are preliminary lists that simply remind you which points to make, formal outlines are detailed, multilevel constructions that indicate the exact order in which you will present your key points and supporting details. The complexity of your assignment determines which type of outline you need. For a short paper, an informal outline like the one on page 43 is usually sufficient. For a longer, more complex essay, however, you may need a formal outline.

One way to construct a formal outline is to copy down the main headings from your informal outline. Then, arrange ideas from your brainstorming notes or cluster diagram as subheadings under the appropriate headings. As you work on your outline, make sure each idea you include supports your thesis. Ideas that don't fit should be reworded or discarded. As you revise your essay, continue to refer to your outline to make sure your thesis and support are logically related. The guidelines that follow will help you prepare a formal outline.

> ☑**CHECKLIST**   Constructing a Formal Outline
> - Write your thesis statement at the top of the page.
> - Group main headings under roman numerals (*I, II, III, IV,* and so on), and place them flush with the left-hand margin.

- Indent each subheading under the first word of the heading above it. Use capital letters before major points and numbers before supporting details.
- Capitalize the first letter of the first word of each heading.
- Make your outline as simple as possible, avoiding overly complex divisions of ideas. (Try not to go beyond third-level headings — *1, 2, 3,* and so on.)
- Construct either a **topic outline**, with headings expressed as short phrases or single words ("Advantages and disadvantages") or a **sentence outline**, with headings expressed as complete sentences ("The advantages of advanced placement chemistry outweigh the disadvantages"). *Never use both phrases and complete sentences in the same outline.*
- Express all headings at the same level in parallel terms. (If roman numeral *I* is a noun, *II, III,* and *IV* should also be nouns.)
- Make sure each heading contains at least two subdivisions. You cannot have a *1* without a *2* or an *A* without a *B.*
- Make sure your headings do not overlap.

A STUDENT WRITER: Constructing a Formal Outline

The topic outline Laura Bobnak constructed follows the guidelines discussed above. Notice that her outline focuses on the body of her paper and does not include the introduction or conclusion: these are usually developed after the body has been drafted. (Compare this formal outline with the informal outline on page 43 where Laura simply grouped her brainstorming notes under three general headings.)

Thesis statement: As I look back at the cheating I witnessed, I wonder why I kept silent and what would have happened if I had acted.

I. The incident
   A. Test situation
   B. My observation
   C. My reactions
      1. Anger
      2. Silence
II. Reasons for keeping silent
   A. Other students' attitudes
   B. My fears
III. Current attitude toward cheating
   A. Effects of cheating on education
   B. Effects of cheating on students

This outline enabled Laura to arrange her points so that they supported her thesis. As she went on to draft her essay, the outline reminded her to emphasize the contrast between her present and former attitudes toward cheating.

TECH TIP: Constructing a Formal Outline

You can use your word-processing program to arrange and rearrange your headings until your outline is logical and complete. (Your word-processing program will have an outline function that automatically indents and numbers items.) If you saved your prewriting notes in computer files, you can refer to them while working on your outline and perhaps add or modify headings to reflect what you find.

Exercise 5

Read the thesis statement you developed in Chapter 2, Exercise 11 (on page 49), as well as all the notes you made for the essay you are planning. Then, make a topic outline that lists the points you will discuss in your essay. When you are finished, check to make sure your outline conforms to the guidelines on the checklist on pages 62–63.

4

Drafting and Revising

After you decide on a thesis and an arrangement for your ideas, you can begin to draft and revise your essay. Keep in mind that even as you carry out these activities, you may have to generate more material or revise your thesis statement.

Writing Your First Draft

The purpose of your **first draft** is to get your ideas down on paper so that you can react to them. Experienced writers know that the first draft is nothing more than a work in progress; it exists to be revised. With this in mind, you should expect to cross out and extensively rearrange material. In addition, don't be surprised if you think of new ideas as you write. If a new idea comes to you, go with it. Some of the best writing comes from unexpected turns or accidents. The following guidelines will help you prepare your first draft.

✔ **CHECKLIST** **Drafting**

- **Begin with the body paragraphs.** Because your essay will probably be revised extensively, don't take the time at this stage to write an introduction or conclusion. Let your thesis statement guide you as you draft the body paragraphs of your essay. Later, when you have finished, you can write an appropriate introduction and conclusion.
- **Get your ideas down quickly.** Don't worry about grammar or word choice, and try not to interrupt the flow of your writing with concerns about style.
- **Take regular breaks as you write.** Don't write until you are so exhausted you can't think straight. Many writers divide their writing into stages, perhaps completing one or two body paragraphs and then taking a short break.

(continued)

This strategy is more efficient than trying to write a complete first draft without stopping.

- **Write with revision in mind.** Leave enough space between lines so that you will have room to make changes by hand on hard copy.
- **Leave yourself time to revise.** Remember, your first draft is a *rough draft*. All writing benefits from revision, so allow enough time to write two or more drafts.

A STUDENT WRITER: Writing a First Draft

Here is the first draft of Laura Bobnak's essay on the following topic: "Write about a time when you, like Henry Louis Gates Jr.'s father, could have spoken out but chose not to. Would you make the same decision today?"

When I was in high school, I had an experience like the one Henry Louis 1
Gates Jr. talks about in his essay. It was then that I saw a close friend cheat in
chemistry class. As I look back at the cheating I witnessed, I wonder why I kept
silent and what would have happened if I had acted.

The incident I am going to describe took place during the final exam for 2
my advanced placement chemistry class. I had studied hard for it, but even
so, I found the test difficult. As I struggled to balance a particularly difficult
equation, I noticed that my friend Jeff, who was sitting across from me, was
acting strangely. I noticed that he was copying material from a paper. After
watching him for a while, I dismissed the incident and got back to my test.

After the test was over, I began to think about what I had seen. The more 3
I thought about it the angrier I got. It seemed unfair that I had studied for
weeks to memorize formulas and equations while all Jeff had done was to copy
them onto a cheat sheet. For a moment I considered going to the teacher, but
I quickly rejected this idea. After all, cheating was something everybody did.
Besides, I was afraid if I told on Jeff, my friends would stop talking to me.

Now that I am in college I see the situation differently. I find it hard to 4
believe that I could ever have been so calm about cheating. Cheating is certainly
something that students should not take for granted. It undercuts the education
process and is unfair to teachers and to the majority of students who spend their
time studying.

If I could go back to high school and relive the experience, I now know 5
that I would have gone to the teacher. Naturally Jeff would have been angry at
me, but at least I would have known I had the courage to do the right thing.

Exercise 1

Write a draft of the essay you have been working on in Chapters 2 and 3. Be sure to look back at all your notes as well as your outline.

Revising Your Essay

Revision is not something you do after your paper is finished. It is a continuing process during which you consider the logic and clarity of your ideas, as well as how effectively they are presented.

Revision is not simply a matter of proofreading or editing, of crossing out one word and substituting another or correcting errors in spelling and punctuation; revision involves reseeing and rethinking what you have written. When you revise, you may find yourself adding and deleting extensively, reordering whole sentences or paragraphs as you reconsider what you want to communicate to your audience.

Revision can take a lot of time, so don't be discouraged if you have to go through three or four drafts before you think your essay is ready to hand in. The following advice can help you when you revise your essay:

- *Give yourself a cooling-off period.*   Put your first draft aside for several hours or even a day or two if you can. This cooling-off period lets you distance yourself from your essay so that you can read it more objectively when you return to it. When you read it again, you will see things you missed the first time.
- *Revise on hard copy.*   Because a printed-out draft shows you all the pages of your paper and enables you to see your handwritten edits, you should revise on hard copy instead of directly on the computer screen.
- *Read your draft aloud.*   Before you revise, read your draft aloud to help you spot choppy sentences, missing words, or phrases that do not sound right.
- *Take advantage of opportunities to get feedback.*   Your instructor may organize peer editing groups, distribute a revision checklist, refer students to a writing center, or schedule one-on-one conferences. Make use of as many of these opportunities for feedback as you can; each offers you a different way of gaining information about what you have written.
- *Try not to get overwhelmed.*   It is easy to become overwhelmed by all the feedback you get about your draft. To avoid this, approach revision systematically. Don't automatically make all the changes people suggest; consider the validity of each change. Also ask yourself whether comments suggest larger issues. For example, does a comment about a series of choppy sentences suggest a need for you to add transitions, or does it mean you need to rethink your ideas?

- *Don't let your ego get in the way.* Everyone likes praise, and receiving negative criticism is never pleasant. Experienced writers know, however, that they must get feedback if they are going to improve their work. Learn to see criticism — whether from an instructor or from your peers — as a necessary part of the revision process.
- *Revise in stages.* Deal with the large elements (essay and paragraph structure) before moving on to the smaller elements (sentence structure and word choice).

How you revise — what specific strategies you decide to use — depends on your own preference, your instructor's instructions, and the time available. Like the rest of the writing process, revision varies from student to student and from assignment to assignment. Four of the most useful revision strategies are *revising with a checklist, revising with an outline, revising with a peer critique,* and *revising with your instructor's comments.*

Revising with a Checklist

If you have time, you can use the following revision checklist, adapting it to your own writing process.

✓ CHECKLIST   Revising

- **Thesis statement** Is your thesis statement clear and specific? Does it indicate the direction your essay is taking? Is it consistent with the body of your essay? If you departed from your essay's original direction while you were writing, you may need to revise your thesis statement so that it accurately reflects the ideas and information now contained in the body.
- **Body Paragraphs** Are the body paragraphs unified? Coherent? Well developed? If not, you might have to add more facts or examples or smoother transitions. Does each body paragraph follow a particular pattern of development? Do the points you make in these paragraphs support your thesis? If not, you may need to delete material that is unrelated to the thesis statement — or revise it so that it *is* relevant.
- **Introduction and conclusion** Are your introduction and your conclusion appropriate for your material, your audience, and your purpose? Are they interesting? Do they reinforce your thesis?
- **Sentences** Are your sentences effective? Interesting? Varied in length and structure? Should any sentences be deleted, combined, or moved?
- **Words** Do your words accurately express your ideas? Should you make any changes?

Revising with an Outline

If you do not have time to consult a detailed checklist, you can check your essay's structure by making a **review outline**. Either an informal outline or a formal one can show you whether you have omitted any important points. An outline can also show you whether your essay follows a particular pattern of development. Finally, an outline can clarify the relationship between your thesis statement and your body paragraphs. (See pages 62-64 for guidelines for constructing an outline.)

Revising in a Peer Editing Group

Another revision strategy involves getting feedback from other students. Sometimes this process is formal: an instructor may require students to exchange papers and evaluate their classmates' work according to certain standards, perhaps by completing a **peer editing worksheet**. (See pages 71-72 for an example.) Often, however, soliciting feedback from others is an informal process. Even if a friend is unfamiliar with your topic, he or she can still tell you whether you are getting your point across — and maybe even advise you about how to communicate more effectively. (Remember, though, that your critic should be only your reader, not your ghostwriter.)

Getting feedback from others mirrors how people in the real world actually write. Businesspeople circulate reports to get feedback from coworkers; scientists and academics routinely collaborate when they write. (And, as you may have realized, even this book is the result of a collaboration.)

Your classmates can be helpful as you write the early drafts of your essay, providing suggestions that can guide you through the revision process. In addition, they can respond to questions you may have about your essay — for example, whether your introduction works or whether one of your supporting points needs more explanation. When friends ask *you* to critique their work, the guidelines on page 70 should help you.

TECH TIP: Revising

When you revise, make sure you do not delete text you may need later. Move this information to the end of the draft or to a separate file. That way, if you change your mind about a deletion or if you find you need information you took out of a draft, you can recover it easily.

☑ CHECKLIST **Guidelines for Peer Critiques**

- **Be positive.** Remember that your purpose is to help other students improve their essays.
- **Be tactful.** Be sure to emphasize the good points about the essay. Mention one or two things the writer has done particularly well before you offer your suggestions.
- **Be specific.** Offer concrete suggestions about what the writer could do better. Vague words like *good* or *bad* provide little help.
- **Be involved.** If you are doing a critique orally, make sure you interact with the writer. Ask questions, listen to responses, and explain your comments.
- **Look at the big picture.** Don't focus exclusively on issues such as spelling and punctuation. At this stage, the clarity of the thesis statement, the effectiveness of the support, and the organization of the writer's ideas are much more important.
- **Be thorough.** When possible, write down and explain your comments, either on a form your instructor provides or in the margins of the draft you are reviewing.

Revising with Your Instructor's Comments

Your instructor's **written comments** on a draft of your essay can also help you revise by suggesting changes in content, arrangement, or style. For example, these comments may question your logic, suggest a clearer thesis statement, ask for more explicit transitions, recommend that a paragraph be relocated, or even propose a new direction for your essay. They may also recommend stylistic changes or ask you to provide more support in one or more of your body paragraphs. You may decide to incorporate these suggestions into the next draft of your essay, or you may decide not to. Whatever the case, you should take your instructor's comments seriously and make reading and responding to them a part of your revision process.

Here is a paragraph from the first draft of Laura Bobnak's essay along with her instructor's comments.

Your tentative thesis statement is good — as far as it goes. It really doesn't address the second half of the assignment — namely, would you make the same decision today?

When I was in high school, I had an experience like the one Henry Louis Gates Jr. talks about in his essay. It was then that I saw a close friend cheat in chemistry class. As I look back at the cheating I witnessed, I wonder why I kept silent and what would have happened if I had acted.

⊞ TECH TIP: Revising

It is usually not a good idea to revise directly on the computer screen. Since most screens show only a portion of a page, the connections between ideas are hard to see and to keep track of. Even with the split-screen option that some word-processing programs offer, you cannot view several pages of a draft at once or easily compare one draft to another. For these reasons, it is a good idea to revise on a hard copy of your essay. Once you have made your handwritten corrections, you can type them into your paper.

Your instructor's **oral comments** at a one-on-one conference can also help you revise. If your instructor encourages (or requires) you to schedule a conference, come to the conference prepared. Read all your drafts carefully and bring a copy of your most recent draft as well as a list of any questions you have. During the conference, ask your instructor to clarify marginal comments or to help you revise a particular section of your essay that is giving you trouble. Make sure you take notes during the conference so that you will have a record of what you and your instructor discussed. Remember that the more prepared for the conference you are, the more you will get out of it. (Some instructors use email or video links to answer questions and to give students feedback.)

A STUDENT WRITER: Revising a First Draft

When she revised the first draft of her essay (page 66), Laura Bobnak followed the revision process discussed above. After writing her rough draft, she put it aside for a few hours and then reread it. Later, her instructor divided the class into pairs and had them read each other's essays and fill out **peer editing worksheets**. After reading and discussing the following worksheet (filled out by one of her classmates), Laura was able to focus on a number of areas that needed revision.

▱ PEER EDITING WORKSHEET

1. What is the essay's thesis? Is it clearly worded? Does it provide a focus for the essay?

   "As I look back at the cheating I witnessed, I wonder why I kept silent and what would have happened if I had acted." The thesis is clear and gives a good idea of what the essay is about.

2. Do the body paragraphs clearly support the essay's thesis? Should any of the topic sentences be revised? Which, if any, could be more clearly worded?

   The topic sentences seem fine — each one seems to tell what the paragraph is about.

(continued)

3. How do the body paragraphs develop the essay's main idea? Where could the writer have used more detail?

> Each of the body paragraphs tells a part of the narrative. You could add more detail about how the exam room was set up — I really can't picture the scene.

4. Can you follow the writer's ideas? Does the essay need transitions?

> I have no problem following your ideas. Maybe you could have added some more transitions, but I think the essay moves OK.

5. Which points are especially clear? What questions do you have that are not answered in the essay?

> I think you clearly explained what you didn't like about Jeff's cheating. I'm not sure what AP chemistry is like, though. Do people cheat because it's so hard?

6. If this were your essay, what would you change before you handed it in?

> I'd add more detail and explain more about AP chemistry. Also, what were the other students doing while the cheating was going on?

7. Overall, do you think the paper is effective? Explain.

> Good paper; cheating is a big issue, and I think your essay really gets this across.

> A peer editing worksheet for each pattern of development appears at the end of the introductions for Chapters 6 through 15.

Points for Special Attention: First Draft

The Introduction

When she wrote her first draft, Laura knew she would eventually have to expand her introduction. At this stage, though, she was more concerned with her thesis statement — which, as her instructor's comments pointed out, didn't address the second half of the assignment: to explain whether or not she would act differently today.

Keeping in mind the feedback she received, Laura rewrote her introduction. First, she created a context for her discussion by specifically linking her story to Gates's essay. Next, she decided to postpone mentioning her subject — cheating — until later in the paper, hoping this strategy would stimulate the curiosity of her readers and make them want to read further. Finally, she revised her thesis statement to reflect the specific wording of the assignment.

The Body Paragraphs

The students in her peer editing group said Laura needed to expand her body paragraphs. Although she had expected most of her readers to be familiar with courses like advanced placement chemistry, she discovered this was not the case. In addition, some students in her group thought she should expand the paragraph in which she described her reaction to the cheating. They wondered what the other students had thought about the incident. Did they know? Did they care? Laura's classmates were curious, and they thought other readers would be, too.

Before revising the body paragraphs, Laura did some brainstorming for additional ideas. She decided to describe the difficulty of advanced placement chemistry and the pressure the students in the class had felt. She also decided to summarize discussions she had had with several of her classmates after the test. In addition, she wanted to explain in more detail her present views on cheating; she felt that the paragraph presenting these ideas did not contrast enough with the paragraphs dealing with her high school experiences.

To make sure her sentences led smoothly into one another, Laura added transitions and rewrote entire sentences when necessary, signaling the progression of her thoughts by adding words and phrases such as *therefore, for this reason, for example,* and *as a result.* In addition, she tried to repeat key words so that important concepts would be reinforced.

The Conclusion

Laura's biggest concern as she revised was to make sure her readers would see the connection between her essay and the assignment. To make this connection clear, she decided to mention in her conclusion a specific effect the incident had on her: its impact on her friendship with Jeff. She also decided to link her reactions to those of Henry Louis Gates Jr. Like him, she had been upset by the actions of someone she knew. By employing this strategy, she was able to bring her essay full circle and develop an idea she had alluded to in her introduction. Thus, rewriting her conclusion helped Laura to reinforce her thesis statement and provide closure to her essay.

A STUDENT WRITER: Revising a Second Draft

The following draft incorporates Laura's revisions, as well as some preliminary editing of grammar and punctuation.

Speaking Out

In his essay "'What's in a Name?'" Henry Louis Gates Jr. recalls an incident 1
from his past in which his father did not speak up. Perhaps he kept silent
because he was afraid or because he knew that nothing he said or did would
change the situation in Piedmont, West Virginia. Although I have never

encountered the kind of prejudice Gates describes, I did have an experience in high school where, like Gates's father, I could have spoken up but did not. As I now look back at the cheating I witnessed, I know I would not make the same decision today.

The incident I am going to describe took place during the final examination in my advanced placement chemistry class. The course was very demanding and required hours of studying every night. Every day after school, I would meet with other students to outline chapters and answer homework questions. Sometimes we would even work on weekends. We would often ask ourselves whether we had gotten in over our heads. As the semester dragged on, it became clear to me, as well as to the other students in the class, that passing the course was not something we could take for granted. Test after test came back with grades that were well below the "As" and "Bs" I was used to getting in the regular chemistry course I took in tenth grade. By the time we were ready to take the final exam, most of us were worried that we would fail the course — despite the teacher's assurances that she would mark on a curve.

The final examination for advanced placement chemistry was given on a Friday morning from nine to twelve o'clock. As I struggled to balance a particularly complex equation, I noticed that the person sitting across from me was acting strangely. I thought I was imagining things, but as I stared I saw Jeff, my friend and study partner, fumbling with his test booklet. I realized that he was copying material from a paper he had taped inside the cuff of his shirt. After watching him for a while, I dismissed the incident and finished my test.

Surprisingly, when I mentioned the incident to others in the class, they all knew what Jeff had done. The more I thought about Jeff's actions, the angrier I got. It seemed unfair that I had studied for weeks to memorize formulas and equations while all Jeff had done was to copy them onto a cheat sheet. For a moment I considered going to the teacher, but I quickly rejected this idea. Cheating was nothing new to me or to others in my school. Many of my classmates cheated at one time or another. Most of us saw school as a war between us and the teachers, and cheating was just another weapon in our arsenal. The worst crime I could commit would be to turn Jeff in. As far as I was concerned, I had no choice. I fell in line with the values of my high school classmates and dismissed the incident as "no big deal."

I find it hard to believe that I could ever have been so complacent about cheating. The issues that were simple in high school now seem complex. I now ask questions that never would have occurred to me in high school. Interestingly, Jeff and I are no longer very close. Whenever I see him, I have the same reaction Henry Louis Gates Jr. had when he met Mr. Wilson after he had insulted his father.

Points for Special Attention: Second Draft

Laura could see that her second draft was stronger than her first, but she decided to schedule a conference with her instructor to help her improve her draft further.

The Introduction

Although Laura was satisfied with her introduction, her instructor identified a problem during a conference. Laura had assumed that everyone reading her essay would be familiar with Gates's essay. However, her instructor pointed out that this might not be the case. So he suggested that she add a brief explanation of the problems Gates's father had faced in order to accommodate readers who didn't know about or remember Gates's comments.

The Body Paragraphs

After rereading her first body paragraph, Laura thought she could sharpen its focus. Her instructor agreed, suggesting she delete the first sentence of the paragraph, which seemed too conversational. She also decided she could delete the sentences that explained how difficult advanced placement chemistry was — even though she had added this material at the suggestion of a classmate. After all, cheating, not advanced placement chemistry, was the subject of her paper. She realized that if she included this kind of detail, she ran the risk of distracting readers from the real subject of her discussion.

Her instructor also pointed out that in the second body paragraph, the first and second sentences did not seem to be connected, so Laura decided to connect these ideas by adding a short discussion of her own reaction to the test. Her instructor also suggested that Laura add more transitional words and phrases to this paragraph to clarify the sequence of events she was describing. Phrases such as *at first* and *about a minute passed* would help readers follow her discussion.

Laura thought the third body paragraph was her best, but, even so, she thought she needed to add more material. She and her instructor decided she should expand her discussion of the students' reactions to cheating. More information — perhaps some dialogue — would help Laura make the point that cheating was condoned by the students in her class.

The Conclusion

Laura's conclusion began by mentioning her present attitude toward cheating and then suddenly shifted to the effect cheating had on her relationship with Jeff. Her instructor suggested that she revise by taking her discussion about her current view of cheating out of her conclusion and putting it in a separate paragraph. By doing this, she could focus her conclusion on the effect cheating had on both Jeff and her. This strategy enabled Laura to present her views about cheating in more detail and also helped her end her essay forcefully.

Working with Sources

Her instructor also suggested that Laura consider adding a quotation from Gates's essay to her conclusion. He thought that Gates's words would clearly connect his experience to Laura's. He reminded her not to forget to document the quotation and to use correct MLA documentation format (as explained and illustrated in Chapter 18 of this text).

The Title

Laura's original title was only a working title, and now she wanted one that would create interest and draw readers into her essay. She knew, however, that a humorous, cute, or catchy title would undermine the seriousness of her essay. After she rejected a number of possibilities, she decided on "The Price of Silence." This title was thought provoking and also descriptive, and it prepared readers for what was to follow in the essay.

CHOOSING A TITLE

Because it is the first thing in your essay that readers see, your title should create interest. Usually, single-word titles and cute ones do little to draw readers into your essay. To be effective, a title should reflect your purpose and your tone. The titles of some of the essays in this book illustrate the various kinds of titles you can use:

Statement of essay's focus: "Grant and Lee: A Study in Contrasts"

Question: "Who Killed Benny Paret?"

Unusual angle: "Thirty-Eight Who Saw Murder Didn't Call the Police"

Controversy: "A Peaceful Woman Explains Why She Carries a Gun"

Provocative wording: "No Wonder They Call Me a Bitch"

Quotation: "The 'Black Table' Is Still There"

Humor: "The Dog Ate My Disk, and Other Tales of Woe"

A STUDENT WRITER: Preparing a Final Draft

Based on the decisions she made during and after her conference, Laura revised and edited her draft and handed in this final version of her essay.

The Price of Silence

Introduction (provides background)

In his essay "'What's in a Name?'" Henry Louis Gates Jr. recalls an incident from his past in which his father encountered prejudice and did not speak up. Perhaps he kept silent because he was afraid or because he knew that nothing he said or did would change the racial situation in Piedmont, West Virginia. Although I have never encountered the kind of prejudice Gates describes, I did have an experience in high school where, like Gates's father, I could have spoken out but did not. As I look back at the cheating incident that I witnessed, I realize that I have outgrown the immaturity and lack of confidence that made me keep silent.

Thesis statement

Narrative begins

In my senior year in high school I, along with fifteen other students, took advanced placement chemistry. The course was very demanding and required hours of studying every night. As the semester dragged on, it became clear to me, as well as to the other students in the class, that passing the course was not something we could take for granted. Test after test came back with grades that were well below the As and Bs I was used to getting in the regular chemistry course I had taken in tenth grade. By the time we were ready to take the final exam, most of us were worried that we would fail the course — despite the teacher's assurances that she would mark on a curve.

Key incident occurs

The final examination for advanced placement chemistry was given on a Friday morning between nine o'clock and noon. I had studied all that week, but, even so, I found the test difficult. I knew the material, but I had a hard time answering the long questions that were asked. As I struggled to balance a particularly complex equation, I noticed that the person sitting across from me was acting strangely. At first I thought I was imagining things, but as I stared I saw Jeff, my friend and study partner, fumbling with his test booklet. About a minute passed before I realized that he was copying material from a paper he had taped to the inside of his shirt cuff. After a short time, I stopped watching him and finished my test.

1

2

3

Narrative continues:
reactions to the
incident

It was not until after the test that I began thinking   4
about what I had seen. Surprisingly, when I mentioned the
incident to others in the class, they all knew what Jeff had done.
Some even thought that Jeff's actions were justified. "After all,"
one student said, "the test was hard." But the more I thought
about Jeff's actions, the angrier I got. It seemed unfair that I had
studied for weeks to memorize formulas and equations while all
Jeff had done was copy them onto a cheat sheet. For a moment I
considered going to the teacher, but I quickly rejected this idea.
Cheating was nothing new to me or to others in my school. Many
of my classmates cheated at one time or another. Most of us saw
school as a war between us and the teachers, and cheating was
just another weapon in our arsenal. The worst crime I could

Narrative ends

commit would be to turn Jeff in. As far as I was concerned, I
had no choice. I fell in line with the values of my high school
classmates and dismissed the incident as "no big deal."

Analysis of key
incident

Now that I am in college, however, I see the situation   5
differently. I find it hard to believe that I could ever have been so
complacent about cheating. The issues that were simple in high
school now seem complex — especially in light of the honor code
that I follow in college. I now ask questions that never would
have occurred to me in high school. What, for example, are the
implications of cheating? What would happen to the educational
system if cheating became the norm? What are my obligations
to all those who are involved in education? Aren't teachers and
students interested in achieving a common goal? The answers to
these questions give me a sense of the far-reaching effects of my
failure to act. If confronted with the same situation today, I know
I would speak out regardless of the consequences.

Jeff is now a first-year student at the state university and,   6
like me, he was given credit for AP chemistry. I feel certain that
by not turning him in, I failed not only myself but also Jeff. I
gave in to peer pressure instead of doing what I knew to be right.
The worst that would have happened to Jeff had I spoken up is
that he would have had to repeat chemistry in summer school.
By doing so, he would have proven to himself that he could, like
the rest of us in the class, pass on his own. In the long run, this
knowledge would have served him better than the knowledge that
he could cheat whenever he faced a difficult situation.

Conclusion
(aftermath
of incident)

Interestingly, Jeff and I are no longer very close. Whenever I   7
see him, I have the same reaction Henry Louis Gates Jr. had when
he met Mr. Wilson after he had insulted his father: "'I never again
looked [him] in the eye'" (7).

Work Cited

Gates, Henry Louis, Jr. "'What's in a Name?'" *Patterns for*
College Writing. 12th ed. Ed. Laurie G. Kirszner and
Stephen R. Mandell. Boston: Bedford, 2012. 2–4. Print.

With each draft of her essay, Laura sharpened the focus of her discussion. In the process, she clarified her thoughts about her subject and
reached some new and interesting conclusions. Although much of Laura's
paper is a narrative, it also includes a contrast between her current ideas
about cheating and the ideas she had in high school. Perhaps Laura could
have explained the reasons behind her current ideas about cheating more
fully. Even so, her paper gives a straightforward account of the incident
and analyzes its significance without drifting off into clichés or simplistic
moralizing. Especially effective is Laura's conclusion, in which she discusses the long-term effects of her experience and quotes Gates. By placing
this discussion at the end of her essay, she makes sure her readers will not
lose sight of the implications of her experience. Finally, Laura documents
the quotation she uses in her conclusion and includes a works-cited page
at the end of her essay.

Exercise 2

Use the checklist on page 68 to help you revise your draft. If you prefer,
outline your draft and use that outline to help you revise.

Exercise 3

Have another student read your second draft. Then, using the student's
peer critique checklist on page 70 as your guide, revise your draft.

Exercise 4

Using the essay on pages 77–79 as your guide, label the final draft of
your own essay. In addition to identifying your introduction, conclusion, and thesis statement, you should also label the main points of your
essay.

5

Editing and Proofreading

When you finish revising your essay, it is tempting to print it out, hand it in, and breathe a sigh of relief. This is one temptation you should resist. You still have to *edit* and *proofread* your paper to correct any problems that may remain after you revise.

When you **edit**, you search for grammatical errors, check punctuation, and look over your sentence style and word choice one last time. When you **proofread**, you look for surface errors, such as spelling errors, typos, incorrect spacing, or problems with your essay's format. The idea is to look carefully for any error, no matter how small, that might weaken your essay's message or undermine your credibility. Remember, this is your last chance to make sure your essay says exactly what you want it to say.

Editing for Grammar

As you edit, keep in mind that certain grammatical errors occur more frequently than others — and even more frequently in particular kinds of writing. By concentrating on these errors, as well as on those errors you yourself are most likely to make, you will learn to edit your essays quickly and efficiently.

Learning the few rules that follow will help you identify the most common errors. Later on, when you practice writing essays in various patterns of development, you can use the **Grammar in Context** section in each chapter to help you correct any errors you find.

Be Sure Subjects and Verbs Agree

Subjects and verbs must agree in number. A singular subject takes a singular verb.

Stephanie Ericsson discusses ten kinds of liars.

A plural subject takes a plural verb.

Chronic liars are different from occasional liars.

Liars and plagiarists have a lot in common.

For information on editing for subject-verb agreement with indefinite pronoun subjects, see the Grammar in Context section of Chapter 15 (page 657).

Be Sure Verb Tenses Are Accurate and Consistent

Unintentional shifts in verb tense can be confusing to readers. Verb tenses in the same passage should be the same unless you are referring to two different time periods.

Single time period:

past tense
Lee surrendered to Grant on April 9, 1865, and then he addressed his men.
past tense

Two different time periods:

In "Two Ways to Belong in America," Bharati Mukherjee compares herself
present tense
and her sister, both of whom emigrated
past tense
from India.

For more information on editing for consistent verb tenses, as well as to eliminate unwarranted shifts in voice, person, and mood, see the Grammar in Context section of Chapter 9 (page 268).

Be Sure Pronoun References Are Clear

A pronoun is a word that takes the place of a noun in a sentence. Every pronoun should clearly refer to a specific **antecedent**, the word (a noun or pronoun) it replaces. Pronouns and antecedents must agree in number.

- Singular pronouns refer to singular antecedents.

When she was attacked, Kitty Genovese was on her way home.

- Plural pronouns refer to plural antecedents.

The people who watched the attack gave different reasons for their failure to help.

For information on editing for pronoun-antecedent agreement with indefinite pronouns, see the Grammar in Context section of Chapter 15 (page 658).

Be Sure Sentences Are Complete

A **sentence** is a group of words that includes a subject and a verb and expresses a complete thought. A **fragment** is an incomplete sentence, one that is missing a subject, a verb, or both a subject and a verb — or that has a subject and a verb but does not express a complete thought.

Sentence:	Although it was written in 1963, Martin Luther King's "Letter from Birmingham Jail" remains powerful today.
Fragment (no subject):	Remains powerful today.
Fragment (no verb):	Martin Luther King's "Letter from Birmingham Jail."
Fragment (no subject or verb):	Written in 1963.
Fragment (includes subject and verb but does not express a complete thought):	Although it was written in 1963.

To correct a sentence fragment, you need to supply the missing part of the sentence (a subject, a verb, or both — or an entire independent clause). Often, you will find that the missing words appear in an adjacent sentence in your essay.

Be Careful Not to Run Sentences Together without Proper Punctuation

There are two kinds of **run-ons**: *comma splices* and *fused sentences.*

A **comma splice** is an error that occurs when two independent clauses are connected by just a comma.

Comma splice:	Women who live alone need to learn to protect themselves, sometimes this means carrying a gun.

A **fused sentence** is an error that occurs when two independent clauses are connected without any punctuation.

Fused sentence:	Residents of isolated rural areas may carry guns for protection sometimes these guns may be used against them.

For more information on editing run-ons, including additional ways to correct them, see the Grammar in Context section of Chapter 6 (page 102).

Be Careful to Avoid Misplaced and Dangling Modifiers

Modifiers are words and phrases that describe other words in a sentence. To avoid confusion, place modifiers as close as possible to the words they modify.

Limited by their illiteracy, millions of Americans are ashamed to seek help.

Hoping to draw attention to their plight, Jonathan Kozol wrote *Illiterate America.*

A **misplaced modifier** appears to modify the wrong word because it is placed incorrectly in the sentence.

Misplaced modifier: Judith Ortiz Cofer wonders why Latin women are so often stereotyped as either "hot tamales" or low-level workers in her essay "The Myth of the Latin Woman: I Just Met a Girl Named Maria" (232). (*Does Cofer's essay stereotype Latin women?*)

Correct: In her essay "The Myth of the Latin Woman: I Just Met a Girl Named Maria," Judith Ortiz Cofer wonders why Latin women are so often stereotyped as either "hot tamales" or low-level workers (232).

A **dangling modifier** "dangles" because it cannot logically describe any word in the sentence.

Dangling modifier: Going back to his old junior high school, the "black table" was still there. (*Who went back to his old school?*)

Correct: Going back to his old junior high school, Graham discovered that the "black table" was still there.

For more information on editing to correct misplaced and dangling modifiers, see the Grammar in Context section of Chapter 7 (page 160).

Be Sure Sentence Elements Are Parallel

Parallelism is the use of matching grammatical elements (words, phrases, clauses) to express similar ideas. Used effectively — for example, with paired items or items in a series — parallelism makes the links between related ideas clear and emphasizes connections.

Paired items: As Deborah Tannen points out, men speak more than women in public but less than women at home (423).

Items in a series: Amy Tan says, "I spend a great deal of my time thinking about the power of language — the way it can evoke an emotion, a visual image, a complex idea, or a simple truth" (466).

Faulty parallelism — using items that are not parallel in a context in which parallelism is expected — makes ideas difficult to follow and will likely confuse your readers.

Faulty parallelism: As Deborah Tannen points out, men speak more than women in public, but at home less talking is done by them (423).

Faulty parallelism: Amy Tan says, "I spend a great deal of my time thinking about the power of language — the way it can evoke an emotion, visual images, or complex ideas can be suggested, or communicate a simple truth" (466).

For more information on using parallelism to strengthen your writing, see the Grammar in Context section of Chapter 11 (page 378).

✔**CHECKLIST**   **Editing for Grammar**

- **Subject-verb agreement** Do all your verbs agree with their subjects? Remember that singular subjects take singular verbs, and plural subjects take plural verbs.
- **Verb tenses** Are all your verb tenses accurate and consistent? Have you avoided unnecessary shifts in tense?
- **Pronoun reference** Do pronouns clearly refer to their antecedents?
- **Fragments** Does each group of words punctuated as a sentence have both a subject and a verb and express a complete thought? If not, can you correct the fragment by adding the missing words or by attaching it to an adjacent sentence?
- **Run-ons** Have you been careful not to connect two independent clauses without the necessary punctuation? Have you avoided comma splices and fused sentences?
- **Modification** Does every modifier point clearly to the word it modifies? Have you avoided misplaced and dangling modifiers?
- **Parallelism** Have you used matching words, phrases, or clauses to express equivalent ideas? Have you avoided faulty parallelism?

For practice in editing for grammar, visit the resources for Chapter 5 at **bedfordstmartins.com/patterns**.

Editing for Punctuation

Like grammatical errors, certain punctuation errors are more common than others, particularly in certain contexts. By understanding a few punctuation rules, you can learn to identify and correct these errors in your writing.

Learn When to Use Commas — and When Not to Use Them

Commas separate certain elements of a sentence. They are used most often in the following situations:

- To separate an introductory phrase or clause from the rest of the sentence

In "Only Daughter," Sandra Cisneros writes about her father.

According to Cisneros, he is very critical of her.

Although her father has six sons, she is the only daughter.

NOTE: Do not use a comma if a dependent clause *follows* an independent clause: She is the only daughter although her father has six sons.

- To separate two independent clauses that are joined by a coordinating conjunction

Cisneros tries to please her father, but he is not impressed.

- To separate elements in a series

Cisneros has written stories, essays, poems, and a novel.

For more information on using commas in a series, see the Grammar in Context section of Chapter 8 (page 217).

- To separate a **nonrestrictive clause** (a clause that does not supply information that is essential to the sentence's meaning) from the rest of the sentence

Cisneros, who is the only daughter, feels her father would prefer her to be a son.

NOTE: Do not use commas to set off a **restrictive clause** (a clause that supplies information that is vital to the sentence's meaning): The child who is overlooked is often the daughter.

Learn When to Use Semicolons

Semicolons, like commas, separate certain elements of a sentence. However, semicolons separate only grammatically equivalent elements — for example, two closely related independent clauses.

In Burma, George Orwell learned something about the nature of imperialism; it was not an easy lesson.

Shirley Jackson's "The Lottery" is fiction; however, many early readers thought it was a true story.

In most cases, commas separate items in a series. However, when one or more of the items in a series already include commas, separate the items with semicolons. This will make the sentence easier to follow.

Orwell set his works in <u>Paris, France</u>; <u>London, England</u>; and <u>Moulmein, Burma</u>.

Learn When to Use Quotation Marks

Quotation marks are used to set off quoted speech or writing.

At the end of his essay, E. B. White feels "the chill of death" (199).

Special rules govern the use of other punctuation marks with quotation marks:

- Commas and periods are always placed before quotation marks.

- Colons and semicolons are always placed after quotation marks.

- Question marks and exclamation points can go either before or after quotation marks, depending on whether or not they are part of the quoted material.

Quotation marks are also used to set off the titles of essays ("Once More to the Lake"), stories ("The Lottery"), and poems ("Sadie and Maud").

NOTE: Italics are used to set off titles of books, periodicals, and plays: *Life on the Mississippi, College English, Hamlet.*

For information on formatting quotations in research papers, see Chapter 17.

Learn When to Use Dashes and Colons

Dashes are occasionally used to set off and emphasize information within a sentence.

Jessica Mitford wrote a scathing critique of the funeral industry — and touched off an uproar. Her book *The American Way of Death* was widely read around the world.

However, because this usage is somewhat informal, dashes should be used in moderation in your college writing.

Colons are used to introduce lists, examples, and clarifications. A colon should always be preceded by a complete sentence.

As Norman Cousins observes in "Who Killed Benny Paret?" one simple cause was ultimately responsible for Paret's death: the fact that spectators came to the fight expecting to see a knockout.

For more information on using colons, see the Grammar in Context section of Chapter 12 (page 441).

> ✔ **CHECKLIST**   **Editing for Punctuation**
>
> - **Commas** Have you used commas when necessary — and only when necessary?
> - **Semicolons** Have you used semicolons only between grammatically equivalent elements?
> - **Quotation marks** Have you used quotation marks to set off quoted speech or writing and to set off titles of essays, stories, and poems? Have you used other punctuation correctly with quotation marks?
> - **Dashes and colons** Have you used dashes in moderation? Is every colon that introduces a list, an example, or a clarification preceded by a complete sentence?

For practice in editing for punctuation, visit the resources for Chapter 5 at **bedfordstmartins.com/patterns**.

Exercise 1

Reread the essay you wrote in Chapters 2–4, and edit it for grammar and punctuation.

🖥 TECH TIP: Editing

Just as you do when you revise, you should edit on a hard copy of your essay. Seeing your work on the printed page makes it easy for you to spot surface-level errors in grammar and punctuation. You can also run a grammar check to help you find grammar and punctuation errors, but you should keep in mind that grammar checkers are far from perfect. They often miss errors (such as faulty modification), and they frequently highlight areas of text (such as a long sentence) that may not contain an error.

Exercise 2

Run a grammar check, and then make any additional corrections you think are necessary.

Editing for Sentence Style and Word Choice

As you edit your essay for grammar and punctuation, you should also be looking one last time at how you construct sentences and choose words. So that your essay is as clear, readable, and convincing as possible, your sentences should be not only correct but also concise and varied. In addition, every word should mean exactly what you want it to mean, and your language should be free of clichés.

Eliminate Awkward Phrasing

As you review your essay's sentences, check carefully for awkward phrasing, and do your best to smooth it out.

Awkward: The reason Jefferson drafted the Declaration of Independence <u>was because</u> he felt the king was a tyrant.

Correct: The reason Jefferson drafted the Declaration of Independence <u>was that</u> he felt the king was a tyrant.

For more information about this error, see the Grammar in Context section of Chapter 10 (page 331).

Awkward: *Work* <u>is where</u> you earn money.

Correct: *Work* <u>is the activity</u> you do to earn money.

For more information about this error, see the Grammar in Context section of Chapter 13 (page 495).

Be Sure Your Sentences Are Concise

A **concise** sentence is efficient; it is not overloaded with extra words and complicated constructions. To make sentences concise, you need to eliminate repetition and redundancy, delete empty words and expressions, and cut everything that is not absolutely necessary.

Wordy: Brent Staples's essay "Just Walk On By" explores his feelings, thoughts, and ideas about various events and experiences that were painful to him as a black man living in a large metropolitan city.

Concise: Brent Staples's essay "Just Walk On By" explores his ideas about his painful experiences as a black man living in a large city.

Be Sure Your Sentences Are Varied

To add interest to your paper, vary the length and structure of your sentences, and vary the way you open them.

- Mix long and short sentences.

  As time went on, and as he saw people's hostile reactions to him, Staples grew more and more uneasy. Then, he had an idea.

- Mix simple, compound, and complex sentences.

  Simple sentence (*one independent clause*): Staples grew more and more uneasy.

  Compound sentence (*two independent clauses*): Staples grew more and more uneasy, but he stood his ground.

Complex sentence (*dependent clause, independent clause*): Although Staples grew more and more uneasy, he continued to walk in the neighborhood.

For more information on how to form compound and complex sentences, see the Grammar in Context section of Chapter 14 (page 543).

• Vary your sentence openings. Instead of beginning every sentence with the subject (particularly with a pronoun like *he* or *this*), begin some sentences with an introductory word, phrase, or clause that ties it to the preceding sentence.

The 1964 murder of Kitty Genovese, discussed in Martin Gansberg's "Thirty-Eight Who Saw Murder Didn't Call the Police," remains relevant today for a number of reasons. For one thing, urban crime remains a problem, particularly for women. Moreover, many people are still reluctant to report crimes. Although nearly fifty years have gone by, the story of Kitty Genovese and the people who watched her die and did nothing still stirs strong emotional responses.

Choose Your Words Carefully

• Choose **specific** words that identify particular examples and details.

Vague: Violence in sports is a bad thing.

Specific: Violence in boxing is a serious problem that threatens not just the lives of the boxers but also the sport itself.

• Avoid **clichés**, overused expressions that rely on tired figures of speech.

Clichés: When he was hit, the boxer stood for a moment like a deer caught in the headlights, and then he fell to the mat like a ton of bricks.

Revised: When he was hit, the boxer stood frozen for a moment, and then he fell to the mat.

✔**CHECKLIST**   Editing for Sentence Style and Word Choice

• **Awkward phrasing** Have you eliminated awkward constructions?
• **Concise sentences** Have you eliminated repetition, empty phrases, and excess words? Is every sentence as concise as it can be?
• **Varied sentences** Have you varied the length and structure of your sentences? Have you varied your sentence openings?
• **Word choice** Have you selected specific words? Have you eliminated clichés?

For practice in editing for sentence style and word choice, visit the resources for Chapter 5 online at **bedfordstmartins.com/patterns**.

<u>Exercise 3</u>

Check your essay's sentence style and word choice.

Proofreading Your Essay

When you proofread, you check your essay for surface errors, such as commonly confused words, misspellings, faulty capitalization, and incorrect italic use; then, you check for typographical errors.

Check for Commonly Confused Words

Even if you have carefully considered your choice of words during the editing stage, you may have missed some errors. As you proofread, look carefully to see if you can spot any **commonly confused words** — *its* for *it's, there* for *their,* or *affect* for *effect,* for example — that a spell check will not catch.

For more information on how to distinguish between *affect* and *effect,* see the Grammar in Context section of Chapter 10 (page 332).

Check for Misspellings and Faulty Capitalization

It makes no sense to work hard on an essay and then undermine your credibility with spelling and mechanical errors. If you have any doubt about how a word is spelled or whether or not to capitalize it, check a dictionary (in print or online).

Check for Typos

The last step in the proofreading process is to read carefully and look for typos. Make sure you have spaced correctly between words and have not accidentally typed an extra letter, omitted a letter, or transposed two letters. Reading your essay *backwards* — one sentence at a time — will help you focus on individual sentences, which in turn will help you see errors more clearly.

✔**CHECKLIST**   Proofreading

- **Commonly confused words** Have you proofread for errors involving words that are often confused with each other?
- **Misspelled words and faulty capitalization** Have you proofread for errors in spelling and capitalization? Have you run a spell check?
- **Typos** Have you checked carefully to eliminate typing errors?

For more practice with proofreading, visit the resources for Chapter 5 online at **bedfordstmartins.com/patterns**.

⬛ TECH TIP: Spell Checkers

You should certainly run a spell check to help you locate misspelled words and incorrect strings of letters caused by typos, but keep in mind that a spell checker will not find every error. For example, it will not identify many misspelled proper nouns or foreign words, nor will it highlight words that are spelled correctly but used incorrectly — *work* for *word* or *form* for *from*, for example. For this reason, you must still proofread carefully — even after you run a spell check.

Exercise 4

Proofread your essay.

Checking Your Paper's Format

The final thing to consider is your paper's **format** — how your paragraphs, sentences, and words look on the page. Your instructor will give you some general guidelines about format — telling you, for example, to type your last name and the page number at the top right of each page — and, of course, you should follow these guidelines. Students writing in the humanities usually follow the format illustrated below. (For information on MLA documentation format, see Chapter 18.)

1″ ↑ ↓ 1/2″

Lau 1 ↑

Last name and page number

Phillip Lau
Professor Carroll
ENG 101
23 Nov. 2011

Double-space

The Limitations of *Wikipedia* ← *Title (centered)*

When they get a research assignment, many students immediately go to the Internet to find sources. Searching the

1″ ←→ Web, they may discover a *Wikipedia* article on their topic. But is ←→ 1″

Wikipedia a reliable reference source for a research paper? There is quite a controversy over the use of *Wikipedia* as a source, but the answer seems to be no. Although *Wikipedia* may be a good starting point for general information about a topic, college-level research papers should rely on authoritative sources.

> **✓CHECKLIST**   **Checking Your Paper's Format**
>
> - **Format** Have you followed your instructor's format guidelines?
> - **Spacing** Have you double-spaced throughout?
> - **Type size** Have you used ten- or twelve-point type?
> - **Paragraphing** Have you indented the first line of every paragraph?
> - **Visuals** If you used one or more visuals in your essay, did you insert each visual as close as possible to where it is discussed?
> - **Documentation** Have you documented each source — and each visual — you used? Have you included a works-cited page?

Exercise 5

Make any necessary corrections to your essay's format, and then print out a final draft.

PART TWO

Readings for Writers

The relationship between reading and writing is a complex one. Sometimes you will write an essay based on your own experience; more often than not, however, you will respond in writing to something you have read. The essays in this book give you a chance to do both.

As you are probably aware, the fact that information appears in print or on the Internet does not mean it should be taken at face value. Of course, many of the books and articles you read will be reliable, but some — especially material found on many Web sites and blogs — will include contradictions, biased ideas, or even inaccurate or misleading information. For this reason, your goal should not be simply to understand what you read but to assess the credibility of the writers and, eventually, to judge the soundness of their ideas.

When you read the essays in this book, you should approach them critically. In other words, you should question (and sometimes challenge) the writer's ideas — and, in the process, try to create new interpretations that you can explore in your writing. Approaching a text in this way is not easy, for it requires you to develop your own analytical and critical skills and your own set of standards to help you judge and interpret what you read. Only after you have read and critically evaluated a text can you begin to draw your ideas together and write about them.

Every reading selection in Chapters 6 through 15 is accompanied by a series of questions intended to guide you through the reading process. In many ways, these questions are a warm-up for the intellectual workout of writing an essay. The more time you devote to them, the more you will be practicing your analytical skills. In a real sense, then, these questions will help you develop the critical thinking skills you will need when you write. In becoming a proficient reader, you will also gain confidence in yourself as a writer.

Each of the reading selections in Chapters 6 through 14 is organized around one dominant pattern of development. In your outside reading, however, you will often find more than one pattern used in a single piece of writing (as in Chapter 15, Combining the Patterns, page 655). When you write, then, do not feel you must follow these patterns blindly; instead, think of them as tools for making your writing more effective, and adapt them to your subject, your audience, and your purpose for writing.

In addition to the reading selections, each chapter also includes a visual text — for example, a piece of fine art, an advertisement, or a photograph. By visually reinforcing the chapter's basic rhetorical concept, each visual text serves as a bridge to the chapter's essays. Following each visual is a set of questions designed to help you understand not just the image but also the rhetorical pattern that is the chapter's focus.

6

Narration

What Is Narration?

Narration tells a story by presenting events in an orderly, logical sequence. In the following paragraph from "The Stone Horse," essayist Barry Lopez recounts the history of the exploration of the California desert.

Topic sentence

Western man did not enter the California desert until the end of the eighteenth century, 250 years after Coronado brought his soldiers into the Zuni pueblos in a bewildered search for the cities of Cibola. The earliest appraisals of the land were cursory, hurried. People traveled *through* it, en route to Santa Fe or the California coastal settlements.

Narrative traces developments through the nineteenth century

Only miners tarried. In 1823 what had been Spain's became Mexico's, and in 1848 what had been Mexico's became America's; but the bare, jagged mountains and dry lake beds, the vast and uniform plains of creosote bush and yucca plants, remained as obscure as the northern Sudan until the end of the nineteenth century.

Narration can be the dominant pattern in many kinds of writing (as well as in speech). Histories, biographies, and autobiographies follow a narrative form, as do personal letters, diaries, journals, and bios on personal Web pages or social networking sites, such as Facebook. Narration is the dominant pattern in many works of fiction and poetry, and it is an essential part of casual conversation. Narration also underlies folk and fairy tales and radio and television news reports. In short, anytime you tell what happened, you are using narration.

Using Narration

Narration can provide the structure for an entire essay, but narrative passages may also appear in essays that are not primarily narrative. In an argumentative essay supporting stricter gun-safety legislation, for example, you might devote one or two paragraphs to the story of a child accidentally killed by a handgun. In this chapter, however, we focus on narration as the dominant pattern of a piece of writing.

During your college career, many of your assignments will call for narration. In an English composition class, you may be asked to write about an experience that was important to your development as an adult; on a European history exam, you may need to relate the events that led to Napoleon's defeat at the Battle of Waterloo; and in a technical writing class, you may be asked to write a letter of complaint tracing a company's negligent actions. In each of these situations (as well as in many additional assignments), your writing has a primarily narrative structure, and the narrative supports a particular thesis.

The skills you develop in narrative writing will also help you in other kinds of writing. A *process essay,* such as an explanation of a laboratory experiment, is like a narrative because it outlines a series of steps in chronological order; a *cause-and-effect essay,* such as your answer to an exam question that asks you to analyze the events that caused the Great Depression, also resembles a narrative in that it traces a sequence of events. Although a process essay explains how to do something and a cause-and-effect essay explains why events occur, writing both these kinds of essays will be easier after you master narration. (Process essays and cause-and-effect essays are dealt with in Chapters 9 and 10, respectively.)

Planning a Narrative Essay

Developing a Thesis Statement

Although the purpose of a narrative may be simply to recount events or to create a particular mood or impression, in college writing a narrative essay is more likely to present a sequence of events for the purpose of supporting a thesis. For instance, in a narrative about your problems with credit card debt, your purpose may be to show your readers that college students should not have easy access to credit cards. Accordingly, you do not simply tell the story of your unwise spending. Rather, you select and arrange details to show your readers why having a credit card encouraged you to spend money you didn't have. Although it is usually best to include an explicit **thesis statement** ("My negative experiences with credit have convinced me that college students should not have access to credit cards"), you may also imply your thesis through your selection and arrangement of events.

Including Enough Detail

Narratives, like other types of writing, need rich, specific details if they are to be convincing. Each detail should help to create a picture for the reader; even exact times, dates, and geographic locations can be helpful.

Look, for example, at the following paragraph from the essay "My Mother Never Worked" by Bonnie Smith-Yackel, which appears later in this chapter:

> In the winter she sewed night after night, endlessly, begging cast-off clothing from relatives, ripping apart coats, dresses, blouses, and trousers to remake them to fit her four daughters and son. Every morning and every evening she milked cows, fed pigs and calves, cared for chickens, picked eggs, cooked meals, washed dishes, scrubbed floors, and tended and loved her children. In the spring she planted a garden once more, dragging pails of water to nourish and sustain the vegetables for the family. In 1936 she lost a baby in her sixth month.

This list of details adds interest and authenticity to the narrative. The central figure in the narrative is a busy, productive woman, and readers know this because they are given an exhaustive catalog of her activities.

Varying Sentence Structure

When narratives present a long series of events, all the sentences can begin to sound alike: "She sewed dresses. She milked cows. She fed pigs. She fed calves. She cared for chickens." Such a predictable string of sentences may become monotonous for your readers. You can eliminate this monotony by varying your sentence structure — for instance, by using a variety of sentence openings or by combining simple sentences as Smith-Yackel does: "In the winter she sewed night after night, endlessly. . . . Every morning and every evening she milked cows, fed pigs and calves, cared for chickens. . . ."

Maintaining Clear Narrative Order

Many narratives present events in the exact order in which they occurred, moving from first event to last. Whether or not you follow a strict **chronological order** depends on the purpose of your narrative. If you are writing a straightforward account of a historical event or summarizing a record of poor management practices, you will probably want to move directly from beginning to end. In a personal-experience essay or a fictional narrative, however, you may want to engage your readers' interest by beginning with an event from the middle of your story, or even from the end, and then presenting the events that led up to it. You may also decide to begin in the present and then use one or more **flashbacks** (shifts into the past) to tell your story. To help readers follow the order of events in your narrative, it is very important to use correct verb tenses and clear transitional words and phrases.

Using Accurate Verb Tenses. Verb tense is extremely important in writing that recounts events in a fixed order because tenses indicate temporal (time) relationships. When you write a narrative, you should be careful to keep verb tenses consistent and accurate so that your readers can follow the sequence of events. Naturally, you must shift tenses to reflect an actual time shift in your narrative. For instance, convention requires that you use present tense when discussing works of literature ("When Hamlet's mother *marries* his uncle . . ."), but a flashback to an earlier point in the story calls for a shift from present to past tense ("Before their marriage, Hamlet *was* . . ."). Nevertheless, you should avoid unwarranted shifts in verb tense; they will make your narrative confusing.

Using Transitions. Transitions — connecting words or phrases — help link events in time, enabling narratives to flow smoothly. Without them, narratives would lack coherence, and readers would be unsure of the correct sequence of events. Transitions indicate the order of events, and they also signal shifts in time. In narrative writing, the transitions commonly used for these purposes include *first, second, next, then, later, at the same time, meanwhile, immediately, soon, before, earlier, after, afterward, now, and finally.* In addition to these transitional words and phrases, specific time markers — such as *three years later, in 1927, after two hours,* and *on January 3* — indicate how much time has passed between events. (A more complete list of transitions appears on page 57.)

Structuring a Narrative Essay

Like other essays, a **narrative** essay has an introduction, a body, and a conclusion. If your essay's thesis is explicitly stated, it will, in most cases, appear in the **introduction**. The **body paragraphs** of your essay will recount the events that make up your narrative, following a clear and orderly plan. Finally, the **conclusion** will give your readers the sense that your narrative is complete, perhaps by restating your thesis or by summarizing key points or events.

Suppose you are assigned a short history paper about the Battle of Waterloo. You plan to support the thesis that if Napoleon had kept more troops in reserve, he might have defeated the British troops serving under Wellington. Based on this thesis, you decide that the best way to organize your paper is to present the five major phases of the battle in chronological order. An informal outline of your essay might look like this:

SAMPLE OUTLINE: Narration

Introduction:	Thesis statement — If Napoleon had kept more troops in reserve, he might have broken Wellington's line with another infantry attack and thus won the Battle of Waterloo.
Phase 1 of the battle:	Napoleon attacked the Château of Hougoumont.
Phase 2 of the battle:	The French infantry attacked the British lines.

Phase 3 of the battle:	The French cavalry staged a series of charges against the British lines that had not been attacked before; Napoleon committed his reserves.
Phase 4 of the battle:	The French captured La Haye Sainte, their first success of the day but an advantage that Napoleon, having committed troops elsewhere, could not maintain without reserves.
Phase 5 of the battle:	The French infantry was decisively defeated by the combined thrust of the British infantry and the remaining British cavalry.
Conclusion:	Restatement of thesis or review of key points or events.

By discussing the five phases of the battle in chronological order, you clearly support your thesis. As you expand your informal outline into a historical narrative, exact details, dates, times, and geographic locations are extremely important. Without them, your statements are open to question. In addition, to keep your readers aware of the order of events, you must select appropriate transitional words and phrases and pay careful attention to verb tenses.

Revising a Narrative Essay

When you revise a narrative essay, consider the items on the revision checklist on page 68. In addition, pay special attention to the items on the following checklist, which apply specifically to revising narrative essays.

✔ REVISION CHECKLIST   **Narration**

- Does your assignment call for narration?
- Does your essay's thesis communicate the significance of the events you discuss?
- Have you included enough specific detail?
- Have you varied your sentence structure?
- Is the order of events clear to readers?
- Have you varied sentence openings and combined short sentences to avoid monotony?
- Do your transitions indicate the order of events and signal shifts in time?

Editing a Narrative Essay

When you edit your narrative essay, follow the guidelines on the editing checklists on pages 85, 88, and 90. In addition, focus on the grammar, mechanics, and punctuation issues that are particularly relevant to narrative essays. One of these issues — avoiding run-on sentences — is discussed below.

GRAMMAR IN CONTEXT　Avoiding Run-ons

When writing narrative essays, particularly personal narratives and essays that include dialogue, writers can easily lose sight of sentence boundaries and create **run-ons**. There are two kinds of run-ons: *fused sentences* and *comma splices*.

A **fused sentence** occurs when two sentences are incorrectly joined without punctuation.

TWO CORRECT SENTENCES:	"The sun came out hot and bright, endlessly, day after day. The crops shriveled and died" (Smith-Yackel 122).
FUSED SENTENCE:	The sun came out hot and bright, endlessly, day after day the crops shriveled and died.

A **comma splice** occurs when two sentences are incorrectly joined with just a comma.

COMMA SPLICE:	The sun came out hot and bright, endlessly, day after day, the crops shriveled and died.

Five Ways to Correct These Errors

1. **Use a period to create two separate sentences.**

   The sun came out hot and bright, endlessly, day after day. The crops shriveled and died.

2. **Join the sentences with a comma and a coordinating conjunction (*and, or, nor, for, so, but, yet*).**

   The sun came out hot and bright, endlessly, day after day, and the crops shriveled and died.

3. **Join the sentences with a semicolon.**

   The sun came out hot and bright, endlessly, day after day; the crops shriveled and died.

4. **Join the sentences with a semicolon and a transitional word or phrase (followed by a comma), such as *however, therefore,* or *for example*. (See page 57 for a list of transitional words and phrases.)**

   The sun came out hot and bright, endlessly, day after day; eventually, the crops shriveled and died.

5. **Create a complex sentence by adding a subordinating conjunction (*although, because, if,* and so on) or a relative pronoun (*who, which, that,* and so on) to one of the sentences.**

   As the sun came out hot and bright, endlessly, day after day, the crops shriveled and died.

For more practice in avoiding run-ons, visit the resources for Chapter 6 at **bedfordstmartins.com/patterns**.

✔**EDITING CHECKLIST**   Narration

- Have you avoided run-ons?
- Do your verb tenses clearly indicate time relationships between events?
- Have you avoided unnecessary tense shifts?
- If you use dialogue, have you punctuated correctly and capitalized where necessary?

A STUDENT WRITER: Narration

The following essay is typical of the informal narrative writing many students are asked to do in English composition classes. It was written by Tiffany Forte in response to the assignment "Write an informal essay about a goal or dream you had when you were a child."

My Field of Dreams

Introduction   When I was young, I was told that when I grew up I could   1
be anything I wanted to be, and I always took for granted that
this was true. I knew exactly what I was going to be, and I would
spend hours dreaming about how wonderful my life would be when

Thesis statement   I grew up. One day, though, when I did grow up, I realized that
things had not turned out the way I had always expected they
would.

Narrative begins   When I was little, I never played with baby dolls or Barbies.   2
I wasn't like other little girls; I was a tomboy. I was the only girl
in the neighborhood where I lived, so I always played with boys.
We would play army or football or (my favorite) baseball.

Almost every summer afternoon, all the boys in my   3
neighborhood and I would meet by the big oak tree to get a
baseball game going. Surprisingly, I was always one of the first to
be picked for a team. I was very fast, and (for my size) I could hit
the ball far. I loved baseball more than anything, and I wouldn't
miss a game for the world.

My dad played baseball too, and every Friday night I would   4
go to the field with my mother to watch him play. It was just like
the big leagues, with lots of people, a snack bar, and lights that
shone so high and bright you could see them a mile away. I loved
to go to my dad's games. When all the other kids would wander

off and play, I would sit and cheer on my dad and his team. My attention was focused on the field, and my heart would jump with every pitch.

Even more exciting than my dad's games were the major league games. The Phillies were my favorite team, and I always looked forward to watching them on television. My dad would make popcorn, and we would sit and watch in anticipation of a Phillies victory. We would go wild, yelling and screaming at all the big plays. When the Phillies would win, I would be so excited I couldn't sleep; when they would lose, I would go to bed angry, just like my dad.

Key experience introduced (pars. 6–7)

It was when my dad took me to my first Phillies game that I decided I wanted to be a major league baseball player. The excitement began when we pulled into the parking lot of the old Veterans Stadium. There were thousands of cars. As we walked from the car to the stadium, my dad told me to hold on to his hand and not to let go no matter what. When we gave the man our tickets and entered the stadium, I understood why. There were mobs of people everywhere. They were walking around the stadium and standing in long lines for hot dogs, beer, and souvenirs. It was the most wonderful thing I had ever seen. When we got to our seats, I looked down at the tiny baseball diamond below and felt as if I were on top of the world.

The cheering of the crowd, the singing, and the chants were almost more than I could stand. I was bursting with enthusiasm. Then, in the bottom of the eighth inning, with the score tied and two outs, Mike Schmidt came up to bat and hit the game-winning home run. The crowd went crazy. Everyone in the whole stadium was standing, and I found myself yelling and screaming along with everyone else. When Mike Schmidt came out of the dugout to receive his standing ovation, I felt a lump in my throat and butterflies in my stomach. He was everyone's hero that night, and I could only imagine the pride he must have felt. I slept the whole way home and dreamed of what it would be like to be the hero of the game.

Narrative continues

The next day, when I met with the boys at the oak tree, I told them that when I grew up, I was going to be a major league baseball player. They all laughed at me and said I could never be a baseball player because I was a girl. I told them that they were all wrong and that I would show them.

Analysis of childhood experiences   In the years to follow, I played girls' softball in a   9
competitive fast-pitch league, and I was very good. I always
wanted to play baseball with the boys, but there were no mixed
leagues. After a few years, I realized that the boys from the oak
tree were right: I was never going to be a major league baseball
player. I realized that what I had been told when I was younger
wasn't the whole truth. What no one had bothered to tell me
was that I could be anything I wanted to be — as long as it was
something that was appropriate for a girl to do.

Conclusion   In time, I would get over the loss of my dream. I found new   10
dreams, acceptable for a young woman, and I moved on to other
things. Still, every time I watch a baseball game and someone hits
a home run, I get those same butterflies in my stomach and think,
for just a minute, about what might have been.

Points for Special Attention

Assignment. Tiffany's assignment was to write about a goal or dream
she had when she was a child. As a nontraditional student, a good deal
older than most of her classmates, Tiffany found this assignment challenging at first. She wondered if her childhood dreams would be different
from those of her classmates, and she was somewhat hesitant to share her
drafts with her peer editing group. As it turned out, though, her childhood
dreams were not very different from those of the other students in her
class.

Introduction. Tiffany's introduction is straightforward, yet it arouses
reader interest by setting up a contrast between what she expected and what
actually happened. Her optimistic expectation — that she could be anything
she wanted to be — is contradicted by her thesis statement, encouraging
readers to read on to learn how things turned out and why.

Thesis Statement. Although the assignment called for a personal
narrative, the instructor made it clear that the essay should have an
explicitly stated thesis that made a point about a childhood goal or dream.
Tiffany knew she wanted to write about her passion for baseball, but she
also knew that just listing a series of events would not fulfill the assignment.
Her thesis statement — "One day, though, when I did grow up, I realized
that things had not turned out the way I had always expected they
would" — puts her memories in context, suggesting that she will use them
to support a general conclusion about the gap between dreams and reality.

Structure. The body of Tiffany's essay traces the chronology of her
involvement with baseball — playing with the neighborhood boys,
watching her father's games, watching baseball on television, and, finally,

attending her first major league game. Each body paragraph introduces a different aspect of her experience with baseball, culminating in the vividly described Phillies game. The balance of the essay (paragraphs 8–10) summarizes the aftermath of that game, gives a brief overview of Tiffany's later years in baseball, and presents her conclusion.

Detail. Personal narratives like Tiffany's need a lot of detail because the writers want readers to see and hear and feel what they did. To present an accurate picture, Tiffany includes all the significant sights and sounds she can remember: the big oak tree, the lights on the field, the popcorn, the excited cheers, the food and souvenir stands, the crowds, and so on. She also names Mike Schmidt ("everyone's hero"), his team, and the stadium where she saw him play. Despite all these details, though, she omits some important information — for example, how old she was at each stage of her essay.

Working with Sources. Tiffany's essay is very personal, and she supports her thesis with experiences and observations from her own childhood. Although she could have consulted sources to find specific information about team standings or players' stats — or even quoted her hero, Mike Schmidt — she decided that her own memories would provide convincing support for her thesis.

Verb Tense. Maintaining clear chronological order is very important in narrative writing, where unwarranted shifts in verb tenses can confuse readers. Knowing this, Tiffany avoids unnecessary tense shifts. In her conclusion, she shifts from past to present tense, but this shift is both necessary and clear. Elsewhere she uses *would* to identify events that recurred regularly. For example, in paragraph 5 she says, "My dad *would* make popcorn" rather than "My dad *made* popcorn," which would have suggested that he did so only once.

Transitions. Tiffany's skillful use of transitional words and expressions links her sentences and moves her readers smoothly through her essay. In addition to transitional words such as *when* and *then,* she uses specific time markers — "When I was little," "Almost every summer afternoon," "every Friday night," "As we walked," "The next day," "In the years to follow," and "After a few years" — to advance the narrative and carry her readers along.

Focus on Revision

In their responses to an earlier draft of Tiffany's essay, several students in her peer editing group recommended that she revise one particularly monotonous paragraph. (As one student pointed out, all its sentences began with the subject, making the paragraph seem choppy and its ideas disconnected.) Here is the paragraph from her draft:

My dad played baseball too. I went to the field with my mother every Friday night to watch him play. It was just like the big leagues. There were lots of people and a snack bar. The lights shone so high and bright you could see them a mile away. I loved to go to my dad's games. All the other kids would wander off and play. I would sit and cheer on my dad and his team. My attention was focused on the field. My heart would jump with every pitch.

In the revised version of the paragraph (now paragraph 4 of her essay), Tiffany varies sentence length and opening strategies:

My dad played baseball too, and every Friday night I would go to the field with my mother to watch him play. It was just like the big leagues, with lots of people, a snack bar, and lights that shone so high and bright you could see them a mile away. I loved to go to my dad's games. When all the other kids would wander off and play, I would sit and cheer on my dad and his team. My attention was focused on the field, and my heart would jump with every pitch.

After reading Tiffany's revised draft, another student suggested that she might still polish her essay a bit. For instance, she could add some dialogue, quoting the boys' taunts and her own reply in paragraph 8. She could also revise to eliminate **clichés** (overused expressions), substituting fresher, more original language for phrases such as "I felt a lump in my throat and butterflies in my stomach" and "felt as if I were on top of the world." In the next draft of her essay, Tiffany followed up on these suggestions.

PEER EDITING WORKSHEET: Narration

1. What point is the writer making about the essay's subject? Is this point explicitly stated in a thesis statement? If so, where? If not, can you state the essay's thesis in one sentence?

2. List some details that enrich the narrative. Where could more detail be added? What kind of detail? Be specific.

3. Does the writer vary sentence structure and avoid monotonous strings of similar sentences? Should any sentences be combined? If so, which ones? Can you suggest different openings for any sentences?

4. Should any transitions be added to clarify the order in which events occurred? If so, where?

5. Do verb tenses establish a clear chronological order? Identify any verb tenses that you believe need to be changed.

6. Does the writer avoid run-on sentences? Point out any fused sentences or comma splices.

7. What could the writer *add* to this essay?

8. What could the writer take out of this essay?

(continued)

9. What is the essay's greatest strength? Why?
10. What is the essay's greatest weakness? What steps should the writer take to correct this problem?

The selections that follow illustrate some of the many possibilities open to writers of narratives. The first selection, a visual text, is followed by questions designed to illustrate how narration can operate in visual form.

MARJANE SATRAPI

The Socks (Graphic Fiction)

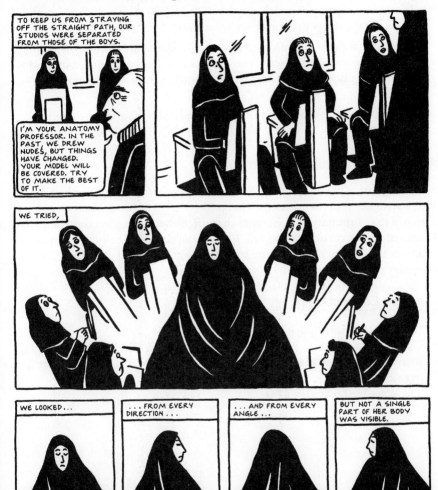

Reading Images

1. The seven panels on page 109 (from the graphic novel *Persepolis II*) tell part of a story about changes in the life of a young girl during Iran's Islamic Revolution, which began in 1979. List the events depicted in the panels in the order in which they are shown.

2. What visual elements link each panel to the one that follows? Can you identify any words that serve as transitions? What additional transitional words and phrases might help to move readers from one panel to the next?

3. What do you think happened right before (and right after) the events depicted here?

Journal Entry

Write a narrative paragraph summarizing the story told in these panels. Begin with a sentence that identifies the characters and the setting. Next, write a sentence that summarizes the events that might have preceded the first panel. Then, tell the story the pictures tell. In your last sentence, bring the sequence of events to a logical close. Be sure to use present tense and to include all necessary transitions.

Thematic Connections

- "Indian Education" (page 142)
- "The Myth of the Latin Woman: I Just Met a Girl Named Maria" (page 232)
- "Just Walk On By: A Black Man Ponders His Power to Alter Public Space" (page 240)
- "The Ways We Lie" (page 474)

SANDRA CISNEROS

Only Daughter

Born into a working-class family in 1954, Sandra Cisneros, the daughter of a Mexican-American mother and a Mexican father, spent much of her childhood shuttling between Chicago and Mexico City. A lonely, bookish child, Cisneros began writing privately at a young age but only began to find her voice when she was a creative-writing student at Loyola University and later at the University of Iowa Writers' Workshop. Her best-known works are the novel *The House on Mango Street* (1983) and the short-story collection *Woman Hollering Creek* (1991); she has also published several collections of poetry. Cisneros's latest novel, *Caramelo,* appeared in 2002.

Background on gender preference In the following essay, which originally appeared in *Glamour* magazine in 1990, Cisneros describes the difficulties of growing up as the only daughter in a Mexican-American family of six sons. Historically, sons have been valued over daughters in most cultures, as reflected in the following proverbs: "A house full of daughters is like a cellar full of sour beer" (Dutch); "Daughters pay nae [no] debts" (Scottish); "A stupid son is better than a crafty daughter" (Chinese); and "A virtuous son is the sun of his family" (Sanskrit). This was largely the case because limited employment opportunities for women meant that sons were more likely to be able to provide financial support for aging parents. Contemporary research suggests that while the preference for male children has diminished considerably in industrialized nations, a distinct preference for sons continues among many cultures in Asia and the Middle East, raising concerns among medical ethicists worldwide. And, even within the more traditional cultures of the industrialized world, old habits of mind regarding the role of women in society can die hard, as the attitudes of Cisneros's father suggest.

Once, several years ago, when I was just starting out my writing career, 1 I was asked to write my own contributor's note for an anthology I was part of. I wrote: "I am the only daughter in a family of six sons. *That* explains everything."

Well, I've thought about that ever since, and yes, it explains a lot to me, 2 but for the reader's sake I should have written: "I am the only daughter in a *Mexican* family of six sons." Or even: "I am the only daughter of a Mexican father and a Mexican-American mother." Or: "I am the only daughter of a working-class family of nine." All of these had everything to do with who I am today.

I was/am the only daughter and *only* a daughter. Being an only daugh- 3 ter in a family of six sons forced me by circumstance to spend a lot of time by myself because my brothers felt it beneath them to play with a *girl* in public. But that aloneness, that loneliness, was good for a would-be writer — it allowed me time to think and think, to imagine, to read and prepare myself.

Being only a daughter for my father meant my destiny would lead me to 4 become someone's wife. That's what he believed. But when I was in the fifth grade and shared my plans for college with him, I was sure he understood. I remember my father saying, "*Que bueno, mi'ja,* that's good." That meant a lot to me, especially since my brothers thought the idea hilarious. What I didn't realize was that my father thought college was good for girls — good for finding a husband. After four years in college and two more in graduate school, and still no husband, my father shakes his head even now and says I wasted all that education.

In retrospect, I'm lucky my father believed daughters were meant for 5 husbands. It meant it didn't matter if I majored in something silly like English. After all, I'd find a nice professional eventually, right? This allowed me the liberty to putter about embroidering my little poems and stories without my father interrupting with so much as a "What's that you're writing?"

But the truth is, I wanted him to interrupt. I wanted my father to 6 understand what it was I was scribbling, to introduce me as "My only daughter, the writer." Not as "This is only my daughter. She teaches." *Es maestra* — teacher. Not even *profesora.*

In a sense, everything I have ever written has been for him, to win his 7 approval even though I know my father can't read English words, even though my father's only reading includes the brown-ink *Esto* sports magazines from Mexico City and the bloody *¡Alarma!* magazines that feature yet another sighting of *La Virgen de Guadalupe* on a tortilla or a wife's revenge on her philandering husband by bashing his skull in with a *molcajete* (a kitchen mortar made of volcanic rock). Or the *fotonovelas,* the little picture paperbacks with tragedy and trauma erupting from the characters' mouths in bubbles.

My father represents, then, the public majority. A public who is un- 8 interested in reading, and yet one whom I am writing about and for, and privately trying to woo.

When we were growing up in Chicago, we moved a lot because of my 9 father. He suffered bouts of nostalgia. Then we'd have to let go of our flat, store the furniture with mother's relatives, load the station wagon with baggage and bologna sandwiches, and head south. To Mexico City.

We came back, of course. To yet another Chicago flat, another Chicago 10 neighborhood, another Catholic school. Each time, my father would seek out the parish priest in order to get a tuition break, and complain or boast: "I have seven sons."

He meant *siete hijos,* seven children, but he translated it as "sons." "I have 11 seven sons." To anyone who would listen. The Sears Roebuck employee who sold us the washing machine. The short-order cook where my father ate his ham-and-eggs breakfasts. "I have seven sons." As if he deserved a medal from the state.

My papa. He didn't mean anything by that mistranslation, I'm sure. 12
But somehow I could feel myself being erased. I'd tug my father's sleeve and
whisper: "Not seven sons. Six! and *one daughter.*"

When my oldest brother graduated from medical school, he fulfilled 13
my father's dream that we study hard and use this — our heads, instead
of this — our hands. Even now my father's hands are thick and yellow,
stubbed by a history of hammer and nails and twine and coils and springs.
"Use this," my father said, tapping his head, "and not this," showing us
those hands. He always looked tired when he said it.

Wasn't college an investment? And hadn't I spent all those years in 14
college? And if I didn't marry, what was it all for? Why would anyone go to
college and then choose to be poor? Especially someone who had always
been poor.

Last year, after ten years of writing professionally, the financial rewards 15
started to trickle in. My second National Endowment for the Arts Fellow-
ship. A guest professorship at the University of California, Berkeley. My
book, which sold to a major New York publishing house.

At Christmas, I flew home to Chicago. The house was throbbing, same 16
as always; hot *tamales* and sweet *tamales* hissing in my mother's pressure
cooker, and everybody — my mother, six brothers, wives, babies, aunts,
cousins — talking too loud and at the same time, like in a Fellini film, because that's just how we are.

I went upstairs to my father's room. One of my stories had just been 17
translated into Spanish and published in an anthology of Chicano writing, and I wanted to show it to him. Ever since he recovered from a stroke
two years ago, my father likes to spend his leisure hours horizontally. And
that's how I found him, watching a Pedro Infante* movie on Galavisión**
and eating rice pudding.

There was a glass filmed with milk on the bedside table. There were 18
several vials of pills and balled Kleenex. And on the floor, one black sock
and a plastic urinal that I didn't want to look at but looked at anyway.
Pedro Infante was about to burst into song, and my father was laughing.

I'm not sure if it was because my story was translated into Spanish, or 19
because it was published in Mexico, or perhaps because the story dealt with
Tepeyac, the *colonia* my father was raised in and the house he grew up in,
but at any rate, my father punched the mute button on his remote control
and read my story.

I sat on the bed next to my father and waited. He read it very slowly. As 20
if he were reading each line over and over. He laughed at all the right places
and read lines he liked out loud. He pointed and asked questions: "Is this
So-and-so?" "Yes," I said. He kept reading.

---

* Eds. note — Mexican actor.
** Eds. note — A Spanish-language cable channel.

When he was finally finished, after what seemed like hours, my father 21 looked up and asked: "Where can we get more copies of this for the relatives?"

Of all the wonderful things that happened to me last year, that was the 22 most wonderful.

●   ●   ●

Comprehension

1. What does Cisneros mean when she writes that being an only daughter in a family of six sons "explains everything" (1)?

2. What distinction does Cisneros make in paragraphs 2 and 3 between being "the only daughter" and being *"only* a daughter"?

3. What advantages does Cisneros see in being "the only daughter"? In being *"only* a daughter"?

4. Why does her father think she has wasted her education? What is her reaction to his opinion?

5. Why is her father's reaction to her story the "most wonderful" (22) thing that happened to Cisneros that year?

Purpose and Audience

1. Although Cisneros uses many Spanish words in her essay, in most cases she defines or explains these words. What does this decision tell you about her purpose and her audience?

2. What is Cisneros's thesis? What incidents and details support this thesis?

3. Do you think Cisneros intends to convey a sympathetic or an unsympathetic impression of her father? Explain.

Style and Structure

1. Where does Cisneros interrupt a narrative passage to comment on or analyze events? What does this strategy accomplish?

2. Are the episodes in this essay presented in chronological order? Explain.

3. What transitional expressions does Cisneros use to introduce new episodes?

4. Cisneros quotes her father several times. What do we learn about him from his words?

5. Why does Cisneros devote so much space to describing her father in paragraphs 17–21? How does this portrait compare to the one she presents in paragraphs 9–11?

Vocabulary Projects

1. Define each of the following words as it is used in this selection.

embroidering (5)   stubbed (13)

2. What is the difference in **connotation** between *sons* and *children?* Between *teacher* and *professor?* Do you think these distinctions are as significant as Cisneros seems to think they are? Explain.

Journal Entry

Recount an incident that illustrates how the number and gender(s) of your siblings "explain[s] everything" about who you are today.

Writing Workshop

1. Write a narrative essay consisting of a series of related episodes that show how you gradually gained the approval and respect of one of your parents, of another relative, or of a friend.

2. **Working with Sources.** In "Only Daughter," Cisneros traces the development of her identity as an adult, as a female, and as a writer. Write a narrative essay tracing the development of your own personal or professional identity. Refer in your essay to "Only Daughter," quoting relevant ideas if possible to help explain your own personal development. Be sure you document all quotations you use, and include a works-cited page. (See Chapter 18 for information on MLA documentation.)

3. Are male and female children treated differently in your family? Have your parents had different expectations for their sons and daughters? Write a narrative essay recounting one or more incidents that illustrate these differences (or the lack of differences). If you and your siblings are all the same gender, or if you are an only child, write about another family you know well.

Combining the Patterns

Cisneros structures her essay as a narrative in which she is the main character and her brothers barely appear. To give her readers a clearer understanding of how her father's attitude toward her differs from his attitude toward her brothers, Cisneros could have added one or more paragraphs of **comparison and contrast**, focusing on the different ways she and her brothers are treated. What specific points of contrast do you think readers would find most useful? Where might such paragraphs be added?

Thematic Connections

- "My Field of Dreams" (page 103)
- "Rice" (page 172)
- "Why Chinese Mothers Are Superior" (page 410)
- Declaration of Sentiments and Resolutions, Seneca Falls Convention, 1848 (page 559)

MARK EDMUNDSON

Pink Floyd Night School

Mark Edmundson was born in 1952 in Malden, Massachusetts. He attended Bennington College in Vermont and earned a Ph.D. in English from Yale University. Edmundson currently teaches at the University of Virginia. While he has published widely in his field of scholarship, Edmundson has also written an educational memoir, *Teacher: The One Who Made a Difference* (2002) as well as books and essays on consumerism and popular culture. He has an abiding interest in rock music, as is evident from the following essay. His most recent book is *The Fine Wisdom and Perfect Teachings of the Kings of Rock and Roll: A Memoir* (2009).

Background on Pink Floyd Pink Floyd was a psychedelic and progressive rock band best known for concept albums like *Dark Side of the Moon, Wish You Were Here,* and *The Wall.* Formed in London in 1965, the band reached the height of its worldwide popularity in the 1970s and early 1980s. Its 1973 release *The Dark Side of the Moon* remained on the *Billboard* charts longer than any other album in history: 741 consecutive weeks. Like other progressive rock bands of the era — Yes; King Crimson; Emerson, Lake, and Palmer — Pink Floyd's work was experimental and complex, both musically and lyrically. As Edmundson's essay makes clear, the group's live shows were also elaborate, highly staged productions. Pink Floyd has sold more than 200 million albums and remains one of the best-selling bands of all time.

"So, what are you doing after graduation?" 1

In the spring of my last year in college I posed that question to at least 2 a dozen fellow graduates-to-be at my little out-of-the-way school in Vermont. The answers they gave me were satisfying in the extreme: not very much, just kick back, hang out, look things over, take it slow. It was 1974. That's what you were supposed to say.

My classmates weren't, strictly speaking, telling the truth. They were, 3 one might even say, lying outrageously. By graduation day, it was clear that most of my contemporaries would be trotting off to law school and graduate school and to cool and unusual internships in New York and San Francisco.

But I *did* take it slow. After graduation, I spent five years wandering 4 around doing nothing — or getting as close to it as I could manage. I was a cab driver, an obsessed moviegoer, a wanderer in the mountains of Colorado, a teacher at a crazy grand hippie school in Vermont, the manager of a movie house (who didn't do much managing), a crewman on a ship, and a doorman at a disco.

The most memorable job of all, though, was a gig on the stage crew for 5 a rock production company in Jersey City. We did our shows at Roosevelt

Stadium, a grungy behemoth that could hold 60,000, counting seats on the grass. I humped amps out of the trucks and onto the stage; six or so hours later I humped them back. I did it for the Grateful Dead and Alice Cooper and the Allman Brothers and Crosby, Stills & Nash on the night that Richard Nixon resigned. But the most memorable night of that most memorable job was the night of Pink Floyd.

Pink Floyd demanded a certain quality of sound. They wanted their 6 amps stacked high, not just on stage, where they were so broad and tall and forbidding that they looked like a barricade in the Paris Commune.* They also wanted amp clusters at three highly elevated points around the stadium, and I spent the morning lugging huge blocks of wood and circuitry up and up and up the stairs of the decayed old bowl.

There was one other assignment: a parachute-like white silken canopy 7 roof that Pink Floyd required over the stage. It took about six hours to get the thing up and in position. We were told that this was the first use of the canopy and Pink's guys were unsteady. They had some blueprints, but those turned out not to be of much use. Eventually the roof did rise and inflate, with American know-how applied. Such know-how involved a lot of spontaneous knot-tying and strategic rope tangling.

Pink Floyd went on at about 10 that night and the amp clusters that 8 we'd expended all that servile sweat to build didn't work — people had sat on them, kicked them, or cut the cords. So Pink made its noise, the towers stayed mute, the mob flicked on lighters at the end, and then we spent three hours breaking the amps down and loading the truck. We refused to go after the speakers all the way up the stadium steps and, after some sharp words, Pink's guys had to scramble up and retrieve them.

There was, for the record, almost always tension between the roadies 9 and the stage crew. One time, at a show by (if memory serves) Queen, their five roadies got into a brawl with a dozen of our stage crew guys; then the house security, mostly Jersey bikers and black-belt karate devotees, heard the noise and jumped in. The roadies held on for a while, but finally they saw it was a lost cause. One of them grabbed a case of champagne from the truck cab and opened a bottle and passed it around — all became drunk and happy.

Pink's road manager wanted the inflatable canopy brought down 10 gently, then folded and packed securely in its wooden boxes. The problem was that the thing was full of helium and no one knew where the release valve was; we'd also secured it to the stage with so many knots of such foolish intricacy that their disentanglement would have given a gang of sailors pause. Everyone was tired. Those once intoxicated were no longer. It was 4 a.m. and time to go home.

---

* Eds. note — A popular left-wing uprising in Paris in 1871 against the national government of France. The Commune held the city for 72 days before it was retaken by the national government.

An hour went into concocting strategies to get the floating pillowy 11
roof down. It became a regular seminar. Then came Jim — Jimbo — our
crew chief, who looked like a good-natured Viking captain and who de-
fended the integrity of his stage crew at every turn, even going so far as to
have screamed at Stevie Nicks, who was yelling at me for having dropped
a guitar case, that he was the only one who had the right to holler at
Edmundson. Faced with the Pink Floyd roof crisis, Jimbo did what he
always could be counted on to do in critical circumstances, which is to say,
he did something.

Jimbo walked softly to a corner of the stage, reached into his pocket, 12
removed a buck knife, and with it began to saw one of the ropes attaching
the holy celestial roof to the earth. Three or four of us, his minions, did
the same. "Hey, what are you doing?" wailed Pink's head roadie. "I'll smash
your — " Only then did he realize that Jimbo had a knife in his hand, and
that some of the rest of us did, too. In the space of a few minutes, we sawed
through the ropes.

There came a great sighing noise as the last thick cord broke apart. For 13
a moment there was nothing; for another moment, more of the same.

Then the canopy rose into the air and began to float away, like a gor- 14
geous cloud, white and soft. The sun at that moment burst above the horizon and the silk bloomed into a soft crimson tinge. Jimbo started to laugh
his big bear-bellied laugh. We all joined. Even Pink's guys did. We were like
little kids on the last day of school. We stood on the naked stage, watching
the silk roof go up and out, wafting over the Atlantic. Some of us waved.

"So, what are you doing after graduation?" Thirty-five years later, a col- 15
lege teacher, I ask my students the old question. They aren't inclined to
dissimulate now. The culture is on their side when they tell me about law
school and med school and higher degrees in journalism and business; or
when they talk about a research grant in China or a well-paying gig teaching English in Japan.

I'm impressed, sure, but I'm worried about them too. Aren't they decid- 16
ing too soon? Shouldn't they hang out a little, learn to take it slow? I can't
help it. I flash on that canopy of white silk floating out into the void. I can
see it as though it were still there. I want to point up to it. I'd like for my
students to see it, too.

· · ·

Comprehension

1. How did Edmundson spend his time during the first five years after his
college graduation? Does he consider this time well spent?

2. What was Edmundson's most memorable job? What made it so memorable?

3. What problem did the "parachute-like white silken canopy roof" (7) present? How did Jimbo solve the problem?

4. In paragraph 16, Edmundson says, "I flash on that canopy of white silk floating out into the void. I can see it as though it were still there. I want to point up to it. I'd like for my students to see it, too." What exactly does he want his students to see?

5. What lessons do you think Edmundson learned in his "night school"?

Purpose and Audience

1. This essay has a persuasive purpose. What does Edmundson want to persuade students to do? How do you react to his proposal? How do you think most other students you know would react?

2. Is this essay's intended audience just students, or do you think it has meaning for parents or college teachers as well? Explain.

3. Edmundson mentions various rock stars. Why? Does he need to mention these figures to get his point across, or does he have some other purpose?

Style and Structure

1. Edmundson's narrative focuses on one night of a memorable job, "the night of Pink Floyd" (5). Where does this narrative begin? Where does it end? What purpose do the paragraphs that precede and follow the narrative serve?

2. What information does paragraph 9 provide? Is it necessary? Is it part of the narrative, or is it a digression?

3. The language of this essay is quite informal. Give examples of colloquial words and expressions. Is this level of diction appropriate for the essay?

4. Reread the description of the floating canopy in paragraph 14. What does this image mean to Edmundson? Why do you think it has stayed in his mind for so many years? Do you think the parachute is a **symbol**? If so, what might it symbolize?

5. In paragraph 15, Edmundson repeats the question he asks in paragraph 1. Why? Is this repetition necessary?

Vocabulary Projects

1. Define each of the following words as it is used in this selection.

   behemoth (5)   concocting (11)
   servile (8)   minions (12)
   intricacy (10)   dissimulate (15)

2. Edmundson uses **jargon** specific to the world of rock-concert tours — for example, *gig* (5) and *roadies* (9). What other jargon does he use? Would synonyms work as well? Explain.

Journal Entry

Do you think Edmundson's proposal that students "hang out a little, learn to take it slow" (16) makes sense for you and for the college students you know? Why or why not?

Writing Workshop

1. Write an essay focusing on an experience that included a memorable image that you still remember. Begin your essay by describing the "parachute-like white silken canopy roof" (7) that is central to Edmundson's's essay. Then, recount your own experience, explaining what you learned from it and what significance the key image had for you.

2. **Working with Sources.** Write a response to Edmundson arguing that in today's economic climate, students cannot afford to "hang out a little" but must look for employment immediately. In your thesis, state that meaningful employment can provide experiences as valuable and memorable as the one Edmundson describes, and recount a particular experience that supports your thesis. Refer to specific portions of Edmundson's essay, and be sure to include parenthetical citations and a works-cited page. (See Chapter 18 for information on MLA documentation.)

3. In paragraphs 1 and 15, Edmundson poses the question, "So, what are you doing after graduation?" Write a narrative essay that answers this question.

Combining the Patterns

This essay is a narrative, but it includes some memorable descriptive details. Identify specific **descriptions** of people, places, and objects. Is the description primarily visual, or does it incorporate other senses (sound, smell, taste, and touch) as well? Do you think any person, setting, or object should be described in greater detail? Explain.

Thematic Connections

- Job Application Letter (page 219)
- "College Pressures" (page 450)
- "'Take This Internship and Shove It'" (page 583)

BONNIE SMITH-YACKEL

My Mother Never Worked

Bonnie Smith-Yackel was born into a farm family in Willmar, Minnesota, in 1937. She began writing as a young homemaker in the early 1960s and for the next fourteen years published short stories, essays, and book reviews in such publications as *Catholic Digest, Minnesota Monthly,* and *Ms.* magazine, as well as in several local newspapers. As Smith-Yackel explains it, "The catalyst for writing the [following] essay shortly after my mother's death was recounting my telephone conversation with Social Security to the lawyer who was helping me settle my mother's estate. When I told him what the SS woman had said, he responded: 'Well, that's right. Your mother didn't work, you know.' At which point I stood and said, 'She worked harder throughout her life than you or a hundred men like you!' and stomped out of his office, drove home, sat down and wrote the essay in one sitting." Although this narrative essay, first published in *Women: A Journal of Liberation* in 1975, is based on personal experience, it also makes a broader statement about how society values "women's work."

Background on Social Security benefits Social Security is a federal insurance program that requires workers to contribute a percentage of their wages to a fund that they may draw benefits from if they become unemployed due to disability. After retirement, workers can receive a monthly income from this fund, which also provides a modest death benefit to survivors. The contribution is generally deducted directly from a worker's paycheck, and employers must contribute a matching amount. According to federal law, a woman who is a homemaker, who has never been a wage earner, is eligible for Social Security benefits only through the earnings of her deceased husband. (The same would be true for a man if the roles were reversed.) Therefore, a homemaker's survivors would not be eligible for the death benefit. Although the law has been challenged in the courts, the survivors of a homemaker who has never been a wage earner are still not entitled to a Social Security death benefit.

"Social Security Office." (The voice answering the telephone sounds 1 very self-assured.)

"I'm calling about . . . my mother just died . . . I was told to call you 2 and see about a . . . death-benefit check, I think they call it. . . ."

"I see. Was your mother on Social Security? How old was she?" 3

"Yes . . . she was seventy-eight. . . ." 4

"Do you know her number?" 5

"No . . . I, ah . . . don't you have a record?" 6

"Certainly. I'll look it up. Her name?" 7

"Smith. Martha Smith. Or maybe she used Martha Ruth 8 Smith? . . . Sometimes she used her maiden name . . . Martha Jerabek Smith?"

"If you'd care to hold on, I'll check our records — it'll be a few minutes." 9
"Yes. . . ."   10

Her love letters — to and from Daddy — were in an old box, tied with 11
ribbons and stiff, rigid-with-age leather thongs: 1918 through 1920; hers
written on stationery from the general store she had worked in full-time
and managed, single-handed, after her graduation from high school in
1913; and his, at first, on YMCA or Soldiers and Sailors Club stationery
dispensed to the fighting men of World War I. He wooed her thoroughly
and persistently by mail, and though she reciprocated all his feelings for
her, she dreaded marriage. . . .

"It's so hard for me to decide when to have my wedding day — that's all 12
I've thought about these last two days. I have told you dozens of times that
I won't be afraid of married life, but when it comes down to setting the date
and then picturing myself a married woman with half a dozen or more kids
to look after, it just makes me sick. . . . I am weeping right now — I hope
that some day I can look back and say how foolish I was to dread it all."

They married in February, 1921, and began farming. Their first baby, 13
a daughter, was born in January, 1922, when my mother was twenty-six
years old. The second baby, a son, was born in March, 1923. They were
renting farms; my father, besides working his own fields, also was a hired
man for two other farmers. They had no capital initially, and had to gain
it slowly, working from dawn until midnight every day. My town-bred
mother learned to set hens and raise chickens, feed pigs, milk cows, plant
and harvest a garden, and can every fruit and vegetable she could scrounge.
She carried water nearly a quarter of a mile from the well to fill her wash
boilers in order to do her laundry on a scrub board. She learned to shuck
grain, feed threshers, shock and husk corn, feed corn pickers. In September,
1925, the third baby came, and in June, 1927, the fourth child — both
daughters. In 1930, my parents had enough money to buy their own farm,
and that March they moved all their livestock and belongings themselves,
fifty-five miles over rutted, muddy roads.

In the summer of 1930 my mother and her two eldest children re- 14
claimed a forty-acre field from Canadian thistles, by chopping them all out
with a hoe. In the other fields, when the oats and flax began to head out,
the green and blue of the crops were hidden by the bright yellow of wild
mustard. My mother walked the fields day after day, pulling each mustard plant. She raised a new flock of baby chicks — five hundred — and she
spaded up, planted, hoed, and harvested a half-acre garden.

During the next spring their hogs caught cholera and died. No cash 15
that fall.

And in the next year the drought hit. My mother and father trudged 16
from the well to the chickens, the well to the calf pasture, the well to the
barn, and from the well to the garden. The sun came out hot and bright,
endlessly, day after day. The crops shriveled and died. They harvested half
the corn, and ground the other half, stalks and all, and fed it to the cattle
as fodder. With the price at four cents a bushel for the harvested crop, they

couldn't afford to haul it into town. They burned it in the furnace for fuel that winter.

In 1934, in February, when the dust was still so thick in the Minnesota air that my parents couldn't always see from the house to the barn, their fifth child — a fourth daughter — was born. My father hunted rabbits daily, and my mother stewed them, fried them, canned them, and wished out loud that she could taste hamburger once more. In the fall the shotgun brought prairie chickens, ducks, pheasant, and grouse. My mother plucked each bird, carefully reserving the breast feathers for pillows.   17

In the winter she sewed night after night, endlessly, begging cast-off clothing from relatives, ripping apart coats, dresses, blouses, and trousers to remake them to fit her four daughters and son. Every morning and every evening she milked cows, fed pigs and calves, cared for chickens, picked eggs, cooked meals, washed dishes, scrubbed floors, and tended and loved her children. In the spring she planted a garden once more, dragging pails of water to nourish and sustain the vegetables for the family. In 1936 she lost a baby in her sixth month.   18

In 1937 her fifth daughter was born. She was forty-two years old. In 1939 a second son, and in 1941 her eighth child — and third son.   19

But the war had come, and prosperity of a sort. The herd of cattle had grown to thirty head; she still milked morning and evening. Her garden was more than a half acre — the rains had come, and by now the Rural Electricity Administration and indoor plumbing. Still she sewed — dresses and jackets for the children, housedresses and aprons for herself, weekly patching of jeans, overalls, and denim shirts. She still made pillows, using feathers she had plucked, and quilts every year — intricate patterns as well as patchwork, stitched as well as tied — all necessary bedding for her family. Every scrap of cloth too small to be used in quilts was carefully saved and painstakingly sewed together in strips to make rugs. She still went out in the fields to help with the haying whenever there was a threat of rain.   20

In 1959 my mother's last child graduated from high school. A year later the cows were sold. She still raised chickens and ducks, plucked feathers, made pillows, baked her own bread, and every year made a new quilt — now for a married child or for a grandchild. And her garden, that huge, undying symbol of sustenance, was as large and cared for as in all the years before. The canning, and now freezing, continued.   21

In 1969, on a June afternoon, mother and father started out for town so that she could buy sugar to make rhubarb jam for a daughter who lived in Texas. The car crashed into a ditch. She was paralyzed from the waist down.   22

In 1970 her husband, my father, died. My mother struggled to regain some competence and dignity and order in her life. At the rehabilitation institute, where they gave her physical therapy and trained her to live usefully in a wheelchair, the therapist told me: "She did fifteen pushups today — fifteen! She's almost seventy-five years old! I've never known a woman so strong!"   23

From her wheelchair she canned pickles, baked bread, ironed clothes, 24
wrote dozens of letters weekly to her friends and her "half dozen or more
kids," and made three patchwork housecoats and one quilt. She made balls
and balls of carpet rags — enough for five rugs. And kept all her love letters.

"I think I've found your mother's records — Martha Ruth Smith; mar- 25
ried to Ben F. Smith?"

"Yes, that's right."   26

"Well, I see that she was getting a widow's pension. . . ."   27

"Yes, that's right."   28

"Well, your mother isn't entitled to our $255 death benefit."   29

"Not entitled! But why?"   30

The voice on the telephone explains patiently: 31

"Well, you see — your mother never worked."   32

• • •

Comprehension

1. What kind of work did Martha Smith do while her children were growing
   up? List some of the chores she performed.

2. Why aren't Martha Smith's survivors entitled to a death benefit when
   their mother dies?

3. How does the government define *work?*

Purpose and Audience

1. What point is the writer trying to make? Why do you suppose her thesis is
   never explicitly stated?

2. This essay appeared in *Ms.* magazine and other publications whose audiences are sympathetic to feminist goals. Could it have appeared in a
   magazine whose audience had a more traditional view of gender roles?
   Explain.

3. Smith-Yackel mentions relatively little about her father in this essay. How
   can you account for this?

4. This essay was first published in 1975. Do you think it is dated, or do you
   think the issues it raises are still relevant today?

Style and Structure

1. Is the essay's title effective? If so, why? If not, what alternate title can you
   suggest?

2. Smith-Yackel could have outlined her mother's life without framing it
   with the telephone conversation. Why do you think she includes this
   frame?

3. What strategies does Smith-Yackel use to indicate the passing of time in
   her narrative?

4. This narrative piles details one on top of another almost like a list. Why does the writer include so many details?

5. In paragraphs 20 and 21, what is accomplished by the repetition of the word *still?*

Vocabulary Projects

1. Define each of the following words as it is used in this selection.

   scrounge (13)   rutted (13)   intricate (20)
   shuck (13)   reclaimed (14)   sustenance (21)
   shock (13)   flax (14)
   husk (13)   fodder (16)

2. Try substituting equivalent words for those italicized in this sentence:

   He *wooed* her *thoroughly* and *persistently* by mail, and though she *reciprocated* all his feelings for her, she *dreaded* marriage . . . (11).

   How do your substitutions change the sentence's meaning?

3. Throughout her narrative, Smith-Yackel uses concrete, specific verbs. Review her choice of verbs, particularly in paragraphs 13–24, and comment on how such verbs serve the essay's purpose.

Journal Entry

Do you believe that a homemaker who has never been a wage earner should be entitled to a Social Security death benefit for her survivors? Explain your reasoning.

Writing Workshop

1. If you can, interview one of your parents or grandparents (or another person you know who reminds you of Smith-Yackel's mother) about his or her work history, and write a chronological narrative based on what you learn. Include a thesis statement that your narrative can support, and quote your family member's responses when possible.

2. Write Martha Smith's obituary as it might have appeared in her hometown newspaper. (If you are not familiar with the form of an obituary, read a few in your local paper or online at Legacy.com or Obituaries.com.)

3. Write a narrative account of a typical day at the worst job you ever had. Include a thesis statement that expresses your negative feelings.

Combining the Patterns

Because of the repetitive nature of the farm chores Smith-Yackel describes in her narrative, some passages come very close to explaining a **process**, a series of repeated steps that always occur in a predictable order. Identify several such passages. If Smith-Yackel's essay were written entirely as a process explanation, what material would have to be left out? How would these omissions change the essay?

Thematic Connections

- "Midnight" (page 221)
- "'Girl'" (page 258)
- "Aristotle" (page 484)
- "I Want a Wife" (page 503)

MARTIN GANSBERG

Thirty-Eight Who Saw Murder Didn't Call the Police

Martin Gansberg (1920–1995), a native of Brooklyn, New York, was a reporter and editor for the *New York Times* for forty-three years. The following article, written for the *Times* two weeks after the 1964 murder it recounts, earned Gansberg an award for excellence from the Newspaper Reporters Association of New York. Gansberg's thesis, though not explicitly stated, still retains its power.

Background on the Kitty Genovese murder case The events reported here took place on March 14, 1964, as contemporary American culture was undergoing a complex transition. The relatively placid years of the 1950s were giving way to more troubling times: the civil rights movement was leading to social unrest in the South and in northern inner cities; the escalating war in Vietnam was creating angry political divisions; President John F. Kennedy had been assassinated just four months earlier; violent imagery was increasing in television and film; crime rates were rising; and a growing drug culture was becoming apparent. The brutal, senseless murder of Kitty Genovese — and, more important, her neighbors' failure to respond immediately to her cries for help — became a nationwide, and even worldwide, symbol for what was perceived as an evolving culture of violence and indifference.

Recently, some of the details Gansberg mentions have been challenged. For example, as the *New York Times* now acknowledges, there were only two attacks on Ms. Genovese, not three; the first attack may have been shorter than first reported; the second attack may have occurred in the apartment house foyer, where neighbors would not have been able to see Genovese; and some witnesses may, in fact, actually *have* called the police. At the time, however, the world was shocked by the incident, and even today social scientists around the world debate the causes of "the Genovese syndrome."

For more than half an hour thirty-eight respectable, law-abiding citizens in Queens watched a killer stalk and stab a woman in three separate attacks in Kew Gardens.

> "Not one person telephoned the police during the assault; one witness called after the woman was dead."

Twice their chatter and the sudden glow of their bedroom lights interrupted him and frightened him off. Each time he returned, sought her out, and stabbed her again. Not one person telephoned the police during the assault; one witness called after the woman was dead.

That was two weeks ago today.

Still shocked is Assistant Chief Inspector Frederick M. Lussen, in 4 charge of the borough's detectives and a veteran of twenty-five years of homicide investigations. He can give a matter-of-fact recitation on many murders. But the Kew Gardens slaying baffles him — not because it is a murder, but because the "good people" failed to call the police.

"As we have reconstructed the crime," he said, "the assailant had three 5 chances to kill this woman during a thirty-five-minute period. He returned twice to complete the job. If we had been called when he first attacked, the woman might not be dead now."

This is what the police say happened beginning at 3:20 A.M. in the staid, 6 middle-class, tree-lined Austin Street area:

Twenty-eight-year-old Catherine Genovese, who was called Kitty by al- 7 most everyone in the neighborhood, was returning home from her job as manager of a bar in Hollis. She parked her red Fiat in a lot adjacent to the Kew Gardens Long Island Rail Road Station, facing Mowbray Place. Like many residents of the neighborhood, she had parked there day after day since her arrival from Connecticut a year ago, although the railroad frowns on the practice.

She turned off the lights of her car, locked the door, and started to 8 walk the one hundred feet to the entrance of her apartment at 82-70 Austin Street, which is in a Tudor building, with stores in the first floor and apartments on the second.

The entrance to the apartment is in the rear of the building because the 9 front is rented to retail stores. At night the quiet neighborhood is shrouded in the slumbering darkness that marks most residential areas.

Miss Genovese noticed a man at the far end of the lot, near a seven- 10 story apartment house at 82-40 Austin Street. She halted. Then, nervously, she headed up Austin Street toward Lefferts Boulevard, where there is a call box to the 102nd Police Precinct in nearby Richmond Hill.

She got as far as a street light in front of a bookstore before the man 11 grabbed her. She screamed. Lights went on in the ten-story apartment house at 82-67 Austin Street, which faces the bookstore. Windows slid open and voices punctuated the early-morning stillness.

Miss Genovese screamed: "Oh, my God, he stabbed me! Please help 12 me! Please help me!"

From one of the upper windows in the apartment house, a man called 13 down: "Let that girl alone!"

The assailant looked up at him, shrugged, and walked down Austin 14 Street toward a white sedan parked a short distance away. Miss Genovese struggled to her feet.

Lights went out. The killer returned to Miss Genovese, now trying to 15 make her way around the side of the building by the parking lot to get to her apartment. The assailant stabbed her again.

"I'm dying!" she shrieked. "I'm dying!"   16

Windows were opened again, and lights went on in many apartments. 17 The assailant got into his car and drove away. Miss Genovese staggered to her feet. A city bus, 0–10, the Lefferts Boulevard line to Kennedy International Airport, passed. It was 3:35 A.M.

The assailant returned. By then, Miss Genovese had crawled to the 18
back of the building, where the freshly painted brown doors to the apartment house held out hope for safety. The killer tried the first door; she wasn't there. At the second door, 82-62 Austin Street, he saw her slumped on the floor at the foot of the stairs. He stabbed her a third time — fatally.

It was 3:50 by the time the police received their first call, from a man 19
who was a neighbor of Miss Genovese. In two minutes they were at the scene. The neighbor, a seventy-year-old woman, and another woman were the only persons on the street. Nobody else came forward.

The man explained that he had called the police after much delibera- 20
tion. He had phoned a friend in Nassau County for advice, and then he had crossed the roof of the building to the apartment of the elderly woman to get her to make the call.

"I didn't want to get involved," he sheepishly told police.   21

Six days later, the police arrested Winston Moseley, a twenty-nine-year- 22
old business machine operator, and charged him with homicide. Moseley had no previous record. He is married, has two children, and owns a home at 133-19 Sutter Avenue, South Ozone Park, Queens. On Wednesday, a court committed him to Kings County Hospital for psychiatric observation.

When questioned by the police, Moseley also said that he had slain 23
Mrs. Annie May Johnson, twenty-four, of 146-12 133d Avenue, Jamaica, on Feb. 29 and Barbara Kralik, fifteen, of 174-17 140th Avenue, Springfield Gardens, last July. In the Kralik case, the police are holding Alvin L. Mitchell, who is said to have confessed to that slaying.

The police stressed how simple it would have been to have gotten 24
in touch with them. "A phone call," said one of the detectives, "would have done it." The police may be reached by dialing "0" for operator or SPring 7-3100.

Today witnesses from the neighborhood, which is made up of one- 25
family homes in the $35,000 to $60,000 range with the exception of the two apartment houses near the railroad station, find it difficult to explain why they didn't call the police.

A housewife, knowingly if quite casually, said, "We thought it was a 26
lovers' quarrel." A husband and wife both said, "Frankly, we were afraid." They seemed aware of the fact that events might have been different. A distraught woman, wiping her hands in her apron, said, "I didn't want my husband to get involved."

One couple, now willing to talk about that night, said they heard the 27
first screams. The husband looked thoughtfully at the bookstore where the killer first grabbed Miss Genovese.

"We went to the window to see what was happening," he said, "but the 28
light from our bedroom made it difficult to see the street." The wife, still apprehensive, added: "I put out the light and we were able to see better."

Asked why they hadn't called the police, she shrugged and replied: "I   29
don't know."

A man peeked out from a slight opening in the doorway to his apart-   30
ment and rattled off an account of the killer's second attack. Why hadn't
he called the police at the time? "I was tired," he said without emotion. "I
went back to bed."

It was 4:25 A.M. when the ambulance arrived to take the body of Miss   31
Genovese. It drove off. "Then," a solemn police detective said, "the people
came out."

• • •

Comprehension

1. According to Gansberg, how much time elapsed between the first stabbing of Kitty Genovese and the time when the people finally came out?

2. What excuses do the neighbors make for not coming to Kitty Genovese's
   aid?

Purpose and Audience

1. This article appeared in 1964. What effect was it intended to have on its
   audience? Do you think it has the same impact today, or has its impact
   changed or diminished?

2. What is the article's main point? Why does Gansberg imply his thesis
   rather than state it explicitly?

3. What is Gansberg's purpose in describing the Austin Street area as "staid,
   middle-class, tree-lined" (6)?

4. Why do you suppose Gansberg provides the police department's phone
   number in his article? (Note that New York City did not have 911 emergency service in 1964.)

Style and Structure

1. Gansberg is very precise in this article, especially in his references to time,
   addresses, and ages. Why?

2. The objective newspaper style is dominant in this article, but the writer's
   anger shows through. Point to words and phrases that reveal his attitude
   toward his material.

3. Because this article was originally set in the narrow columns of a newspaper, it has many short paragraphs. Would the narrative be more effective if some of these brief paragraphs were combined? If so, why? If not,
   why not? Give examples to support your answer.

4. Review the dialogue. Does it strengthen Gansberg's narrative? Would the
   article be more compelling with additional dialogue? Without dialogue?
   Explain.

5. This article does not have a formal conclusion; nevertheless, the last paragraph sums up the writer's attitude. How?

Vocabulary Projects

1. Define each of the following words as it is used in this selection.

stalk (1)   adjacent (7)   distraught (26)
baffles (4)   punctuated (11)   apprehensive (28)
staid (6)   sheepishly (21)

2. The word *assailant* appears frequently in this article. Why is it used so often? What impact is this repetition likely to have on readers? What other words could have been used?

Journal Entry

In a similar situation, would you have called the police? Would you have gone outside to help? What factors do you think might have influenced your decision?

Writing Workshop

1. In your own words, write a ten-sentence **summary** (see page 712) of the article. Try to reflect Gansberg's order and emphasis, as well as his ideas, and be sure to include all necessary transitions.

2. Rewrite the article as if it were a blog post by one of the thirty-eight people who watched the murder. Summarize what you saw, and explain why you decided not to call for help. (You may invent details that Gansberg does not include.) If you like, you can first visit the Web site oldkewgardens.com, which includes a detailed critique of Gansberg's article as well as photos of the area in which the crime took place.

3. **Working with Sources.** If you have ever been involved in or witnessed a situation in which someone was in trouble, write a narrative essay about the incident. If people failed to help the person in trouble, explain why you think no one acted. If people did act, tell how. Be sure to account for your own actions. In your essay's introduction, refer to Gansberg's account of Kitty Genovese's murder. If you quote Gansberg, be sure to include documentation and a works-cited page. (See Chapter 18 for information on MLA documentation.)

Combining the Patterns

Because the purpose of this newspaper article is to give basic factual information, it has no extended descriptions of the victim, the witnesses, or the crime scene. It also does not explain *why* those who watched did not act. Where might passages of **description** or **cause and effect** be added? How might such additions change the article's impact on readers? Do you think they would strengthen the article?

Thematic Connections

- "Shooting an Elephant" (page 133)
- "The Lottery" (page 311)
- "Who Killed Benny Paret?" (page 339)
- "A Peaceful Woman Explains Why She Carries a Gun" (page 354)

GEORGE ORWELL

Shooting an Elephant

George Orwell (1903–1950) was born Eric Blair in Bengal, India, where his father was a British civil servant. Rather than attend university, Orwell joined the Imperial Police in neighboring Burma (now renamed Myanmar), where he served from 1922 to 1927. Finding himself increasingly opposed to British colonial rule, Orwell left Burma to live and write in Paris and London. A political liberal and a fierce moralist, Orwell is best known today for his novels *Animal Farm* (1945) and *1984* (1949), which portray the dangers of totalitarianism. In "Shooting an Elephant," written in 1936, he recalls an incident from his days in Burma that clarified his thinking about British colonial rule.

Background on British imperialism The British had gradually taken over Burma through a succession of wars beginning in 1824; by 1885, the domination was complete. Like a number of other European countries, Britain had forcibly established colonial rule in countries throughout the world during the eighteenth and nineteenth centuries, primarily to exploit their natural resources. This empire building, known as *imperialism,* was justified by the belief that European culture was superior to the cultures of the indigenous peoples, particularly in Asia and Africa. Therefore, imperialist nations claimed, it was "the white man's burden" to bring civilization to these "heathen" lands. In most cases, such control could be achieved only through force. Anti-imperialist sentiment began to grow in the early twentieth century, but colonial rule continued until the mid-twentieth century in much of the less-developed world. Not until the late 1940s did many European colonies begin to gain independence. The British ceded home rule to Burma in 1947.

In Moulmein, in Lower Burma, I was hated by large numbers of 1 people — the only time in my life that I have been important enough for this to happen to me. I was sub-divisional police officer of the town, and in an aimless, petty kind of way anti-European feeling was very bitter. No one had the guts to raise a riot, but if a European woman went through the bazaars alone somebody would probably spit betel juice over her dress. As a police officer I was an obvious target and was baited whenever it seemed safe to do so. When a nimble Burman tripped me up on the football field and the referee (another Burman) looked the other way, the crowd yelled with hideous laughter. This happened more than once. In the end the sneering yellow faces of young men that met me everywhere, the insults hooted after me when I was at a safe distance, got badly on my nerves. The young Buddhist priests were the worst of all. There were several thousands of them in the town and none of them seemed to have anything to do except stand on street corners and jeer at Europeans.

All this was perplexing and upsetting. For at that time I had already 2 made up my mind that imperialism was an evil thing and the sooner I chucked up my job and got out of it the better. Theoretically — and secretly, of course — I was all for the Burmese and all against their oppressors, the British. As for the job I was doing, I hated it more bitterly than I can perhaps make clear. In a job like that you see the dirty work of Empire at close quarters. The wretched prisoners huddling in the stinking cages of the lockups, the grey, cowed faces of the long-term convicts, the scarred buttocks of the men who had been flogged with bamboos — all these oppressed me with an intolerable sense of guilt. But I could get nothing into perspective. I was young and ill-educated and I had had to think out my problems in the utter silence that is imposed on every Englishman in the East. I did not even know that the British Empire is dying, still less did I know that it is a great deal better than the younger empires that are going to supplant it.* All I knew was that I was stuck between my hatred of the empire I served and my rage against the evil-spirited little beasts who tried to make my job impossible. With one part of my mind I thought of the British Raj** as an unbreakable tyranny, as something clamped down, in *saecula saeculorum*,*** upon the will of prostrate peoples; with another part I thought that the greatest joy in the world would be to drive a bayonet into a Buddhist priest's guts. Feelings like these are the normal by-products of imperialism; ask any Anglo-Indian official, if you can catch him off duty.

One day something happened which in a roundabout way was enlight- 3 ening. It was a tiny incident in itself, but it gave me a better glimpse than I had had before of the real nature of imperialism — the real motives for which despotic governments act. Early one morning the sub-inspector at a police station the other end of the town rang me up on the phone and said that an elephant was ravaging the bazaar. Would I please come and do something about it? I did not know what I could do, but I wanted to see what was happening and I got on to a pony and started out. I took my rifle, an old .44 Winchester and much too small to kill an elephant, but I thought the noise might be useful *in terrorem*.† Various Burmans stopped me on the way and told me about the elephant's doings. It was not, of course, a wild elephant, but a tame one which had gone "must."‡ It had been chained up, as tame elephants always are when their attack of "must" is due, but on the previous night it had broken its chain and escaped. Its mahout,§ the only person who could manage it when it was in that state, had set out in pursuit, but had taken the wrong direction and was now

---

* Eds. note — Orwell was writing in 1936, when Hitler and Stalin were in power and World War II was only three years away.
** Eds. note — The former British rule of the Indian subcontinent.
*** Eds. note — From time immemorial.
† Eds. note — For the purpose of frightening.
‡ Eds. note — Was in heat, a condition likely to wear off.
§ Eds. note — A keeper and driver of an elephant.

twelve hours' journey away, and in the morning the elephant had suddenly reappeared in the town. The Burmese population had no weapons and were quite helpless against it. It had already destroyed somebody's bamboo hut, killed a cow, and raided some fruit-stalls and devoured the stock; also it had met the municipal rubbish van and, when the driver jumped out and took to his heels, had turned the van over and inflicted violences upon it.

The Burmese sub-inspector and some Indian constables were waiting for me in the quarter where the elephant had been seen. It was a very poor quarter, a labyrinth of squalid bamboo huts, thatched with palm-leaf, winding all over a steep hillside. I remember that it was a cloudy, stuffy morning at the beginning of the rains. We began questioning people as to where the elephant had gone, and, as usual, failed to get any definite information. That is invariably the case in the East; a story always sounds clear enough at a distance, but the nearer you get to the scene of events the vaguer it becomes. Some of the people said that the elephant had gone in one direction, some said that he had gone in another, some professed not even to have heard of an elephant. I had almost made up my mind that the whole story was a pack of lies, when we heard yells a little distance away. There was a loud, scandalized cry of "Go away, child! Go away this instant!" and an old woman with a switch in her hand came round the corner of a hut, violently shooing away a crowd of naked children. Some more women followed, clicking their tongues and exclaiming; evidently there was something that the children ought not to have seen. I rounded the hut and saw a man's dead body sprawling in the mud. He was an Indian, a black Dravidian coolie,* almost naked, and he could not have been dead many minutes. The people said that the elephant had come suddenly upon him round the corner of the hut, caught him with its trunk, put its foot on his back, and ground him into the earth. This was the rainy season and the ground was soft, and his face had scored a trench a foot deep and a couple of yards long. He was lying on his belly with arms crucified and head sharply twisted to one side. His face was coated with mud, the eyes wide open, the teeth bared and grinning with an expression of unendurable agony. (Never tell me, by the way, that the dead look peaceful. Most of the corpses I have seen looked devilish.) The friction of the great beast's foot had stripped the skin from his back as neatly as one skins a rabbit. As soon as I saw the dead man I sent an orderly to a friend's house nearby to borrow an elephant rifle. I had already sent back the pony, not wanting it to go mad with fright and throw me if it smelled the elephant.

The orderly came back in a few minutes with a rifle and five cartridges, and meanwhile some Burmans had arrived and told us that the elephant was in the paddy** fields below, only a few hundred yards away. As I started

---

* Eds. note — An unskilled laborer.
** Eds. note — Wet land for growing rice.

forward practically the whole population of the quarter flocked out of the houses and followed me. They had seen the rifle and were all shouting excitedly that I was going to shoot the elephant. They had not shown much interest in the elephant when he was merely ravaging their homes, but it was different now that he was going to be shot. It was a bit of fun to them, as it would be to an English crowd; besides they wanted the meat. It made me vaguely uneasy. I had no intention of shooting the elephant — I had merely sent for the rifle to defend myself if necessary — and it is always unnerving to have a crowd following you. I marched down the hill, looking and feeling a fool, with the rifle over my shoulder and an ever-growing army of people jostling at my heels. At the bottom, when you got away from the huts, there was a metalled road and beyond that a miry waste of paddy fields a thousand yards across, not yet ploughed but soggy from the first rains and dotted with coarse grass. The elephant was standing eight yards from the road, his left side towards us. He took not the slightest notice of the crowd's approach. He was tearing up bunches of grass, beating them against his knees to clean them and stuffing them into his mouth.

I had halted on the road. As soon as I saw the elephant I knew with perfect certainty that I ought not to shoot him. It is a serious matter to shoot a working elephant — it is comparable to destroying a huge and costly piece of machinery — and obviously one ought not to do it if it can possibly be avoided. And at that distance, peacefully eating, the elephant looked no more dangerous than a cow. I thought then and I think now that his attack of "must" was already passing off; in which case he would merely wander harmlessly about until the mahout came back and caught him. Moreover, I did not in the least want to shoot him. I decided that I would watch him for a little while to make sure that he did not turn savage again, and then go home.

But at that moment I glanced round at the crowd that had followed me. It was an immense crowd, two thousand at the least and growing every minute. It blocked the road for a long distance on either side. I looked at the sea of yellow faces above the garish clothes — faces all happy and excited over this bit of fun, all certain that the elephant was going to be shot. They were watching me as they would watch a conjurer about to perform a trick. They did not like me, but with the magical rifle in my hands I was momentarily worth watching. And suddenly I realized that I should have to shoot the elephant after all. The people expected it of me and I had got to do it; I could feel their two thousand wills pressing me forward, irresistibly. And it was at this moment, as I stood there with the rifle in my hands, that I first grasped the hollowness, the futility of the white man's dominion in the East. Here was I, the white man with his gun, standing in front of the unarmed native crowd — seemingly the leading actor of the piece; but in reality I was only an absurd puppet pushed to and fro by the will of those yellow faces behind. I perceived in this moment that when the white man turns tyrant it is his own freedom that he destroys. He becomes a sort of hollow, posing dummy, the conventionalized figure of a sahib.* For it is the condition of his rule that he shall spend his life in trying to impress the "natives," and so in every crisis he has got to do what the "natives" expect of him. He wears a mask, and his face grows to fit it. I had got to shoot the elephant. I had committed myself to doing it when I sent for the rifle. A sahib has got to act like a sahib; he has got to appear resolute, to know his own mind and do definite things. To come all that way, rifle in hand, with two thousand people marching at my heels, and then to trail feebly away, having done nothing — no, that was impossible. The crowd would laugh at me. And my whole life, every white man's life in the East, was one long struggle not to be laughed at.

But I did not want to shoot the elephant. I watched him beating his 8 bunch of grass against his knees, with the preoccupied grandmotherly air that elephants have. It seemed to me that it would be murder to shoot him. At that age I was not squeamish about killing animals, but I had never shot an elephant and never wanted to. (Somehow it always seems worse to kill a *large* animal.) Besides, there was the beast's owner to be considered. Alive, the elephant was worth at least a hundred pounds; dead, he would only be worth the value of his tusks, five pounds, possibly. But I had got to act quickly. I turned to some experienced-looking Burmans who had been there when we arrived, and asked them how the elephant had been behaving. They all said the same thing: he took no notice of you if you left him alone, but he might charge if you went too close to him.

It was perfectly clear to me what I ought to do. I ought to walk up to 9 within, say, twenty-five yards of the elephant and test his behavior. If he charged I could shoot, if he took no notice of me it would be safe to leave him until the mahout came back. But also I knew that I was going to do no such thing. I was a poor shot with a rifle and the ground was soft mud into which one would sink at every step. If the elephant charged and I missed him, I should have about as much chance as a toad under a steamroller. But even then I was not thinking particularly of my own skin, only of the watchful yellow faces behind. For at that moment, with the crowd watching me, I was not afraid in the ordinary sense, as I would have been if I had been alone. A white man mustn't be frightened in front of "natives"; and so, in general, he isn't frightened. The sole thought in my mind was that if anything went wrong those two thousand Burmans would see me pursued, caught, trampled on, and reduced to a grinning corpse like that Indian up the hill. And if that happened it was quite probable that some of them would laugh. That would never do. There was only one alternative. I shoved the cartridges into the magazine and lay down on the road to get a better aim.

---

* Eds. note — An official. The term was used among Hindus and Muslims in colonial India.

The crowd grew very still, and a deep, low, happy sigh, as of people who   10
see the theatre curtain go up at last, breathed from innumerable throats.
They were going to have their bit of fun after all. The rifle was a beautiful
German thing with cross-hair sights. I did not then know that in shooting an elephant one would shoot to cut an imaginary bar running from
ear-hole to ear-hole. I ought, therefore, as the elephant was sideways on, to
have aimed straight at his ear-hole; actually I aimed several inches in front
of this, thinking the brain would be further forward.

   When I pulled the trigger I did not hear the bang or feel the kick — one   11
never does when a shot goes home — but I heard the devilish roar of glee
that went up from the crowd. In that instant, in too short a time, one
would have thought, even for the bullet to get there, a mysterious, terrible
change had come over the elephant. He neither stirred nor fell, but every
line on his body had altered. He looked suddenly stricken, shrunken, immensely old, as though the frightful impact of the bullet had paralyzed him
without knocking him down. At last, after what seemed a long time — it
might have been five seconds, I dare say — he sagged flabbily to his knees.
His mouth slobbered. An enormous senility seemed to have settled upon
him. One could have imagined him thousands of years old. I fired again
into the same spot. At the second shot he did not collapse but climbed
with desperate slowness to his feet and stood weakly upright, with legs
sagging and head drooping. I fired a third time. That was the shot that
did for him. You could see the agony of it jolt his whole body and knock
the last remnant of strength from his legs. But in falling he seemed for a
moment to rise, for as his hind legs collapsed beneath him he seemed to
tower upwards like a huge rock toppling, his trunk reaching skywards like
a tree. He trumpeted, for the first and only time. And then down he came,
his belly towards me, with a crash that seemed to shake the ground even
where I lay.

   I got up. The Burmans were already racing past me across the mud.   12
It was obvious that the elephant would never rise again, but he was not
dead. He was breathing very rhythmically with long rattling gasps, his great
mound of a side painfully rising and falling. His mouth was wide open — I
could see far down into the caverns of pale pink throat. I waited a long time
for him to die, but his breathing did not weaken. Finally I fired my two remaining shots into the spot where I thought his heart must be. The thick
blood welled out of him like red velvet, but still he did not die. His body
did not even jerk when the shots hit him, the tortured breathing continued
without a pause. He was dying, very slowly and in great agony, but in some
world remote from me where not even a bullet could damage him further. I
felt that I had got to put an end to that dreadful noise. It seemed dreadful
to see the great beast lying there, powerless to move and yet powerless to
die, and not even to be able to finish him. I sent back for my small rifle and
poured shot after shot into his heart and down his throat. They seemed to
make no impression. The tortured gasps continued as steadily as the ticking of a clock.

In the end I could not stand it any longer and went away. I heard later 13
that it took him half an hour to die. Burmans were bringing dahs* and
baskets even before I left, and I was told they had stripped his body almost
to the bones by the afternoon.

Afterwards, of course, there were endless discussions about the shoot- 14
ing of the elephant. The owner was furious, but he was only an Indian and
could do nothing. Besides, legally I had done the right thing, for a mad
elephant has to be killed, like a mad dog, if its owner fails to control it.
Among the Europeans opinion was divided. The older men said I was right,
the younger men said it was a damn shame to shoot an elephant for killing
a coolie, because an elephant was worth more than any damn Coringhee
coolie. And afterwards I was very glad that the coolie had been killed; it put
me legally in the right and it gave me a sufficient pretext for shooting the
elephant. I often wondered whether any of the others grasped that I had
done it solely to avoid looking a fool.

· · ·

Comprehension

1. Why is Orwell "hated by large numbers of people" (1) in Burma? Why
   does he have mixed feelings toward the Burmese people?

2. Why do the local officials want something done about the elephant? Why
   does the crowd want Orwell to shoot the elephant?

3. Why does Orwell finally decide to kill the elephant? What makes him hes-
   itate at first?

4. Why does Orwell say at the end that he was glad the coolie had been
   killed?

Purpose and Audience

1. One of Orwell's purposes in telling his story is to show how it gave him a
   glimpse of "the real nature of imperialism" (3). What does he mean? How
   does his essay illustrate this purpose?

2. Do you think Orwell wrote this essay to inform or to persuade his audience? How did Orwell expect his audience to react to his ideas? How can
   you tell?

3. What is the essay's thesis?

Style and Structure

1. What does Orwell's first paragraph accomplish? Where does the introduction end and the narrative itself begin?

---

* Eds. note — Heavy knives.

2. The essay includes almost no dialogue. Why do you think Orwell's voice as narrator is the only one readers hear? Is the absence of dialogue a strength or a weakness? Explain.

3. Why do you think Orwell devotes so much attention to the elephant's misery (11–12)?

4. Orwell's essay includes a number of editorial comments, which appear within parentheses or dashes. How would you characterize these comments? Why are they set off from the text?

5. Consider the following statements: "Some of the people said that the elephant had gone in one direction, some said that he had gone in another" (4); "Among the Europeans opinion was divided. The older men said I was right, the younger men said it was a damn shame to shoot an elephant" (14). How do these comments reinforce the idea expressed in paragraph 2 ("All I knew was that I was stuck between my hatred of the empire I served and my rage against the evil-spirited little beasts")? What other comments reinforce this idea?

Vocabulary Projects

1. Define each of the following words as it is used in this selection.

baited (1)	despotic (3)	conjurer (7)
perplexing (2)	labyrinth (4)	dominion (7)
oppressors (2)	squalid (4)	magazine (9)
lockups (2)	professed (4)	cross-hair (10)
flogged (2)	ravaging (5)	remnant (11)
supplant (2)	miry (5)	trumpeted (11)
prostrate (2)	garish (7)	pretext (14)

2. Because Orwell is British, he frequently uses words or expressions that an American writer would not likely use. Substitute a contemporary American word or phrase for each of the following, making sure it is appropriate in Orwell's context.

raise a riot (1)	rubbish van (3)	a bit of fun (5)
rang me up (3)	inflicted violences (3)	I dare say (11)

What other expressions in Orwell's essay might need to be "translated" for a contemporary American audience?

Journal Entry

Do you think Orwell is a coward? Do you think he is a racist? Explain your feelings.

Writing Workshop

1. **Working with Sources.** Orwell says that even though he hated British imperialism and sympathized with the Burmese people, he found himself

a puppet of the system. Write a narrative essay about a time when you had to do something that went against your beliefs or convictions. Begin by summarizing Orwell's situation in Burma, and go on to show how your situation was similar to his. If you quote Orwell, be sure to include documentation and a works-cited page. (See Chapter 18 for information on MLA documentation.)

2. Orwell's experience taught him something not only about himself but also about something beyond himself — the way British imperialism worked. Write a narrative essay that reveals how an incident in your life taught you something about some larger social or political force as well as about yourself.

3. Write an objective, factual newspaper article recounting the events Orwell describes.

Combining the Patterns

Implicit in this narrative essay is an extended **comparison and contrast** that highlights the differences between Orwell and the Burmese people. Review the essay, and list the most obvious differences Orwell perceives between himself and them. Do you think his perceptions are accurate? If all of the differences were set forth in a single paragraph, how might such a paragraph change your perception of Orwell's dilemma? Of his character?

Thematic Connections

- "Thirty-Eight Who Saw Murder Didn't Call the Police" (page 127)
- "Just Walk On By: A Black Man Ponders His Power to Alter Public Space" (page 240)
- "The Untouchable" (page 496)
- "The Shame Game" (page 680)

Indian Education (Fiction)

Sherman Alexie, the son of a Coeur d'Alene Indian father and a Spokane Indian mother, was born in 1966 and grew up on the Spokane Reservation in Wellpinit, Washington, home to some eleven hundred Spokane tribal members. Realizing as a teenager that his educational opportunities there were extremely limited, Alexie made the unusual decision to attend high school off the reservation in nearby Reardon. Later a scholarship student at Gonzaga University, he received a bachelor's degree in American studies from Washington State University at Pullman. While in college, he began publishing poetry; within a year of graduation, his first collection, *The Business of Fancydancing* (1992), appeared. This was followed by *The Lone Ranger and Tonto Fistfight in Heaven* (1993), a short-story collection, and the novels *Reservation Blues* (1995) and *Indian Killer* (1996), all of which garnered numerous awards and honors. Alexie also wrote the screenplay for the film *Smoke Signals* (1998) and wrote and directed *The Business of Fancydancing* (2002). His most recent novel, *The Absolutely True Diary of a Part-Time Indian*, won the 2007 National Book Award for Young People's Literature. *War Dances*, a collection of his stories and poems, was published in 2009 and received the PEN/Faulkner Award for Fiction in 2010.

Background on the U.S. government's "Indian schools" By the mid-1800s, most Native American tribes had been overwhelmed by the superior weapons of the U.S. military and confined to reservations. Beginning in the late 1800s and continuing into the 1950s, government policymakers established boarding schools for Native American youth to help them assimilate into the dominant culture and thus become "civilized." To this end, children were forcibly removed from their homes for long periods to separate them from native traditions. At the boarding schools, they were given a cursory academic education and spent most of their time studying Christian teachings and working to offset the cost of their schooling. Students were punished for speaking their own language or practicing their own religion. Responding to protests from the American Indian movement in the 1970s, the U.S. government began to send fewer Native Americans to boarding schools and retreated from its goal of assimilation at boarding schools and at newly established reservation schools. However, such schools still exist. Today, government funding for Native American schools remains considerably lower than for other public schools, and students often make do with inadequate and antiquated facilities, equipment, and textbooks. In part because of such educational failures, few Native American students go on to college, and the incidence of alcohol and drug abuse among Native Americans is higher than in any other U.S. population.

First Grade

My hair was too short and my U.S. Government glasses were horn- 1
rimmed, ugly, and all that first winter in school, the other Indian boys
chased me from one corner of the playground to the other. They pushed
me down, buried me in the snow until I couldn't breathe, thought I'd never
breathe again.

They stole my glasses and threw them over my head, around my out- 2
stretched hands, just beyond my reach, until someone tripped me and sent
me falling again, facedown in the snow.

I was always falling down; my Indian name was Junior Falls Down. 3
Sometimes it was Bloody Nose or Steal-His-Lunch. Once, it was Cries-Like-
a-White-Boy, even though none of us had seen a white boy cry.

Then it was a Friday morning recess and Frenchy SiJohn threw snow- 4
balls at me while the rest of the Indian boys tortured some other *top-yogh-
yaught* kid, another weakling. But Frenchy was confident enough to tor-
ment me all by himself, and most days I would have let him.

But the little warrior in me roared to life that day and knocked Frenchy 5
to the ground, held his head against the snow, and punched him so hard
that my knuckles and the snow made symmetrical bruises on his face. He
almost looked like he was wearing war paint.

But he wasn't the warrior. I was. And I chanted *It's a good day to die, it's a* 6
good day to die, all the way down to the principal's office.

Second Grade

Betty Towle, missionary teacher, redheaded and so ugly that no one 7
ever had a puppy crush on her, made me stay in for recess fourteen days
straight.

"Tell me you're sorry," she said. 8

"Sorry for what?" I asked. 9

"Everything," she said and made me stand straight for fifteen minutes, 10
eagle-armed with books in each hand. One was a math book; the other was
English. But all I learned was that gravity can be painful.

For Halloween I drew a picture of her riding a broom with a scrawny 11
cat on the back. She said that her God would never forgive me for that.

Once, she gave the class a spelling test but set me aside and gave me a 12
test designed for junior high students. When I spelled all the words right,
she crumpled up the paper and made me eat it.

"You'll learn respect," she said. 13

She sent a letter home with me that told my parents to either cut my 14
braids or keep me home from class. My parents came in the next day and
dragged their braids across Betty Towle's desk.

"Indians, indians, indians." She said it without capitalization. She 15
called me "indian, indian, indian."

And I said, *Yes, I am. I am Indian. Indian, I am.* 16

Third Grade

My traditional Native American art career began and ended with my 17
very first portrait: *Stick Indian Taking a Piss in My Backyard.*

As I circulated the original print around the classroom, Mrs. Schluter 18
intercepted and confiscated my art.

Censorship, I might cry now. *Freedom of expression,* I would write in edito- 19
rials to the tribal newspaper.

In third grade, though, I stood alone in the corner, faced the wall, and 20
waited for the punishment to end.

I'm still waiting.   21

Fourth Grade

"You should be a doctor when you grow up," Mr. Schluter told me, 22
even though his wife, the third grade teacher, thought I was crazy beyond
my years. My eyes always looked like I had just hit-and-run someone.

"Guilty," she said. "You always look guilty."   23

"Why should I be a doctor?" I asked Mr. Schluter.   24

"So you can come back and help the tribe. So you can heal people."   25

That was the year my father drank a gallon of vodka a day and the same 26
year that my mother started two hundred different quilts but never finished
any. They sat in separate, dark places in our HUD house and wept savagely.

I ran home after school, heard their Indian tears, and looked in the 27
mirror. *Doctor Victor,* I called myself, invented an education, talked to my
reflection. *Doctor Victor to the emergency room.*

Fifth Grade

I picked up a basketball for the first time and made my first shot. No. I 28
missed my first shot, missed the basket completely, and the ball landed in
the dirt and sawdust, sat there just like I had sat there only minutes before.

But it felt good, that ball in my hands, all those possibilities and 29
angles. It was mathematics, geometry. It was beautiful.

At that same moment, my cousin Steven Ford sniffed rubber cement 30
from a paper bag and leaned back on the merry-go-round. His ears rang,
his mouth was dry, and everyone seemed so far away.

But it felt good, that buzz in his head, all those colors and noises. It was 31
chemistry, biology. It was beautiful.

Oh, do you remember those sweet, almost innocent choices that the Indian 32
boys were forced to make?

Sixth Grade

Randy, the new Indian kid from the white town of Springdale, got into 33
a fight an hour after he first walked into the reservation school.

Stevie Flett called him out, called him a squawman, called him a pussy, 34
and called him a punk.

Randy and Stevie, and the rest of the Indian boys, walked out into the 35
playground.

"Throw the first punch," Stevie said as they squared off. 36

"No," Randy said. 37

"Throw the first punch," Stevie said again. 38

"No," Randy said again. 39

"Throw the first punch!" Stevie said for the third time, and Randy 40
reared back and pitched a knuckle fastball that broke Stevie's nose.

We all stood there in silence, in awe. 41

That was Randy, my soon-to-be first and best friend, who taught me 42
the most valuable lesson about living in the white world: *Always throw the
first punch.*

Seventh Grade

I leaned through the basement window of the HUD house and kissed 43
the white girl who would later be raped by her foster-parent father, who
was also white. They both lived on the reservation, though, and when the
headlines and stories filled the papers later, not one word was made of their
color.

Just Indians being Indians, someone must have said somewhere and they 44
were wrong.

But on the day I leaned through the basement window of the HUD 45
house and kissed the white girl, I felt the good-byes I was saying to my entire tribe. I held my lips tight against her lips, a dry, clumsy, and ultimately
stupid kiss.

But I was saying good-bye to my tribe, to all the Indian girls and women 46
I might have loved, to all the Indian men who might have called me cousin,
even brother.

I kissed that white girl and when I opened my eyes, she was gone from 47
the reservation, and when I opened my eyes, I was gone from the reservation, living in a farm town where a beautiful white girl asked my name.

"Junior Polatkin," I said, and she laughed. 48

After that, no one spoke to me for another five hundred years. 49

Eighth Grade

At the farm town junior high, in the boys' bathroom, I could hear 50
voices from the girls' bathroom, nervous whispers of anorexia and bulimia.
I could hear the white girls' forced vomiting, a sound so familiar and natural to me after years of listening to my father's hangovers.

"Give me your lunch if you're just going to throw it up," I said to one 51
of those girls once.

I sat back and watched them grow skinny from self-pity. 52

• • •

Back on the reservation, my mother stood in line to get us commodities. 53
We carried them home, happy to have food, and opened the canned beef
that even the dogs wouldn't eat.

But we ate it day after day and grew skinny from self-pity. 54

There is more than one way to starve. 55

Ninth Grade

At the farm town high school dance, after a basketball game in an over- 56
heated gym where I had scored twenty-seven points and pulled down thirteen rebounds, I passed out during a slow song.

As my white friends revived me and prepared to take me to the emer- 57
gency room where doctors would later diagnose my diabetes, the Chicano
teacher ran up to us.

"Hey," he said. "What's that boy been drinking? I know all about these 58
Indian kids. They start drinking real young."

Sharing dark skin doesn't necessarily make two men brothers. 59

Tenth Grade

I passed the written test easily and nearly flunked the driving, but still 60
received my Washington State driver's license on the same day that Wally
Jim killed himself by driving his car into a pine tree.

No traces of alcohol in his blood, good job, wife and two kids. 61

"Why'd he do it?" asked a white Washington State trooper. 62

All the Indians shrugged their shoulders, looked down at the ground. 63

"Don't know," we all said, but when we look in the mirror, see the his- 64
tory of our tribe in our eyes, taste failure in the tap water, and shake with
old tears, we understand completely.

Believe me, everything looks like a noose if you stare at it long enough. 65

Eleventh Grade

Last night I missed two free throws which would have won the game 66
against the best team in the state. The farm town high school I play for is
nicknamed the "Indians," and I'm probably the only actual Indian ever to
play for a team with such a mascot.

This morning I pick up the sports page and read the headline: INDIANS 67
LOSE AGAIN.

Go ahead and tell me none of this is supposed to hurt me very much. 68

Twelfth Grade

I walk down the aisle, valedictorian of this farm town high school, and 69
my cap doesn't fit because I've grown my hair longer than it's ever been.

Later, I stand as the school-board chairman recites my awards, accomplishments, and scholarships.

I try to remain stoic for the photographers as I look toward the future.   70

Back home on the reservation, my former classmates graduate: a few can't   71
read, one or two are just given attendance diplomas, most look forward to
the parties. The bright students are shaken, frightened, because they don't
know what comes next.

They smile for the photographer as they look back toward tradition.   72

The tribal newspaper runs my photograph and the photograph of my for-   73
mer classmates side by side.

Postscript: Class Reunion

Victor said, "Why should we organize a reservation high school re-   74
union? My graduating class has a reunion every weekend at the Powwow
Tavern."

•   •   •

Reading Literature

1. Instead of linking events with transitional phrases that establish chronology, Alexie uses headings to move readers through his story. How do these headings indicate the passage of time? Are these headings enough, or do you think Alexie should have opened each section of the story with a transitional phrase? (Try to suggest some possibilities.)

2. The narrator's experiences in each grade in school are illustrated by specific incidents. What do these incidents have in common? What do they reveal about the narrator? About his schools?

3. Explain the meaning of each of these statements in the context of the story:

   • "There is more than one way to starve" (55).
   • "Sharing dark skin doesn't necessarily make two men brothers" (59).
   • "Believe me, everything looks like a noose if you stare at it long enough" (65).

Journal Entry

What does the "Postscript: Class Reunion" section (74) tell readers about Indian education? Is this information consistent with what we have learned in the rest of the story, or does it come as a surprise? Explain.

Thematic Connections

• "College Pressures" (page 450)
• "The Dog Ate My Disk, and Other Tales of Woe" (page 460)
• The Declaration of Independence (page 553)

Writing Assignments for Narration

1. Trace the path you expect to follow to establish yourself in your chosen profession, considering possible obstacles you may face and how you expect to deal with them. Include a thesis statement that conveys the importance of your goals. If you like, you may refer to some readings in this book that focus on work — for example, the two essays in the debate "Are Internships Fair to Students?" (page 582).

2. Write a personal narrative looking back from some point in the far future on your own life as you hope others will see it. Use third person if you like, and write your own obituary; or, use first person, assessing your life in a letter to your great-grandchildren.

3. Write a news article recounting in objective terms the events described in an essay that appears anywhere in this text — for example, "Who Killed Benny Paret?" (page 339) or "Grant and Lee: A Study in Contrasts" (page 393). Include a descriptive headline.

4. Write the introductory narrative for the home page of your family's (or community's) Web site. In this historical narrative, trace the roots of your family or your hometown or community. Be sure to include specific detail, dialogue, and descriptions of people and places. (You may also include visuals if you like.)

5. Write an account of one of these "firsts": your first serious argument with your parents; your first experience with physical violence or danger; your first extended stay away from home; your first encounter with someone whose culture was very different from your own; or your first experience with the serious illness or death of a close friend or relative. Make sure your essay includes a thesis statement your narrative can support.

Can be on any first not just these one?

6. **Working with Sources.** Both George Orwell and Martin Gansberg deal with the consequences of failing to act. Write an essay or story recounting what would have happened if Orwell had *not* shot the elephant or if one of the eyewitnesses *had* called the police right away. Be sure to document references to Orwell or Gansberg and to include a works-cited page. (See Chapter 18 for information on MLA documentation.)

7. A Pink Floyd concert was Mark Edmundson's "night school." Write an essay about a place where you developed into the person you are today. What did you learn from this place, and how did this knowledge serve you later?

8. **Working with Sources.** Write a narrative about a time when you were an outsider, isolated because of social, intellectual, or ethnic differences between you and others. Did you resolve the problems your isolation created? Explain. If you like, you may refer to the Orwell essay in this chapter or to "Just Walk On By" (page 240), taking care to include parenthetical documentation and a works-cited page. (See Chapter 18 for information on MLA documentation.)

9. Imagine a meeting between any two people who appear in this chapter's reading selections. Using dialogue and narrative, write an account of this meeting.

10. Using Alexie's story as a model, write the story of your own education.

11. List the five books you have read that most influenced you at important stages of your life. Then, write your literary autobiography, tracing your personal development through these books. (Or, write your wardrobe autobiography — discussing what you wore at different times of your life — or your music autobiography.)

Collaborative Activity for Narration

Working with a group of students of about your own age, write a history of your television-viewing habits. Start by working individually to list all your most-watched television shows in chronological order, beginning as far back as you can remember. Then, compile a single list that reflects a consensus of the group's preferences, perhaps choosing one or two representative programs for each stage of your life (preschool, elementary school, and so on). Have a different student write a paragraph on each stage, describing the chosen programs in as much detail as possible and using "we" as the subject. Finally, combine the individual paragraphs to create a narrative essay that traces the group's changing tastes in television shows. The essay's thesis statement should express what your group's television preferences reveal about your generation's development.

7

Description

What Is Description?

You use **description** to tell readers about the physical characteristics of a person, place, or thing. Description relies on the five senses —
sight, hearing, taste, touch, and smell. In the following paragraph from
"Knoxville: Summer 1915," James Agee uses sight, touch, and sound to re-
create a summer's evening for his audience.

Topic sentence

It is not of games children play in the evening
that I want to speak now, it is of a contemporane-
ous atmosphere that has little to do with them; that
of fathers and families, each in his space of lawn, his

Description using sight

shirt fishlike pale in the unnatural light and his face
nearly anonymous, hosing their lawns. The hoses
were attached to spigots that stood out of the brick
foundations of the houses. The nozzles were vari-
ously set but usually so there was a long sweet

Description using touch

stream of spray, the nozzle wet in the hand, the
water trickling the right forearm and the peeled-back
cuff, and the water whishing out a long loose and
low-curved cone, and so gentle a sound. First an in-

Description using sound

sane noise of violence in the nozzle, then the still
irregular sound of adjustment, then the smoothing
into steadiness and a pitch as accurately tuned to
the size and style of stream as any violin. So many
qualities of sound out of one hose: so many cho-
ral differences out of those several hoses that were
in earshot. Out of any one hose, the almost dead
silence of the release, and the short still arch of
the separate big drops, silent as a held breath, and
the only noise the flattering noise on leaves and the
slapped grass at the fall of each big drop. That, and
the intense hiss with the intense stream; that, and
the same intensity not growing less but growing
more quiet and delicate with the turn of the nozzle,

up to that extreme tender whisper when the water was just a wide bell of film.

A descriptive essay tells what something looks like or what it feels like, sounds like, smells like, or tastes like. However, description often goes beyond personal sense impressions: novelists can create imaginary landscapes, historians can paint word pictures of historical figures, and scientists can describe physical phenomena they have never actually seen. When you write description, you use language to create a vivid impression for your readers.

Using Description

In your college writing, you use description in many different kinds of assignments. In a comparison-and-contrast essay, for example, you may describe the designs of two proposed buildings to show that one is more desirable than the other. In an argumentative essay, you may describe a fish kill in a local river to make the point that industrial waste dumping is a problem. Through description, you communicate your view of the world to your readers. If your readers come to understand or share your view, they are more likely to accept your observations, your judgments, and, eventually, your conclusions. Therefore, in almost every essay you write, knowing how to write effective description is important.

Understanding Objective Description

Description can be objective or subjective. In an **objective description**, you focus on the object itself rather than on your personal reactions to it. Your purpose is to present a precise, literal picture of your subject. Many writing situations require exact descriptions of apparatus or conditions, and in these cases your goal is to construct an accurate picture for your audience. A biologist describing what he sees through a microscope and a historian describing a Civil War battlefield would both write objectively. The biologist would not, for instance, say how exciting his observations were, nor would the historian say how disappointed she was at the outcome of the battle. Many newspaper reporters also try to achieve this objectivity, as do writers of technical reports, scientific papers, and certain types of business correspondence. Still, objectivity is an ideal that writers strive for but never fully achieve. In fact, in selecting some details and leaving out others, writers are making subjective decisions.

In the following descriptive passage, Shakespearean scholar Thomas Marc Parrott aims for objectivity by giving his readers the factual information they need to visualize Shakespeare's theater:

The main or outer stage [of Shakespeare's theater] was a large platform, which projected out into the audience. Sections of the floor could be removed to make such things as the grave in the grave digger's scene in *Hamlet*, or they could be transformed into trapdoors through which characters could disappear, as in *The Tempest*. The players referred to the space beneath the platform as the Hell. At the rear of the platform and at the same level was the smaller, inner stage, or alcove. . . . Above the alcove at the level of the second story, there was another curtained stage, the chamber. . . . The action of the play would move from one scene to another, using one, two, or all of them. Above the chamber was the music gallery; . . . and above this were the windows, "The Huts," where characters and lookouts could appear.

Artist's rendering of the Globe Theatre, London.

Note that Parrott is not interested in responding to or evaluating the theater he describes. Instead, he chooses words that convey sizes and directions, such as *large* and *above*.

Objective descriptions are sometimes accompanied by **visuals**, such as diagrams, drawings, or photographs. A well-chosen visual can enhance a description by enabling writers to avoid tedious passages of description that might confuse readers. To be effective, a visual should clearly illustrate what is being discussed and not introduce new material.

The illustration on page 153, which accompanies Parrott's description of Shakespeare's theater, makes the passage much easier to understand, helping readers to visualize the multiple stages where Shakespeare's plays were performed.

✔**CHECKLIST**   Using Visuals Effectively

If your instructor permits you to use visuals, ask the following questions to make sure that you have used them responsibly and effectively.

- **Does your visual add something to your paper?** For example, you could use a diagram to help explain a process, a chart or graph to clarify statistics, or a photograph to show an unusual structure.
- **Is your visual located as close as possible to where it is discussed in the paper?** This placement will establish the context for the visual and ensure that readers understand the reason why you have included it.
- **Have you documented your visual?** Like all material you borrow from a source, visuals must be documented. (For more on documentation, see Chapter 18.)

TECH TIP: Finding Visuals

You can find visuals on the Internet, on DVDs, or on clip-art compilations. You can also scan pictures you find in print sources or download pictures you take with a digital camera. Once the visual is downloaded onto your computer as a file, you can cut and paste it into your essay. Remember, however, that all visual material you get from a source — whether print or Internet — must be documented.

Understanding Subjective Description

In contrast to objective description, **subjective description** conveys your personal response to your subject. Here your perspective is not necessarily stated explicitly; often it is revealed indirectly, through your choice of words and phrasing. If an English composition assignment asks you to describe a place that has special meaning to you, you could give a subjective reaction to your topic by selecting and emphasizing details that show your feelings about the place. For example, you could write a subjective description of your room by focusing on particular objects — your desk, your window, and your bookshelves — and explaining the meanings these things have for you. Thus, your desk could be a "warm brown rectangle of wood whose surface reveals the scratched impressions of a thousand school assignments."

A subjective description should convey not just a literal record of sights and sounds but also their significance. For example, if you objectively described a fire that destroyed a house in your neighborhood, you might include its temperature, duration, and scope. In addition, you might describe, as accurately as possible, the fire's movement and intensity. If you subjectively described the fire, however, you would try to re-create for your audience a sense of how the fire made you feel — your reactions to the noise, to the dense smoke, to the destruction.

In the following passage, notice how Mark Twain subjectively describes a sunset on the Mississippi River:

> I still kept in mind a certain wonderful sunset which I witnessed when steamboating was new to me. A broad expanse of the river was turned to blood; in the middle distance the red hue brightened into gold, through which a solitary log came floating, black and conspicuous; in one place a long, slanting mark lay sparkling upon the water; in another the surface was broken by boiling, tumbling rings, that were as many-tinted as an opal.

In this passage, Twain conveys his strong emotional reaction to the sunset by using vivid, powerful images, such as the river "turned to blood," the "solitary log . . . black and conspicuous," and the "boiling, tumbling rings." He also chooses words that suggest great value, such as *gold* and *opal*.

Neither objective nor subjective description exists independently. Objective descriptions usually include some subjective elements, and subjective descriptions need some objective elements to convey a sense of reality. The skillful writer adjusts the balance between objectivity and subjectivity to suit the topic, thesis, audience, and purpose as well as occasion for writing.

Using Objective and Subjective Language

As the passages by Parrott and Twain illustrate, both objective and subjective descriptions rely on language that appeals to readers' senses. But these two types of description use language differently. Objective descriptions rely on precise, factual language that presents a writer's observations without conveying his or her attitude toward the subject. Subjective descriptions, however, often use richer and more suggestive language than objective descriptions do. They are more likely to rely on the **connotations** of words, their emotional associations, than on their **denotations**, or more direct meanings (such as those found in a dictionary). In addition, they may deliberately provoke the reader's imagination with striking phrases or vivid language, including **figures of speech** such as *simile, metaphor, personification,* and *allusion.*

- A **simile** uses *like* or *as* to compare two dissimilar things. These comparisons occur frequently in everyday speech — for example, when someone claims to be "happy as a clam," "free as a bird," or "hungry as a bear." As a rule, however, you should avoid overused expressions like these in your writing. Effective writers constantly strive to create original similes. In his essay "Once More to the Lake" (page 194), for instance, E. B. White uses a striking simile to describe the annoying sound of boats on a lake when he says that in the evening "they whined around one's ears *like mosquitoes.*" Later in the same essay, he describes a thunderstorm as being "*like the revival of an old melodrama* that I had seen long ago with childish awe."

- A **metaphor** compares two dissimilar things without using *like* or *as.* Instead of saying that something is *like* something else, a metaphor says it *is* something else. Mark Twain uses a metaphor when he says, "A broad expanse of the river was turned to blood."

- **Personification** speaks of concepts or objects as if they had life or human characteristics. If you say that the wind whispered or that an engine died, you are using personification.

- An **allusion** is a reference to a person, place, event, or quotation that the writer assumes readers will recognize. In "Letter from Birmingham Jail" (page 566), for example, Martin Luther King Jr. enriches his argument by alluding to biblical passages and proverbs that he expects his audience of clergy to be familiar with.

Your purpose and audience determine whether you should use objective or subjective description. An assignment that specifically asks for reactions calls for a subjective description. Legal, medical, technical, business, and scientific writing assignments, however, usually require objective descriptions because their primary purpose is to give the audience factual information. Even in these areas, though, figures of speech are often used to describe an unfamiliar object or concept. For example, in their pioneering article on the structure of DNA, scientists James Watson and Francis Crick use a simile when they describe a molecule of DNA as looking like two spiral staircases winding around each other.

Selecting Details

Sometimes inexperienced writers pack their descriptions with general words such as *nice, great, terrific,* or *awful,* substituting their own reactions to an object for the qualities of the object itself. To produce an effective description, however, you must do more than just *say* something is wonderful — you must use details that evoke this response in your readers, as Twain does with the sunset. (Twain does use the word *wonderful* at the beginning of his description, but he then goes on to supply many specific details that make the scene he describes vivid and specific.)

All good descriptive writing, whether objective or subjective, relies on **specific details**. Your aim is not simply to *tell* readers what something looks like but to *show* them. Every person, place, or thing has its special characteristics, and you should use your powers of observation to detect them. Then, you need to select the specific words that will enable your readers to imagine what you describe. Don't be satisfied with "He looked angry" when you can say, "His face flushed, and one corner of his mouth twitched as he tried to control his anger." What's the difference? In the first case, you simply identify the man's emotional state. In the second, you provide enough detail so that readers can tell not only that he was angry but also how he revealed the intensity of his anger.

Of course, you could have provided even more detail by describing the man's beard, his wrinkles, or any number of other features. Keep in mind, however, that not all details are equally useful or desirable. You should include only those that contribute to the dominant impression you wish to create. Thus, in describing a man's face to show how angry he was, you would probably not include the shape of his nose or the color of his hair. (After all, a person's hair color does not change when he or she gets angry.) In fact, the number of particulars you use is less important than their quality and appropriateness. You should select and use only those details relevant to your purpose.

Factors such as the level, background, and knowledge of your audience also influence the kinds of details you include. For example, a description of a DNA molecule written for high school students would contain more basic descriptive details than a description written for college biology majors. In addition, the more advanced description would contain details — the sequence of amino acid groups, for instance — that might be inappropriate for high school students.

Planning a Descriptive Essay

Developing a Thesis Statement

Writers of descriptive essays often use an **implied thesis** when they describe a person, place, or thing. This technique allows them to convey an essay's main idea subtly, through the selection and arrangement of details. When they use description to support a particular point, however, many writers prefer to use an **explicitly stated thesis**. This strategy lets readers see immediately what point the writer is making — for example, "The sculptures that adorn Philadelphia's City Hall are a catalog of nineteenth-century artistic styles."

Whether you state or imply your thesis, the details of your descriptive essay must work together to create a single **dominant impression** — the mood or quality emphasized in the piece of writing. In many cases, your thesis may be just a statement of the dominant impression; sometimes, however, your thesis may go further and make a point about that dominant impression.

Organizing Details

When you plan a descriptive essay, you usually begin by writing down descriptive details in no particular order. You then arrange these details in a way that supports your thesis and communicates your dominant impression. As you consider how to arrange your details, keep in mind that you have a number of options. For example, you can move from a specific description of an object to a general description of other things around it. Or you can reverse this order, beginning with the general and proceeding to the specific. You can also progress from the least important feature to the most important one, from the smallest to the largest item, from the least unusual to the most unusual detail, or from left to right, right to left, top to bottom, or bottom to top. Another option is to combine approaches, using different organizing schemes in different parts of the essay. The strategy you choose depends on the dominant impression you want to convey, your thesis, and your purpose and audience.

Using Transitions

Be sure to include all the transitional words and phrases readers need to follow your description. Without them, readers will have difficulty understanding the relationship between one detail and another. Throughout your description, especially in the topic sentences of your body paragraphs, use words or phrases indicating the spatial arrangement of details. In descriptive essays, the transitions commonly used include *above, adjacent to, at the bottom, at the top, behind, below, beyond, in front of, in the middle, next to, over, under, through,* and *within.* (A more complete list of transitions appears on page 57.)

Structuring a Descriptive Essay

Descriptive essays begin with an **introduction** that presents the **thesis** or establishes the **dominant impression** that the rest of the essay will develop. Each **body paragraph** includes details that support the thesis or convey the dominant impression. The **conclusion** reinforces the thesis or dominant impression, perhaps echoing an idea stated in the introduction or using a particularly effective simile or metaphor.

Suppose your English composition instructor has asked you to write a short essay describing a person, place, or thing. After thinking about the assignment for a day or two, you decide to write an objective description of the National Air and Space Museum in Washington, DC, because you have visited it recently and many details are fresh in your mind. The museum is large and has many different exhibits, so you know you cannot describe them all. Therefore, you decide to concentrate on one, the heavier-than-air flight exhibit, and you choose as your topic the display you remember most vividly — Charles Lindbergh's airplane, *The Spirit of St. Louis*. You begin by brainstorming to recall all the details you can. When you read over your notes, you realize that you could present the details of the airplane in the order in which your eye took them in, from front to rear. The dominant impression you wish to create is how small and fragile *The Spirit of St. Louis* appears, and your thesis statement communicates this impression. An informal outline for your essay might look like this.

SAMPLE OUTLINE: Description

Introduction:	Thesis statement — It is startling that a plane as small as *The Spirit of St. Louis* could fly across the Atlantic.
Front of plane:	Single engine, tiny cockpit
Middle of plane:	Short wingspan, extra gas tanks
Rear of plane:	Limited cargo space filled with more gas tanks
Conclusion:	Restatement of thesis or review of key points or details

Revising a Descriptive Essay

When you revise a descriptive essay, consider the items on the revision checklist on page 68. In addition, pay special attention to the items on the following checklist, which apply specifically to descriptive essays.

✔ REVISION CHECKLIST   Description

- Does your assignment call for description?
- Does your descriptive essay clearly communicate its thesis or dominant impression?
- Is your description primarily objective or subjective?
- If your description is primarily objective, have you used precise, factual language? Would your essay be enriched by a visual?
- If your description is primarily subjective, have you used figures of speech as well as words that convey your feelings and emotions?
- Have you included enough specific details?
- Have you arranged your details in a way that supports your thesis and communicates your dominant impression?
- Have you used the transitional words and phrases that readers need to follow your description?

Editing a Descriptive Essay

When you edit your descriptive essay, follow the guidelines in the editing checklists on pages 85, 88, and 90. In addition, focus on the grammar, mechanics, and punctuation issues particularly relevant to descriptive essays. One of these issues — avoiding misplaced and dangling modifiers — is discussed below.

GRAMMAR IN CONTEXT   Avoiding Misplaced and Dangling Modifiers

When writing descriptive essays, you use **modifying words** and **phrases** to describe people, places, and objects. Because these modifiers are important in descriptive essays, you need to place them correctly to ensure they clearly refer to the words they describe.

Avoiding Misplaced Modifiers   A **misplaced modifier** appears to modify the wrong word because it is placed incorrectly in the sentence. Sentences that contain misplaced modifiers are always illogical and frequently humorous.

MISPLACED: E. B. White's son swam in the lake wearing an old bathing suit. (*Was the lake wearing a bathing suit?*)

MISPLACED: From the cabin, the sounds of the woods were heard by E. B. White and his son. (*Were the sounds of the woods inside the cabin?*)

In these sentences, the phrases *wearing an old bathing suit* and *from the cabin* appear to modify words that they cannot logically modify. You can correct these errors and avoid confusion by moving each modifier as close as possible to the word it is supposed to modify.

CORRECT: Wearing an old bathing suit, E. B. White's son swam in the lake.

CORRECT: From the cabin, E. B. White and his son heard the sounds of the woods.

Avoiding Dangling Modifiers   A modifier "dangles" when it cannot logically modify any word that appears in the sentence. Often, these **dangling modifiers** come at the beginning of sentences (as present or past participle phrases), where they illogically seem to modify the words that come immediately after them.

DANGLING: Determined to get a better look, the viewing platform next to St. Paul's Chapel was crowded. (*Who was determined to get a better look?*)

DANGLING: <u>Standing on the corner,</u> the cranes, jackhammers, and
bulldozers worked feverishly at ground zero. (*Who was
standing on the corner?*)

In the preceding sentences, the phrases *determined to get a better look* and
standing on the corner seem to modify *the viewing platform* and *cranes, jackham-mers, and bulldozers,* respectively. However, these sentences make no sense.
How can a viewing platform get a better look? How can cranes, jackham-mers, and bulldozers stand on a corner? In addition, the two sentences do
not contain the words that the modifying phrases are supposed to describe.
In each case, you can correct the problem by supplying the missing word
and rewriting the sentence accordingly.

CORRECT: <u>Determined to get a better look,</u> people crowded the
viewing platform next to St. Paul's Chapel.

CORRECT: <u>Standing on the corner,</u> people watched the cranes, jack-hammers, and bulldozers work feverishly at ground zero.

For more practice in avoiding misplaced and dangling modifiers, visit the resources
for Chapter 7 at **bedfordstmartins.com/patterns**.

☑ **EDITING CHECKLIST**   Description

- Have you avoided misplaced modifiers?
- Have you avoided dangling modifiers?
- Have you used figures of speech effectively?
- Have you avoided general words such as *nice, great,* and *terrific?*

A STUDENT WRITER: Objective Description

The following essay, an objective description of a globe from 1939, was
written by Mallory Cogan for a composition class. The assignment was to
write a description of an object that has special meaning for her.

My Grandfather's Globe

Introduction   Each afternoon, sunlight slants through the windows of   1
my grandfather's bedroom. Slowly, slowly, it sweeps over the
bookshelves. Late in the day, just before the light disappears
altogether, it rests sleepily on a globe in the corner. My
grandfather bought this globe in 1939, just before World War II.
Thesis   The world has changed since then, and the globe is a record of
statement   what it looked like at that time.

Description of Western Hemisphere

Turning the globe left, I begin my world tour. The blue   2
of the Pacific Ocean gives way to the faded pinks, browns, and
oranges of North and South America. In the north is a large area
dotted with lakes and bays. This is the Dominion of Canada, now
simply Canada. In the far north, the Canadian mainland breaks
into islands that extend into the Arctic Ocean. Below it is the
multicolored United States. To the north, Canada sprawls and
breaks apart; to the south, Mexico narrows, then curves east,
extended by the uneven strip of land that is Central America.
This strip of land is connected to the northernmost part of South
America. South America, in the same colors as the United States,
looks like a face in profile looking east, with a nose extending
into the Atlantic Ocean and a long neck that narrows as it reaches
toward Antarctica at the South Pole.

Description of Africa

As I trace the equator east across the Atlantic Ocean, I   3
come to French Equatorial Africa. The huge African continent, like
a fat boomerang, is labeled with names of European countries. A
large, kidney-shaped purple area to the northwest is called French
West Africa. To the east, about halfway down the continent, is
the Belgian Congo, a substantial orange splotch that straddles
the equator. On the eastern coast just above the equator is a
somewhat smaller, almost heart-shaped yellow area called Italian
East Africa. These regions, once European colonies, are now
divided into dozens of independent countries.

Description of Europe

Moving north, I follow the thick blue ribbon of the   4
Mediterranean Sea until I reach Western Europe. I pause on yellow,
boot-shaped Italy and glance to the west and southwest at purple
France and orange Spain. The northwestern coasts of both countries
extend slightly into the Atlantic. To the northwest of France, the
pink clusters of the British Isles droop like bunches of grapes.

Description of Europe and changes since 1939

Looking eastward, I see a water stain on Germany. It   5
extends down through Italy and across the Mediterranean, ending
in the Sahara Desert on the African continent. Following the stain
back into Europe, I look north, where Norway, Sweden, and Finland
reach toward the rest of Europe. Returning to Germany, I move
east, through Poland. On a modern globe, I would find Belarus
and Ukraine on Poland's eastern border. On this globe, however,
my finger passes directly into a vast area called the Union of
Soviet Socialist Republics. The U.S.S.R. (today called the Russian
Federation) cuts a wide swath across the northern part of the

Asian continent; there is plenty of room for its long name to be
displayed horizontally across the country's light-brown surface.
Still in the southern half of the country, I travel east, crossing
the landlocked Caspian Sea into a region of the U.S.S.R. called
Turkistan, now the country of Turkmenistan. To the southeast,
green Afghanistan sits between light-purple Iran to the west and
pink India to the east. India is cone shaped, but with a pointed
top, and green rectangular Nepal sits atop its western border.

*Description of
China and
additional changes*

Looking north again, I continue moving east. In Tibet, there   6
is a small tear in the globe. I continue into China's vast interior.
Just as the U.S.S.R. blankets the northern part of the Asian
continent, China spreads over much of the southeast. I notice
that China's borders on this globe are different from what they are
today. On my grandfather's globe, China includes Mongolia but
not a purple region to the northwest labeled Manchoukuo,
also known as Manchuria. Following Manchoukuo to its
southern border, I see a strip of land that extends into the sea,
surrounded by water on three sides. The area is small, so its
name — Chosen — has been printed in the Sea of Japan to the
east. Today, it is called Korea.

*Description of
Southeast Asia*

Backtracking west and dropping south, past China's   7
southern border, I see Siam, now called Thailand. Siam is a
three-leaf clover with a stem that hangs down. Wrapped along its
eastern border, bordering two of its "leaves," is a purple country
called French Indo-China. Today, this region is divided into the
countries of Cambodia, Laos, and Vietnam. Bordering Siam on the
west is the larger country of Burma, in pink. Like Siam, Burma is
top-heavy, like a flower or a clover with a thin stem.

*Description of
Indonesia and
Australia*

Tracing that stem south, I come to the numerous islands of   8
Indonesia, splashes of yellow spreading east-west along, above, and
below the equator. I do not need to travel much farther before I
arrive at an island bigger than any other on this globe: Australia.
This country is pink and shaped like half of a very thick doughnut.
On Australia's eastern coast is the Pacific; on its western coast is the
Indian Ocean.

Conclusion

Of course, it is not surprising that I would end where I   9
started, with the ocean, since water covers seventy percent of the
Earth. Still, countries — not oceans — are what interest me most
about this globe. The shifting names and borders of countries that
no longer exist remind me that although the world seems fixed,

just as it did to the people of 1939, it is always changing. The change happens slowly, like the sun crossing my grandfather's room. Caught at any single moment, the world, like the afternoon light, appears still and mysterious.

Points for Special Attention

Objective Description. Because her essay is primarily an objective description, Mallory keeps her description straightforward. She uses concrete language and concentrates on the shapes, colors, and surroundings of the countries she describes.

This objective description does include a few subjective elements. For example, in her introduction, Mallory says that the sunlight rests "sleepily" on her grandfather's globe. In her conclusion, she observes that the world represented by her grandfather's globe is "still and mysterious." (Her instructor had told the class that they could include a few subjective comments to convey the special meaning that the items they describe have for them.)

Figurative Language. In order to give readers a clear sense of what the countries on the globe look like, Mallory uses figurative language. For example, she uses **similes** when she describes South America as "like a face in profile" and Africa as looking "like a fat boomerang." She also uses **metaphor** when she says that the Mediterranean Sea is a "thick blue ribbon" and Siam is "a three-leaf clover with a stem that hangs down." Finally, Mallory uses **personification** when she says that the Belgian Congo "straddles the equator." By using these figures of speech, Mallory creates a vivid and striking picture of her grandfather's globe.

Structure. Mallory structures her description by moving from north to south as she moves east around the globe. She begins by describing the colors of North America, and then she describes South America. She directs her readers' attention to specific areas – for example, Central America. She then moves east, to Africa, and repeats the process of describing the regions in the north (Western Europe) and then in the south (Africa). As she does so, she notes that some countries, such as the U.S.S.R., have changed names since the globe was made in 1939. She repeats the pattern of moving east, north, and south and ends by describing Australia. Mallory frames her description of the globe with a description of her grandfather's bedroom. In her conclusion, she connects the sunlight in her grandfather's room to the world pictured on the globe by observing that both seem "still and mysterious."

Selection of Detail. Mallory's instructor defined her audience as people who know about the world today but have never seen her grandfather's globe and do not know much about the world in 1939. For this reason,

Mallory includes details such as the tear in Tibet and the water stain that runs through Germany and Italy. In addition, she explains how some countries' names and borders differ from those that exist today.

Working with Sources. Before she wrote her essay, Mallory thought about looking at old atlases or history books. She decided that because her assignment called for a description of an object — not an analysis of how the world changed due to war or to the decline of colonialism — she did not have to consult these sources. She did, however, look up a few facts, such as the current name of Manchoukuo, but since facts are considered common knowledge, she did not have to document her sources for this information.

Focus on Revision

Mallory's peer editing group suggested three changes. One student said Mallory should include descriptions of more countries, such as Japan in Asia and Chile, Argentina, and Brazil in South America. This student thought that without these descriptions, readers would not fully appreciate how much information the globe contained. Another student suggested that Mallory add more detail about the globe itself, such as its size, whether it was on a table or on the floor, and the materials from which it was constructed. A third student suggested that Mallory include a picture of the globe in her essay. He thought that this picture would give students a clear idea of what the globe looked like and would eliminate the need to add more description.

Mallory decided to write a short paragraph (and insert it between paragraphs 1 and 2) that provided a general description of the globe. She decided to add a picture because even with all the vivid description she included, she thought that the globe might be hard to picture. However, she decided that she had mentioned enough countries in her essay and that adding more would be repetitious and might cause readers to lose interest. (A sample peer editing worksheet for description appears on page 168.)

A STUDENT WRITER: Subjective Description

The essay that follows, a subjective description of an area in Burma (renamed Myanmar after a military coup in 1989), was written by Mary Lim for her composition class. Her assignment was to write an essay about a place that had a profound effect on her. Mary's essay uses **subjective description** so that readers can share, as well as understand, her experience.

The Valley of Windmills

Introduction   In my native country of Burma, strange happenings and   1

exotic scenery are not unusual, for Burma is a mysterious land that in some areas seems to have been ignored by time. Mountains stand jutting their rocky peaks into the clouds as they have for thousands of years. Jungles are so dense with exotic vegetation that human beings or large animals cannot even enter. But

Description (identifying the scene)

one of the most fascinating areas in Burma is the Valley of Windmills, nestled between the tall mountains near the fertile and beautiful city of Taungaleik. In this valley there is beautiful and breathtaking scenery, but there are also old, massive, and gloomy structures that can disturb a person deeply.

Description (moving toward the valley)

The road to Taungaleik twists out of the coastal flatlands   2
into those heaps of slag, shale, and limestone that are the Tennesserim Mountains in the southern part of Burma. The air grows rarer and cooler, and stones become grayer, the highway a little more precarious at its edges, until, ahead, standing in ghostly sentinel across the lip of a pass, is a line of squat forms.

Description (immediate view)

They straddle the road and stand at intervals up hillsides on either side. Are they boulders? Are they fortifications? Are they broken wooden crosses on graves in an abandoned cemetery?

These dark figures are windmills standing in the misty   3
atmosphere. They are immensely old and distinctly evil, some merely turrets, some with remnants of arms hanging derelict from their snouts, and most of them covered with dark green moss. Their decayed but still massive forms seem to turn and sneer

Description (more distant view)

at visitors. Down the pass on the other side is a circular green plateau that lies like an arena below, where there are still more windmills. Massed in the plain behind them, as far as the eye can see, in every field, above every hut, stand ten thousand iron windmills, silent and sailless. They seem to await only a call from a watchman to clank, whirr, flap, and groan into action. Visitors suddenly feel cold. Perhaps it is a sense of loneliness, the cool air, the desolation, or the weirdness of the arcane windmills — but something chills them.

Conclusion

As you stand at the lip of the valley, contrasts rush as if   4
to overwhelm you. Beyond, glittering on the mountainside like a

Description (windmills contrasted with city)

solitary jewel, is Taungaleik in the territory once occupied by the Portuguese. Below, on rolling hillsides, are the dark windmills,

Thesis statement

still enveloped in morning mist. These ancient windmills can remind you of the impermanence of life and the mystery that still surrounds these hills. In a strange way, the scene in the valley can disturb you, but it also can give you an insight into the contrasts that seem to define our lives here in my country.

Points for Special Attention

Subjective Description. One of the first things her classmates noticed when they read Mary's essay was her use of vivid details. The road to Taungaleik is described in specific terms: it twists "out of the coastal flatlands" into the mountains, which are "heaps of slag, shale, and limestone." The iron windmills are decayed and stand "silent and sailless" on a green plateau that "lies like an arena." Through her use of detail, Mary creates her dominant impression of the Valley of Windmills as dark, mysterious, and disquieting. The point of her essay — the thesis — is stated in the last paragraph: the Valley of Windmills embodies the contrasts that characterize life in Burma.

Subjective Language. By describing the windmills, Mary conveys her sense of foreboding. When she first introduces them, she questions whether these "squat forms" are "boulders," "fortifications," or "broken wooden crosses," each of which has a menacing connotation. After telling readers what they are, she uses **personification**, describing the windmills as dark, evil, sneering figures with "arms hanging derelict." She sees them as ghostly sentinels awaiting "a call from a watchman" to spring into action. With this figure of speech, Mary skillfully re-creates the unearthly quality of the scene.

Structure. Mary's purpose in this paper was to give her readers the experience of being in the Valley of Windmills. She uses an organizing scheme that takes readers along the road to Taungaleik, up into the Tennesserim Mountains, and finally to the pass where the windmills wait. From her perspective on the lip of the valley, she describes the details closest to her and then those farther away, as if following the movement of her eyes. She ends by bringing her readers back to the lip of the valley, contrasting Taungaleik "glittering on the mountainside" with the windmills "enveloped in morning mist." With her description, Mary builds up to her thesis about the nature of life in her country. She withholds the explicit statement of her main point until her last paragraph, when readers are fully prepared for it.

Focus on Revision

One of Mary's classmates thought that her essay's thesis about life in Burma needed additional support. The student pointed out that although Mary's description is quite powerful, it does not fully convey the contrasts she alludes to in her conclusion.

Mary decided that adding another paragraph discussing something about her life (perhaps her reasons for visiting the windmills) could help supply this missing information. She could, for example, tell her readers that right after her return from the valley, she found out that a friend had been accidentally shot by border guards and that this event caused her to characterize the windmills as she did. Such information would help explain the passage's somber mood and underscore the ideas presented in the conclusion.

Working with Sources. Another one of Mary's classmates suggested that she add some information about the political situation in Burma. He pointed out that few, if any, students in the class knew much about Burma — for example, that after a coup in 1989, the military threw out the civilian government and changed the name of Burma to Myanmar. In addition, he said that he had no idea how repressive the current government of Burma was. For this reason, the student thought that readers would benefit from a paragraph that gave a short history of Burma. Mary considered this option but decided that such information would distract readers from the main point of her description.

PEER EDITING WORKSHEET: Description

1. What is the essay's dominant impression or thesis?
2. What points does the writer emphasize in the introduction? Should any other points be included? If so, which ones?
3. Would you characterize the essay as primarily an objective or subjective description? What leads you to your conclusion?
4. Point out some examples of figures of speech. Could the writer use figures of speech in other places? If so, where?
5. What specific details does the writer use to help readers visualize what is being described? Where could the writer have used more details? Would a visual have helped readers understand what is being described?
6. Are all the details necessary? Can you identify any that seem excessive or redundant? Where could the writer have provided more details to support the thesis or convey the dominant impression?
7. How are the details in the essay arranged? What other arrangement could the writer have used?
8. List some transitional words and phrases the writer uses to help readers follow the discussion. Which sentences need transitional words or phrases to link them to other sentences?
9. Do any sentences contain misplaced or dangling modifiers? If so, which ones?
10. How effective is the essay's conclusion? Does the conclusion reinforce the dominant impression?

The following selections illustrate various ways description can shape an essay. As you read them, pay particular attention to the differences between objective and subjective description. The first selection, a visual text, is followed by questions designed to illustrate how description can operate in visual form.

MARY HOOVER AIKEN

Café Fortune Teller (Painting)

• • •

Reading Images

1. The painting is a self-portrait showing the artist, Mary Hoover Aiken, reading her own fortune in a café on Ibiza, an island off the coast of Spain. Describe what you see in the picture, starting with the image of the artist and moving from near to far (or far to near).

2. What details does the painting include? What determines how these details are arranged?

3. What dominant impression do you think Aiken wants to create? How do the details in the painting communicate this dominant impression?

Journal Entry

Go to Google Images and find Caravaggio's *The Fortune Teller.* Write a one-paragraph description of this painting. What dominant impression do you think Caravaggio was trying to create? How is it different from the dominant impression created by Aiken in *Café Fortune Teller*?

Thematic Connections

- "The Lottery" (page 311)
- "Why Vampires Never Die" (page 361)
- "The Ways We Lie" (page 474)

JHUMPA LAHIRI

Rice

The daughter of Indian immigrants, Jhumpa Lahiri was born in London in 1967. Her family moved to the United States, where she attended Barnard College and received multiple graduate degrees, including a Ph.D. in Renaissance studies from Boston University. She is the author of three books, including *Interpreter of Maladies* (1999) and *The Namesake* (2003), as well as many short stories. Lahiri has won several literary awards, including a Pulitzer Prize and a PEN/Hemingway Award. Her fiction often explores Indian and Indian-American life and culture — as does this personal essay, which originally appeared in the *New Yorker* magazine.

Background on rice Along with corn and wheat, rice remains one of the most important crops in the world, especially in Asia, where it has been cultivated for thousands of years. Rice accounts for between 35 percent and 85 percent of the calories consumed by billions of people living in India, China, and other Asian countries. Indeed, the ancient Indian word for rice ("dhanya") means "sustainer of the human race." But rice can be symbolic as well: we throw rice at weddings because it suggests fertility and prosperity. For Lahiri, the significance of rice is personal rather than universal. She describes her father's pulao dish as both an expression of his idiosyncratic personality and a symbol that binds her family together.

My father, seventy-eight, is a methodical man. For thirty-nine years, he 1 has had the same job, cataloguing books for a university library. He drinks two glasses of water first thing in the morning, walks for an hour every day, and devotes almost as much time, before bed, to flossing his teeth. "Winging it" is not a term that comes to mind in describing my father. When he's driving to new places, he does not enjoy getting lost.

In the kitchen, too, he walks a deliberate line, counting out the raisins 2 that go into his oatmeal (fifteen) and never boiling even a drop more water than required for tea. It is my father who knows how many cups of rice are necessary to feed four, or forty, or a hundred and forty people. He has a reputation for *andaj* — the Bengali word for "estimate" — accurately gauging quantities that tend to baffle other cooks. An oracle of rice, if you will.

But there is another rice that my father is more famous for. This is not 3 the white rice, boiled like pasta and then drained in a colander, that most Bengalis eat for dinner. This other rice is pulao, a baked, buttery, sophisticated indulgence, Persian in origin, served at festive occasions. I have often watched him make it. It involves sautéing grains of basmati in butter, along with cinnamon sticks, cloves, bay leaves, and cardamom pods. In go halved cashews and raisins (unlike the oatmeal raisins, these must be golden, not black). Ginger, pulverized into a paste, is incorporated, along with salt and sugar, nutmeg and mace, saffron threads if they're available, ground turmeric if not. A certain amount of water is added, and the rice simmers until most of the water evaporates. Then it is spread out in a baking tray. (My father prefers disposable aluminum ones, which he recycled long before recycling laws were passed.) More water is flicked on top with his fingers, in the ritual and cryptic manner of Catholic priests. Then the tray, covered with foil, goes into the oven, until the rice is cooked through and not a single grain sticks to another.

Despite having a superficial knowledge of the ingredients and the 4 technique, I have no idea how to make my father's pulao, nor would I ever dare attempt it. The recipe is his own, and has never been recorded. There has never been an unsuccessful batch, yet no batch is ever identical to any other. It is a dish that has become an extension of himself, that he has perfected, and to which he has earned the copyright. A dish that will die with him when he dies.

In 1968, when I was seven months old, my father made pulao for the 5 first time. We lived in London, in Finsbury Park, where my parents shared the kitchen, up a steep set of stairs in the attic of the house, with another Bengali couple. The occasion was my *annaprasan,* a rite of passage in which Bengali children are given solid food for the first time; it is known colloquially as a *bhath,* which happens to be the Bengali word for "cooked rice." In the oven of a stove no more than twenty inches wide, my father baked pulao for about thirty-five people. Since then, he has made pulao for the *annaprasans* of his friends' children, for birthday parties and anniversaries, for bridal and baby showers, for wedding receptions, and for my sister's Ph.D. party. For a few decades, after we moved to the United States, his pulao fed crowds of up to four hundred people, at events organized by Prabasi, a Bengali cultural institution in New England, and he found himself at institutional venues — schools and churches and community centers — working with industrial ovens and stoves. This has never unnerved him. He could probably rig up a system to make pulao out of a hot-dog cart, were someone to ask.

There are times when certain ingredients are missing, when he must 6 use almonds instead of cashews, when the raisins in a friend's cupboard are the wrong color. He makes it anyway, with exacting standards but a sanguine hand.

When my son and daughter were infants, and we celebrated their 7 *annaprasans,* we hired a caterer, but my father made the pulao, preparing it at home in Rhode Island and transporting it in the trunk of his car to Brooklyn. The occasion, both times, was held at the Society for Ethical Culture, in Park Slope. In 2002, for my son's first taste of rice, my father warmed the trays on the premises, in the giant oven in the basement. But by 2005, when it was my daughter's turn, the representative on duty would not permit my father to use the oven, telling him that he was not a licensed cook. My father transferred the pulao from his aluminum trays into glass baking dishes, and microwaved, batch by batch, rice that fed almost a hundred people. When I asked my father to describe that experience, he expressed no frustration. "It was fine," he said. "It was a big microwave."

• • •

Comprehension

1. How does Lahiri describe her father? What is his most important character trait?
2. According to Lahiri, what is special about pulao? Why is it served just on festive occasions?
3. What is an *annaprasan*? Why is this occasion so important to Bengalis?
4. Why, according to Lahiri, would she never try to make pulao?
5. What does Lahiri mean when she says that pulao is a dish for which her father "has earned the copyright" (4)?

Purpose and Audience

1. How much does Lahiri assume her readers know about Bengali culture? How can you tell?
2. Is this essay simply about rice — more specifically pulao — or is it also about something else? Explain.
3. Does this essay have an explicitly stated or an implied thesis? What dominant impression do you think Lahiri wants to convey?

Style and Structure

1. Why does Lahiri begin her essay by describing her father?
2. This essay is divided into three parts: the first describes Lahiri's father; the second describes the making of pulao; and the third describes the occasions on which her father cooked pulao. How does Lahiri signal the shift from one part of the essay to another? What other strategies could she have used?
3. Why does Lahiri go into so much detail about her father's pulao recipe?
4. What does pulao mean to Lahiri? Does it have the same meaning for her father? Explain.
5. Why does Lahiri end her essay with a quotation? Is this an effective closing strategy? What other strategies could she have used?

Vocabulary Projects

1. Define each of the following words as it is used in this selection.

   methodical (1)   colander (3)
   deliberate (2)   sanguine (6)
   oracle (2)

2. Throughout her essay, Lahiri uses several Bengali words. What might she have gained or lost if she had used English equivalents?

Journal Entry

What food do you associate with a specific member of your family? Why do you think this food has the association it does?

Writing Workshop

1. **Working with Sources.** Write an essay in which you describe a food that is as meaningful for you as pulao is for Lahiri. Make sure that your essay has a clear thesis and that it includes at least one reference to Lahiri's essay. Be sure that you document all material that you borrow from Lahiri's essay and that you include a works-cited page. (See Chapter 18 for information on MLA documentation.)

2. Write an email to a friend in another country in which you describe the foods you traditionally eat on a particular holiday. Assume that the person is not familiar with the foods you describe. Be sure your email conveys a clear dominant impression.

3. Write an essay in which you describe a parent or grandparent (or any other older person) who has (or had) a great deal of influence on you. Make sure you include basic biographical information as well as a detailed physical description.

Combining the Patterns

In addition to describing Lahiri's experience with pulao, this essay contains an explanation of a **process** in paragraph 3. What purpose does this process explanation serve?

Thematic Connections

- "The Myth of the Latin Woman: I Just Met a Girl Named Maria" (page 232)
- "Two Ways to Belong in America" (page 404)
- "Tortillas" (page 507)

ANN HODGMAN

No Wonder They Call Me a Bitch

Ann Hodgman, who was born in 1956, is a humorist, food writer, and children's author. She has published many books, including *You Know You're 40 When . . .* (2005), *The House of a Million Pets* (2007), and *How to Die of Embarrassment Every Day* (2011). A former contributing editor at *Spy*, an influential humor magazine in the 1980s, Hodgman has also written for *Good Housekeeping* and the *New York Times*.

Background on pet food Ohioan James Spratt created Spratt's Meat Fibrine Dog Cakes, the first commercially prepared dog food, in 1860. However, the industry truly boomed during the first half of the twentieth century, with products like Milk-Bones and Ken-L Ration, the first canned dog food. Ken-L Ration was also a pioneer in advertising dog food, first as a sponsor for the radio show *The Adventures of Rin Tin Tin* and then on television, advertising on programs like *The Adventures of Ozzie and Harriet*. The food's commercial tagline at the time is instructive: "This dog food uses only USDA, government-inspected horse meat." Indeed, while dog-food advertising has long relied on images of satisfied and healthy dogs with shiny coats, as well as on claims of appetizing ingredients ("Real beef!"), the product's contents have long been the subject of curiosity and even satire. Now, the dog-food business is largely an extension of the industrial food system of humans, as it makes use of offal, waste, and animal by-products deemed unfit for human consumption. Still, through a "miracle of beauty and packaging" (in Hodgman's words), it is also a $10 billion industry.

I've always wondered about dog food. Is a Gaines-burger really like a 1 hamburger? Can you fry it? Does dog food "cheese" taste like real cheese? Does Gravy Train actually make gravy in a dog's bowl, or is that brown liquid just dissolved crumbs? And what exactly *are* by-products?

Having spent the better part of a week eating dog food, I'm sorry 2 to say that I now know the answers to these questions. While my dachshund, Shortie, watched in agonies of yearning, I gagged my way through can after can of stinky, white-flecked mush and bag after bag of stinky, fat-drenched nuggets. And now I understand exactly why Shortie's breath is so bad.

Of course, Gaines-burgers are neither mush nor nuggets. They are, 3 rather, a miracle of beauty and packaging — or at least that's what I thought when I was little. I used to beg my mother to get them for our dogs, but she always said they were too expensive. When I finally bought a box of cheese-flavored Gaines-burgers — after twenty years of longing — I felt deliciously wicked.

"Dogs love real beef," the back of the box proclaimed proudly. "That's 4 why Gaines-burgers is the only beef burger for dogs with real beef and no meat by-products!" The copy was accurate: meat by-products did not appear in the list of ingredients. Poultry by-products did, though — right there next to preserved animal fat.

One Purina spokesman told me that poultry by-products consist of 5 necks, intestines, undeveloped eggs, and other "carcass remnants," but not feathers, heads, or feet. When I told him I'd been eating dog food, he said, "Oh, you're kidding! Oh, *no!*" (I came to share his alarm when, weeks later, a second Purina spokesman said that Gaines-burgers *do* contain poultry heads and feet — but *not* undeveloped eggs.)

Up close my Gaines-burger didn't much resemble chopped beef. 6 Rather, it looked — and felt — like a single long, extruded piece of redness that had been chopped into segments and formed into a patty. You could make one at home if you had a Play-Doh Fun Factory.

I turned on the skillet. While I waited for it to heat up I pulled out a 7 shred of cheese-colored material and palpated it. Again, like Play-Doh, it was quite malleable. I made a little cheese bird out of it; then I counted to three and ate the bird.

There was a horrifying rush of cheddar taste, followed immediately by the dull tang of soybean flour — the main ingredient in Gaines-burgers. Next I tried a piece of red extrusion. The main difference between the meat-flavored and cheese-flavored extrusions is one of texture. The "cheese" chews like fresh Play-Doh, whereas the "meat" chews like Play-Doh that's been sitting out on the rug for a couple of hours.

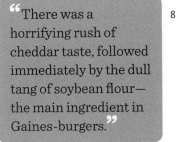

"There was a 8 horrifying rush of cheddar taste, followed immediately by the dull tang of soybean flour— the main ingredient in Gaines-burgers."

Frying only turned the Gaines-burger black. There was no melting, no 9 sizzling, no warm meat smells. A cherished childhood illusion was gone. I flipped the patty into the sink, where it immediately began leaking rivulets of red dye.

As alarming as the Gaines-burgers were, their soy meal began to seem 10 like an old friend when the time came to try some *canned* dog foods. I decided to try the Cycle foods first. When I opened them, I thought about how rarely I use can openers these days, and I was suddenly visited by a long-forgotten sensation of can-opener distaste. *This* is the kind of unsavory place can openers spend their time when you're not watching! Every time you open a can of, say, Italian plum tomatoes, you infect them with invisible particles of by-product.

I had been expecting to see the usual homogeneous scrapple inside, 11 but each can of Cycle was packed with smooth, round, oily nuggets. As if someone at Gaines had been tipped off that a human would be tasting the stuff, the four Cycles really were different from one another. Cycle-1, for puppies, is wet and soyish. Cycle-2, for adults, glistens nastily with fat, but it's passably edible — a lot like some canned Swedish meatballs I once got in a Care package at college. Cycle-3, the "lite" one, for fatties, had no specific flavor; it just tasted like dog food. But at least it didn't make me fat.

Cycle-4, for senior dogs, had the smallest nuggets. Maybe old dogs can't 12
open their mouths as wide. This kind was far sweeter than the other three
Cycles — almost like baked beans. It was also the only one to contain "dried
beef digest," a mysterious substance that the Purina spokesman defined as
"enzymes" and my dictionary defined as "the products of digestion."

Next on the menu was a can of Kal Kan Pedigree with Chunky Chicken. 13
Chunky *chicken*? There were chunks in the can, certainly — big, purplish-
brown chunks. I forked one chunk out (by now I was becoming callous)
and found that while it had no discernible chicken flavor, it wasn't bad
except for its texture — like meat loaf with ground-up chicken bones.

In the world of canned dog food, a smooth consistency is a sign of low 14
quality — lots of cereal. A lumpy, frightening, bloody, stringy horror is a
sign of high quality — lots of meat. Nowhere in the world of wet dog foods
was this demonstrated better than in the fanciest I tried — Kal Kan's Pedigree Select Dinners. These came not in a can but in a tiny foil packet with
a picture of an imperious Yorkie. When I pulled open the container, juice
spurted all over my hand, and the first chunk I speared was trailing a long
gray vein. I shrieked and went instead for a plain chunk, which I was able
to swallow only after taking a break to read some suddenly fascinating office equipment catalogues. Once again, though, it tasted no more alarming
than, say, canned hash.

Still, how pleasant it was to turn to *dry* dog food! Gravy Train was the 15
first I tried, and I'm happy to report that it really does make a "thick, rich,
real beef gravy" when you mix it with water. Thick and rich, anyway. Except
for a lingering rancid-fat flavor, the gravy wasn't beefy, but since it tasted
primarily like tap water, it wasn't nauseating either.

My poor dachshund just gets plain old Purina Dog Chow, but Purina 16
also makes a dry food called Butcher's Blend that comes in Beef, Bacon &
Chicken flavor. Here we see dog food's arcane semiotics at its best: a red
triangle with a *T* stamped into it is supposed to suggest beef; a tan curl,
chicken; and a brown *S*, a piece of bacon. Only dogs understand these messages. But Butcher's Blend does have an endearing slogan: "Great Meaty
Tastes — without bothering the Butcher!" *You know, I wanted to buy some
meat, but I just couldn't bring myself to bother the butcher.*

Purina O.N.E. ("Optimum Nutritional Effectiveness") is targeted at 17
people who are unlikely ever to worry about bothering a tradesperson. "We
chose chicken as a primary ingredient in Purina O.N.E. for several reasonings [sic]," the long, long essay on the back of the bag announces. Chief
among these reasonings, I'd guess, is the fact that chicken appeals to people
who are — you know — *like us*. Although our dogs do nothing but spend
eighteen-hour days alone in the apartment, we still want them to be *premium* dogs. We want them to cut down on red meat, too. We also want dog
food that comes in a bag with an attractive design, a subtle typeface, and no
kitschy pictures of slobbering golden retrievers.

Besides that, we want a list of the Nutritional Benefits of our dog 18
food — and we get it on O.N.E. One thing I especially like about this list

is its constant references to a dog's "hair coat," as in "Beef tallow is good for the dog's skin and hair coat." (On the other hand, beef tallow merely provides palatability, while the dried beef digest in Cycle provides palatability *enhancement*.)

I hate to say it, but O.N.E. was pretty palatable. Maybe that's because 19 it has about 100 percent more fat than, say, Butcher's Blend. Or maybe I'd been duped by the packaging; that's been known to happen before.

As with people food, dog snacks taste much better than dog meals. 20 They're better looking, too. Take Milk-Bone Flavor Snacks. The loving-hands-at-home prose describing each flavor is colorful; the writers practically choke on their own exuberance. Of bacon they say, "It's so good, your dog will think it's hot off the frying pan." Of liver: "The only taste your dog wants more than liver — is even more liver!" Of poultry: "All those farm fresh flavors deliciously mixed in one biscuit. Your dog will bark with delight!" And of vegetable: "Gardens of taste! Specially blended to give your dog that vegetable flavor he wants — but can rarely get!"

Well, I may be a sucker, but advertising *this* emphatic just doesn't con- 21 vince me. I lined up all seven flavors of Milk-Bone Flavor Snacks on the floor. Unless my dog's palate is a lot more sensitive than mine — and considering that she steals dirty diapers out of the trash and eats them, I'm loath to think it is — she doesn't detect any more difference in the seven flavors than I did when I tried them.

I much preferred Bonz, the hard-baked, bone-shaped snack stuffed 22 with simulated marrow. I liked the bone part, that is; it tasted almost exactly like the cornmeal it was made of. The mock marrow inside was a bit more problematic: in addition to looking like the sludge that collects in the treads of my running shoes, it was bursting with tiny hairs.

I'm sure you have a few dog food questions of your own. To save us 23 time, I've answered them in advance.

Q. *Are those little cans of Mighty Dog actually branded with the sizzling word* 24 BEEF, *the way they show in the commercials?*

A. You should know by now that that kind of thing never happens.   25

Q. *Does chicken-flavored dog food taste like chicken-flavored cat food?*   26

A. To my surprise, chicken cat food was actually a little better — 27 more chickeny. It tasted like inferior canned pâté.

Q. *Was there any dog food that you just couldn't bring yourself to try?*   28

A. Alas, it was a can of Mighty Dog called Prime Entree with Bone Mar- 29 row. The meat was dark, dark brown, and it was surrounded by gelatin that was almost black. I knew I would die if I tasted it, so I put it outside for the raccoons.

• • •

Comprehension

1. Why did Hodgman decide to try eating dog food? Do you find her reasons convincing?

2. According to Hodgman, how does the packaging of dog food contrast with its taste?

3. Which brand of dog food does Hodgman like best? Which does she like least?

4. How does Hodgman describe the advertising copy that appears on the packages of dog food? What message does this advertising try to convey to purchasers?

Purpose and Audience

1. Does "No Wonder They Call Me a Bitch" have an explicitly stated thesis? If so, where? If not, why not?

2. What dominant impression is Hodgman trying to create in her essay? How successful is she?

3. How do you think Hodgman expects readers to react to her essay? How can you tell? How do these expectations affect Hodgman's treatment of her subject?

Style and Structure

1. What is your reaction to the title of this essay? What are the advantages and disadvantages of using a word like *bitch* in this title?

2. What determines how the details in this description are arranged? Would another organizing principle have been more effective?

3. Does Hodgman develop her description of the various dog foods fully enough? Where could she have provided more detail? Where, if anywhere, do you think she gives too much detail?

4. What figures of speech does Hodgman use to help readers understand her description? How do these figures of speech help Hodgman make her points?

5. Why does Hodgman end her essay by answering questions that readers may have? Do you think this is an effective strategy? Explain.

Vocabulary Projects

1. Define each of the following words as it is used in this selection.

by-products (1)	unsavory (10)
carcass (5)	imperious (14)
palpated (7)	rancid (15)
malleable (7)	arcane (16)
extrusions (8)	semiotics (16)
rivulets (9)	kitschy (17)

2. Make a list of the adjectives Hodgman uses to describe the dog foods she tasted. How effectively do these adjectives convey the look, feel, taste, and smell of the various foods?

Journal Entry

Why do you think Hodgman uses humor so extensively in this essay? Include some specific examples to support your answer.

Writing Workshop

1. **Working with Sources.** Hodgman uses original research to find out about her subject and then writes an essay that describes the results of her research. Conduct your own food-tasting on a type of food product — for example, kinds of energy drinks, snack foods, or fast-food burgers. Then, write an essay that describes the results of your research. Be sure to document all material that you borrow from Hodgman's essay and to include a works-cited page. (See Chapter 18 for information on MLA documentation.)

2. Make a list of products that make claims that could be considered exaggerated or false — in TV infomercials or on natural food labels, for example. Then, write an essay in which you describe several of these products. Like Hodgman, use concrete sensory details to convey your dominant impression.

3. In addition to writing essays, Hodgman writes a food column. Read a few food columns online, and then write one that describes the food served in your school cafeteria. Make sure your description supports your thesis statement (or the dominant impression you wish to convey).

Combining the Patterns

At various points in her essay — for example, in paragraphs 7 and 13 — Hodgman uses **narration**. What do these narrative paragraphs add to her essay?

Thematic Connections

- "The Embalming of Mr. Jones" (page 303)
- "Tortillas" (page 507)
- "On Dumpster Diving" (page 664)

SUZANNE BERNE

Ground Zero

Suzanne Berne has worked as a journalist and has also published book reviews and personal essays as well as three well-received novels, including *The Ghost at the Table* (2006) and *Lucille* (2010). She currently teaches English at Boston College. In the following essay, which appeared on the *New York Times* op-ed page in April 2002, Berne describes a personal pilgrimage to the former site of the World Trade Center in New York City.

Background on the terrorist attacks of 9/11 The September 11, 2001, terrorist attacks that destroyed the twin towers of New York's World Trade Center and severely damaged the Pentagon stunned the nation and the world. People watched in horror as camera crews recorded the collapse of the towers while victims jumped to their deaths. The three hijacked aircraft that crashed into these targets, and a fourth that crashed into a field in rural Pennsylvania, caused the deaths of some three thousand people. An outpouring of grief, outrage, fear, and patriotism consumed the nation in the ensuing months. While many, like Berne, have felt drawn to visit "ground zero" (as it has come to be called), some family members of the victims — particularly of those whose unidentified remains are still at the site — have expressed concern that it not become a tourist attraction. A memorial at the site includes two huge reflecting pools where the original twin towers stood. The names of the nearly three thousand people who were killed in the September 11 attacks in New York City, Pennsylvania, and Washington, DC (as well as those killed in the 1993 World Trade Center bombings) are inscribed around the edges of the pools. An underground museum, scheduled to open in 2012, will house exhibits that convey the experiences of responders, victims, and witnesses.

On a cold, damp March morning, I visited Manhattan's financial district, a place I'd never been, to pay my respects at what used to be the World Trade Center. Many other people had chosen to do the same that day, despite the raw wind and spits of rain, and so the first thing I noticed when I arrived on the corner of Vesey and Church Streets was a crowd.

Standing on the sidewalk, pressed against aluminum police barricades, wearing scarves that flapped into their faces and woolen hats pulled over their ears, were people apparently from everywhere. Germans, Italians, Japanese. An elegant-looking Norwegian family in matching shearling coats. People from Ohio and California and Maine. Children, middle-aged couples, older people. Many of them were clutching cameras and video recorders, and they were all craning to see across the street, where there was nothing to see.

At least, nothing is what it first looked like, the space that is now ground zero. But once your eyes adjust to what you are looking at, "nothing" becomes something much more potent, which is absence.

But to the out-of-towner, ground zero looks at first simply like a con-   4
struction site. All the familiar details are there: the wooden scaffolding; the
cranes, the bulldozers, and forklifts; the trailers and construction workers
in hard hats; even the dust. There is the pound of jackhammers, the steady
beep-beep-beep of trucks backing up, the roar of heavy machinery.

So much busyness is reassuring, and it is possible to stand looking at   5
the cranes and trucks and feel that mild curiosity and hopefulness so often
inspired by construction sites.

Then gradually your eyes do adjust, exactly as if you have stepped from   6
a dark theater into a bright afternoon, because what becomes most striking
about this scene is the light itself.

Ground zero is a great bowl of light, an emptiness that seems weirdly   7
spacious and grand, like a vast plaza amid the dense tangle of streets in
lower Manhattan. Light reflecting off the Hudson River vaults into the site,
soaking everything — especially on an overcast morning — with a watery
glow. This is the moment when absence begins to assume a material form,
when what is not there becomes visible.

Suddenly you notice the periphery, the skyscraper shrouded in black   8
plastic, the boarded windows, the steel skeleton of the shattered Winter
Garden. Suddenly there are the broken steps and cracked masonry in front
of Brooks Brothers. Suddenly there are the firefighters, the waiting ambulance on the other side of the pit, the police on every corner. Suddenly there
is the enormous cross made of two rusted girders.

And suddenly, very suddenly, there is the little cemetery attached to   9
St. Paul's Chapel, with tulips coming up, the chapel and grounds miraculously undamaged except for a few plastic-sheathed gravestones. The iron
fence is almost invisible beneath a welter of dried pine wreaths, banners,
ribbons, laminated poems and prayers and photographs, swags of paper
cranes, withered flowers, baseball hats, rosary beads, teddy bears. And
flags, flags everywhere, little American flags fluttering in the breeze, flags
on posters drawn by Brownie troops, flags on T-shirts, flags on hats, flags
streaming by, tied to the handles of baby strollers.

It takes quite a while to see all of this; it takes even longer to come up   10
with something to say about it.

An elderly man standing next to me had been staring fixedly across   11
the street for some time. Finally he touched his son's elbow and said: "I
watched those towers being built. I saw this place when they weren't there."
Then he stopped, clearly struggling with, what for him, was a double negative, recalling an absence before there was an absence. His son, waiting patiently, took a few photographs. "Let's get out of here," the man said at last.

Again and again I heard people say, "It's unbelievable." And then they   12
would turn to each other, dissatisfied. They wanted to say something more
expressive, more meaningful. But it *is* unbelievable, to stare at so much
devastation, and know it for devastation, and yet recognize that it does
not look like the devastation one has imagined.

Like me, perhaps, the people around me had in mind images from tele-   13
vision and newspaper pictures: the collapsing buildings, the running office

workers, the black plume of smoke against a bright blue sky. Like me, they were probably trying to superimpose those terrible images onto the industrious emptiness right in front of them. The difficulty of this kind of mental revision is measured, I believe, by the brisk trade in World Trade Center photograph booklets at tables set up on street corners.

Determined to understand better what I was looking at, I decided to get a ticket for the viewing platform beside St. Paul's. This proved no easy task, as no one seemed to be able to direct me to South Street Seaport, where the tickets are distributed. Various police officers whom I asked for directions waved me vaguely toward the East River, differing degrees of boredom and resignation on their faces. Or perhaps it was a kind of incredulousness. Somewhere around the American Stock Exchange, I asked a security guard for help and he frowned at me, saying, "You want tickets to the disaster?"   14

Finally I found myself in line at a cheerfully painted kiosk, watching a young juggler try to entertain the crowd. He kept dropping the four red balls he was attempting to juggle, and having to chase after them. It was noon; the next available viewing was at 4 P.M.   15

Back I walked, up Fulton Street, the smell of fish in the air, to wander again around St. Paul's. A deli on Vesey Street advertised a view of the World Trade Center from its second-floor dining area. I went in and ordered a pastrami sandwich, uncomfortably aware that many people before me had come to that same deli for pastrami sandwiches who would never come there again. But I was here to see what I could, so I carried my sandwich upstairs and sat down beside one of the big plate-glass windows.   16

And there, at last, I got my ticket to the disaster.   17

I could see not just into the pit now, but also its access ramp, which trucks had been traveling up and down since I had arrived that morning. Gathered along the ramp were firefighters in their black helmets and black coats. Slowly they lined up, and it became clear that this was an honor guard, and that someone's remains were being carried up the ramp toward the open door of an ambulance.   18

Everyone in the dining room stopped eating. Several people stood up, whether out of respect or to see better, I don't know. For a moment, everything paused.   19

Then the day flowed back into itself. Soon I was outside once more, joining the tide of people washing around the site. Later, as I huddled with a little crowd on the viewing platform, watching people scrawl their names or write "God Bless America" on the plywood walls, it occurred to me that a form of repopulation was taking effect, with so many visitors to this place, thousands of visitors, all of us coming to see the wide emptiness where so many were lost. And by the act of our visiting — whether we are motivated by curiosity or horror or reverence or grief, or by something confusing that combines them all — that space fills up again.   20

• • •

Comprehension

1. What does Berne mean when she says that as her eyes adjust to what she is seeing, "'nothing' becomes something much more potent, which is absence" (3)?

2. Why does it take "quite a while" (10) to see all the details at ground zero? Why does it take "even longer" (10) to think of something to say about it?

3. According to Berne, how were the television pictures of ground zero different from the actual experience of seeing it?

4. How does the area around ground zero contrast with the site itself? How does Berne react to this contrast?

5. What does Berne mean in her conclusion when she says that with so many visitors coming to see ground zero, a form of "repopulation" (20) is taking place? Do you think she is being **sarcastic**?

Purpose and Audience

1. Does Berne state or imply her thesis? Why do you think she makes the decision she does? State Berne's thesis in your own words.

2. What is Berne's purpose in writing her essay?

3. What assumptions does Berne make about her readers' ideas about ground zero? How can you tell?

Style and Structure

1. Why does Berne begin her essay by saying she had never before visited Manhattan's financial district?

2. What organizational scheme does Berne use? What are the advantages and disadvantages of this scheme?

3. In paragraph 3, Berne says that ground zero at first looks like "nothing"; in paragraph 4, she says that it looks like a construction site. Then, in paragraph 7, she describes ground zero as "a great bowl of light." And finally, in her conclusion, she refers to it as a pit (18). Why do you think Berne describes ground zero in so many different ways?

4. Berne leaves a space between paragraphs 17 and 18. In what way does the space (as well as paragraph 17) reinforce a shift in her essay's focus?

5. Why does Berne end her essay with a description of the crowd standing on the viewing platform? Why do you suppose she feels the need to include these observations?

6. In paragraphs 8 and 9, Berne repeats the word *suddenly*. What is the effect of this repetition? Could she have achieved this effect some other way?

Vocabulary Projects

1. Define each of the following words as it is used in this selection.

   shearling (2)   devastation (12)
   potent (3)   incredulousness (14)
   periphery (8)   repopulation (20)
   laminated (9)

2. A **paradox** is a seemingly contradictory statement that may nonetheless be true. Find examples of paradoxes in "Ground Zero." Why do you think Berne uses these paradoxes?

3. List ten striking visual details Berne uses to describe people and objects. Can you think of other details she could have used?

4. Go to dictionary.com and look up the meaning of the term *ground zero*. What connotations does this term have? Do you think this is an appropriate title for Berne's essay?

Journal Entry

Go to the Web site wtc.vjs.org and look at film clips of ground zero after the twin towers collapsed. Are your reactions to these images similar to or different from Berne's?

Writing Workshop

1. **Working with Sources.** Write an essay describing what you saw in the film clips you watched for your journal entry. Be sure to include an explicitly stated thesis and use descriptive details to convey your reactions to the event. If you can, include a quotation from Berne's essay in your paper. Be sure to document the quotation and to include a works-cited page. (See Chapter 18 for information on MLA documentation.)

2. Write a description of a place from several different vantage points, as Berne does. Make sure each of your perspectives provides different information about the place you are describing.

3. Write a subjective description of a scene you remember from your childhood. In your thesis statement and in your conclusion, explain how your adult impressions of the scene differ from those of your childhood.

Combining the Patterns

In addition to containing a great deal of description, this essay also uses **comparison and contrast**. In paragraphs 1 through 10, what two ways of seeing

ground zero does Berne compare? What points about each view of ground
zero does she contrast?

Thematic Connections

- "The Socks" (page 109)
- "Shooting an Elephant" (page 133)
- "Once More to the Lake" (page 194)

HEATHER ROGERS

The Hidden Life of Garbage

Journalist Heather Rogers has written articles on the environmental effects of mass production and consumption for the *New York Times Magazine,* the *Utne Reader, Architecture,* and a variety of other publications. Her 2002 documentary film *Gone Tomorrow: The Hidden Life of Garbage* has been screened at festivals around the world and served as the basis for a book of the same title. Named an Editor's Choice by the *New York Times* and the *Guardian,* the book, published in 2005, traces the history and politics of household garbage in the United States, drawing connections between modern industrial production, consumer culture, and our contemporary throwaway lifestyle. In the following excerpt from the book, Rogers provides a detailed description of a giant landfill in central Pennsylvania and asks readers to think about the ramifications of accumulating so much trash. Her most recent book is *Green Gone Wrong: How Our Economy Is Undermining the Environmental Revolution* (2010).

Background on waste disposal Human beings have always faced the question of how to dispose of garbage. The first city dump was established in ancient Athens, and the government of Rome had begun the collection of municipal trash by 200 C.E. Even as late as the 1800s, garbage was, at worst, simply thrown out into the streets of U.S. cities or dumped into rivers and ditches; in more enlightened communities, it might have been carted to foul-smelling open dumps or burned in incinerators, creating clouds of dense smoke. Experiments with systematically covering the garbage in dumps began as early as the 1920s, and the first true "sanitary landfill," as it was called, was created in Fresno, California, in 1937. Today, more than 60 percent of the solid waste in the United States ends up in landfills, and the amount of waste seems to keep growing. According to the Energy Information Administration, the amount of waste produced in the United States has more than doubled in the past thirty years, and it is estimated that the average American generates an astounding 4.5 pounds of trash every day.

In the dark chill of early morning, heavy steel garbage trucks chug and creep along neighborhood collection routes. A worker empties the contents of each household's waste bin into the truck's rear compaction unit. Hydraulic compressors scoop up and crush the dross, cramming it into the enclosed hull. When the rig is full, the collector heads to a garbage depot called a "transfer station" to unload. From there the rejectamenta is taken to a recycling center, an incinerator or, most often, to what's called a "sanitary landfill." 1

Land dumping has long been the favored disposal method in the U.S. thanks to the relative low cost of burial and North America's abundant supply of unused acreage. Although the great majority of our castoffs go 2 to landfills, they are places the public is not meant to see. Today's garbage graveyards are sequestered, guarded, veiled. They are also high-tech, and, increasingly, located in rural areas that receive much of their rubbish from urban centers that no longer bury their own wastes.

There's a reason landfills are tucked away, on the edge of town, in 3 otherwise untraveled terrain, camouflaged by hydroseeded, neatly tiered slopes. If people saw what happened to their waste, lived with the stench, witnessed the scale of destruction, they might start asking difficult questions. Waste Management Inc., the largest rubbish handling corporation in the world, operates its Geological Reclamation Operations and Waste Systems (GROWS) landfill just outside Morrisville, Pennsylvania — in the docile river valley near where Washington momentously crossed the Delaware leading his troops into Trenton in 1776. Sitting atop the landfill's 300-foot-high butte composed entirely of garbage, the logic of our society's unrestrained consuming and wasting quickly unravels.

Up here is where the dumping takes place; it is referred to as the fill's 4 "working face." Clusters of trailer trucks, yellow earthmovers, compacting machines, steamrollers, and water tankers populate this bizarre, thirty-acre nightmare. Churning in slow motion through the surreal landscape, these machines are remaking the earth in the image of garbage. Scores of seagulls hover overhead then suddenly drop into the rotting piles. The ground underfoot is torn from the metal treads of the equipment. Potato chip wrappers, tattered plastic bags, and old shoes poke through the dirt as if floating to the surface. The smell is sickly and sour.

The aptly named GROWS landfill is part of Waste Management Inc.'s 5 (WMI) 6,000-acre garbage treatment complex, which includes a second landfill, an incinerator, and a state-mandated leaf composting lot. GROWS is one of a new breed of waste burial sites referred to as "mega-fills." These high-tech, high-capacity dumps are comprised of a series of earth-covered "cells" that can be ten to one hundred acres across and up to hundreds of feet deep — or tall, as is the case at GROWS. (One Virginia whopper has disposal capacity equivalent to the length of one thousand football fields and the height of the Washington Monument.) As of 2002, GROWS was the single largest recipient of New York City's garbage in Pennsylvania, a state that is the country's biggest depository for exported waste.

WMI's Delaware-side operation sits on land that has long served the 6 interests of industry. Overlooking a rambling, mostly decommissioned US Steel factory, WMI now occupies the former grounds of the Warner Company. In the previous century, Warner surface mined the area for gravel and sand, much of which was shipped to its cement factory in Philadelphia. The area has since been converted into a reverse mine of sorts; instead of extraction, workers dump, pack, and fill the earth with almost forty million pounds of municipal wastes daily.

Back on top of the GROWS landfill, twenty-ton dump trucks gather 7 at the low end of the working face, where they discharge their fetid cargo. Several feet up a dirt bank, a string of large trailers are being detached from semi trucks. In rapid succession each container is tipped almost vertical by a giant hydraulic lift and, within seconds, twenty-four tons of putrescence cascades down into the day's menacing valley of trash. In the middle of the dumping is a "landfill compactor" — which looks like a bulldozer on steroids with mammoth metal spiked wheels — that pitches back and forth, its fifty tons crushing the detritus into the earth. A smaller vehicle called a "track loader" maneuvers on tank treads, channeling the castoffs from kitchens and offices into the compactor's path. The place runs like a well-oiled machine, with only a handful of workers orchestrating the burial.

Get a few hundred yards from the landfill's working face and it's hard 8 to smell the rot or see the debris. The place is kept tidy with the help of thirty-five-foot-tall fencing made of "litter netting" that surrounds the perimeter of the site's two landfills. As a backup measure, teams of "paper pickers" constantly patrol the area retrieving discards carried off by the wind. Small misting machines dot fence tops, roads, and hillsides, spraying a fine, invisible chemical-water mixture into the air, which binds with odor molecules and pulls them to the ground.

In new state-of-the-art landfills, the cells that contain the trash are 9 built on top of what is called a "liner." The liner is a giant underground bladder intended to prevent contamination of groundwater by collecting leachate — liquid wastes and the rainwater that seeps through buried trash — and channeling it to nearby water treatment facilities. WMI's two Morrisville landfills leach on average 100,000 gallons daily. If this toxic stew contaminated the site's groundwater it would be devastating.

Once a cell is filled, which might take years, it is closed off or "capped." 10 The capping process entails covering the garbage with several feet of dirt, which gets graded, then packed by steamrollers. After that, layers of clay-embedded fabric, synthetic mesh, and plastic sheeting are draped across the top of the cell and joined with the bottom liner (which is made of the same materials) to encapsulate all those outmoded appliances, dirty diapers, and discarded wrappers.

Today's landfill regulations, ranging from liner construction to post- 11 capping oversight, mean that disposal areas like WMI's GROWS are potentially less dangerous than the dumps of previous generations. But the fact remains that these systems are short-term solutions to the garbage problem. While they may not seem toxic now, all those underground cells packed with plastics, solvents, paints, batteries, and other hazardous materials will someday have to be treated since the liners won't last forever. Most liners are expected to last somewhere between thirty and fifty years. That time frame just happens to coincide with the post-closure liability private landfill operators are subject to: thirty years after a site is shuttered, its owner is no longer responsible for contamination, the public is.

There is a palpable tension at waste treatment facilities, as though at 12 any minute the visitor will uncover some illegal activity. But what's most striking at these places isn't what they might be hiding; it's what's in plain view. The lavish resources dedicated to destroying used commodities and making that obliteration acceptable, even "green," is what's so astounding. Each landfill (not to mention garbage collection systems, transfer stations, recycling centers, and incinerators) is an expensive, complex operation that uses the latest methods developed and perfected at laboratories, universities, and corporate campuses across the globe.

The more state-of-the-art, the more "environmentally responsible" the 13 operation, the more the repressed question pushes to the surface: what if we didn't have so much trash to get rid of?

• • •

Comprehension

1. According to Rogers, why are landfills "tucked away, on the edge of town, in otherwise untraveled terrain" (3)?

2. What is the landfill's "working face" (4)? How does it compare with other parts of the landfill?

3. Why does Rogers think that the GROWS landfill is "aptly named" (5)? What **connotations** do you think Waste Management Inc. intended the name GROWS to have? What connotations does Rogers think the name has?

4. What are the dangers of the "new state-of-the-art landfills" (9)? What point does Rogers make about liners being "expected to last somewhere between thirty and fifty years" (11)?

5. According to Rogers, what is the "repressed question" (13) that is not being asked?

Purpose and Audience

1. At what point in the essay does Rogers state her thesis? Why do you think she places the thesis where she does?

2. What dominant impression does Rogers try to create in her description? Is she successful?

3. What is Rogers's attitude toward waste disposal in general — and toward disposal companies like Waste Management Inc. in particular? Do you share her feelings?

Style and Structure

1. Rogers begins her essay with a description of garbage trucks collecting trash. What specific things does she describe? How does this description establish the context for the rest of the essay?

2. What determines the order in which details are arranged in Rogers's essay?

3. Is this essay a subjective or objective description of the landfill? Explain.

4. In paragraph 13, why does Rogers put the phrase *environmentally responsible* in quotation marks? What impression is she trying to convey?

5. Rogers never offers a solution to the problems she writes about. Should she have done so? Is her failure to offer a solution a shortcoming of the essay?

Vocabulary Projects

1. Define each of the following words as it is used in this selection.

hydraulic (1)	putrescence (7)
rejectamenta (1)	cascades (7)
sequestered (2)	leach (9)
hydroseeded (3)	encapsulate (10)
butte (3)	palpable (12)
aptly (5)	lavish (12)
fetid (7)	obliteration (12)

2. Some critics of waste disposal methods accuse both municipalities and waste disposal companies of "environmental racism." Research this term on the Web. Do you think the methods described by Rogers are examples of environmental racism? Explain.

3. Underline the adjectives Rogers uses when she describes garbage in paragraph 7. How do these adjectives help her make her point?

Journal Entry

What do you think you and your family could do to reduce the amount of garbage you produce? How realistic are your suggestions?

Writing Workshop

1. **Working with Sources.** Write an essay in which you describe the waste that you see generated at your school, home, or job. Like Rogers, write your description in a way that will motivate people to do something about the problem. In your essay, use a quotation from Rogers's essay. Make sure you document the quotation and include a works-cited page. (See Chapter 18 for information on MLA documentation.)

2. **Working with Sources.** In 1986, the city of Philadelphia hired a company to dispose of waste from a city incinerator. Over thirteen thousand tons of waste — some of which was hazardous — was loaded onto a ship called the *Khian Sea,* which unsuccessfully tried to dispose of it. After two years, the cargo mysteriously disappeared. Go to Google Images and find several pictures of the *Khian Sea.* Then, write a description of the ship and its cargo. Make sure the thesis statement of your description clearly conveys your dominant impression. If you wish, you may insert one of the images you found into your essay. Make sure that you document the image and

include a works-cited page. (See Chapter 18 for information on MLA documentation.)

3. Describe a place that has played an important role in your life. Include a narrative passage that conveys the place's significance to you.

Combining the Patterns

In paragraphs 9 and 10, Rogers includes a **definition** as well as a **process** description. Explain how these paragraphs help Rogers develop her description.

Thematic Connections

- "The Case against Air Conditioning" (page 344)
- "Environmentalism as Religion" (page 399)
- "On Dumpster Diving" (page 664)

E. B. WHITE

Once More to the Lake

Elwyn Brooks White was born in 1899 in Mount Vernon, New York. He joined the newly founded *New Yorker* in 1925 and was associated with the magazine until his death in 1985. In 1937, White moved his family to a farm in Maine and began a monthly column for *Harper's* magazine titled "One Man's Meat." A collection of some of these essays appeared under the same title in 1942. In addition to this and other essay collections, White published two popular children's books, *Stuart Little* (1945) and *Charlotte's Web* (1952). He also wrote a classic writer's handbook, *The Elements of Style* (1959), a revision of a text by one of his Cornell professors, William Strunk.

Background on continuity and change In a sense, White's essay is a reflection on continuity and change. While much had remained the same at the Maine lake since 1904, the year White first began coming with his parents, the world outside had undergone a significant transformation by the time he returned years later with his son. Auto and air travel had become commonplace; the invention of innumerable electrical appliances and machines had revolutionized the home and the workplace; movies had gone from primitive, silent, black-and-white shorts to sophisticated productions with sound and sometimes color; and the rise of national advertising had spurred a new and greatly expanded generation of consumer products. Moreover, the country had suffered through World War I, enjoyed a great economic expansion, experienced a period of social revolution, and been devastated by a great economic depression. Within this context, White relives his childhood through his son's eyes.

One summer, along about 1904, my father rented a camp on a lake in 1 Maine and took us all there for the month of August. We all got ringworm from some kittens and had to rub Pond's Extract on our arms and legs night and morning, and my father rolled over in a canoe with all his clothes on; but outside of that the vacation was a success and from then on none of us ever thought there was any place in the world like that lake in Maine. We returned summer after summer — always on August 1st for one month. I have since become a salt-water man, but sometimes in summer there are days when the restlessness of the tides and the fearful cold of the sea water and the incessant wind which blows across the afternoon and into the evening make me wish for the placidity of a lake in the woods. A few weeks ago this feeling got so strong I bought myself a couple of bass hooks and a spinner and returned to the lake where we used to go, for a week's fishing and to revisit old haunts.

I took along my son, who had never had any fresh water up his nose 2 and who had seen lily pads only from train windows. On the journey over to the lake I began to wonder what it would be like. I wondered how time would have marred this unique, this holy spot — the coves and streams, the hills that the sun set behind, the camps and the paths behind the camps. I was sure that the tarred road would have found it out and I wondered in what other ways it would be desolated. It is strange how much you can remember about places like that once you allow your mind to return into the grooves which lead back. You remember one thing, and that suddenly reminds you of another thing. I guess I remembered clearest of all the early mornings, when the lake was cool and motionless, remembered how the bedroom smelled of the lumber it was made of and the wet woods whose scent entered through the screen. The partitions in the camp were thin and did not extend clear to the top of the rooms, and as I was always the first up I would dress softly so as not to wake the others, and sneak out into the sweet outdoors and start out in the canoe, keeping close along the shore in the long shadows of the pines. I remembered being very careful never to rub my paddle against the gunwale for fear of disturbing the stillness of the cathedral.

The lake had never been what you would call a wild lake. There were 3 cottages sprinkled around the shores, and it was in farming country although the shores of the lake were quite heavily wooded. Some of the cottages were owned by nearby farmers, and you would live at the shore and eat your meals at the farmhouse. That's what our family did. But although it wasn't wild, it was a fairly large and undisturbed lake and there were places in it which, to a child at least, seemed infinitely remote and primeval.

I was right about the tar: it led to within half a mile of the shore. But 4 when I got back there, with my boy, and we settled into a camp near a farmhouse and into the kind of summertime I had known, I could tell that it was going to be pretty much the same as it had been before — I knew it, lying in bed the first morning, smelling the bedroom, and hearing the boy sneak quietly out and go off along the shore in a boat. I began to sustain the illusion that he was I, and therefore, by simple transposition, that I was my father. This sensation persisted, kept cropping up all the time we were there. It was not an entirely new feeling, but in this setting it grew much stronger. I seemed to be living a dual existence. I would be in the middle of some simple act, I would be picking up a bait box or laying down a table fork, or I would be saying something, and suddenly it would be not I but my father who was saying the words or making the gesture. It gave me a creepy sensation.

We went fishing the first morning. I felt the same damp moss covering 5 the worms in the bait can, and saw the dragonfly alight on the tip of my rod as it hovered a few inches from the surface of the water. It was the arrival of this fly that convinced me beyond any doubt that everything was as it always had been, that the years were a mirage and there had been no years. The small waves were the same, chucking the rowboat under the chin as we fished at anchor, and the boat was the same boat, the same color green and the ribs broken in the same places, and under the floor-boards the same freshwater leavings and débris — the dead helgramite,* the wisps of moss, the rusty discarded fishhook, the dried blood from yesterday's catch. We stared silently at the tips of our rods, at the dragonflies that came and went. I lowered the tip of mine into the water, tentatively, pensively dislodging the fly, which darted two feet away, poised, darted two feet back, and came to rest again a little farther up the rod. There had been no years between the ducking of this dragonfly and the other one — the one that was part of memory. I looked at the boy, who was silently watching his fly, and it was my hands that held his rod, my eyes watching. I felt dizzy and didn't know which rod I was at the end of.

We caught two bass, hauling them in briskly as though they were 6 mackerel, pulling them over the side of the boat in a businesslike manner without any landing net, and stunning them with a blow on the back of the head. When we got back for a swim before lunch, the lake was exactly where we had left it, the same number of inches from the dock, and there was only the merest suggestion of a breeze. This seemed an utterly enchanted sea, this lake you could leave to its own devices for a few hours and come back to, and find that it had not stirred, this constant and trustworthy body of water. In the shallows, the dark, water-soaked sticks and twigs, smooth and old, were undulating in clusters on the bottom against the clean ribbed sand, and the track of the mussel was plain. A school of minnows swam by, each minnow with its small individual shadow, doubling the attendance, so clear and sharp in the sunlight. Some of the other campers were in swimming, along the shore, one of them with a cake of soap, and the water felt thin and clear and unsubstantial. Over the years there had been this person with the cake of soap, this cultist, and here he was. There had been no years.

Up to the farmhouse to dinner through the teeming, dusty field, the 7 road under our sneakers was only a two-track road. The middle track was missing, the one with the marks of the hooves and the splotches of dried, flaky manure. There had always been three tracks to choose from in choosing which track to walk in; now the choice was narrowed down to two. For a moment I missed terribly the middle alternative. But the way led past the tennis court, and something about the way it lay there in the sun reassured me; the tape had loosened along the backline, the alleys were green with plantains and other weeds, and the net (installed in June and removed in September) sagged in the dry noon, and the whole place steamed with midday heat and hunger and emptiness. There was a choice of pie for dessert, and one was blueberry and one was apple, and the waitresses were the same country girls, there having been no passage of time, only the illusion of it as in a dropped curtain — the waitresses were still fifteen; their hair had been washed, that was the only difference — they had been to the movies and seen the pretty girls with the clean hair.

Summertime, oh summertime, pattern of life indelible, the fade-proof 8 lake, the woods unshatterable, the pasture with the sweetfern and the

---

* Eds. note — An insect larva often used as bait.

juniper forever and ever, summer without end; this was the background, and the life along the shore was the design, the cottages with their innocent and tranquil design, their tiny docks with the flagpole and the American flag floating against the white clouds in the blue sky, the little paths over the roots of the trees leading from camp to camp and the paths leading back to the outhouses and the can of lime for sprinkling, and at the souvenir counters at the store the miniature birch-bark canoes and the post cards that showed things looking a little better than they looked. This was the American family at play, escaping the city heat, wondering whether the newcomers in the camp at the head of the cove were "common" or "nice," wondering whether it was true that the people who drove up for Sunday dinner at the farmhouse were turned away because there wasn't enough chicken.

It seemed to me, as I kept remembering all this, that those times and those summers had been infinitely precious and worth saving. There had been jollity and peace and goodness. The arriving (at the beginning of August) had been so big a business in itself, at the railway station the farm wagon drawn up, the first smell of the pine-laden air, the first glimpse of the smiling farmer, and the great importance of the trunks and your father's enormous authority in such matters, and the feel of the wagon under you for the long ten-mile haul, and at the top of the last long hill catching the first view of the lake after eleven months of not seeing this cherished body of water. The shouts and cries of the other campers when they saw you, and the trunks to be unpacked, to give up their rich burden. (Arriving was less exciting nowadays, when you sneaked up in your car and parked it under a tree near the camp and took out the bags and in five minutes it was all over, no fuss, no loud wonderful fuss about trunks.)

Peace and goodness and jollity. The only thing that was wrong now, really, was the sound of the place, an unfamiliar nervous sound of the outboard motors. This was the note that jarred, the one thing that would sometimes break the illusion and set the years moving. In those other summertimes all motors were inboard; and when they were at a little distance, the noise they made was a sedative, an ingredient of summer sleep. They were one-cylinder and two-cylinder engines, and some were make-and-break and some were jump-spark, but they all made a sleepy sound across the lake. The one-lungers throbbed and fluttered, and the twin-cylinder ones purred and purred, and that was a quiet sound too. But now the campers all had outboards. In the daytime, in the hot mornings, these motors made a petulant, irritable sound; at night, in the still evening when the afterglow lit the water, they whined about one's ears like mosquitoes. My boy loved our rented outboard, and his great desire was to achieve singlehanded mastery over it, and authority, and he soon learned the trick of choking it a little (but not too much), and the adjustment of the needle valve. Watching him I would remember the things you could do with the old one-cylinder engine with the heavy flywheel, how you could have it eating out of your hand if you got really close to it spiritually. Motor boats in those days didn't have clutches, and you would make a landing by shutting off the motor at the proper time and coasting in with a dead rudder. But there was a way of reversing them, if you learned the trick, by cutting the switch and putting it on again exactly on the final dying revolution of the flywheel, so that it would kick back against compression and begin reversing. Approaching a dock in a strong following breeze, it was difficult to slow up sufficiently by the ordinary coasting method, and if a boy felt he had complete mastery over his motor, he was tempted to keep it running beyond its time and then reverse it a few feet from the dock. It took a cool nerve, because if you threw the switch a twentieth of a second too soon you could catch the flywheel when it still had speed enough to go up past center, and the boat would leap ahead, charging bull-fashion at the dock.

We had a good week at the camp. The bass were biting well and the 11 sun shone endlessly, day after day. We would be tired at night and lie down in the accumulated heat of the little bedrooms after the long hot day and the breeze would stir almost imperceptibly outside and the smell of the swamp drift in through the rusty screens. Sleep would come easily and in the morning the red squirrel would be on the roof, tapping out his gay routine. I kept remembering everything, lying in bed in the mornings — the small steamboat that had a long rounded stern like the lip of a Ubangi,* how quietly she ran on the moonlight sails, when the older boys played their mandolins and the girls sang and we ate doughnuts dipped in sugar, and how sweet the music was on the water in the shining night, and what it had felt like to think about girls then. After breakfast we would go up to the store and the things were in the same place — the minnows in a bottle, the plugs and spinners disarranged and pawed over by the youngsters from the boys' camp, the fig newtons and the Beeman's gum. Outside, the road was tarred and cars stood in front of the store. Inside, all was just as it had always been, except there was more Coca-Cola and not so much Moxie** and root beer and birch beer and sarsaparilla.*** We would walk out with a bottle of pop apiece and sometimes the pop would backfire up our noses and hurt. We explored the streams, quietly, where the turtles slid off the sunny logs and dug their way into the soft bottom; and we lay on the town wharf and fed worms to the tame bass. Everywhere we went I had trouble making out which was I, the one walking at my side, the one walking in my pants.

One afternoon while we were there at that lake a thunderstorm came 12 up. It was like the revival of an old melodrama that I had seen long ago with childish awe. The second-act climax of the drama of the electrical disturbance over a lake in America had not changed in any important respect.

---

* Eds. note — A member of an African tribe known for wearing mouth ornaments that stretch the lips into a saucerlike shape.
** Eds. note — A soft drink that was popular in the early twentieth century.
*** Eds. note — A sweetened carbonated beverage flavored with birch oil and sassafras.

This was the big scene, still the big scene. The whole thing was so familiar, the first feeling of oppression and heat and a general air around camp of not wanting to go very far away. In midafternoon (it was all the same) a curious darkening of the sky, and a lull in everything that had made life tick; and then the way the boats suddenly swung the other way at their moorings with the coming of a breeze out of the new quarter, and the premonitory rumble. Then the kettle drum, then the snare, then the bass drum and cymbals, then crackling light against the dark, and the gods grinning and licking their chops in the hills. Afterward the calm, the rain steadily rustling in the calm lake, the return of light and hope and spirits, and the campers running out in joy and relief to go swimming in the rain, their bright cries perpetuating the deathless joke about how they were getting simply drenched, and the children screaming with delight at the new sensation of bathing in the rain, and the joke about getting drenched linking the generations in a strong indestructible chain. And the comedian who waded in carrying an umbrella.

When the others went swimming my son said he was going in too. He ¹³ pulled his dripping trunks from the line where they had hung all through the shower, and wrung them out. Languidly, and with no thought of going in, I watched him, his hard little body, skinny and bare, saw him wince slightly as he pulled up around his vitals the small, soggy, icy garment. As he buckled the swollen belt suddenly my groin felt the chill of death.

· · ·

Comprehension

1. How are the writer and his son alike? How are they different? What does White mean when he says, "I seemed to be living a dual existence" (4)?

2. In paragraph 5, White says that "no years" seemed to have gone by between past and present; elsewhere, he senses that things are different. How do you account for these conflicting feelings?

3. Why does White feel disconcerted when he discovers that the road to the farmhouse has two tracks, not three? What do you make of his comment that "now the choice was narrowed down to two" (7)?

4. How does sound "break the illusion and set the years moving" (10)?

5. What is White referring to in the essay's last sentence?

Purpose and Audience

1. What is the thesis of this essay? Is it stated or implied?

2. Do you think White expects the ending of his essay to surprise his audience? Explain.

3. What age group do you think this essay would appeal to most? Why?

Style and Structure

1. List the specific changes that have taken place on the lake. Does White emphasize these changes or play them down? Explain.
2. What ideas and images does White repeat throughout his essay? What is the purpose of this repetition?
3. White goes to great lengths to describe how things look, feel, smell, taste, and sound. How does this help him achieve his purpose in this essay?
4. How does White's conclusion echo the first paragraph of the essay?

Vocabulary Projects

1. Define each of the following words as it is used in this selection.

   placidity (1)   pensively (5)   melodrama (12)
   gunwale (2)   jollity (9)   premonitory (12)
   primeval (3)   petulant (10)   perpetuating (12)
   transposition (4)   imperceptibly (11)   languidly (13)

2. Underline ten words in the essay that refer to one of the five senses, and make a list of synonyms you could use for these words. How close do your substitutions come to capturing White's meaning?

Journal Entry

Do you identify more with the father or with the son in this essay? Why?

Writing Workshop

1. Write a description of a scene you remember from your childhood. In your essay, discuss how your current view of the scene differs from the view you had when you were a child. ,
2. **Working with Sources.** Assume you are a travel agent. Write a descriptive brochure designed to bring tourists to the lake. Be specific, and stress the benefits White mentions in his essay. In your essay, use a quotation from White's essay. (See Chapter 18 for information on MLA documentation.)
3. Write an essay describing yourself from the perspective of one of your parents. Make sure your description conveys both the qualities your parent likes and the qualities he or she would want to change.

Combining the Patterns

White opens his essay with a short narrative about his first trip to the lake in 1904. How does this use of **narration** provide a context for the entire essay?

Thematic Connections

- "Only Daughter" (page 111)
- "The Case against Air Conditioning" (page 344)

KATE CHOPIN

The Storm (Fiction)

Kate Chopin (1851–1904) was born Catherine O'Flaherty. In 1870, she married Oscar Chopin and moved with him to New Orleans. After suffering business reversals, the Chopins relocated to Cloutierville, Louisiana, to be closer to Oscar's extended Creole family. Oscar Chopin died suddenly in 1882, and Kate Chopin, left with six children to raise, returned to St. Louis. There she began writing short stories, many set in the colorful Creole country of central Louisiana. Her first collection, *Bayou Folk,* was published in 1894, followed by *A Night in Arcadie* in 1897. Her literary success was cut short, however, with the publication of her first novel, *The Awakening* (1899), a story of adultery that outraged many of her critics and readers because it was told sympathetically from a woman's perspective. Her work languished until the middle of the twentieth century, when it was rediscovered, largely by feminist literary scholars.

Background on Creole culture The following story was probably written about the same time as *The Awakening,* but Chopin never attempted to publish it. Its frank sexuality — franker than that depicted in her controversial novel — and its focus on a liaison between two lovers (Calixta and Alcée) married to others would have been too scandalous for middle-class readers of the day. Even within the more liberal Creole culture in which the story is set, Calixta's actions would have been outrageous. While Creole men were expected to have mistresses (usually black or mixed-race women), Creole wives were expected to remain true to their wedding vows. The Creoles themselves were descendants of the early Spanish and French settlers in Louisiana, and they lived lives quite separate from — and, they believed, superior to — those whose ancestors were British. Their language became a mix of French and English, as did their mode of dress and cuisine. A strong Creole influence can still be found in New Orleans and the surrounding Louisiana countryside; Mardi Gras, for example, is a Creole tradition.

I

The leaves were so still that even Bibi thought it was going to rain. 1
Bobinôt, who was accustomed to converse on terms of perfect equality with his little son, called the child's attention to certain sombre clouds that were rolling with sinister intention from the west, accompanied by a sullen, threatening roar. They were at Friedheimer's store and decided to remain there till the storm had passed. They sat within the door on two empty kegs. Bibi was four years old and looked very wise.

"Mama'll be 'fraid, yes," he suggested with blinking eyes. 2
"She'll shut the house. Maybe she got Sylvie helpin' her this evenin'," 3
Bobinôt responded reassuringly.
"No; she ent got Sylvie. Sylvie was helpin' her yistiday," piped Bibi. 4

Bobinôt arose and going across to the counter purchased a can of 5
shrimps, of which Calixta was very fond. Then he returned to his perch
on the keg and sat stolidly holding the can of shrimps while the storm
burst. It shook the wooden store and seemed to be ripping great furrows
in the distant field. Bibi laid his little hand on his father's knee and was
not afraid.

II

Calixta, at home, felt no uneasiness for their safety. She sat at a side 6
window sewing furiously on a sewing machine. She was greatly occupied
and did not notice the approaching storm. But she felt very warm and often stopped to mop her face on which the perspiration gathered in beads.
She unfastened her white sacque at the throat. It began to grow dark, and
suddenly realizing the situation she got up hurriedly and went about closing windows and doors.

Out on the small front gallery she had hung Bobinôt's Sunday clothes 7
to air and she hastened out to gather them before the rain fell. As she
stepped outside, Alcée Laballière rode in at the gate. She had not seen
him very often since her marriage, and never alone. She stood there with
Bobinôt's coat in her hands, and the big rain drops began to fall. Alcée rode
his horse under the shelter of a side projection where the chickens had
huddled and there were plows and a harrow piled up in the corner.

"May I come and wait on your gallery till the storm is over, Calixta?" 8
he asked.

"Come 'long in, M'sieur Alcée." 9

His voice and her own startled her as if from a trance, and she seized 10
Bobinôt's vest. Alcée, mounting to the porch, grabbed the trousers and
snatched Bibi's braided jacket that was about to be carried away by a sudden gust of wind. He expressed an intention to remain outside, but it was
soon apparent that he might as well have been out in the open: the water
beat in upon the boards in driving sheets, and he went inside, closing the
door after him. It was even necessary to put something beneath the door
to keep the water out.

"My! what a rain! It's good two years since it rain' like that," exclaimed 11
Calixta as she rolled up a piece of bagging and Alcée helped her to thrust it
beneath the crack.

She was a little fuller of figure than five years before when she mar- 12
ried; but she had lost nothing of her vivacity. Her blue eyes still retained
their melting quality; and her yellow hair, dishevelled by the wind and rain,
kinked more stubbornly than ever about her ears and temples.

The rain beat upon the low, shingled roof with a force and clatter that 13
threatened to break an entrance and deluge them there. They were in the
dining room — the sitting room — the general utility room. Adjoining was
her bed room, with Bibi's couch along side her own. The door stood open,
and the room with its white, monumental bed, its closed shutters, looked
dim and mysterious.

Alcée flung himself into a rocker and Calixta nervously began to gather 14 up from the floor the lengths of a cotton sheet which she had been sewing. "If this keeps up, *Dieu sait** if the levees goin' to stan' it!" she exclaimed. 15 "What have you got to do with the levees?" 16 "I got enough to do! An' there's Bobinôt with Bibi out in that storm — if 17 he only didn't left Friedheimer's!" "Let us hope, Calixta, that Bobinôt's got sense enough to come in out 18 of a cyclone." She went and stood at the window with a greatly disturbed look on her 19 face. She wiped the frame that was clouded with moisture. It was stiflingly hot. Alcée got up and joined her at the window, looking over her shoulder. The rain was coming down in sheets obscuring the view of far-off cabins and enveloping the distant wood in a gray mist. The playing of the lightning was incessant. A bolt struck a tall chinaberry tree at the edge of the field. It filled all visible space with a blinding glare and the crash seemed to invade the very boards they stood upon.

Calixta put her hands to her eyes, and with a cry, staggered backward. 20 Alcée's arm encircled her, and for an instant he drew her close and spasmodically to him.

"*Bonté!*"** she cried, releasing herself from his encircling arm and 21 retreating from the window, "the house'll go next! If I only knew w'ere Bibi was!" She would not compose herself; she would not be seated. Alcée clasped her shoulders and looked into her face. The contact of her warm, palpitating body when he had unthinkingly drawn her into his arms, had aroused all the old-time infatuation and desire for her flesh.

"Calixta," he said, "don't be frightened. Nothing can happen. The house 22 is too low to be struck, with so many tall trees standing about. There! aren't you going to be quiet? say, aren't you?" He pushed her hair back from her face that was warm and steaming. Her lips were as red and moist as pomegranate seed. Her white neck and a glimpse of her full, firm bosom disturbed him powerfully. As she glanced up at him the fear in her liquid blue eyes had given place to a drowsy gleam that unconsciously betrayed a sensuous desire. He looked down into her eyes and there was nothing for him to do but to gather her lips in a kiss. It reminded him of Assumption.***

"Do you remember — in Assumption, Calixta?" he asked in a low voice 23 broken by passion. Oh! she remembered; for in Assumption he had kissed her and kissed and kissed her; until his senses would well nigh fail, and to save her he would resort to a desperate flight. If she was not an immaculate dove in those days, she was still inviolate; a passionate creature whose very defenselessness had made her defense, against which his honor forbade him to prevail. Now — well, now — her lips seemed in a manner free to be tasted, as well as her round, white throat and her whiter breasts.

---

* Eds. note — God knows.
** Eds. note — Goodness!
*** Eds. note — A parish near New Orleans.

They did not heed the crashing torrents, and the roar of the elements 24 made her laugh as she lay in his arms. She was a revelation in that dim, mysterious chamber; as white as the couch she lay upon. Her firm, elastic flesh that was knowing for the first time its birthright, was like a creamy lily that the sun invites to contribute its breath and perfume to the undying life of the world.

The generous abundance of her passion, without guile or trickery, was 25 like a white flame which penetrated and found response in depths of his own sensuous nature that had never yet been reached.

When he touched her breasts they gave themselves up in quivering ec- 26 stasy, inviting his lips. Her mouth was a fountain of delight. And when he possessed her, they seemed to swoon together at the very borderland of life's mystery.

He stayed cushioned upon her, breathless, dazed, enervated, with his 27 heart beating like a hammer upon her. With one hand she clasped his head, her lips lightly touching his forehead. The other hand stroked with a soothing rhythm his muscular shoulders.

The growl of the thunder was distant and passing away. The rain beat 28 softly upon the shingles, inviting them to drowsiness and sleep. But they dared not yield.

The rain was over; and the sun was turning the glistening green world 29 into a palace of gems. Calixta, on the gallery, watched Alcée ride away. He turned and smiled at her with a beaming face; and she lifted her pretty chin in the air and laughed aloud.

III

Bobinôt and Bibi, trudging home, stopped without at the cistern to 30 make themselves presentable.

"My! Bibi, w'at will yo' mama say! You ought to be asham'. You oughtn' 31 put on those good pants. Look at 'em! An' that mud on yo' collar! How you got that mud on yo' collar, Bibi? I never saw such a boy!" Bibi was the picture of pathetic resignation. Bobinôt was the embodiment of serious solicitude as he strove to remove from his own person and his son's the signs of their tramp over heavy roads and through wet fields. He scraped the mud off Bibi's bare legs and feet with a stick and carefully removed all traces from his heavy brogans. Then, prepared for the worst — the meeting with an over-scrupulous housewife, they entered cautiously at the back door.

Calixta was preparing supper. She had set the table and was dripping 32 coffee at the hearth. She sprang up as they came in.

"Oh, Bobinôt! You back! My! but I was uneasy. W'ere you been during 33 the rain? An' Bibi? he ain't wet? he ain't hurt?" She had clasped Bibi and was kissing him effusively. Bobinôt's explanations and apologies which he had been composing all along the way, died on his lips as Calixta felt him to see if he were dry, and seemed to express nothing but satisfaction at their safe return.

"I brought you some shrimps, Calixta," offered Bobinôt, hauling the 34 can from his ample side pocket and laying it on the table.

"Shrimps! Oh, Bobinôt! you too good fo' anything!" and she gave him 35 a smacking kiss on the cheek that resounded. "*J'vous réponds,** we'll have a feas' tonight! umph-umph!"

Bobinôt and Bibi began to relax and enjoy themselves, and when the 36 three sated themselves at table they laughed much and so loud that anyone might have heard them as far away as Laballière's.

IV

Alcée Laballière wrote to his wife, Clarisse, that night. It was a loving 37 letter, full of tender solicitude. He told her not to hurry back, but if she and the babies liked it at Biloxi, to stay a month longer. He was getting on nicely; and though he missed them, he was willing to bear the separation a while longer — realizing that their health and pleasure were the first things to be considered.

V

As for Clarisse, she was charmed upon receiving her husband's letter. 38 She and the babies were doing well. The society was agreeable; many of her old friends and acquaintances were at the bay. And the first free breath since her marriage seemed to restore the pleasant liberty of her maiden days. Devoted as she was to her husband, their intimate conjugal life was something which she was more than willing to forego for a while.

So the storm passed and everyone was happy. 39

• • •

Reading Literature

1. How does the storm help set in motion the action of the story? List the events caused by the storm.

2. Is the last line of the story to be taken literally, or is it meant to be **ironic** (that is, does it actually suggest the opposite meaning)? Explain.

3. What do the story's specific descriptive details tell us about Calixta?

Journal Entry

On one level, the story's title refers to the storm that takes place through much of the story. To what else could the story's title refer?

---

* Eds. note — I tell you.

Thematic Connections

Writing Assignments for Description

1. Choose a character from a book or movie who you think is interesting. Write a descriptive essay conveying what makes this character so special.

2. Several of the essays in this chapter deal with the way journeys change how the writers see themselves. For example, in "Once More to the Lake," a visit to a campground forces E. B. White to confront his own mortality, and in "The Hidden Life of Garbage," a visit to a landfill outside Morrisville, Pennsylvania, enables Heather Rogers to grasp the enormity of the task of disposing of garbage in the United States. Write an essay describing a place that you traveled to. Make sure that, in addition to describing the place, you explain how it has taught you something about yourself.

3. Locate some photographs of your relatives. Describe three of these pictures, including details that provide insight into the lives of the people you discuss. Use your descriptive passages to support a thesis about your family.

4. **Working with Sources.** Visit an art museum (or go to a museum site on the Web), and select a painting that interests you. Study it carefully, and then write an essay-length description of it. Before you write, decide how you will organize your details and whether you will write a subjective or an objective description. If possible, include a photograph of the painting in your essay. Be sure to document the photograph and to include a works-cited page. (See Chapter 18 for information on MLA documentation.)

5. Select an object you are familiar with, and write an objective description of it. Include a diagram.

6. Assume you are writing an email to someone in another country who knows little about life in the United States. Describe to this person something you consider typically American — for example, a baseball stadium or a food court in a shopping mall.

7. Visit your college library, and write a brochure in which you describe the reference area. Be specific, and select an organizing scheme before you begin your description. Your purpose is to acquaint students with some of the reference materials they will use. If possible, include a diagram that will help orient students to this section of the library.

8. Describe your neighborhood to a visitor who knows nothing about it. Include as much specific detail as you can.

9. After reading "Ground Zero," write a description of a sight or scene that fascinated, surprised, or shocked you. Your description should explain why you were so deeply affected by what you saw.

10. Write an essay describing an especially frightening horror film. What specific sights and sounds make this film so horrifying? Include a thesis statement assessing the film's success as a horror film. (Be careful not to simply summarize the plot of the film.)

Collaborative Activity for Description

Working in groups of three or four students, select a famous person — one you can reasonably expect your classmates to recognize. Then, work as a group to write a description of that individual, including as much physical detail as possible. (Avoid any details that will be an instant giveaway.) Give your description a general title — *politician, television star,* or *person in the news,* for example. Finally, have one person read the description aloud to the class, and see whether your classmates can guess the person's identity.

8

Exemplification

What Is Exemplification?

Exemplification uses one or more particular cases, or **examples**, to illustrate or explain a general point or an abstract concept. In the following paragraph from *Sexism and Language,* Alleen Pace Nilsen uses a number of well-chosen examples to illustrate her statement that the armed forces use words that have positive masculine connotations to encourage recruitment.

Topic sentence

The armed forces, particularly the Marines, use the positive masculine connotation as part of their recruitment psychology. They promote the idea that to join the Marines (or the Army, Navy, or Air Force) guarantees that you will become a man. But this brings up a problem, because much of the work that is necessary to keep a large organization running is what is traditionally thought of as *woman's work.* Now, how can the Marines ask someone who has signed up for a *man-sized job* to do *woman's work?* Since they can't, they euphemize and give the jobs titles that are more prestigious or, at least, don't make people think of females. Wait-

Series of related examples

resses are called *orderlies,* secretaries are called *clerk-typists,* nurses are called *medics,* assistants are called *adjutants,* and cleaning up an area is called *policing* the area. The same kind of word glorification is used in civilian life to bolster a man's ego when he is doing such tasks as cooking and sewing. For example, a *chef* has higher prestige than a *cook* and a *tailor* has higher prestige than a *seamstress.*

Using Exemplification

You have probably noticed, when watching television talk shows or listening to classroom discussions, that the most effective exchanges occur when participants support their points with specific examples. Sweeping generalizations and vague statements are not nearly as effective as specific observations, anecdotes, details, and opinions. It is one thing to say, "The mayor is corrupt and should not be reelected" and another to illustrate your point by saying, "The mayor should not be reelected because he has fired two city workers who refused to contribute to his campaign fund, has put his family and friends on the city payroll, and has used public employees to make improvements to his home." The same principle applies to writing: many of the most effective essays use examples extensively. Exemplification is used in every kind of writing situation to explain and clarify, to add interest, and to persuade.

Using Examples to Explain and Clarify

On a midterm exam in a film course, you might write, "Even though horror movies seem modern, they really aren't." You may think your statement is perfectly clear, but if this is all you say about horror movies, you should not be surprised if your exam comes back with a question mark in the margin next to this sentence. After all, you have only made a general statement about your subject. It is not specific, nor does it anticipate readers' questions about how horror movies are not modern. To be certain your audience knows exactly what you mean, state your point precisely: "Despite the fact that horror movies seem modern, two of the most memorable ones are adaptations of nineteenth-century Gothic novels." Then, use examples to ensure clarity and avoid ambiguity. For example, you could illustrate your point by discussing two films — *Frankenstein,* directed by James Whale, and *Dracula,* directed by Todd Browning — and linking them to the nineteenth-century novels they are based on. With the benefit of these specific examples, readers would know what you mean — that the literary roots of such movies are in the past, not that their cinematic techniques or production methods are dated. Moreover, readers would know which particular horror movies you are discussing.

Using Examples to Add Interest

Writers use well-chosen examples to add interest as well as to clarify their points. Brent Staples does this in his essay "Just Walk On By," which appears later in this chapter. In itself, the claim that during his time away from home, Staples became "thoroughly familiar with the language of fear" is not very interesting. This statement becomes compelling, however, when Staples illustrates it with specific examples — experiences he had while walking the streets at night. For example, his presence apparently inspired so much fear in people that they locked their car doors as he walked past or crossed to the other side of the street when they saw him approaching.

When you use exemplification, look for examples that are interesting as well as pertinent. Test the effectiveness of your examples by putting yourself in your readers' place. If you don't find your essay lively and absorbing, chances are your readers won't either. If this is the case, try to add more thought-provoking and spirited examples. After all, your goal is to communicate ideas to your readers, and imaginative examples can make the difference between an engrossing essay and one that is a chore to read.

Using Examples to Persuade

Although you may use examples to explain or to add interest, examples are also an effective way of persuading people that what you are saying is reasonable and worth considering. A few well-chosen examples can provide effective support for otherwise unconvincing general statements. For instance, a broad statement that school districts across the country cannot cope with the numerous students with limited English skills is one that needs support. If you make such a statement on an exam, you need to back it up with appropriate examples — such as that in Massachusetts alone, the number of students who speak English as a second language has increased by more than 20 percent over the past ten years. In other words, in 2010, 57,000 students lacked proficiency in English. Similarly, a statement in a biology paper that DDT should continue to be banned is unconvincing without persuasive examples such as these to support it:

- Although DDT has been banned since December 31, 1972, scientists are finding traces in the eggs of various fish and waterfowl.
- Certain lakes and streams cannot be used for sport and recreation because DDT levels are dangerously high, presumably because of farmland runoff.
- Because of its stability as a compound, DDT does not degrade quickly; therefore, existing residues will threaten the environment well into the twenty-first century.

Planning an Exemplification Essay

Developing a Thesis Statement

The **thesis statement** of an exemplification essay makes a point that the rest of the essay will support with examples. This statement usually identifies your topic as well as the main point you want to make about it.

The examples you gather during the invention stage of the writing process can help you develop your thesis. By doing so, they can help you test your ideas as well as the ideas of others. For instance, suppose you plan to write a paper for a composition class about students' writing skills. Your tentative thesis is that writing well is an inborn talent and that teachers can do little to help people write better. But is this really true? Has it been true in your own life? To test your point, you brainstorm about the various teachers you have had who tried to help you improve your writing.

As you assemble your list, you remember a teacher you had in high school. She was strict, required lots of writing, and seemed to accept nothing less than perfection. At the time, neither you nor your classmates liked her. But looking back, you recall her one-on-one conferences, her organized lessons, and her helpful comments on your essays. You realize that after completing her class, you felt much more comfortable writing. When examining some papers you saved, you are surprised to see how much your writing actually improved during that year. These examples lead you to reevaluate your ideas and to revise your thesis:

> Even though some people seem to have a natural flair for writing, a good teacher can make a difference.

Providing Enough Examples

Unfortunately, no general rule exists to tell you when you have enough examples to support your ideas. The number you use depends on your thesis statement. If, for instance, your thesis is that an educational institution, like a business, needs careful financial management, a single detailed examination of one college or university could provide all the information you need to make your point.

If, however, your thesis is that conflict between sons and fathers is a major theme in Franz Kafka's writing, more than one example would be necessary. A single example would show only that the theme is present in *one* of Kafka's works. In this case, the more examples you include, the more effectively you support your point.

For some thesis statements, however, even several examples would not be enough. Examples alone, for instance, could not demonstrate convincingly that children from small families have more successful careers than children from large families. This thesis would have to be supported with a **statistical study** — that is, by collecting and interpreting numerical data representing a great many examples.

Choosing a Fair Range of Examples

Selecting a sufficient **range of examples** is just as important as choosing an appropriate number. If you want to persuade readers that Colin Powell was an able general, you should choose examples from several stages of his military career. Likewise, if you want to convince readers that outdoor advertising ruins the scenic views from major highways, you should discuss an area larger than your immediate neighborhood. Your objective in each case is to choose a cross section of examples to represent the full range of your topic.

Similarly, if you want to argue for a ban on smoking in all public buildings, you should not limit your examples to restaurants. To be convincing, you should include examples involving many public places, such as office buildings, hotel lobbies, and sports stadiums. For the same reason, one person's experience is not enough to support a general conclusion involving many people unless you can establish that the experience is typical.

If you decide you cannot cite a fair range of examples that support your thesis, reexamine it. Rather than switching to a new topic, try to narrow your thesis. After all, the only way your paper will be convincing is if your readers believe that your thesis is supported by your examples and that your examples fairly represent the scope of your topic.

Of course, to be convincing you must not only *choose* examples effectively but also *use* them effectively. You should keep your thesis statement in mind as you write, taking care not to get so involved with one example that you digress from your main point. No matter how carefully developed, no matter how specific, lively, and appropriate, your examples accomplish nothing if they do not support your essay's main idea.

Using Transitions

Be sure to use transitional words and phrases to introduce your examples. Without them, readers will have difficulty seeing the connection between an example and the general statement it is illustrating. In some cases, transitions will help you connect examples to your thesis statement ("*Another* successful program for the homeless provides telephone answering services for job seekers"). In other cases, transitions will link examples to topic sentences ("*For instance,* I have written articles for my college newspaper"). In exemplification essays, the most frequently used transitions include *for example, for instance, in fact, namely, specifically, that is,* and *thus.* (A more complete list of transitions appears on page 57.)

Structuring an Exemplification Essay

Exemplification essays usually begin with an **introduction** that includes the **thesis statement**, which is supported by examples in the body of the essay. Each **body paragraph** may develop a separate example, present a point illustrated by several brief examples, or explore one aspect of a single extended example that is developed throughout the essay. The **conclusion** reinforces the essay's main idea, perhaps restating the thesis. At times, however, variations of this basic pattern are advisable and even necessary. For instance, beginning your paper with a striking example might stimulate your reader's interest and curiosity; ending with one might vividly reinforce your thesis.

Exemplification presents one special organizational problem. If you do not select your examples carefully and arrange them effectively, your paper can become a thesis statement followed by a list or by ten or fifteen brief, choppy paragraphs. One way to avoid this problem is to develop your best examples fully in separate paragraphs and to discard the others. Another effective strategy is to group related examples together in one paragraph.

Within each paragraph, you can arrange examples **chronologically**, beginning with those that occurred first and moving to those that occurred later. You can also arrange examples **in order of increasing complexity**, beginning with the simplest and moving to the most difficult or complex. Finally, you can arrange examples **in order of importance**, beginning with those that are less significant and moving to those that are most significant or persuasive.

The following informal outline for an essay evaluating the nursing care at a hospital illustrates one way to arrange examples. Notice how the writer presents his examples in order of increasing importance under three general headings — *patient rooms, emergency room,* and *clinics.*

SAMPLE OUTLINE: Exemplification

Introduction:	Thesis statement — Because of its focus on the patient, the nursing care at Montgomery Hospital can serve as a model for other medical facilities.

In Patient Rooms

Example 1:	Being responsive
Example 2:	Establishing rapport
Example 3:	Delivering bedside care

In Emergency Room

Example 4:	Staffing treatment rooms
Example 5:	Circulating among patients in the waiting room
Example 6:	Maintaining good working relationships with physicians

In Clinics

Example 7:	Preparing patients
Example 8:	Assisting during treatment
Example 9:	Instructing patients after treatment
Conclusion:	Restatement of thesis or review of key points or examples

Revising an Exemplification Essay

When you revise an exemplification essay, consider the items on the revision checklist on page 68. In addition, pay special attention to the items on the following checklist, which apply specifically to exemplification essays.

✔ **REVISION CHECKLIST**   **Exemplification**

- Does your assignment call for exemplification?
- Does your essay have a clear thesis statement that identifies the point you will illustrate?
- Do your examples explain and clarify your thesis statement?
- Have you provided enough examples?

- Have you used a range of examples?
- Are your examples persuasive?
- Do your examples add interest?
- Have you used transitional words and phrases that reinforce the connection between your examples and your thesis statement?

Editing an Exemplification Essay

When you edit your exemplification essay, follow the guidelines on the editing checklists on pages 85, 88, and 90. In addition, focus on the grammar, mechanics, and punctuation issues that are most relevant to exemplification essays. One of these issues — using commas in a series — is discussed here.

GRAMMAR IN CONTEXT **Using Commas in a Series**

When you write an exemplification essay, you often use a **series of examples** to support a statement or to illustrate a point. When you use a series of three or more examples in a sentence, you must remember to separate them with commas.

- Always use commas to separate three or more items — words, phrases, or clauses — in a series.

In "Just Walk On By," Brent Staples says, "I was <u>surprised</u>, <u>embarrassed</u>, and <u>dismayed</u> all at once" (241).

In "Just Walk On By," Staples observes that the woman thought she was being stalked <u>by a mugger</u>, <u>by a rapist</u>, or <u>by something worse</u> (241).

In "The Catbird Seat," David J. Birnbaum describes what happened when he moved his wheelchair toward an elevator: "<u>The 'L' on the display lighted</u>, <u>the ding went off</u>, <u>the doors opened</u>, and <u>I swiftly pushed my chair forward into the car</u>" (229).

NOTE: Although newspaper and magazine writers routinely leave out the comma before the last item in a series of three or more items, you should always include this comma in your college writing.

- Do not use a comma after the final element in a series of three or more items.

INCORRECT: Staples was <u>shocked</u>, <u>horrified</u>, and <u>disillusioned</u>, to be taken for a mugger.

CORRECT: Staples was <u>shocked</u>, <u>horrified</u>, and <u>disillusioned</u> to be taken for a mugger.

- Do not use commas if all the elements in a series of three or more items are separated by coordinating conjunctions (*and, or, but,* and so on).

David J. Birnbaum believes that there is a pecking order: <u>being blind beats being in a wheelchair</u> and <u>being in a wheelchair beats being pregnant</u> and <u>being pregnant beats being old</u>. (*no commas*)

For more practice in using commas in a series, visit the resources for Chapter 8 at **bedfordstmartins.com/patterns.**

✔**EDITING CHECKLIST**   Exemplification

- Have you used commas to separate three or more items in a series?
- Have you made sure not to use a comma after the last element in a series?
- Have you made sure not to use a comma in a series with items separated by coordinating conjunctions?
- Are all the elements in a series stated in **parallel** terms (see page 378)?

A STUDENT WRITER: Exemplification

Exemplification is frequently used in nonacademic writing situations, such as business reports, memos, and proposals. One of the most important situations for using exemplification is in a letter you write to apply for a job.* Kristy Bredin's letter of application to a prospective employer follows.

---

* Eds. note — In business letters, paragraphs are not indented and extra space is added between paragraphs.

1028 Geissinger Street
Bethlehem, PA 18018
September 7, 2011

Kim Goldstein
Rolling Stone
1290 Avenue of the Americas
New York, NY 10104

Dear Ms. Goldstein:

Introduction

I am writing to apply for the editorial internship with *Rolling*   1
Stone magazine that you posted on Moravian College's employment

Thesis statement Web site. I believe that both my education and my experience in
publishing qualify me for the position you advertised.

Examples

I am currently a senior at Moravian College, where I am majoring   2
in English (with a concentration in creative writing) and music.
Throughout my college career, I have maintained a 3.4 average.
After I graduate in May, I would like to find a full-time job
in publishing. For this reason, I am very interested in your
internship. It would not only give me additional editorial and
administrative experience, but it would also give me insight into
a large-scale publishing operation. An internship at *Rolling Stone*
would also enable to me to read, edit, and possibly write articles
about popular music — a subject I know a lot about.

Examples

Throughout college, I have been involved in writing and editing. I   3
have served as both secretary and president of the Literary Society
and have written, edited, and published its annual newsletter.
I have also worked as a tutor in Moravian's Writing Center; as a
literature editor for the *Manuscript*, Moravian's literary magazine;
and as a features editor for the *Comeneian*, the student newspaper.
In these jobs I have gained a good deal of practical experience in
publishing as well as insight into dealing with people. In addition,
I acquired professional editing experience this past semester when
I worked as an intern for Taylor and Francis (Routledge) Publishing
in New York.

Conclusion   I believe that my education and my publishing experience make   4
me a good candidate for your position. As your ad requested, I
have enclosed my résumé, three letters of reference, information
on Moravian's internship program, and several writing samples
for your consideration. You can contact me by phone at (484)
625-6731 or by e-mail at stkab@moravian.edu. I will be available
for an interview anytime after September 23. I look forward to
meeting with you to discuss my qualifications.

Sincerely,

Kristy Bredin

Kristy Bredin

Points for Special Attention

Organization. Exemplification is ideally suited for letters of application. The best way Kristy Bredin can support her claims about her qualifications for the internship at *Rolling Stone* is to give examples of her educational and professional qualifications. For this reason, the body of her letter is divided into two categories — her educational record and her editorial experience.

Each of the body paragraphs has a clear purpose and function. The second paragraph contains two examples pertaining to Kristy's educational record. The third paragraph contains examples of her editorial experience. These examples tell the prospective employer what qualifies Kristy for the internship. Within these two body paragraphs, she arranges her examples in order of increasing importance. Because her practical experience as an editor relates directly to the position she is applying for, Kristy considers this her strongest point and presents it last.

Kristy ends her letter on a strong note, expressing her willingness to be interviewed and giving the first date she will be available for an interview. Because people remember best what they read last, a strong conclusion is essential here, just as it is in other writing situations.

Persuasive Examples. To support a thesis convincingly, examples should convey specific information, not generalizations. Saying "I am a good student who is not afraid of responsibility" means very little. It is far better to say, as Kristy does, "Throughout my college career, I have maintained a 3.4 average" and "I have served as both secretary and president of the Literary Society." A letter of application should specifically show a prospective employer how your strengths and background correspond to the employer's needs; well-chosen examples can help you accomplish this goal.

Focus on Revision

After reading her letter, the students in Kristy's peer editing group identified several areas that they thought needed work.

One student thought Kristy should have mentioned her computer experience: she had taken a desktop publishing course as an elective and worked with publishing and graphics software when she was the features editor of the student newspaper. Kristy agreed that this expertise would make her a more attractive candidate for the job and thought she could work these examples into her third paragraph.

Another student asked Kristy to explain how her experience as secretary and president of the Literary Society relates to the job she is applying for. If her purpose is to show that she can assume responsibility, she should say so; if it is to illustrate that she can supervise others, she should make this clear.

A third student suggested that she expand the discussion of her internship with Taylor and Francis Publishing in New York. Examples of her duties there would be persuasive because they would give her prospective employer a clear idea of her editorial experience. (A peer editing worksheet for exemplification can be found on pages 224–225.)

Working with Sources. Kristy's instructor recommended that she include excerpts from the ad to which she was responding. He said that this strategy would help her readers — potential employers — to see that she was tailoring her letter to the specific job at *Rolling Stone*. Kristy considered this suggestion and decided to quote the language of the ad in her letter.

A STUDENT WRITER: Exemplification

The following essay by Grace Ku was written for a composition class in response to the following assignment: "Write an essay about the worst job you (or someone you know) ever had. If you can, include a quotation from one of the essays in your textbook. Make sure you include documentation as well as a works-cited page."

Midnight

Introduction   It was eight o'clock, and I was staring at the television   1
set wondering what kind of lesson Dr. Huxtable would teach his
children on a rerun of *The Cosby Show*. I was glued to the set
like an average eleven-year-old while leisurely eating cold Chef
Boyardee spaghetti out of the can. As I watched the show, I fell
asleep on the floor fully clothed in a pair of jeans and a T-shirt,
wondering when my parents would come home. Around midnight
I woke up to a rustling noise: my parents had finally arrived from
Thesis statement   a long day at work. I could see in their tired faces the grief and
hardship of working at a dry-cleaning plant.

*Transitional
paragraph
provides
background*

Although my parents lived in the most technologically   2
advanced country in the world, their working conditions were
like those of nineteenth-century factory workers. Because they
were immigrants with little formal education and spoke broken
English, they could get jobs only as laborers. Therefore, they
worked at a dry-cleaning plant that was as big as a factory, a
place where hundreds of small neighborhood cleaners sent their
clothes to be processed. Like Bonnie Smith-Yackel's mother in
the essay "My Mother Never Worked," my parents constantly

*Quotation from
essay
in textbook*

"struggled to regain some competence and dignity and order" in
their lives (123).

*Series of brief
examples: physical
demands*

At work, my parents had to meet certain quotas. Each day   3
they had to clean and press several hundred garments — shirts,
pants, and other clothing. By themselves, every day, they did the
work of four laborers. The muscles of my mother's shoulders and
arms grew hard as iron from working with the press, a difficult
job even for a man. In addition to pressing, my father serviced
the washing machines. As a result, his work clothes always
smelled of oil.

*Example: long
hours*

Not only were my parents' jobs physically demanding, but   4
they also required long hours. My parents went to work at five
o'clock in the morning and came home between nine o'clock at
night and midnight. Each day they worked over twelve hours
at the dry-cleaning plant, where eight-hour workdays and labor
unions did not exist. They were allowed to take only two ten- to
twenty-minute breaks — one for lunch and one for dinner. They

*Example:
frequent burns*

did not stop even when they were burned by a hot iron or by
steam from a press. The scars on their arms made it obvious
that they worked at a dry-cleaning plant. My parents' burned
skin would blister and later peel off, exposing raw flesh. In
time, these injuries would heal, but other burns would soon
follow.

Example: low pay

In addition to having to work long hours and suffering   5
painful injuries, my parents were paid below minimum wage.
Together their paychecks were equal to that of a single unionized
worker (even though they did the work of four). They used this
money to feed and care for a household of five people.

Conclusion

As my parents silently entered our home around midnight,   6
they did not have to complain about their jobs. I could see their
anguish in their faces and their fatigue in the slow movements of

Restatement of thesis   their bodies. Even though they did not speak, their eyes said, "We hate our jobs, but we work so that our children will have better lives than we do."

Work Cited

Smith-Yackel, Bonnie. "My Mother Never Worked." *Patterns for College Writing*. 12th ed. Ed. Laurie G. Kirszner and Stephen R. Mandell. Boston: Bedford, 2012. 121–24. Print.

Points for Special Attention

Organization. Grace Ku begins her introduction by describing herself as an eleven-year-old sitting on the floor watching television. At first, her behavior seems typical of many American children, but two things suggest problems: first, she is eating her cold dinner out of a can, and, second, even though it is late in the evening, she is still waiting for her parents to return from work. This opening prepares readers for her thesis that her parents' jobs produce only grief and hardship.

In the body of her essay, Grace presents the examples that support her thesis statement. In paragraph 2, she sets the stage for the discussion to follow, explaining that her parents' working conditions were similar to those of nineteenth-century factory workers. In paragraph 3, she presents a series of examples that illustrate how physically demanding her parents' jobs were. In the remaining body paragraphs, she gives three other examples to show how unpleasant the jobs were — how long her parents worked, how often they were injured, and how little they were paid.

Grace concludes her essay by returning to the scene in her introduction, using a quotation that she wants to stay with her readers after they have finished the essay.

Working with Sources. Because her assignment asked students to include a quotation from an essay in their textbook, Grace looked for essays that had to do with work. After reading three of them, she decided that the sentiments expressed by Bonnie Smith-Yackel in "My Mother Never Worked" most closely mirrored her own. For this reason, at the end of paragraph 2, she included a quotation from Smith-Yackel's essay that helped her put her parents' struggles into perspective. Grace was careful to include quotation marks as well as MLA documentation. She also included bibliographic information for the essay in a works-cited section at the end of her essay. (See Chapter 18 for information on MLA documentation.)

Enough Examples. Certainly no single example, no matter how graphic, could adequately support the thesis of this essay. To establish the pain and difficulty of her parents' jobs, Grace uses several examples. Although additional examples would have added even more depth to the essay, the ones she uses are vivid and compelling enough to reinforce her thesis that her parents had to endure great hardship to make a living.

Range of Examples. Grace selects examples that illustrate the full range of her subject. She draws from her parents' daily experience and does not include atypical examples. She also includes enough detail so that her readers, who she assumes do not know much about working in a dry-cleaning plant, will understand her points. She does not, however, provide so much detail that her readers get bogged down and lose interest.

Effective Examples. All of Grace's examples support her thesis statement. While developing these examples, she never loses sight of her main idea; consequently, she does not get sidetracked in irrelevant discussions. She also avoids the temptation to preach to her readers about the injustice of her parents' situation. By allowing her examples to speak for themselves, Grace paints a powerful portrait of her parents and their hardships.

Focus on Revision

After reading this draft, a classmate thought Grace could go into more detail about her parents' situation and could explain her examples in more depth — perhaps writing about the quotas her parents had to meet or the other physical dangers of their jobs.

Grace herself thought she should expand the discussion in paragraph 5 about her parents' low wages, perhaps anticipating questions some of her readers might have about working conditions. For example, was it legal for her parents' employer to require them to work overtime without compensation or to pay them less than the minimum wage? If not, how was the employer able to get away with such practices?

Grace also thought she should move the information about her parents' work-related injuries from paragraph 4 to paragraph 3, where she discusses the physical demands of their jobs.

Finally, she decided to follow the advice of another student and include comments by her parents to make their experiences more immediate to readers.

PEER EDITING WORKSHEET: Exemplification

1. What strategy does the writer use in the essay's introduction? Would another strategy be more effective?
2. What is the essay's thesis? Does it make a point that the rest of the essay will support with examples?
3. What specific points do the body paragraphs make?
4. Does the writer use one example or several to illustrate each point? Should the writer use more examples? Fewer? Explain.
5. Does the writer use a sufficient range of examples? Are they explained in enough depth?

6. Do the examples add interest? How persuasive are they? List a few other examples that might be more persuasive.

7. What transitional words and phrases does the writer use to introduce examples? What other transitional words and phrases should be added? Where?

8. In what order are the examples presented? Would another order be more effective? Explain.

9. Has the writer used a series of three or more examples in a single sentence? If so, are these examples separated by commas?

10. What strategy does the writer use in the conclusion? What other strategy could be used?

The selections in this chapter all depend on exemplification to explain and clarify, to add interest, or to persuade. The first selection, a visual text, is followed by questions designed to illustrate how exemplification can operate in visual form.

ALEX WILLIAMS, JOEL GORDON, CHARLES GATEWOOD, AND BOB DAEMMRICH*

Four Tattoos (Photos)

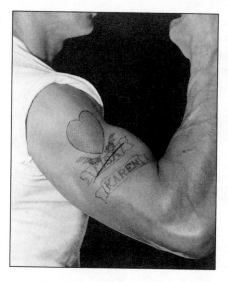

Alex Williams, "~~Lisa~~, Karen"

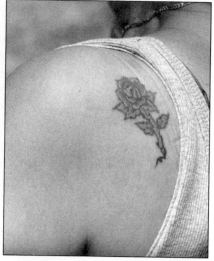

Joel Gordon, "Rose"

Bob Daemmrich, "Jiminy Cricket"

Charles Gatewood, "Body Art"

---

* Photos shown clockwise from top left.

Reading Images

1. How would you describe each of the four tattoos pictured on the previous page? List the prominent features of each, and then write two or three sentences that describe each of them.

2. After studying the four pictures (and reviewing your answer to question 1), write a one-sentence general statement that sums up your ideas about tattoos. For example, why do you think people get tattoos? Do you see them as a way for people to express themselves? As a way of demonstrating individuality? As a form of rebellion? As an impulsive act? As something else?

3. List several examples that support the general statement you made in question 2. What examples could you use to support this general statement?

Journal Entry

Would you ever get a tattoo? Write a paragraph answering this question. Use your answers to the questions above to support the main idea in your topic sentence. (If you have a tattoo, give several reasons why you decided to get it.)

Thematic Connections

- "Medium Ash Brown" (page 275)
- "My First Conk" (page 281)
- "The Wife-Beater" (page 516)
- "Inked Well" (page 685)

DAVID J. BIRNBAUM

The Catbird Seat

David J. Birnbaum was born in 1963 in Brooklyn, New York. Vice president of a real estate company, he also contributes essays to a number of publications. As he explains in the following essay, he lost the use of his legs in an auto accident and now uses a wheelchair to move about. The essay originally appeared in 1998 in the *New York Times Magazine*'s "Lives" column, where people from a variety of backgrounds write about their experiences.

Background on the 1990 Americans with Disabilities Act Approximately 19 percent of Americans, representing about 49 million people, have some form of disability, and almost half of these are considered severely disabled. An estimated 15 percent (about 38 million people) have disabilities that limit their physical activity.

The 1990 Americans with Disabilities Act, which Birnbaum refers to in paragraph 11, requires that reasonable accommodation be made in areas of educational opportunity, employment, government services, and access to businesses open to the general public, and it further prohibits discrimination against people with disabilities. Noncompliance with the act can result in fines, and perceived noncompliance has resulted in a number of lawsuits, which have raised questions about who can legitimately be considered disabled and what, in fact, constitutes "reasonable" accommodation. As Birnbaum suggests, due to various ambiguities in the wording of the act and to some of the loopholes contained in it, many establishments are still not in full compliance.

I wasn't in a hurry to get back to my hospital room, but I had a lot on 1 my mind. I was adjusting to my new fate, quadriplegia. Besides, I had been waiting at least three minutes for the elevator, which in teenage time is three years. When I heard the ding, I dashed into the car, unintentionally cutting off the handful of other riders.

"What's the big hurry?" a pregnant woman asked. An elderly Asian 2 man chimed in: "Leave the young man alone. He's in a wheelchair!"

That was the first time I felt my new place in society. A few months 3 later, my friend Roy and I were in the back of a ticketholders' line that was clogging 34th Street waiting to see *The Empire Strikes Back* at the Murray Hill cinema. Suddenly an usher appeared and asked us to follow him into the theater. Despite the drizzle, the other patrons didn't seem to mind that we were cutting ahead. I was the only one in line that had a chair to sit in. Yet I didn't have to wait. Thereafter, I began to cut ahead often. Cashing a check at Chase, I'd ignore the velvet ropes and go straight to a teller. Registering for classes at N.Y.U., I cut three lines in one day: department approval, course selection, and, finally, registrar payment. Older people who only a few months earlier would have ignored a teenager with long hair began acting very friendly. Senior citizens still smile at me seventeen years after I crashed my car in Park Slope, breaking my neck, just days before my eighteenth birthday. Are they trying to cheer me up? Maybe they just see me as nonthreatening. They're probably thinking, "This guy is less than half my age, but I can still beat him up."

Soon after leaving the hospital, I realized I could now break rules. I 4 would sneak cans of beer into concerts at Madison Square Garden. At the queue where teenagers are routinely patted down, the guards held up the process for me: "Please step back, we gotta wheelchair coming through!"

When I leave Staples, I tell the security guard that I need the plastic 5 shopping basket to carry my goods to my van. He nods his head trustingly, on the assumption that I'll unload and return it. I have five of these red baskets in my hallway closet. I don't know what I'm going to do with them. I just get a kick driving them home.

Before I left Jamaica last January, I hid a box of Cuban cigars in my 6 canvas case. As I passed through customs at Newark International Airport, a woman in a brown uniform looked at my two large bags suspiciously. Perusing the card I filled out on the plane, she asked, "Nothing to declare?"

"Nothing."   7

"What's the canvas bag for?"   8

"It's a portable handicap shower seat," I replied truthfully.   9

"Oh . . . I'm so sorry. Go ahead."   10

Cutting the lines at the Department of Motor Vehicles to renew my 11 driver's license, getting out of speeding tickets, and arriving late to work without a reprimand are my "even uppers" for my physical limitations and for the difficulties caused by establishments not complying with the Americans with Disabilities Act. I had to sit behind the last row in a theater, separated from my college friends, only once before I stopped being too proud to accept the senior citizens' discount offered by sympathetic employees. When the purser offered to bump me up into first class on that flight from Jamaica, I didn't say: "No, thank you. I've accepted my disability, I have a successful career and live independently. Please treat me like everyone else." I didn't care whether she was condescending, sympathizing, or patronizing. I was just glad to be in "2B" sipping Chardonnay while I eyed the coach passengers frantically seeking space for their carry-on luggage and duty-free rum.

After sneaking my cigars through customs, I headed upstairs to get a 12 taxi. Three carloads of tired travelers, dragging luggage with and without wheels, were waiting for a single elevator to arrive. I waited like an Olympic sprinter anticipating the starting gun. I began inching my wheelchair forward, but accidentally wheeled over some guy's foot.

"Oww!" he turned around, saw my wheelchair, and then followed ner- 13 vously with, "Oh, I'm ss . . . sss . . . sorry." He stepped to the side, leaving me perfectly positioned in front of the sliding aluminum doors. The "L" on the display lighted, the ding went off, the doors opened, and I swiftly pushed my chair forward into the car.

"What's wrong with you?" A well-tanned girl asked me angrily. I looked 14 her in the eye with cockiness, expecting my usual support from others. But it didn't come.

"Have some respect, for God's sake!" she continued, holding the door 15 open for a middle-aged man with dark glasses and a white cane.

There in the elevator, as everyone looked at me in disgust, I learned 16 the pecking order: blind trumps wheelchair; wheelchair trumps pregnant; pregnant trumps old; old trumps whatever is left.

· · ·

Comprehension

1. What "new place in society" does Birnbaum occupy after his accident (3)?
2. How does Birnbaum take advantage of his new status?
3. According to Birnbaum, how are cutting in line, avoiding speeding tickets, and getting to work late his "even uppers" (11)?
4. What incident causes Birnbaum to realize that the advantages he gets from his disability have limitations?

Purpose and Audience

1. What preconceptions about the disabled does Birnbaum assume his readers have? How can you tell?
2. Why does Birnbaum wait until paragraph 16 to state his thesis? Should he have stated it sooner? Explain.
3. Birnbaum is aiming his essay at a general audience. How would his essay be different if he were addressing health-care professionals? Other people with disabilities?
4. What is Birnbaum's purpose in writing this essay? For example, does he want to educate his readers? To persuade them? Or does he have some other purpose?

Style and Structure

1. Birnbaum begins his essay with an example. Is this an effective introductory strategy? Should he have used a more formal introduction?
2. All of Birnbaum's examples are drawn from his own experience. Does this reliance on personal experience make his essay more (or less) convincing? Explain.
3. How does Birnbaum arrange his examples? Is this arrangement effective? Explain.
4. How are the ideas in Birnbaum's first example (1–2) echoed in his conclusion?

Vocabulary Projects

1. Define each of the following words as it is used in this selection.

   quadriplegia (1)   patronizing (11)
   reprimand (11)   Chardonnay (11)
   purser (11)   trumps (16)
   condescending (11)

2. What terms does Birnbaum use to refer to his physical condition? What other terms could he have used? What different connotations do these terms have?

3. Someone in a positon of power or prominence is said to be "in the catbird seat." Why does Birnbaum use this expression as his title? Is he being serious or **ironic**?

Journal Entry

Do you think people with disabilities have advantages that others do not have? Do you think Birnbaum should have special privileges because of his disability?

Writing Workshop

1. Write an email to Birnbaum agreeing or disagreeing with his actions. Do you think he should reject the benefits conferred on him because he has a disability? Or do you think these benefits are justified given his physical limitations?

2. A **stereotype** is an oversimplified concept or image of a person or thing. Write an essay discussing three stereotypes of people with disabilities that many people share. How accurate are these stereotypes? What could (or should) be done to eliminate them?

3. Write an editorial for your school newspaper discussing how your school could do more to help students with physical disabilities. To support your thesis, include specific examples of changes that could be made. You might begin by visiting the Americans with Disabilities Web site at ada.gov.

Combining the Patterns

Identify four or five examples that Birnbaum uses in his essay. What other patterns of development does he use in presenting these examples? Does any single pattern predominate? If so, why?

Thematic Connections

- "The 'Black Table' Is Still There" (page 349)
- "On Dumpster Diving" (page 664)
- "The Shame Game" (page 680)

JUDITH ORTIZ COFER

The Myth of the Latin Woman: I Just Met a Girl Named Maria

Born in Puerto Rico in 1952, Judith Ortiz Cofer moved to New Jersey with her family when she was four. She is now Regents' and Franklin Professor of English and Creative Writing at the University of Georgia. Widely anthologized, Cofer has published three collections of poetry, including *A Love Story Beginning in Spanish* (2005); three essay collections, including *Silent Dancing* (1990) and *The Latin Deli* (1993); three novels, including the young adult novel *Call Me Maria* (2006); and the short-story collection *An Island Like You: Stories of the Barrio* (1995). In a recent interview, she commented on her early writing: "Poetry allowed me to become intimate with English. And it allowed me to master the one skill that I try to teach my students — and if that's the only thing I accomplish, I consider it a success — and that is succinctness: economy and concentration of language. Why use fifteen words when one clear, elegant sentence will do it?"

Background on images of Hispanic women in film During the era of silent film, Hispanic performers found a particular niche with the popularity of the stereotypical "Latin lover." Although Hispanic actors enjoyed success, just a handful of Hispanic actresses, such as Myrtle Gonzalez and Beatriz Michelena, played in leading roles that did not always cast them as Latina. For example, Mexican-born Dolores del Rio, the only Hispanic actress to achieve international stardom during the period, played characters named Evelyn Iffield and Jeanne Lamont as well as Carlotta de Silva and Carmelita de Granados. However, in the late 1920s, the advent of sound brought many fewer movie roles for Hispanic actresses. Some who found success during the thirties and forties conformed to broad stereotypes — for example, "Mexican Spitfire" Lupe Vélez, Carmen "the Lady in the Tutti-Frutti Hat" Miranda, and Maria Montez's hot-blooded seductresses. Others concealed their Hispanic identities on-screen (as was the case for Margarita Carmen Cansino, whose hair was dyed, eyebrows heavily plucked, and skin lightened to make her into the movie star Rita Hayworth). In the fifties and sixties, actresses such as Katy Jurado and Rita Moreno (who won a supporting actress Academy Award for her performance in *West Side Story*) rarely played leads. The sixties saw the stardom of Raquel Welch (born Jo Raquel Tejada), who, like Hayworth, played down her Hispanic roots; but it was not really until the nineties that young performers such as Jessica Alba, Jennifer Lopez, Penelope Cruz, and Salma Hayek came into their own, playing Latinas who are more than stereotypes or characters whose ethnicity is not important.

On a bus trip to London from Oxford University where I was earning 1 some graduate credits one summer, a young man, obviously fresh from a pub, spotted me and as if struck by inspiration went down on his knees in the aisle. With both hands over his heart he broke into an Irish tenor's rendition of "Maria" from *West Side Story*.* My politely amused fellow passengers gave his lovely voice the round of gentle applause it deserved. Though I was not quite as amused, I managed my version of an English smile: no show of teeth, no extreme contortions of the facial muscles — I was at this time of my life practicing reserve and cool. Oh, that British control, how I coveted it. But "Maria" had followed me to London, reminding me of a prime fact of my life: you can leave the island, master the English language, and travel as far as you can, but if you are a Latina, especially one like me who so obviously belongs to Rita Moreno's** gene pool, the island travels with you.

This is sometimes a very good thing — it may win you that extra minute of someone's attention. But with some people, the same things can make *you* an island — not a tropical paradise but an Alcatraz, a place nobody wants to visit. As a Puerto Rican girl living in the United States[†] and wanting like most children to "belong," I resented the stereotype that my Hispanic appearance called forth from many people I met.

Growing up in a large urban center in New Jersey during the 1960s, I suffered from what I think of as "cultural schizophrenia." Our life was designed by my parents as a microcosm of their *casas*[‡] on the island. We spoke in Spanish, ate Puerto Rican food bought at the *bodega*,[§] and practiced strict Catholicism at a church that allotted us a one-hour slot each week for mass, performed in Spanish by a Chinese priest trained as a missionary for Latin America.

As a girl I was kept under strict surveillance by my parents, since my virtue and modesty were, by their cultural equation, the same as their honor. As a teenager I was lectured constantly on how to behave as a proper *señorita*. But it was a conflicting message I received, since the Puerto Rican mothers also encouraged their daughters to look and act like women and to dress in clothes our Anglo friends and their mothers found too "mature" and flashy. The difference was, and is, cultural; yet I often felt humiliated when I appeared at an American friend's party wearing a dress more suitable to a semi-formal than to a playroom birthday celebration. At Puerto Rican festivities, neither the music nor the colors we wore could be too loud.

I remember Career Day in our high school, when teachers told us to come dressed as if for a job interview. It quickly became obvious that to the Puerto Rican girls "dressing up" meant wearing their mother's ornate

2

3

4

5

---

* Eds. note — A Broadway musical, based on *Romeo and Juliet*, about two rival New York street gangs, one Anglo and one Puerto Rican.
** Eds. note — Puerto Rico–born actress who won an Oscar for her role in the 1960 movie version of *West Side Story*.
[†] Eds. note — Although it is an island, Puerto Rico is part of the United States.
[‡] Eds. note — Homes.
[§] Eds. note — Small grocery store.

jewelry and clothing, more appropriate (by mainstream standards) for the company Christmas party than as daily office attire. That morning I had agonized in front of my closet, trying to figure out what a "career girl" would wear. I knew how to dress for school (at the Catholic school I attended, we all wore uniforms), I knew how to dress for Sunday mass, and I knew what dresses to wear for parties at my relatives' homes. Though I do not recall the precise details of my Career Day outfit, it must have been a composite of these choices. But I remember a comment my friend (an Italian American) made in later years that coalesced my impressions of that day. She said that at the business school she was attending, the Puerto Rican girls always stood out for wearing "everything at once." She meant, of course, too much jewelry, too many accessories. On that day at school we were simply made the negative models by the nuns, who were themselves not credible fashion experts to any of us. But it was painfully obvious to me that to the others, in their tailored skirts and silk blouses, we must have seemed "hopeless" and "vulgar." Though I now know that most adolescents feel out of step much of the time, I also know that for the Puerto Rican girls of my generation that sense was intensified. The way our teachers and classmates looked at us that day in school was just a taste of the cultural clash that awaited us in the real world, where prospective employers and men on the street would often misinterpret our tight skirts and jingling bracelets as a "come-on."

Mixed cultural signals have perpetuated certain stereotypes — for example, that of the Hispanic woman as the "hot tamale" or sexual firebrand. It is a one-dimensional view that the media have found easy to promote. In their special vocabulary, advertisers have designated "sizzling" and "smoldering" as the adjectives of choice for describing not only the foods but also the women of Latin America. From conversations in my house I recall hearing about the harassment that Puerto Rican women endured in factories where the "boss-men" talked to them as if sexual innuendo was all they understood, and worse, often gave them the choice of submitting to their advances or being fired.

It is custom, however, not chromosomes, that leads us to choose scarlet over pale pink. As young girls, it was our mothers who influenced our decisions about clothes and colors — mothers who had grown up on a tropical island where the natural environment was a riot of primary colors, where showing your skin was one way to keep cool as well as to look sexy. Most important of all, on the island, women perhaps felt freer to dress and move more provocatively since, in most cases, they were protected by the traditions, mores, and laws of a Spanish/Catholic system of morality and machismo whose main rule was: *You may look at my sister, but if you touch her I will kill you.* The extended family and church structure could provide a young woman with a circle of safety in her small pueblo on the island; if a man "wronged" a girl, everyone would close in to save her family honor.

My mother has told me about dressing in her best party clothes on Saturday nights and going to the town's plaza to promenade with her girl-

friends in front of the boys they liked. The males were thus given an opportunity to admire the women and to express their admiration in the form
of *piropos*: erotically charged street poems they composed on the spot. (I
have myself been subjected to a few *piropos* while visiting the island, and
they can be outrageous, although custom dictates that they must never
cross into obscenity.) This ritual, as I understand it, also entails a show
of studied indifference on the woman's part; if she is "decent," she must
not acknowledge the man's impassioned words. So I do understand how
things can be lost in translation. When a Puerto Rican girl dressed in her
idea of what is attractive meets a man from the mainstream culture who
has been trained to react to certain types of clothing as a sexual signal, a
clash is likely to take place. I remember the boy who took me to my first
formal dance leaning over to plant a sloppy, over-eager kiss painfully on my
mouth; when I didn't respond with sufficient passion, he remarked resent-
fully: "I thought you Latin girls were supposed to mature early," as if I were
expected to *ripen* like a fruit or vegetable, not just grow into womanhood
like other girls.

It is surprising to my professional friends that even today some people,
including those who should know better, still put others "in their place."
It happened to me most recently during a stay at a classy metropolitan hotel favored by young professional couples for weddings. Late one evening
after the theater, as I walked toward my room with a colleague (a woman
with whom I was coordinating an arts program), a middle-aged man in a
tuxedo, with a young girl in satin and lace on his arm, stepped directly into
our path. With his champagne glass extended toward me, he exclaimed
"Evita!"*

Our way blocked, my companion and I listened as the man half- 10
recited, half-bellowed "Don't Cry for Me, Argentina." When he finished,
the young girl said: "How about a round of applause for my daddy?" We
complied, hoping this would bring the silly spectacle to a close. I was becoming aware that our little group was attracting the attention of the other
guests. "Daddy" must have perceived this too, and he once more barred the
way as we tried to walk past him. He began to shout-sing a ditty to the tune
of "La Bamba" — except the lyrics were about a girl named Maria whose
exploits rhymed with her name and gonorrhea. The girl kept saying "Oh,
Daddy" and looking at me with pleading eyes. She wanted me to laugh
along with the others. My companion and I stood silently waiting for the
man to end his offensive song. When he finished, I looked not at him but at
his daughter. I advised her calmly never to ask her father what he had done
in the army. Then I walked between them and to my room. My friend com-
plimented me on my cool handling of the situation, but I confessed that
I had really wanted to push the jerk into the swimming pool. This same
man — probably a corporate executive, well-educated, even worldly by most

---

* Eds. note — A Broadway musical about Eva Duarte de Perón, the former first lady
of Argentina.

standards — would not have been likely to regale an Anglo woman with a dirty song in public. He might have checked his impulse by assuming that she could be somebody's wife or mother, or at least *somebody* who might take offense. But, to him, I was just an Evita or a Maria: merely a character in his cartoon-populated universe. ?

Another facet of the myth of the Latin woman in the United States is 11 the menial, the domestic — Maria the housemaid or countergirl. It's true that work as domestics, as waitresses, and in factories is all that's available to women with little English and few skills. But the myth of the Hispanic menial — the funny maid, mispronouncing words and cooking up a spicy storm in a shiny California kitchen — has been perpetuated by the media in the same way that "Mammy" from *Gone with the Wind* became America's idea of the black woman for generations. Since I do not wear my diplomas around my neck for all to see, I have on occasion been sent to that "kitchen" where some think I obviously belong.

One incident has stayed with me, though I recognize it as a minor of- 12 fense. My first public poetry reading took place in Miami, at a restaurant where a luncheon was being held before the event. I was nervous and excited as I walked in with notebook in hand. An older woman motioned me to her table, and thinking (foolish me) that she wanted me to autograph a copy of my newly published slender volume of verse, I went over. She ordered a cup of coffee from me, assuming that I was the waitress. (Easy enough to mistake my poems for menus, I suppose.) I know it wasn't an intentional act of cruelty. Yet of all the good things that happened later, I remember that scene most clearly, because it reminded me of what I had to overcome before anyone would take me seriously. In retrospect I understand that my anger gave my reading fire. In fact, I have almost always taken any doubt in my abilities as a challenge, the result most often being the satisfaction of winning a convert, of seeing the cold, appraising eyes warm to my words, the body language change, the smile that indicates I have opened some avenue for communication. So that day as I read, I looked directly at that woman. Her lowered eyes told me she was embarrassed at her faux pas, and when I willed her to look up at me, she graciously allowed me to punish her with my full attention. We shook hands at the end of the reading and I never saw her again. She has probably forgotten the entire incident, but maybe not.

Yet I am one of the lucky ones. There are thousands of Latinas without 13 the privilege of an education or the entrees into society that I have. For them life is a constant struggle against the misconceptions perpetuated by the myth of the Latina. My goal is to try to replace the old stereotypes with a much more interesting set of realities. Every time I give a reading, I hope the stories I tell, the dreams and fears I examine in my work, can achieve some universal truth that will get my audience past the particulars of my skin color, my accent, or my clothes.

I once wrote a poem in which I called all Latinas "God's brown daugh- 14 ters." This poem is really a prayer of sorts, offered upward, but also, through the human-to-human channel of art, outward. It is a prayer for communication and for respect. In it, Latin women pray "in Spanish to an Anglo God/with a Jewish heritage," and they are "fervently hoping/that if not omnipotent,/at least He be bilingual."

. . .

Comprehension

1. What does Cofer mean by "cultural schizophrenia" (3)?
2. What "conflicting message" (4) did Cofer receive from her family?
3. What points does Cofer make by including each of the following in her essay?
   - The story about the young man in Oxford (1)
   - The story about Career Day (5)
   - The story about the poetry reading (12)
4. According to Cofer, what stereotypes are commonly applied to Latinas?
5. How does Cofer explain why she and other Puerto Rican women like to dress as they do? Why do outsiders think they dress this way?
6. What exactly is "the myth of the Latin woman" (11)?
7. How does Cofer hope to help people see beyond the stereotypes she describes? Is she successful?

Purpose and Audience

1. Which of the following do you think is Cofer's thesis? Why?
   - "[I]f you are a Latina, especially one like me who so obviously belongs to Rita Moreno's gene pool, the island travels with you" (1).
   - "As a Puerto Rican girl living in the United States . . . I resented the stereotype that my Hispanic appearance called forth from many people I met" (2).
   - "My goal is to try to replace the old stereotypes with a much more interesting set of realities" (13).
2. Why does Cofer begin paragraph 13 with "Yet I am one of the lucky ones"? How do you think she expects her audience to react to this statement?
3. Despite its use of Spanish words, this essay is directed at an Anglo audience. How can you tell?

Style and Structure

1. Cofer opens her essay with a story about an incident in her life. Considering her subject matter and her audience, is this an effective opening strategy? Why or why not?

2. In paragraphs 1–2, Cofer uses the word *island* to suggest several different things. What positive connotations — and what negative ones — does this word have for her?

3. What do you think Cofer means to suggest with these expressions in paragraph 8?
   - "erotically charged"
   - "studied indifference"
   - "lost in translation"
   - "mainstream culture"

4. Cofer does not introduce the stereotype of the Latina as "the menial, the domestic" until paragraph 11, when she devotes two paragraphs to this part of the stereotype. Why does she wait so long? Should this discussion have appeared earlier? Should it have been deleted altogether? Explain your reasoning.

5. Cofer uses exemplification to support her thesis. Does she provide enough examples? Are they the right kinds of examples?

6. How do you interpret the lines of poetry that Cofer quotes in her conclusion? Is this an effective concluding strategy? Why or why not?

Vocabulary Projects

1. Define each of the following words as it is used in this selection.

coveted (1)	innuendo (6)	complied (10)
microcosm (3)	machismo (7)	regale (10)
coalesced (5)	pueblo (7)	faux pas (12)
firebrand (6)	promenade (8)	

2. Cofer uses Spanish words throughout this essay, and she does not define them. Find definitions of these words in a Spanish/English dictionary, such as SpanishDict.com, or at Google Language Tools. Would the English equivalents be just as effective as — or even more effective than — the Spanish words?

Journal Entry

On the basis of what she writes here, it seems as if Cofer does not confront the people who stereotype her and does not show anger, even in the incident described in paragraphs 9–10. Do you think she should have acted differently, or do you admire her restraint?

Writing Workshop

1. What stereotypes are applied by outsiders to your racial or ethnic group (or to people of your gender, intended profession, or geographic region)? Write an exemplification essay in which you argue that these stereotypes

are untrue and potentially harmful. Support your thesis with passages of narration, comparison and contrast, and cause and effect.

2. Think of some books, films, advertisements, or TV shows that feature characters of your own racial or ethnic group. Write a classification essay in which you discuss the different ways in which these characters are portrayed. Use exemplification and description to explain your categories. In your thesis, evaluate the accuracy of these characterizations.

3. **Working with Sources.** In paragraph 1 of her essay, Cofer says that "you can leave the island, master the English language, and travel as far as you can, but if you are a Latina, especially one like me who so obviously belongs to Rita Moreno's gene pool, the island travels with you." Editing this statement to suit your own "gene pool," use it as the thesis of an essay about the problems you have fitting in to some larger segment of society. Be sure to acknowledge Cofer as your source and to document your version of her statement as well as any words you quote. (See Chapter 18 for information on MLA documentation.)

Combining the Patterns

The examples Cofer uses are personal narratives — stories of her own experience. What are the advantages and disadvantages of using **narration** here? Would other kinds of examples be more effective? Explain.

Thematic Connections

- "Only Daughter" (page 111)
- "Just Walk On By: A Black Man Ponders His Power to Alter Public Space" (page 240)
- "Two Ways to Belong in America" (page 404)
- "The Case for Birthright Citizenship" (page 595)

BRENT STAPLES

Just Walk On By: A Black Man Ponders His Power to Alter Public Space

Born in Chester, Pennsylvania, in 1951, Brent Staples joined the staff of the *New York Times* in 1985, writing on culture and politics, and he became a member of its editorial board in 1990. His columns appear regularly on the paper's op-ed pages. Staples has also written a memoir, *Parallel Time: Growing Up in Black and White* (1994), about his escape from the poverty and violence of his childhood.

Background on racial profiling "Just Walk On By" can be read in the light of current controversies surrounding racial profiling of criminal suspects, which occurs, according to the American Civil Liberties Union, "when the police target someone for investigation on the basis of that person's race, national origin, or ethnicity. Examples of profiling are the use of race to determine which drivers to stop for minor traffic violations ('driving while black') and the use of race to determine which motorists or pedestrians to search for contraband." Although law enforcement officials have often denied that they profile criminals solely on the basis of race, studies have shown a high prevalence of police profiling directed primarily at African and Hispanic Americans. A number of states have enacted laws barring racial profiling, and some people have won court settlements when they objected to being interrogated by police solely because of their race. Since the terrorist attacks of September 11, 2001, however, people of Arab descent have been targets of heightened interest at airports and elsewhere. In addition, the passage of a strict anti-illegal immigration law in Arizona in 2010 caused many Hispanics to fear that they would be singled out for scrutiny solely on the basis of race. (Just before the bill was scheduled to take effect, a federal judge blocked sections that required police to check immigration status during traffic violations, detentions, and arrests. Currently, the ruling is under appeal and will most likely be settled by the United States Supreme Court.) Clearly, these events have added to the continuing controversy surrounding the association of criminal behavior with particular ethnic groups.

My first victim was a woman — white, well dressed, probably in her early 1 twenties. I came upon her late one evening on a deserted street in Hyde Park, a relatively affluent neighborhood in an otherwise mean, impoverished section of Chicago. As I swung onto the avenue behind her, there seemed to be a discreet, uninflammatory distance between us. Not so. She cast back a worried glance. To her, the youngish black man — a broad six feet two inches with a beard and billowing hair, both hands shoved into the pockets of a bulky military jacket — seemed menacingly close. After a few more quick glimpses, she picked up her pace and was soon running in earnest. Within seconds she disappeared into a cross street.

That was more than a decade ago. I was twenty-two years old, a graduate student newly arrived at the University of Chicago. It was in the echo of that terrified woman's footfalls that I first began to know the unwieldy inheritance I'd come into — the ability to alter public space in ugly ways. It was clear that she thought herself the quarry of a mugger, rapist, or worse. Suffering a bout of insomnia, however, I was stalking sleep, not defenseless wayfarers. As a softy who is scarcely able to take a knife to a raw chicken — let alone hold it to a person's throat — I was surprised, embarrassed, and dismayed all at once. Her flight made me feel like an accomplice in tyranny. It also made it clear that I was indistinguishable from the muggers who occasionally seeped into the area from the surrounding ghetto. That first encounter, and those that followed, signified that a vast, unnerving gulf lay between nighttime pedestrians — particularly women — and me. And I soon gathered that being perceived as dangerous is a hazard in itself. I only needed to turn a corner into a dicey situation, or crowd some frightened, armed person in a foyer somewhere, or make an errant move after being pulled over by a policeman. Where fear and weapons meet — and they often do in urban America — there is always the possibility of death.

> **"It was in the echo of that terrified woman's footfalls that I first began to know the unwieldy inheritance I'd come into — the ability to alter public space in ugly ways."**

In that first year, my first away from my hometown, I was to become thoroughly familiar with the language of fear. At dark, shadowy intersections in Chicago, I could cross in front of a car stopped at a traffic light and elicit the *thunk, thunk, thunk, thunk* of the driver — black, white, male, or female — hammering down the door locks. On less traveled streets after dark, I grew accustomed to but never comfortable with people who crossed to the other side of the street rather than pass me. Then there were the standard unpleasantries with police, doormen, bouncers, cab drivers, and others whose business it is to screen out troublesome individuals *before* there is any nastiness.

I moved to New York nearly two years ago and I have remained an avid night walker. In central Manhattan, the near-constant crowd cover minimizes tense one-on-one street encounters. Elsewhere — visiting friends in SoHo, where sidewalks are narrow and tightly spaced buildings shut out the sky — things can get very taut indeed.

Black men have a firm place in New York mugging literature. Norman Podhoretz in his famed (or infamous) 1963 essay, "My Negro Problem — and Ours," recalls growing up in terror of black males; they "were tougher than we were, more ruthless," he writes — and as an adult on the Upper West Side of Manhattan, he continues, he cannot constrain his nervousness when he meets black men on certain streets. Similarly, a decade later, the essayist and novelist Edward Hoagland extols a New York where once "Negro bitterness bore down mainly on other Negroes." Where some see mere panhandlers, Hoagland sees "a mugger who is clearly screwing up his nerve to do more than just *ask* for money." But Hoagland has "the New Yorker's quick-hunch posture for broken-field maneuvering," and the bad guy swerves away.

I often witness that "hunch posture," from women after dark on the 6 warrenlike streets of Brooklyn where I live. They seem to set their faces on neutral and, with their purse straps strung across their chests bandolier style, they forge ahead as though bracing themselves against being tackled. I understand, of course, that the danger they perceive is not a hallucination. Women are particularly vulnerable to street violence, and young black males are drastically overrepresented among the perpetrators of that violence. Yet these truths are no solace against the kind of alienation that comes of being ever the suspect, against being set apart, a fearsome entity with whom pedestrians avoid making eye contact.

It is not altogether clear to me how I reached the ripe old age of twenty- 7 two without being conscious of the lethality nighttime pedestrians attributed to me. Perhaps it was because in Chester, Pennsylvania, the small, angry industrial town where I came of age in the 1960s, I was scarcely noticeable against a backdrop of gang warfare, street knifings, and murders. I grew up one of the good boys, had perhaps a half-dozen fist fights. In retrospect, my shyness of combat has clear sources.

Many things go into the making of a young thug. One of those things 8 is the consummation of the male romance with the power to intimidate. An infant discovers that random flailings send the baby bottle flying out of the crib and crashing to the floor. Delighted, the joyful babe repeats those motions again and again, seeking to duplicate the feat. Just so, I recall the points at which some of my boyhood friends were finally seduced by the perception of themselves as tough guys. When a mark cowered and surrendered his money without resistance, myth and reality merged — and paid off. It is, after all, only manly to embrace the power to frighten and intimidate. We, as men, are not supposed to give an inch of our lane on the highway; we are to seize the fighter's edge in work and in play and even in love; we are to be valiant in the face of hostile forces.

Unfortunately, poor and powerless young men seem to take all this 9 nonsense literally. As a boy, I saw countless tough guys locked away; I have since buried several, too. They were babies, really — a teenage cousin, a brother of twenty-two, a childhood friend in his mid-twenties — all gone down in episodes of bravado played out in the streets. I came to doubt the virtues of intimidation early on. I chose, perhaps even unconsciously, to remain a shadow — timid, but a survivor.

The fearsomeness mistakenly attributed to me in public places often 10 has a perilous flavor. The most frightening of these confusions occurred in the late 1970s and early 1980s when I worked as a journalist in Chicago. One day, rushing into the office of a magazine I was writing for with a deadline story in hand, I was mistaken for a burglar. The office manager called security and, with an ad hoc posse, pursued me through the labyrinthine halls, nearly to my editor's door. I had no way of proving who I was. I could only move briskly toward the company of someone who knew me.

Another time I was on assignment for a local paper and killing 11
time before an interview. I entered a jewelry store on the city's affluent
Near North Side. The proprietor excused herself and returned with an
enormous red Doberman pinscher straining at the end of a leash. She
stood, the dog extended toward me, silent to my questions, her eyes
bulging nearly out of her head. I took a cursory look around, nodded, and
bade her good night. Relatively speaking, however, I never fared as badly
as another black male journalist. He went to nearby Waukegan, Illinois, a
couple of summers ago to work on a story about a murderer who was born
there. Mistaking the reporter for the killer, police hauled him from his car
at gunpoint and but for his press credentials would probably have tried to
book him. Such episodes are not uncommon. Black men trade tales like
this all the time.

In "My Negro Problem — and Ours," Podhoretz writes that the ha- 12
tred he feels for blacks makes itself known to him through a variety of
avenues — one being his discomfort with that "special brand of paranoid
touchiness" to which he says blacks are prone. No doubt he is speaking
here of black men. In time, I learned to smother the rage I felt at so often
being taken for a criminal. Not to do so would surely have led to madness — via that special "paranoid touchiness" that so annoyed Podhoretz
at the time he wrote the essay.

I began to take precautions to make myself less threatening. I move 13
about with care, particularly late in the evening. I give a wide berth to nervous people on subway platforms during the wee hours, particularly when
I have exchanged business clothes for jeans. If I happen to be entering a
building behind some people who appear skittish, I may walk by, letting
them clear the lobby before I return, so as not to seem to be following them.
I have been calm and extremely congenial on those rare occasions when I've
been pulled over by the police.

And on late-evening constitutionals along streets less traveled by, I 14
employ what has proved to be an excellent tension-reducing measure: I
whistle melodies from Beethoven and Vivaldi and the more popular classical composers. Even steely New Yorkers hunching toward nighttime desti-
nations seem to relax, and occasionally they even join in the tune. Virtually
everybody seems to sense that a mugger wouldn't be warbling bright, sunny
selections from Vivaldi's *Four Seasons*. It is my equivalent of the cowbell that
hikers wear when they know they are in bear country.

· · ·

Comprehension

1. Why does Staples characterize the woman he encounters in paragraph 1
   as a "victim"?

2. What does Staples mean when he says he has the power to "alter public
   space" (2)?

3. Why does Staples walk the streets at night?

4. What things, in Staples's opinion, contribute to "the making of a young thug" (8)? According to Staples, why are young, poor, and powerless men especially likely to become thugs?

5. How does Staples attempt to make himself less threatening?

Purpose and Audience

1. What is Staples's thesis? Does he state it or imply it?

2. Does Staples use logic, emotion, or a combination of the two to appeal to his readers? How appropriate is his strategy?

3. What preconceptions does Staples assume his audience has? How does he challenge these preconceptions?

4. What is Staples trying to accomplish with his first sentence? Do you think he succeeds? Why or why not?

Style and Structure

1. Why does Staples mention Norman Podhoretz? Could he make the same points without referring to Podhoretz's essay?

2. Staples begins his essay with an anecdote. How effective is this strategy? Do you think another opening strategy would be more effective? Explain.

3. Does Staples present enough examples to support his thesis? Are they representative? Would other types of examples be more convincing? Explain.

4. In what order does Staples present his examples? Would another order be more effective? Explain.

Vocabulary Projects

1. Define each of the following words as it is used in this selection.

discreet (1)	quarry (2)	constrain (5)
uninflammatory (1)	insomnia (2)	bravado (9)
billowing (1)	wayfarers (2)	constitutionals (14)

2. In his essay, Staples uses the word *thug*. List as many synonyms as you can for this word. Do all these words convey the same idea, or do they differ in their connotations? Explain. (If you like, consult an online thesaurus at thesaurus.com.)

Journal Entry

Have you ever been in a situation such as the ones Staples describes, where you perceived someone (or someone perceived you) as threatening? How did you react? After reading Staples's essay, do you think you would react the same way now?

Writing Workshop

1. Use your journal entry to help you write an essay using a single long example to support this statement: "When walking alone at night, you can (or cannot) be too careful."

2. **Working with Sources.** Relying on examples from your own experience and from Staples's essay, write an essay discussing what part you think race plays in people's reactions to Staples. Do you think his perceptions are accurate? Make sure that you document Staples's words and ideas and that you include a works-cited page. (See Chapter 18 for information on MLA documentation.)

3. How accurate is Staples's observation concerning the "male romance with the power to intimidate" (8)? What does he mean by this statement? What examples from your own experience support (or do not support) the idea that this "romance" is an element of male upbringing in our society?

Combining the Patterns

In paragraph 8, Staples uses **cause and effect** to demonstrate what goes "into the making of a young thug." Would several **examples** have better explained how a youth becomes a thug?

Thematic Connections

- "The 'Black Table' Is Still There" (page 349)
- "A Peaceful Woman Explains Why She Carries a Gun" (page 354)
- "The Ways We Lie" (page 474)
- "The Wife-Beater" (page 516)

DEBORAH L. RHODE

Why Looks Are the Last Bastion of Discrimination

Deborah L. Rhode (b. 1952) is the Ernest McFarland Professor of Law and the Director of the Center on the Legal Profession at Stanford University. She earned her undergraduate and law degrees at Yale University; she also served as a law clerk for former Supreme Court Justice Thurgood Marshall. She has published many books on gender, legal ethics, and professional responsibility, including *The Difference "Difference" Makes: Women and Leadership* (2002) and *The Beauty Bias: The Injustice of Appearance in Life and Law* (2010). A columnist for the *National Law Journal,* Rhode has also written for the *New York Times, Slate,* the *Boston Globe,* and other publications. The following essay originally appeared in the *Washington Post.*

Background on appearance-based discrimination The Constitution bars discrimination on the basis of race, sex, religion, national origin, and ethnicity. Although some see "lookism" as a civil rights issue similar to racism and sexism, others worry that addressing the issue with legislation encroaches on individual freedom and unnecessarily creates another legally protected group. As Rhode notes, however, the state of Michigan and six local jurisdictions throughout the United States have already enacted legal prohibitions on appearance discrimination. In Michigan, for example, a Hooters waitress sued the chain after she was told to lose weight and improve her looks. Lawyers for Hooters argued that employees at the restaurant — who wear tank tops and tight shorts — are entertainers as much as servers, but a circuit court judge has allowed the case to proceed, placing the eventual decision in the hands of a jury.

In the nineteenth century, many American cities banned public appearances by "unsightly" individuals. A Chicago ordinance was typical: "Any person who is diseased, maimed, mutilated, or in any way deformed, so as to be an unsightly or disgusting subject . . . shall not . . . expose himself to public view, under the penalty of a fine of $1 for each offense." 1

Although the government is no longer in the business of enforcing such discrimination, it still allows businesses, schools and other organizations to indulge their own prejudices. Over the past half-century, the United States has expanded protections against discrimination to include race, religion, sex, age, disability and, in a growing number of jurisdictions, sexual orientation. Yet bias based on appearance remains perfectly permissible in all but one state and six cities and counties. Across the rest of the country, looks are the last bastion of acceptable bigotry. 2

We all know that appearance matters, but the price of prejudice can be steeper than we often assume. In Texas in 1994, an obese woman was 3 rejected for a job as a bus driver when a company doctor assumed she was not up to the task after watching her, in his words, "waddling down the hall." He did not perform any agility tests to determine whether she was, as the company would later claim, unfit to evacuate the bus in the event of an accident.

In New Jersey in 2005, one of the Borgata Hotel Casino's "Borgata 4 babe" cocktail waitresses went from a Size 4 to a Size 6 because of a thyroid condition. When the waitress, whose contract required her to keep "an hourglass figure" that was "height and weight appropriate," requested a larger uniform, she was turned down. "Borgata babes don't go up in size," she was told. (Unless, the waitress noted, they have breast implants, which the casino happily accommodated with paid medical leave and a bigger bustier.)

And in California in 2001, Jennifer Portnick, a 240-pound aerobics 5 instructor, was denied a franchise by Jazzercise, a national fitness chain. Jazzercise explained that its image demanded instructors who are "fit" and "toned." But Portnick was both: She worked out six days a week, taught back-to-back classes, and had no shortage of willing students.

Such cases are common. In a survey by the National Association to 6 Advance Fat Acceptance, 62 percent of its overweight female members and 42 percent of its overweight male members said they had been turned down for a job because of their weight.

And it isn't just weight that's at issue; it's appearance overall. Accord- 7 ing to a national poll by the Employment Law Alliance in 2005, 16 percent of workers reported being victims of appearance discrimination more generally — a figure comparable to the percentage who in other surveys say they have experienced sex or race discrimination.

Conventional wisdom holds that beauty is in the eye of the beholder, 8 but most beholders tend to agree on what is beautiful. A number of researchers have independently found that, when people are asked to rate an individual's attractiveness, their responses are quite consistent, even across race, sex, age, class, and cultural background. Facial symmetry and unblemished skin are universally admired. Men get a bump for height, women are favored if they have hourglass figures, and racial minorities get points for light skin color, European facial characteristics, and conventionally "white" hairstyles.

Yale's Kelly Brownell and Rebecca Puhl and Harvard's Nancy Etcoff 9 have each reviewed hundreds of studies on the impact of appearance. Etcoff finds that unattractive people are less likely than their attractive peers to be viewed as intelligent, likable, and good. Brownell and Puhl have documented that overweight individuals consistently suffer disadvantages at school, at work, and beyond.

Among the key findings of a quarter-century's worth of research: Un- 10 attractive people are less likely to be hired and promoted, and they earn lower salaries, even in fields in which looks have no obvious relationship to professional duties. (In one study, economists Jeff Biddle and Daniel Hamermesh estimated that for lawyers, such prejudice can translate to a pay cut of as much as 12 percent.) When researchers ask people to evaluate written essays, the same material receives lower ratings for ideas, style, and creativity when an accompanying photograph shows a less attractive author. Good-looking professors get better course evaluations from students; teachers in turn rate good-looking students as more intelligent.

Not even justice is blind. In studies that simulate legal proceedings, 11 unattractive plaintiffs receive lower damage awards. And in a study released this month, Stephen Ceci and Justin Gunnell, two researchers at Cornell University, gave students case studies involving real criminal defendants and asked them to come to a verdict and a punishment for each. The students gave unattractive defendants prison sentences that were, on average, 22 months longer than those they gave to attractive defendants.

Just like racial or gender discrimination, discrimination based on irrel- 12 evant physical characteristics reinforces invidious stereotypes and undermines equal-opportunity principles based on merit and performance. And when grooming choices come into play, such bias can also restrict personal freedom.

Consider Nikki Youngblood, a lesbian who in 2001 was denied a photo 13 in her Tampa high school yearbook because she would not pose in a scoop-necked dress. Youngblood was "not a rebellious kid," her lawyer explained. "She simply wanted to appear in her yearbook as herself, not as a fluffed-up stereotype of what school administrators thought she should look like." Furthermore, many grooming codes sexualize the workplace and jeopardize employees' health. The weight restrictions at the Borgata, for example, reportedly contributed to eating disorders among its waitresses.

Appearance-related bias also exacerbates disadvantages based on gen- 14 der, race, ethnicity, age, sexual orientation, and class. Prevailing beauty standards penalize people who lack the time and money to invest in their appearance. And weight discrimination, in particular, imposes special costs on people who live in communities with shortages of healthy food options and exercise facilities.

So why not simply ban discrimination based on appearance?   15

Employers often argue that attractiveness is job-related; their workers' 16 appearance, they say, can affect the company's image and its profitability. In this way, the Borgata blamed its weight limits on market demands. Customers, according to a spokesperson, like being served by an attractive waitress. The same assumption presumably motivated the L'Oreal executive who was sued for sex discrimination in 2003 after allegedly ordering a store manager to fire a salesperson who was not "hot" enough.

Such practices can violate the law if they disproportionately exclude 17 groups protected by civil rights statutes — hence the sex discrimination suit. Abercrombie & Fitch's notorious efforts to project what it called a "classic American" look led to a race discrimination settlement on behalf of minority job-seekers who said they were turned down for positions on the sales floor. But unless the victims of appearance bias belong to groups already protected by civil rights laws, they have no legal remedy.

As the history of civil rights legislation suggests, customer preferences 18 should not be a defense for prejudice. During the early civil rights era, employers in the South often argued that hiring African Americans would be financially ruinous; white customers, they said, would take their business elsewhere. In rejecting this logic, Congress and the courts recognized that customer preferences often reflect and reinforce precisely the attitudes that society is seeking to eliminate. Over the decades, we've seen that the most effective way of combating prejudice is to deprive people of the option to indulge it.

Similarly, during the 1960s and 1970s, major airlines argued that the 19 male business travelers who dominated their customer ranks preferred attractive female flight attendants. According to the airlines, that made sex a bona fide occupational qualification and exempted them from anti-discrimination requirements. But the courts reasoned that only if sexual allure were the "essence" of a job should employers be allowed to select workers on that basis. Since airplanes were not flying bordellos, it was time to start hiring men.

Opponents of a ban on appearance-based discrimination also warn 20 that it would trivialize other, more serious forms of bias. After all, if the goal is a level playing field, why draw the line at looks? "By the time you've finished preventing discrimination against the ugly, the short, the skinny, the bald, the knobbly-kneed, the flat-chested, and the stupid," Andrew Sullivan wrote in the London *Sunday Times* in 1999, "you're living in a totalitarian state." Yet intelligence and civility are generally related to job performance in a way that appearance isn't.

We also have enough experience with prohibitions on appearance 21 discrimination to challenge opponents' arguments. Already, one state (Michigan) and six local jurisdictions (the District of Columbia; Howard County, Md.; San Francisco; Santa Cruz, Calif.; Madison, Wis.; and Urbana, Ill.) have banned such discrimination. Some of these laws date back to the 1970s and 1980s, while some are more recent; some cover height and weight only, while others cover looks broadly; but all make exceptions for reasonable business needs.

Such bans have not produced a barrage of loony litigation or an ero- 22 sion of support for civil rights remedies generally. These cities and counties each receive between zero and nine complaints a year, while the entire state of Michigan totals about 30, with fewer than one a year ending up in court.

Although the laws are unevenly enforced, they have had a positive ef- 23 fect by publicizing and remedying the worst abuses. Because Portnick, the aerobics instructor turned away by Jazzercise, lived in San Francisco, she was able to bring a claim against the company. After a wave of sympathetic media coverage, Jazzercise changed its policy.

This is not to overstate the power of legal remedies. Given the stigma 24 attached to unattractiveness, few will want to claim that status in public litigation. And in the vast majority of cases, the cost of filing suit and the difficulty of proving discrimination are likely to be prohibitive. But stricter anti-discrimination laws could play a modest role in advancing healthier and more inclusive ideals of attractiveness. At the very least, such laws could reflect our principles of equal opportunity and raise our collective consciousness when we fall short.

• • •

Comprehension

1. Why, according to Rhode, are looks "the last bastion of acceptable bigotry" (2)?
2. Why does the government allow organizations to engage in appearance discrimination?
3. What forms of discrimination do unattractive people face?
4. Why do some people object to banning discrimination based on appearance? How does Rhode address these objections?
5. According to Rhode, how effective are laws that prohibit appearance discrimination? What positive effects might they have?

Purpose and Audience

1. Does Rhode assume that her readers are aware of the problem she discusses? How can you tell?
2. What preconceived attitudes about appearance does Rhode assume her readers have?
3. Where does Rhode state her thesis? Why does she state it where she does instead of earlier in her essay?
4. Is Rhode's purpose simply to inform her readers or to persuade them? Explain.

Style and Structure

1. The first half of Rhode's essay contains a series of short examples. What do these examples illustrate? Do you think she should have made her point with fewer examples developed in more depth?
2. Paragraph 15 is a **rhetorical question**. What is the purpose of this rhetorical question? How effective is it?
3. The second half of Rhode's essay addresses objections to laws banning appearance discrimination. How effectively does Rhode respond to these objections?
4. At several points in her essay, Rhode cites statistics. Is this kind of evidence convincing? Is it more convincing than additional examples would be?
5. What strategy does Rhode use in her conclusion? What other strategy could she have used?

Vocabulary Projects

1. Define each of the following words as it is used in this selection.

   maimed (1)   bona fide (19)
   jurisdictions (2)   trivialize (20)
   symmetry (8)   totalitarian (20)
   invidious (12)   stigma (24)

2. What words or phrases convey Rhode's feelings toward her subject? Do you think these emotional words and phrases undercut her essay in any way? What other language could she have used instead of these words and phrases?

Journal Entry

Do you believe, as Rhode does, that "stricter anti-discrimination laws could play a modest role in advancing healthier and more inclusive ideals of attractiveness" (24)?

Writing Workshop

1. Do you think Rhode overstates her case? Write an email to her in which you agree or disagree with her position. Make sure you address the specific points she makes in her essay.

2. Write an essay that shows how Rhode's ideas apply (or do not apply) to a school, a business, or an organization that you know well.

3. **Working with Sources.** According to an article on the HRM Guide Web site, unattractive people are not the only ones who face discrimination. "Regardless of who the real person may be," says the article, "stereotypes associated with piercings and tattoos can and do affect others. In general, individuals with tattoos and body piercings are often viewed as 'rougher' or 'less educated.'" Does your own experience support this observation? Go to the HRM Guide Web site hrmguide.com/diversity/appearance-at-work.htm, and read the information you find there. Then, write an essay in which you agree or disagree with the statement above. Be sure that your essay includes at least one reference to Rhode's essay. Document all material that you borrow from your sources, and include a works-cited page. (See Chapter 18 for information on MLA documentation.)

Combining the Patterns

In paragraphs 1 and 2, Rhode uses **comparison and contrast**. In these paragraphs, she compares nineteenth-century laws that penalized "'unsightly' individuals" to the actions of government today. How does this comparison help Rhode prepare her readers for her thesis?

Thematic Connections

- "Indian Education" (page 142)
- "Four Tattoos" (page 226)
- "The Myth of the Latin Woman: I Just Met a Girl Named Maria" (page 232)
- "My First Conk" (page 281)
- "The Shame Game" (page 680)
- "Inked Well" (page 685)

ZEV CHAFETS

Let Steroids into the Hall of Fame

A versatile journalist and novelist, American-Israeli writer Zev Chafets was born in Pontiac, Michigan, in 1947. After graduating from the University of Michigan, he moved to Israel, where he worked for the Government Press Office and founded the *Jerusalem Report* magazine. He has written for many publications, including the *New York Times Sunday Magazine* and the *Los Angeles Times*. Chafets writes regularly about sports, politics, and the Middle East; he has also written five works of fiction. His most recent books are *Cooperstown Confidential: Heroes, Rogues, and the Inside Story of the Baseball Hall of Fame* (2009) and *Rush Limbaugh: Army of One* (2010).

Background on steroids In 1991, then-Commissioner of Baseball Fay Vincent added steroids to the list of banned substances under Major League Baseball's drug policy — although the league instituted no testing program at the time. The 1990s and early 2000s witnessed an explosion of home-run hitting, highlighted in 1998 by the home-run race between Sammy Sosa and Mark McGwire, both of whom used steroids. In the years since, Major League Baseball has cracked down on steroid use under scrutiny and pressure from Congress. Steroids, which increase muscle mass and endurance, can have dangerous side effects, including depression, mood swings, liver damage, and cancer.

When the Baseball Hall of Fame commemorates its 70th anniversary 1 with an exhibition game in Cooperstown, N.Y., on Sunday, five of its members will play on the national field of dreams. At least two of them — Paul Molitor and Ferguson Jenkins — were busted in the 1980s for using cocaine. Molitor later said he was sure he wasn't the only player on the team using drugs.

Given what we now know about baseball's drug habit, the remark 2 sounds quaint. This week's report that Sammy Sosa tested positive for performance-enhancing drugs in 2003 is only the latest in a long string of revelations. Barry Bonds, Roger Clemens, Alex Rodriguez, Manny Ramirez, Mark McGwire — what great players haven't been linked to drug use?

Since the dawn of baseball, players have used whatever substances they 3 believed would help them perform better, heal faster, or relax during a long and stressful season. As far back as 1889, the pitcher Pud Galvin ingested monkey testosterone. During Prohibition, Grover Cleveland Alexander, also a pitcher, calmed his nerves with federally banned alcohol, and no less an expert than Bill Veeck, who owned several major-league teams, said that Alexander was a better pitcher drunk than sober.

In 1961, during his home run race with Roger Maris, Mickey Mantle 4 developed a sudden abscess that kept him on the bench. It came from an infected needle used by Max Jacobson, a quack who injected Mantle with a home-brew containing steroids and speed. In his autobiography, Hank Aaron admitted once taking an amphetamine tablet during a game. The Pirates' John Milner testified at a drug dealer's trial that his teammate, Willie Mays, kept "red juice," a liquid form of speed, in his locker. (Mays denied it.) After he retired, Sandy Koufax admitted that he was often "half high" on the mound from the drugs he took for his ailing left arm.

For decades, baseball beat writers — the Hall of Fame's designated elec- 5 toral college — shielded the players from scrutiny. When the Internet (and exposés by two former ballplayers, Jim Bouton and Jose Canseco) allowed fans to see what was really happening, the baseball writers were revealed as dupes or stooges. In a rage, they formed a posse to drive the drug users out of the game.

But today's superstars have lawyers and a union. They know how to use 6 the news media. And they have plenty of money. The only way to punish them is to deny them a place in Cooperstown. The punishment has already been visited on Mark McGwire, and many more are on deck.

This makes no sense. On any given day, the stands are packed with 7 youngsters on Adderall and Ritalin (stimulants used to treat attention deficit hyperactivity disorder) and college students who use Provigil (an anti-narcolepsy drug) as a study aid. The guy who sings the national anthem has probably taken a beta blocker to calm his stage fright. Like it or not, chemical enhancement is here to stay. And it is as much a part of the national game as $5.50 hot dogs, free agency, and Tommy John elbow surgery.

Purists say that steroids alter the game. But since the Hall opened its 8 doors, baseball has never stopped changing. Batters now wear body padding and helmets. The pitcher's mound has risen and fallen. Bats have more pop. Night games affect visibility. Players stay in shape in the off-season. Expansion has altered the game's geography. And its demography has changed beyond recognition. Babe Ruth never faced a black pitcher. As Chris Rock put it, Ruth's record consisted of "714 affirmative-action home runs." This doesn't diminish Ruth's accomplishment, but it puts it into context.

Statistics change, too. In 1908, Ed Walsh pitched 464 innings; in 2008, 9 C. C. Sabathia led the majors with 253. So what? They were both first under the prevailing conditions of the time.

Despite these changes, or because of them, Americans continue to love 10 baseball. Fans will accept anything except the sense that they are being lied to. Chemical enhancement won't kill the game; it is the cover-up that could be fatal.

Baseball, led by the Hall of Fame, needs to accept this and replace my- 11 thology and spin with realism and honesty. If everyone has access to the same drugs and training methods, and the fans are told what these are, then the field is level and fans will be able to interpret what they are seeing on the diamond and in the box scores.

The purists' last argument is that players' use of performance-enhancing 12 drugs sets a bad example for young athletes. But baseball players aren't children; they are adults in a very stressful and competitive profession. If they want to use anabolic steroids, or human growth hormone or bull's testosterone, it should be up to them. As for children, the government can regulate their use of these substances as they do with tobacco, alcohol, and prescription medicine.

The Baseball Hall of Fame, which started as a local tourist attraction 13 and a major-league publicity stunt, has since become a national field of dreams — and now, a battlefield. If it surrenders to the moralists who want to turn back the clock to some imagined golden era, and excommunicates the greatest stars anyone has ever seen, it will suffer the fate of all battlefields located on the wrong side of history. Obscurity.

• • •

Comprehension

1. According to Chafets, how widespread is drug abuse among professional baseball players?
2. Why do players take performance-enhancing drugs?
3. What is Chafets's response to the charge that "steroids alter the game" (8)?
4. What does Chafets mean when he says that both baseball and the Hall of Fame need to "replace mythology and spin with realism and honesty" (11)?
5. What is Chafets's response to the charge that if it allowed players to use performance-enhancing drugs, the Baseball Hall of Fame would set a bad example for children — especially young athletes?

Purpose and Audience

1. At what point in the essay does Chafets state his thesis? Why does he wait so long to do so?
2. Is this essay aimed primarily at baseball fans, or does Chafets have a wider audience in mind? Explain.
3. Why does Chafets believe he has to defend the use of performance-enhancing drugs? What preconceptions does he think his readers have?

Style and Structure

1. Chafets begins his essay by discussing the upcoming Baseball Hall of Fame exhibition game. What are the advantages of this opening strategy?
2. Does Chafets include enough examples to support his thesis? Should he have used more?

3. Does Chafets present a fair range of examples, or does he seem to be "stacking the deck" in favor of his position?

4. Do you think Chafets makes a strong case? Can you think of any arguments either for or against his position that he fails to mention?

5. Chafets's essay includes a number of short sentences. Rewrite paragraph 6, combining two or more short sentences into longer ones. Is the rewritten paragraph better than the original? Explain.

6. What points does Chafets emphasize in his conclusion? How does the conclusion help him reinforce his essay's main idea?

Vocabulary Projects

1. Define each of the following words as it is used in this selection.

testosterone (3)   posse (5)
quack (4)   beta blocker (7)
dupes (5)   anabolic steroids (12)

2. In paragraph 8, Chafets refers to those who oppose his ideas as *purists*. What is a *purist*? Do you think this characterization is fair? Do you think it is accurate?

Journal Entry

In paragraph 7, Chafets implies that baseball players should be allowed to use performance-enhancing drugs because everyone does it. Do you agree? Should this line of reasoning apply to players who violated other rules as well — for example, Pete Rose, who was permanently suspended from baseball in 1989 for gambling?

Writing Workshop

1. **Working with Sources.** Write an essay in which you agree or disagree with Chafets. In addition to using information from his essay, use information from the Baseball Hall of Fame Web site, baseballhall.org. Be sure to document all material that you borrow from your sources and to include a works-cited page. (See Chapter 18 for information on MLA documentation.)

2. Do you think it is possible to regulate performance-enhancing drugs in sports? Write an essay in which you present your opinion. Give some examples from your own experience to support your thesis.

3. If you were on the board of the Baseball Hall of Fame, would you vote for or against banning players with a history of drug abuse? Write an email to Jane Ford Clark, Chair of the Board of Directors for the National Baseball Hall of Fame, in which you explain your vote. Be sure to support your points with specific examples.

Combining the Patterns

In paragraphs 3 and 4, Chafets uses **narration**. How does this narrative section help Chafets set up the rest of his essay?

Thematic Connections

- "Major League Baseball Brawl" (page 337)
- "College Pressures" (page 450)
- "The Shame Game" (page 680)

JAMAICA KINCAID

"Girl" (Fiction)

Jamaica Kincaid's novels, short stories, and nonfiction frequently reflect on race, colonialism, adolescence, gender, and the weight of family relationships and personal history. Born Elaine Potter Johnson in St. John's, Antigua, in 1949, she changed her name to Jamaica Kincaid in 1973 partly to avoid a negative response from her family, who disapproved of her writing. She moved to New York City at 17 and worked as a nanny. She began college but dropped out to write for *Ingenue*, a teen magazine, as well as the *Village Voice*. In 1985, she became a staff writer for the *New Yorker*, where she worked until 1995. Her first published work of fiction, "Girl," appeared in the magazine in 1978. Kincaid credits *New Yorker* editor William Shawn for "show[ing] me what my voice was. . . . He made me feel that what I thought, my inner life, my thoughts as I organized them, were important." The author of *Annie John* (1985), *My Brother* (1997), *Among the Flowers: A Walk in the Himalayas* (2005), and several other books, Kincaid is a visiting lecturer at Harvard University.

Background on slavery and colonialism in the West Indies Europeans brought Africans to the Caribbean islands in the sixteenth and seventeenth centuries to work as slaves, primarily on sugar plantations. In her nonfiction book *A Small Place*, Kincaid writes searingly of her native island's dark colonial history, the "large ships filled up with human cargo." The human beings, she says, were "forced to work under conditions that were cruel and inhuman, they were beaten, they were murdered, they were sold, their children were taken from them and these separations lasted forever. . . ." Although the British outlawed slavery in the 1830s, blacks remained the largest percentage of the population in the British Caribbean colonies. Antigua remained a British colony until 1981.

Wash the white clothes on Monday and put them on the stone heap; 1 wash the color clothes on Tuesday and put them on the clothesline to dry; don't walk barehead in the hot sun; cook pumpkin fritters in very hot sweet oil; soak your little cloths right after you take them off; when buying cotton to make yourself a nice blouse, be sure that it doesn't have gum on it, because that way it won't hold up well after a wash; soak salt fish overnight before you cook it; is it true that you sing benna* in Sunday school?; always eat your food in such a way that it won't turn someone else's stomach; on Sundays try to walk like a lady and not like the slut you are so bent on becoming; don't sing benna in Sunday school; you mustn't speak to wharf-rat boys, not even to give directions; don't eat fruits on the street — flies will follow you; *but I don't sing benna on Sundays at all and never in Sunday school;* this is how to sew on a button; this is how to make a button-hole

---

* Eds. note — Form of popular music.

for the button you have just sewed on; this is how to hem a dress when you see the hem coming down and so to prevent yourself from looking like the slut I know you are so bent on becoming; this is how you iron your father's khaki shirt so that it doesn't have a crease; this is how you iron your father's khaki pants so that they don't have a crease; this is how you grow okra — far from the house, because okra tree harbors red ants; when you are growing dasheen, make sure it gets plenty of water or else it makes your throat itch when you are eating it; this is how you sweep a corner; this is how you sweep a whole house; this is how you sweep a yard; this is how you smile to someone you don't like too much; this is how you smile to someone you don't like at all; this is how you smile to someone you like completely; this is how you set a table for tea; this is how you set a table for dinner; this is how you set a table for dinner with an important guest; this is how you set a table for lunch; this is how you set a table for breakfast; this is how to behave in the presence of men who don't know you very well, and this way they won't recognize immediately the slut I have warned you against becoming; be sure to wash every day, even if it is with your own spit; don't squat down to play marbles — you are not a boy, you know; don't pick people's flowers — you might catch something; don't throw stones at blackbirds, because it might not be a blackbird at all; this is how to make a bread pudding; this is how to make doukona;* this is how to make pepper pot; this is how to make a good medicine for a cold; this is how to make a good medicine to throw away a child before it even becomes a child; this is how to catch a fish; this is how to throw back a fish you don't like, and that way something bad won't fall on you; this is how to bully a man; this is how a man bullies you; this is how to love a man, and if this doesn't work there are other ways, and if they don't work don't feel too bad about giving up; this is how to spit up in the air if you feel like it, and this is how to move quick so that it doesn't fall on you; this is how to make ends meet; always squeeze bread to make sure it's fresh; *but what if the baker won't let me feel the bread?*; you mean to say that after all you are really going to be the kind of woman who the baker won't let near the bread?

. . .

Reading Literature

1. Who is the speaker in the story? To whom is she speaking?

2. What do the speaker's remarks suggest about being female? Do the speaker's ideas correspond to your own ideas about being female? Explain.

3. Do you think this story has political or social implications? For example, what does the speaker's list suggest about the status of working-class women in the West Indies?

---

* Eds. note — A spiced pudding.

Journal Entry

Write a journal entry in which you record the duties of a woman (or a man) in your family.

Thematic Connections

* " 'What's in a Name?' " (page 2)
* "Only Daughter" (page 111)
* "My Mother Never Worked" (page 121)
* "I Want a Wife" (page 503)

Writing Assignments for Exemplification

1. Write a humorous essay about a ritual, ceremony, or celebration you experienced and the types of people who participated in it. Make a point about the event, and use the participants as examples to support your point.
2. Write an essay establishing that you are an optimistic (or pessimistic) person. Use examples to support your case.
3. If you could change three or four things at your school, what would they be? Use examples from your own experience to support your recommendations, and tie your recommendations together in your thesis statement.
4. **Working with Sources.** Write an essay discussing two or three of the greatest challenges facing the United States today. If you like, you may refer to essays in this chapter, such as "Just Walk On By" (page 240), or to essays elsewhere in this book, such as "Two Ways to Belong in America" (page 404) or "On Dumpster Diving" (page 664). Make sure that you document any material you get from your sources and that you include a works-cited page. (See Chapter 18 for information on MLA documentation.)
5. Using your family and friends as examples, write an essay suggesting some of the positive or negative characteristics of Americans.
6. Write an essay presenting your formula for achieving success in college. You may, if you wish, talk about things such as scheduling time, maintaining a high energy level, and learning how to relax. Use examples from your own experience to make your point. You may wish to refer to "College Pressures" (page 450).
7. Write an exemplification essay discussing how cooperation has helped you achieve some important goal. Support your thesis with a single well-developed example.
8. Choose an event that you believe illustrates a less-than-admirable moment in your life. Then, write an essay explaining your feelings.
9. The popularity of the TV show *American Idol* has revealed once again Americans' long-standing infatuation with music icons. Choose several pop groups or stars, old and new — such as Elvis Presley, the Beatles, Michael Jackson, Alicia Keys, 50 Cent, Beyoncé Knowles, Amy Winehouse, Lady Gaga, and Taylor Swift, to name only a few — and use them to illustrate the characteristics that you think make pop stars so appealing.

Collaborative Activity for Exemplification

The following passage appeared in a handbook given to parents of entering students at a midwestern university:

The freshman experience is like no other — at once challenging, exhilarating, and fun. Students face academic challenges as they are exposed to many new ideas. They also face personal challenges as they meet many new people from diverse backgrounds. It is a time to mature and grow. It is an opportunity to explore new subjects and familiar ones. There may be no more challenging and exciting time of personal growth than the first year of university study.

Working in groups of four, brainstorm to identify examples that support or refute the idea that there "may be no more challenging and exciting time of personal growth" than the first year of college. Then, choose one person from each group to tell the class the position the group took and explain the examples you collected. Finally, work together to write an essay that presents your group's position. Have one student write the first draft, two others revise this draft, and the last student edit and proofread the revised draft.

9

Process

What Is Process?

A **process** essay explains how to do something or how something occurs. It presents a sequence of steps and shows how those steps lead to a particular result. In the following paragraph from *Language in Thought and Action,* the semanticist S. I. Hayakawa uses process to explain how a dictionary editor decides on a word's definition.

Process presents series of steps in chronological order

To define a word, then, the dictionary-editor places before him the stack of cards illustrating that word; each of the cards represents an actual use of the word by a writer of some literary or historical importance. He reads the cards carefully, discards some, rereads the rest, and divides up the stack according to what he thinks are the several senses of the word. Finally, he writes his definitions, following the hard-and-fast rule that each definition *must* be based on what the quotations in front of him reveal about the meaning of the word. The editor cannot be influenced by what *he* thinks a given word *ought* to mean. He must work according to the cards or not at all.

Topic sentence

Process, like narration, presents events in chronological order. Unlike a narrative, however, a process essay explains a particular series of events that produces the same outcome whenever it is duplicated. Because these events form a sequence with a fixed order, clarity is extremely important. Whether your readers will actually perform the process or are simply trying to understand how it occurs, your essay must make clear the exact order of the individual steps, as well as their relationships to one another and to the process as a whole. This means that you need to provide clear, logical transitions between the steps in a process and that you need to present the steps in *strict* chronological order — that is, in the exact order in which they occur or are to be performed.

Depending on its purpose, a process essay can be either a set of *instructions* or a *process explanation.*

Understanding Instructions

The purpose of **instructions** is to enable readers to perform a process. A recipe, a handout about using your library's online databases, and the individual sections of the user's guide that comes with your cell phone are all written in the form of instructions. So are directions for locating an office building in Washington, DC, or for driving from Houston to Pensacola. Instructions use the present tense and, like commands, they use the imperative mood, speaking directly to readers: "*Disconnect* the system, and *check* the electrical source."

Understanding Process Explanations

The purpose of a **process explanation** is not to enable readers to perform a process but rather to help them understand how it is carried out. Such essays may examine anything from how silkworms spin their cocoons to how Michelangelo and Leonardo da Vinci painted their masterpieces on plaster walls and ceilings.

A process explanation may use the first person (*I, we*) or the third (*he, she, it, they*), the past tense or the present. Because its readers need to understand the process, not perform it, a process explanation does not use the second person (*you*) or the imperative mood (commands). The style of a process explanation varies, depending on whether a writer is explaining a process that takes place regularly or one that occurred in the past and also depending on whether the writer or someone else carries out the steps. The following chart suggests the stylistic options available to writers of process explanations.

	First Person	Third Person
Present tense	"After I place the chemicals in the tray, I turn out the lights in the darkroom." *(habitual process performed by the writer)*	"After photographers place the chemicals in the tray, they turn out the lights in the darkroom." *(habitual process performed by someone other than the writer)*
Past tense	"After I placed the chemicals in the tray, I turned out the lights in the darkroom." *(process performed in the past by the writer)*	"After the photographer placed the chemicals in the tray, she turned out the lights in the darkroom." *(process performed in the past by someone other than the writer)*

Using Process

College writing frequently calls for instructions or process explanations. In a biology paper on genetic testing, you might devote a paragraph to an explanation of the process of amniocentesis; in an editorial about the negative side of fraternity life, you might include a brief account of the process of pledging. You can also organize an entire paper around a process pattern: in a literature essay, you might trace a fictional character's progress toward some new insight; on a finance midterm, you might explain the procedure for approving a commercial loan.

Planning a Process Essay

As you plan a process essay, remember that your primary goal is to depict the process accurately. This means you need to distinguish between what usually or always happens and what occasionally or rarely happens, between necessary steps and optional ones. You should also mentally test all the steps in sequence to be sure the process really works as you say it does, checking carefully for omitted steps or incorrect information. If you are writing about a process you observed, try to test the accuracy of your explanation by observing the process again.

Accommodating Your Audience

As you write, remember to keep your readers' needs in mind. When necessary, explain the reasons for performing the steps, describe unfamiliar materials or equipment, define terms, and warn readers about possible problems that may occur during the process. (Sometimes you may want to include illustrations.) Besides complete information, your readers need a clear and consistent discussion, without ambiguities or digressions. For this reason, you should avoid unnecessary shifts in tense, person, voice, and mood. You should also be careful not to omit articles (*a, an,* and *the*); you want your discussion to move smoothly, like an essay — not abruptly, like a cookbook.

Developing a Thesis Statement

Both instructions and process explanations can be written either to persuade or simply to present information. If its purpose is persuasive, a process essay may take a strong stand in a **thesis statement**, such as "Applying for food stamps is a needlessly complex process that discourages many qualified recipients" or "The process of slaughtering baby seals is inhumane and sadistic." Many process essays, however, communicate nothing more debatable than the procedure for blood typing. Even in such a case, though, a process should have a clear thesis statement that identifies the process and perhaps tells why it is performed: "Typing their own blood can familiarize students with some basic laboratory procedures."

Using Transitions

Throughout your essay, be sure to use transitional words and phrases to ensure that each step, each stage, and each paragraph leads logically to the next. Transitions such as *first, second, meanwhile, after this, next, then, at the same time, when you have finished,* and *finally* help to establish sequential and chronological relationships so that readers can follow the process. (A more complete list of transitions appears on page 57.)

Structuring a Process Essay

Like other essays, a process essay generally consists of three sections. The **introduction** identifies the process and indicates why and under what circumstances it is performed. This section may include information about materials or preliminary preparations, or it may present an overview of the process, perhaps even listing its major stages. The paper's thesis is also usually stated in the introduction.

Each paragraph in the **body** of the essay typically treats one major stage of the process. Each stage may group several steps, depending on the nature and complexity of the process. These steps are presented in chronological order, interrupted only for essential definitions, explanations, or cautions. Every step must be included and must appear in its proper place.

A short process essay may not need a formal **conclusion**. If an essay does have a conclusion, however, it will often briefly review the procedure's major stages. Such an ending is especially useful if the paper has outlined a technical procedure that may seem complicated to general readers. The conclusion may also reinforce the thesis by summarizing the results of the process or explaining its significance.

Suppose you are taking a midterm examination in a course in childhood and adolescent behavior. One essay question calls for a process explanation: "Trace the stages that children go through in acquiring language." After thinking about the question, you formulate the following thesis statement: "Although individual cases may differ, most children acquire language in a predictable series of stages." You then plan your essay and develop an informal outline, which might look like this:

SAMPLE OUTLINE: Process

Introduction:	Thesis statement — Although individual cases may differ, most children acquire language in a predictable series of stages.
First stage (two to twelve months):	Prelinguistic behavior, including "babbling" and appropriate responses to nonverbal cues.

Second stage (end of first year):	Single words as commands or requests; infant catalogs his or her environment.
Third stage (beginning of second year):	Expressive jargon (flow of sounds that imitates adult speech); real words along with jargon.
Fourth and final stage (middle of second year to beginning of third year):	Two-word phrases; longer strings; missing parts of speech.
Conclusion:	Restatement of thesis or review of major stages of process.

This essay, when completed, will show not only what the stages of the process are but also how they relate to one another. In addition, it will support the thesis that children learn language through a well-defined process.

Revising a Process Essay

When you revise a set of instructions or a process explanation, consider the items on the revision checklist on page 68. In addition, pay special attention to the items on the following checklist, which apply specifically to revising process essays.

✔ REVISION CHECKLIST   Process

- Does your assignment call for a set of instructions or a process explanation?
- Is your essay's style appropriate for the kind of process essay (instructions or process explanation) you are writing?
- Does your essay have a clearly stated thesis that identifies the process and perhaps tells why it is (or was) performed?
- Have you included all necessary steps?
- Are the steps presented in strict chronological order?
- Do transitions clearly indicate where one step ends and the next begins?
- Have you included all necessary reminders and cautions?

Editing a Process Essay

When you edit your process essay, follow the guidelines on the editing checklists on pages 85, 88, and 90. In addition, focus on the grammar, mechanics, and punctuation issues that are particularly relevant to process essays. One of these issues — avoiding unnecessary shifts in tense, person, voice, and mood — is discussed on pages 268–269.

GRAMMAR IN CONTEXT   Avoiding Unnecessary Shifts

To explain a process to readers, you need to use consistent verb **tense** (past or present), **person** (first, second, or third), **voice** (active or passive), and **mood** (statements or commands). Unnecessary shifts in tense, person, voice, or mood can confuse readers and make it difficult for them to follow your process.

Avoiding Shifts in Tense Use present tense for a process that is performed regularly.

"The body is first laid out in the undertaker's morgue — or rather, Mr. Jones is reposing in the preparation room — to be readied to bid the world farewell" (Mitford 304).

Use past tense for a process that was performed in the past.

"He peeled the potatoes and thin-sliced them into a quart-sized Mason fruit jar" (Malcolm X 281).

Shift from present to past tense only when you need to indicate a change in time: Usually, I study several days before a test, but this time I studied the night before.

Avoiding Shifts in Person In process explanations, use first or third person.

FIRST PERSON (*I*):   "I reached for the box of Medium Ash Brown hair color just as my friend Veronica grabbed the box labeled Sparkling Sherry" (Hunt 275).

FIRST PERSON (*WE*):   "We decided to use my bathroom to color our hair" (Hunt 275).

THIRD PERSON (*HE*):   "The embalmer, having allowed an appropriate interval to elapse, returns to the attack, but now he brings into play the skill and equipment of sculptor and cosmetician" (Mitford 306).

In instructions, use second person.

SECOND PERSON   "If you sometimes forget to pay bills, or if you
(*YOU*):   have large student loans, you may have a problem" (McGlade 270).

When you give instructions, be careful not to shift from third to second person.

INCORRECT: If a person sometimes forgets to pay bills, or if someone has large student loans, you may have a problem. (shift from third to second person)

CORRECT: If you sometimes forget to pay bills, or if you have large student loans, you may have a problem. (second person used consistently)

Avoiding Shifts in Voice   Use active voice when you want to emphasize the person performing the action.

"In the last four years, I <u>have moved</u> eight times, living in three dorm rooms, two summer sublets, and three apartments in three different cities." (McGlade 270).

Use passive voice to emphasize the action itself, not the person performing it.

"The patching and filling completed, Mr. Jones <u>is</u> now <u>shaved</u>, <u>washed</u>, and <u>dressed</u>" (Mitford 307).

Do not shift between the active and the passive voice, especially within a sentence, unless your intent is to change your emphasis.

INCORRECT: The first draft of my essay <u>was completed</u>, and then <u>I started</u> the second draft. (shift from passive to active voice)

CORRECT: <u>I completed</u> the first draft of my essay, and then <u>I started</u> the second draft. (active voice used consistently)

Avoiding Shifts in Mood   Use the indicative mood (statements) for process explanations.

"<u>He draped</u> the towel around my shoulders, over my rubber apron, and <u>began</u> again vaselining my hair" (Malcolm X 282).

Use the imperative mood (commands) only in instructions.

"<u>Turn</u> the crate upside down" (Piven et al. 291).

Be careful not to shift from the imperative mood to the indicative mood.

INCORRECT: First, <u>check</u> your credit report for errors, and <u>you should report</u> any errors you find. (shift from imperative to indicative mood)

CORRECT: First, <u>check</u> your credit report for errors, and <u>report</u> any errors you find. (imperative mood used consistently)

CORRECT: First, <u>you should check</u> your credit report for errors, and <u>you should report</u> any errors you find. (indicative mood used consistently)

For more practice in avoiding unnecessary shifts, visit the resources for Chapter 9 at **bedfordstmartins.com/patterns**.

A STUDENT WRITER: Instructions

The following student essay, "The Search," by Eric McGlade, gives readers **instructions** on how to find an apartment. It was written for a composition class in response to the assignment "Write an essay giving practical instructions for doing something most people you know will need to do at one time or another."

The Search

Introduction

In the last four years, I have moved eight times, living in three dorm rooms, two summer sublets, and three apartments in three different cities. I would not recommend this experience to anyone. Finding an apartment is time consuming, stressful, and *Thesis statement* expensive, so the best advice is to stay where you are. However, if you must move, here are a few tips to help you survive the search. 1

First major stage of process: before the search

Before you begin your search, take some time to plan. First, figure out what you can afford. (Here's a hint — you can afford less than you think.) Most experts say you should spend no more *First step: review your finances* than one-third of your net income on rent. Find a budgeting worksheet online, and see for yourself how car insurance, electricity, and cable can add up. Remember, your new landlord may charge a security deposit and the first month's rent, and there may be pet, parking, cleaning, or moving-in fees. 2

Second step: check your credit history

Next, consider your credit history. If you sometimes forget to pay bills, or if you have large student loans, you may have a problem. Landlords usually run a credit check on potential renters. If you are particularly concerned about your credit rating, order a credit report from one of the three main credit bureaus: TransUnion, Equifax, or Experian. If you find that your credit isn't perfect, don't panic. First, check your credit report for errors, and report any errors you find to the credit bureau. Second, adopt good financial habits immediately. Start paying bills on time, and 3 try to consolidate any debts at a lower interest rate. If a landlord does question your credit, be prepared to explain any extenuating circumstances in the past and to point out your current good behavior.

Third step: consider where to live

After you know what you can afford, you need to figure   4 out where you want to (and can afford to) live. Keep in mind important factors such as how close the apartment is to your school or workplace and how convenient the neighborhood is. Is public transportation located nearby? Is on-street parking available? Can you easily get to a supermarket, coffee shop, convenience store, and Laundromat? If possible, visit each potential neighborhood both during the day and at night. A business district may be bustling during the day but deserted (and even dangerous) at night. If you visit both early and late, you will get a more accurate impression of how safe the neighborhood feels.

Fourth step: consider a roommate

During this stage, consider whether or not you are willing   5 to live with a roommate. You will sacrifice privacy, but you will be able to afford a better apartment. If you do decide to live with a roommate, the easiest way to proceed is to find a friend who also needs an apartment. If this isn't possible, try to find an apartment that comes with a roommate — one with one roommate moving out but the other roommate remaining in the apartment. The third option is to find another apartment seeker and go apartment hunting together. Some Web sites, such as www.roommates.com, cater to this type of search, but, unfortunately, most require a fee. However, your school housing office might have a list of students looking for roommates.

Transitional paragraph

Now, you are ready to start looking. You can find the perfect   6 apartment through a real estate agent, by checking your local newspaper or school's housing listings, by asking your friends and family, or by visiting Web sites such as Craigslist.

Second major stage of process: during the search

Each of these methods has pros and cons. A real estate   7 agent might help you find your dream apartment quickly, but you will usually have to pay for this speedy service. As for newspaper listings, stick to your local paper; unless you are looking for a

First step: do research

second vacation home in Maui, national newspapers are not your best bet. An even better idea is to check your school's housing listings, where you are likely to find fellow students in search of apartments in your price range.

Second step: spread
the word

Meanwhile, spread the word. Tell everyone you know that 8
you are apartment hunting. After all, your stepsister's uncle's
mother-in-law may live in a building with a newly vacant
apartment. This method isn't the most efficient, but the results
can be amazing. As a bonus, you will receive practical advice
about your neighborhood, such as what to watch out for and what
problems other renters have had.

Third step: try
Craigslist

Finally, if you are hunting in a major city, I have but one 9
word: Craigslist. Craigslist.org has free apartment listings arranged
by city and neighborhood. You can hunt for an apartment by
price, by number of bedrooms, or by length of lease. If you are
on a tight moving schedule and need a place immediately, this
Web site is especially helpful because of the sheer volume of its
listings. Craigslist also has the added benefit of providing a general
price range for your ideal neighborhood.

Fourth step: visit
apartments

Once you have identified some possibilities, it's time to visit 10
the apartments. Get a good look at each one. Is it furnished or
unfurnished? Look closely at the kitchen. Are all the appliances in
good working order? Will your bed fit in the bedroom? How much
closet space will you have? Are there phone, cable, and Internet
hookups? Is it a sunny apartment (south facing), or is it dark (north
facing)? In the bathroom, turn on the faucets in the sink and shower;
check for rust and poor water pressure. As you walk through the
apartment, check the cell-phone reception (leaning out the window
of your bathroom to talk on the phone is not fun). Most important,
do not forget to take notes. After seeing fourteen apartments, you
may confuse Apartment A, with the six pets and funny smell, with
Apartment G, with the balcony and renovated kitchen.

Third major stage
of process: after
the search

And now, at last, the search is over: you have found your 11
apartment. Congratulations! Unfortunately, your work is not yet
over. Now, it is time to read your lease. It will be long and boring,

First step: check
your lease

but it is a very important document. Among other things, your
lease should specify the length of the lease, a rent due date, fees
for late rent payments, the amount of the security deposit, and
the conditions required for the return of the security deposit.
If you have decided to live with a roommate, you might ask
the landlord to divide the rent on your lease. This way, if your
roommate moves to Brazil, you will not have to pay his or her
share of the rent. Be sure to read your lease thoroughly and bring
up any concerns with your landlord.

Second step: get insurance and activate utilities	Before you move in, you have a few more things to do: get 12 renter's insurance to protect you from theft or damage to your possessions; arrange to get your utilities hooked up; submit a change-of-address form at the post office; and inform your bank or credit-card company about your future move. Finally, start packing!
Conclusion	If you plan ahead and shop smart, you can find your 13 perfect apartment. Remember to figure out what you can afford, check out the neighborhoods, consider a roommate, use multiple search methods, and take careful notes when you visit potential apartments. Yes, happy endings do occur. I am now in the third month of a two-year lease, and I have no plans to move anytime soon.

Points for Special Attention

Introduction. Eric McGlade's essay begins by giving readers some background on his own experience as an apartment hunter. This strategy gives him some credibility, establishing him as an "expert" who can explain the process. Eric then narrows his focus to the difficulties of apartment hunting and ends his introduction with a thesis statement telling readers that the process can be made easier.

Structure. Eric divides his essay into the three major stages of apartment hunting: what to do before, during, and after the search. After his introduction, Eric includes four paragraphs that explain what to do before the search gets under way. In paragraphs 6 through 10, he explains how to go about the actual hunt for an apartment. Then, in paragraphs 11 and 12, he tells readers what they should do after they locate an apartment (but before they move in). In his conclusion, he restates his thesis, summarizes the steps in the process, and returns to his own experience to reassure readers that a positive outcome is possible.

Purpose and Style. Because Eric's assignment asked him to give practical advice for a process readers could expect to perform, he decided to write the essay as a set of instructions. Therefore, he uses the second person ("If *you* find that *your* credit isn't perfect, don't panic") and the present tense, with many of his verbs in the form of commands ("First, *figure* out what you can afford").

Transitions. To make his essay clear and easy to follow, Eric includes transitions that indicate the order in which each step is to be performed ("First," "Next," "Now," "Meanwhile," "Finally," and so on), as well as expressions such as "During this stage." He also includes transitional sentences to move his essay from one stage of the process to the next:

- "Before you begin your search, take some time to plan" (2).
- "Now, you are ready to start looking" (6).
- "Once you have identified some possibilities, it's time to visit the apartments" (10).
- "And now, at last, the search is over: you have found your apartment" (11).

Finally, paragraph 6 serves as a transitional paragraph, moving readers from the preliminary steps to the start of the actual search for an apartment.

Focus on Revision

When he met with his peer editing group, Eric found that they had all gone through the apartment-hunting process and therefore had some practical suggestions to make. In the draft they reviewed, Eric included a good deal of information about his own experiences, but his readers felt those narratives, although amusing, were distracting and got in the way of the process. Eric agreed, and he deleted these anecdotes. His readers thought that mentioning his experiences briefly in his introduction would be sufficient, but Eric decided to also return briefly to his own story in his conclusion, adding the two "happy ending" sentences that now conclude his essay. In addition, he followed his readers' suggestion to add a review of the steps of the process to his conclusion to help readers remember what they had read. These additions gave him a fully developed conclusion.

In terms of his essay's content, his fellow students were most concerned with paragraph 10, which they felt seemed to rush through a very important part of the process: visiting the apartments. They also observed that the information in this paragraph was not arranged in any logical order and that Eric had failed to mention other considerations (for example, whether the apartment needed repairs or painting, whether it was noisy, whether it included air conditioning). One reader suggested that Eric expand his discussion and divide the information into two separate paragraphs, one on the apartment's mechanical systems (plumbing, electricity, and so on) and another on its physical appearance (size of rooms, light, and so on). In the final draft of his essay, Eric did just that. (A sample peer editing worksheet for process appears on page 278.)

Working with Sources. Although the students in his peer editing group did not suggest any specific revisions to his introductory paragraph, Eric thought his essay needed a more interesting opening. So, in his final draft, he planned to quote key phrases from some of the Craigslist ads he rejected. He thought this might add some humor to an otherwise straightforward essay.

A STUDENT WRITER: Process Explanation

The essay that follows, "Medium Ash Brown," by Melany Hunt, is a **process explanation**. It was written for a composition class in response to the assignment "Write an essay explaining a process that changed your appearance in some way."

Medium Ash Brown

Introduction   The beautiful chestnut-haired woman pictured on the box   1
seemed to beckon to me. I reached for the box of Medium Ash
Brown hair color just as my friend Veronica grabbed the box
labeled Sparkling Sherry. I can't remember our reasons for wanting
to change our hair color, but they seemed to make sense at the
time. Maybe we were just bored. I do remember that the idea of
transforming our appearance came up unexpectedly. Impulsively,
we decided to change our hair color — and, we hoped, ourselves —

Thesis statement   that very evening. The process that followed taught me that some
impulses should definitely be resisted.

Materials   We decided to use my bathroom to color our hair. Inside   2
assembled   each box of hair color, we found two little bottles and a small tube
wrapped in a page of instructions. Attached to the instruction
page itself were two very large, one-size-fits-all plastic gloves,
which looked and felt like plastic sandwich bags. The directions
recommended having some old towels around to soak up any spills
or drips that might occur. Under the sink we found some old,
frayed towels that I figured my mom had forgotten about, and we

First stage of   spread them around the bathtub. After we put our gloves on, we
process: preparing   began the actual coloring process. First we poured the first bottle
the color   into the second, which was half-full of some odd-smelling liquid.
The smell was not much better after we combined the two bottles.
The directions advised us to cut off a small section of hair to use
as a sample. For some reason, we decided to skip this step.

Second stage of   At this point, Veronica and I took turns leaning over the tub   3
process: applying   to wet our hair for the color. The directions said to leave the color
the color   on the hair for fifteen to twenty minutes, so we found a little
timer and set it for fifteen minutes. Next, we applied the color to
our hair. Again, we took turns, squeezing the bottle in order to
cover all our hair. We then wrapped the old towels around our
sour-smelling hair and went outside to get some fresh air.

Third stage of   After the fifteen minutes were up, we rinsed our hair.   4
process: rinsing   According to the directions, we were to add a little water and

scrub as if we were shampooing our hair. The color lathered up, and we rinsed our hair until the water ran clear. So far, so good.

Last stage of process: applying conditioner

The last part of the process involved applying the small   5
tube of conditioner to our hair (because colored hair becomes brittle and easily damaged). We used the conditioner as directed, and then we dried our hair so that we could see the actual color. Even before I looked in the mirror, I heard Veronica's gasp.

Outcome of process

"Nice try," I said, assuming she was just trying to make me   6
nervous, "but you're not funny."

"Mel," she said, "look in the mirror." Slowly, I turned   7
around. My stomach turned into a lead ball when I saw my reflection. My hair was the putrid greenish-brown color of a winter lawn, dying in patches yet still a nice green in the shade.

The next day in school, I wore my hair tied back under a   8
baseball cap. I told only my close friends what I had done. After they were finished laughing, they offered their deepest, most heartfelt condolences. They also offered many suggestions — none very helpful — on what to do to get my old hair color back.

Conclusion

It is now three months later, and I still have no idea what   9
prompted me to color my hair. My only consolation is that I resisted my first impulse: to use a wild color, like blue or fuchsia. Still, as I wait for my hair to grow out, and as I assemble a larger and larger collection of baseball caps, it is small consolation indeed.

Points for Special Attention

Structure. In Melany's opening paragraph, her thesis statement makes it very clear that the experience she describes is not one she would recommend to others. The temptation she describes in her introduction's first few sentences lures readers into her essay, just as the picture on the box lured her. Her second paragraph lists the contents of the box and explains how she and her friend assembled the other necessary materials. Then, she explains the first stage in the process: preparing the color. Paragraphs 3–5 describe the other stages in the process in chronological order, and paragraphs 6–8 record Melany's and Veronica's reactions to their experiment. In paragraph 9, Melany sums up the impact of her experience and once again expresses her annoyance with herself for her impulsive act.

Purpose and Style. Melany's purpose is not to enable others to duplicate the process she explains; on the contrary, she wants to discourage readers from doing what she did. Consequently, she presents her process not as a set of instructions but as a process explanation, using first person and past tense to explain her and her friend's actions. She also largely eliminates cautions and reminders that her readers, who are not likely to undertake the process, will not need to know.

Detail. Melany's essay includes vivid descriptive detail that gives readers a clear sense of the process and its outcome. Throughout, her emphasis is on the negative aspects of the process — the "odd-smelling liquid" and the "putrid greenish-brown color" of her hair, for instance — and this emphasis is consistent with her essay's purpose.

Transitions. To move readers smoothly through the process, Melany includes clear transitions ("First," "At this point," "Next," "then") and clearly identifies the beginning of the process ("After we put our gloves on, we began the actual coloring process") and the end ("The last part of the process").

Focus on Revision

Students who read Melany's essay thought it was clearly written and structured and that its ironic, self-mocking tone was well suited to her audience and purpose. They felt, however, that some minor revisions would make her essay even more effective. Specifically, they thought that paragraph 2 began too abruptly: paragraph 1 recorded the purchase of the hair color, and paragraph 2 opened with the sentence "We decided to use my bathroom to color our hair," leaving readers wondering how much time had passed between purchase and application. Because the thesis rests on the idea of the foolishness of an impulsive gesture, it is important for readers to understand that the girls presumably went immediately from the store to Melany's house.

After thinking about this criticism, Melany decided to write a clearer opening for paragraph 2: "As soon as we paid for the color, we returned to my house, where, eager to begin our transformation, we locked ourselves in my bathroom. Inside each box . . ." She also decided to divide paragraph 2 into two paragraphs, one describing the materials and another beginning with "After we put our gloves on," which introduces the first step in the process.

Another possible revision Melany considered was developing Veronica's character further. Although both girls purchase and apply hair color, readers never learn what happens to Veronica. Melany knew she could easily add a brief paragraph after paragraph 7, describing Veronica's "Sparkling Sherry" hair in humorous terms, and she planned to do so in her paper's final draft.

Working with Sources. One student suggested that Melany refer in her essay to Malcolm X's "My First Conk" (page 281). After all, Malcolm X had also tried to change his appearance and had also been sorry afterward. (In fact, the class's assignment — "Write an essay explaining a process that changed your appearance in some way" — was inspired by their reading of "My First Conk.") Melany considered this suggestion but ultimately decided not to take her classmate's advice. For one thing, she realized that Malcolm X's initial response to his transformation (unlike hers) was positive; only later did he realize that his desire to transform his looks to conform to a white ideal was "ridiculous" (page 283), a "step toward self-degradation" (page 283). More important, Melany thought Malcolm X's serious analysis would not be a good fit for her lighthearted essay. So, even though the topic of Malcolm X's essay was similar to hers, Melany decided that referring to his experience would trivialize his ideas and be out of place in her essay.

PEER EDITING WORKSHEET: Process

1. What process does this essay describe?

2. Does the writer include all the information the audience needs? Is any vital step or piece of information missing? Is any step or piece of information irrelevant? Is any necessary definition, explanation, or caution missing or incomplete?

3. Is the essay a set of instructions or a process explanation? How can you tell? Why do you think the writer chose this strategy rather than the alternative? Do you think this was the right choice?

4. Does the writer consistently follow the stylistic conventions for the strategy — instructions or process explanation — he or she has chosen?

5. Are the steps presented in a clear, logical order? Are they grouped logically into paragraphs? Should any steps be combined or relocated? If so, which ones?

6. Does the writer use enough transitions to move readers through the process? Should any transitions be added? If so, where?

7. Does the writer need to revise to correct confusing shifts in tense, person, voice, or mood? If so, where?

8. Is the essay interesting? What descriptive details would add interest to the essay? Would a visual be helpful?

9. How would you characterize the writer's opening strategy? Is it appropriate for the essay's purpose and audience? What alternative strategy might be more effective?

10. How would you characterize the writer's closing strategy? Would a different conclusion be more effective? Explain.

The reading selections that follow illustrate how varied the uses of process writing can be. The first selection, a visual text, is followed by questions designed to illustrate how process can operate in visual form.

RUBIN RODRIGUES

Growth of Facebook and Privacy "Events"

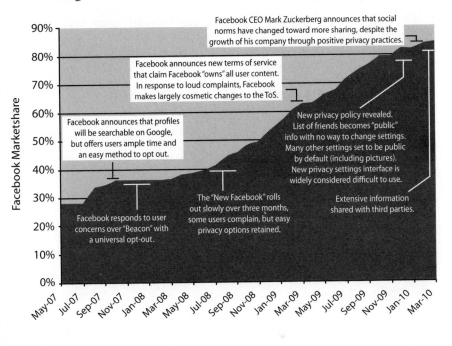

Facebook CEO Mark Zuckerberg announces that social norms have changed toward more sharing, despite the growth of his company through positive privacy practices.

Facebook announces new terms of service that claim Facebook "owns" all user content. In response to loud complaints, Facebook makes largely cosmetic changes to the ToS.

Facebook announces that profiles will be searchable on Google, but offers users ample time and an easy method to opt out.

New privacy policy revealed. List of friends becomes "public" info with no way to change settings. Many other settings set to be public by default (including pictures). New privacy settings interface is widely considered difficult to use.

The "New Facebook" rolls out slowly over three months, some users complain, but easy privacy options retained.

Extensive information shared with third parties.

Facebook responds to user concerns over "Beacon" with a universal opt-out.

Reading Images

1. How easy (or difficult) is it to understand the information on Rodrigues's chart? Should Rodrigues have presented the information in some other way? Explain.

2. Some recent studies suggest that Facebook users are most concerned with protecting their contact and birthday information and less concerned with protecting their names, their network connections (including Facebook friends), and their profile pictures. According to Rodrigues's chart, do Facebook's privacy policies address these user concerns?

3. How has Facebook's policy toward user privacy changed from 2007 to 2010? Has this process moved steadily in one direction? Explain.

continued

Journal Entry

How secure is your Facebook data? What restrictions do you have in place? Why?

Thematic Connections

- "I'm Your Teacher, Not Your Internet-Service Provider" (page 417)
- "College Pressures" (page 450)
- "The Dog Ate My Disk, and Other Tales of Woe" (page 460)
- "The Ways We Lie" (page 474)

MALCOLM X

My First Conk

Malcolm X was born Malcolm Little in Omaha, Nebraska, in 1925. As a young man, he had a number of run-ins with the law, and he wound up in prison on burglary charges before he was twenty-one. There he pursued his education and was influenced by the writings of Elijah Muhammad, the founder of the Black Muslims (now known as the Nation of Islam), a black separatist organization. On his release from prison, Malcolm X became a highly visible member of this group and a disciple of its leader. He left the movement in 1963, later converting to orthodox Islam and founding a rival African-American political organization. He was assassinated in 1965.

Background on conks and other African-American hair styles *The Autobiography of Malcolm X* (written with Alex Haley) was published in 1964. The following excerpt from that book describes the painful and painstaking process many African-American men once endured to achieve a style of straight hair called a "conk." (The term probably comes from Congolene, the brand name of one commercial hair straightener.) First popularized in the 1920s by black entertainers such as Cab Calloway, the style continued to be fashionable until the 1960s, when more natural styles, including the Afro, became a symbol of black pride and conked hair came to be seen as a self-loathing attempt to imitate whites. Ironically, perhaps, some African Americans still distinguish between "good" (that is, naturally straight) and "bad" (that is, naturally curly) hair. Today, cosmetically straightened hair (a process that is no longer so arduous) is considered one fashion option among many, including shaved heads, closely cropped hair, braids, cornrows, and dreadlocks.

Shorty soon decided that my hair was finally long enough to be conked. 1 He had promised to school me in how to beat the barber shops' three- and four-dollar price by making up congolene, and then conking ourselves.

I took the little list of ingredients he had printed out for me, and went 2 to a grocery store, where I got a can of Red Devil lye, two eggs, and two medium-sized white potatoes. Then at a drugstore near the poolroom, I asked for a large jar of vaseline, a large bar of soap, a large-toothed comb and a fine-toothed comb, one of those rubber hoses with a metal spray-head, a rubber apron, and a pair of gloves.

"Going to lay on that first conk?" the drugstore man asked me. I 3 proudly told him, grinning, "Right!"

Shorty paid six dollars a week for a room in his cousin's shabby apart- 4 ment. His cousin wasn't at home. "It's like the pad's mine, he spends so much time with his woman," Shorty said. "Now, you watch me —"

He peeled the potatoes and thin-sliced them into a quart-sized Mason 5 fruit jar, then started stirring them with a wooden spoon as he gradually poured in a little over half the can of lye. "Never use a metal spoon; the lye will turn it black," he told me.

A jelly-like, starchy-looking glop resulted from the lye and potatoes, 6 and Shorty broke in the two eggs, stirring real fast — his own conk and dark face bent down close. The congolene turned pale-yellowish. "Feel the jar," Shorty said. I cupped my hand against the outside, and snatched it away. "Damn right, it's hot, that's the lye," he said. "So you know it's going to burn when I comb it in — it burns bad. But the longer you can stand it, the straighter the hair."

He made me sit down, and he tied the string of the new rubber apron 7 tightly around my neck, and combed up my bush of hair. Then, from the big vaseline jar, he took a handful and massaged it hard all through my hair and into the scalp. He also thickly vaselined my neck, ears, and forehead. "When I get to washing out your head, be sure to tell me anywhere you feel any little stinging," Shorty warned me, washing his hands, then pulling on the rubber gloves, and tying on his own rubber apron. "You always got to remember that any congolene left in burns a sore into your head."

The congolene just felt warm when Shorty started combing it in. But 8 then my head caught fire.

I gritted my teeth and tried to pull the sides of the kitchen table to- 9 gether. The comb felt as if it was raking my skin off.

My eyes watered, my nose was running. I couldn't stand it any lon- 10 ger; I bolted to the washbasin. I was cursing Shorty with every name I could think of when he got the spray going and started soap lathering my head.

He lathered and spray-rinsed, lathered and spray-rinsed, maybe ten or 11 twelve times, each time gradually closing the hot-water faucet, until the rinse was cold, and that helped some.

"You feel any stinging spots?" 12

"No," I managed to say. My knees were trembling. 13

"Sit back down, then. I think we got it all out okay." 14

The flame came back as Shorty, with a thick towel, started drying my 15 head, rubbing hard. *"Easy, man, easy!"* I kept shouting.

"The first time's always worst. You get used to it better before long. You 16 took it real good, homeboy. You got a good conk."

When Shorty let me stand up and see in the mirror, my hair hung down 17 in limp, damp strings. My scalp still flamed, but not as badly; I could bear it. He draped the towel around my shoulders, over my rubber apron, and began again vaselining my hair.

I could feel him combing, straight back, first the big comb, then the 18 fine-tooth one.

Then, he was using a razor, very delicately, on the back of my neck. 19 Then, finally, shaping the sideburns.

My first view in the mirror blotted out the hurting. I'd seen some pretty 20 conks, but when it's the first time, on your *own* head, the transformation, after the lifetime of kinks, is staggering.

The mirror reflected Shorty behind me. We both were grinning and 21 sweating. And on top of my head was this thick, smooth sheen of shining red hair — real red — as straight as any white man's.

How ridiculous I was! Stupid enough to stand there simply lost in ad- 22 miration of my hair now looking "white," reflected in the mirror in Shorty's room. I vowed that I'd never again be without a conk, and I never was for many years.

This was my first really big step toward self-degradation: when I en- 23 dured all of that pain, literally burning my flesh to have it look like a white man's hair. I had joined that multitude of Negro men and women in America who are brainwashed into believing that the black people are "inferior" — and white people "superior" — that they will even violate and mutilate their God-created bodies to try to look "pretty" by white standards.

Look around today, in every small town and big city, from two-bit cat- 24 fish and soda-pop joints into the "integrated" lobby of the Waldorf-Astoria, and you'll see conks on black men. And you'll see black women wearing these green and pink and purple and red and platinum-blonde wigs. They're all more ridiculous than a slapstick comedy. It makes you wonder if the Negro has completely lost his sense of identity, lost touch with himself.

You'll see the conk worn by many, many so-called "upper class" Negroes, 25 and, as much as I hate to say it about them, on all too many Negro entertainers. One of the reasons that I've especially admired some of them, like Lionel Hampton and Sidney Poitier, among others, is that they have kept their natural hair and fought to the top. I admire any Negro man who has never had himself conked, or who has had the sense to get rid of it — as I finally did.

I don't know which kind of self-defacing conk is the greater shame — the 26 one you'll see on the heads of the black so-called "middle class" and "upper class," who ought to know better, or the one you'll see on the heads of the poorest, most downtrodden, ignorant black men. I mean the legal-minimum-wage ghetto-dwelling kind of Negro, as I was when I got my first one. It's generally among these poor fools that you'll see a black kerchief over the man's head, like Aunt Jemima; he's trying to make his conk last longer, between trips to the barbershop. Only for special occasions is this kerchief-protected conk exposed — to show off how "sharp" and "hip" its owner is. The ironic thing is that I have never heard any woman, white or black, express any admiration for a conk. Of course, any white woman with a black man isn't thinking about his hair. But I don't see how on earth a black woman with any race pride could walk down the street with any black man wearing a conk — the emblem of his shame that he is black.

To my own shame, when I say all of this, I'm talking first of all about 27 myself — because you can't show me any Negro who ever conked more faithfully than I did. I'm speaking from personal experience when I say of any black man who conks today, or any white-wigged black woman, that if they gave the brains in their heads just half as much attention as they do their hair, they would be a thousand times better off.

• • •

Comprehension

1. What exactly is a conk? Why does Malcolm X want to get his hair conked? What does the conk symbolize to him at the time he gets it? What does it symbolize at the time he writes about it?
2. List the materials Shorty asks Malcolm X to buy. Is the purpose of each explained? If so, where?
3. Outline the major stages in the procedure Malcolm X describes. Are they presented in chronological order? Which, if any, of the major stages are out of place?

Purpose and Audience

1. Why was this selection written as a process explanation instead of as a set of instructions?
2. This selection has an explicitly stated thesis that makes its purpose clear. What is this thesis?
3. *The Autobiography of Malcolm X* was published in 1964, when many African Americans regularly straightened their hair. Is the thesis of this excerpt from the book still relevant today?
4. Why do you think Malcolm X includes so many references to the pain and discomfort he endured as part of the process?
5. What is the relationship between Malcolm X's personal experience and his universal statement about the process he discusses?

Style and Structure

1. Identify some of the transitional words Malcolm X uses to move from step to step.
2. Only about half of this selection is devoted to the process explanation. Where does the process begin? Where does it end?
3. In paragraphs 22–26, Malcolm X encloses several words in quotation marks, occasionally prefacing them with the phrase *so-called.* What is the effect of these quotation marks?

Vocabulary Projects

1. Define each of the following words as it is used in this selection.

   vowed (22)   mutilate (23)   downtrodden (26)
   self-degradation (23)   slapstick (24)   emblem (26)
   multitude (23)   self-defacing (26)

2. Because this is an informal piece of writing, Malcolm X uses many **colloquialisms** and **slang** terms. Substitute a more formal word for each of the following.

   beat (1)   glop (6)   "sharp" (26)
   pad (4)   real (6)   "hip" (26)

Evaluate the possible impact of your substitutions. Do they improve the essay or weaken it?

Journal Entry

Did you ever engage in behavior that you later came to view as unacceptable as your beliefs changed or as your social consciousness developed? What made you change your attitude toward this behavior?

Writing Workshop

1. Write a process explanation of an unpleasant experience you or someone you know has gone through to conform to someone else's standard of physical beauty (for instance, dieting or getting a tattoo). Include a thesis statement that conveys your disapproval of the process.

2. **Working with Sources.** Rewrite Malcolm X's process explanation as he might have written it when he still considered conking a desirable process, worth all the trouble. Include all his steps, but change his thesis and choose words that make the process sound painless and worthwhile. If you quote Malcolm X's words, be sure to include parenthetical documentation and a works-cited page. (See Chapter 18 for information on MLA documentation.)

3. Rewrite this essay as a set of instructions that Shorty might have written for a friend about to help someone conk his hair. Begin by telling the friend what materials to purchase. Be sure to include all necessary cautions and reminders.

Combining the Patterns

Although "My First Conk" is very detailed, it does not include an extended **definition** of a conk. Do you think a definition paragraph should be added? If so, where could it be inserted? What patterns could be used to develop such a definition?

Thematic Connections

- "Four Tattoos" (page 226)
- "Just Walk On By: A Black Man Ponders His Power to Alter Public Space" (page 240)
- "Medium Ash Brown" (page 275)
- "The Shame Game" (page 680)
- "Inked Well" (page 685)

STANLEY FISH

Getting Coffee Is Hard to Do

Literary critic and legal scholar Stanley Fish (b. 1938) has had a long and distinguished academic career. He is currently Davidson-Kahn Distinguished Professor of Humanities and a professor of law at Florida International University in Miami. An authority on the seventeenth-century poet John Milton, Fish is also widely recognized for his revolutionary approach to literary criticism, as summarized in his groundbreaking book *Is There a Text in This Class?: The Authority of Interpretive Communities* (1980). A regular contributor to popular journals and op-ed pages in newspapers nationwide, Fish has also been a guest columnist for the *New York Times,* where the following essay originally appeared. His most recent book is *The Fugitive in Flight: Faith, Liberalism, and Law in a Classic TV Show* (2010).

Background on U.S. coffee-drinking trends Coffee consumption in the United States goes back to the earliest English settlers. In fact, the British tax imposed on tea that led to the rebellious Boston Tea Party resulted in coffee's becoming the most popular American drink. However, the popularity of gourmet coffees can be traced back to 1966, when Dutch immigrant Alfred Peet, a coffee importer who was unhappy with the general quality of coffee in the United States, opened a shop in Berkeley, California, where he sold his own special roast. Trained in coffee roasting by Peet, the founders of Starbucks opened their first outlet in Seattle in 1971, selling quality coffee beans and coffeemaking equipment. Returning from a buying trip to Italy in 1985, then-marketing director Howard Schultz suggested that Starbucks become a true coffeehouse in the Italian tradition, a gathering spot where people could enjoy freshly roasted and brewed coffee. Despite being met with skepticism, Schultz would eventually take over the business and turn it into a worldwide phenomenon.

A coordination problem (a term of art in economics and management) occurs when you have a task to perform, the task has multiple and shifting components, the time for completion is limited, and your performance is affected by the order and sequence of the actions you take. The trick is to manage it so that the components don't bump into each other in ways that produce confusion, frustration, and inefficiency. 1

You will face a coordination problem if you are a general deploying troops, tanks, helicopters, food, tents, and medical supplies, or if you are the CEO of a large company juggling the demands of design, personnel, inventory, and production. 2

And these days, you will face a coordination problem if you want to get a cup of coffee. 3

It used to be that when you wanted a cup of coffee you went into a nondescript place fitted out largely in linoleum, Formica, and neon, sat 4 down at a counter, and, in response to a brisk "What'll you have, dear?" said, "Coffee and a cheese Danish." Twenty seconds later, tops, they arrived, just as you were settling into the sports page.

Now it's all wood or concrete floors, lots of earth tones, soft, high-style 5 lighting, open barrels of coffee beans, folk-rock and indie music, photographs of urban landscapes, and copies of *The Onion*. As you walk in, everything is saying, "This is very sophisticated, and you'd better be up to it."

It turns out to be hard. First you have to get in line, and you may have 6 one or two people in front of you who are ordering a drink with more parts than an internal combustion engine, something about "double shot," "skinny," "breve," "grande," "au lait," and a lot of other words that never pass my lips. If you are patient and stay in line (no bathroom breaks), you get to put in your order, but then you have to find a place to stand while you wait for it. There is no such place. So you shift your body, first here and then there, trying not to get in the way of those you can't help get in the way of.

Finally, the coffee arrives.   7

But then your real problems begin when you turn, holding your prize, 8 and make your way to where the accessories — things you put in, on, and around your coffee — are to be found. There is a staggering array of them, and the order of their placement seems random in relation to the order of your needs. There is no "right" place to start, so you lunge after one thing and then after another with awkward reaches.

Unfortunately, two or three other people are doing the same thing, and 9 each is doing it in a different sequence. So there is an endless round of "excuse me," "no, excuse me," as if you were in an old Steve Martin routine.

But no amount of politeness and care is enough. After all, there are so 10 many items to reach for — lids, cup jackets, straws, napkins, stirrers, milk, half and half, water, sugar, Splenda, the wastepaper basket, spoons. You and your companions may strive for a ballet of courtesy, but what you end up performing is more like bumper cars. It's just a question of what will happen first — getting what you want or spilling the coffee you are trying to balance in one hand on the guy reaching over you.

I won't even talk about the problem of finding a seat.   11

And two things add to your pain and trouble. First, it costs a lot, $3 12 and up. And worst of all, what you're paying for is the privilege of doing the work that should be done by those who take your money. The coffee shop experience is just one instance of the growing practice of shifting the burden of labor to the consumer — gas stations, grocery and drug stores, bagel shops (why should I put on my own cream cheese?), airline check-ins, parking lots. It's insert this, swipe that, choose credit or debit, enter your PIN, push the red button, error, start again. At least when you go on a "vacation" that involves working on a ranch, the work is something you've chosen. But none of us has chosen to take over the jobs of those we pay to serve us.

Well, it's Sunday morning, and you're probably reading this with a cup 13 of coffee. I hope it was easy to get.

• • •

Comprehension

1. How does Fish describe the traditional process of getting a cup of coffee (4)? What does he see as the main difference between getting a cup of coffee in a diner or coffee shop and getting coffee in today's coffee bars?
2. According to Fish, how do the two kinds of coffee shops differ in terms of their physical setting?
3. List some of the obstacles Fish says customers face in a modern-day coffee bar.
4. Whom, or what, does Fish blame for the situation he describes?
5. Note that Fish does not mention paying for the coffee. Do you think the fact that this step is missing is significant in any way?

Purpose and Audience

1. What purpose do the first two paragraphs of this essay serve? Are they necessary, or could the essay begin with paragraph 3?
2. What is the point of this essay? Is Fish simply trying to explain how difficult it has become to get a cup of coffee (as his title suggests), or does he have a more specific — and perhaps more serious — purpose in mind? (Read paragraph 12 carefully before you answer this question.)
3. In one sentence, state this essay's thesis. Does this thesis statement appear in the essay? If so, where?
4. Do you think Fish is exaggerating the difficulty of getting a cup of coffee? If so, what might be his purpose for doing so?
5. Who is the "you" Fish addresses in this essay?

Style and Structure

1. This essay includes several one-sentence paragraphs. Locate each one, and explain why you think it is so short. Should any of these one-sentence paragraphs be developed further? If so, how? Should any be combined with an adjacent paragraph?
2. List the steps in the process Fish describes. Then, group the steps into stages in the process.
3. Where does Fish include cautions and reminders? Give some examples. Given his audience's likely familiarity with the process he describes, are these tips necessary? If not, why do you think he includes them?
4. This essay is a process explanation. Do you think it would have been more effective if Fish had written it in the form of instructions? Explain.
5. Would you characterize Fish's tone as amused? Annoyed? Puzzled? What is his attitude toward the process he describes?

Vocabulary Projects

1. Define each of the following words as it is used in this selection.

   deploying (2)   nondescript (4)   staggering (8)

2. As Fish illustrates, the world of the coffee bar has its own vocabulary. List and define five words that are part of this specialized vocabulary. (You can define words Fish includes here, or you can make your own list.)

Journal Entry

Do you agree with Fish that the process he describes is a problem? Why or why not?

Writing Workshop

1. **Working with Sources.** Write an essay describing another process that is "hard to do" — specifically, something that is more complicated today than it used to be. For possible topics, see paragraph 12 of Fish's essay. If you like, you may quote the fourth sentence of this essay in your essay — but if you do, be sure to include parenthetical documentation and a works-cited page. (See Chapter 18 for information on MLA documentation.)
2. Write a set of instructions for ordering, eating, and cleaning up after a meal in a fast-food restaurant. Assume your audience has never eaten in a fast-food restaurant before. Use "Getting Fast Food Is Easy to Do" as your essay's title.

Combining the Patterns

Fish includes several other patterns of development in his process essay. Locate examples of **definition, comparison and contrast, description, exemplification**, and **narration**. How do these passages support the process explanation?

Thematic Connections

- "Rice" (page 172)
- "Tortillas" (page 507)
- " 'Take This Internship and Shove It' " (page 583)

JOSHUA PIVEN, DAVID BORGENICHT,
AND JENNIFER WORICK

How to Decorate Your Room
When You're Broke

Joshua Piven and David Borgenicht are the authors of the best-seller *The Worst-Case Scenario Survival Handbook* (1999), which provides expert advice on such dilemmas as "How to Break into a Parked Car" and "How to Escape from a Mountain Lion." The book's success sparked a series that now includes *The Worst-Case Scenario Survival Handbook: Weddings* (2004) and *The Complete Worst-Case Scenario Survival Handbook: Man Skills* (2010). Piven and Borgenicht have collaborated with Jennifer Worick on some books in the series, including *The Worst-Case Scenario Survival Handbook: Dating and Sex* (2001) and *The Worst-Case Scenario Survival Handbook: College* (2004). Worick is also the author of *Nancy Drew's Guide to Life* (2001) and *Backcountry Betty: Roughing It in Style* (2007).

Background on the history of college housing The residential college in America was modeled largely on its English predecessor. Dating back to the thirteenth century, universities like Oxford and Cambridge traditionally placed a high value on the scholarly community: life on campus — especially shared housing — encouraged closely knit ties between faculty and students. Harvard, the first American university (founded in 1636), and other colonial colleges followed suit. These early schools lacked financial resources for elaborate student housing: their dormitories were spare and rustic. Well into the nineteenth century, Harvard students — male only — were still buying, chopping, and hauling their own firewood to heat their dorms. But a more modern American university system emerged following the Civil War. Influenced by the German rather than the English model of higher education, these institutions placed more importance on specialized training, research, and practical knowledge. Newly founded state universities placed less emphasis on residential life — or even disparaged it altogether. "In our country we have ever begun at the wrong end," claimed Henry Phillip Tappan, the first president of the University of Michigan. "We have erected vast dormitories for the night's sleep, instead of creating libraries and laboratories for the day's work." Others worried that this communal living encouraged bad habits, disorderly conduct, and even rebellion. Both views of residential life coexisted as the number of colleges and universities increased and higher education became more democratic and accessible. In the twentieth century, especially after the influx of students on the GI Bill and the introduction of women to campuses, colleges saw even more changes to residential life, such as the introduction of coed residence halls and special housing for ethnic minorities, athletes, foreign-language students, vegetarians, and other groups.

Milk Crate Chair

You will need a square, stackable milk crate; a cloth placemat or your favorite fabric in a similar size; an old magazine; 6 large car-wash sponges; heavy upholstery thread; an upholstery sewing needle; and scissors.

1. **Turn the crate upside down.**

2. **Create the base of the cushion.**
   Place the magazine on top of the bottom of the crate. Use the scissors to trim the magazine pages so that the magazine rests about ¾ inch from the inside edge of the crate.

3. **Arrange 4 sponges on top of the magazine.**
   Lay the sponges next to one another to form the cushion. You may have to use the scissors to trim them to fit squarely to the top of the crate.

4. **Lay the remaining sponges on top of the existing row.**
   Create a second layer of cushion by centering 2 sponges on top of the first layer.

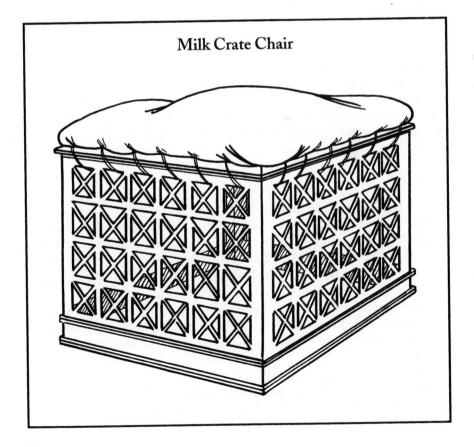

Milk Crate Chair

5. **Anchor the placemat to the crate.**   6
Position the placemat on top of the sponges. Using the needle and thread, secure both shorter sides of the placemat to the crate by hooking a single loop stitch through the edge and around a crate grid square.

6. **Push down on the placemat.**   7
Compress the sponges until the longer sides of the fabric reach the edges of the crate.

7. **Sew the placemat to the crate.**   8
Secure the placemat with a continuous loop stitch around the perimeter of the crate.

8. **Sit.**   9
You can also use the crate as an ottoman or low stool, or stack it on top of another crate for a desk-height chair.

Be Aware

If you're using your own fabric rather than a placemat, lay a strip of mask- 10
ing tape ¼ inch from the edges around the perimeter of the fabric to prevent fraying before securing the fabric to the crate.

T-Shirt Curtains

To accommodate a window of approximately 4 feet × 4 feet, you will need 11
13 of your favorite old T-shirts; 1 spool of thread in any color; 1 to 2 spools of iron-on hem tape; 1 spool of picture-hanging wire; 2 medium-weight eyehole screws; 1 manila folder (or similarly stiff paper); a medium-tipped marking pen; a sharp pair of scissors; and a sewing machine.

1. **Make a stencil.**   12
Cut the manila folder into a rectangle (9 inches × 12 inches) or a square (10 inches × 10 inches) to make a stencil.

2. **Cut the T-shirts into pieces.**   13
Lay a T-shirt on a flat surface for cutting. Put the stencil on the center of the shirt body. Trace the outline of the stencil with the marker on the T-shirt. Lift the stencil off the shirt. With the scissors, cut through both layers of the T-shirt, following the drawn cut-line. Perform this step on all the shirts.

3. **Arrange the pieces to make a curtain.** On the floor or your bed, arrange 14
the pieces next to one another in a pattern you like. Use as many pieces as you need to create a covering a little bit longer and wider than your window.

4. **Disassemble the curtain.**   15
Collect your horizontal rows into piles and set them down next to your sewing machine.

T-Shirt Curtains

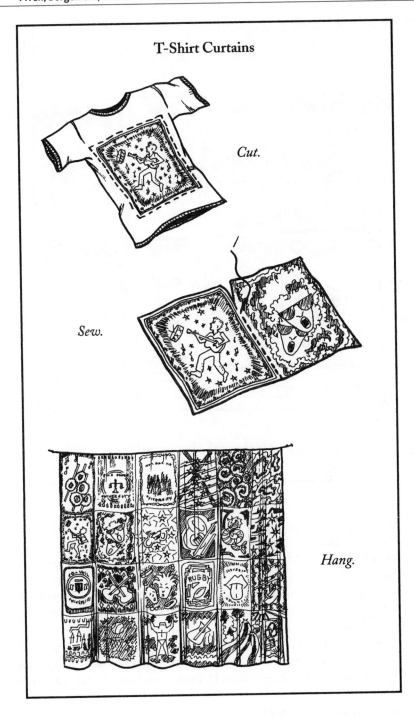

Cut.

Sew.

Hang.

T-Shirt Curtains (Alternate Method)

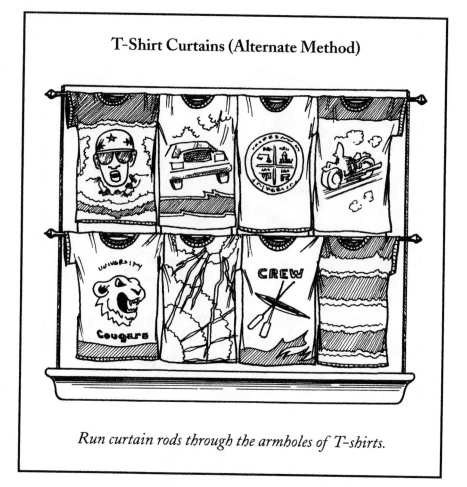

Run curtain rods through the armholes of T-shirts.

5. **Sew the pieces together.**
   Place the front faces of two pieces together and sew, using a medium straight stitch ¼ inch from the edge of the mated pieces.

6. **Connect the rows.**
   Sew front face to front face. Make sure any design on the T-shirt pieces is right-side up.

7. **Finish the edges.**
   Once you have sewn the window covering to the desired size, cut the hem tape to size for the perimeter of the covering. Iron on the hem tape along the sides so the tape wraps around the edge, covering the front and back of the edge.

8. **Prepare the curtain for hanging.**
   Facing the front of your window piece, fold back 2 inches of the top edge to form the place to string the picture-hanging wire through. Secure the

folded portion by sewing ¼ inch along the edge. Cut the wire 1 foot longer than the width of your window opening. Thread the wire through the pipeline you created.

9. **Hang the curtain.**   20
With your hand, screw in the eyehole screws at either edge of your window. Hang the window covering by wrapping 6 inches of excess wire through the eyehole hooks.

Be Aware

If you do not have a sewing machine, hem tape, or a needle and thread, use   21
a stapler or duct tape to secure the T-shirt pieces together.

Alternate Method:

If you would rather keep your T-shirts intact, run a curtain rod straight   22
through the armholes of as many T-shirts as it takes to cover the width of
the window. Repeat this procedure, adding more rows until the window is
covered. Smelly, worn T-shirts can be put on the rods to be aired out, thus
saving you from having to wash them.

Picture Frame

You will need an empty, transparent jewel case from a CD; a photo; and   23
scissors.

1. **Detach the cover of the jewel case at its hinge.**   24

2. **Reattach the cover, wrong-side out.**   25
This will form a wide V shape that can stand up on a flat surface.

3. **Insert your photo on top of the outer half of the case.**   26
Use the scissors to trim the photo to fit. Add colored paper behind the
photo for a more sophisticated look.

4. **Display.**   27

• • •

Comprehension

1. What three decorative items do these instructions focus on? Which is simplest to make? Which is most difficult?

2. About how much time do you think it would take to complete each project?

3. What kind of room do the writers seem to be imagining? For example, how big is it? What is its condition? How is it furnished? How can you tell?

Purpose and Audience

1. What thesis is implied in this set of instructions? Write a sentence that could serve as the thesis statement. Should such a sentence be added to the essay? If so, where?

2. Does this essay seem to be directed at an audience of male students, female students, or both? What other kinds of readers might find this essay useful?

3. In addition to helping to explain how to perform the process, what other purpose do the visuals serve?

4. Do you think the writers actually expect readers to construct the three items they discuss? If not, what other purpose might the writers have in mind?

Style and Structure

1. This selection is neither structured nor formatted like most of the other essays in this text. What does it include that other essays do not? What elements are missing that other essays include? Should any of these missing elements be added?

2. What stylistic features tell you that this is a set of instructions rather than a process explanation?

3. Instructions are directed at people who will actually perform a process. Is that the case here? (Before you answer this question, look carefully at the lists of materials required for the first two projects.)

4. Where do the writers include the cautions and reminders that often characterize instructions? Do you think readers need any additional warnings or reminders?

5. Look carefully at the steps listed in each of the essay's three sections. How do the writers move readers from one step to the next? Would transitional words and expressions be helpful additions? Suggest some transitions that could be added.

6. This essay explains how to make three different items. Do you think the writers need to add sentences or paragraphs to connect the three sets of instructions? Should they rearrange the three discussions to put the simplest process first?

Vocabulary Projects

1. Define each of the following words as it is used in this selection.

upholstery (1)   fraying (10)
ottoman (9)

2. The writers of this straightforward "how-to" selection do not use very descriptive language. If you were a campus tour guide showing prospective students a dorm room, what adjectives would you use to describe the milk crate chair, T-shirt curtains, and picture frame?

Journal Entry

What furnishings and decorative items do you consider essential to your comfort and well-being? Discuss the items that any room you live in must have, and explain why they are essential.

Writing Workshop

1. Write a short speech that presents instructions for decorating a room in a children's hospital, a women's shelter, or a veterans' hospital. Begin your speech by enumerating the particular needs of the people who will use the room, and then present a plan for meeting these needs — for example, interviewing residents, shopping, and decorating.

2. Expand the writers' instructions for creating a picture frame into an essay. Add an introductory paragraph (with a thesis statement) and a conclusion. Expand steps 1–3 into three body paragraphs, adding descriptive detail, cautions and reminders, and transitions to link sentences and paragraphs. Include a visual of the finished product.

3. Write a set of instructions titled "How to Decorate Your Room When Money Is No Object." Your essay will be a step-by-step guide to designing your ideal room, shopping for furnishings and decorative items, and arranging the items in your room. Be sure to include a thesis statement.

Combining the Patterns

Two of the three sets of instructions are illustrated with pictures that show the finished product, but the essay does not provide **descriptions** of what the finished milk crate chair, T-shirt curtains, or picture frame looks like. Should such descriptive passages be added? If so, where?

Thematic Connections

- "The Search" (page 270)
- "College Pressures" (page 450)
- "The Wife-Beater" (page 516)

ARTHUR MILLER

Get It Right: Privatize Executions

One of the leading playwrights of the twentieth century, Arthur Miller (1915–2005) had his first play produced on Broadway in 1944. Though it was not a success, his next Broadway production, *All My Sons* (1947), received positive reviews and the New York Drama Critics' Circle Award. However, it was his 1949 play *Death of a Salesman* that established Miller as a major voice in the American theater: opening to ecstatic reviews, it went on to win the Pulitzer Prize. Another important play, *The Crucible* (1953), was set during the Salem witch trials of the late seventeenth century but was written as an allegory for the persecution of suspected Communists in the 1950s. (Miller himself was called before the House Un-American Activities Committee and convicted of contempt of Congress because he refused to testify.) While his plays from the 1960s on did not achieve the success of his earlier works, Miller's artistic legacy is assured; his moral vision, as evidenced in the following 1992 essay, continues to move readers and playgoers around the world.

Background on public executions Public executions of convicted felons can be traced back at least as far as the ancient civilizations of Greece and Rome and were common in European countries until well into the nineteenth century (public executions were conducted in England, for example, until 1868). Over time, they have been carried out by crucifixion, stoning, burning at the stake, and beheading, among other methods. However, by the 1600s in England and in the American colonies, public executions were most often accomplished by hanging, usually in a public square. These hangings, which were meant to teach spectators a moral lesson, ironically took on a festive, carnival-like air and were considered a form of free entertainment. By the early 1800s, authorities in a number of states began to require that hangings be performed in the privacy of prisons — in part because the crowds witnessing them had become so rowdy and in part because it was felt that public executions could stir sentiments against capital punishment. Still, public executions persisted in some areas of the United States until the twentieth century; the last was performed in 1936 in Owensboro, Kentucky. Today, public executions continue in countries operating under Muslim law and under repressive regimes, such as that of North Korea. In this essay, Miller makes the somewhat radical suggestion that execution be "privatized" — that is, run not by the government but by private companies — and public.

The time has come to consider the privatization of executions. 1

There can no longer be any doubt that government — society itself — is 2 incapable of doing anything right, and this certainly applies to the executions of convicted criminals.

At present, the thing is a total loss, to the convicted person, to his fam- 3
ily, and to society. It need not be so.

People can be executed in places like Shea Stadium before immense 4
paying audiences. The income from the spectacle could be distributed to
the prison that fed and housed him or to a trust fund for prisoner rehabilitation and his own family and/or girlfriend, as he himself chose.

The condemned would of course get a percentage of the gate, to be 5
negotiated by his agent or a promoter, if he so desired.

The take would, without question, be sizable, considering the immense 6
number of Americans in favor of capital punishment. A $200 to $300 ring-
side seat would not be excessive, with bleachers going for, say, $25.

As with all sports events, a certain ritual would seem inevitable and 7
would quickly become an expected part of the occasion. The electric chair
would be set on a platform, like a boxing ring without the rope, around
second base.

Once the audience was seated, a soprano would come forward and 8
sing "The Star-Spangled Banner." When she stepped down, the governor,
holding a microphone, would appear and describe the condemned man's
crimes in detail, plus his many failed appeals.

Then the governor would step aside and a phalanx of police officers or 9
possibly National Guard or Army troops would mount the platform and
surround the condemned. This climactic entrance might be accompanied
by a trumpet fanfare or other musical number by the police or Army band,
unless it was thought to offend good taste.

Next, a minister or priest would appear and offer a benediction, asking 10
God's blessing on the execution.

The condemned, should he desire, could make a short statement and 11
even a plea of innocence. This would only add to the pathos of the occasion
and would of course not be legally binding. He would then be strapped
into the chair.

Finally, the executioner, hooded to protect himself from retaliation, 12
would proceed to the platform. He would walk to a console where, on a
solemn signal from the governor, he would pull the switch.

The condemned man would instantly surge upward against his bind- 13
ings, with smoke emitting from his flesh. This by itself would provide a
most powerful lesson for anyone contemplating murder. For those not
contemplating murder, it would be a reminder of how lucky they are to
have been straight and honest in America.

For the state, this would mean additional income; for the audience, an 14
intense and educational experience — people might, for example, wish to
bring their children.

And for the condemned, it would have its achievement aspect, because 15
he would know that he had not lived his life for nothing.

Some might object that such proceedings are so fundamentally attrac- 16
tive that it is not too much to imagine certain individuals contemplating
murder in order to star in the program. But no solution to any profound
social problem is perfect.

Finally, and perhaps most important, it is entirely possible that after 17 witnessing a few dozen privatized executions, the public might grow tired of the spectacle — just as it seizes on all kinds of entertainment only to lose interest once their repetitiousness becomes too tiresomely apparent.

Then perhaps we might be willing to consider the fact that in execut- 18 ing prisoners we merely add to the number of untimely dead without diminishing the number of murders committed.

At that point, the point of boredom, we might begin asking why it is 19 that Americans commit murder more often than any other people. At the moment, we are not bored enough with executions to ask this question; instead, we are apparently going to demand more and more of them, most probably because we never get to witness any in person.

My proposal would lead us more quickly to boredom and away from 20 our current gratifying excitement — and ultimately perhaps to a wiser use of alternating current.

• • •

Comprehension

1. What process does Miller describe? List the individual steps in this process.

2. Which of Miller's recommendations are most outrageous? Is any part of his scheme actually plausible?

3. In paragraph 6, Miller notes that many Americans support capital punishment. Do you think Miller is one of these people? Why or why not?

4. Why, according to Miller, do executions need to be privatized rather than performed by the government?

5. What specific benefits does Miller say will result from his scheme?

6. In paragraph 20, Miller suggests that his proposal might ultimately lead to "a wiser use of alternating current." What does he mean by "alternating current"?

Purpose and Audience

1. This essay begins with an abrupt statement of a very controversial thesis. Why does Miller choose this approach? How successful is it?

2. What kind of reaction do you think Miller would like to get from his audience? For instance, does he want them to be amused? Shocked? Guilty? Angry? Explain.

3. What is Miller's primary purpose in writing this essay? What do you think he hopes to accomplish?

Style and Structure

1. Because this essay was first published in a newspaper and set in columns, it has relatively short paragraphs. Which paragraphs, if any, could be

combined? Which would you leave as they are? Are there any advantages to using one- or two-sentence paragraphs in this essay?

2. Where does the actual process begin? Where does it end?

3. What words and phrases does Miller use to link the steps in the process? Do you think he needs any additional transitions? If so, where?

4. Much of this essay's tone is ironic, and Miller clearly intends that many of his statements not be taken literally. How do you suppose he expects readers to react to each of the following?

   - "unless it was thought to offend good taste" (9)
   - "he would know that he had not lived his life for nothing" (15)
   - "no solution to any profound social problem is perfect" (16)

5. Miller seems to suggest that executions are not unlike sporting events. How, according to Miller, are they alike? Is this a valid **analogy**?

Vocabulary Projects

1. Define each of the following words as it is used in this selection.

privatization (1)	fanfare (9)
phalanx (9)	pathos (11)
climactic (9)	emitting (13)

2. Miller repeats variations of the word *execution* many times. What alternatives does he have? What different connotations does each of these possible alternatives suggest?

Journal Entry

Many people who support capital punishment see it as a deterrent to crime. Do you think Miller's scheme, if enacted, would be a deterrent?

Writing Workshop

1. Using past tense, rewrite the process section of Miller's essay from the point of view of someone who has just witnessed a public execution. Give the condemned person an identity, a history, and a family, and explain the crime for which he or she is being punished. In your thesis, take a stand on whether or not this person deserves to be executed.

2. **Working with Sources.** Write an email to the editor of a newspaper expressing your strong disapproval of the idea of public executions. Quoting Miller where necessary, use the steps in the process he describes to support your position. To convince readers this practice is inhumane, add descriptive details — for example, information about the observers' reactions and the sensationalist TV news coverage. Be sure to cite Miller as the source of your quoted material and to include a works-cited page. (See Chapter 18 for information on MLA documentation.)

Combining the Patterns

Although the body of this essay is structured as a process, the essay as a whole makes a powerful **argument**. Does Miller have a debatable thesis? Do you think he needs more evidence to support his thesis, or is the process itself enough? Does he consider the possible objections of his audience? Does he refute these objections?

Thematic Connections

- "Shooting an Elephant" (page 133)
- "The Lottery" (page 311)
- "Who Killed Benny Paret?" (page 339)
- "A Modest Proposal" (page 692)

The Embalming of Mr. Jones

Jessica Mitford (1917–1996) was born in Batsford Mansion, England, to a wealthy, aristocratic family. Rebelling against her sheltered upbringing, she became involved in left-wing politics and eventually immigrated to the United States. Mitford wrote two volumes of autobiography — *Daughters and Rebels* (1960), about her eccentric family, and *A Fine Old Conflict* (1976). In the 1950s, she began a career in investigative journalism, which produced the books *The American Way of Death* (1963), about abuses in the funeral business; *Kind and Usual Punishment* (1973), about the U.S. prison system; and *The American Way of Birth* (1992), about the crisis in American obstetrical care.

Background on the funeral industry "The Embalming of Mr. Jones" is excerpted from *The American Way of Death,* a scathing critique of the funeral industry in the United States. The book prompted angry responses from morticians but also led to increased governmental regulation, culminating in a 1984 Federal Trade Commission ruling requiring funeral homes to disclose in writing the prices for all goods and services, as well as certain consumer rights; barring funeral homes from forcing consumers to purchase more than they really want; and forbidding funeral directors from misleading consumers regarding state laws governing the disposal of bodies. Still, industry critics charge that many abuses continue. While funeral services can be purchased for less than a thousand dollars, the standard rate is between two and four thousand dollars — and it can go much higher. The difference in cost is based largely on the price of a casket, and grieving family members are often strongly pressured into buying the most expensive caskets, which may be marked up as much as 500 percent. Advocates for reform suggest that consumers choose cremation over burial (of the approximately 2.5 million people who died in the United States in 2006, only some 800,000 were cremated) and that they hold memorial services in churches or other settings, where costs are much lower than in funeral homes.

Embalming is indeed a most extraordinary procedure, and one must 1 wonder at the docility of Americans who each year pay hundreds of millions of dollars for its perpetuation, blissfully ignorant of what it is all about, what is done, how it is done. Not one in ten thousand has any idea of what actually takes place. Books on the subject are extremely hard to come by. They are not to be found in most libraries or bookshops.

In an era when huge television audiences watch surgical operations in 2 the comfort of their living rooms, when, thanks to the animated cartoon, the geography of the digestive system has become familiar territory even to the nursery school set, in a land where the satisfaction of curiosity about almost all matters is a national pastime, the secrecy surrounding embalming can, surely, hardly be attributed to the inherent gruesomeness of the subject. Custom in this regard has within this century suffered a complete reversal. In the early days of American embalming, when it was performed in the home of the deceased, it was almost mandatory for some relative to stay by the embalmer's side and witness the procedure. Today, family members who might wish to be in attendance would certainly be dissuaded by the funeral director. All others, except apprentices, are excluded by law from the preparation room.

A close look at what does actually take place may explain in large mea-   3
sure the undertaker's intractable reticence concerning a procedure that has become his major *raison d'être.** Is it possible he fears that public information about embalming might lead patrons to wonder if they really want this service? If the funeral men are loath to discuss the subject outside the trade, the reader may, understandably, be equally loath to go on reading at this point. For those who have the stomach for it, let us part the formaldehyde curtain. . . .

> "For those who have the stomach for it, let us part the formaldehyde curtain."

The body is first laid out in the undertaker's morgue — or rather,   4
Mr. Jones is reposing in the preparation room — to be readied to bid the world farewell.

The preparation room in any of the better funeral establishments has   5
the tiled and sterile look of a surgery, and indeed the embalmer-restorative artist who does his chores there is beginning to adopt the term "derma-surgeon" (appropriately corrupted by some mortician-writers as "demi-surgeon") to describe his calling. His equipment, consisting of scalpels, scissors, augers, forceps, clamps, needles, pumps, tubes, bowls, and basin, is crudely imitative of the surgeon's, as is his technique, acquired in a nine- or twelve-month post-high-school course in an embalming school. He is supplied by an advanced chemical industry with a bewildering array of fluids, sprays, pastes, oils, powders, creams, to fix or soften tissue, shrink or distend it as needed, dry it here, restore the moisture there. There are cosmetics, waxes, and paints to fill and cover features, even plaster of Paris to replace entire limbs. There are ingenious aids to prop and stabilize the cadaver: a Vari-Pose Head Rest, the Edwards Arm and Hand Positioner, the Repose Block (to support the shoulders during the embalming), and the Throop Foot Positioner, which resembles an old-fashioned stocks.

Mr. John H. Eckels, president of the Eckels College of Mortuary Science,   6
thus describes the first part of the embalming procedure: "In the hands of a skilled practitioner, this work may be done in a comparatively short time and without mutilating the body other than by slight incision — so slight that it scarcely would cause serious inconvenience if made upon a living

---

* Eds. note — Reason for being (French).

person. It is necessary to remove all the blood, and doing this not only helps in the disinfecting, but removes the principal cause of disfigurements due to discoloration."

Another textbook discusses the all-important time element: "The 7 earlier this is done, the better, for every hour that elapses between death and embalming will add to the problems and complications encountered. . . ." Just how soon should one get going on the embalming? The author tells us, "On the basis of such scanty information made available to this profession through its rudimentary and haphazard system of technical research, we must conclude that the best results are to be obtained if the subject is embalmed before life is completely extinct — that is, before cellular death has occurred. In the average case, this would mean within an hour after somatic death." For those who feel that there is something a little rudimentary, not to say haphazard, about this advice, a comforting thought is offered by another writer. Speaking of fears entertained in early days of premature burial, he points out, "One of the effects of embalming by chemical injection, however, has been to dispel fears of live burial." How true; once the blood is removed, chances of live burial are indeed remote.

To return to Mr. Jones, the blood is drained out through the veins and 8 replaced by embalming fluid pumped in through the arteries. As noted in *The Principles and Practices of Embalming,* "every operator has a favorite injection and drainage point — a fact which becomes a handicap only if he fails or refuses to forsake his favorites when conditions demand it." Typical favorites are the carotid artery, femoral artery, jugular vein, subclavian vein. There are various choices of embalming fluid. If Flextone is used, it will produce a "mild, flexible rigidity. The skin retains a velvety softness, the tissues are rubbery and pliable. Ideal for women and children." It may be blended with B. and G. Products Company's Lyf-Lyk tint, which is guaranteed to reproduce "nature's own skin texture . . . the velvety appearance of living tissue." Suntone comes in three separate tints: Suntan; Special Cosmetic Tint, a pink shade "especially indicated for young female subjects"; and Regular Cosmetic Tint, moderately pink.

About three to six gallons of a dyed and perfumed solution of form- 9 aldehyde, glycerin, borax, phenol, alcohol, and water is soon circulating through Mr. Jones, whose mouth has been sewn together with a "needle directed upward between the upper lip and gum and brought out through the left nostril," with the corners raised slightly "for a more pleasant expression." If he should be buck-toothed, his teeth are cleaned with Bon Ami and coated with colorless nail polish. His eyes, meanwhile, are closed with flesh-tinted eye caps and eye cement.

The next step is to have at Mr. Jones with a thing called a trocar. This 10 is a long, hollow needle attached to a tube. It is jabbed into the abdomen, poked around the entrails and chest cavity, the contents of which are pumped out and replaced with "cavity fluid." This done, and the hole in the abdomen sewed up, Mr. Jones's face is heavily creamed (to protect the skin from burns which may be caused by leakage of the chemicals), and he is covered with a sheet and left unmolested for a while. But not for long — there is more, much more, in store for him. He has been embalmed, but not yet restored, and the best time to start restorative work is eight to ten hours after embalming, when the tissues have become firm and dry.

The object of all this attention to the corpse, it must be remembered, 11 is to make it presentable for viewing in an attitude of healthy repose. "Our customs require the presentation of our dead in the semblance of normality . . . unmarred by the ravages of illness, disease, or mutilation," says Mr. J. Sheridan Mayer in his *Restorative Art*. This is rather a large order since few people die in the full bloom of health, unravaged by illness and unmarked by some disfigurement. The funeral industry is equal to the challenge: "In some cases the gruesome appearance of a mutilated or disease-ridden subject may be quite discouraging. The task of restoration may seem impossible and shake the confidence of the embalmer. This is the time for intestinal fortitude and determination. Once the formative work is begun and affected tissues are cleaned or removed, all doubts of success vanish. It is surprising and gratifying to discover the results which may be obtained."

The embalmer, having allowed an appropriate interval to elapse, re- 12 turns to the attack, but now he brings into play the skill and equipment of sculptor and cosmetician. Is a hand missing? Casting one in plaster of Paris is a simple matter. "For replacement purposes, only a cast of the back of the hand is necessary; this is within the ability of the average operator and is quite adequate." If a lip or two, a nose or an ear should be missing, the embalmer has at hand a variety of restorative waxes with which to model replacements. Pores and skin texture are simulated by stippling with a little brush, and over this cosmetics are laid on. Head off? Decapitation cases are rather routinely handled. Ragged edges are trimmed, and head joined to torso with a series of splints, wires, and sutures. It is a good idea to have a little something at the neck — a scarf or high collar — when time for viewing comes. Swollen mouth? Cut out tissue as needed from inside the lips. If too much is removed, the surface contour can easily be restored by padding with cotton. Swollen necks and cheeks are reduced by removing tissue through vertical incisions made down each side of the neck. "When the deceased is casketed, the pillow will hide the suture incisions. . . . as an extra precaution against leakage, the suture may be painted with liquid sealer."

The opposite condition is more likely to present itself — that of 13 emaciation. His hypodermic syringe now loaded with massage cream, the embalmer seeks out and fills the hollowed and sunken areas by injection. In this procedure the backs of the hands and fingers and the underchin area should not be neglected.

Positioning the lips is a problem that recurrently challenges the in- 14 genuity of the embalmer. Closed too tightly, they tend to give a stern, even disapproving expression. Ideally, embalmers feel, the lips should give the impression of being ever so slightly parted, the upper lip protruding slightly for a more youthful appearance. This takes some engineering, however, as the lips tend to drift apart. Lip drift can sometimes be remedied by pushing one or two straight pins through the inner margin of the lower lip and then inserting them between the two front upper teeth. If Mr. Jones happens to have no teeth, the pins can just as easily be anchored in his Armstrong Face Former and Denture Replacer. Another method to maintain lip closure is to dislocate the lower jaw, which is then held in its new position by a wire run through holes which have been drilled through the upper jaws at the midline. As the French are fond of saying, *il faut souf-frir pour être belle.* *

If Mr. Jones has died of jaundice, the embalming fluid will very likely 15 turn him green. Does this deter the embalmer? Not if he has intestinal fortitude. Masking pastes and cosmetics are heavily laid on, burial garments and casket interiors are color-correlated with particular care, and Jones is displayed beneath rose-colored lights. Friends will say, "How *well* he looks." Death by carbon monoxide, on the other hand, can be rather a good thing from an embalmer's viewpoint: "One advantage is the fact that this type of discoloration is an exaggerated form of a natural pink coloration." This is nice because the healthy glow is already present and needs but little attention.

The patching and filling completed, Mr. Jones is now shaved, washed, 16 and dressed. Cream-based cosmetic, available in pink, flesh, suntan, brunette, and blonde, is applied to his hands and face, his hair is shampooed and combed (and, in the case of Mrs. Jones, set), his hands manicured. For the horny-handed son of toil special care must be taken; cream should be applied to remove ingrained grime, and the nails cleaned. "If he were not in the habit of having them manicured in life, trimming and shaping is advised for better appearance — never questioned by kin."

Jones is now ready for casketing (this is the present participle of the 17 verb "to casket"). In this operation his right shoulder should be depressed slightly "to turn the body a bit to the right and soften the appearance of lying flat on the back." Positioning the hands is a matter of importance, and special rubber positioning blocks may be used. The hands should be cupped slightly for a more lifelike, relaxed appearance. Proper placement of the body requires a delicate sense of balance. It should lie as high as possible in the casket, yet not so high that the lid, when lowered, will hit the nose. On the other hand, we are cautioned, placing the body too low "creates the impression that the body is in a box."

Jones is next wheeled into the appointed slumber room where a few 18 last touches may be added — his favorite pipe placed in his hand or, if

---

* Eds. note — It is necessary to suffer in order to be beautiful.

he was a great reader, a book propped into position. (In the case of little Master Jones a Teddy bear may be clutched.) Here he will hold open house for a few days, visiting hours 10 A.M. to 9 P.M.

• • •

Comprehension

1. How, according to Mitford, has the public's knowledge of embalming changed? How does she explain this change?

2. To what other professionals does Mitford compare the embalmer? Are these analogies flattering or critical? Explain.

3. What are the major stages in the process of embalming and restoration?

Purpose and Audience

1. Mitford's purpose in this essay is to convince her audience of something. What is her thesis?

2. Do you think Mitford expects her audience to agree with her thesis? How can you tell?

3. In one of her books, Mitford refers to herself as a *muckraker*, one who informs the public of misconduct. Does she achieve this status here? Cite specific examples.

4. Mitford's tone in this essay is subjective, even judgmental. What effect does her tone have on you? Does it encourage you to trust her? Should she have presented her facts in a more objective way? Explain.

Style and Structure

1. Identify the stylistic features that distinguish this process explanation from a set of instructions.

2. In this selection, as in many process essays, a list of necessary materials comes before the procedure. What additional details does Mitford include in her list in paragraph 5? How do these additions affect you?

3. Locate Mitford's remarks about the language of embalming. How do her comments about euphemisms, newly coined words, and other aspects of language help to support her thesis?

4. Throughout the essay, Mitford quotes various experts. How does she use their remarks to support her thesis?

5. Give examples of phrases that serve as transitions that link the various stages of Mitford's process.

6. Mitford uses a good deal of sarcasm and biased language in this essay. Identify some examples. Do you think her use of this kind of language strengthens or weakens her essay? Why?

Vocabulary Projects

1. Define each of the following words as it is used in this selection.

perpetuation (1)   rudimentary (7)   stippling (12)
inherent (2)   haphazard (7)   emaciation (13)
mandatory (2)   entertained (7)   recurrently (14)
dissuaded (2)   pliable (8)   jaundice (15)
intractable (3)   repose (11)   toil (16)
reticence (3)   unravaged (11)
loath (3)   fortitude (11)

2. Substitute another word for each of the following.

territory (2)   ingenious (5)   presentable (11)
gruesomeness (2)   jabbed (10)

How does each of your substitutions change Mitford's meaning?

3. Reread paragraphs 5–9 carefully. Then, list all the words in this section of the essay that suggest surgical technique and all the words that suggest cosmetic artistry. What do your lists tell you about Mitford's intent in these paragraphs?

Journal Entry

What are your thoughts about how your religion or culture deals with death and dying? What practices, if any, make you uncomfortable? Why?

Writing Workshop

1. Use the information in this process explanation to help you prepare a two-page set of instructions for undertakers. Unlike Mitford, keep your essay objective.

2. **Working with Sources.** In the role of a funeral director, write a blog post taking issue with Mitford's essay. As you explain the process of embalming, paraphrase or quote two or three of Mitford's statements and argue against them, making sure to identify the source of these quotations. Your objective is to defend the practice of embalming as necessary and practical. Be sure to cite Mitford as your source, and include a works-cited page. (See Chapter 18 for information on MLA documentation.)

3. Write an explanation of a process you personally find disgusting — or delightful. Make your attitude clear in your thesis statement and in your choice of words.

Combining the Patterns

Although Mitford structures this essay as a process, many passages rely heavily on subjective **description**. Where is her focus on descriptive details most obvious? What is her purpose in describing particular individuals and objects as she does? How do these descriptive passages help to support her essay's thesis?

Thematic Connections

- "My First Conk" (page 281)
- "Why Vampires Never Die" (page 361)
- "The Ways We Lie" (page 474)
- "The Case for Mandatory Organ Donation" (page 614)
- "A Modest Proposal" (page 692)

The Lottery (Fiction)

Shirley Jackson (1919–1965) is best known for her subtly macabre stories of horror and suspense, most notably her best-selling novel *The Haunting of Hill House* (1959), which Stephen King has called "one of the greatest horror stories of all time." She also published wryly humorous reflections on her experiences as a wife and mother of four children. Many of her finest stories and novels were not anthologized until after her death.

Background on the initial reaction to "The Lottery" "The Lottery" first appeared in the *New Yorker* in 1948, three years after the end of World War II. Jackson was living somewhat uneasily in the New England college town of Bennington, Vermont, a village very similar to the setting of "The Lottery." She felt herself an outsider there, a sophisticated intellectual in an isolated, closely knit community that was suspicious of strangers. Here, Jackson (whose husband was Jewish) experienced frequent encounters with anti-Semitism. At the time, the full atrocity of Germany's wartime program to exterminate Jews, now called the Holocaust, had led many social critics to contemplate humanity's terrible capacity for evil. Most Americans, however, wished to put the horrors of the war behind them, and many readers reacted with outrage to Jackson's tale of an annual small-town ritual, calling it "nasty," "nauseating," and even "perverted." Others, however, immediately recognized its genius, its power, and its many layers of meaning. This classic tale is now one of the most widely anthologized of all twentieth-century short stories.

The morning of June 27th was clear and sunny, with the fresh warmth 1 of a full-summer day; the flowers were blossoming profusely and the grass was richly green. The people of the village began to gather in the square, between the post office and the bank, around ten o'clock; in some towns there were so many people that the lottery took two days and had to be started on June 26th, but in this village, where there were only about three hundred people, the whole lottery took less than two hours, so it could begin at ten o'clock in the morning and still be through in time to allow the villagers to get home for noon dinner.

The children assembled first, of course. School was recently over for the 2 summer, and the feeling of liberty sat uneasily on most of them; they tended to gather together quietly for a while before they broke into boisterous play, and their talk was still of the classroom and the teacher, of books and reprimands. Bobby Martin had already stuffed his pockets full of stones, and the other boys soon followed his example, selecting the smoothest and roundest stones; Bobby and Harry Jones and Dickie Delacroix — the villagers pronounced his name "Dellacroy" — eventually made a great pile of stones in one corner of the square and guarded it against the raids of the other boys. The girls stood aside, talking among themselves, looking over their shoulders at the boys, and the very small children rolled in the dust or clung to the hands of their older brothers or sisters.

Soon the men began to gather, surveying their own children, speak- 3 ing of planting and rain, tractors and taxes. They stood together, away from the pile of stones in the corner, and their jokes were quiet and they smiled rather than laughed. The women, wearing faded house dresses and sweaters, came shortly after their menfolk. They greeted one another and exchanged bits of gossip as they went to join their husbands. Soon the women, standing by their husbands, began to call to their children, and the children came reluctantly, having to be called four or five times. Bobby Martin ducked under his mother's grasping hand and ran, laughing, back to the pile of stones. His father spoke up sharply, and Bobby came quickly and took his place between his father and his oldest brother.

The lottery was conducted — as were the square dances, the teenage 4 club, the Halloween program — by Mr. Summers, who had time and energy to devote to civic activities. He was a round-faced, jovial man and he ran the coal business, and people were sorry for him, because he had no children and his wife was a scold. When he arrived in the square, carrying the black wooden box, there was a murmur of conversation among the villagers, and he waved and called "Little late today, folks." The postmaster, Mr. Graves, followed him, carrying a three-legged stool, and the stool was put in the center of the square and Mr. Summers set the black box down on it. The villagers kept their distance, leaving a space between themselves and the stool, and when Mr. Summers said, "Some of you fellows want to give me a hand?" there was a hesitation before two men, Mr. Martin and his oldest son, Baxter, came forward to hold the box steady on the stool while Mr. Summers stirred up the papers inside it.

The original paraphernalia for the lottery had been lost long ago, and 5 the black box now resting on the stool had been put into use even before Old Man Warner, the oldest man in town, was born. Mr. Summers spoke frequently to the villagers about making a new box, but no one liked to upset even as much tradition as was represented by the black box. There was a story that the present box had been made with some pieces of the box that had preceded it, the one that had been constructed when the first people settled down to make a village here. Every year, after the lottery, Mr. Summers began talking about a new box, but every year the subject was allowed to fade off without anything's being done. The black box grew shabbier each year; by now it was no longer completely black but splintered badly along one side to show the original wood color, and in some places faded and stained.

Mr. Martin and his oldest son, Baxter, held the black box securely on 6 the stool until Mr. Summers had stirred the papers thoroughly with his hand. Because so much of the ritual had been forgotten or discarded, Mr. Summers had been successful in having slips of paper substituted for the chips of wood that had been used for generations. Chips of wood, Mr. Summers had argued, had been all very well when the village was tiny, but now that the population was more than three hundred and likely to keep on growing, it was necessary to use something that would fit more easily into the black box. The night before the lottery, Mr. Summers and Mr. Graves made up the slips of paper and put them in the box, and it was then taken to the safe of Mr. Summers' coal company and locked up until Mr. Summers was ready to take it to the square the next morning. The rest of the year, the box was put away, sometimes one place, sometimes another; it had spent one year in Mr. Graves' barn and another year underfoot in the post office, and sometimes it was set on a shelf in the Martin grocery and left there.

There was a great deal of fussing to be done before Mr. Summers de- 7 clared the lottery open. There were the lists to make up — of heads of families, heads of households in each family, members of each household in each family. There was the proper swearing-in of Mr. Summers by the postmaster, as the official of the lottery; at one time, some people remembered, there had been a recital of some sort, performed by the official of the lottery, a perfunctory, tuneless chant that had been rattled off duly each year; some people believed that the official of the lottery used to stand just so when he said or sang it, others believed that he was supposed to walk among the people, but years and years ago this part of the ritual had been allowed to lapse. There had been, also, a ritual salute, which the official of the lottery had had to use in addressing each person who came up to draw from the box, but this also had changed with time, until now it was felt necessary only for the official to speak to each person approaching. Mr. Summers was very good at all this; in his clean white shirt and blue jeans, with one hand resting carelessly on the black box, he seemed very proper and important as he talked interminably to Mr. Graves and the Martins.

Just as Mr. Summers finally left off talking and turned to the as- 8 sembled villagers, Mrs. Hutchinson came hurriedly along the path to the square, her sweater thrown over her shoulders, and slid into place in the back of the crowd. "Clean forgot what day it was," she said to Mrs. Delacroix, who stood next to her, and they both laughed softly. "Thought my old man was out back stacking wood," Mrs. Hutchinson went on, "and then I looked out the window and the kids were gone, and then I remembered it was the twenty-seventh and came a-running." She dried her hands on her apron, and Mrs. Delacroix said, "You're in time, though. They're still talking away up there."

Mrs. Hutchinson craned her neck to see through the crowd and 9 found her husband and children standing near the front. She tapped Mrs. Delacroix on the arm as a farewell and began to make her way through the crowd. The people separated good-humoredly to let her through; two or three people said, in voices just loud enough to be heard across the crowd, "Here comes your Missus, Hutchinson," and "Bill, she made it after all." Mrs. Hutchinson reached her husband, and Mr. Summers, who had been waiting, said cheerfully, "Thought we were going to have to get on without you, Tessie." Mrs. Hutchinson said, grinning, "Wouldn't have me leave m'dishes in the sink, now, would you, Joe?" and soft laughter ran through the crowd as the people stirred back into position after Mrs. Hutchinson's arrival.

"Well, now," Mr. Summers said soberly, "guess we better get started, 10 get this over with, so's we can go back to work. Anybody ain't here?"

"Dunbar," several people said. "Dunbar, Dunbar." 11

Mr. Summers consulted his list. "Clyde Dunbar," he said. "That's right. 12 He's broke his leg, hasn't he? Who's drawing for him?"

"Me, I guess," a woman said, and Mr. Summers turned to look at her. 13 "Wife draws for her husband," Mr. Summers said. "Don't you have a grown boy to do it for you, Janey?" Although Mr. Summers and everyone else in the village knew the answer perfectly well, it was the business of the official of the lottery to ask such questions formally. Mr. Summers waited with an expression of polite interest while Mrs. Dunbar answered.

"Horace's not but sixteen yet," Mrs. Dunbar said regretfully. "Guess I 14 gotta fill in for the old man this year."

"Right," Mr. Summers said. He made a note on the list he was holding. 15 Then he asked, "Watson boy drawing this year?"

A tall boy in the crowd raised his hand. "Here," he said. "I'm draw- 16 ing for m'mother and me." He blinked his eyes nervously and ducked his head as several voices in the crowd said things like "Good fellow, Jack," and "Glad to see your mother's got a man to do it."

"Well," Mr. Summers said, "guess that's everyone. Old Man Warner 17 make it?"

"Here," a voice said, and Mr. Summers nodded. 18

A sudden hush fell on the crowd as Mr. Summers cleared his throat and 19 looked at the list. "All ready?" he called. "Now, I'll read the names — heads of families first — and the men come up and take a paper out of the box. Keep the paper folded in your hand without looking at it until everyone has had a turn. Everything clear?"

The people had done it so many times that they only half listened to 20 the directions; most of them were quiet, wetting their lips, not looking around. Then Mr. Summers raised one hand high and said, "Adams." A man disengaged himself from the crowd and came forward. "Hi, Steve," Mr. Summers said, and Mr. Adams said, "Hi, Joe." They grinned at one another humorlessly and nervously. Then Mr. Adams reached into the black box and took out a folded paper. He held it firmly by one corner as he turned and went hastily back to his place in the crowd, where he stood a little apart from his family, not looking down at his hand.

"Allen," Mr. Summers said. "Anderson. . . . Betham." 21

"Seems like there's no time at all between lotteries any more," Mrs. 22 Delacroix said to Mrs. Graves in the back row. "Seems like we got through the last one only last week."

"Time sure goes fast," Mrs. Graves said. 23

"Clark. . . . Delacroix." 24

"There goes my old man," Mrs. Delacroix said. She held her breath 25 while her husband went forward.

"Dunbar," Mr. Summers said, and Mrs. Dunbar went steadily to the 26
box while one of the women said, "Go on, Janey," and another said, "There
she goes."

"We're next," Mrs. Graves said. She watched while Mr. Graves came 27
around from the side of the box, greeted Mr. Summers gravely, and selected
a slip of paper from the box. By now, all through the crowd there were
men holding the small folded papers in their large hands, turning them
over and over nervously. Mrs. Dunbar and her two sons stood together,
Mrs. Dunbar holding the slip of paper.

"Harburt. . . . Hutchinson." 28

"Get up there, Bill," Mrs. Hutchinson said, and the people near her 29
laughed.

"Jones." 30

"They do say," Mr. Adams said to Old Man Warner, who stood next to 31
him, "that over in the north village they're talking of giving up the lottery."

Old Man Warner snorted. "Pack of crazy fools," he said. "Listening to 32
the young folks, nothing's good enough for *them*. Next thing you know,
they'll be wanting to go back to living in caves, nobody work any more,
live *that* way for a while. Used to be a saying about 'Lottery in June, corn be
heavy soon.' First thing you know, we'd all be eating stewed chickweed and
acorns. There's *always* been a lottery," he added petulantly. "Bad enough to
see young Joe Summers up there joking with everybody."

"Some places have already quit lotteries," Mrs. Adams said. 33

"Nothing but trouble in *that*," Old Man Warner said stoutly. "Pack of 34
young fools."

"Martin." And Bobby Martin watched his father go forward. 35
"Overdyke. . . . Percy."

"I wish they'd hurry," Mrs. Dunbar said to her older son. "I wish they'd 36
hurry."

"They're almost through," her son said. 37

"You get ready to run tell Dad," Mrs. Dunbar said. 38

Mr. Summers called his own name and then stepped forward precisely 39
and selected a slip from the box. Then he called, "Warner."

"Seventy-seventh year I been in the lottery," Old Man Warner said as he 40
went through the crowd. "Seventy-seventh time."

"Watson." The tall boy came awkwardly through the crowd. Someone 41
said, "Don't be nervous, Jack," and Mr. Summers said, "Take your time, son."

"Zanini." 42

After that, there was a long pause, a breathless pause, until 43
Mr. Summers, holding his slip of paper in the air, said, "All right fellows."
For a minute, no one moved, and then all the slips of paper were opened.
Suddenly, all the women began to speak at once, saying, "Who is it?,"
"Who's got it?," "Is it the Dunbars?," "Is it the Watsons?" Then the voices
began to say, "It's Hutchinson. It's Bill," "Bill Hutchinson's got it."

"Go tell your father," Mrs. Dunbar said to her older son. 44

People began to look around to see the Hutchinsons. Bill Hutchinson 45
was standing quiet, staring down at the paper in his hand. Suddenly, Tessie

Hutchinson shouted to Mr. Summers, "You didn't give him time enough to take any paper he wanted. I saw you. It wasn't fair!"

"Be a good sport, Tessie," Mrs. Delacroix called, and Mrs. Graves said, 46 "All of us took the same chance."

"Shut up, Tessie," Bill Hutchinson said.   47

"Well, everyone," Mr. Summers said, "That was done pretty fast, and 48 now we've got to be hurrying a little more to get it done in time." He consulted his next list. "Bill," he said, "you draw for the Hutchinson family. You got any other households in the Hutchinsons?"

"There's Don and Eva," Mrs. Hutchinson yelled. "Make *them* take their 49 chance!"

"Daughters draw with their husbands' families, Tessie," Mr. Summers 50 said gently. "You know that as well as anyone else."

"It wasn't *fair*," Tessie said.   51

"I guess not, Joe," Bill Hutchinson said regretfully. "My daughter draws 52 with her husband's family, that's only fair. And I've got no other family except the kids."

"Then, as far as drawing for families is concerned, it's you," Mr. 53 Summers said in explanation, "and as far as drawing for households is concerned, that's you, too. Right?"

"Right," Bill Hutchinson said.   54

"How many kids, Bill?" Mr. Summers asked formally.   55

"Three," Bill Hutchinson said. "There's Bill, Jr., and Nancy, and little 56 Dave. And Tessie and me."

"All right, then," Mr. Summers said. "Harry, you got their tickets back?" 57

Mr. Graves nodded and held up the slips of paper. "Put them in the 58 box, then," Mr. Summers directed. "Take Bill's and put it in."

"I think we ought to start over," Mrs. Hutchinson said, as quietly as she 59 could. "I tell you it wasn't *fair*. You didn't give him time enough to choose. *Every*body saw that."

Mr. Graves had selected the five slips and put them in the box, and he 60 dropped all the papers but those onto the ground, where the breeze caught them and lifted them off.

"Listen, everybody," Mrs. Hutchinson was saying to the people around 61 her.

"Ready, Bill?" Mr. Summers asked, and Bill Hutchinson, with one 62 quick glance around at his wife and children, nodded.

"Remember," Mr. Summers said, "take the slips and keep them folded 63 until each person has taken one. Harry, you help little Dave." Mr. Graves took the hand of the little boy, who came willingly with him up to the box. "Take a paper out of the box, Davy," Mr. Summers said. Davy put his hand into the box and laughed. "Take just *one* paper," Mr. Summers said. "Harry, you hold it for him." Mr. Graves took the child's hand and removed the folded paper from the tight fist and held it while little Dave stood next to him and looked up at him wonderingly.

"Nancy next," Mr. Summers said. Nancy was twelve, and her school 64 friends breathed heavily as she went forward, switching her skirt, and took a slip daintily from the box. "Bill, Jr.," Mr. Summers said, and Billy, his face red and his feet over-large, nearly knocked the box over as he got a paper out. "Tessie," Mr. Summers said. She hesitated for a minute, looking around defiantly, and then set her lips and went up to the box. She snatched a paper out and held it behind her.

"Bill," Mr. Summers said, and Bill Hutchinson reached into the box 65 and felt around, bringing his hand out at last with the slip of paper in it.

The crowd was quiet. A girl whispered, "I hope it's not Nancy," and the 66 sound of the whisper reached the edges of the crowd.

"It's not the way it used to be," Old Man Warner said clearly. "People 67 ain't the way they used to be."

"All right," Mr. Summers said. "Open the papers. Harry, you open little 68 Dave's."

Mr. Graves opened the slip of paper and there was a general sigh 69 through the crowd as he held it up and everyone could see that it was blank. Nancy and Bill, Jr., opened theirs at the same time, and both beamed and laughed, turning around to the crowd and holding their slips of paper above their heads.

"Tessie," Mr. Summers said. There was a pause, and then Mr. Summers 70 looked at Bill Hutchinson, and Bill unfolded his paper and showed it. It was blank.

"It's Tessie," Mr. Summers said, and his voice was hushed. "Show us 71 her paper, Bill."

Bill Hutchinson went over to his wife and forced the slip of paper out 72 of her hand. It had a black spot on it, the black spot Mr. Summers had made the night before with the heavy pencil in the coal-company office. Bill Hutchinson held it up, and there was a stir in the crowd.

"All right, folks," Mr. Summers said. "Let's finish quickly."   73

Although the villagers had forgotten the ritual and lost the original 74 black box, they still remembered to use stones. The pile of stones the boys had made earlier was ready; there were stones on the ground with the blowing scraps of paper that had come out of the box. Mrs. Delacroix selected a stone so large she had to pick it up with both hands and turned to Mrs. Dunbar. "Come on," she said. "Hurry up."

Mrs. Dunbar had small stones in both hands, and she said, gasping for 75 breath, "I can't run at all. You'll have to go ahead and I'll catch up with you."

The children had stones already, and someone gave little Davy 76 Hutchinson a few pebbles.

Tessie Hutchinson was in the center of a cleared space by now, and she 77 held her hands out desperately as the villagers moved in on her. "It isn't fair," she said. A stone hit her on the side of the head.

Old Man Warner was saying, "Come on, come on, everyone." Steve 78 Adams was in the front of the crowd of villagers, with Mrs. Graves beside him.

"It isn't fair, it isn't right," Mrs. Hutchinson screamed, and then they 79 were upon her.

• • •

Reading Literature

1. List the stages in the process of the lottery. Then, identify passages explaining the reasons behind each step. How logical are these explanations?

2. What is the significance of the fact that the process has continued essentially unchanged for so many years? What does this fact suggest about the people in the town?

3. Do you see this story as an explanation of a brutal process carried out in one town, or do you see it as a universal statement about dangerous tendencies in modern society — or in human nature? Explain your reasoning.

Journal Entry

What do you think it would take to stop a process like this lottery? What would have to be done — and who would have to do it?

Thematic Connections

- "Thirty-Eight Who Saw Murder Didn't Call the Police" (page 127)
- "Shooting an Elephant" (page 133)
- "Get It Right: Privatize Executions" (page 298)

Writing Assignments for Process

1. Jessica Mitford describes the process of doing a job. Write an essay summarizing the steps you took in applying for, performing, or quitting a job.
2. Write a set of instructions explaining in objective terms how the lottery Shirley Jackson describes should be conducted. Imagine you are setting these steps down in writing for generations of your fellow townspeople to follow.
3. Write a consumer-oriented article for your school newspaper explaining how to apply for financial aid, a work-study job, or an internship.
4. List the steps in the process you follow when you study for an important exam. Then, interview two friends about how they study, and take notes about their usual routine. Finally, combine the most helpful strategies into a set of instructions aimed at students entering your school.
5. Think of a series of steps in a bureaucratic process, a process you had to go through to accomplish something — getting a driver's license or becoming a U.S. citizen, for instance. Write an essay explaining that process, and include a thesis statement that evaluates the process's efficiency.
6. Imagine you have encountered a visitor from another country (or another planet) who is not familiar with a social ritual you take for granted. Try to outline the steps involved in the ritual you are familiar with — for instance, choosing sides for a game or pledging a fraternity or sorority.
7. Write a process essay explaining how you went about putting together a collection, a scrapbook, a writing portfolio, or an album of some kind. Be sure your essay makes clear why you collected or compiled your materials.
8. Explain how a certain ritual or ceremony is conducted in your religion. Make sure someone of another faith could understand the process, and include a thesis statement that explains why the ritual is important.
9. Think of a process you believe should be modified or discontinued. Formulate a thesis that presents your negative feelings, and then explain the process so that you make your objections clear to your readers.
10. Write an essay explaining a process you experienced but would not recommend to others — for example, getting a tattoo or a body piercing.
11. Give readers instructions for the process of participating in a potentially dangerous but worthwhile physical activity — for example, skydiving, rock climbing, or white-water rafting. Be sure to include all necessary cautions.

Collaborative Activity for Process

Working with three other students, create an illustrated instructional pamphlet to help new students survive four of your college's first "ordeals" — for example, registering for classes, purchasing textbooks, eating in the cafeteria, and moving into a dorm. Before beginning, decide as a group which processes to write about, whether you want your pamphlet to be practical and serious or humorous and irreverent, and what kinds of illustrations it should include. Then, decide who will write about which process — each student should do one — and who will provide the illustrations. When all of you are ready, assemble your individual efforts into a single unified piece of writing.

10

Cause and Effect

What Is Cause and Effect?

Process describes *how* something happens; **cause and effect** analyzes *why* something happens. Cause-and-effect essays examine causes, describe effects, or do both. In the following paragraph, journalist Tom Wicker considers the effects of a technological advance on a village in India.

Cause

Effects

Topic sentence

When a solar-powered water pump was provided for a well in India, the village headman took it over and sold the water, until stopped. The new liquid abundance attracted hordes of unwanted nomads. Village boys who had drawn water in buckets had nothing to do, and some became criminals. The gap between rich and poor widened, since the poor had no land to benefit from irrigation. Finally, village women broke the pump, so they could gather again around the well that had been the center of their social lives. Moral: technological advances have social, cultural, and economic consequences, often unanticipated.

Cause and effect, like narration, links situations and events together in time, with causes preceding effects. But causality involves more than sequence: cause-and-effect analysis explains why something happened — or is happening — and predicts what probably will happen.

Sometimes many different causes can be responsible for one effect. For example, as the following diagram illustrates, many elements may contribute to an individual's decision to leave his or her country of origin for the United States.

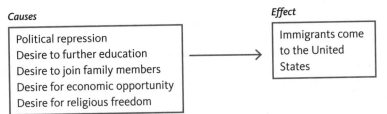

Causes

Political repression
Desire to further education
Desire to join family members
Desire for economic opportunity
Desire for religious freedom

Effect

Immigrants come to the United States

Similarly, a single cause can produce many different effects. Immigration, for instance, has had a variety of effects on the United States.

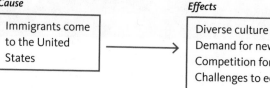

Cause   *Effects*

| Immigrants come to the United States | → | Diverse culture
Demand for new goods and services
Competition for jobs
Challenges to educational system
New political agendas |

Using Cause and Effect

Of course, causal relationships are rarely as neat as the boxes above suggest; in fact, such relationships are often subtle and complex. As you examine situations that seem suited to cause-and-effect analysis, you will discover that most complex situations involve numerous causes and many different effects.

Consider the two examples that follow.

The Case of the Losing Team. Suppose a professional basketball team, recently stocked with the best players money can buy, has had a mediocre season. Because the individual players are talented and were successful under other coaches, fans blame the current coach for the team's losing streak and want him fired. But is the coach alone responsible? Maybe the inability of the players to function well as a team contributed to their poor performance. Perhaps some of the players are suffering from injuries, personal problems, or drug dependency. Or maybe the lack of support among fans has affected the team's morale. Clearly, other elements besides the new coach could have caused the losing streak. (And, of course, the team's losing streak might have any number of consequences, from declining attendance at games to the city's refusal to build a new arena.)

The Case of the Declining SAT Scores. For more than twenty years, from the 1960s to the 1980s, the college-board scores of high school seniors steadily declined, and educators began to look for causes.* The decline began soon after television became popular, and therefore many people concluded that the two events were connected. This idea is plausible

---

* More recently, with 2006 SAT scores showing their biggest decline since 1975 and the average SAT verbal scores falling five points, educators have continued to search for causes, including changes in the test itself and the fact that fewer students are taking the test more than once. (In 2009, average reading and writing scores declined by one point, while average math scores stayed the same.)

because children did seem to be reading less to watch television more, and reading comprehension is one of the chief skills the tests evaluate.

But many other elements might have contributed to the decline of test scores. During the same period, for example, many schools reduced the number of required courses and deemphasized traditional subjects and skills, such as reading. Adults were reading less than they used to, and perhaps they were not encouraging their children to read. Furthermore, during the 1960s and 1970s, many colleges changed their policies and admitted students who previously would not have qualified. These new admission standards encouraged students who would not have taken college boards in earlier years to take the tests. Therefore, the scores may have been lower because they measured the top third of high school seniors rather than the top fifth. In any case, the reason for the lower scores during that twenty-year period remains unclear. Perhaps television was the main cause after all, but nobody knows for sure. In such a case, it is easy — too easy — to claim a cause-and-effect relationship without the evidence to support it.

And just as the drop in scores may have had many causes, television watching may have had many effects. For instance, it may have made those same students better observers and listeners even if they did less well on standardized written tests. It may have encouraged them to have a national or even international outlook instead of a narrower local perspective. In other words, even if watching television did limit young people in some ways, it might also have expanded their horizons in other ways.

Remember, when you write about situations such as those described above, you need to give a balanced analysis. This means that you should try to consider all possible causes and effects, not just the most obvious ones or the first ones you think of.

Understanding Main and Contributory Causes

Even when you have identified several causes of a particular effect, one — the *main cause* — is always more important than the others, the *contributory causes*. Understanding the distinction between the **main** (most important) **cause** and the **contributory** (less important) **causes** is vital for planning a cause-and-effect paper because once you identify the main cause, you can emphasize it in your paper and downplay the other causes. How, then, can you tell which cause is most important? Sometimes the main cause is obvious, but often it is not, as the following example shows.

The Case of the Hartford Roof Collapse. During one winter a number of years ago, an unusually large amount of snow accumulated on the roof of the Civic Center Auditorium in Hartford, Connecticut, and the roof fell in. Newspapers reported that the weight of the snow had caused the collapse, and they were partly right. Other buildings, however, had not been flattened by the snow, so the main cause seemed to lie elsewhere. Insurance investigators eventually determined that the roof design, not the weight of the snow (which was a contributory cause), was the main cause of the collapse.

These cause-and-effect relationships are shown in this diagram:

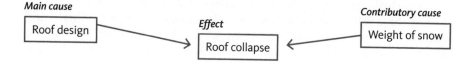

Because the main cause is not always the most obvious one, you should be sure to consider the significance of each cause very carefully as you plan your essay — and to continue to evaluate the importance of each cause as you write and revise.

Understanding Immediate and Remote Causes

Another important distinction is the difference between an immediate cause and a remote cause. An **immediate cause** closely precedes an effect and is therefore relatively easy to recognize. A **remote cause** is less obvious, perhaps because it involves something in the past or far away. Assuming that the most obvious cause is always the most important can be dangerous as well as shortsighted.

Reconsidering the Hartford Roof Collapse. Most people agreed that the snow was the immediate, or most obvious, cause of the roof collapse. But further study by insurance investigators suggested remote causes that were not so apparent. The design of the roof was the most important remote cause of the collapse, but other remote causes were also examined. Perhaps the materials used in the roof's construction were partly to blame. Maybe maintenance crews had not done their jobs properly, or necessary repairs had not been made. If you were the insurance investigator analyzing the causes of this event, you would want to assess all possible contributing factors rather than just the most obvious. If you did not consider the remote as well as the immediate causes, you would reach an oversimplified and perhaps incorrect conclusion.

This diagram shows the cause-and-effect relationships just summarized.

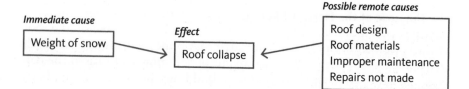

Remember, remote causes can be extremely important. In the roof-collapse situation, as we have seen, a remote cause — the roof design — was actually the main cause of the accident.

Understanding Causal Chains

Sometimes an effect can also be a cause. This is true in a **causal chain**, where A causes B, B causes C, C causes D, and so on, as shown here.

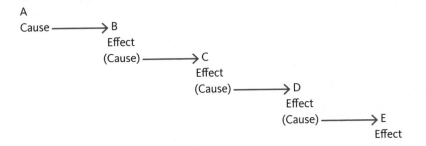

In causal chains, the result of one action is the cause of another. Leaving out any link in the chain, or failing to put any link in its proper order, destroys the logic and continuity of the chain.

A simple example of a causal chain is the recent suggestion by a group of retired generals that global warming might be a threat to U.S. national security. According to these generals, global warming causes worldwide climate changes, such as droughts, which in turn create a refugee crisis as people leave their homelands in search of clean water. The resulting refugee camps, the generals claim, become a breeding ground for terrorists, and it is these terrorists who threaten our nation's security.

Here is another example of a causal chain.

The Case of the Disappearing Bicycle. In the past thirty-five years, the bicycle as a form of transportation for children has become increasingly rare, with fewer than one percent of children now riding bicycles to school. In addition, fewer children ride bicycles for recreation. Causes cited for this decline include the absence of sidewalks in many newer suburban communities, parents' rising fears about crime and traffic accidents, the rise in the number of students who schedule back-to-back after-school activities (perhaps due in part to the increased number of households with both parents working), the growing popularity of social media and video games, and the increased availability of after-school jobs for teenagers (who often need cars, not bikes, to get to work). The decreasing number of children who ride bikes has contributed to a corresponding steady decline, since the 1970s, in the sale of bicycles.

As a result of the decline in bicycle sales, bicycle thefts have decreased sharply, and bicycle deaths involving children under sixteen have also dropped dramatically (although this is due in part to the increased use of helmets). However, the number of American children who are obese has doubled since the mid-1980s — in part because children get less and less exercise. So, factors such as fewer sidewalks and more working teenagers may have led to a decline in bicycle sales, which in turn seems to have had a far-reaching impact on children's health.

If your analysis of a situation reveals a causal chain, this discovery can be useful as you plan your essay. The very operation of a causal chain suggests an organizational pattern for a paper, and following the chain helps you to discuss items in their logical order. Be careful, however, to keep your emphasis on the causal connections and not to lapse into narration.

Avoiding *Post Hoc* Reasoning

When developing a cause-and-effect paper, you should not assume that just because event A *precedes* event B, event A has *caused* event B. This illogical assumption, called *post hoc* **reasoning**, equates a chronological sequence with causality. When you fall into this trap — assuming, for instance, that you failed an exam because a black cat crossed your path the day before — you are mistaking coincidence for causality.

Consider a classic example of *post hoc* reasoning.

The Case of the Magical Maggots. Until the late nineteenth century, many scientists accepted the notion of spontaneous generation — that is, they believed living things could arise directly from nonliving matter. To support their beliefs, they pointed to specific situations. For instance, they observed that maggots, the larvae of the housefly, seemed to arise directly from the decaying flesh of dead animals.

These scientists were confusing sequence with causality, assuming that because the presence of decaying meat preceded the appearance of maggots, the two were connected in a causal relationship. In fact, because the dead animals were exposed to the air, flies were free to lay eggs in the animals' bodies, and these eggs hatched into maggots. Therefore, the living maggots were not a direct result of the presence of nonliving matter. Although these scientists were applying the best technology and scientific theory of their time, hindsight reveals that their conclusions were not valid.

Here is a more recent example of *post hoc* reasoning.

The Case of the Female Centenarians. Several years ago, medical researchers published findings reporting that female centenarians — women who reached the age of one hundred — were four times as likely to have given birth when they were past forty as were women in a control group who died at the age of seventy-three. Researchers saw no causal connection between childbirth after forty and long life, suggesting only that the centenarians might have been predisposed to live longer because they reached menopause later than the other women. Local television newscasts and tabloid newspapers, however, misinterpreted the study's implications, presenting the relationship between late childbearing and long life as a causal one. In a vivid example of *post hoc* reasoning, one promotional spot for a local television newscast proclaimed, "Having kids late in life can help you live longer."

In your writing, as well as in your observations, it is neither logical nor fair to assume that a causal relationship exists unless clear, strong evidence supports the connection. When you revise a cause-and-effect paper, make sure you have not confused words such as *because, therefore,* and *consequently* (words that indicate a causal relationship) with words such as *then, next, subsequently, later,* and *afterward* (words that indicate a chronological relationship). When you use a word like *because,* you are signaling to readers that you are telling *why* something happened; when you use a word like *later,* you are only showing *when* it happened.

The ability to identify and analyze cause-and-effect relationships; to distinguish causes from effects and recognize causal chains; and to distinguish immediate from remote, main from contributory, and logical from illogical causes are all skills that will improve your writing. Understanding the nature of various cause-and-effect relationships will help you decide when and how to use this pattern in a paper.

Planning a Cause-and-Effect Essay

After you have sorted out the cause-and-effect relationships you will write about, you are ready to plan your paper. You have three basic options — to discuss causes, to discuss effects, or to discuss both causes and effects. Often your assignment will suggest which of these options to use. Here are a few likely topics for cause-and-effect treatment.

Focus on finding causes	Discuss the factors that contributed to the declining population of state mental hospitals in the 1960s. (social work paper)
	Identify some possible causes of collective obsessional behavior. (psychology exam)
Focus on describing or predicting effects	Evaluate the probable effects of moving elementary school children from a highly structured classroom to a relatively open classroom. (education paper)
	Discuss the impact of World War I on two of Ernest Hemingway's characters. (literature exam)

Focus on both causes and effects { The 1840s were volatile years in Europe. Choose one social, political, or economic event that occurred during those years, analyze its causes, and briefly note how the event influenced later developments in European history. (history exam)

Developing a Thesis Statement

Of course, a cause-and-effect essay usually does more than just enumerate causes or effects; more often, it presents and supports a particular thesis. For example, an economics paper treating the major effects of the Vietnam War on the U.S. economy could be just a straightforward presentation of factual information — an attempt to inform readers of the war's economic impact. It is more likely, however, that the paper would not just list the war's effects but also indicate their significance. In fact, cause-and-effect analysis often requires you to judge various factors so that you can assess their relative significance.

When you formulate a **thesis statement**, be sure it identifies the relationships among the specific causes or effects you will discuss. This thesis statement should tell your readers three things: the issues you plan to consider, the position you will take, and whether your emphasis is on causes, effects, or both. Your thesis statement may also indicate explicitly or implicitly the cause or effect you consider most important and the order in which you will present your points.

Arranging Causes and Effects

When deciding on the sequence in which you will present causes or effects, you have several options. One option, of course, is chronological order: you can present causes or effects in the order in which they occurred. Another option is to introduce the main cause first and then the contributory causes — or you can do just the opposite. If you want to stress positive consequences, begin by briefly discussing the negative ones; if you plan to emphasize negative results, summarize the less important positive effects first. Still another possibility is to begin by dismissing any events that were *not* causes and then explain what the real causes were. (This method is especially effective if you think your readers are likely to jump to *post hoc* conclusions.) Finally, you can begin with the most obvious causes or effects and move on to more subtle factors — and then to your analysis and conclusion.

Using Transitions

Cause-and-effect essays rely on clear transitions — *the first cause, the second cause; one result, another result* — to distinguish causes from effects and to help move readers through the discussion. In essays that analyze complex causal relationships, transitions are even more important because they can help readers distinguish main from contributory causes (*the most important cause, another cause*) and immediate from remote causes (*the most obvious cause, a less apparent cause*). Transitions are also essential in a causal chain, where they can help readers sort out the sequence (*then, next*) as well as the causal relationships (*because, as a result, for this reason*). A more complete list of transitions appears on page 57.

Structuring a Cause-and-Effect Essay

Finding Causes

Suppose you are planning the social work paper mentioned earlier: "Discuss the factors that contributed to the declining population of state mental hospitals in the 1960s." Your assignment specifies an effect — the declining population of state mental hospitals — and asks you to discuss possible causes, which might include the following:

- An increasing acceptance of mental illness in our society
- Prohibitive costs of in-patient care
- Increasing numbers of mental health professionals, which made it possible to treat patients outside of hospitals

Many health professionals, however, believe that the most important cause was the development and use of psychotropic drugs, such as chlorpromazine (Thorazine), which can alter behavior. To emphasize this cause in your paper, you could formulate the following thesis statement.

Less important causes	Although society's increasing acceptance of the mentally ill, the high cost of in-patient care, and the rise in the number of mental health profession-
Effect	als were all influential in reducing the population of state mental hospitals in the 1960s, the most im-
Most important cause	portant cause of this decline was the development and use of psychotropic drugs.

This thesis statement fully prepares your readers for your essay. It identifies the points you will consider, and it reveals your position — your assessment of the relative significance of the causes you identify. It states the less important causes first and indicates their secondary importance with *although*. In the body of your essay, the less important causes would come first so that the essay could gradually build up to the most convincing material. An informal outline for your paper might look like the one that follows.

SAMPLE OUTLINE: Finding Causes

Introduction:	Thesis statement — Although society's increasing acceptance of the mentally ill, the high cost of in-patient care, and the rise in the number of mental health professionals were all influential in reducing the population of state mental hospitals in the 1960s, the most important cause of this decline was the development and use of psychotropic drugs.
First cause:	Increasing acceptance of the mentally ill
Second cause:	High cost of in-patient care
Third cause:	Rise in the number of mental health professionals
Fourth (and most important) cause:	Development and use of psychotropic drugs
Conclusion:	Restatement of thesis or summary of key points

Describing or Predicting Effects

Suppose you were planning the education paper mentioned earlier: "Evaluate the probable effects of moving elementary school children from a highly structured classroom to a relatively open classroom." Here you would focus on effects rather than on causes. After brainstorming and deciding which specific points to discuss, you might formulate this thesis statement.

Cause	Moving children from a highly structured classroom to a relatively open one is desirable because it is likely to encourage
Effects	more independent play, more flexibility in forming friendship groups, and, ultimately, more creativity.

This thesis statement clearly tells readers the stand you will take and the main points you will consider in your essay. The thesis also clearly indicates that these points are *effects* of the open classroom. After introducing the cause, your essay would treat these three effects in the order they are presented in the thesis statement, building up to the most important point. An informal outline of your paper might look like this.

SAMPLE OUTLINE: Describing or Predicting Effects

Introduction:	Thesis statement — Moving children from a highly structured classroom to a relatively open one is desirable because it is likely to encourage more independent play, more flexibility in forming friendship groups, and, ultimately, more creativity.
First effect:	More independent play
Second effect:	More flexibility in forming friendship groups
Third (and most important) effect:	More creativity
Conclusion:	Restatement of thesis or summary of key points

Revising a Cause-and-Effect Essay

When you revise a cause-and-effect essay, consider the items on the revision checklist on page 68. In addition, pay special attention to the items on the following checklist, which apply specifically to cause-and-effect essays.

> ✔ **REVISION CHECKLIST**   **Cause and Effect**
>
> - Does your assignment call for a discussion of causes, of effects, or of both causes and effects?
> - Does your essay have a clearly stated thesis that indicates whether you will focus on causes, effects, or both?
> - Have you considered all possible causes and all possible effects?
> - Have you distinguished between the main (most important) cause and the contributory (less important) causes?
> - Have you distinguished between immediate and remote causes?
> - Have you identified a causal chain in your reasoning?
> - Have you avoided *post hoc* reasoning?
> - Have you used transitional words and phrases to show how the causes and effects you discuss are related?

Editing a Cause-and-Effect Essay

When you edit your cause-and-effect essay, follow the guidelines on the editing checklists on pages 85, 88, and 90. In addition, focus on the grammar, mechanics, and punctuation issues that are particularly relevant to cause-and-effect essays. Two of these issues — avoiding faulty "the reason is because" constructions and using *affect* and *effect* correctly — are discussed here.

> **GRAMMAR IN CONTEXT**   Avoiding "The reason is because";
> Using *Affect* and *Effect* Correctly

Avoiding "the reason is because" When you discuss causes and effects, you may find yourself using the phrase "the reason is." If you follow this phrase with *because* ("the reason is *because*"), you will create an error.

The word *because* means "for the reason that." Therefore, it is redundant to say "the reason is because" (which literally means "the reason is for the reason that"). You can correct this error by substituting *that* for *because* ("the reason is *that*").

INCORRECT: Lawrence Otis Graham believes that one <u>reason</u> he did not sit with other African-American students in the cafeteria <u>was</u> <u>because</u> he was afraid of losing his white friends (350).

CORRECT: Lawrence Otis Graham believes that one <u>reason</u> he did not sit with other African-American students in the cafeteria <u>was</u> <u>that</u> he was afraid of losing his white friends (350).

Using *Affect* and *Effect* Correctly   When you write a cause-and-effect essay, you will probably use the words *affect* and *effect* quite often. For this reason, it is important that you know the difference between *affect* and *effect*.

• *Affect,* usually a verb, means "to influence."

  Linda M. Hasselstrom believes that carrying a gun has <u>affected</u> her life in a positive way (354).

• *Effect,* usually a noun, means "a result."

  Linda M. Hasselstrom believes that carrying a gun has had a positive <u>effect</u> on her life (354).

NOTE: *Effect* can also be a verb meaning "to bring about" ("She worked hard to <u>effect</u> change in the community").

For more practice in avoiding faulty constructions and commonly confused words, visit the resources for Chapter 10 at **bedfordstmartins.com/patterns**.

✔ EDITING CHECKLIST   **Cause and Effect**

• Have you used verb tenses correctly to distinguish among events that happened earlier, at the same time, and later?
• Have you placed a comma after every dependent clause introduced by *because* ("Because the rally was so crowded, we left early") but not used a comma before a dependent clause introduced by *because* ("We left early because the rally was so crowded")?
• Have you used "the reason is that" (not "the reason is because")?
• Have you used *affect* and *effect* correctly?

A STUDENT WRITER: Cause and Effect

The following midterm exam, written for a history class, analyzes both the causes and the effects of the famine that occurred in Ireland during the 1840s. Notice how the writer, Evelyn Pellicane, concentrates on causes but also discusses briefly the effects of this tragedy, just as the exam question directs.

Question: The 1840s were volatile years in Europe. Choose one social, political, or economic event that occurred during those years, analyze its causes, and briefly note how the event influenced later developments in European history.

The Irish Famine, 1845-1849

Thesis statement   The Irish famine, which brought hardship and tragedy to   1
Ireland during the 1840s, was caused and prolonged by four basic
factors: the failure of the potato crop, the landlord-tenant system,
errors in government policy, and the long-standing prejudice of
the British toward Ireland.

First cause   The immediate cause of the famine was the failure of the   2
potato crop. In 1845, potato disease struck the crop, and potatoes
rotted in the ground. The 1846 crop also failed, and before long
people were eating weeds. The 1847 crop was healthy, but there were
not enough potatoes to go around, and in 1848 the blight struck
again, leading to more and more evictions of tenants by landlords.

Second cause   The tenants' position on the land had never been very secure.   3
Most had no leases and could be turned out by their landlords at
any time. If a tenant owed rent, he was evicted—or, worse, put
in prison, leaving his family to starve. The threat of prison caused
many tenants to leave their land; those who could leave Ireland
did so, sometimes with money provided by their landlords. Some
landlords did try to take care of their tenants, but most did not.
Many were absentee landlords who spent their rent money abroad.

Third cause   Government policy errors, although not an immediate cause   4
of the famine, played an important role in creating an unstable
economy and perpetuating starvation. In 1846, the government
decided not to continue selling corn, as it had during the first year
of the famine, claiming that low-cost purchases of corn by Ireland
had paralyzed British trade by interfering with free enterprise.
Therefore, 1846 saw a starving population, angry demonstrations,
and panic; even those with money were unable to buy food. Still,
the government insisted that if it sent food to Ireland, prices would
rise in the rest of the United Kingdom and that this would be
unfair to hardworking English and Scots. As a result, no food was
sent. Throughout the years of the famine, the British government
aggravated an already grave situation: they did nothing to improve
agricultural operations, to help people adjust to another crop, to
distribute seeds, or to reform the landlord-tenant system that made
the tenants' position so insecure.

Fourth cause   At the root of this poor government policy was the   5
long-standing British prejudice against the Irish. Hostility between
the two countries went back some six hundred years, and the
British were simply not about to inconvenience themselves to save

the Irish. When the Irish so desperately needed grain to replace the damaged potatoes, it was clear that grain had to be imported from England. This meant, however, that the Corn Laws, which had been enacted to keep the price of British corn high by taxing imported grain, had to be repealed. The British were unwilling to repeal the Corn Laws. Even when they did supply cornmeal, they made no attempt to explain to the Irish how to cook this unfamiliar food. Moreover, the British government was determined to make Ireland pay for its own poor, so it forced the collection of taxes. Since many landlords could not collect the tax money, they were forced to evict their tenants. The British government's callous and indifferent treatment of the Irish has been called genocide.

Effects   As a result of this devastating famine, the population of   6
Ireland was reduced from about nine million to about six and one-half million. During the famine years, men roamed the streets looking for work, begging when they found none. Epidemics of "famine fever" and dysentery reduced the population drastically. The most important historical result of the famine, however, was the massive immigration to the United States, Canada, and Great Britain of poor, unskilled people who had to struggle to fit into a skilled economy and who brought with them a deep-seated hatred of the British. (This same hatred remained strong in Ireland itself—so strong that during World War II, Ireland, then independent, remained neutral rather than coming to England's aid.) Irish immigrants faced slums, fever epidemics, joblessness, and hostility—even anti-Catholic and anti-Irish riots—in Boston, New York, London, Glasgow, and Quebec. In Ireland itself, poverty and discontent continued, and by 1848 those emigrating from Ireland included a more highly skilled class of farmers, the ones Ireland needed to recover and to survive.

Conclusion   The Irish famine, one of the great tragedies of the   7
(includes
restatement   nineteenth century, was a natural disaster compounded by the
of thesis)   insensitivity of the British government and the archaic agricultural system of Ireland. Although the deaths that resulted depleted Ireland's resources even more, the men and women who immigrated to other countries permanently enriched those nations.

Points for Special Attention

Structure. This is a relatively long essay; if it were not so clearly organized, it would be difficult to follow. Because the essay was to focus primarily on causes, Evelyn first introduces the effect — the famine itself — and then considers its causes. After she examines the causes, she moves on to the results of the famine, treating the most important result last. In this essay, then, the famine is first treated as an effect and then, toward the end, as a cause. In fact, it is the central link in a causal chain.

Evelyn devotes one paragraph to her introduction and one to each cause; she sums up the famine's results in a separate paragraph and devotes the final paragraph to her conclusion. (Depending on a particular paper's length and complexity, more — or less — than one paragraph may be devoted to each cause or effect.) An informal outline for her paper might look like this:

> The Irish Famine
>
> Introduction (including thesis statement)
>
> First cause: Failure of the potato crop
>
> Second cause: The landlord-tenant system
>
> Third cause: Errors in government policy
>
> Fourth cause: British prejudice
>
> Results of the famine
>
> Conclusion

Because Evelyn saw all the causes as important and interrelated, she did not present them in order of increasing importance. Instead, she begins with the immediate cause of the famine — the failure of the potato crop — and then digs more deeply until she arrives at the most remote cause, British prejudice. The immediate cause is also the main (most important) cause; the other situations had existed before the famine began.

Transitions. Because Evelyn considers a series of relationships as well as an intricate causal chain, the cause-and-effect relationships in this essay are both subtle and complex. Throughout the essay, many words suggest cause-and-effect connections: *brought, caused, leading to, therefore, as a result, so, since,* and the like. These words help readers sort out the causal connections.

Answering an Exam Question. Before planning and writing her answer, Evelyn read the exam question carefully. She saw that it asked for both causes and effects but that its wording directed her to spend more time on causes ("analyze") than on effects ("briefly note"), so she organized her discussion to conform to these directions. In addition, she indicated *explicitly* which were the causes ("government policy . . . played an important role") and which were the effects ("The most important historical result").

Evelyn's purpose was to convey factual information and, in doing so, to demonstrate her understanding of the course material. Rather than waste her limited time choosing a clever opening strategy or making elaborate attempts to engage her audience, she began her essay with a direct statement of her thesis.

Working with Sources. Evelyn was obviously influenced by outside sources; the ideas in the essay are not completely her own. Because this was an exam, however, and because the instructor expected that students would base their essays on class notes and assigned readings, Evelyn was not required to document her sources.

Focus on Revision

Because this essay was written as an exam answer, Evelyn had no time — and no need — to revise it further. If she had been preparing this assignment outside of class, however, she might have done more. For example, she could have added a more arresting opening, such as a brief eyewitness account of the famine's effects. Her conclusion — appropriately brief and straightforward for an exam answer — could also have been developed further, perhaps with the addition of information about the nation's eventual recovery. Finally, adding statistics, quotations by historians, or a brief summary of Irish history before the famine could have further enriched the essay.

PEER EDITING WORKSHEET: Cause and Effect

1. Paraphrase the essay's thesis. Is it explicitly stated? Should it be?

2. Does the essay focus on causes, effects, or both? Does the thesis statement clearly identify this focus? If not, how should the thesis statement be revised?

3. Does the writer consider *all* relevant causes or effects? Are any key causes or effects omitted? Are any irrelevant causes or effects included?

4. Make an informal outline of the essay. What determines the order of the causes or effects? Is this the most effective order? If not, what revisions do you suggest?

5. List the transitional words and phrases used to indicate causal connections. Are any additional transitions needed? If so, where?

6. Does the writer use *post hoc* reasoning? Point out any examples of illogical reasoning.

7. Are more examples or details needed to help readers understand causal connections? If so, where?

8. Do you agree with the writer's conclusions? Why or why not?

9. Has the writer used any "the reason is because" constructions? If so, suggest revisions.

10. Are *affect* and *effect* used correctly? Point out any errors.

All the selections that follow focus on cause-and-effect relationships. Some readings focus on causes, others on effects. The first selection, a visual text, is followed by questions designed to illustrate how cause and effect can operate in visual form.

LOUIS REQUENA

Major League Baseball Brawl (Photo)

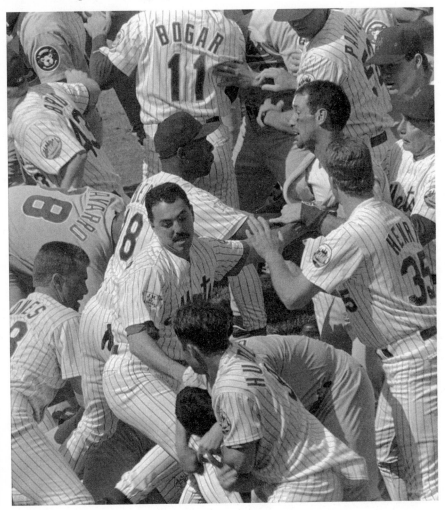

. . .

Reading Images

1. Study the photo above. What might have caused the situation on the field? Consider remote as well as immediate causes.

continued

2. What outcomes might you expect from this fight? Consider the effects on the players on the field, on the players waiting in the dugout, and on the fans in the stands.

3. Consider the fight on the field as part of a causal chain. Diagram that chain of events, using arrows to point from one event to the next.

Journal Entry

Write a paragraph suggesting ways to prevent situations such as the one shown in the picture. For example, would high fines deter players from losing their tempers?

Thematic Connections

- "My Field of Dreams" (page 103)
- "Let Steroids into the Hall of Fame" (page 253)
- "Who Killed Benny Paret?" (page 339)

NORMAN COUSINS

Who Killed Benny Paret?

Norman Cousins (1915–1990) began his career in journalism writing for the *New York Evening Post* and *Current History* magazine. In 1940, Cousins joined the *Saturday Review*, where he served as editor from 1942 to 1978. A noted social critic, Cousins lectured widely on world affairs. An adjunct professor in the department of psychiatry at the UCLA School of Medicine from 1978 until his death, he is particularly remembered for his many books urging a positive outlook to combat illness, including *Anatomy of an Illness* (1979).

Background on the hazards of boxing Cousins's classic 1962 essay "Who Killed Benny Paret?" focuses on a brutal boxing match at Madison Square Garden between Emile Griffith and Benny (Kid) Paret — a fight that led to Paret's death after nine days in a coma. The event, witnessed by millions of shocked television viewers, is the subject of a 2004 documentary, *Ring of Fire*. The fight went twelve rounds and ended with Griffith driving Paret onto the ropes and relentlessly beating him. Some newspapers reported that Griffith was angry because Paret had questioned his manhood, calling him, in Spanish (Paret was Cuban), a *maricón* (a derogatory name for a gay man). In the aftermath of the fight, many demanded that boxing be banned altogether. As a result of Paret's death, a number of rules for professional boxing were changed, but boxing remains an inherently dangerous sport. More than five hundred ring deaths have occurred in the past century; as recently as 2005, a professional boxer died following a knockout in the ring. In addition, many boxers suffer from chronic latent brain damage, known medically as *dementia pugilistica*. In answering the question posed by his essay's title, Cousins takes a strong stand against violence in boxing.

Sometime about 1935 or 1936 I had an interview with Mike Jacobs, the 1 prize-fight promoter. I was a fledgling reporter at that time; my beat was education but during the vacation season I found myself on varied assignments, all the way from ship news to sports reporting. In this way I found myself sitting opposite the most powerful figure in the boxing world.

There was nothing spectacular in Mr. Jacobs' manner or appearance; 2 but when he spoke about prize fights, he was no longer a bland little man but a colossus who sounded the way Napoleon must have sounded when he reviewed a battle. You knew you were listening to Number One. His saying something made it true.

We discussed what to him was the only important element in suc- 3 cessful promoting — how to please the crowd. So far as he was concerned, there was no mystery to it. You put killers in the ring and the people filled your arena. You hire boxing artists — men who are adroit at feinting, parrying, weaving, jabbing, and dancing, but who don't pack dynamite in their fists — and you wind up counting your empty seats. So you searched for the killers and sluggers and maulers — fellows who could hit with the force of a baseball bat.

I asked Mr. Jacobs if he was speaking literally when he said people came 4 out to see the killer.

"They don't come out to see a tea party," he said evenly. "They come 5 out to see the knockout. They come out to see a man hurt. If they think anything else, they're kidding themselves."

Recently, a young man by the name of Benny Paret was killed in the 6 ring. The killing was seen by millions; it was on television. In the twelfth round, he was hit hard in the head several times, went down, was counted out, and never came out of the coma.

The Paret fight produced a flurry of investigations. Governor Rocke- 7 feller was shocked by what happened and appointed a committee to assess the responsibility. The New York State Boxing Commission decided to find out what was wrong. The District Attorney's office expressed its concern. One question that was solemnly studied in all three probes concerned the action of the referee. Did he act in time to stop the fight? Another question had to do with the role of the examining doctors who certified the physical fitness of the fighters before the bout. Still another question involved Mr. Paret's manager; did he rush his boy into the fight without adequate time to recuperate from the previous one?

In short, the investigators looked into every possible cause except the 8 real one. Benny Paret was killed because the human fist delivers enough impact, when directed against the head, to produce a massive hemorrhage in the brain. The human brain is the most delicate and complex mechanism in all creation. It has a lacework of millions of highly fragile nerve connections. Nature attempts to protect this exquisitely intricate machinery by encasing it in a hard shell. Fortunately, the shell is thick enough to withstand a great deal of pounding. Nature, however, can protect a man against everything except man himself. Not every blow to the head will kill a man — but there is always the risk of concussion and damage to the brain. A prize fighter may be able to survive even repeated brain concussions and go on fighting, but the damage to his brain may be permanent.

In any event, it is futile to investigate the referee's role and seek to de- 9 termine whether he should have intervened to stop the fight earlier. That is not where the primary responsibility lies. The primary responsibility lies with the people who pay to see a man hurt. The referee who stops a fight too soon from the crowd's viewpoint can expect to be booed. The crowd wants the knockout; it wants to see a man stretched out on the canvas. This is the supreme moment in boxing. It is nonsense to talk about prize fighting as a test of boxing skills. No crowd was ever brought to its feet scream- ing and cheering at the sight of two men beautifully dodging and weaving out of each other's jabs. The time the crowd comes alive is when a man is hit hard over the heart or the head, when his mouthpiece flies out, when the blood squirts out of his nose or eyes, when he wobbles under the attack and his pursuer continues to smash at him with pole-axe impact.

Don't blame it on the referee. Don't even blame it on the fight manag- 10
ers. Put the blame where it belongs — on the prevailing mores that regard
prize fighting as a perfectly proper enterprise and vehicle of entertainment.
No one doubts that many people enjoy prize fighting and will miss it if it
should be thrown out. And that is precisely the point.

· · ·

Comprehension

1. Why, according to Mike Jacobs, do people come to see a prize fight? Does
   Cousins agree with him?
2. What was the immediate cause of Paret's death? What remote causes did
   the investigators consider? What, according to Cousins, was the main
   cause — that is, where does the "primary responsibility" (9) lie?
3. Why does Cousins believe "it is futile to investigate the referee's role" (9)?
4. Cousins ends his essay with "And that is precisely the point." What is the
   "point" he refers to?

Purpose and Audience

1. This persuasive essay has a strong thesis. What is it?
2. This essay appeared on May 5, 1962, a month after Paret died. What do
   you suppose its impact was on its audience? Do you think the impact on
   readers is the same today?
3. At whom is this essay aimed — boxing enthusiasts, sportswriters, or a general audience? On what do you base your conclusion?
4. Does Cousins expect his audience to agree with his thesis? How does he
   try to win sympathy for his position?

Style and Structure

1. Do you think Cousins includes enough detail to convince readers? Where,
   if anywhere, might more detail be helpful?
2. Explain the complex cause-and-effect relationships discussed in paragraph 9.
3. What strategy does Cousins use in his conclusion? Is it effective? Explain
   your reasoning.

Vocabulary Projects

1. Define each of the following words as it is used in this selection.

promoter (1)	feinting (3)	lacework (8)
fledgling (1)	parrying (3)	encasing (8)
colossus (2)	maulers (3)	intervened (9)

2. The specialized vocabulary of boxing is prominent in this essay, but the facts Cousins presents would apply equally well to any sport in which violence is a potential problem.

    a. Imagine you are writing a similar essay about football, hockey, rugby, or another sport. Think about your audience, and substitute an appropriate equivalent word or phrase for each of the following.

promoter (1)	feinting, parrying, weaving,	knockout (5)
prize fights (2)	jabbing, and dancing (3)	referee (7)
in the ring (3)	killers and sluggers	fighters/fight (7)
boxing artists (3)	and maulers (3)	

    b. Rewrite this sentence so that it suits the sport you have chosen: "The crowd wants the knockout; it wants to see a man stretched out on the canvas. . . . It is nonsense to talk about prize fighting as a test of boxing skills. No crowd was ever brought to its feet screaming and cheering at the sight of two men beautifully dodging and weaving out of each other's jabs" (9).

Journal Entry

Do Cousins's graphic descriptions convince you that boxing should be outlawed? Explain.

Writing Workshop

1. **Working with Sources.** Write a cause-and-effect essay examining how the pressure to excel affects professional athletes. For example, you might examine steroid use in baseball or violence in hockey or football. In your first paragraph, quote Cousins on this issue, citing your source; be sure to include a works-cited page. (See Chapter 18 for information on MLA documentation.)

2. Write a cause-and-effect essay about a time when, in response to peer pressure, you encouraged someone to do something you felt was dishonest or unwise. Be sure to identify what caused your actions.

3. Why do you think a young person might turn to a career in boxing? Write a cause-and-effect essay examining the possible motives.

Combining the Patterns

This essay begins with five paragraphs of **narration** that summarize a meeting between Cousins and Mike Jacobs. What function does this narrative introduction serve in the essay? Once Paret's death is mentioned and the persuasive portion of the essay begins, Cousins never resumes the narrative. Do you think he should have returned to this narrative? If so, where might he have continued the story?

Thematic Connections

- "Thirty-Eight Who Saw Murder Didn't Call the Police" (page 127)
- "Shooting an Elephant" (page 133)
- "Let Steroids into the Hall of Fame" (page 253)
- "Get It Right: Privatize Executions" (page 298)
- "The Lottery" (page 311)

STAN COX

The Case against Air Conditioning

Stan Cox (b. 1955) writes regularly about sustainability, ecology, and agriculture. After earning a Ph.D. from Iowa State University in 1983, he spent thirteen years working for the U.S. Department of Agriculture as a geneticist. He is now a senior scientist at the Land Institute, an agricultural research and policy organization in Salina, Kansas. His essays and opinion columns have appeared in the *Baltimore Sun, San Jose Mercury News, Counterpunch.org, Progressive Populist,* and many other outlets. Cox is the author of *Sick Planet: Corporate Food and Medicine* (2008) and *Losing Our Cool: Uncomfortable Truths about Our Air-Conditioned World (and Finding New Ways to Get through the Summer)* (2010).

Background on air conditioning In the opening pages of Harper Lee's acclaimed 1961 novel *To Kill a Mockingbird,* the narrator says of her childhood in a small southern town, "Somehow, it was hotter then. . . ." She may have been reflecting on the changes brought about by air conditioning. The first modern air conditioner was built in 1903 by Willis Carrier, an engineer who created a device that chilled and dehumidified air by forcing it over coolant-filled coils. For the first decades of the twentieth century, air conditioning mostly served industrial purposes, cooling factories, textile mills, and printing plants. Gradually, the technology spread to hospitals, hotels, and movie theaters. The boom in residential air-conditioning came with the development of smaller units after World War II: by 1953, over a million had been sold. The invention had an enormous demographic effect on the United States: the spread of air conditioning in the 1960s and 1970s made possible the large shifts in people — and businesses — to the American "Sun Belt."

Washington didn't grind to a sweaty halt last week under triple-digit temperatures. People didn't even slow down. Instead, the three-day, 100-plus-degree, record-shattering heat wave prompted Washingtonians to crank up their favorite humidity-reducing, electricity-bill-busting, fluorocarbon-filled appliance: the air conditioner.

This isn't smart. In a country that's among the world's highest greenhouse-gas emitters, air conditioning is one of the worst power-guzzlers. The energy required to air-condition American homes and retail spaces has doubled since the early 1990s. Turning buildings into refrigerators burns fossil fuels, which emits greenhouse gases, which raises global temperatures, which creates a need for — you guessed it — more air-conditioning.

A.C.'s obvious public-health benefits during severe heat waves do not justify its lavish use in everyday life for months on end. Less than half a century ago, America thrived with only the spottiest use of air conditioning. It could again. While central air will always be needed in facilities such as hospitals, archives, and cooling centers for those who are vulnerable to heat, what would an otherwise A.C.-free Washington look like?

> " Less than half a century ago, America thrived with only the spottiest use of air conditioning. It could again. "   4

At Work

In a world without air conditioning, a warmer, more flexible, more relaxed work-place helps make summer a time to slow down again. Three-digit temperatures prompt siestas. Code-orange days mean offices are closed. Shorter summer business hours and month-long clos-ings — common in pre-air-conditioned America — return.

Business suits are out, for both sexes. And with the right to open a 5 window, office employees no longer have to carry sweaters or space heaters to work in the summer. After a long absence, ceiling fans, window fans, and desk fans (and, for that matter, paperweights) take back the American office.

Best of all, Washington's biggest business — government — is trans- 6 formed. In 1978, 50 years after air conditioning was installed in Congress, *New York Times* columnist Russell Baker noted that, pre-A.C., Congress was forced to adjourn to avoid Washington's torturous summers, and "the nation enjoyed a respite from the promulgation of more laws, the depredations of lobbyists, the hatching of new schemes for Federal expansion and, of course, the cost of maintaining a government running at full blast."

Post-A.C., Congress again adjourns for the summer, giving "tea par- 7 tiers" the smaller government they seek. During unseasonably warm spring and fall days, hearings are held under canopies on the Capitol lawn. What better way to foster open government and prompt politicians to focus on climate change?

At Home

Homeowners from Ward 8 to the Palisades* pry open double-hung 8 windows that were painted shut decades ago. In the air-conditioned age, fear of crime was often cited by people reluctant to open their homes to night breezes. In Washington, as in most of the world's warm cities, win-dow grilles (not "bars," please) are now standard.

In renovation and new construction alike, high ceilings, better cross- 9 ventilation, whole-house fans, screened porches, basements, and white "cool roofs" to reflect solar rays become de rigueur. Home utility bills plummet.

---

* Eds. note — *Ward 8 to the Palisades:* Two neighborhoods in Washington, DC.

Families unplug as many heat-generating appliances as possible. For- 10
get clothes dryers — post-A.C. neighborhoods are crisscrossed with clothes-
lines. The hot stove is abandoned for the grill, and dinner is eaten on the
porch.

Around Town

Saying goodbye to A.C. means saying hello to the world. With more 11
people spending more time outdoors — particularly in the late afternoon and evening, when temperatures fall more quickly outside than
they do inside — neighborhoods see a boom in spontaneous summertime
socializing.

Rather than cowering alone in chilly home-entertainment rooms, 12
neighbors get to know one another. Because there are more people outside,
streets in high-crime areas become safer. As a result of all this, a strange
thing happens: Deaths from heat decline. Elderly people no longer die
alone inside sweltering apartments, too afraid to venture outside for help
and too isolated to be noticed. Instead, people look out for one another
during heat waves, checking in on their most vulnerable neighbors.

Children — and others — take to bikes and scooters, because of the 13
cooling effect of air movement. Calls for more summer school and even
year-round school cease. Our kids don't need more time inside, everyone
agrees; they need the shady playgrounds and water sprinklers that spring
up in every neighborhood.

"Green roofs" of grass, ivy, and even food crops sprout on the flat tops 14
of government and commercial buildings around the city, including the
White House. These layers of soil and vegetation (on top of a crucially leak-
proof surface) insulate interiors from the pounding sun, while water from
the plants' leaves provides evaporative cooling. More trees than ever appear
in both private and public spaces.

And the Mall is reborn as the National Grove.   15

• • •

Comprehension

1. What does Cox think is wrong with air conditioning?

2. According to Cox, what would be the results of a largely "A.C.-free
   Washington" (3)? Does the scenario he outlines apply only to Washington,
   DC? Only to urban areas? Does it apply to other parts of the country as
   well?

3. Beginning in paragraph 4, Cox discusses the positive effects of reducing
   the use of air conditioning. What negative effects does he ignore?

4. Aside from "hospitals, archives, and cooling centers for those who are vulnerable to heat" (3), what other facilities and groups do you think need
   air conditioning?

5. What does Cox mean in paragraph 5 when he says that the end of air-conditioning will bring paperweights back to American offices?

Purpose and Audience

1. When Cox's article was published, during a record-breaking national heat wave, he received more than sixty pages of angry emails, including at least one death threat. Why do you suppose his essay generated such strong reactions?

2. What specific event or situation prompted Cox to write this essay? What other, less immediate causes might have inspired him?

3. Cox states his thesis in the first sentence of paragraph 3: "A.C.'s obvious public-health benefits during severe heat waves do not justify its lavish use in everyday life for months on end." Do you agree? How does his use of the word *lavish* reveal his bias? Does this word weaken his thesis?

4. In paragraph 6, Cox quotes Russell Baker. What does this quotation add to his essay?

5. Do you think Cox is really trying to persuade readers to live in a world without air conditioning, or do you think he has some other, less extreme purpose in mind?

Style and Structure

1. Does this essay focus on causes or on effects? What specific words does Cox use to indicate this focus?

2. In his discussion of a future air-conditioning-free environment, Cox uses present tense (for example, "Three-digit temperatures *prompt* siestas," paragraph 4). Why? What other tense could he have used? Do you think he made the right choice?

3. Paragraph 12 describes a **causal chain**. Diagram this causal chain. What other causal chains can you identify in this essay?

4. Evaluate the effectiveness of Cox's one-sentence conclusion. Does it make sense to close the essay this way? Is it consistent in tone and content with the discussion that precedes it?

Vocabulary Projects

1. Define each of the following words as it is used in this selection.

   lavish (3)   de rigueur (9)
   depredations (6)   plummet (9)

2. Cox uses many hyphenated compounds as adjectives to modify nouns — for example, "month-long closings" (4). Identify these compounds, and then identify the nouns they modify. Try to substitute single-word adjectives for these compound modifiers.

Journal Entry

Do you think Cox is overly optimistic about the "good old days" before air conditioning was widely available? Explain.

Writing Workshop

1. **Working with Sources.** Cox's essay focuses on the positive effects of drastically reducing the use of air conditioning. Write an essay in which you make a case for the continued high use of air conditioning, pointing out the *negative* effects of the adjustments Cox describes. Be sure to document your references to Cox's essay and to include a works-cited page. (See Chapter 18 for information on MLA documentation.)

2. Write an essay called "The Case against Air Conditioning on Campus." In your essay, describe the positive effects of reducing or eliminating air conditioning in your school's classrooms, library, residence halls, labs, and so on.

3. Imagine you have just moved to your first air-conditioned residence after years of suffering without it. Write an essay explaining how air conditioning has changed your life.

Combining the Patterns

Cox's essay is an **argument**. Does he identify and refute opposing arguments here? Should he do so? He supports the thesis of his argument with **exemplification**. Does he include enough examples? Are all his examples relevant?

Thematic Connections

- "My Mother Never Worked" (page 121)
- "Once More to the Lake" (page 194)
- "Environmentalism as Religion" (page 399)

LAWRENCE OTIS GRAHAM

The "Black Table" Is Still There

Lawrence Otis Graham was born in 1962 into one of the few African-American families then living in an upper-middle-class community in Westchester County, near New York City. A graduate of Princeton University and Harvard Law School, Graham works as a corporate attorney in Manhattan and teaches at Fordham University. He is the author of some dozen books, most recently *Our Kind of People: Inside America's Black Upper Class* (1999) and *The Senator and the Socialite: The True Story of America's First Black Dynasty* (2007). The following essay, originally published in the *New York Times* in 1991, is included in Graham's 1995 essay collection, *Member of the Club: Reflections on Life in a Racially Polarized World*.

Background on school segregation In "The 'Black Table' Is Still There," Graham returns to his largely white junior high school and discovers to his dismay how little has changed since the 1970s. Since the 1950s, the United States government has strongly supported integration of public schools. For example, the Supreme Court in 1954 found segregation of public schools unconstitutional; the Civil Rights Act of 1964 required public school systems to implement integration programs; and in 1971, the Supreme Court upheld court-ordered busing as a means of achieving integration. The results of these policies were dramatic. From the mid-1960s to 1972, the number of African-American students attending desegregated schools jumped from 12 percent to 44 percent. By the 1990s, however, this had begun to change as the Supreme Court began to lift desegregation orders in response to local school boards' promises to desegregate voluntarily through magnet schools and the like. A study published in 2003 showed that two-thirds of African-American students attend schools that are predominantly minority and more than 15 percent attend schools that are 99 to 100 percent minority, a significant rise since 1989. Ironically, as Graham observes, when students are given the choice, self-segregation seems to be the norm.

During a recent visit to my old junior high school in Westchester 1 County, I came upon something that I never expected to see again, something that was a source of fear and dread for three hours each school morning of my early adolescence: the all-black lunch table in the cafeteria of my predominantly white suburban junior high school.

As I look back on twenty-seven years of often being the first and only 2 black person integrating such activities and institutions as the college newspaper, the high school tennis team, summer music camps, our all-white suburban neighborhood, my eating club at Princeton, or my private social club at Harvard Law School, the one scenario that puzzled me the most then and now is the all-black lunch table.

Why was it there? Why did the black kids separate themselves? What did the table say about the integration that was supposedly going on in homerooms and gym classes? What did it say about the black kids? The white kids? What did it say about me when I refused to sit there, day after day, for three years? 3

Each afternoon, at 12:03 P.M., after the fourth period ended, I found myself among six hundred 12-, 13-, and 14-year-olds who marched into the brightly-lit cafeteria and dashed for a seat at one of the twenty-seven blue formica lunch tables. 4

No matter who I walked in with — usually a white friend — no matter what mood I was in, there was one thing that was certain: I would not sit at the black table. 5

I would never consider sitting at the black table. 6

What was wrong with me? What was I afraid of? 7

I would like to think that my decision was a heroic one, made in order to express my solidarity with the theories of integration that my community was espousing. But I was just twelve at the time, and there was nothing heroic in my actions. 8

I avoided the black table for a very simple reason: I was afraid that by sitting at the black table I'd lose all my white friends. I thought that by sitting there I'd be making a racist, anti-white statement. 9

Is that what the all-black table means? Is it a rejection of white people? I no longer think so. 10

At the time, I was angry that there was a black lunch table. I believed that the black kids were the reason why other kids didn't mix more. I was ready to believe that their self-segregation was the cause of white bigotry. 11

Ironically, I even believed this after my best friend (who was white) told me I probably shouldn't come to his bar mitzvah because I'd be the only black and people would feel uncomfortable. I even believed this after my Saturday afternoon visit, at age ten, to a private country club pool prompted incensed white parents to pull their kids from the pool in terror. 12

In the face of this blatantly racist (anti-black) behavior I still somehow managed to blame only the black kids for being the barrier to integration in my school and my little world. What was I thinking? 13

I realize now how wrong I was. During that same time, there were at least two tables of athletes, an Italian table, a Jewish girls' table, a Jewish boys' table (where I usually sat), a table of kids who were into heavy metal music and smoking pot, a table of middle-class Irish kids. Weren't these tables just as segregationist as the black table? At the time, no one thought so. At the time, no one even acknowledged the segregated nature of these other tables. 14

Maybe it's the color difference that makes all-black tables or all-black groups attract the scrutiny and wrath of so many people. It scares and angers people; it exasperates. It did those things to me, and I'm black. 15

As an integrating black person, I know that my decision *not* to join the black lunch table attracted its own kinds of scrutiny and wrath from my classmates. At the same time that I heard angry words like "Oreo" and 16 "white boy" being hurled at me from the black table, I was also dodging impatient questions from white classmates: "Why do all those black kids sit together?" or "Why don't you ever sit with the other blacks?"

The black lunch table, like those other segregated tables, is a comment 17 on the superficial inroads that integration has made in society. Perhaps I should be happy that even this is a long way from where we started. Yet, I can't get over the fact that the twenty-seventh table in my junior high school cafeteria is still known as the "black table" — fourteen years after my adolescence.

· · ·

Comprehension

1. What exactly is the "black table"?

2. In paragraph 1, Graham says that on a recent visit to his old junior high school he "came upon something that [he] never expected to see again." Why do you think the sight of the all-black lunch table was such a surprise to him?

3. In Graham's junior high school, what factors determined where students sat?

4. Why didn't Graham sit at the "black table" when he was in junior high?

5. When he was a junior high school student, whom did Graham blame for the existence of the exclusively black lunch table? Whom or what does he now see as the cause of the table's existence?

Purpose and Audience

1. What is Graham's thesis?

2. Rather than introducing outside supporting information — such as statistics, interviews with educators, or sociological studies — Graham relies on his own opinions and on anecdotal evidence to support his thesis. Do you think this is enough? Explain your reasoning.

3. Why does Graham give background information about himself in this essay — for example, in paragraphs 2 and 12? How does this information affect your reaction to him as a person? Your reaction to his essay? Do you think he needs to supply additional information about himself or about his junior high school? If so, what kind of information would be helpful?

4. Do you think Graham's primary purpose here is to criticize a system he despises, to change his audience's views about segregated lunch tables, or to justify his own behavior? Explain your conclusion.

5. In paragraph 5, Graham tells readers that he usually entered the cafeteria with a white friend; in paragraph 12, he reveals that his best friend was white. Why do you suppose he wants his audience to know these facts?

Style and Structure

1. Throughout his essay, Graham asks **rhetorical questions**. Identify as many of these questions as you can. Are they necessary? Provocative? Distracting? Explain.

2. In paragraph 16, Graham quotes his long-ago classmates. What do these quotations reveal? Should he have included more of them?

3. Is Graham's focus on finding causes, describing effects, or both? Explain.

4. This essay uses first-person pronouns and contractions. Do you think Graham would have more credibility if he used a less personal and more formal style?

Vocabulary Projects

1. Define each of the following words as it is used in this selection.

   scenario (2)   incensed (12)   scrutiny (15)
   espousing (8)   blatantly (13)   inroads (17)

2. Does the phrase *black table* have a negative connotation for you? Do you think Graham intends it to? What other names could he give to the table that might present it in a more neutral, even positive, light? What names could he give to the other tables he lists in paragraph 14?

Journal Entry

Graham sees the continued presence of the "black table" as a serious problem. Do you agree?

Writing Workshop

1. **Working with Sources.** In paragraph 14, Graham mentions other lunch tables that were limited to certain groups and asks, "Weren't these tables just as segregationist as the black table?" Answer his question in a cause-and-effect essay explaining why you believe "black tables" still exist. In your introduction, quote Graham's question, and be sure to include parenthetical documentation and a works-cited page. (See Chapter 18 for information on MLA documentation.)

2. In addition to self-segregated lunch tables, many colleges also have single-race social clubs, dormitories, fraternities, and even graduation ceremonies. Do you see such self-segregation as something that divides our society (that is, as a cause) or as something that reflects divisions that already exist (that is, as an effect)? Write an essay discussing this issue, supporting your thesis with examples from your own experience.

3. Do the people at your school or workplace tend to segregate themselves according to race, gender, or some other principle? Do you see a problem in such behavior? Write an email to your school's dean of students or to

your employer explaining what you believe causes this pattern and what effects, positive or negative, you have observed.

Combining the Patterns

In paragraph 14, Graham uses **classification and division**. What is he categorizing? What categories does he identify? What other categories might he include? Why is this pattern of development particularly appropriate for this essay?

Thematic Connections

- "Indian Education" (page 142)
- "The Myth of the Latin Woman: I Just Met a Girl Named Maria" (page 232)
- "Just Walk On By: A Black Man Ponders His Power to Alter Public Space" (page 240)
- "College Pressures" (page 450)

LINDA M. HASSELSTROM

A Peaceful Woman Explains Why She Carries a Gun

Linda M. Hasselstrom (b. 1943) grew up in rural South Dakota in a cattle ranching family. After receiving a master's degree in journalism from the University of Missouri, she returned to South Dakota to run her own ranch and now divides her time between South Dakota and Cheyenne, Wyoming. A highly respected poet, essayist, and writing teacher, she often focuses on everyday life in the American West in her work. Her publications include the poetry collections *Caught by One Wing* (1984), *Roadkill* (1987), and *Dakota Bones* (1991); the essay collection *Land Circle* (1991); and several books about ranching, including *Feels Like Far: A Rancher's Life on the Great Plains* (1999) and *Between Grass and Sky: Where I Live and Work* (2002). Her most recent book is *No Place Like Home: Notes from a Western Life* (2010). In this essay from *Land Circle*, Hasselstrom explains her reluctant decision to become licensed to carry a concealed handgun.

Background on incidences of sexual assault Hasselstrom's gun ownership can certainly be considered in the context of the ongoing debate over how (and even whether) stricter gun safety measures should be enacted in the United States. In 2008, the Supreme Court overturned a thirty-two-year ban on handguns in Washington, DC, concluding that the ban violated individuals' right to keep and bear arms. In a ruling in 2010, it extended Second Amendment protection to every jurisdiction in the nation. Equally important, however, is the fact that Hasselstrom's reason for carrying a gun is to protect herself from sexual assault. According to the 2008 National Crime Victimization survey, more than 200,000 women reported being sexually assaulted in this country in that year. It is estimated that only one in six instances of sexual assault is actually reported to the police, so the number of such attacks is, in reality, much higher. A 2009 study conducted by the National Shooting Sports Foundation found that gun purchases by women were increasing and that 80 percent of the female gun buyers who responded to the survey had purchased a gun for self-defense.

I am a peace-loving woman. But several events in the past ten years 1 have convinced me I'm safer when I carry a pistol. This was a personal decision, but because handgun possession is a controversial subject, perhaps my reasoning will interest others.

I live in western South Dakota on a ranch twenty-five miles from the 2 nearest town: for several years I spent winters alone here. As a freelance writer, I travel alone a lot — more than 100,000 miles by car in the last four years. With women freer than ever before to travel alone, the odds of our encountering trouble seem to have risen. Distances are great, roads are deserted, and the terrain is often too exposed to offer hiding places.

A woman who travels alone is advised, usually by men, to protect her- 3 self by avoiding bars and other "dangerous situations," by approaching her car like an Indian scout, by locking doors and windows. But these precautions aren't always enough. I spent years following them and still found myself in dangerous situations. I began to resent the idea that just because I am female, I have to be extra careful.

A few years ago, with another woman, I camped for several weeks in 4 the West. We discussed self-defense, but neither of us had taken a course in it. She was against firearms, and local police told us Mace was illegal. So we armed ourselves with spray cans of deodorant tucked into our sleeping bags. We never used our improvised Mace because we were lucky enough to camp beside people who came to our aid when men harassed us. But on one occasion we visited a national park where our assigned space was less than fifteen feet from other campers. When we returned from a walk, we found our closest neighbors were two young men. As we gathered our cooking gear, they drank beer and loudly discussed what they would do to us after dark. Nearby campers, even families, ignored them: rangers strolled past, unconcerned. When we asked the rangers point-blank if they would protect us, one of them patted my shoulder and said, "Don't worry, girls. They're just kidding." At dusk we drove out of the park and hid our camp in the woods a few miles away. The illegal spot was lovely, but our enjoyment of that park was ruined. I returned from the trip determined to reconsider the options available for protecting myself.

At that time, I lived alone on the ranch and taught night classes in 5 town. Along a city street I often traveled, a woman had a flat tire, called for help on her CB radio, and got a rapist who left her beaten. She was afraid to call for help again and stayed in her car until morning. For that reason, as well as because CBs work best along line-of-sight, which wouldn't help much in the rolling hills where I live, I ruled out a CB.

As I drove home one night, a car followed me. It passed me on a narrow 6 bridge while a passenger flashed a blinding spotlight in my face. I braked sharply. The car stopped, angled across the bridge, and four men jumped out. I realized the locked doors were useless if they broke the windows of my pickup. I started forward, hoping to knock their car aside so I could pass. Just then another car appeared, and the men hastily got back in their car. They continued to follow me, passing and repassing. I dared not go home because no one else was there. I passed no lighted houses. Finally they pulled over to the roadside, and I decided to use their tactic: fear. Speeding, the pickup horn blaring, I swerved as close to them as I dared as I roared past. It worked: they turned off the highway. But I was frightened and angry. Even in my vehicle I was too vulnerable.

Other incidents occurred over the years. One day I glanced out at a 7 field below my house and saw a man with a shotgun walking toward a pond full of ducks. I drove down and explained that the land was posted. I politely asked him to leave. He stared at me, and the muzzle of the shotgun began to rise. In a moment of utter clarity I realized that I was alone on the ranch, and that he could shoot me and simply drive away. The moment passed: the man left.

One night, I returned home from teaching a class to find deep tire ruts 8
in the wet ground of my yard, garbage in the driveway, and a large gas tank empty. A light shone in the house: I couldn't remember leaving it on. I was too embarrassed to drive to a neighboring ranch and wake someone up. An hour of cautious exploration convinced me the house was safe, but once inside, with the doors locked, I was still afraid. I kept thinking of how vulnerable I felt, prowling around my own house in the dark.

My first positive step was to take a kung fu class, which teaches eva- 9
sive or protective action when someone enters your space without permission. I learned to move confidently, scanning for possible attackers. I learned how to assess danger and techniques for avoiding it without combat.

I also learned that one must practice several hours every day to be good 10
at kung fu. By that time I had married George: when I practiced with him, I learned how *close* you must be to your attacker to use martial arts, and decided a 120-pound woman dare not let a six-foot, 220-pound attacker get that close unless she is very, very good at self-defense. I have since read articles by several women who were extremely well trained in the martial arts, but were raped and beaten anyway.

I thought back over the times in my life when I had been attacked or 11
threatened and tried to be realistic about my own behavior, searching for anything that had allowed me to become a victim. Overall, I was convinced that I had not been at fault. I don't believe myself to be either paranoid or a risk-taker, but I wanted more protection.

With some reluctance I decided to try carrying a pistol. George had al- 12
ways carried one, despite his size and his training in martial arts. I practiced shooting until I was sure I could hit an attacker who moved close enough to endanger me. Then I bought a license from the county sheriff, making it legal for me to carry the gun concealed.

But I was not yet ready to defend myself. George taught me that the 13
most important preparation was mental: convincing myself I could actually *shoot a person.* Few of us wish to hurt or kill another human being. But there is no point in having a gun — in fact, gun possession might increase your danger — unless you know you can use it. I got in the habit of rehearsing, as I drove or walked, the precise conditions that would be required before I would shoot someone.

People who have not grown up with the idea that they are capable of 14
protecting themselves — in other words, most women — might have to work hard to convince themselves of their ability, and of the necessity. Handgun ownership need not turn us into gunslingers, but it can be part of believing in, and relying on, *ourselves* for protection.

To be useful, a pistol has to be available. In my car, it's within instant 15
reach. When I enter a deserted rest stop at night, it's in my purse, with my hand on the grip. When I walk from a dark parking lot into a motel, it's in

my hand, under a coat. At home, it's on the headboard. In short, I take it with me almost everywhere I go alone.

Just carrying a pistol is not protection; avoidance is still the best ap- 16 proach to trouble. Subconsciously watching for signs of danger, I believe I've become more alert. Handgun use, not unlike driving, becomes instinctive. Each time I've drawn my gun — I have never fired it at another human being — I've simply found it in my hand.

I was driving the half-mile to the highway mailbox one day when I saw 17 a vehicle parked about midway down the road. Several men were standing in the ditch, relieving themselves. I have no objection to emergency urination, but I noticed they'd dumped several dozen beer cans in the road. Besides being ugly, cans can slash a cow's feet or stomach.

The men noticed me before they finished and made quite a perfor- 18 mance out of zipping their trousers while walking toward me. All four of them gathered around my small foreign car, and one of them demanded what the hell I wanted.

"This is private land. I'd appreciate it if you'd pick up the beer cans." 19

"What beer cans?" said the belligerent one, putting both hands on the 20 car door and leaning in my window. His face was inches from mine, and the beer fumes were strong. The others laughed. One tried the passenger door, locked; another put his foot on the hood and rocked the car. They circled, lightly thumping the roof, discussing my good fortune in meeting them and the benefits they were likely to bestow upon me. I felt very small and very trapped and they knew it.

"The ones you just threw out," I said politely. 21

"I don't see no beer cans. Why don't you get out here and show them 22 to me, honey?" said the belligerent one, reaching for the handle inside my door.

"Right over there," I said, still being polite. " — there, and over there." I 23 pointed with the pistol, which I'd slipped under my thigh. Within one minute the cans and the men were back in the car and headed down the road.

I believe this incident illustrates several important principles. The men 24 were trespassing and knew it: their judgment may have been impaired by alcohol. Their response to the polite request of a woman alone was to use their size, numbers, and sex to inspire fear. The pistol was a response in the same language. Politeness didn't work: I couldn't match them in size or number. Out of the car, I'd have been more vulnerable. The pistol just changed the balance of power. It worked again recently when I was driving in a desolate part of Wyoming. A man played cat-and-mouse with me for thirty miles, ultimately trying to run me off the road. When his car passed mine with only two inches to spare, I showed him my pistol, and he disappeared.

When I got my pistol, I told my husband, revising the old Colt slogan, 25 "God made men *and women*, but Sam Colt made them equal." Recently I have seen a gunmaker's ad with a similar sentiment. Perhaps this is an idea whose time has come, though the pacifist inside me will be saddened if the only way women can achieve equality is by carrying weapons.

We must treat a firearm's power with caution. "Power tends to corrupt,   26
and absolute power corrupts absolutely," as a man (Lord Acton) once said.
A pistol is not the only way to avoid being raped or murdered in today's
world, but, intelligently wielded, it can shift the balance of power and provide a measure of safety.

·   ·   ·

Comprehension

1. According to Hasselstrom, why does she carry a gun? In one sentence,
   summarize her rationale.

2. List the specific events that led Hasselstrom to her decision to carry a gun.

3. Other than carrying a gun, what means of protecting herself did
   Hasselstrom try? Why did she find them unsatisfactory? Can you think
   of other strategies she could have adopted instead of carrying a gun?

4. Where in the essay does Hasselstrom express her reluctance to carry a
   gun?

5. In paragraph 13, Hasselstrom says, "gun possession might increase your
   danger—unless you know you can use it." Where else does she touch on
   the possible pitfalls of carrying a gun?

6. What does Hasselstrom mean when she says, "The pistol just changed the
   balance of power" (24)?

Purpose and Audience

1. How does paragraph 1 establish Hasselstrom's purpose for writing this
   essay? What other purpose might she have?

2. What purpose does paragraph 5 serve? Is it necessary?

3. Do you think this essay is aimed at a particular gender? If so, do you think
   it is directed at men or at women? Why?

4. Do you think Hasselstrom expects her readers to agree with her position?
   Where does she indicate that she expects them to challenge her? How
   does she address this challenge?

Style and Structure

1. This essay is written in the first person, and it relies heavily on personal
   experience. Do you see this as a strength or a weakness? Explain.

2. What is the main cause in this cause-and-effect essay — that is, what is the
   most important reason Hasselstrom gives for carrying a gun? Can you
   identify any contributory causes?

3. Could you argue that simply being a woman is justification enough for
   carrying a gun? Do you think this is Hasselstrom's position? Explain.

4. Think of Hasselstrom's essay as the first step in a possible causal chain. What situations might result from her decision to carry a gun?

5. In paragraph 25, Hasselstrom says, "the pacifist inside me will be saddened if the only way women can achieve equality is by carrying weapons." In her title and elsewhere in the essay, Hasselstrom characterizes herself as a "peaceful woman." Do you think she is successful in portraying herself as a peace-loving woman who only reluctantly carries a gun?

Vocabulary Projects

1. Define each of the following words as it is used in this selection.

posted (7)   belligerent (20)   wielded (26)
muzzle (7)   bestow (20)

2. Some of the words and phrases Hasselstrom uses in this essay suggest that she sees her pistol as an equalizer, something that helps to compensate for her vulnerability. Identify the words and phrases she uses to characterize her gun in this way.

Journal Entry

Do you agree that carrying a gun is Hasselstrom's only choice, or do you think she could take other steps to ensure her safety? Explain.

Writing Workshop

1. Hasselstrom lives in a rural area, and the scenarios she describes apply to rural life. Rewrite this essay as "A Peaceful Urban (or Suburban) Woman Explains Why She Carries a Gun."

2. **Working with Sources.** What reasons might a "peace-loving" man have for carrying a gun? Write a cause-and-effect essay outlining such a man's motives, using any of Hasselstrom's reasons that might apply to him as well. If you quote Hasselstrom in your essay, be sure to include parenthetical documentation and a works-cited page. (See Chapter 18 for information on MLA documentation.)

3. Write a cause-and-effect essay presenting reasons to support a position that opposes Hasselstrom's: "A Peaceful Woman (or Man) Explains Why She (or He) Refuses to Carry a Gun."

Combining the Patterns

Several times in her essay, Hasselstrom uses **narration** to support her position. Identify these narrative passages. Are they absolutely essential to the essay? Could they be briefer? Could some be deleted? Explain.

Thematic Connections

- "Shooting an Elephant" (page 133)
- "Just Walk On By: A Black Man Ponders His Power to Alter Public Space" (page 240)
- "The Wife-Beater" (page 516)

Why Vampires Never Die

Born in Guadalajara, Mexico, in 1964, Guillermo del Toro is a writer, producer, and director best known for films like the supernatural thriller *Pan's Labyrinth* (2006) and the *Hellboy* superhero series. In 2009, del Toro published his first novel, *The Strain*, cowritten with Chuck Hogan. This book is the first in a vampire trilogy by the two authors. Chuck Hogan is a crime fiction and horror novelist whose books include *The Blood Artists* (1999), *Prince of Thieves* (2004), and *The Killing Moon* (2008).

Background on vampire movies As generations of filmmakers have reinvented the Dracula myth on-screen, movie vampires have ranged from the handsome and romantic to the grotesque and even comical. The most famous early depiction was German director F. W. Murnau's influential and expressionistic *Nosferatu* (1922), in which actor Max Schreck played a repulsive, toothy, and rat-like version of the creature. With actors Bela Lugosi in *Dracula* (1931) and Christopher Lee in *The Horror of Dracula* (1958), the vampire became a more romantic figure. In the years since, the character has proven very versatile, featured in blaxploitation films like *Blacula* (1972) and campy comedy horror movies such as *Fright Night* (1985) as well as in director Francis Ford Coppola's *Dracula* (1992), a faithful adaptation of Bram Stoker's original novel. More recently, the television show *Buffy the Vampire Slayer* (1997–2003), the *Twilight* book and movie series, and HBO's *True Blood* have reaffirmed the enduring appeal of vampires.

Tonight, you or someone you love will likely be visited by a vampire — on cable television or the big screen, or in the bookstore. Our own novel describes a modern-day epidemic that spreads across New York City. 1

It all started nearly 200 years ago. It was the "Year Without a Summer" of 1816, when ash from volcanic eruptions lowered temperatures around the globe, giving rise to widespread famine. A few friends gathered at the Villa Diodati on Lake Geneva and decided to engage in a small competition to see who could come up with the most terrifying tale — and the two great monsters of the modern age were born. 2

One was created by Mary Godwin, soon to become Mary Shelley, whose Dr. Frankenstein gave life to a desolate creature. The other monster was less created than fused. John William Polidori stitched together folklore, personal resentment, and erotic anxieties into "The Vampyre," a story that is the basis for vampires as they are understood today. 3

With "The Vampyre," Polidori gave birth to the two main branches of vampiric fiction: the vampire as romantic hero, and the vampire as undead monster. This ambivalence may reflect Polidori's own, as it is widely accepted that Lord Ruthven, the titular creature, was based upon Lord 4

Byron* — literary superstar of the era and another resident of the lakeside villa that fateful summer. Polidori tended to Byron day and night, both as his doctor and most devoted groupie. But Polidori resented him as well: Byron was dashing and brilliant, while the poor doctor had a rather drab talent and unremarkable physique.

But this was just a new twist to a very old idea. The myth, established 5 well before the invention of the word "vampire," seems to cross every culture, language, and era. The Indian Baital, the Ch'ing Shih in China, and the Romanian Strigoi are but a few of its names. The creature seems to be as old as Babylonia and Sumer. Or even older.

The vampire may originate from a repressed memory we had as pri- 6 mates. Perhaps at some point we were — out of necessity — cannibalistic. As soon as we became sedentary, agricultural tribes with social boundaries, one seminal myth might have featured our ancestors as primitive beasts who slept in the cold loam of the earth and fed off the salty blood of the living.

Monsters, like angels, are invoked by our individual and collective 7 needs. Today, much as during that gloomy summer in 1816, we feel the need to seek their cold embrace.

Herein lies an important clue: in contrast to timeless creatures like the 8 dragon, the vampire does not seek to obliterate us, but instead offers a peculiar brand of blood alchemy. For as his contagion bestows its nocturnal gift, the vampire transforms our vile, mortal selves into the gold of eternal youth, and instills in us something that every social construct seeks to quash: primal lust. If youth is desire married with unending possibility, then vampire lust creates within us a delicious void, one we long to fulfill.

In other words, whereas other monsters emphasize what is mortal in 9 us, the vampire emphasizes the eternal in us. Through the panacea of its blood it turns the lead of our toxic flesh into golden matter.

In a society that moves as fast as ours, where every week a new "block- 10 buster" must be enthroned at the box office, or where idols are fabricated by consensus every new television season, the promise of something everlasting, something truly eternal, holds a special allure. As a seductive figure, the vampire is as flexible and polyvalent as ever. Witness its slow mutation from the pansexual, decadent Anne Rice** creatures to the current permutations — promising anything from chaste eternal love to wild nocturnal escapades — and there you will find the true essence of immortality: adaptability.

Vampires find their niche and mutate at an accelerated rate now — in 11 the past one would see, for decades, the same variety of fiend, repeated in multiple storylines. Now, vampires simultaneously occur in all forms and tap into our every need: soap opera storylines, sexual liberation, noir detec-

---

* Eds. note — British poet and major figure of the Romantic era (1788–1824).
** Eds. note — American writer known for her gothic and erotic vampire fiction (b. 1941).

tive fiction, etc. The myth seems to be twittering promiscuously to serve all avenues of life, from cereal boxes to romantic fiction. The fast pace of technology accelerates its viral dispersion in our culture.

But if Polidori remains the roots in the genealogy of our creature, the 12 most widely known vampire was birthed by Bram Stoker* in 1897.

Part of the reason for the great success of his *Dracula* is generally ac- 13 knowledged to be its appearance at a time of great technological revolu- tion. The narrative is full of new gadgets (telegraphs, typing machines), various forms of communication (diaries, ship logs), and cutting-edge sci- ence (blood transfusions) — a mash-up of ancient myth in conflict with the world of the present.

Today as well, we stand at the rich uncertain dawn of a new level of 14 scientific innovation. The wireless technology we carry in our pockets to- day was the stuff of the science fiction in our youth. Our technological ar- rogance mirrors more and more the Wellsian** dystopia of dissatisfaction, while allowing us to feel safe and connected at all times. We can call, see, or hear almost anything and anyone no matter where we are. For most people then, the only remote place remains within. "Know thyself" we do not.

Despite our obsessive harnessing of information, we are still ultimately 15 vulnerable to our fates and our nightmares. We enthrone the deadly virus in the very same way that *Dracula* allowed the British public to believe in monsters: through science. Science becomes the modern man's supersti- tion. It allows him to experience fear and awe again, and to believe in the things he cannot see.

And through awe, we once again regain spiritual humility. The current 16 vampire pandemic serves to remind us that we have no true jurisdiction over our bodies, our climate, or our very souls. Monsters will always provide the possibility of mystery in our mundane "reality show" lives, hinting at a larger spiritual world; for if there are demons in our midst, there surely must be angels lurking nearby as well. In the vampire we find Eros and Thanatos*** fused together in archetypal embrace, spiraling through the ages, undying.

Forever. 17

. . .

Comprehension

1. What is the "modern-day epidemic" to which the writers refer in para- graph 1? In what sense is this an "epidemic"?

2. Who are the "two great monsters of the modern age" (2)? What two branches of vampire fiction do the writers identify?

---

* Eds. note — Irish writer best known for the novel *Dracula* (1847–1912).
** Eds. note — Referring to the work of science fiction writer H. G. Wells (1866–1946), author of the dystopian novel *The Time Machine* (1895).
*** Eds. note — Erotic love and death.

3. What are the origins of the vampire?

4. In paragraphs 8 and 9, the writers explain the appeal of vampires. In your own words, summarize these two paragraphs.

5. How, according to the writers, has the depiction of the vampire changed in recent years? How does it continue to change? Why is it constantly changing?

6. How is the world we live in today like the world at the time *Dracula* was published? How does this kind of world encourage the proliferation of vampires in popular culture?

7. Why is it that vampires will "never die"?

Purpose and Audience

1. What is this essay's thesis? Is it explicitly stated? If so, where? If not, state it in one sentence.

2. The writers mention their new novel in paragraph 1. What, if anything, does this tell you about their essay's purpose?

3. At what kind of audience do you think this essay is aimed? Consider the writers' topic as well as the essay's vocabulary and its literary and historical allusions.

Style and Structure

1. Evaluate the essay's introduction — in particular, the writers' opening sentence.

2. This essay's focus is on examining causes of vampires' continuing popularity. Do the writers also consider effects? If so, where?

3. In the second sentence of paragraph 13, the writers give a series of parenthetical examples. Write a similar sentence for paragraph 14 that provides examples of modern-day "gadgets," "forms of communication," and "cutting-edge science."

4. Why do the writers set off the essay's last word as a separate paragraph? Do you think it should be part of paragraph 16?

Vocabulary Projects

1. Define each of the following words as it is used in this selection.

seminal (6)	permutations (10)
loam (6)	genealogy (12)
alchemy (8)	dystopia (14)
quash (8)	enthrone (15)
panacea (9)	pandemic (16)
polyvalent (10)	archetypal (16)

2. Search the Web to identify Eros and Thanatos. Why do the writers mention these figures in paragraph 16? Why do you think they do not explain who they are?

Journal Entry

Do you see the tremendous recent popularity of vampires as a positive or a negative development? Why?

Writing Workshop

1. **Working with Sources.** How do you account for the current popularity of books and films about vampires? Write a cause-and-effect essay explaining why vampires continue to live on in the popular imagination. Consider del Toro and Hogan's characterization of the vampire as both "romantic hero" and "undead monster" (4), and quote these terms in your essay. Be sure to cite your source and to include a works-cited page. (See Chapter 18 for information on MLA documentation.)

2. Write an essay explaining the popularity of another icon or character — for example, the avatar or the transformer — in films, television, or novels. Or, explain why the popularity of a typical hero of years ago — for example, the cowboy or the superhero — has declined.

3. What effects do you think the proliferation of vampires in popular culture is having on young teenagers? Write a cause-and-effect essay discussing ways in which this emphasis is a positive or a negative influence on young people.

Combining the Patterns

In paragraphs 13–14, the writers use **comparison and contrast**. What are they comparing? How does this comparison support their thesis?

Thematic Connections

- "The Embalming of Mr. Jones" (page 303)
- "Aristotle" (page 484)
- "The Case for Mandatory Organ Donation" (page 614)

Suicide Note (Poetry)

Janice Mirikitani, a third-generation Japanese American, was born in San Francisco in 1942 and graduated from the University of California at Los Angeles in 1962. In her poetry, Mirikitani often considers how racism in the United States affects Asian Americans, particularly the thousands of Japanese Americans held in internment camps during World War II. Her collections include *Awake in the River* (1978), *Shedding Silence* (1987), and *We, the Dangerous: New and Selected Poems* (1995). She has also edited anthologies of Japanese-American and developing-nation literature, as well as several volumes giving voice to children living in poverty. For many years, she has been president of the Glide Foundation, which sponsors outreach programs for the poor and homeless of San Francisco.

Background on teenage suicide The following poem, which appears in *Shedding Silence,* takes the form of a suicide note written by a young Asian-American college student to her family and reveals the extreme pressure to excel placed on her by her parents and her culture. The theme, however, has considerable relevance beyond the Asian-American community. Tragically, some five thousand teenagers and young adults commit suicide annually in the United States (there are ten times as many attempts), and suicide is the third leading cause of death among fifteen- to twenty-four-year-olds. Among college students, suicide is the second leading cause of death; approximately one thousand college students take their own lives every year. The number of suicides by college students has tripled since the 1950s. Nationally there are 7.29 suicides per year for every 100,000 students. Recent extensive media coverage of a number of youth suicides caused by bullying has increased awareness of this problem and has led to proposals for stronger anti-harassment legislation.

> How many notes written . . .
> ink smeared like birdprints in snow.
>
>   not good enough   not pretty enough   not smart enough
> dear mother and father.
> I apologize
> for disappointing you.
> I've worked very hard,
>
>   not good enough
>
> harder, perhaps to please you.
> If only I were a son, shoulders broad
> as the sunset threading through pine,
> I would see the light in my mother's
> eyes, or the golden pride reflected

5

10

in my father's dream
of my wide, male hands worthy of work   15
and comfort.
I would swagger through life
muscled and bold and assured,
drawing praises to me
like currents in the bed of wind, virile   20
with confidence.

    not good enough   not pretty enough   not smart enough

I apologize.
Tasks do not come easily.
Each failure, a glacier.   25
Each disapproval, a bootprint.
Each disappointment,
ice above my river.
So I have worked hard.

            not good enough   30

My sacrifice I will drop
bone by bone, perched
on the ledge of my womanhood,
fragile as wings.

            not strong enough   35

It is snowing steadily
surely not good weather
for flying — this sparrow
sillied and dizzied by the wind
on the edge.   40

            not smart enough

I make this ledge my altar
to offer penance.
This air will not hold me,
the snow burdens my crippled wings,   45
my tears drop like bitter cloth
softly into the gutter below.

    not good enough   not pretty enough   not smart enough

            Choices thin as shaved
            ice. Notes shredded   50
            drift like snow

on my broken body,
cover me like whispers
of sorries

sorries.   55
Perhaps when they find me
they will bury
my bird bones beneath
a sturdy pine
and scatter my feathers like   60
unspoken song
over this white and cold and silent
breast of earth.

· · ·

Reading Literature

1. An author's note that originally introduced this poem explained the main cause of the student's death.

   An Asian-American college student was reported to have jumped to her death from her dormitory window. Her body was found two days later under a deep cover of snow. Her suicide note contained an apology to her parents for having received less than a perfect four-point grade average.

   What other causes might have contributed to her suicide?

2. Why does the speaker believe her life would be happier if she were male? Do you think she is correct?

3. What words, phrases, and images are repeated in this poem? What effect do these repetitions have on you?

Journal Entry

Whom (or what) do you blame for teenage suicides such as the one the poem describes? How might such deaths be eliminated?

Thematic Connections

- "Only Daughter" (page 111)
- "College Pressures" (page 450)
- "Aristotle" (page 484)

Writing Assignments for Cause and Effect

1. **Working with Sources.** "Thirty-Eight Who Saw Murder Didn't Call the Police" (page 127), "Who Killed Benny Paret?" (page 339), and "On Dumpster Diving" (page 664) all encourage readers, either directly or indirectly, to take action rather than remain uninvolved. Using information gleaned from these essays (or from others in the text) as support for your thesis, write an essay exploring either the possible consequences of apathy, the possible causes of apathy, or both. Be sure to provide parenthetical documentation for any words or ideas that are not your own, and include a works-cited page. (See Chapter 18 for more information on MLA documentation.)

2. Write an updated version of one of this chapter's essays. For example, you might explore the kinds of pressure Lawrence Otis Graham ("The 'Black Table' Is Still There," page 349) might face as junior high school student today.

3. Various technological and social developments have contributed to the decline of formal letter writing. One of these is the telephone; others include text-messaging, blogs, and email. Consider some other possible causes, and write an essay explaining why letter writing has all but disappeared. You may also consider the *effects* (both positive and negative) of this development.

4. How do you account for the popularity of one of the following: Twitter, Facebook, hip-hop, video games, home schooling, reality TV, fast food, flash mobs, or sensationalist tabloids such as the *Star*? Write an essay considering remote as well as immediate causes for the success of the phenomenon you choose.

5. Between 1946 and 1964, the U.S. birthrate increased considerably. Some of the effects attributed to this "baby boom" include the 1960s antiwar movement, an increase in the crime rate, and the development of the women's movement. Write an essay exploring some possible effects on the nation's economy and politics of the baby-boom generation's growing older. What trends would you expect to find now that the first baby boomers have turned sixty-five?

6. Write an essay tracing a series of events in your life that constitutes a causal chain. Indicate clearly both the sequence of events and the causal connections among them, and be careful not to confuse coincidence with causality.

7. In recent years, almost half of American marriages ended in divorce. However, among married couples of "Generation X," born between 1965 and 1980, the divorce rate is considerably lower. To what do you attribute this decline in divorce rate? Be as specific as possible, citing "case studies" of families you are familiar with.

8. What do you see as the major cause of any one of these problems: binge drinking among college students, voter apathy, school shootings, childhood obesity, or academic cheating? Based on your identification

of its cause, formulate some specific solutions for the problem you select.

9. Write an essay considering the likely effects of a severe, protracted shortage of one of the following commodities: clean water, rental housing, cell phones, flu vaccine, books, or gasoline. You may consider a community-, city-, or statewide shortage or a nation- or worldwide crisis.

10. Write an essay exploring the causes, effects, or both of increased violence among children in the United States.

Collaborative Activity for Cause and Effect

Working in groups of four, discuss your thoughts about the increasing homeless population, and then list four effects the presence of homeless people is having on you, your community, and our nation. Assign each member of your group to write a paragraph explaining one of the effects the group identifies. Then, arrange the paragraphs by increasing importance, moving from the least to the most significant consequence. Finally, work together to turn your individual paragraphs into an essay: write an introduction, a conclusion, and transitions between paragraphs, and include a thesis statement in paragraph 1.

Comparison and Contrast

11

What Is Comparison and Contrast?

In the narrowest sense, *comparison* shows how two or more things are similar, and *contrast* shows how they are different. In most writing situations, however, the two related processes of **comparison and contrast** are used together. In the following paragraph from *Disturbing the Universe,* scientist Freeman Dyson compares and contrasts two different styles of human endeavor, which he calls "the gray and the green."

Topic sentence (outlines elements of comparison)

Point-by-point comparison

In everything we undertake, either on earth or in the sky, we have a choice of two styles, which I call the gray and the green. The distinction between the gray and green is not sharp. Only at the extremes of the spectrum can we say without qualification, this is green and that is gray. The difference between green and gray is better explained by examples than by definitions. Factories are gray, gardens are green. Physics is gray, biology is green. Plutonium is gray, horse manure is green. Bureaucracy is gray, pioneer communities are green. Self-reproducing machines are gray, trees and children are green. Human technology is gray, God's technology is green. Clones are gray, clades* are green. Army field manuals are gray, poems are green.

A special form of comparison, called **analogy**, explains one thing by comparing it to a second, more familiar thing. In the following paragraph from *The Shopping Mall High School,* Arthur G. Powell, Eleanor Farrar, and David K. Cohen use analogy to shed light on the nature of contemporary American high schools.

* Eds. note — A group of organisms that evolved from a common ancestor.

If Americans want to understand their high schools at work, they should imagine them as shopping malls. Secondary education is another consumption experience in an abundant society. Shopping malls attract a broad range of customers with different tastes and purposes. Some shop at Target, others at Bloomingdale's. In high schools a broad range of students also shop. They too can select from an astonishing variety of products and services conveniently assembled in one place with ample parking. Furthermore, in malls and schools many different kinds of transactions are possible. Both institutions bring hopeful purveyors and potential purchasers together. The former hope to maximize sales but can take nothing for granted. Shoppers have a wide discretion not only about what to buy but also about whether to buy.

Using Comparison and Contrast

Throughout our lives, we are bombarded with information from newspapers, television, radio, the Internet, and personal experience: the police strike in Memphis; city workers walk out in Philadelphia; the Senate debates government spending; taxes are raised in New Jersey. Somehow we must make sense of the jumbled facts and figures that surround us. One way we have of understanding information like this is to put it side by side with other data and then to compare and contrast. Do the police in Memphis have the same complaints as the city workers in Philadelphia? What are the differences between the two situations? Is the national debate on spending analogous to the New Jersey debate on taxes? How do they differ?

We apply comparison and contrast every day to matters that directly affect us. When we make personal decisions, we consider alternatives, asking ourselves whether one option seems better than another. Should I major in history or business? What job opportunities will each major offer me? Should I register as a Democrat, a Republican, or an Independent? What are the positions of each political party on government spending, health care, and taxes? To answer questions like these, we use comparison and contrast.

Planning a Comparison-and-Contrast Essay

Because comparison and contrast is central to our understanding of the world, this way of thinking is often called for in papers and on essay exams.

Compare and contrast the attitudes toward science and technology expressed in Fritz Lang's *Metropolis* and George Lucas's *Star Wars*. (film)

What are the similarities and differences between mitosis and meiosis? (biology)

Discuss the relative merits of establishing a partnership or setting up a corporation. (business law)

Discuss the advantages and disadvantages of bilingual education. (education)

Recognizing Comparison-and-Contrast Assignments

You are not likely to sit down and say to yourself, "I think I'll write a comparison-and-contrast essay today. Now what can I write about?" Instead, your assignment will suggest comparison and contrast, or you will decide comparison and contrast suits your purpose. In the preceding examples, for instance, the instructors phrased their questions to tell students how to treat the material. When you read these questions, certain key words and phrases — *compare and contrast, similarities and differences, relative merits, advantages and disadvantages* — indicate you should use a comparison-and-contrast pattern to organize your essay. Sometimes you may not even need a key phrase. Consider the question "Which of the two Adamses, John or Samuel, had the greater influence on the timing and course of the American Revolution?" Here the word *greater* is enough to suggest a contrast.

Even when your assignment is not worded to suggest comparison and contrast, your purpose may indicate this pattern of development. For instance, when you **evaluate**, you frequently use comparison and contrast. If, as a student in a management course, you are asked to evaluate two health-care systems, you can begin by researching the standards experts use in their evaluations. You can then compare each system's performance with those standards and contrast the systems with each other, concluding perhaps that both systems meet minimum standards but that one is more cost-efficient than the other. Or, if you are evaluating two of this year's new cars for a consumer newsletter, you can establish some criteria — fuel economy, safety features, reliability, handling, style — and compare and contrast the cars on each criterion. If each of the cars is better in different categories, your readers will have to decide which features matter most to them.

Establishing a Basis for Comparison

Before you can compare and contrast two things, you must be sure a **basis for comparison** exists — that the two things have enough in common to justify the comparison. For example, although cats and dogs are very different, they share several significant elements: they are mammals, they make good pets, and they are intelligent. Without these shared elements, there would be no basis for analysis and nothing of importance to discuss.

A comparison should lead you beyond the obvious. For instance, at first the idea of a comparison-and-contrast essay based on an analogy between bees and people might seem absurd: after all, these two creatures differ in species, physical structure, and intelligence. In fact, their differences are so obvious that an essay based on them might seem pointless. But after further analysis, you might decide that bees and people have quite a few similarities. Both are social animals that live in complex social structures, and both have tasks to perform and roles to fulfill in their respective societies. Therefore, you *could* write about them, but you would focus on the common elements that seem most provocative — social structures and roles — rather than on dissimilar elements. If you tried to draw an analogy between bees and SUVs or humans and golf tees, however, you would run into trouble. Although some points of comparison could be found, they would be trivial. Why bother to point out that both bees and SUVs can travel great distances or that both people and tees are needed to play golf? Neither statement establishes a significant basis for comparison.

When two subjects are very similar, the contrast may be worth writing about. And when two subjects are not very much alike, you may find that the similarities are worth considering.

Selecting Points for Discussion

After you decide which subjects to compare and contrast, you need to select the points you want to discuss. You do this by determining your emphasis — on similarities, differences, or both — and the major focus of your paper. If your purpose in comparing two types of houseplants is to explain that one is easier to grow than the other, you would select points having to do with plant care, not those having to do with plant biology.

When you compare and contrast, make sure you treat the same (or at least similar) elements for each subject you discuss. For instance, if you were going to compare and contrast two novels, you might consider the following elements in both works.

NOVEL A	NOVEL B
Minor characters	Minor characters
Major characters	Major characters
Themes	Themes

Try to avoid the common error of discussing entirely different elements for each subject. Such an approach obscures any basis for comparison that might exist. The two novels, for example, could not be meaningfully compared or contrasted if you discussed dissimilar elements.

NOVEL A	NOVEL B
Minor characters	Author's life
Major characters	Plot
Themes	Symbolism

Developing a Thesis Statement

After selecting the points you want to discuss, you are ready to develop your thesis statement. This **thesis statement** should tell readers what to expect in your essay, identifying not only the subjects to be compared and contrasted but also the point you will make about them. Your thesis statement should also indicate whether you will concentrate on similarities or differences or both. In addition, it may list the points of comparison and contrast in the order in which they will be discussed in the essay.

The structure of your thesis statement can indicate the emphasis of your essay. As the following sentences illustrate, a thesis statement should highlight the essay's central concern by presenting it in the independent, rather than the dependent, clause of the sentence. Notice that the structure of the first thesis statement emphasizes similarities, while the structure of the second highlights differences.

> Despite the fact that television and radio are distinctly different media, they use similar strategies to appeal to their audiences.

> Although Melville's *Moby-Dick* and London's *The Sea Wolf* are both about the sea, the minor characters, major characters, and themes of *Moby-Dick* establish its greater complexity.

Structuring a Comparison-and-Contrast Essay

Like every other type of essay in this book, a comparison-and-contrast essay has an **introduction**, several **body paragraphs**, and a **conclusion**. Within the body of your paper, you can use either of two basic comparison-and-contrast strategies — **subject by subject** or **point by point**.

As you might expect, each organizational strategy has advantages and disadvantages. In general, you should use subject-by-subject comparison when your purpose is to emphasize overall similarities or differences, and you should use point-by-point comparison when your purpose is to emphasize individual points of similarity or difference.

Using Subject-by-Subject Comparison

In a **subject-by-subject comparison**, you essentially write a separate essay about each subject, but you discuss the same points for both subjects. Use your basis for comparison to guide your selection of points, and arrange these points in some logical order, usually in order of their increasing significance. The following informal outline illustrates a subject-by-subject comparison.

Introduction: Thesis statement — Despite the fact that television and radio are distinctly different media, they use similar strategies to appeal to their audiences.

Television audiences

Point 1:	Men
Point 2:	Women
Point 3:	Children

Radio audiences

Point 1:	Men
Point 2:	Women
Point 3:	Children
Conclusion:	Restatement of thesis or review of key points

Subject-by-subject comparisons are most appropriate for short, uncomplicated papers. In longer papers, where you might make many points about each subject, this organizational strategy demands too much of your readers, requiring them to keep track of all your points throughout your paper. In addition, because of the length of each section, your paper may seem like two completely separate essays. For longer or more complex papers, then, it is often best to use point-by-point comparison.

Using Point-by-Point Comparison

In a **point-by-point comparison**, you make a point about one subject and then follow it with a comparable point about the other. This alternating pattern continues throughout the body of your essay until all your points have been made. The following informal outline illustrates a point-by-point comparison.

Introduction:	Thesis statement — Although Melville's *Moby-Dick* and London's *The Sea Wolf* are both about the sea, the minor characters, major characters, and themes of *Moby-Dick* establish its greater complexity.

Minor characters

Book 1:	*The Sea Wolf*
Book 2:	*Moby-Dick*

Major characters

Book 1:	*The Sea Wolf*
Book 2:	*Moby-Dick*

Themes

Book 1:	*The Sea Wolf*
Book 2:	*Moby-Dick*
Conclusion:	Restatement of thesis or review of key points

Point-by-point comparisons are useful for longer, more complicated essays in which you discuss many different points. (If you treat only one or two points of comparison, you should consider a subject-by-subject organization.) In a point-by-point essay, readers can follow comparisons or contrasts more easily and do not have to wait several paragraphs to find out, for example, the differences between minor characters in *Moby-Dick* and *The Sea Wolf* or to remember on page five what was said on page three. Nevertheless, it is easy to fall into a monotonous, back-and-forth movement between points when you write a point-by-point comparison. To avoid this problem, vary your sentence structure as you move from point to point—and be sure to use clear transitions.

Using Transitions

Transitions are especially important in comparison-and-contrast essays because you must supply readers with clear signals that identify individual similarities and differences. Without these cues, readers will have trouble following your discussion and may lose track of the significance of the points you are making. Some transitions indicating comparison and contrast are listed in the following box. (A more complete list of transitions appears on page 57.)

USEFUL TRANSITIONS FOR COMPARISON AND CONTRAST

COMPARISON

in comparison	like
in the same way	likewise
just as . . . so	similarly

CONTRAST

although	nevertheless
but	nonetheless
conversely	on the contrary
despite	on the one hand . . . on the other hand
even though	still
however	unlike
in contrast	whereas
instead	yet

Longer essays frequently include **transitional paragraphs** that connect one part of an essay to another. A transitional paragraph can be a single sentence that signals a shift in focus or a longer paragraph that provides a concise summary of what was said before. In either case, transitional paragraphs enable readers to pause and consider what has already been said before moving on to a new subject.

Revising a Comparison-and-Contrast Essay

When you revise your comparison-and-contrast essay, consider the items on the revision checklist on page 68. In addition, pay special attention to the items on the following checklist, which apply specifically to comparison-and-contrast essays.

> ✔ **REVISION CHECKLIST**   **Comparison and Contrast**
>
> - Does your assignment call for comparison and contrast?
> - What basis for comparison exists between the two subjects you are comparing?
> - Does your essay have a clear thesis statement that identifies both the subjects you are comparing and the points you are making about them?
> - Do you discuss the same or similar points for both subjects?
> - If you have written a subject-by-subject comparison, have you included a transition paragraph that connects the two sections of the essay?
> - If you have written a point-by-point comparison, have you included appropriate transitions and varied your sentence structure to indicate your shift from one point to another?
> - Have you included transitional words and phrases that indicate whether you are discussing similarities or differences?

Editing a Comparison-and-Contrast Essay

When you edit your comparison-and-contrast essay, follow the guidelines on the editing checklists on pages 85, 88, and 90. In addition, focus on the grammar, mechanics, and punctuation issues that are particularly relevant to comparison-and-contrast essays. One of these issues — using parallel structure — is discussed below.

GRAMMAR IN CONTEXT   **Using Parallelism**

Parallelism — the use of matching nouns, verbs, phrases, or clauses to express the same or similar ideas — is often used in comparison-and-contrast essays to emphasize the similarities or differences between one point or subject and another.

- Use parallel structure with paired items or with items in a series.

"I am an American citizen and she is not" (Mukherjee 404).

"For women, as for girls, intimacy is the fabric of relationships, and talk is the thread from which it is woven" (Tannen 424).

"Lee was tidewater Virginia, and in his background were family, culture, and tradition . . . the age of chivalry transplanted to a New World which was making its own legends and its own myths" (Catton 394).

According to Bruce Catton, Lee was strong, aristocratic, and dedicated to the Confederacy (393).

- Use parallel structure with paired items linked by correlative conjunctions (*not only/but also, both/and, neither/nor, either/or,* and so on).

  "In everything we undertake, **either** <u>on earth</u> **or** <u>in the sky</u>, we have a choice of two styles, which I call the gray and the green" (Dyson 371).

  Not only <u>does Catton admire Grant,</u> **but** <u>he</u> **also** <u>respects him.</u>

- Use parallel structure to emphasize the contrast between paired items linked by *as* or *than*.

  According to Deborah Tannen, conversation between men and women is **as** much <u>a problem for men</u> **as** <u>a problem for women</u> (426).

  As Deborah Tannen observes, most men are socialized <u>to communicate through actions</u> **rather than** <u>to communicate through conversation</u> (424).

For more practice in using parallelism, visit the resources for Chapter 11 at **bedfordstmartins.com/patterns**.

✓EDITING CHECKLIST   **Comparison and Contrast**

- Have you used parallel structure with parallel elements in a series?
- Have you used commas to separate three or more parallel elements in a series?
- Have you used parallel structure with paired items linked by correlative conjunctions?
- Have you used parallel structure with paired items linked by *as* or *than*?

A STUDENT WRITER: Subject-by-Subject Comparison

The following essay, by Mark Cotharn, is a subject-by-subject comparison. It was written for a composition class whose instructor asked students to write an essay comparing two educational experiences.

Brains versus Brawn

Introduction   When people think about discrimination, they usually   1
associate it with race or gender. But discrimination can take other
forms. For example, a person can gain an unfair advantage at a
job interview by being attractive, by knowing someone who works
at the company, or by being able to talk about something (like

sports) that has nothing to do with the job. Certainly, the people who do not get the job would claim that they were discriminated against, and to some extent they would be right. As a high school athlete, I experienced both sides of discrimination. When I was a sophomore, I benefited from discrimination. When I was a junior, however, I was penalized by it, treated as if there were no place for me in a classroom. As a result, I learned that discrimination, whether it helps you or hurts you, is wrong.

Thesis statement (emphasizing differences)

First subject: Mark helped by discrimination

At my high school, football was everything, and the entire   2
town supported the local team. In the summer, merchants would run special football promotions. Adults would wear shirts with the team's logo, students would collect money to buy equipment, and everyone would go to the games and cheer the team on. Coming out of junior high school, I was considered an exceptional athlete who was eventually going to start as varsity quarterback. Because of my status, I was enthusiastically welcomed by the high school. Before I entered the school, the varsity coach visited my home, and the principal called my parents and told them how well I was going to do.

Status of football

Treatment by teachers

I knew that high school would be different from junior   3
high, but I wasn't prepared for the treatment I received from my teachers. Many of them talked to me as if I were their friend, not their student. My math teacher used to keep me after class just to talk football; he would give me a note so I could be late for my next class. My biology teacher told me I could skip the afternoon labs so that I would have some time for myself before practice. Several of my teachers told me that during football season, I didn't have to hand in homework because it might distract me during practice. My Spanish teacher even told me that if I didn't do well on a test, I could take it over after the season. Everything I did seemed to be perfect.

Mark's reaction to treatment

Despite this favorable treatment, I continued to study hard.   4
I knew that if I wanted to go to a good college, I would have to get good grades, and I resented the implication that the only way I could get good grades was by getting special treatment. I had always been a good student, and I had no intention of changing my study habits now that I was in high school. Each night after practice, I stayed up late outlining my notes and completing my class assignments. Any studying I couldn't do during the week, I would complete on the weekends. Of course my social life suffered,

but I didn't care. I was proud that I never took advantage of the special treatment my teachers were offering me.

Transitional paragraph: signals shift from one subject to another

Then, one day, the unthinkable happened. The township 5 redrew the school-district lines, and I suddenly found myself assigned to a new high school — one that was academically more demanding than the one I attended and, worse, one that had a weak football team. When my parents appealed to the school board to let me stay at my current school, they were told that if the board made an exception for me, it would have to make exceptions for others, and that would lead to chaos. My principal and my coach also tried to get the board to change its decision, but they got the same response. So, in my junior year, at the height of my career, I changed schools.

Second subject: Mark hurt by discrimination

Status of football

Unlike the people at my old school, no one at my new 6 school seemed to care much about high school football. Many of the students attended the games, but their primary focus was on getting into college. If they talked about football at all, they usually discussed the regional college teams. As a result, I didn't have the status I had when I attended my former school. When I met with the coach before school started, he told me the football team was weak. He also told me that his main goal was to make sure everyone on the team had a chance to play. So, even though I would start, I would have to share the quarterback position with two seniors. Later that day, I saw the principal, who told me that although sports were an important part of school, academic achievement was more important. He made it clear that I would play football only as long as my grades did not suffer.

Treatment by teachers

Unlike the teachers at my old school, the teachers at my 7 new school did not give any special treatment to athletes. When I entered my new school, I was ready for the challenge. What I was not ready for was the hostility of most of my new teachers. From the first day, in just about every class, my teachers made it obvious that they had already made up their minds about what kind of student I was going to be. Some teachers told me I shouldn't expect any special consideration just because I was the team's quarterback. One even said in front of the class that I would have to study as hard as the other students if I expected

Mark's reaction to treatment

to pass. I was hurt and embarrassed by these comments. I didn't expect anyone to give me anything, and I was ready to get the grades I deserved. After all, I had gotten good grades up to this point, and I had no reason to think that the situation would change. Even so, my teachers' preconceived ideas upset me.

Just as I had in my old school, I studied hard, but I didn't   8
know how to deal with the prejudice I faced. At first, it really bothered me and even affected my performance on the football field. However, after awhile, I decided that the best way to show my teachers that I was not the stereotypical jock was to prove to them what kind of student I really was. In the long run, far from discouraging me, their treatment motivated me, and I decided to work as hard in the classroom as I did on the football field. By the end of high school, not only had the team won half of its games (a record season), but I had also proved to my teachers that I was a good student. (I still remember the surprised look on the face of my chemistry teacher when she handed my first exam back to me and told me that I had received the second highest grade in the class.)

Conclusion   Before I graduated, I talked to the teachers about how they   9
had treated me during my junior year. Some admitted they had been harder on me than on the rest of the students, but others denied they had ever discriminated against me. Eventually, I realized that some of them would never understand what they had done. Even so, my experience did have some positive effects. I learned that you should judge people on their merits, not by your own set of assumptions. In addition, I learned that although some people are talented intellectually, others have special skills

Restatement of thesis   that should also be valued. And, as I found out, discriminatory treatment, whether it helps you or hurts you, is no substitute for fairness.

Points for Special Attention

Basis for Comparison. Mark knew he could easily compare his two experiences. Both involved high school, and both focused on the treatment he had received as an athlete. In one case, Mark was treated better than other students because he was the team's quarterback; in the other, he was stereotyped as a "dumb jock" because he was a football player. Mark also knew that his comparison would make an interesting (and perhaps unexpected) point — that discrimination is unfair even when it gives a person an advantage.

Selecting Points for Comparison. Mark wanted to make certain that he would discuss the same (or at least similar) points for the two experiences he was going to compare. As he planned his essay, he consulted his brainstorming notes and made the following informal outline.

EXPERIENCE 1	EXPERIENCE 2
(gained an advantage)	(was put at a disadvantage)
Status of football	Status of football
Treatment by teachers	Treatment by teachers
My reaction	My reaction

Structure. Mark's essay makes three points about each of the two experiences he compares. Because his purpose was to convey the differences between the two experiences, he decided to use a subject-by-subject strategy. In addition, Mark thought he could make his case more convincingly if he discussed the first experience fully before moving on to the next one, and he believed readers would have no trouble keeping his individual points in mind as they read. Of course, Mark could have decided to do a point-by-point comparison. He rejected this strategy, though, because he thought that shifting back and forth between subjects would distract readers from his main point.

Transitions. Without adequate transitions, a subject-by-subject comparison can read like two separate essays. Notice that in Mark's essay, paragraph 5 is a **transitional paragraph** that connects the two sections of the essay. In it, Mark sets up the comparison by telling how he suddenly found himself assigned to another high school.

In addition to connecting the sections of an essay, transitional words and phrases can identify individual similarities or differences. Notice, for example, how the transitional word *however* emphasizes the contrast between the following sentences from paragraph 1.

WITHOUT TRANSITION

When I was a sophomore, I benefited from discrimination. When I was a junior, I was penalized by it.

WITH TRANSITION

When I was a sophomore, I benefited from discrimination. When I was a junior, *however,* I was penalized by it.

Topic Sentences. Like transitional phrases, topic sentences help to guide readers through an essay. When reading a comparison-and-contrast essay, readers can easily forget the points being compared, especially if the paper is long or complex. Direct, clearly stated topic sentences act as guideposts, alerting readers to the comparisons and contrasts you are making. For example, Mark's straightforward topic sentence at the beginning of paragraph 5 dramatically signals the movement from one experience to the other ("Then, one day, the unthinkable happened"). In addition, as in any effective comparison-and-contrast essay, each point discussed in connection with one subject is also discussed in connection with the other. Mark's topic sentences reinforce this balance.

FIRST SUBJECT

At my high school, football was everything, and the entire town supported the local team.

SECOND SUBJECT

Unlike the people at my old school, no one at my new school seemed to care much about high school football.

Focus on Revision

In general, Mark's classmates thought he could have spent more time talking about what he did to counter the preconceptions about athletes that teachers in *both* his schools had.

One student in his peer editing group pointed out that the teachers at both schools seemed to think athletes were weak students. The only difference was that the teachers at Mark's first school were willing to make allowances for athletes, while the teachers at his second school were not. The student thought that although Mark alluded to this fact, he should have made his point more explicitly.

Another classmate thought Mark should acknowledge that some student athletes *do* fit the teachers' stereotypes (although many do not). This information would reinforce his thesis and help him demonstrate how unfair his treatment was.

After rereading his essay, along with his classmates' comments, Mark decided to add information about how demanding football practice was. Without this information, readers would have a hard time understanding how difficult it was for him to keep up with his studies. He also decided to briefly acknowledge the fact that though he did not fit the negative stereotype of student athletes, some other student athletes do. This fact, however, did not justify the treatment he received at the two high schools he attended. (A sample peer editing worksheet for comparison and contrast appears on page 390.)

Working with Sources. One of Mark's classmates suggested that he add a quotation from David J. Birnbaum's essay "The Catbird Seat" (page 228) to his essay. The student pointed out that Birnbaum, like Mark, was given an advantage that he considered unfair. By referring to Birnbaum's essay, Mark would widen the focus of his remarks and show how his experience was similar to that of someone who is physically challenged. Mark agreed and decided to refer to Birnbaum's essay in the next draft of his paper. (Adding this reference would require him to include MLA parenthetical documentation as well as a works-cited page.)

A STUDENT WRITER: Point-by-Point Comparison

The following essay, by Maria Tecson, is a point-by-point comparison. It was written for a class in educational psychology whose instructor asked students to compare two Web sites about a health issue and to determine which is the more reliable information source.

A Comparison of Two Web Sites on Attention Deficit Disorder

Introduction

At first glance, the National Institute of Mental Health (NIMH) Web site on Attention Deficit Hyperactivity Disorder (nimh.nih.gov) and AdultADD.com — two Web sites on Attention Deficit Disorder (ADD) — look a lot alike. Both have good designs, informative headings, and links to other Web sites. Because anyone can publish on the Internet, however, Web sites cannot be judged simply on how they look. Colorful graphics and an appealing layout can often hide shortcomings that make sites *Thesis statement* unsuitable for use as research sources. As a comparison of the *(emphasizing* NIMH and AdultADD.com Web sites shows, one site is definitely a *differences)* more reliable source of information than the other. 1

First point: comparing home pages

The first difference between the two Web sites is the design of their home pages. The nimh.nih.gov home page looks clear and professional. For example, the logos, tabs, links, search boxes, and *NIMH home page* text columns are placed carefully on the page (see fig. 1). Words are spelled correctly; tabs help users to navigate; and content is arranged topically, with headers such as "What is Attention Deficit Hyperactivity Disorder?" and "Signs & Symptoms." The text, set in columns, looks like a newspaper page. Throughout the Web site, links connect to a reference page that lists sources for articles, and footnotes document information. In addition, the nimh.nih.gov site contains links to other reliable Web sites, both governmental and academic. Finally, the site accommodates sight-disabled people by giving them the option of viewing enlarged text. 2

Adult ADD home page

The AdultADD.com home page is more open than the NIMH home page; it has less text and contains fewer design elements (see fig. 2). Even so, the arrangement of text on the page, the no-nonsense style, and the lack of misspellings indicate that it has been carefully designed. The home page is straightforward and businesslike and looks like a PowerPoint slide. It is easy to navigate and contains simple headings, such as "Find a Physician" and "Treatment for Adults." Despite the clean, direct design, however, the layout raises a question: why isn't this site linked to 3

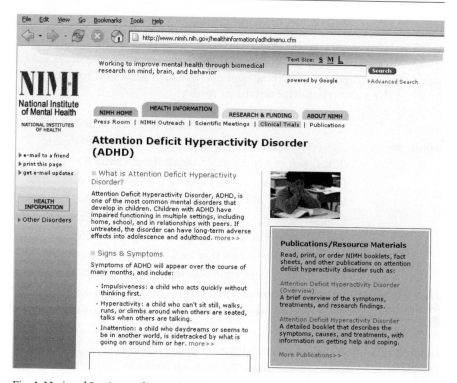

Fig. 1. National Institute of Mental Health. *Attention Deficit Hyperactivity Disorder (ADHD).* NIMH, 16 Nov. 2010. Web. 16 Nov. 2010.

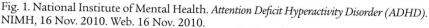

any other Web sites about ADD or ADHD? Unlike nimh.nih.gov, the AdultADD.com Web site has no reference page and no footnotes. In addition, it does not accommodate sight-disabled users.

Second point: comparing sponsors   Another difference between the two Web sites is who posted 4 them. One look at the URL for the NIMH Web site indicates that it is a *.gov* — a Web site created by a branch of the United States government. The logo in the upper left-hand corner of the home *NIMH site sponsor* page identifies the National Institute of Mental Health (NIMH) as the sponsor of the site. In addition, every article on the Web site has a listed author, so users know exactly who is responsible for the content. The "About NIMH" tab on the upper right of the home page takes users to a description of NIMH, as well as to contact information. Here visitors to the site find out that NIMH is part of the National Institutes of Health, which is, in turn, a part of the U.S. Department of Health and Human Services. Furthermore, NIMH is the "lead Federal agency for research on mental and behavioral disorders." This description also makes

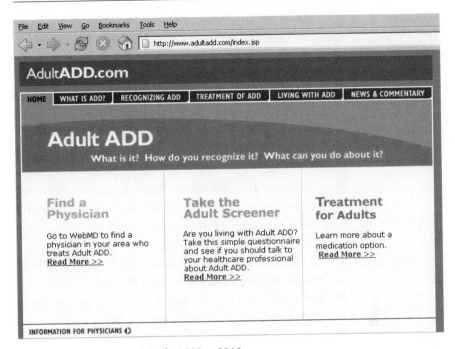

Fig. 2. *AdultADD.* N.p. n.d. Web. 16 Nov. 2010.

clear the NIMH Web site's purpose: to give the American public the latest information about ADHD. For this reason, the Web site lists all the medications used to treat ADHD and evaluates the various treatment options available to patients.

Adult ADD site sponsor   The URL for the AdultADD.com Web site ends with *.com,*   5 indicating that it is a commercial site that promotes a product. It is not immediately clear, however, who (or what) sponsors the Web site. The home page has no corporate logo and no identifying information. Across the top of the home page are a series of links — "What is ADD?" "Recognizing ADD," and so on. Each of these links leads to a page that contains a video clip of a television commercial that promotes Strattera, a drug manufactured by the Eli Lilly pharmaceutical company for the treatment of ADD. If you click on the links in the middle of the page, however, you never encounter this information. For this reason, there is a possibility that much of the information these links lead to is biased. In other words, Lilly could be highlighting treatments that involve its own product and disregarding treatments that involve products made by other pharmaceutical companies.

Third point: comparing frequency of updates

NIMH updates

A final difference between the two Web sites is how   6
frequently they are updated. The NIMH Web site makes a point of
staying up-to-date, presenting the most current information on
its subject. The bottom left-hand corner of the NIMH home page
contains the exact date the site was last updated, and each page
on the Web site has a different date, so it is clear when every
article on the site was written and posted.

Adult ADD updates

The AdultADD.com Web site, however, is less clear about   7
updates. The date on the bottom of the home page indicates only
when the Web site was copyrighted; it does not indicate when the
Web site itself was updated. This omission makes it very difficult
for a visitor to the site to determine how current the information
on the site actually is.

Conclusion

A comparison of the NIMH Web site and AdultADD.com Web   8
site shows some clear differences between the two. The NIMH
Web site makes it easy for users to find out who posted the site,
who wrote material on it, and when the site was last updated.
The AdultADD.com Web site, however, hides its commercial
purpose and makes it difficult for visitors to the site to find
out who posted the material and when it was last updated. For

Restatement of thesis

these reasons, the NIMH Web site is a more trustworthy source of
information than the AdultADD.com Web site.

Points for Special Attention

Structure. Maria's purpose in writing this essay was to compare two
Web sites that deal with Attention Deficit Hyperactivity Disorder and to
determine which is the better, more reliable source of information. She
structured her essay as a point-by-point comparison, carefully discussing
the same points for each subject. With this method of organization, she
can be sure her readers will understand the specific differences between the
NIMH Web site and the AdultADD.com Web site. Had Maria used a
subject-by-subject comparison, her readers would have had to keep turning
back to match the points she made about one Web site with those she made
about the other.

Topic Sentences. Without clear topic sentences, Maria's readers would
have had difficulty determining where each discussion of the NIMH Web
site ended and each one about the AdultADD.com Web site began. Maria
uses topic sentences to distinguish the two subjects of her comparison and
to make the contrast between them clear.

Point 1
⌐ The nimh.nih.gov home page looks clear and professional.
The AdultADD.com home page is more open than the NIMH
home page; it has less text and contains fewer design elements. ⌐

Point 2
⌐ One look at the URL for the NIMH Web site indicates that it
is a *.gov* — a Web site created by a branch of the United States
government.
The URL for the AdultADD.com Web site ends with *.com,* indicating that it is a commercial site that promotes a product. ⌐

Point 3
⌐ The NIMH Web site makes a point of staying up-to-date, presenting the most current information on its subject.
The AdultADD.com Web site, however, is less clear about updates. ⌐

Transitions. In addition to clear and straightforward topic sentences, Maria included **transitional sentences** to help readers move through the essay. These sentences identify the three points of contrast in the essay and, by establishing a parallel structure, they form a pattern that reinforces the essay's thesis.

The first difference between the two Web sites is the design of their home pages.

Another difference between the two Web sites is who posted them.

A final difference between the two Web sites is how frequently they are updated.

Working with Sources. Maria knew that it would be easier for her to compare the NIMH and AdultADD.com Web sites if she included visuals in her paper. Because readers would be able to see the home pages of both Web sites, Maria would not have to include long passages of description. She could then concentrate on making specific points about the sites and not get sidetracked describing their physical features. Her instructor pointed out that if she added these two visuals, she would have to include a label (*Fig. 1, Fig. 2,* and so on) along with a caption under each one. He also told her that if the caption included complete source information, there was no need to list the source on her works-cited page. (See Chapter 18 for a discussion of MLA documentation.)

Focus on Revision

Maria's classmates thought the greatest strength of her essay was its use of detail, which made the contrast between the two Web sites clear, but they thought that even more detail would improve her essay. For example, in paragraph 6, Maria could include a few titles of the articles the NIMH Web site lists, along with their dates of publication. In paragraph 7, she could also list some of the specific information on the AdultADD.com Web site and explain why it is necessary to know when the information was written and posted.

Maria agreed with these suggestions. She also thought she could improve her conclusion: although it summed up the main points of her essay, it contained little that would stay with readers after they finished. A sentence or two to caution readers about the need to carefully evaluate the information they find on Web sites would be an improvement.

PEER EDITING WORKSHEET: Comparison and Contrast

1. Does the essay have a clearly stated thesis? What is it?

2. What two things are being compared? What basis for comparison exists between the two?

3. Does the essay treat the same or similar points for each of its two subjects? List the points discussed.

FIRST SUBJECT	SECOND SUBJECT
a.	a.
b.	b.
c.	c.
d.	d.

Are these points discussed in the same order for both subjects? Are the points presented in parallel terms?

4. Does the essay use a point-by-point or subject-by-subject strategy? Is this the best choice? Why?

5. Are transitional words and phrases used appropriately to identify points of comparison and contrast? List some of the transitions used.

6. Are additional transitions needed? If so, where?

7. How could the introductory paragraph be improved?

8. How could the concluding paragraph be improved?

The selections that follow illustrate both subject-by-subject and point-by-point comparisons. The first selection, a pair of visual texts, is followed by questions designed to illustrate how comparison and contrast can operate in visual form.

AUGUSTE RODIN

The Kiss (Sculpture)

ROBERT INDIANA

LOVE (Sculpture)

. . .

Reading Images

1. What characteristics do the two sculptures pictured above and on the preceding page share? Do they share enough characteristics to establish a basis for comparison? Explain.

2. Make a list of points you could discuss if you were comparing the two sculptures.

3. What general statement could you make about these two sculptures? Do the points you listed in question 2 provide enough support for this general statement?

Journal Entry

How does each sculpture convey the idea of love? Which one do you believe conveys this idea more effectively? Why?

Thematic Connections

- "The Storm" (page 202)
- "Sex, Lies, and Conversation" (page 423)
- "Love and Other Catastrophes: A Mix Tape" (page 520)

BRUCE CATTON

Grant and Lee: A Study in Contrasts

Bruce Catton (1899–1978) was a respected journalist and an authority on the American Civil War. His studies were interrupted by his service during World War I, after which he worked as a journalist and then for various government agencies. Catton edited *American Heritage* magazine from 1954 until his death. Among his many books are *Mr. Lincoln's Army* (1951); *A Stillness at Appomattox* (1953), which won both a Pulitzer Prize and a National Book Award; and *Gettysburg: The Final Fury* (1974). Catton also wrote a memoir, *Waiting for the Morning Train* (1972), in which he recalls listening as a young boy to the reminiscences of Union Army veterans.

Background on Grant and Lee "Grant and Lee: A Study in Contrasts," which first appeared in a collection of historical essays titled *The American Story*, focuses on the two generals who headed the opposing armies during the Civil War (1861–1865). Robert E. Lee led the Army of Northern Virginia, the backbone of the Confederate forces, throughout much of the war. Ulysses S. Grant was named commander in chief of the Union troops in March 1864. By the spring of 1865, although it seemed almost inevitable that the Southern forces would be defeated, Lee made an attempt to lead his troops to join another Confederate army in North Carolina. Finding himself virtually surrounded by Grant's forces near the small town of Appomattox Court House, Lee chose to surrender to Grant. The following essay considers these two great generals in terms of both their differences and their important similarities.

When Ulysses S. Grant and Robert E. Lee met in the parlor of a modest house at Appomattox Court House, Virginia, on April 9, 1865, to work out the terms for the surrender of Lee's Army of Northern Virginia, a great chapter in American life came to a close, and a great new chapter began. 1

These men were bringing the Civil War to its virtual finish. To be sure, other armies had yet to surrender, and for a few days the fugitive Confederate government would struggle desperately and vainly, trying to find some way to go on living now that its chief support was gone. But in effect it was all over when Grant and Lee signed the papers. And the little room where they wrote out the terms was the scene of one of the poignant, dramatic contrasts in American history. 2

They were two strong men, these oddly different generals, and they represented the strengths of two conflicting currents that, through them, had come into final collision. 3

Back of Robert E. Lee was the notion that the old aristocratic concept might somehow survive and be dominant in American life. 4

Lee was tidewater Virginia, and in his background were family, culture, 5
and tradition . . . the age of chivalry transplanted to a New World which
was making its own legends and its own myths. He embodied a way of
life that had come down through the age of knighthood and the English
country squire. America was a land that was beginning all over again, dedicated to nothing much more complicated than the rather hazy belief that
all men had equal rights and should have an equal chance in the world.
In such a land Lee stood for the feeling that it was somehow of advantage
to human society to have pronounced inequality in the social structure.
There should be a leisure class, backed by ownership of land; in turn, society itself should be keyed to the land as the chief source of wealth and
influence. It would bring forth (according to this ideal) a class of men with
a strong sense of obligation to the community; men who lived not to gain
advantage for themselves, but to meet the solemn obligations which had
been laid on them by the very fact that they were privileged. From them the
country would get its leadership; to them it could look for the higher values — of thought, of conduct, of personal deportment — to give it strength
and virtue.

Lee embodied the noblest elements of this aristocratic ideal. Through 6
him, the landed nobility justified itself. For four years, the Southern states
had fought a desperate war to uphold the ideals for which Lee stood. In
the end, it almost seemed as if the Confederacy fought for Lee; as if he
himself was the Confederacy . . . the best thing that the way of life for
which the Confederacy stood could ever have to offer. He had passed into
legend before Appomattox. Thousands of tired, underfed, poorly clothed
Confederate soldiers, long since past the simple enthusiasm of the early
days of the struggle, somehow considered Lee the symbol of everything for
which they had been willing to die. But they could not quite put this feeling
into words. If the Lost Cause, sanctified by so much heroism and so many
deaths, had a living justification, its justification was General Lee.

Grant, the son of a tanner on the Western frontier, was everything Lee 7
was not. He had come up the hard way and embodied nothing in particular except the eternal toughness and sinewy fiber of the men who grew up
beyond the mountains. He was one of a body of men who owed reverence
and obeisance to no one, who were self-reliant to a fault, who cared hardly
anything for the past but who had a sharp eye for the future.

These frontier men were the precise opposites of the tidewater aristo- 8
crats. Back of them, in the great surge that had taken people over the Al-
leghenies and into the opening Western country, there was a deep, implicit
dissatisfaction with a past that had settled into grooves. They stood for
democracy, not from any reasoned conclusion about the proper ordering
of human society, but simply because they had grown up in the middle of
democracy and knew how it worked. Their society might have privileges,
but they would be privileges each man had won for himself. Forms and
patterns meant nothing. No man was born to anything, except perhaps to
a chance to show how far he could rise. Life was competition.

Yet along with this feeling had come a deep sense of belonging to a 9 national community. The Westerner who developed a farm, opened a shop, or set up in business as a trader, could hope to prosper only as his own community prospered — and his community ran from the Atlantic to the Pacific and from Canada down to Mexico. If the land was settled, with towns and highways and accessible markets, he could better himself. He saw his fate in terms of the nation's own destiny. As its horizons expanded, so did his. He had, in other words, an acute dollars-and-cents stake in the continued growth and development of his country.

And that, perhaps, is where the contrast between Grant and Lee be- 10 comes most striking. The Virginia aristocrat, inevitably, saw himself in relation to his own region. He lived in a static society which could endure almost anything except change. Instinctively, his first loyalty would go to the locality in which that society existed. He would fight to the limit of endurance to defend it, because in defending it he was defending everything that gave his own life its deepest meaning.

The Westerner, on the other hand, would fight with an equal tenac- 11 ity for the broader concept of society. He fought so because everything he lived by was tied to growth, expansion, and a constantly widening horizon. What he lived by would survive or fall with the nation itself. He could not possibly stand by unmoved in the face of an attempt to destroy the Union. He would combat it with everything he had, because he could only see it as an effort to cut the ground out from under his feet.

So Grant and Lee were in complete contrast, representing two diametri- 12 cally opposed elements in American life. Grant was the modern man emerging; beyond him, ready to come on the stage, was the great age of steel and machinery, of crowded cities and a restless burgeoning vitality. Lee might have ridden down from the old age of chivalry, lance in hand, silken banner fluttering over his head. Each man was the perfect champion of his cause, drawing both his strengths and his weaknesses from the people he led.

Yet it was not all contrast, after all. Different as they were — in back- 13 ground, in personality, in underlying aspiration — these two great soldiers had much in common. Under everything else, they were marvelous fighters. Furthermore, their fighting qualities were really very much alike.

Each man had, to begin with, the great virtue of utter tenacity and 14 fidelity. Grant fought his way down the Mississippi Valley in spite of acute personal discouragement and profound military handicaps. Lee hung on in the trenches at Petersburg after hope itself had died. In each man there was an indomitable quality . . . the born fighter's refusal to give up as long as he can still remain on his feet and lift his two fists.

Daring and resourcefulness they had, too; the ability to think faster 15 and move faster than the enemy. These were the qualities which gave Lee the dazzling campaigns of Second Manassas and Chancellorsville and won Vicksburg for Grant.

Lastly, and perhaps greatest of all, there was the ability, at the end, to 16 turn quickly from war to peace once the fighting was over. Out of the way these two men behaved at Appomattox came the possibility of a peace of reconciliation. It was a possibility not wholly realized, in the years to come, but which did, in the end, help the two sections to become one nation again . . . after a war whose bitterness might have seemed to make such a reunion wholly impossible. No part of either man's life became him more than the part he played in this brief meeting in the McLean house at Appomattox. Their behavior there put all succeeding generations of Americans in their debt. Two great Americans, Grant and Lee — very different, yet under everything very much alike. Their encounter at Appomattox was one of the great moments of American history.

• • •

Comprehension

1. What took place at Appomattox Court House on April 9, 1865? Why did the meeting at Appomattox signal the closing of "a great chapter in American life" (1)?

2. How does Robert E. Lee represent aristocracy? How does Ulysses S. Grant represent Lee's opposite?

3. According to Catton, where is it that "the contrast between Grant and Lee becomes most striking" (10)?

4. What similarities does Catton see between the two men?

5. Why, according to Catton, are "succeeding generations of Americans" (16) in debt to Grant and Lee?

Purpose and Audience

1. Catton's purpose in contrasting Grant and Lee is to make a statement about the differences between two currents in American history. Summarize these differences. Do you think the differences still exist today? Explain.

2. Is Catton's purpose in comparing Grant and Lee the same as his purpose in contrasting them? That is, do their similarities also make a statement about U.S. history? Explain.

3. State the essay's thesis in your own words.

Style and Structure

1. Does Catton use subject-by-subject or point-by-point comparison? Why do you think he chooses the strategy he does?

2. In this essay, topic sentences are extremely helpful to the reader. Explain the functions of the following sentences: "Grant . . . was everything Lee was not" (7); "So Grant and Lee were in complete contrast" (12); "Yet it was not all contrast, after all" (13); and "Lastly, and perhaps greatest of all . . ." (16).

3. Catton uses transitions skillfully in his essay. Identify the transitional words or expressions that link each paragraph to the preceding one.

4. Why do you suppose Catton provides the background for the meeting at Appomattox but presents no information about the dramatic meeting itself?

Vocabulary Projects

1. Define each of the following words as it is used in this selection.

poignant (2)	obeisance (7)	tenacity (14)
chivalry (5)	implicit (8)	fidelity (14)
deportment (5)	inevitably (10)	indomitable (14)
sanctified (6)	diametrically (12)	reconciliation (16)
embodied (7)	burgeoning (12)	
sinewy (7)	aspiration (13)	

2. Go to the online thesaurus at dictionary.com, and look up **synonyms** for each of the following words. Then, determine whether each synonym would be as effective as the word used in this essay.

deportment (5)	obeisance (7)	indomitable (14)
sanctified (6)	diametrically (12)	

Journal Entry

Compare your attitudes about the United States with those held by Grant and by Lee. With which man do you agree?

Writing Workshop

1. Write a "study in contrasts" about two people you know well — two teachers, your parents, two relatives, two friends — or about two fictional characters you are very familiar with. Be sure to include a thesis statement.

2. Write a dialogue between two people you know that reveals their contrasting attitudes toward school, work, or any other subject.

3. **Working with Sources.** Write an essay about two individuals from a period of American history other than the Civil War to make the same points Catton makes. If you do research, make sure you document your sources and include a works-cited page. (See Chapter 18 for information on MLA documentation.)

Combining the Patterns

In several places, Catton uses **exemplification** to structure a paragraph. For instance, in paragraph 7, he uses examples to support the topic sentence "Grant, the son of a tanner on the Western frontier, was everything Lee was not." Identify three paragraphs that use examples to support the topic sentence, and bracket the examples. How do these examples in these paragraphs reinforce the similarities and differences between Grant and Lee?

Thematic Connections

- "Ground Zero" (page 182)
- "Fame-iness" (page 511)
- The Declaration of Independence (page 553)
- "Letter from Birmingham Jail" (page 566)

PAUL H. RUBIN

Environmentalism as Religion

Paul H. Rubin (b. 1942) is the Samuel Candler Dobbs Professor of Economics at Emory University. He has published widely in the fields of economics, law, and politics, and has written *Darwinian Politics: The Evolutionary Origin of Freedom* (2002). His essays and opinion columns have appeared in the *Wall Street Journal, Washington Times,* and other publications.

Background on the environmental movement in the United States The history of environmental awareness in the United States stretches back to the country's founding: Thomas Jefferson was a naturalist, botanist, and farmer who envisioned the United States as an agrarian republic. In the nineteenth century, industrialization and urbanization spurred both skepticism about progress and a more urgent sense that nature needed protection. Henry David Thoreau wrote *Walden,* a philosophical manifesto about the advantages of living close to nature, in 1854; President Ulysses S. Grant established Yellowstone National Park as protected wilderness in 1872. Twenty years later, author and activist John Muir, the most important American conservationist of the late nineteenth and early twentieth centuries, founded the Sierra Club, which remains the largest environmental organization in the United States. In subsequent years, President Theodore Roosevelt created the United States Forest Service and established several national parks, forests, and reserves. Writers have also played a significant role in conservation and environmentalism. For example, ecologist Aldo Leopold's *Sand County Almanac* (1949) and Rachel Carson's *Silent Spring* (1962) shaped public attitudes about nature and influenced government policies toward the environment. In 1970, Wisconsin senator Gaylord Nelson established Earth Day, which ushered in a decade that witnessed the creation of the Environmental Protection Agency, the Clean Air Act, and other environmental initiatives.

Many observers have made the point that environmentalism is eerily 1 close to a religious belief system, since it includes creation stories and ideas of original sin. But there is another sense in which environmentalism is becoming more and more like a religion: It provides its adherents with an identity.

Scientists are understandably uninterested in religious stories because 2 they do not meet the basic criterion for science: They cannot be tested. God may or may not have created the world — there is no way of knowing, although we do know that the biblical creation story is scientifically incorrect. Since we cannot prove or disprove the existence of God, science can't help us answer questions about the truth of religion as a method of understanding the world.

But scientists, particularly evolutionary psychologists, have identified 3
another function of religion in addition to its function of explaining the
world. Religion often supplements or replaces the tribalism that is an innate part of our evolved nature.

Original religions were tribal rather than universal. Each tribe had its 4
own god or gods, and the success of the tribe was evidence that their god
was stronger than others.

But modern religions have largely replaced tribal gods with univer- 5
sal gods and allowed unrelated individuals from outside the tribe to join.
Identification with a religion has replaced identification with a tribe. While
many decry religious wars, modern religion has probably not reduced human conflict because there are fewer tribal wars. (Anthropologists have
shown that tribal wars are even more lethal per capita than modern wars.)

It is this identity-creating function that environmentalism provides. 6
As the world becomes less religious, people can define themselves as being
Green rather than being Christian or Jewish.

Consider some of the ways in which environmental behaviors echo re- 7
ligious behaviors and thus provide meaningful rituals for Greens:

- There is a holy day — Earth Day.
- There are food taboos. Instead of eating fish on Friday, or avoiding
  pork, Greens now eat organic foods and many are moving towards
  eating only locally grown foods.
- There is no prayer, but there are self-sacrificing rituals that are not
  particularly useful, such as recycling. Recycling paper to save trees,
  for example, makes no sense since the effect will be to reduce the
  number of trees planted in the long run.
- Belief systems are embraced with no logical basis. For example, en-
  vironmentalists almost universally believe in the dangers of global
  warming but also reject the best solution to the problem, which is
  nuclear power. These two beliefs co-exist based on faith, not reason.
- There are no temples, but there are sacred structures. As I walk
  around the Emory campus, I am continually confronted with recycling bins, and instead of one trash can I am faced with several for
  different sorts of trash. Universities are centers of the environmental religion, and such structures are increasingly common. While
  people have worshipped many things, we may be the first to build
  shrines to garbage.
- Environmentalism is a proselytizing religion. Skeptics are not
  merely people unconvinced by the evidence: They are treated as
  evil sinners. I probably would not write this article if I did not have
  tenure.

Some conservatives spend their time criticizing the way Darwin is 8
taught in schools. This is pointless and probably counterproductive. These
same efforts should be spent on making sure that the schools only teach
those aspects of environmentalism that pass rigorous scientific testing. By

making the point that Greenism is a religion, perhaps we environmental skeptics can enlist the First Amendment on our side.

. . .

Comprehension

1. According to Rubin, why are scientists uninterested in religious stories?

2. What does Rubin mean when he says that modern religion "often supplements or replaces the tribalism that is an innate part of our evolved nature" (3)?

3. According to Rubin, in what ways is environmentalism like a religion? Do all the parallels he identifies make sense to you? Why or why not?

4. Why does Rubin think it is "pointless and probably counterproductive" for conservatives to criticize the way that Darwin is being taught in schools (8)? What does Rubin believe conservatives should focus on instead? Why?

Purpose and Audience

1. What is the thesis of this essay? Where is it stated? Paraphrase this thesis.

2. What is Rubin's purpose in writing this essay? Do you think he achieves this purpose? Explain.

3. Does Rubin seem to assume that his readers will agree with his ideas, or does he expect them to be skeptical? How can you tell?

4. Do you think Rubin is being serious here? Does anything in the essay's content or language suggest that he does not intend his comparison to be taken seriously?

5. This article appeared in the *Wall Street Journal,* a newspaper whose readers tend to be politically conservative and interested in business issues. Does the article seem to be directed at these readers or at a general audience? Explain.

Style and Structure

1. Rubin's introduction is short and very direct. What are the advantages and disadvantages of this approach? What other kind of introduction could he have used?

2. Rubin does not begin listing specific parallels between environmentalism and religion until paragraph 7 of his essay. What does he do in paragraphs 1–6?

3. In comparing his two subjects (environmentalism and religion), does Rubin use a point-by-point or a subject-by-subject organization? What are the advantages of the arrangement he chooses?

4. Rubin presents his points of comparison as a bulleted list. What does he gain and what does he lose with this approach?

5. What is the basis for comparison between environmentalism and religion? Where does Rubin present this basis for comparison?

6. What point does Rubin reinforce in his conclusion? Should he have emphasized something else? Explain.

Vocabulary Projects

1. Define each of the following words as it is used in this selection.

eerily (1)	anthropologists (5)
adherents (1)	taboos (7)
criterion (2)	proselytizing (7)
tribalism (3)	counterproductive (8)
decry (5)	skeptics (8)

2. Rubin uses words that are associated with religion — *holy day, prayer,* and *temples,* for example. What do these terms add to the essay? What other religious terms could he have used? Where?

Journal Entry

Can you think of any ways in which environmentalism is *not* like religion?

Writing Workshop

1. Write an essay in which you tell how being environmentally conscious has changed the way you live. Be sure to compare your life before you became environmentally conscious with your life now. Your essay can be either humorous or serious.

2. **Working with Sources.** Write an email to Rubin in which you support or challenge his thesis. Include at least one quotation from his essay. Be sure to document the quotation and to include a works-cited page. (See Chapter 18 for information on MLA documentation.)

3. Write an essay in which you consider how something else — for example, a sport or other activity — is like a religion. Give your essay a title that makes your comparison clear — for example, "Baseball as Religion." Your essay can be humorous or serious.

Combining the Patterns

Paragraph 2 of this essay is an **argumentation** paragraph, which follows a chain of reasoning to its logical conclusion. What point does this paragraph make? What does this paragraph add to the essay?

Thematic Connections

BHARATI MUKHERJEE

Two Ways to Belong in America

Born in 1940 in Calcutta, India, novelist Bharati Mukherjee immigrated to the United States in 1961. Now a naturalized U.S. citizen, she teaches at the University of California at Berkeley. Mukherjee's novels include *Tiger's Daughter* (1972), *Jasmine* (1989), *Leave It to Me* (1997), *Desirable Daughters* (2002), and *The Tree Bride* (2004); her story collections are *Darkness* (1975) and the prize-winning *The Middleman and Other Stories* (1988). Her fiction often explores the tensions between the traditional role of women in Indian society and their very different role in the United States.

Background on U.S. immigration policy   The following essay, originally published in 1996, was written in response to proposals in Congress (eventually defeated) to enact legislation denying government benefits, such as Social Security, to resident aliens. Not to be confused with illegal immigrants, resident aliens — also called *legal permanent residents* — are immigrants who live in the United States legally, sometimes for their whole lives, but do not apply for citizenship. Most work and pay taxes like any citizen. According to the census bureau, the United States population includes more than 38 million foreign-born residents, accounting for about 12 percent of the population. Of these, 12.5 million are legal permanent residents, 12.6 million are naturalized citizens, and an estimated 11.1 million are in the country illegally (some experts think this number is much higher); most of the rest are refugees seeking political asylum and students and temporary workers with visas. Although various issues related to immigration policy have been hotly debated for many years, particularly as large numbers of immigrants entered the country in the 1990s, the terrorist attacks of September 2001 have led to closer screenings of foreigners who want to enter the United States, especially those applying for student visas.

This is a tale of two sisters from Calcutta, Mira and Bharati, who have 1 lived in the United States for some 35 years, but who find themselves on different sides in the current debate over the status of immigrants. I am an American citizen and she is not. I am moved that thousands of long-term residents are finally taking the oath of citizenship. She is not.

Mira arrived in Detroit in 1960 to study child psychology and pre- 2 school education. I followed her a year later to study creative writing at the University of Iowa. When we left India, we were almost identical in appearance and attitude. We dressed alike, in saris; we expressed identical views on politics, social issues, love, and marriage in the same Calcutta convent-school accent. We would endure our two years in America, secure our degrees, then return to India to marry the grooms of our father's choosing.

Instead, Mira married an Indian student in 1962 who was getting his 3 business administration degree at Wayne State University. They soon acquired the labor certifications necessary for the green card of hassle-free residence and employment.

Mira still lives in Detroit, works in the Southfield, Mich., school sys- 4 tem, and has become nationally recognized for her contributions in the fields of pre-school education and parent-teacher relationships. After 36 years as a legal immigrant in this country, she clings passionately to her Indian citizenship and hopes to go home to India when she retires.

In Iowa City in 1963, I married a fellow student, an American of Ca- 5 nadian parentage. Because of the accident of his North Dakota birth, I bypassed labor-certification requirements and the race-related "quota" system that favored the applicant's country of origin over his or her merit. I was prepared for (and even welcomed) the emotional strain that came with marrying outside my ethnic community. In 33 years of marriage, we have lived in every part of North America. By choosing a husband who was not my father's selection, I was opting for fluidity, self-invention, blue jeans and T-shirts, and renouncing 3,000 years (at least) of caste-observant, "pure culture" marriage in the Mukherjee family. My books have often been read as unapologetic (and in some quarters overenthusiastic) texts for cultural and psychological "mongrelization." It's a word I celebrate.

Mira and I have stayed sisterly close by phone. In our regular Sunday 6 morning conversations, we are unguardedly affectionate. I am her only blood relative on this continent. We expect to see each other through the looming crises of aging and ill health without being asked. Long before Vice President Gore's "Citizenship U.S.A." drive, we'd had our polite arguments over the ethics of retaining an overseas citizenship while expecting the permanent protection and economic benefits that come with living and working in America.

Like well-raised sisters, we never said what was really on our minds, 7 but we probably pitied one another. She, for the lack of structure in my life, the erasure of Indianness, the absence of an unvarying daily core. I, for the narrowness of her perspective, her uninvolvement with the mythic depths or the superficial pop culture of this society. But, now, with the scapegoatings of "aliens" (documented or illegal) on the increase, and the targeting of long-term legal immigrants like Mira for new scrutiny and new self-consciousness, she and I find ourselves unable to maintain the same polite discretion. We were always unacknowledged adversaries, and we are now, more than ever, sisters.

"I feel used," Mira raged on the phone the other night. "I feel manipu- 8 lated and discarded. This is such an unfair way to treat a person who was invited to stay and work here because of her talent. My employer went to the I.N.S. and petitioned for the labor certification. For over 30 years, I've invested my creativity and professional skills into the improvement of *this* country's pre-school system. I've obeyed all the rules, I've paid my taxes, I love my work, I love my students, I love the friends I've made. How dare

America now change its rules in midstream? If America wants to make new rules curtailing benefits of legal immigrants, they should apply only to immigrants who arrive after those rules are already in place."

To my ears, it sounded like the description of a long-enduring, comfortable yet loveless marriage, without risk or recklessness. Have we the right to demand, and to expect, that we be loved? (That, to me, is the subtext of the arguments by immigration advocates.) My sister is an expatriate, professionally generous and creative, socially courteous and gracious, and that's as far as her Americanization can go. She is here to maintain an identity, not to transform it. 9

I asked her if she would follow the example of others who have decided to become citizens because of the anti-immigration bills in Congress. And here, she surprised me. "If America wants to play the manipulative game, I'll play it, too," she snapped. "I'll become a U.S. citizen for now, then change back to India when I'm ready to go home. I feel some kind of irrational attachment to India that I don't to America. Until all this hysteria against legal immigrants, I was totally happy. Having my green card meant I could visit any place in the world I wanted to and then come back to a job that's satisfying and that I do very well." 10

In one family, from two sisters alike as peas in a pod, there could not be a wider divergence of immigrant experience. America spoke to me — I married it — I embraced the demotion from expatriate aristocrat to immigrant nobody, surrendering those thousands of years of "pure culture," the saris, the delightfully accented English. She retained them all. Which of us is the freak? 11

Mira's voice, I realize, is the voice not just of the immigrant South Asian community but of an immigrant community of the millions who have stayed rooted in one job, one city, one house, one ancestral culture, one cuisine, for the entirety of their productive years. She speaks for greater numbers than I possibly can. Only the fluency of her English and the anger, rather than fear, born of confidence from her education, differentiate her from the seamstresses, the domestics, the technicians, the shop owners, the millions of hard-working but effectively silenced documented immigrants as well as their less fortunate "illegal" brothers and sisters. 12

Nearly 20 years ago, when I was living in my husband's ancestral homeland of Canada, I was always well-employed but never allowed to feel part of the local Quebec or larger Canadian society. Then, through a Green Paper that invited a national referendum on the unwanted side effects of "nontraditional" immigration, the Government officially turned against its immigrant communities, particularly those from South Asia. 13

I felt then the same sense of betrayal that Mira feels now. I will never forget the pain of that sudden turning, and the casual racist outbursts the Green Paper elicited. That sense of betrayal had its desired effect and drove me, and thousands like me, from the country. 14

Mira and I differ, however, in the ways in which we hope to interact with the country that we have chosen to live in. She is happier to live in America as an expatriate Indian than as an immigrant American. I need to 15 feel like a part of the community I have adopted (as I tried to feel in Canada as well). I need to put roots down, to vote and make the difference that I can. The price that the immigrant willingly pays, and that the exile avoids, is the trauma of self-transformation.

· · ·

Comprehension

1. At first, how long did Mukherjee and her sister intend to stay in America? Why did they change their plans?

2. What does Mukherjee mean when she says she welcomed the "emotional strain" of "marrying outside [her] ethnic community" (5)?

3. In what ways is Mukherjee different from her sister? What kind of relationship do they have?

4. Why does Mukherjee's sister feel used? Why does she say that America has "'change[d] its rules in midstream'" (8)?

5. According to Mukherjee, how is her sister like all immigrants who "have stayed rooted in one job, one city, one house, one ancestral culture, one cuisine, for the entirety of their productive years" (12)?

Purpose and Audience

1. What is Mukherjee's thesis? At what point does she state it?

2. At whom is Mukherjee aiming her remarks? Immigrants like herself? Immigrants like her sister? General readers? Explain.

3. What is Mukherjee's purpose? Is she trying to inform? To move readers to action? To accomplish something else? Explain.

Style and Structure

1. What basis for comparison exists between Mukherjee and her sister? Where in the essay does Mukherjee establish this basis?

2. Is this essay a point-by-point or a subject-by-subject comparison? Why do you think Mukherjee chose the strategy she did?

3. What points does Mukherjee discuss for each subject? Should she have discussed any other points?

4. What transitional words and phrases does Mukherjee use to signal shifts from one point to another?

5. How effective is Mukherjee's conclusion? Does it summarize the essay's major points? Would another strategy be more effective? Explain.

Vocabulary Projects

1. Define each of the following words as it is used in this selection.

saris (2)	mythic (7)	curtailing (8)
certifications (3)	superficial (7)	divergence (11)
mongrelization (5)	scrutiny (7)	expatriate (11)
perspective (7)	discretion (7)	trauma (15)

2. What, according to Mukherjee, is the difference between an *immigrant* and an *exile* (15)? What are the connotations of these two words? Do you think the distinction Mukherjee makes is valid?

Journal Entry

Do you think Mukherjee respects her sister's decision? From your perspective, which sister has made the right choice?

Writing Workshop

1. Assume that her sister, Mira, has just read Mukherjee's essay and wants to respond to it. Write an email from Mira comparing her position about assimilation to that of Mukherjee. Make sure you explain Mira's position and address Mukherjee's points about assimilation.

2. Have you ever moved from one town or city to another? Write an essay comparing the two places. Your thesis statement should indicate whether you are emphasizing similarities or differences and convey your opinion of the new area. (If you have never moved, write an essay comparing two places you are familiar with — your college and your high school, for example.)

3. **Working with Sources.** Assume you had to move to another country. Where would you move? Would you, like Mukherjee, assimilate into your new culture, or would you, like her sister, retain your own cultural values? Write an essay comparing life in your new country with life in the United States. (If you have already moved from another country, compare your life in the United States with your life in your country of origin.) Include at least one quotation from Mukherjee's essay in your introduction, and be sure to document the quotation and to include a works-cited page. (See Chapter 18 for information on MLA documentation.)

Combining the Patterns

Do you think Mukherjee should have used **cause and effect** to structure a section explaining why she and her sister are so different? Explain what such a section would add to or take away from the essay.

Thematic Connections

- "Only Daughter" (page 111)
- "Rice" (page 172)
- "The Myth of the Latin Woman: I Just Met a Girl Named Maria" (page 232)
- "The Untouchable" (page 496)

AMY CHUA

Why Chinese Mothers Are Superior

Amy Chua was born in Champaign, Illinois, in 1962. She graduated from Harvard College and earned her J.D. at Harvard Law School, where she was an executive editor of the *Harvard Law Review*. Chua is now the John M. Duff Professor of Law at Yale Law School, where she focuses on international law and business, ethnic conflict, and globalization and the law. She has written two scholarly books, *World on Fire: How Exporting Free Market Democracy Breeds Ethnic Hatred and Global Instability* (2003) and *Days of Empire: How Hyperpowers Rise to Global Dominance — and Why They Fall* (2007). Today, however, Chua is best known for her parenting memoir, *Battle Hymn of the Tiger Mother* (2011).

Background on parenting styles Chua writes disapprovingly about contemporary "Western" parents who, she claims, are "extremely anxious about their children's self-esteem." Such anxieties are relatively new, especially when one surveys the history of parenting — from the ancient Greeks, who commonly left unwanted children in the woods to die of exposure, to seventeenth-century American Puritans, who practiced a philosophy of "Better whipt than damned." French Enlightenment figure Jean-Jacques Rousseau (1712–1778) proposed a more sympathetic view of the child, writing that when "children's wills are not spoiled by our fault, children want nothing uselessly." But in the nineteenth and early twentieth centuries, American parenting philosophies usually focused on discipline, emotional detachment, and the wisdom of experts. As Dr. Luther Emmett Holt wrote in *The Care and Feeding of Children* (1894), "instinct and maternal love are too often assumed to be a sufficient guide for a mother." Pediatrician Benjamin Spock, who published his enormously influential *Baby and Child Care* in 1946, is often credited with — or blamed for — a social shift toward more permissive child-rearing, especially in the context of the baby-boom generation. Spock urged parents to trust their own judgment and to meet their children's needs rather than worrying about "spoiling" the child. In the decades that followed, this parenting approach accompanied an increasing emphasis on children's self-esteem, both at home and in school.

A lot of people wonder how Chinese parents raise such stereotypically 1 successful kids. They wonder what these parents do to produce so many math whizzes and music prodigies, what it's like inside the family, and whether they could do it too. Well, I can tell them, because I've done it. Here are some things my daughters, Sophia and Louisa, were never allowed to do:

- attend a sleepover
- have a playdate
- be in a school play

- complain about not being in a school play
- watch TV or play computer games
- choose their own extracurricular activities
- get any grade less than an A
- not be the No. 1 student in every subject except gym and drama
- play any instrument other than the piano or violin
- not play the piano or violin.

I'm using the term "Chinese mother" loosely. I know some Korean, In- 2
dian, Jamaican, Irish, and Ghanaian parents who qualify too. Conversely, I
know some mothers of Chinese heritage, almost always born in the West,
who are not Chinese mothers, by choice or otherwise. I'm also using the
term "Western parents" loosely. Western parents come in all varieties.

When it comes to parenting, the Chinese seem to produce children 3
who display academic excellence, musical mastery, and professional success — or so the stereotype goes. *WSJ's** Christina Tsuei speaks to two
moms raised by Chinese immigrants who share what it was like growing
up and how they hope to raise their children.

All the same, even when Western parents think they're being strict, they 4
usually don't come close to being Chinese mothers. For example, my Western friends who consider themselves strict make their children practice their
instruments 30 minutes every day. An hour at most. For a Chinese mother,
the first hour is the easy part. It's hours two and three that get tough.

Despite our squeamishness about cultural stereotypes, there are tons 5
of studies out there showing marked and quantifiable differences between
Chinese and Westerners when it comes to parenting. In one study of 50
Western American mothers and 48 Chinese immigrant mothers, almost
70 percent of the Western mothers said either that "stressing academic success is not good for children" or that "parents need to foster the idea that
learning is fun." By contrast, roughly 0 percent of the Chinese mothers
felt the same way. Instead, the vast majority of the Chinese mothers said
that they believe their children can be "the best" students, that "academic
achievement reflects successful parenting," and that if children did not excel at school then there was "a problem" and parents "were not doing their
job." Other studies indicate that compared to Western parents, Chinese
parents spend approximately 10 times as long every day drilling academic
activities with their children. By contrast, Western kids are more likely to
participate in sports teams.

What Chinese parents understand is that nothing is fun until you're 6
good at it. To get good at anything you have to work, and children on their
own never want to work, which is why it is crucial to override their preferences. This often requires fortitude on the part of the parents because the
child will resist; things are always hardest at the beginning, which is where
Western parents tend to give up. But if done properly, the Chinese strategy
produces a virtuous circle. Tenacious practice, practice, practice is crucial

---

* Eds. note — *Wall Street Journal.*

for excellence; rote repetition is underrated in America. Once a child starts to excel at something — whether it's math, piano, pitching, or ballet — he or she gets praise, admiration, and satisfaction. This builds confidence and makes the once not-fun activity fun. This in turn makes it easier for the parent to get the child to work even more.

Chinese parents can get away with things that Western parents can't. 7 Once when I was young — maybe more than once — when I was extremely disrespectful to my mother, my father angrily called me "garbage" in our native Hokkien dialect. It worked really well. I felt terrible and deeply ashamed of what I had done. But it didn't damage my self-esteem or anything like that. I knew exactly how highly he thought of me. I didn't actually think I was worthless or feel like a piece of garbage.

As an adult, I once did the same thing to Sophia, calling her "garbage" 8 in English when she acted extremely disrespectfully toward me. When I mentioned that I had done this at a dinner party, I was immediately ostracized. One guest named Marcy got so upset she broke down in tears and had to leave early. My friend Susan, the host, tried to rehabilitate me with the remaining guests.

The fact is that Chinese parents can do things that would seem un- 9 imaginable — even legally actionable — to Westerners. Chinese mothers can say to their daughters, "Hey fatty — lose some weight." By contrast, Western parents have to tiptoe around the issue, talking in terms of "health" and never ever mentioning the f-word, and their kids still end up in therapy for eating disorders and negative self-image. (I also once heard a Western father toast his adult daughter by calling her "beautiful and incredibly competent." She later told me that made her feel like garbage.)

Chinese parents can order their kids to get straight As. Western parents 10 can only ask their kids to try their best. Chinese parents can say, "You're lazy. All your classmates are getting ahead of you." By contrast, Western parents have to struggle with their own conflicted feelings about achievement, and try to persuade themselves that they're not disappointed about how their kids turned out.

I've thought long and hard about how Chinese parents can get away 11 with what they do. I think there are three big differences between the Chinese and Western parental mind-sets.

First, I've noticed that Western parents are extremely anxious about 12 their children's self-esteem. They worry about how their children will feel if they fail at something, and they constantly try to reassure their children about how good they are notwithstanding a mediocre performance on a test or at a recital. In other words, Western parents are concerned about their children's psyches. Chinese parents aren't. They assume strength, not fragility, and as a result they behave very differently.

For example, if a child comes home with an A-minus on a test, a West- 13 ern parent will most likely praise the child. The Chinese mother will gasp in horror and ask what went wrong. If the child comes home with a B on the test, some Western parents will still praise the child. Other Western parents will sit their child down and express disapproval, but they will be careful not to make their child feel inadequate or insecure, and they will not call their child "stupid," "worthless," or "a disgrace." Privately, the Western parents may worry that their child does not test well or have aptitude in the subject or that there is something wrong with the curriculum and possibly the whole school. If the child's grades do not improve, they may eventually schedule a meeting with the school principal to challenge the way the subject is being taught or to call into question the teacher's credentials.

If a Chinese child gets a B — which would never happen — there would 14 first be a screaming, hair-tearing explosion. The devastated Chinese mother would then get dozens, maybe hundreds of practice tests and work through them with her child for as long as it takes to get the grade up to an A.

Chinese parents demand perfect grades because they believe that their 15 child can get them. If their child doesn't get them, the Chinese parent assumes it's because the child didn't work hard enough. That's why the solution to substandard performance is always to excoriate, punish, and shame the child. The Chinese parent believes that their child will be strong enough to take the shaming and to improve from it. (And when Chinese kids do excel, there is plenty of ego-inflating parental praise lavished in the privacy of the home.)

Second, Chinese parents believe that their kids owe them everything. 16 The reason for this is a little unclear, but it's probably a combination of Confucian filial piety and the fact that the parents have sacrificed and done so much for their children. (And it's true that Chinese mothers get in the trenches, putting in long grueling hours personally tutoring, training, interrogating, and spying on their kids.) Anyway, the understanding is that Chinese children must spend their lives repaying their parents by obeying them and making them proud.

By contrast, I don't think most Westerners have the same view of chil- 17 dren being permanently indebted to their parents. My husband, Jed, actually has the opposite view. "Children don't choose their parents," he once said to me. "They don't even choose to be born. It's parents who foist life on their kids, so it's the parents' responsibility to provide for them. Kids don't owe their parents anything. Their duty will be to their own kids." This strikes me as a terrible deal for the Western parent.

Third, Chinese parents believe that they know what is best for their 18 children and therefore override all of their children's own desires and preferences. That's why Chinese daughters can't have boyfriends in high school and why Chinese kids can't go to sleepaway camp. It's also why no Chinese kid would ever dare say to their mother, "I got a part in the school play! I'm Villager Number Six. I'll have to stay after school for rehearsal every day from 3:00 to 7:00, and I'll also need a ride on weekends." God help any Chinese kid who tried that one.

Don't get me wrong: It's not that Chinese parents don't care about 19 their children. Just the opposite. They would give up anything for their children. It's just an entirely different parenting model.

. . . Western parents worry a lot about their children's self-esteem. But 20 as a parent, one of the worst things you can do for your child's self-esteem is to let them give up. On the flip side, there's nothing better for building confidence than learning you can do something you thought you couldn't.

There are all these new books out there portraying Asian mothers as 21 scheming, callous, overdriven people indifferent to their kids' true interests. For their part, many Chinese secretly believe that they care more about their children and are willing to sacrifice much more for them than Westerners, who seem perfectly content to let their children turn out badly. I think it's a misunderstanding on both sides. All decent parents want to do what's best for their children. The Chinese just have a totally different idea of how to do that.

Western parents try to respect their children's individuality, encour- 22 aging them to pursue their true passions, supporting their choices, and providing positive reinforcement and a nurturing environment. By contrast, the Chinese believe that the best way to protect their children is by preparing them for the future, letting them see what they're capable of, and arming them with skills, work habits, and inner confidence that no one can ever take away.

· · ·

Comprehension

1. What does Chua mean when she says, "What Chinese parents understand is that nothing is fun until you're good at it" (6)? Do you agree with her?

2. Does Chua's husband agree or disagree with her child-rearing methods? Why does he react the way he does?

3. According to Chua, why are Chinese parents able to do things that Western parents cannot?

4. How does Chua respond to the charge that Chinese parents don't care about their children?

5. According to Chua, how do Chinese child-rearing practices prepare children for life?

Purpose and Audience

1. What preconceptions about Chinese mothers does Chua think Westerners have? Do you think she is right about this?

2. Does Chua seem to expect her readers to be receptive, hostile, or neutral to her ideas? What evidence can you find to support your impression? How do you know?

3. What is Chua's thesis? Where does she state it?

4. In an interview, Chua said that the editors of the *Wall Street Journal*, not she, chose the title of her essay. Why do you think the editors chose the title they did? What title do you think Chua would have chosen? What title would you give the essay?

Style and Structure

1. Why does Chua begin her essay with a list of things her two daughters were not allowed to do as they were growing up? How do you think she expects readers to react to this list? How do you react?

2. Is this essay a point-by-point comparison, a subject-by-subject comparison, or a combination of the two organizational strategies? Why does Chua arrange her comparison the way she does?

3. What evidence does Chua present to support her view that there are marked differences between the parenting styles of Chinese and Western parents?

4. Chua was born in the United States. Does this fact undercut her conclusions about the differences between Western and Chinese child-rearing? Explain.

5. What points does Chua emphasize in her conclusion? How else could she have ended her essay?

Vocabulary Projects

1. Define each of the following words as it is used in this selection.

   stereotypically (1)   ostracized (8)
   prodigies (1)   mediocre (12)
   squeamishness (5)   fragility (12)
   foster (5)   aptitude (13)
   fortitude (6)   interrogating (16)
   tenacious (6)   callous (21)

2. In paragraph 2, Chua says she is using the terms "Chinese mother" and "Western parents" loosely. What does she mean? How does she define these two terms? How would you define them?

Journal Entry

Do you think Chua's essay perpetuates a cultural stereotype? Why or why not?

Writing Workshop

1. Write an essay in which you compare your upbringing to that of Chua's daughters. Were your parents "Western" or "Chinese" parents (or, were they a combination of the two)? In your thesis, take a stand on the question of which kind of parent is "superior." Use examples from your childhood to support your thesis.

2. **Working with Sources.** Read the poem "Suicide Note" by Janice Mirikitani (page 366). Then, write an essay in which you compare Chua's positive view of Asian child-rearing practices with the feelings expressed by the

speaker in Mirikitani's poem. Be sure to document any material that you borrow from the two sources and to include a works-cited page. (See Chapter 18 for information on MLA documentation.)

3. When Chua's essay was published, it elicited thousands of responses, many of which were negative. For example, some readers thought that her parenting methods were tantamount to child abuse, while some readers admired Chua for her resolve and her emphasis on hard work, and others said that her methods reminded them of their own upbringings. Chua herself responded to readers' comments by saying that her "tough love" approach was grounded in her desire to make sure her children were the best that they could be. Write an email to Chua in which you respond to her essay. Be sure to address each of her major points and to compare your opinions to hers.

Combining the Patterns

Throughout her essay, Chua includes **exemplification** paragraphs. Identify two exemplification paragraphs, and explain how they help Chua make her point about the superiority of Chinese mothers.

Thematic Connections

- "Pink Floyd Night School" (page 116)
- "Rice" (page 172)
- "Suicide Note" (page 366)
- "Mother Tongue" (page 466)

ELLEN LAIRD

I'm Your Teacher, Not Your Internet-Service Provider

An educator and essayist for over thirty years, Ellen Laird believes that technology has forever changed both teaching and learning, as the following essay, originally published in the *Chronicle of Higher Education*, suggests. Laird teaches at Hudson Valley Community College in New York.

Background on "distance learning" Correspondence schools began to appear in the United States in the late nineteenth century, facilitated to a large degree by an extensive and efficient national postal service. These schools allowed students to receive study materials by mail and to complete examinations and other written work that they then submitted, again by mail, to a central departmental office for response and grading by instructors. For the most part, correspondence schools tended to focus on technical curricula, although some programs were geared toward a more traditional liberal arts curriculum. By the 1930s, correspondence schools had entered a period of decline as an increase in the number of high school graduates and the rise of junior colleges meant that students were more likely to have hands-on educational opportunities close to home. Then, beginning in the 1960s, the concept was revived through the broadcast of publicly funded televised courses, again with a mail-based system for transmitting written materials. Today, many universities have Internet-based distance-learning programs.

The honeymoon is over. My romance with distance teaching is losing its spark. Gone are the days when I looked forward to each new online encounter with students, when preparing and posting a basic assignment was a thrilling adventure, when my colleagues and friends were well-wishers, cautiously hopeful about my new entanglement. What remains is this instructor, alone, often in the dark of night, facing the reality of my online class and struggling to make it work. [1]

> "The honeymoon is over. My romance with distance teaching is losing its spark."

After four years of Internet teaching, I must pause. When pressed to demonstrate that my online composition class is the equivalent of my classroom-based composition sections, I can do so professionally and persuasively. On the surface, course goals, objectives, standards, outlines, texts, Web materials, and so forth, are identical. But my fingers are crossed. [2]

The two experiences are as different as a wedding reception and a rave. The nonlinear nature of online activity and the well-ingrained habits of Web use involve behavior vastly different from that which fosters success [3] in the traditional college classroom. Last fall, my online students ranged from ages fifteen to fifty, from the home-schooled teen to the local union president. Yet all brought to class assumptions and habits that sometimes interfered with learning and often diminished the quality of the experience for all of us. As a seasoned online instructor, I knew what to expect and how to help students through the inevitable. But for the uninitiated, the reality of online teaching can be confounding and upsetting. It can make a talented teacher feel like an unmitigated failure.

If faculty members, whether well established or new, are to succeed in 4 online teaching, they must be prepared for attitudes and behaviors that permeate Web use but undermine teaching and learning in the Web classroom. Potential online instructors are generally offered technical training in file organization, course-management software use, and the like. But they would be best served by an unfiltered look at what really happens when the student logs into class, however elegantly designed the course may be. A few declarative sentences drafted for my next online syllabus may suffice:

The syllabus is not a restaurant menu.

In sections offered in campus classrooms, my students regard the syl- 5 labus as a fixed set of requirements, not as a menu of choices. They accept the sequence and format in which course material is provided for them. They do not make selections among course requirements according to preference.

Online? Not so. Each semester, online students howl electronically 6 about having to complete the same assignments in the same sequence required of my face-to-face students. Typical Internet users, these students are accustomed to choices online. They enjoy the nonlinear nature of Web surfing; they would be hard pressed to replicate the sequence of their activity without the down arrow beside the URL box on their browsers.

To their detriment, many of these students fail to consider that Web 7 learning is different from Web use, particularly in a skills-based course like composition. They find it hard to accept, for example, that they must focus on writing a solid thesis before tackling a research paper. Most would prefer to surf from one module of material to the next and complete what appeals to them rather than what is required of them.

The difference between students' expectations and reality frustrates us 8 all. In traditional classrooms, students do not pick up or download only the handouts that appeal to them; most do not try to begin the semester's final project without instruction in the material on which it is based. Yet, online students expect such options.

Even Cinderella had a deadline.

Students in my traditional classes certainly miss deadlines. But they 9 generally regard deadlines as real, if not observable; they recognize an instructor's right to set due dates; and they accept the consequences of missing them to be those stated on the syllabus.

Not so with my online students. Neither fancy font nor flashing bullet 10 can stir the majority to submit work by the published deadline. Students seem to extend the freedom to choose the time and place of their course work to every aspect of the class. Few request extensions in the usual manner. Instead, they announce them. One student, for example, emailed me days after a paper was due, indicating that he had traveled to New York for a Yankees' game and would submit the essay in a couple of weeks.

All course components do not function at the speed of the Internet.

As relaxed as my online students are about meeting deadlines, they be- 11 gin the course expecting instantaneous service. The speed of Internet transmission seduces them into seeking and expecting speed as an element of the course. Naturally, students' emphasis on rapidity works against them. The long, hard, eventually satisfying work of thinking, doing research, reading, and writing has no relationship to bandwidth, processor speed, or cable modems.

At the same time, it takes me a long time to respond thoughtfully to 12 students' work, particularly their writing. Each semester, online students require help in understanding that waiting continues to be part of teaching and learning, that the instructor is not another version of an Internet-service provider, to be judged satisfactory or not by processing speed and 24/7 availability.

There are no sick or personal days in cyberspace.

In my traditional classes, I refrain from informing students that I will 13 be out of town for a weekend, that I need a root canal, or that my water heater failed before work. My face-to-face students can read my expression and bearing when they see me; thus, I can usually keep personal explanations to a professional minimum.

In my online class, however, students cannot see the bags under my 14 eyes or the look of exuberance on my face. They cannot hear the calm or the shake in my voice. Thus, for the smooth functioning of the course, I willingly provide details about where I am and what I am doing, so students can know what to expect.

However, I am still troubled by the email message from an online stu- 15 dent that began, "I know you are at your father's funeral right now, but I just wondered if you got my paper." Surely, he hesitated before pushing "send," but his need for reassurance prevailed. And so it goes, all semester long. There simply isn't room in an online class for the messiness of ordinary life, the students' or mine. Nor is there room for the extraordinary — the events of September 11, for example. As long as the server functions, the course is always on, bearing down hard on both students and instructor.

Still, students will register for online classes under circumstances that 16 would prohibit them from enrolling in a course on the campus. The welder compelled to work mandatory overtime, the pregnant woman due before midsemester, and the newly separated security guard whose wife will not surrender the laptop all arrive online with the hope and the illusion that, in cyberspace, they can accomplish what is temporarily impossible for them on campus.

I am not on your buddy list.

The egalitarian atmosphere of the Internet chat room transfers rap- 17 idly and inappropriately to the online classroom. Faceless and ageless on-line, I am, at first, addressed as a peer. If students knew that I dress like many of their mothers, or that my hair will soon be more gray than brown, would their exchanges with me be different? I reveal what I want them to know — the date of my marathon, my now-deceased dog's consumption of a roll of aluminum foil, my one gig as a cocktail-lounge pianist — but little of what one good look at me, in my jumper and jewelry, would tell them.

They, on the other hand, hold back nothing. Confessional writing, al- 18 ways a challenge in composition, can easily become the norm online. So can racist, sexist, and otherwise offensive remarks — even admissions of crimes. The lack of a face to match with a rhetorical voice provides the illusion of anonymity, and thus the potential for a no-holds-barred qual-ity to every discussion thread. The usual restraint characterizing conversa-tion among classroom acquaintances evaporates online within about two weeks. Private conversations fuse with academic discussion before an in-structor can log in.

Are there strategies to manage these and similar difficulties? Of course 19 there are. Thus, I continue with online teaching and welcome both its chal-lenges and its rewards. But educators considering online teaching need to know that instruction in person and online are day and night. They must brace themselves for a marriage of opposites, and build large reserves of commitment, patience, and wherewithal if the relationship is to succeed.

• • •

Comprehension

1. Why does Laird say that her "honeymoon" with distance learning is over (1)?

2. According to Laird, why are Internet teaching and classroom-based teach-ing different? How does she explain the differences?

3. What does Laird mean when she says that potential online instructors "would be best served by an unfiltered look at what really happens when the student logs into class" (4)?

4. In what way does classroom-based teaching limit students' choices? How is Internet teaching different?

5. In paragraph 11, Laird says, "The long, hard, eventually satisfying work of thinking, doing research, reading, and writing has no relationship to bandwidth, processor speed, or cable modems." What does she mean?

Purpose and Audience

1. What is the thesis of this essay?
2. To whom do you think Laird is addressing her essay? Instructors? Students? Both?
3. What do you think Laird is trying to accomplish in her essay? Is she successful?
4. Does Laird assume that her readers are familiar with Internet-based teaching, or does she assume they are relatively unfamiliar with it? How can you tell?

Style and Structure

1. Is this essay a point-by-point or subject-by-subject comparison? Why do you think Laird chose this strategy?
2. Laird highlights "a few declarative sentences" (4) as boldfaced headings throughout her essay. What is the function of these headings?
3. Does Laird seem to favor one type of teaching over another? Is she optimistic or pessimistic about the future of Internet teaching? Explain.
4. Does Laird indicate how students feel about Internet teaching? Should she have spent more time exploring this issue?
5. In her conclusion, Laird asks, "Are there strategies to manage these and similar difficulties?" Her answer: "Of course there are." Should she have listed some of these strategies in her conclusion? Why do you think she does not?

Vocabulary Projects

1. Define each of the following words as it is used in this selection.

   nonlinear (3)   permeate (4)
   inevitable (3)   declarative (4)
   uninitiated (3)   consequences (9)
   unmitigated (3)   wherewithal (19)

2. Laird spends four paragraphs introducing the points she intends to discuss. What words and phrases in these paragraphs indicate that she intends to write a comparison?
3. In paragraph 3, Laird says, "The two experiences are as different as a wedding reception and a rave." What are the denotations and connotations of *wedding reception* and *rave*? What point is Laird trying to make with this comparison?

Journal Entry

Do you agree or disagree with Laird's assessment of Internet learning and classroom-based learning? (If you have never taken an Internet course, discuss only her analysis of classroom-based learning.)

Writing Workshop

1. Write an essay in which you discuss whether you would like to take a distance-learning writing course. How do you think such a course would compare with a traditional classroom-based course? (If you are already taking such a course, compare it with a traditional writing course.)

2. **Working with Sources.** Write an email to Laird in which you explain that like her, students also have difficulty adapting to Internet instruction. Address the specific difficulties that students encounter in such courses, and compare these difficulties with those they experience when they take a classroom-based course. Include at least one quotation from Laird's essay, and be sure to document the quotation and to include a works-cited page. (See Chapter 18 for information on MLA documentation.)

3. Read the following list of advantages of taking online courses:

   - A student who is ill will not miss classes.
   - Students who are employed and cannot come to campus can take courses.
   - Nontraditional students — the elderly and disabled, for example — can take courses.
   - Courses are taken at any time, day or night.
   - Guest speakers who cannot travel to campus can be integrated into the course.

   Then, make a list of disadvantages (for example, students never have face-to-face contact with an instructor). Finally, write an essay in which you discuss whether the advantages of online instruction outweigh the disadvantages.

Combining the Patterns

Laird begins her essay with two **narrative** paragraphs. What is the purpose of these paragraphs? What other strategy could Laird have used to introduce her essay?

Thematic Connections

- "Pink Floyd Night School" (page 116)
- "College Pressures" (page 450)
- "The Dog Ate My Disk, and Other Tales of Woe" (page 460)

DEBORAH TANNEN

Sex, Lies, and Conversation

Deborah Tannen was born in Brooklyn, New York, in 1945 and currently teaches at Georgetown University. Tannen has written and edited several scholarly books on the problems of communicating across cultural, class, ethnic, and sexual divides. She has also presented her research to the general public in newspapers and magazines and in her best-selling books *That's Not What I Meant!* (1986), *You Just Don't Understand: Women and Men in Conversation* (1990), and *Talking from 9 to 5* (1994). Her most recent book is *You Were Always Mom's Favorite: Sisters in Conversation throughout Their Lives* (2010).

Background on men's and women's communication styles Tannen wrote "Sex, Lies, and Conversation" because the chapter in *That's Not What I Meant!* on the difficulties men and women have communicating with one another got such a strong response. She realized the chapter might raise some controversy — that discussing their different communication styles might be used to malign men or to put women at a disadvantage — and indeed, some critics have seen her work as reinforcing stereotypes. Still, her work on the subject, along with that of other writers (most notably John Gray in his *Men Are from Mars, Women Are from Venus* series), has proved enormously popular. Much of the research about male and female differences in terms of brain function, relational styles and expectations, and evolutionary roles is controversial and continues to stir debate.

I was addressing a small gathering in a suburban Virginia living 1 room — a women's group that had invited men to join them. Throughout the evening, one man had been particularly talkative, frequently offering ideas and anecdotes, while his wife sat silently beside him on the couch. Toward the end of the evening, I commented that women frequently complain that their husbands don't talk to them. This man quickly concurred. He gestured toward his wife and said, "She's the talker in our family." The room burst into laughter; the man looked puzzled and hurt. "It's true," he explained. "When I come home from work I have nothing to say. If she didn't keep the conversation going, we'd spend the whole evening in silence."

This episode crystallizes the irony that although American men tend 2 to talk more than women in public situations, they often talk less at home. And this pattern is wreaking havoc with marriage.

The pattern was observed by political scientist Andrew Hacker in 3 the late '70s. Sociologist Catherine Kohler Riessman reports in her new book *Divorce Talk* that most of the women she interviewed — but only a few of the men — gave lack of communication as the reason for their divorces. Given the current divorce rate of nearly 50 percent, that amounts to millions of cases in the United States every year — a virtual epidemic of failed conversation.

In my own research, complaints from women about their husbands 4 most often focused not on tangible inequities such as having given up the chance for a career to accompany a husband to his, or doing far more than their share of daily life-support work like cleaning, cooking, social arrangements, and errands. Instead, they focused on communication: "He doesn't listen to me," "He doesn't talk to me." I found, as Hacker observed years before, that most wives want their husbands to be, first and foremost, conversational partners, but few husbands share this expectation of their wives.

In short, the image that best represents the current crisis is the stereo- 5 typical cartoon scene of a man sitting at the breakfast table with a newspaper held up in front of his face, while a woman glares at the back of it, wanting to talk.

Linguistic Battle of the Sexes

How can women and men have such different impressions of commu- 6 nication in marriage? Why the widespread imbalance in their interests and expectations?

In the April issue of *American Psychologist,* Stanford University's Eleanor 7 Maccoby reports the results of her own and others' research showing that children's development is most influenced by the social structure of peer interactions. Boys and girls tend to play with children of their own gender, and their sex-separate groups have different organizational structures and interactive norms.

I believe these systematic differences in childhood socialization make 8 talk between women and men like cross-cultural communication, heir to all the attraction and pitfalls of that enticing but difficult enterprise. My research on men's and women's conversations uncovered patterns similar to those described for children's groups.

For women, as for girls, intimacy is the fabric of relationships, and talk 9 is the thread from which it is woven. Little girls create and maintain friendships by exchanging secrets; similarly, women regard conversation as the cornerstone of friendship. So a woman expects her husband to be a new and improved version of a best friend. What is important is not the individual subjects that are discussed but the sense of closeness, of a life shared, that emerges when people tell their thoughts, feelings, and impressions.

Bonds between boys can be as intense as girls', but they are based less 10 on talking, more on doing things together. Since they don't assume talk is the cement that binds a relationship, men don't know what kind of talk women want, and they don't miss it when it isn't there.

Boys' groups are larger, more inclusive, and more hierarchical, so boys 11 must struggle to avoid the subordinate position in the group. This may play a role in women's complaints that men don't listen to them. Some men really don't like to listen, because being the listener makes them feel one-down, like a child listening to adults or an employee to a boss.

But often when women tell men, "You aren't listening," and the men 12
protest, "I am," the men are right. The impression of not listening results
from misalignments in the mechanics of conversation. The misalignment
begins as soon as a man and a woman take physical positions. This became
clear when I studied videotapes made by psychologist Bruce Dorval of children and adults talking to their same-sex best friends. I found that at every
age, the girls and women faced each other directly, their eyes anchored on
each other's faces. At every age, the boys and men sat at angles to each other
and looked elsewhere in the room, periodically glancing at each other.
They were obviously attuned to each other, often mirroring each other's
movements. But the tendency of men to face away can give women the
impression they aren't listening even when they are. A young woman in
college was frustrated: Whenever she told her boyfriend she wanted to talk
to him, he would lie down on the floor, close his eyes, and put his arm over
his face. This signaled to her, "He's taking a nap." But he insisted he was
listening extra hard. Normally, he looks around the room, so he is easily
distracted. Lying down and covering his eyes helped him concentrate on
what she was saying.

Analogous to the physical alignment that women and men take in 13
conversation is their topical alignment. The girls in my study tended to
talk at length about one topic, but the boys tended to jump from topic to
topic. The second-grade girls exchanged stories about people they knew.
The second-grade boys teased, told jokes, noticed things in the room, and
talked about finding games to play. The sixth-grade girls talked about
problems with a mutual friend. The sixth-grade boys talked about 55 different topics, none of which extended over more than a few turns.

Listening to Body Language

Switching topics is another habit that gives women the impression 14
men aren't listening, especially if they switch to a topic about themselves.
But the evidence of the 10th-grade boys in my study indicates otherwise.
The 10th-grade boys sprawled across their chairs with bodies parallel and
eyes straight ahead, rarely looking at each other. They looked as if they
were riding in a car, staring out the windshield. But they were talking
about their feelings. One boy was upset because a girl had told him he
had a drinking problem, and the other was feeling alienated from all his
friends.

Now, when a girl told a friend about a problem, the friend responded 15
by asking probing questions and expressing agreement and understanding. But the boys dismissed each other's problems. Todd assured Richard
that his drinking was "no big problem" because "sometimes you're funny
when you're off your butt." And when Todd said he felt left out, Richard
responded, "Why should you? You know more people than me."

Women perceive such responses as belittling and unsupportive. But 16
the boys seemed satisfied with them. Whereas women reassure each other
by implying, "You shouldn't feel bad because I've had similar experiences,"

men do so by implying, "You shouldn't feel bad because your problems aren't so bad."

There are even simpler reasons for women's impression that men don't 17 listen. Linguist Lynette Hirschman found that women make more listener-noise, such as "mhm," "uhuh," and "yeah," to show "I'm with you." Men, she found, more often give silent attention. Women who expect a stream of listener-noise interpret silent attention as no attention at all.

Women's conversational habits are as frustrating to men as men's are 18 to women. Men who expect silent attention interpret a stream of listener-noise as overreaction or impatience. Also, when women talk to each other in a close, comfortable setting, they often overlap, finish each other's sentences, and anticipate what the other is about to say. This practice, which I call "participatory listenership," is often perceived by men as interruption, intrusion, and lack of attention.

A parallel difference caused a man to complain about his wife, "She 19 just wants to talk about her own point of view. If I show her another view, she gets mad at me." When most women talk to each other, they assume a conversationalist's job is to express agreement and support. But many men see their conversational duty as pointing out the other side of an argument. This is heard as disloyalty by women, and refusal to offer the requisite support. It is not that women don't want to see other points of view, but that they prefer them phrased as suggestions and inquiries rather than as direct challenges.

In his book *Fighting for Life*, Walter Ong points out that men use "ago- 20 nistic," or warlike, oppositional formats to do almost anything; thus discussion becomes debate, and conversation a competitive sport. In contrast, women see conversation as a ritual means of establishing rapport. If Jane tells a problem and June says she has a similar one, they walk away feeling closer to each other. But this attempt at establishing rapport can backfire when used with men. Men take too literally women's ritual "troubles talk," just as women mistake men's ritual challenges for real attack.

The Sounds of Silence

These differences begin to clarify why women and men have such dif- 21 ferent expectations about communication in marriage. For women, talk creates intimacy. Marriage is an orgy of closeness: you can tell your feelings and thoughts, and still be loved. Their greatest fear is being pushed away. But men live in a hierarchical world, where talk maintains independence and status. They are on guard to protect themselves from being put down and pushed around.

This explains the paradox of the talkative man who said of his silent 22 wife, "She's the talker." In the public setting of a guest lecture, he felt challenged to show his intelligence and display his understanding of the lecture. But at home, where he has nothing to prove and no one to defend against, he is free to remain silent. For his wife, being home means she is free from the worry that something she says might offend someone, or spark disagreement, or appear to be showing off; at home she is free to talk.

The communication problems that endanger marriage can't be fixed 23 by mechanical engineering. They require a new conceptual framework about the role of talk in human relationships. Many of the psychological explanations that have become second nature may not be helpful, because they tend to blame either women (for not being assertive enough) or men (for not being in touch with their feelings). A sociolinguistic approach by which male-female conversation is seen as cross-cultural communication allows us to understand the problem and forge solutions without blaming either party.

Once the problem is understood, improvement comes naturally, as 24 it did to the young woman and her boyfriend who seemed to go to sleep when she wanted to talk. Previously, she had accused him of not listening, and he had refused to change his behavior, since that would be admitting fault. But then she learned about and explained to him the differences in women's and men's habitual ways of aligning themselves in conversation. The next time she told him she wanted to talk, he began, as usual, by lying down and covering his eyes. When the familiar negative reaction bubbled up, she reassured herself that he really was listening. But then he sat up and looked at her. Thrilled, she asked why. He said, "You like me to look at you when we talk, so I'll try to do it." Once he saw their differences as cross-cultural rather than right and wrong, he independently altered his behavior.

Women who feel abandoned and deprived when their husbands won't 25 listen to or report daily news may be happy to discover their husbands trying to adapt once they understand the place of small talk in women's relationships. But if their husbands don't adapt, the women may still be comforted that for men, this is not a failure of intimacy. Accepting the difference, the wives may look to their friends or family for that kind of talk. And husbands who can't provide it shouldn't feel their wives have made unreasonable demands. Some couples will still decide to divorce, but at least their decisions will be based on realistic expectations.

In these times of resurgent ethnic conflicts, the world desperately 26 needs cross-cultural understanding. Like charity, successful cross-cultural communication should begin at home.

•   •   •

Comprehension

1. What pattern of communication does Tannen identify at the beginning of her essay?

2. According to Tannen, what do women complain about most in their marriages?

3. What gives women the impression that men do not listen?

4. What characteristics of women's speech do men find frustrating?

5. According to Tannen, what can men and women do to remedy the communication problems that exist in most marriages?

Purpose and Audience

1. What is Tannen's thesis?

2. What is Tannen's purpose in writing this essay? Do you think she wants to inform or to persuade? On what do you base your conclusion?

3. Is Tannen writing for an expert audience or for an audience of general readers? To men, women, or both? How can you tell?

Style and Structure

1. What does Tannen gain by stating her thesis in paragraph 2 of the essay? Would there be any advantage in postponing the thesis statement until the end? Explain.

2. Is this essay a subject-by-subject or a point-by-point comparison? What does Tannen gain by organizing her essay the way she does?

3. Throughout her essay, Tannen cites scholarly studies and quotes statistics. How effectively does this information support her points? Could she have made a strong case without this material? Why or why not?

4. Would you say Tannen's tone is hopeful, despairing, sarcastic, angry, or something else? Explain.

5. Tannen concludes her essay with a far-reaching statement. What do you think she hopes to accomplish with this conclusion? Is she successful? Explain your reasoning.

Vocabulary Projects

1. Define each of the following words as it is used in this selection.

concurred (1)	pitfalls (8)	rapport (20)
crystallizes (2)	subordinate (11)	ritual (20)
inequities (4)	misalignment (12)	orgy (21)
imbalance (6)	analogous (13)	sociolinguistic (23)
peer (7)	alienated (14)	forge (23)
organizational (7)	intrusion (18)	

2. Where does Tannen use professional **jargon** in this essay? Would the essay be more or less effective without these words? Explain.

Journal Entry

Based on your own observations of male-female communication, how accurate is Tannen's analysis? Can you relate an anecdote from your own life that illustrates (or contradicts) her thesis?

Writing Workshop

1. **Working with Sources.** In another essay, Tannen contrasts the communication patterns of male and female students in classroom settings. After observing students in a few of your own classes, write an essay also drawing a comparison between the communication patterns of your male and female classmates. Include quotations from both male and female students. Be sure to document these quotations, using the format for "A personal interview" (page 734), and to include a works-cited page. (See Chapter 18 for information on MLA documentation.)

2. Write an essay comparing the way male and female characters speak in films or on television. Use examples to support your points.

3. Write an essay comparing the vocabulary used in two different sports. Does one sport use more violent language than the other? For example, baseball uses the terms *bunt* and *sacrifice,* and football uses the terms *blitz* and *bomb.* Use as many examples as you can to support your points.

Combining the Patterns

Tannen begins her essay with an anecdote. Why does she begin with a paragraph of **narration**? How does this story set the tone for the rest of the essay?

Thematic Connections

- "Only Daughter" (page 111)
- "I Want a Wife" (page 503)
- "The Wife-Beater" (page 516)
- Declaration of Sentiments and Resolutions, Seneca Falls Convention, 1848 (page 559)

Sadie and Maud (Poetry)

Poet Gwendolyn Brooks (1917–2000) was born in Topeka, Kansas, and graduated from Wilson Junior College in Chicago, where she lived most of her life. She was on the faculty of Columbia College and Northeastern Illinois State College, and she was named the poet laureate of Illinois. Her first volume of poetry was *A Street in Bronzeville* (1945), named for the African-American neighborhood on the South Side of Chicago where she grew up. Among her many later collections are *Annie Allen* (1949), for which she was the first African American to win a Pulitzer Prize; *Riot* (1969), based on the violent unrest that gripped many inner-city neighborhoods following the assassination of Martin Luther King Jr.; and *Blacks* (1987). She also published books for children, a novel, and two volumes of her memoirs. The following poem is from *A Street in Bronzeville*.

Background on African Americans in the 1940s Because deed restrictions in Chicago in the 1940s prevented blacks from buying property outside of Bronzeville, the area was home to African Americans from all income levels as well as to many thriving black-owned businesses. Still, the opportunities available to women like Sadie and Maud in the 1940s were limited. Only about 12 percent of African Americans completed four years of high school (although numbers were higher in the North than in the South), and many fewer went on to college. Six out of ten African-American women were employed in low-paying domestic service positions, while fewer than one percent held professional positions, primarily as teachers in segregated schools.

Maud went to college.
Sadie stayed at home.
Sadie scraped life
With a fine-tooth comb.

She didn't leave a tangle in.   5
Her comb found every strand.
Sadie was one of the livingest chits
In all the land.

Sadie bore two babies
Under her maiden name.   10
Maud and Ma and Papa
Nearly died of shame.

When Sadie said her last so-long
Her girls struck out from home.
(Sadie had left as heritage   15
Her fine-tooth comb.)

Maud, who went to college,
Is a thin brown mouse.
She is living all alone
In this old house.   20

. . .

Reading Literature

1. What two ideas is Brooks comparing in the poem? How does the speaker let readers know when she is shifting her focus from one subject to another?
2. How accurate do you think the speaker's portrayals are? Is the speaker stereotyping the two women?
3. What comment do you think the poem is making about education? About society? About women? About African-American women?

Journal Entry

Brooks wrote "Sadie and Maud" in 1945. What changes do you think she would have to make if she wrote her poem today?

Thematic Connections

- "Only Daughter" (page 111)
- "Indian Education" (page 142)
- "The Myth of the Latin Woman: I Just Met a Girl Named Maria" (page 232)
- "'Girl'" (page 258)
- Declaration of Sentiments and Resolutions, Seneca Falls Convention, 1848 (page 559)

Writing Assignments for Comparison and Contrast

1. Find a description of the same news event in two different magazines or newspapers. Write a comparison-and-contrast essay discussing the similarities and differences between the two stories.

2. **Working with Sources.** In your local public library, locate two children's books on the same subject — one written in the 1950s and one written within the past ten years. Write an essay discussing which elements are the same and which are different. Include a thesis statement about the significance of the differences between the two books. Make sure that you document all material you take from the two books and that you include a works-cited page. (See Chapter 18 for information on MLA documentation.)

3. Write an essay about a relative or friend you have known since you were a child. Consider how your opinion of this person is different now from what it was then.

4. Write an essay comparing and contrasting the expectations that college professors and high school teachers have for their students. Cite your own experiences as examples.

5. Since you started college, how have you changed? Write an essay that answers this question.

6. Taking careful notes, watch a local television news program and then a national news broadcast. Write an essay comparing the two programs, paying particular attention to the news content and to the journalists' broadcasting styles.

7. Write an essay comparing your own early memories of school with those of a parent or an older relative.

8. How are the attitudes toward education different among students who work to finance their own education and students who do not? Your thesis statement should indicate what differences exist and why.

9. Compare and contrast the college experiences of commuters and students who live in dorms on campus. Interview people in your classes to use as examples.

10. Write an essay comparing any two groups that have divergent values — vegetarians and meat eaters or smokers and nonsmokers, for example.

11. How is being a participant — playing a sport or acting in a play, for instance — different from being a spectator? Write a comparison-and-contrast essay in which you answer this question.

Collaborative Activity for Comparison and Contrast

Form groups of four students each. Assume your college has hired these groups as consultants to suggest solutions for several problems students have been complaining about. Select the four areas — food, campus safety, parking, and class scheduling, for example — you think need improvement. Then, as a group, write a short report to your college describing the present conditions in these areas, and compare them to the improvements you envision. (Be sure to organize your report as a comparison-and-contrast essay.) Finally, have one person from each group read the group's report to the class. Decide as a class which group has the best suggestion.

Classification and Division

What Is Classification and Division?

Division is the process of breaking a whole into parts; **classification** is the process of sorting individual items into categories. In the following paragraph from "Pregnant with Possibility," Gregory J. E. Rawlins divides Americans into categories based on their access to computer technology.

Topic sentence identifies categories

Today's computer technology is rapidly turning us into three completely new races: the superpoor, the rich, and the superrich. The superpoor are perhaps eight thousand in every ten thousand of us. The rich — me and you — make up most of the remaining two thousand, while the superrich are perhaps the last two of every ten thousand. Roughly speaking, the decisions of two superrich people control what almost two thousand of us do, and our decisions, in turn, control what the remaining eight thousand do. These groups are really like races since the group you're born into often determines which group your children will be born into.

Through **classification and division**, we can make sense of seemingly random ideas by putting scattered bits of information into useful, coherent order. By breaking a large group into smaller categories and assigning individual items to larger categories, we can identify relationships between a whole and its parts and relationships among the parts themselves. Keep in mind, though, that classification involves more than simply comparing two items or enumerating examples; when you classify, you sort individual examples into a variety of different categories.

In countless practical situations, classification and division bring order to chaos. For example, your iPod will *classify* your music, sorting individual songs into distinct genres — alternative rock, hip-hop, country,

Ranchera, and so on. Similarly, phone numbers listed in your cell phone's address book are *divided* into three clearly defined categories: home, work, and mobile. Thus, order can be brought to your music and your phone numbers — just as it is brought to newspapers, department stores, supermarkets, biological hierarchies, and libraries — when a whole is divided into categories or sections and individual items are assigned to one or another of these subgroups.

Understanding Classification

Even though the interrelated processes of classification and division invariably occur together, they are two separate operations. When you **classify**, you begin with individual items and sort them into categories. Since a given item invariably has several different attributes, it can be classified in various ways. For example, the most obvious way to classify the students who attend your school might be according to their year in college. But you could also classify students according to their major, racial or ethnic background, home state, grade-point average, or any number of other principles. The **principle of classification** you choose — the quality your items have in common — would depend on how you wish to approach the members of this large and diverse group.

Understanding Division

Division is the opposite of classification. When you **divide**, you start with a whole (an entire class) and break it into its individual parts. For example, you might start with the large general class *television shows* and divide it into categories: *sitcoms, action/adventure, reality shows,* and so forth. You could then divide each of these still further. *Action/adventure programs,* for example, might include *Westerns, crime dramas, spy dramas,* and so on — and each of these categories could be further divided as well. Eventually, you would need to identify a particular principle of classification to help you assign specific programs to one category or another — that is, to classify them.

Using Classification and Division

Whenever you write an essay, you use classification and division to bring order to the invention stage of the writing process. For example, when you brainstorm, as Chapter 2 explains, you begin with your paper's topic and list all the ideas you can think of. Next, you *divide* your topic into logical categories and *classify* the items in your brainstorming notes into one category or another, perhaps narrowing, expanding, or eliminating some categories — or some ideas — as you go along. This sorting and grouping enables you to condense and shape your material until it eventually suggests a thesis and the main points your essay will develop.

More specifically, certain topics and questions, because of the way they are worded, immediately suggest a classification-and-division pattern. Suppose, for example, you are asked, "What kinds of policies can government implement to reduce the nation's budget deficit?" Here the word *kinds* suggests classification and division. Other words — such as *types, varieties, aspects,* and *categories* — can also indicate that this pattern of development is called for.

Planning a Classification-and-Division Essay

Once you decide to use a classification-and-division pattern, you need to identify a **principle of classification**. Every group of people, things, or ideas can be categorized in many different ways. When you are at your college bookstore with limited funds, the cost of different books may be the only principle of classification you use when deciding which ones to buy. As you consider which books to carry across campus, however, weight may matter more. Finally, as you study and read, the usefulness of the books will determine which ones you concentrate on. Similarly, when you organize an essay, the principle of classification you choose is determined by your writing situation — your assignment, your purpose, your audience, and your special knowledge and interests.

Selecting and Arranging Categories

After you define your principle of classification and apply it to your topic, you should select your categories by dividing a whole class into parts and grouping a number of different items together within each part. Next, you should decide how you will treat the categories in your essay. Just as a comparison-and-contrast essay makes comparable points about its subjects, so your classification-and-division essay should treat all categories similarly. When you discuss comparable points for each category, your readers are able to understand your distinctions among categories as well as your definition of each category.

Finally, you should arrange your categories in some logical order so that readers can see how the categories are related and what their relative importance is. Whatever order you choose, it should be consistent with your purpose and with your essay's thesis.

✓**CHECKLIST**   Establishing Categories

- **All the categories should derive from the same principle.** If you decide to divide *television shows* into *sitcoms*, *reality shows*, and the like, it is not logical to include *children's programs*, for this category results from one principle (target audience) while the others result from another principle (genre). Similarly, if you were classifying undergraduates at your school according to their year, you would not include the category *students receiving financial aid.*
- **All the categories should be at the same level.** In the series *sitcoms*, *action/adventure*, and *Westerns*, the last item, *Westerns*, does not belong because it is at a lower level — that is, it is a subcategory of *action/adventure.* Likewise, *sophomores* (a subcategory of *undergraduates*) does not belong in the series *undergraduates, graduate students, continuing education students.*
- **You should treat all categories that are significant and relevant to your discussion.** Include enough categories to make your point, with no important omissions and no overlapping categories. In a review of a network's fall television lineup, the series *sitcoms, reality shows, crime shows*, and *detective shows* is incomplete because it omits important categories such as *news programs, game shows*, and *documentaries;* moreover, *detective shows* may overlap with *crime shows.* In the same way, the series *freshmen, sophomores, juniors*, and *transfers* is illogical: the important group *seniors* has been omitted, and *transfers* may include *freshmen, sophomores*, and *juniors.*

Developing a Thesis Statement

Like other kinds of essays, a classification-and-division essay should have a thesis. Your **thesis statement** should identify your subject, introduce the categories you will discuss, and perhaps show readers the relationships of your categories to one another and to the subject as a whole. In addition, your thesis statement should tell your readers why your categories are significant or establish their relative value. For example, simply listing different kinds of investments would be pointless. Instead, your thesis statement might note their relative strengths and weaknesses and perhaps make recommendations based on your assessment. Similarly, a research paper about a writer's major works would accomplish little if it merely categorized his or her writings. Instead, your thesis statement should communicate your evaluation of these works, perhaps demonstrating that some deserve higher public regard than others.

Using Transitions

When you write a classification-and-division essay, you use transitional words and phrases both to introduce your categories (*the first category, one category*, and so on) and to move readers from one category to the next (*the second category, another category*, and so on). In addition, transitional words

and expressions can show readers the relationships between categories —
for example, whether one category is more important than another (*a more
important category*, the *most important category*, and so on). A more complete
list of transitions appears on page 57.

Structuring a Classification-and-Division Essay

Once you have formulated your essay's thesis and established your
categories, you should plan your classification-and-division essay around
the same three major sections that other essays have: *introduction, body,* and
conclusion. Your **introduction** should orient your readers by identifying
your topic, the principle for classifying your material, and the individual
categories you plan to discuss; your thesis is also usually stated in the introduction. In the **body paragraphs**, you should discuss your categories one
by one, in the same order in which you mentioned them in your introduction. Finally, your **conclusion** should restate your thesis, summing up the
points you have made and perhaps considering their implications.

Suppose you are preparing a research paper on Mark Twain's nonfiction works for an American literature course. You have read selections from
Roughing It, Life on the Mississippi, and *The Innocents Abroad.* Besides these travel
narratives, you have read parts of Twain's autobiography and some of
his correspondence and essays. When you realize that the works you have
studied can easily be classified as four different types of Twain's nonfiction — travel narratives, essays, letters, and autobiography — you decide
to use classification and division to structure your essay. So, you first divide
the large class *Twain's nonfiction prose* into major categories — his travel narratives, essays, autobiography, and letters. Then, you classify the individual
works, assigning each work to one of these categories, which you will discuss one at a time. Your purpose is to persuade readers to reconsider the
reputations of some of these works, and you word your thesis statement
accordingly. You might then prepare a formal outline like the one that follows for the body of your paper.

SAMPLE OUTLINE: Classification and Division

Thesis statement: Most readers know Mark Twain as a novelist, but his nonfiction
works — his travel narratives, essays, letters, and especially his autobiography —
deserve more attention.

    I. Travel narratives

       A. *Roughing It*

       B. *The Innocents Abroad*

       C. *Life on the Mississippi*

II. Essays

    A. "Fenimore Cooper's Literary Offenses"

    B. "How to Tell a Story"

    C. "The Awful German Language"

III. Letters

    A. To W. D. Howells

    B. To his family

IV. Autobiography

Because this will be a long essay, each of the outline's divisions will have several subdivisions, and each subdivision might require several paragraphs.

This outline illustrates the characteristics of an effective classification-and-division essay. First, Twain's nonfiction works are classified according to a single principle of classification — literary genre. (Depending on your purpose, of course, another principle — such as theme or subject matter — could work just as well.) The outline also reveals that the paper's four categories are on the same level (each is a different literary genre) and that all relevant categories are included. Had you left out *essays*, for example, you would have been unable to classify several significant works of nonfiction.

This outline also arranges the four categories so that they will support your thesis most effectively. Because you believe Twain's travel narratives are somewhat overrated, you plan to discuss them early in your paper. Similarly, because you think the autobiography would make your best case for the merit of the nonfiction works as a whole, you decide it should be placed last. (Of course, you could arrange your categories in several other orders, such as from shorter to longer works or from least to most popular, depending on the thesis your paper will support.)

Finally, this outline reminds you to treat all categories comparably in your paper. Your case would be weakened if, for example, you inadvertently skipped style in your discussion of Twain's letters while discussing style for every other category. This omission might lead your readers to suspect that you had not done enough research on the letters or that the style of Twain's letters did not measure up to the style of his other works.

Revising a Classification-and-Division Essay

When you revise a classification-and-division essay, consider the items on the revision checklist on page 68. In addition, pay special attention to the items on the following checklist, which apply specifically to revising classification-and-division essays.

✔ **REVISION CHECKLIST**   Classification and Division

- Does your assignment call for classification and division?
- Have you identified a principle of classification for your material?
- Have you identified the categories you plan to discuss and decided how you will treat them?
- Have you arranged your categories in a logical order?
- Have you treated all categories similarly?
- Does your essay have a clearly stated thesis that identifies your subject and the categories you will discuss and indicates the significance of your classification?
- Have you used transitional words and phrases to show the relationships among categories?

Editing a Classification-and-Division Essay

When you edit your classification-and-division essay, you should follow the guidelines on the editing checklists on pages 85, 88, and 90. In addition, you should focus on the grammar, mechanics, and punctuation issues that are particularly relevant to classification-and-division essays. One of these issues — using a colon to introduce your categories — is discussed below.

GRAMMAR IN CONTEXT   Using a Colon to Introduce Your Categories

When you state the thesis of a classification-and-division essay, you often give readers an overview by listing the categories you will discuss. You introduce this list of categories with a **colon**, a punctuation mark whose purpose is to direct readers to look ahead for a series, list, clarification, or explanation.

When you use a colon to introduce your categories, the colon must be preceded by a complete sentence.

CORRECT: "I see four kinds of pressure working on college students today: economic pressure, parental pressure, peer pressure, and self-induced pressure" (Zinsser 452).

INCORRECT: Four kinds of pressure working on college students today are: economic pressure, parental pressure, peer pressure, and self-induced pressure.

In any list or series of three or more categories, the categories should be separated by commas, with a comma preceding the *and* that separates the last two items. This last comma prevents confusion by ensuring that readers will be able to see at a glance exactly how many categories you are discussing.

CORRECT: economic pressure, parental pressure, peer pressure, and self-induced pressure (four categories)

INCORRECT: economic pressure, parental pressure, peer pressure and self-induced pressure (without the final comma, it might appear you are only discussing three categories)

NOTE: Items on a list or in a series are always expressed in **parallel** terms.

For more practice in using colons correctly, visit the resources for Chapter 12 at **bedfordstmartins.com/patterns**.

✔ **EDITING CHECKLIST**   Classification and Division

- Do you introduce your list of categories with a colon preceded by a complete sentence?
- Are the items on your list of categories separated by commas?
- Do you include a comma before the *and* that connects the last two items on your list?
- Do you express the items on your list in parallel terms?

A STUDENT WRITER: Classification and Division

The following classification-and-division essay was written by Josie Martinez for an education course. Her assignment was to look back at her own education and to consider what she had learned so far, referring in her essay to William Zinsser's "College Pressures" (page 450). Josie's essay divides a whole — college classes — into four categories.

What I Learned (and Didn't Learn) in College

Introduction   In "College Pressures," William Zinsser notes the   1
disappearance of a time when college students "journeyed through college with a certain relaxation, sampling a wide variety of courses — music, art, philosophy, classics, anthropology, poetry, religion — that would send them out as liberally educated men and women" (452). The change in college students' focus is even more noticeable today than when Zinsser wrote his essay, and it represents a real loss for students. Taking a variety of different kinds of courses can educate students about a wide range of subjects, and it can also teach them about themselves.

Despite the variety of experiences that different students   2
have with different courses, most college classes can be classified
into one of four categories: ideal classes, worthless classes,

Categories listed disappointing classes, and unexpectedly valuable classes. First are
and explained courses that students love — ideal learning environments in which
they enjoy both the subject matter and the professor-student
interaction. Far from these ideal courses are those that students
find completely worthless in terms of subject matter, atmosphere,
and teaching style. Somewhere between these two extremes are
two kinds of courses that can be classified into another pair of
opposites: courses that students expect to enjoy and to learn
much from but are disappointing and courses that students are
initially not interested in but that exceed their expectations.

Thesis statement Understanding these four categories can help students accept
the fact that one disappointing class is not a disaster and can
encourage them to try classes with different kinds of subjects,
class sizes, and instructors.

First category: One of the best courses I have taken so far as a college   3
ideal class student was my Shakespeare class. The professor who taught it
had a great sense of humor and was liberal in terms of what she
allowed in her classroom — for example, controversial Shakespeare
adaptations and virtually any discussion, relevant or irrelevant.
The students in the class — English majors and non-English majors,
those who were interested in the plays as theater and those who
preferred to study them as literature — shared an enthusiasm for
Shakespeare, and they were eager to engage in lively discussions.
This class gave us a thorough knowledge of Shakespeare's plays
(tragedies, histories, comedies) as well as an understanding
of his life. We also developed our analytical skills through our
discussions of the plays and films as well as through special
projects — for example, a character profile presentation and an
abstract art presentation relating a work of art to one of the plays.
This class was an ideal learning environment not only because
of the wealth of material we were exposed to but also because
of the respect with which our professor treated us: we were her
colleagues, and she was as willing to learn from us as we were to
learn from her.

Second category: In contrast to this ideal class, one of the most worthless   4
worthless class courses I have taken in college was Movement Education. As an

education major, I expected to like this class, and several other students who had taken it told me it was both easy and enjoyable. The class consisted of playing children's games and learning what made certain activities appropriate and inappropriate for children of various ages. The only requirement for this class was that we had to write note cards explaining how to play each game so that we could use them for reference in our future teaching experiences. Unfortunately, I never really enjoyed the games we played, and I have long since discarded my note cards and forgotten how to play the games — or even what they were.

Third category: disappointing class

Although I looked forward to taking Introduction to Astronomy, I was very disappointed in this class. I had hoped to satisfy my curiosity about the universe outside our solar system, but the instructor devoted most of the semester to a detailed study of the Earth and the other bodies in our own solar system. In addition, a large part of our work included charting orbits and processing distance equations — work that I found both difficult and boring. Furthermore, we spent hardly any class time learning how to use a telescope and how to locate objects in the sky. In short, I gained little information from the class, learning only how to solve equations I would never confront again and how to chart orbits that had already been charted.   5

Fourth category: unexpectedly valuable class

In direct contrast to my astronomy class, a religion class called Paul and the Early Church was much more rewarding than I had anticipated. Having attended Catholic school for thirteen years, I assumed this course would offer me little that was new to me. However, because the class took a historical approach to studying Paul's biblical texts, I found that I learned more about Christianity than I had in all my previous religion classes. We learned about the historical validity of Paul and other texts in the Bible and how they were derived from various sources and passed orally through several generations before being written down and translated into different languages. We approached the texts from a linguistic perspective, determining the significance of certain words and learning how various meanings can be derived from different translations of the same passage. This class was unlike any of my other religion classes in that it encouraged me to study the texts objectively, leaving me with a new and valuable understanding of material I had been exposed to for most of my life.   6

Conclusion   Although each student's learning experience in college   7
will be different — because every student has a different learning
style, is interested in different subjects, and takes courses at
different schools taught by different professors — all college

Summary of four   students' experiences are similar in one respect. All students
categories   will encounter the same kinds of courses: those that are ideal,
those that are worthless, those that they learn little from despite
their interest in the subject, and those that they learn from and

Restatement of   become engaged in despite their low expectations. Understanding
thesis   that these categories exist is important because it gives students
the freedom and courage to try new things, as college students
did years ago. After all, even if one course is a disappointment,
another may be more interesting — or even exciting. For this
reason, college students should not be discouraged by a course
they do not like; the best classes are almost certainly still in their
future.

Work Cited

Works-cited list   Zinsser, William. "College Pressures." *Patterns for College*
(begins new page)   *Writing: A Rhetorical Reader and Guide*. 12th ed.
Ed. Laurie G. Kirszner and Stephen R. Mandell.
Boston: Bedford, 2012. 450–56. Print.

Points for Special Attention

Working with Sources. Josie's teacher asked students to cite William
Zinsser's "College Pressures," which they had just discussed, somewhere in
their own essays. Josie knew that the passage she chose to quote or
paraphrase would have to be directly relevant to her own paper's subject, so
she knew it would have to focus on academic (rather than economic or
social) pressures. When she discovered Zinsser's comments on students'
tendency not to experiment with a wide variety of courses, she knew she
had found material that could give her essay a more global, less personal
focus. For this reason, she decided to refer to Zinsser in her essay's first
paragraph. (Note that she includes parenthetical documentation and a
separate work-cited page.)

Thesis and Support. Josie's purpose in writing this essay was to
communicate to her professor and the other students in her education
class what she had learned from the classes she had taken so far in college,
and both the thesis she states in paragraph 2 and the restatement of this
thesis in her conclusion make this clear: what she has learned is to take a
wide variety of courses. Knowing that few, if any, students in her class

would have taken any of the courses she took, Josie realized she had to provide a lot of detail to show what these classes taught her.

Organization. As she reviewed the various courses she had taken and took stock of their strengths and weaknesses, Josie saw a classification scheme emerging. As soon as she noticed this, she organized her material into four categories. Rather than discuss the four kinds of classes from best to worst or from worst to best, Josie decided to present them as two opposing pairs: ideal class and worthless class, surprisingly disappointing class and unexpectedly worthwhile class. In paragraph 2, Josie lists the four categories she plans to discuss in her essay and gives readers an overview of these categories to help prepare them for her thesis.

Transitions between Categories. Josie uses clear topic sentences to move readers from one category to the next and indicate the relationship of each category to another.

"One of the best courses I have taken so far as a college student was my Shakespeare class." (3)

"In contrast to this ideal class, one of the most worthless courses I have taken in college was Movement Education." (4)

"Although I looked forward to taking Introduction to Astronomy, I was very disappointed in this class." (5)

"In direct contrast to my astronomy class, a religion class called Paul and the Early Church was much more rewarding than I had anticipated." (6)

These four sentences distinguish the four categories from one another and also help to communicate Josie's direction and emphasis.

Focus on Revision

An earlier draft of Josie's essay, which she discussed with her classmates in a peer editing session, did not include very helpful topic sentences. Instead, the sentences were vague and unfocused:

"One class I took in college was a Shakespeare course."

"Another class I took was Movement Education."

"I looked forward to taking Introduction to Astronomy."

"My experience with a religion class was very different."

Although her essay's second paragraph listed the categories and explained how they differed, Josie's classmates advised her to revise her topic sentences so that it would be clear which category she was discussing in each body paragraph. Josie took the advice of her peer editing group and revised these topic sentences. After reading her next draft, she felt confident that her categories — listed in paragraph 2 and repeated in her topic sentences and again in her conclusion — were clear and distinct.

Even after making these revisions, however, Josie felt her paper needed some additional fine-tuning. For example, in her final draft, she planned to add some material to paragraphs 4 and 5. At first, because she had dismissed Movement Education as completely worthless and Introduction to Astronomy as disappointing, Josie felt she did not have to say much about them. When she reread her paper, however, she realized she needed to explain the shortcomings of the two classes more fully so that her readers would understand why these classes had little value for her.

PEER EDITING WORKSHEET: Classification and Division

1. Paraphrase the essay's thesis.
2. What whole is being divided into parts in this essay? Into what general categories is the whole divided?
3. Is each category clearly identified and explained? If not, what revisions can you suggest? (For example, can you suggest a different title for a particular category? A different topic sentence to introduce it?)
4. Where does the writer list the categories to be discussed? Is the list introduced by a colon (preceded by a complete sentence)? If not, suggest revisions.
5. Are the categories arranged in a logical order, one that indicates their relationships to one another and their relative importance? If not, how could they be rearranged?
6. Does the writer treat all relevant categories and no irrelevant ones? Which categories, if any, should be added, deleted, or combined?
7. Does the writer include all necessary items, and no unnecessary ones, within each category? What additional items could be added? Should any items be located elsewhere?
8. Does the writer treat all categories similarly, discussing comparable points for each? Should any additional points be discussed? If so, where?
9. Do topic sentences clearly signal the movement from one category to the next? Should any topic sentences be strengthened to mark the boundaries between categories more clearly? If so, which ones?
10. Could the writer use another pattern of development to structure this essay, or is classification and division the best choice? Explain.

Each of the following selections is developed by means of classification and division. In some cases, the pattern is used to explain ideas; in others, it is used to persuade the reader. The first selection, a visual text, is followed by questions designed to illustrate how classification and division can operate in visual form.

Key to Chalk Marks Designating Medical Conditions of Immigrants, Ellis Island (Chart)

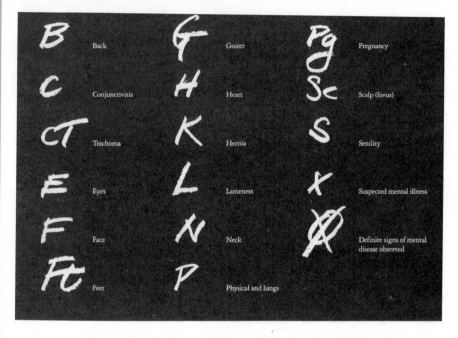

B	Back	*G*	Goiter	*Pg*	Pregnancy
C	Conjunctivitis	*H*	Heart	*Sc*	Scalp (favus)
CT	Trachoma	*K*	Hernia	*S*	Senility
E	Eyes	*L*	Lameness	*X*	Suspected mental illness
F	Face	*N*	Neck	*Ⓧ*	Definite signs of mental disease observed
Ft	Feet	*P*	Physical and lungs		

• • •

Reading Images

1. The photo above shows symbols, written in chalk on early-twentieth-century immigrants' clothing, representing medical conditions that could disqualify them from entry into the United States. What different principles of classification might be used to sort these symbols into categories? Which principle of classification seems to make the most sense? Why?

2. Guided by the principle of classification you selected in question 1, arrange the various symbols into three or four distinct categories. Are there any that do not fit into your classification scheme?

3. The chalk mark system illustrated here is no longer in use, but visitors' health is still a consideration. What medical conditions do you think should disqualify a visitor for entry into the United States today? List some possible criteria for exclusion, and arrange these criteria into categories.

Journal Entry

Do you think the United States should exclude any potential immigrants solely for medical reasons? Why or why not?

Thematic Connections

- "The Catbird Seat" (page 228)
- "Why Looks Are the Last Bastion of Discrimination" (page 246)
- "Does This Tax Make Me Look Fat?" (page 647)
- "The Shame Game" (page 680)

WILLIAM ZINSSER

College Pressures

William Zinsser has worked as a newspaper and magazine writer and has taught English at Yale University. He is also author of numerous books on writing, including *On Writing Well: The Classic Guide to Writing Nonfiction* (twenty-fifth anniversary edition, 2001) and *Writing about Your Life: A Journey into the Past* (2004). His works on American culture include *Spring Training* (1989), about the culture of baseball, and *Easy to Remember: Great American Songwriters and Their Songs* (2001). Zinsser also writes a weekly online column for *The American Scholar* called Zinsser on Friday.

Background on college pressures today   Although the following essay focuses on the kinds of pressures facing Yale students in 1979, many of these remain relevant (and, in some cases, even more relevant) for college students today. These pressures include the need to develop time management and study skills appropriate for college work, the desire for good grades, the desire to meet parents' expectations, and the need to find employment in a competitive job market after graduation. In addition, many college students today face pressures unknown to most students in the late 1970s. According to the U.S. Department of Education's National Center for Education Statistics, only about 25 percent of current undergraduates fit the "traditional" model of eighteen- to twenty-two-year-old full-time students still supported primarily by their parents. Increasingly, college undergraduates are adults, supporting themselves — and sometimes familiess — and funding their own education through full- or part-time employment in addition to loans. A 2010 report by the Project on Student Debt found that college students averaged $24,000 in student loans in 2009, an increase of 6 percent from 2008. The report also found that unemployment for recent college graduates had increased from a rate of 5.8 percent in 2008 to 8.7 percent in 2009, the highest annual rate on record for college graduates aged 20 to 24. This increase is consistent with the high rate of unemployment in the workforce as a whole.

Dear Carlos: I desperately need a dean's excuse for my chem midterm which will begin in about one hour. All I can say is that I totally blew it this week. I've fallen incredibly, inconceivably behind.   1

Carlos: Help! I'm anxious to hear from you. I'll be in my room and won't leave it until I hear from you. Tomorrow is the last day for . . .   2

Carlos: I left town because I started bugging out again. I stayed up all night to finish a take home make-up exam and am typing it to hand in on the 10th. It was due on the 5th. P.S. I'm going to the dentist. Pain is pretty bad.   3

Carlos: Probably by Friday I'll be able to get back to my studies. Right   4
now I'm going to take a long walk. This whole thing has taken a lot out
of me.

Carlos: I'm really up the proverbial creek. The problem is I really *bombed*   5
the history final. Since I need that course for my major . . .

Carlos: Here follows a tale of woe. I went home this weekend, had to   6
help my Mom, & caught a fever so didn't have much time to study. My
professor . . .

Carlos: Aargh! Nothing original but everything's piling up at once. To be   7
brief, my job interview . . .

Hey Carlos, good news! I've got mononucleosis.   8

Who are these wretched supplicants, scribbling notes so laden with   9
anxiety, seeking such miracles of postponement and balm? They are men
and women who belong to Bradford College, one of the twelve residential
colleges at Yale University, and the messages are just a few of the hundreds
that they left for their dean, Carlos Hortas — often slipped under his door
at 4 A.M. — last year.

But students like the ones who wrote those notes can also be found on   10
campuses from coast to coast — especially in New England and at many
other private colleges across the country that have high academic standards and highly motivated students. Nobody could doubt that the notes
are real. In their urgency and their gallows humor they are authentic voices
of a generation that is panicky to succeed.

My own connection with the message writers is that I am master of   11
Bradford College. I live in its Gothic quadrangle and know the students
well. (We have 485 of them.) I am privy to their hopes and fears — and also
to their stereo music and their piercing cries in the dead of night ("Does
anybody *ca-a-are?*"). If they went to Carlos to ask how to get through tomorrow, they come to me to ask how to get through the rest of their lives.

Mainly I try to remind them that the road ahead is a long one and that   12
it will have more unexpected turns than they think. There will be plenty of
time to change jobs, change careers, change whole attitudes and approaches.
They don't want to hear such liberating news. They want a map — right
now — that they can follow unswervingly to career security, financial security, Social Security, and, presumably, a prepaid grave.

What I wish for all students is some release from the clammy grip of   13
the future. I wish them a chance to savor each segment of their education
as an experience in itself and not as a grim preparation for the next step. I
wish them the right to experiment, to trip and fall, to learn that defeat is as
instructive as victory and is not the end of the world.

My wish, of course, is naive. One of the few rights that America does   14
not proclaim is the right to fail. Achievement is the national god, venerated in our media — the million-dollar athlete, the wealthy executive — and

glorified in our praise of possessions. In the presence of such a potent state religion, the young are growing up old.

I see four kinds of pressure working on college students today: eco- 15 nomic pressure, parental pressure, peer pressure, and self-induced pressure. It is easy to look around for villains — to blame the colleges for charging too much money, the professors for assigning too much work, the parents for pushing their children too far, the students for driving themselves too hard. But there are no villains, only victims.

"In the late 1960s," one dean told me, "the typical question that I 16 got from students was 'Why is there so much suffering in the world?' or 'How can I make a contribution?' Today it's 'Do you think it would look better for getting into law school if I did a double major in history and political science, or just majored in one of them?'" Many other deans confirmed this pattern. One said: "They're trying to find an edge — the intangible something that will look better on paper if two students are about equal."

Note the emphasis on looking better. The transcript has become a sa- 17 cred document, the passport to security. How one appears on paper is more important than how one appears in person. *A* is for Admirable and *B* is for Borderline, even though, in Yale's official system of grading, *A* means "excellent" and *B* means "very good." Today, looking very good is no longer good enough, especially for students who hope to go on to law school or medical school. They know that entrance into the better schools will be an entrance into the better law firms and better medical practices where they will make a lot of money. They also know that the odds are harsh. Yale Law School, for instance, matriculates 170 students from an applicant pool of 3,700; Harvard enrolls 550 from a pool of 7,000.

It's all very well for those of us who write letters of recommendation 18 for our students to stress the qualities of humanity that will make them good lawyers or doctors. And it's nice to think that admission officers are really reading our letters and looking for the extra dimension of commit-ment or concern. Still, it would be hard for a student not to visualize these officers shuffling so many transcripts studded with *A*s that they regard a *B* as positively shameful.

The pressure is almost as heavy on students who just want to graduate 19 and get a job. Long gone are the days of the "gentleman's *C*," when stu-dents journeyed through college with a certain relaxation, sampling a wide variety of courses — music, art, philosophy, classics, anthropology, po-etry, religion — that would send them out as liberally educated men and women. If I were an employer I would rather employ graduates who have this range and curiosity than those who narrowly pursued safe subjects and high grades. I know countless students whose inquiring minds exhilarate me. I like to hear the play of their ideas. I don't know if they're getting *A*s or *C*s, and I don't care. I also like them as people. The country needs them, and they will find satisfying jobs. I tell them to relax. They can't.

Nor can I blame them. They live in a brutal economy. Tuition, room, 20 and board at most private colleges now comes to at least $7,000, not counting books and fees.* This might seem to suggest that the colleges are getting rich. But they are equally battered by inflation. Tuition covers only 60 percent of what it costs to educate a student, and ordinarily the remainder comes from what colleges receive in endowments, grants, and gifts. Now the remainder keeps being swallowed by cruel costs — higher every year — of just opening the doors. Heating oil is up. Insurance is up. Postage is up. Health-premium costs are up. Everything is up. Deficits are up. We are witnessing in America the creation of a brotherhood of paupers — colleges, parents, and students, joined by the common bond of debt.

Today it is not unusual for a student, even if he works part-time at   21 college and full-time during the summer, to accrue $5,000 in loans after four years — loans that he must start to repay within one year after graduation. Exhorted at commencement to go forth into the world, he is already behind as he goes forth. How could he not feel under pressure throughout college to prepare for this day of reckoning? I have used "he" incidentally, only for brevity. Women at Yale are under no less pressure to justify their expensive education to themselves, their parents, and society. In fact, they are probably under more pressure. For although they leave college superbly equipped to bring fresh leadership to traditionally male jobs, society hasn't yet caught up with this fact.

Along with economic pressure goes parental pressure. Inevitably, the   22 two are deeply intertwined.

I see many students taking pre-medical courses with joyless tenacity.   23 They go off to their labs as if they were going to the dentist. It saddens me because I know them in other corners of their life as cheerful people.

"Do you want to go to medical school?" I ask them.   24

"I guess so," they say, without conviction, or "Not really."   25

"Then why are you going?"   26

"Well, my parents want me to be a doctor. They're paying all this   27 money and . . ."

Poor students, poor parents. They are caught in one of the oldest webs   28 of love and duty and guilt. The parents mean well; they are trying to steer their sons and daughters toward a secure future. But the sons and daughters want to major in history or classics or philosophy — subjects with no "practical" value. Where's the payoff on the humanities? It's not easy to persuade such loving parents that the humanities do indeed pay off. The intellectual faculties developed by studying subjects like history and classics — an ability to synthesize and relate, to weigh cause and effect, to see events in perspective — are just the faculties that make creative leaders in business or almost any general field. Still, many fathers would rather put their money on courses that point toward a specific profession — courses that are pre-law, pre-medical, pre-business, or, as I sometimes heard it put, "pre-rich."

---

* Eds. note — Zinsser's essay was published in 1979; the figures quoted for tuition and other expenses would be much higher today.

But the pressure on students is severe. They are truly torn. One part 29 of them feels obliged to fulfill their parents' expectations; after all, their parents are older and presumably wiser. Another part tells them that the expectations that are right for their parents are not right for them.

I know a student who wants to be an artist. She is very obviously an 30 artist and will be a good one — she has already had several modest exhibits. Meanwhile she is growing as a well-rounded person and taking humanistic subjects that will enrich the inner resources out of which her art will grow. But her father is strongly opposed. He thinks that an artist is a "dumb" thing to be. The student vacillates and tries to please everybody. She keeps up with her art somewhat furtively and takes some of the "dumb" courses her father wants her to take — at least they are dumb courses for her. She is a free spirit on a campus of tense students — no small achievement in itself — and she deserves to follow her muse.

Peer pressure and self-induced pressure are also intertwined, and they 31 begin almost at the beginning of freshman year.

"I had a freshman student I'll call Linda," one dean told me, "who came 32 in and said she was under terrible pressure because her roommate, Barbara, was much brighter and studied all the time. I couldn't tell her that Barbara had come in two hours earlier to say the same thing about Linda."

The story is almost funny — except that it's not. It's symptomatic of all 33 the pressures put together. When every student thinks every other student is working harder and doing better, the only solution is to study harder still. I see students going off to the library every night after dinner and coming back when it closes at midnight. I wish they could sometimes forget about their peers and go to a movie. I hear the clacking of typewriters in the hours before dawn. I see the tension in their eyes when exams are approaching and papers are due: *Will I get everything done?*

Probably they won't. They will get sick. They will get "blocked." They 34 will sleep. They will oversleep. They will bug out. *Hey Carlos, help!*

Part of the problem is that they do more than they are expected to do. 35 A professor will assign five-page papers. Several students will start writing ten-page papers to impress him. Then more students will write ten-page papers, and a few will raise the ante to fifteen. Pity the poor student who is still just doing the assignment.

"Once you have twenty or thirty percent of the student population 36 deliberately overexerting," one dean points out, "it's bad for everybody. When a teacher gets more and more effort from his class, the student who is doing normal work can be perceived as not doing well. The tactic works, psychologically."

Why can't the professor just cut back and not accept longer papers? 37 He can, and he probably will. But by then the term will be half over and the damage done. Grade fever is highly contagious and not easily reversed. Besides, the professor's main concern is with his course. He knows his students only in relation to the course and doesn't know that they are also overexerting in their other courses. Nor is it really his business. He didn't sign up for dealing with the student as a whole person and with all the emotional baggage the student brought along from home. That's what deans, masters, chaplains, and psychiatrists are for.

To some extent this is nothing new: a certain number of professors 38 have always been self-contained islands of scholarship and shyness, more comfortable with books than with people. But the new pauperism has widened the gap still further, for professors who actually like to spend time with students don't have as much time to spend. They also are overexerting. If they are young, they are busy trying to publish in order not to perish, hanging by their fingernails onto a shrinking profession. If they are old and tenured, they are buried under the duties of administering departments — as departmental chairmen or members of committees — that have been thinned out by the budgetary axe.

Ultimately it will be the students' own business to break the circles in 39 which they are trapped. They are too young to be prisoners of their parents' dreams and their classmates' fears. They must be jolted into believing in themselves as unique men and women who have the power to shape their own future.

"Violence is being done to the undergraduate experience," says Carlos 40 Hortas. "College should be open-ended: at the end it should open many, many roads. Instead, students are choosing their goal in advance, and their choices narrow as they go along. It's almost as if they think that the country has been codified in the type of jobs that exist — that they've got to fit into certain slots. Therefore, fit into the best-paying slot.

"They ought to take chances. Not taking chances will lead to a life of 41 colorless mediocrity. They'll be comfortable. But something in the spirit will be missing."

I have painted too drab a portrait of today's students, making them 42 seem a solemn lot. That is only half of their story; if they were so dreary I wouldn't so thoroughly enjoy their company. The other half is that they are easy to like. They are quick to laugh and to offer friendship. They are not introverts. They are usually kind and are more considerate of one another than any student generation I have known.

Nor are they so obsessed with their studies that they avoid sports and 43 extracurricular activities. On the contrary, they juggle their crowded hours to play on a variety of teams, perform with musical and dramatic groups, and write for campus publications. But this in turn is one more cause of anxiety. There are too many choices. Academically, they have 1,300 courses to select from; outside class they have to decide how much spare time they can spare and how to spend it.

This means that they engage in fewer extracurricular pursuits than 44 their predecessors did. If they want to row on the crew and play in the symphony they will eliminate one; in the '60s they would have done both. They also tend to choose activities that are self-limiting. Drama, for instance, is flourishing in all twelve of Yale's residential colleges as it never has before. Students hurl themselves into these productions — as actors, directors, carpenters, and technicians — with a dedication to create the best possible play, knowing that the day will come when the run will end and they can get back to their studies.

They also can't afford to be the willing slave of organizations like the   45 *Yale Daily News.* Last spring at the one-hundredth anniversary banquet of that paper — whose past chairmen include such once and future kings as Potter Stewart, Kingman Brewster, and William F. Buckley Jr.* — much was made of the fact that the editorial staff used to be small and totally committed and that "newsies" routinely worked fifty hours a week. In effect they belonged to a club; Newsies is how they defined themselves at Yale. Today's student will write one or two articles a week, when he can, and he defines himself as a student. I've never heard the word Newsie except at the banquet.

If I have described the modern undergraduate primarily as a driven   46 creature who is largely ignoring the blithe spirit inside who keeps trying to come out and play, it's because that's where the crunch is, not only at Yale but throughout American education. It's why I think we should all be worried about the values that are nurturing a generation so fearful of risk and so goal-obsessed at such an early age.

I tell students that there is no one "right" way to get ahead — that each   47 of them is a different person, starting from a different point and bound for a different destination. I tell them that change is a tonic and that all the slots are not codified nor the frontiers closed. One of my ways of telling them is to invite men and women who have achieved success outside the academic world to come and talk informally with my students during the year. They are heads of companies or ad agencies, editors of magazines, politicians, public officials, television magnates, labor leaders, business executives, Broadway producers, artists, writers, economists, photographers, scientists, historians — a mixed bag of achievers.

I ask them to say a few words about how they got started. The students   48 assume that they started in their present profession and knew all along that it was what they wanted to do. Luckily for me, most of them got into their field by a circuitous route, to their surprise, after many detours. The students are startled. They can hardly conceive of a career that was not preplanned. They can hardly imagine allowing the hand of God or chance to nudge them down some unforeseen trail.

• • •

Comprehension

1. What advice does Zinsser give students when they bring their problems to him?

2. What does Zinsser wish for his students? Why does he believe his wish is naive?

---

* Eds. note — Stewart was a U.S. Supreme Court justice, Brewster was a president of Yale, and Buckley was a conservative editor and columnist.

3. What four kinds of pressure does Zinsser identify?

4. Whom does Zinsser blame for the existence of these pressures? Explain.

5. How, according to Zinsser, is his evaluation of students different from their own and from their potential employers' assessments?

6. Why does Zinsser believe that women are probably under even more pressure than men? Do you think this is true today?

7. How does what Zinsser calls the "new pauperism" (38) affect professors?

8. Who, according to Zinsser, is ultimately responsible for eliminating college pressures? Explain.

9. In what sense are sports and other extracurricular activities another source of anxiety for students? How do students adapt to this pressure?

Purpose and Audience

1. In your own words, state Zinsser's thesis. Is his intent in this essay simply to expose a difficult situation or does he want to effect change? What makes you think so?

2. On what kind of audience do you think this essay would have the most significant impact: students, teachers, parents, potential employers, graduate school admissions committees, or college administrators? Why?

3. What do you think Zinsser hopes to accomplish in paragraphs 42–46? How would the essay be different without this section?

4. What assumptions does Zinsser make about his audience? Do you think these assumptions are valid? Explain.

Style and Structure

1. Evaluate the essay's introductory strategy. What impact do you think including the notes to Carlos is likely to have on readers?

2. Identify the boundaries of Zinsser's actual classification. How does he introduce the first category? How does he indicate that his treatment of the final category is complete?

3. What function do paragraphs 22 and 31 serve in the essay?

4. Zinsser is careful to explain that when he refers to students as *he,* he includes female students as well. However, he also refers to professors as *he* (for example, in paragraphs 35–37). Assuming that not all professors at Yale are male, what other stylistic options does Zinsser have?

5. At various points in the essay, Zinsser quotes deans and students at Yale. What is the effect of these quotations?

6. Zinsser notes that his categories are "intertwined" (22, 31). In what ways do the categories overlap? Does this overlap weaken the essay? Explain.

7. What, if anything, seems to determine the order in which Zinsser presents categories? Is this order effective? Why or why not?

Vocabulary Projects

1. Define each of the following words as it is used in this selection.

   proverbial (5)   intangible (16)   blithe (46)
   supplicants (9)   accrue (21)   tonic (47)
   balm (9)   exhorted (21)   codified (47)
   privy (11)   tenacity (23)
   venerated (14)   faculties (28)

2. At times Zinsser uses religious language — *national god, sacred document* — to describe the students' quest for success. Identify other examples of such language, and explain why it is used.

Journal Entry

Which of the pressures Zinsser identifies has the greatest impact on you? Why? Do you have any pressures Zinsser does not mention?

Writing Workshop

1. Zinsser describes problems faced by students at an elite private college in the late 1970s. Are the pressures you experience as a college student similar to or different from the ones Zinsser identifies? Classify your own college pressures, and write an email to your academic adviser or dean. Include a thesis statement that takes a strong stand against the forces responsible for these pressures.

2. **Working with Sources.** Write a classification essay supporting a thesis about college students' drive for success. Categorize students you know either by the degree of their need to succeed or by the different ways in which they wish to succeed. Include a reference to Zinsser's essay — or to Carolyn Foster Segal's essay on page 460 — to support your thesis. Be sure to include parenthetical documentation and a works-cited page. (See Chapter 18 for information on MLA documentation.)

3. Zinsser takes a negative view of the college pressures he identifies. Using his four categories, write an essay arguing that, in the long run, these pressures are not only necessary but also valuable.

Combining the Patterns

Exemplification is an important secondary pattern in this classification-and-division essay. Identify as many passages of exemplification as you can. What do these examples add to Zinsser's essay? What other kinds of examples might be helpful to readers?

Thematic Connections

- "Suicide Note" (page 366)
- "Why Chinese Mothers Are Superior" (page 410)
- "I'm Your Teacher, Not Your Internet-Service Provider" (page 417)
- "The Dog Ate My Disk, and Other Tales of Woe" (page 460)

CAROLYN FOSTER SEGAL

The Dog Ate My Disk, and Other Tales of Woe

Carolyn Foster Segal (b. 1950) teaches English at Cedar Crest College in Allentown, Pennsylvania. Segal has published poetry, fiction, and essays in a number of publications, including the *Chronicle of Higher Education,* where the following essay originally appeared. She sums up her ideas about writing as follows: "Writing — and it does not matter if it is writing about a feature of the landscape, an aspect of human nature, or a work of literature — begins with observation. The other parts are curiosity, imagination, and patience." She has received hundreds of responses from other instructors corroborating the experiences she describes here.

Background on academic integrity and honor codes While making up an excuse for being unprepared for class may seem like a minor infraction, it may still be considered a breach of academic integrity. At many colleges, honor codes define academic integrity and set penalties for those who violate its rules. The concept of college honor codes in the United States goes back to one developed by students at the University of Virginia in 1840, but reports of widespread cheating on college campuses in the early 1990s brought renewed interest in such codes. (Surveys show that more than three-quarters of college students have cheated at least once during their schooling, and an even greater number see cheating as the norm among successful students.) In 1992, the Center for Academic Integrity was established to help colleges and universities find ways to promote "honesty, trust, fairness, respect, and responsibility" among students and faculty members. Its original twenty-five-member group has grown to include more than two hundred institutions, and many other colleges have adopted its goals as well. The main focus of most honor codes is on discouraging plagiarism — copying the work of others and presenting the work of others as one's own — and various forms of cheating on tests. The Center for Academic Integrity sees promoting individual honesty as the fundamental issue underlying all of these concerns.

Taped to the door of my office is a cartoon that features a cat explaining to his feline teacher, "The dog ate my homework." It is intended as a gently humorous reminder to my students that I will not accept excuses for late work, and it, like the lengthy warning on my syllabus, has had absolutely no effect. With a show of energy and creativity that would be admirable if applied to the (missing) assignments in question, my students persist, week after week, semester after semester, year after year, in offering excuses about why their work is not ready. Those reasons fall into several broad categories: the family, the best friend, the evils of dorm life, the evils of technology, and the totally bizarre.

The Family

The death of the grandfather/grandmother is, of course, the grand- 2 mother of all excuses. What heartless teacher would dare to question a student's grief or veracity? What heartless student would lie, wishing death on a revered family member, just to avoid a deadline? Creative students may win extra extensions (and days off) with a little careful planning and fuller plot development, as in the sequence of "My grandfather/grandmother is sick"; "Now my grandfather/grandmother is in the hospital"; and finally, "We could all see it coming — my grandfather/grandmother is dead."

Another favorite excuse is "the family emergency," which (always) goes 3 like this: "There was an emergency at home, and I had to help my family." It's a lovely sentiment, one that conjures up images of Louisa May Alcott's* little women rushing off with baskets of food and copies of *Pilgrim's Progress,*** but I do not understand why anyone would turn to my most irresponsible students in times of trouble.

The Best Friend

This heartwarming concern for others extends beyond the family to 4 friends, as in, "My best friend was up all night and I had to (a) stay up with her in the dorm, (b) drive her to the hospital, or (c) drive to her college because (1) her boyfriend broke up with her, (2) she was throwing up blood [no one catches a cold anymore; everyone throws up blood], or (3) her grandfather/grandmother died."

At one private university where I worked as an adjunct, I heard an in- 5 teresting spin that incorporated the motifs of both best friend and dead relative: "My best friend's mother killed herself." One has to admire the cleverness here: A mysterious woman in the prime of her life has allegedly committed suicide, and no professor can prove otherwise! And I admit I was moved, until finally I had to point out to my students that it was amazing how the simple act of my assigning a topic for a paper seemed to drive large numbers of otherwise happy and healthy middle-aged women to their deaths. I was careful to make that point during an off week, during which no deaths were reported.

The Evils of Dorm Life

These stories are usually fairly predictable; almost always feature the 6 evil roommate or hallmate, with my student in the role of the innocent

---

* Eds. note — Nineteenth-century sentimental novelist, author of *Little Women.*
** Eds. note — Eighteenth-century allegory by John Bunyan describing a Christian's journey from the City of Destruction to the Celestial City.

victim; and can be summed up as follows: My roommate, who is a horrible person, likes to party, and I, who am a good person, cannot concentrate on my work when he or she is partying. Variations include stories about the two people next door who were running around and crying loudly last night because (a) one of them had boyfriend/girlfriend problems; (b) one of them was throwing up blood; or (c) someone, somewhere, died. A friend of mine in graduate school had a student who claimed that his roommate attacked him with a hammer. That, in fact, was a true story; it came out in court when the bad roommate was tried for killing his grandfather.

The Evils of Technology

The computer age has revolutionized the student story, inspiring al-   7
most as many new excuses as it has Internet businesses. Here are just a few
electronically enhanced explanations:

- The computer wouldn't let me save my work.
- The printer wouldn't print.
- The printer wouldn't print this disk.
- The printer wouldn't give me time to proofread.
- The printer made a black line run through all my words, and I know you can't read this, but do you still want it, or wait, here, take my disk. File name? I don't know what you mean.
- I swear I attached it.
- It's my roommate's computer, and she usually helps me, but she had to go to the hospital because she was throwing up blood.
- I did write to the newsgroup, but all my messages came back to me.
- I just found out that all my other newsgroup messages came up under a diferent name. I just want you to know that its really me who wrote all those messages, you can tel which ones our mine because I didnt use the spelcheck! But it was yours truely :) Anyway, just in case you missed those messages or dont belief its my writting. I'll repeat what I sad: I thought the last movie we watched in clas was borring.

The Totally Bizarre

I call the first story "The Pennsylvania Chain Saw Episode." A com-   8
muter student called to explain why she had missed my morning class. She
had gotten up early so that she would be wide awake for class. Having a
bit of extra time, she walked outside to see her neighbor, who was cutting
some wood. She called out to him, and he waved back to her with the saw.
Wouldn't you know it, the safety catch wasn't on or was broken, and the
blade flew right out of the saw and across his lawn and over her fence and
across her yard and severed a tendon in her right hand. So she was calling me from the hospital, where she was waiting for surgery. Luckily, she
reassured me, she had remembered to bring her paper and a stamped envelope

(in a plastic bag, to avoid bloodstains) along with her in the ambulance, and a nurse was mailing everything to me even as we spoke.

That wasn't her first absence. In fact, this student had missed most 9 of the class meetings, and I had already recommended that she withdraw from the course. Now I suggested again that it might be best if she dropped the class. I didn't harp on the absences (what if even some of this story were true?). I did mention that she would need time to recuperate and that making up so much missed work might be difficult. "Oh, no," she said, "I can't drop this course. I had been planning to go on to medical school and become a surgeon, but since I won't be able to operate because of my accident, I'll have to major in English, and this course is more important than ever to me." She did come to the next class, wearing — as evidence of her recent trauma — a bedraggled Ace bandage on her left hand.

You may be thinking that nothing could top that excuse, but in fact 10 I have one more story, provided by the same student, who sent me a letter to explain why her final assignment would be late. While recuperating from her surgery, she had begun corresponding on the Internet with a man who lived in Germany. After a one-week, whirlwind Web romance, they had agreed to meet in Rome, to rendezvous (her phrase) at the papal Easter Mass. Regrettably, the time of her flight made it impossible for her to attend class, but she trusted that I — just this once — would accept late work if the pope wrote a note.

· · ·

Comprehension

1. What is Segal's thesis? Does she state it in her essay? What exactly is she classifying here?

2. In paragraph 3, Segal says, "I do not understand why anyone would turn to my most irresponsible students in times of trouble." Do you see this comment as fair?

3. Which of the excuses Segal discusses do you see as valid? Which do you see as just excuses? Why?

4. Do you see Segal as rigid and unsympathetic, or do you think her frustration is justified? Do you think her students are irresponsible procrastinators or simply overworked?

5. What lessons do you think Segal would like her students to learn from her? Would reading this essay teach them what she wants them to learn?

Purpose and Audience

1. This essay was originally published in the *Chronicle of Higher Education,* a periodical for college teachers and administrators. How do you think these readers responded to the essay? How do you respond?

2. Do you see Segal's purpose here as being to entertain, to let off steam, to warn, to criticize, or to change students' habits? Explain.

3. In paragraph 7, Segal lists some specific excuses in the "evils of technology" category, paraphrasing students' remarks and even imitating their grammar and style. Why does she do this? Considering her likely audience, is this an effective strategy?

Style and Structure

1. In paragraph 1, Segal lists the five categories she plans to discuss. Is this list necessary?

2. Are Segal's categories mutually exclusive, or do they overlap? Could she combine any categories? Can you think of any categories she does not include?

3. What determines the order in which Segal introduces her categories? Is this order logical, or should she present her categories in a different order?

4. Does Segal discuss comparable points for each category? What points, if any, need to be added?

5. Segal frequently uses **sarcasm** in this essay. Give some examples. Given her intended audience, do you think this tone is appropriate? How do you react to her sarcasm?

6. Throughout her essay, Segal returns again and again to two excuses: "my grandfather/grandmother died" and "throwing up blood." Locate different versions of these excuses in the essay. Why do you think she singles out these two excuses?

7. Although Segal deals with a serious academic problem, she includes many expressions — such as "Wouldn't you know it" (8) — that give her essay an informal tone. Identify some other examples. What is your reaction to the essay's casual, offhand tone?

8. Review the category Segal calls "The Evils of Technology." Can you add to (and update) her list? Can you create subcategories?

Vocabulary Projects

1. Define each of the following words as it is used in this selection.

feline (1)	adjunct (5)
veracity (2)	harp (9)
revered (2)	bedraggled (9)
conjures (3)	rendezvous (10)

2. Every profession has its own unique terms. What terms in this essay characterize the writer as a college professor?

Journal Entry

Do you think this essay is funny? Explain your reaction.

Writing Workshop

1. **Working with Sources.** Write an email to Segal explaining why your English paper will be late, presenting several different kinds of original excuses for your paper's lateness. Before you present your own superior excuses, be sure to acknowledge the inadequacies of the excuses Segal lists, quoting a few and including parenthetical documentation and a works-cited page. (See Chapter 18 for information about MLA documentation.)

2. Write an essay identifying four or five categories of legitimate excuses for handing in work late. If you like, you can use narrative examples from your own life as a student to explain each category.

3. Using a humorous (or even sarcastic) tone, write an essay identifying several different categories of teachers in terms of their shortcomings — for instance, teachers who do not cover the assigned work or teachers who do not grade papers in a timely fashion. Be sure to give specific examples of teachers in each category.

Combining the Patterns

In paragraphs 8–10, Segal uses **narration** to tell two stories. What do these stories add to her essay? Do you think she should have added more stories like these to her essay? If so, where?

Thematic Connections

- "Cutting and Pasting: A Senior Thesis by (Insert Name)" (page 24)
- "I'm Your Teacher, Not Your Internet-Service Provider" (page 417)
- "College Pressures" (page 450)
- "The Ways We Lie" (page 474)

AMY TAN

Mother Tongue

Amy Tan was born in 1952 in Oakland, California, the daughter of recent Chinese immigrants. In 1984, when she began to write fiction, she started to explore the contradictions she faced as a Chinese American who was also the daughter of immigrant parents. Three years later, she published *The Joy Luck Club* (1987), a best-selling novel about four immigrant Chinese women and their American-born daughters. Her later works include the novel *The Bonesetter's Daughter* (2001), two children's books, *The Opposite of Fate: A Book of Musings* (2003), and *Saving Fish from Drowning* (2005). In the following 1990 essay, Tan considers her mother's heavily Chinese-influenced English, as well as the different "Englishes" she herself uses, especially in communicating with her mother. She then discusses the potential limitations of growing up with immigrant parents who do not speak fluent English.

Background on Asian Americans and standardized tests The children of Asian immigrants tend to be highly assimilated and are often outstanding students, in part because their parents expect them to work hard and do well. Most who were born in the United States speak and read English fluently. Yet on standardized tests, they have generally scored much higher in math than in English. For example, the average SAT scores nationally in 2009 were 515 in math, 501 in critical reading, and 493 in writing. Asian-American students had average scores of 587 in math, 516 in critical reading, and 520 in writing. The verbal scores represent a recent improvement over previous years, in which Asian-American students generally scored lower than average in the verbal sections of the SAT. In some cases, as Tan suggests, the perception that Asian-American students have greater skill in math than in reading and writing, based on average standardized test scores, may lead teachers to discourage these students from pursuing degrees in fields outside of math and science.

I am not a scholar of English or literature. I cannot give you much 1 more than personal opinions on the English language and its variations in this country or others.

I am a writer. And by that definition, I am someone who has always 2 loved language. I am fascinated by language in daily life. I spend a great deal of my time thinking about the power of language — the way it can evoke an emotion, a visual image, a complex idea, or a simple truth. Language is the tool of my trade. And I use them all — all the Englishes I grew up with.

Recently, I was made keenly aware of the different Englishes I do use. 3 I was giving a talk to a large group of people, the same talk I had already given to half a dozen other groups. The nature of the talk was about my writing, my life, and my book, *The Joy Luck Club*. The talk was going along well enough, until I remembered one major difference that made the whole talk sound wrong. My mother was in the room. And it was perhaps the first time she had heard me give a lengthy speech, using the kind of English I have never used with her. I was saying things like, "The intersection of memory upon imagination" and "There is an aspect of my fiction that relates to thus-and-thus" — a speech filled with carefully wrought grammatical phrases, burdened, it suddenly seemed to me, with nominalized forms, past perfect tenses, conditional phrases, all the forms of standard English that I had learned in school and through books, the forms of English I did not use at home with my mother.

Just last week, I was walking down the street with my mother, and I 4 again found myself conscious of the English I was using, and the English I do use with her. We were talking about the price of new and used furniture and I heard myself saying this: "Not waste money that way." My husband was with us as well, and he didn't notice any switch in my English. And then I realized why. It's because over the twenty years we've been together I've often used that same kind of English with him, and sometimes he even uses it with me. It has become our language of intimacy, a different sort of English that relates to family talk, the language I grew up with.

So you'll have some idea of what this family talk I heard sounds like, 5 I'll quote what my mother said during a recent conversation which I videotaped and then transcribed. During this conversation my mother was talking about a political gangster in Shanghai who had the same last name as her family's, Du, and how the gangster in his early years wanted to be adopted by her family, which was rich by comparison. Later, the gangster became more powerful, far richer than my mother's family, and one day showed up at my mother's wedding to pay his respects. Here's what she said in part:

"Du Yusong having business like fruit stand. Like off the street kind. 6 He is Du like Du Zong — but not Tsung-ming Island people. The local people call putong, the river east side, he belong to that side local people. The man want to ask Du Zong father take him in like become own family. Du Zong father wasn't looking down on him, but didn't take seriously, until that man big like become a mafia. Now important person very hard to inviting him. Chinese way, come only to show respect, don't stay for dinner. Respect for making big celebration, he shows up. Mean gives lots of respect. Chinese custom. Chinese social life that way. If too important won't have to stay too long. He come to my wedding. I didn't see. I heard it. I gone to boy's side, they have YMCA dinner. Chinese age I was nineteen."

You should know that my mother's expressive command of English 7 belies how much she actually understands. She reads the *Forbes* report, listens to *Wall Street Week*, converses daily with her stockbroker, reads all of Shirley MacLaine's books with ease — all kinds of things I can't begin to understand. Yet some of my friends tell me they understand 50 percent of what my mother says. Some say they understand 80 to 90 percent. Some say they understand none of it, as if she were speaking pure Chinese. But to me, my mother's English is perfectly clear, perfectly natural. It's my mother's tongue. Her language, as I hear it, is vivid, direct, full of observation and imagery. This was the language that helped shape the way I saw things, expressed things, made sense of the world.

Lately, I've been giving more thought to the kind of English my mother 8
speaks. Like others, I have described it to people as "broken" or "fractured" English. But I wince when I say that. It has always bothered me that I can think of no way to describe it other than "broken," as if it were damaged and needed to be fixed, as if it lacked a certain wholeness and soundness. I've heard other terms used, "limited English," for example. But they seem just as bad, as if everything is limited, including people's perceptions of the limited English speaker.

I know this for a fact, because when I was growing up, my mother's 9
"limited" English limited *my* perception of her. I was ashamed of her English. I believed that her English reflected the quality of what she had to say. That is, because she expressed them imperfectly her thoughts were imperfect. And I had plenty of empirical evidence to support me: the fact that people in department stores, at banks, and at restaurants did not take her seriously, did not give her good service, pretended not to understand her, or even acted as if they did not hear her.

My mother has long realized the limitations of her English as well. 10
When I was fifteen, she used to have me call people on the phone to pretend I was she. In this guise, I was forced to ask for information or even complain and yell at people who had been rude to her. One time it was a call to her stockbroker in New York. She had cashed out her small portfolio and it just so happened we were going to go to New York the next week, our very first trip outside California. I had to get on the phone and say in an adolescent voice that was not very convincing, "This is Mrs. Tan."

And my mother was standing in the back whispering loudly, "Why he 11
don't send me check, already two weeks late. So mad he lie to me, losing me money."

And then I said in perfect English, "Yes, I'm getting rather concerned. 12
You had agreed to send the check two weeks ago, but it hasn't arrived."

Then she began to talk more loudly. "What he want, I come to New 13
York tell him front of his boss, you cheating me?" And I was trying to calm her down, make her be quiet, while telling the stockbroker, "I can't tolerate any more excuses. If I don't receive the check immediately I am going to have to speak to your manager when I'm in New York next week." And sure enough, the following week there we were in front of this astonished stockbroker, and I was sitting there red-faced and quiet, and my mother, the real Mrs. Tan, was shouting at his boss in her impeccable broken English.

We used a similar routine just five days ago, for a situation that was far 14
less humorous. My mother had gone to the hospital for an appointment, to find out about a benign brain tumor a CAT scan had revealed a month ago. She said she had spoken very good English, her best English, no mistakes. Still, she said, the hospital did not apologize when they said they had lost the CAT scan and she had come for nothing. She said they did not

seem to have any sympathy when she told them she was anxious to know the exact diagnosis, since her husband and son had both died of brain tumors. She said they would not give her any more information until the next time and she would have to make another appointment for that. So she said she would not leave until the doctor called her daughter. She wouldn't budge. And when the doctor finally called her daughter, me, who spoke in perfect English — lo and behold — we had assurances the CAT scan would be found, promises that a conference call on Monday would be held, and apologies for any suffering my mother had gone through for a most regrettable mistake.

I think my mother's English almost had an effect on limiting my pos- 15 sibilities in life as well. Sociologists and linguists probably will tell you that a person's developing language skills are more influenced by peers. But I do think that the language spoken in the family, especially in immigrant families which are more insular, plays a large role in shaping the language of the child. And I believe that it affected my results on achievement tests, IQ tests, and the SAT. While my English skills were never judged as poor, compared to math, English could not be considered my strong suit. In grade school I did moderately well, getting perhaps B's, sometimes B-pluses, in English and scoring perhaps in the sixtieth or seventieth percentile on achievement tests. But those scores were not good enough to override the opinion that my true abilities lay in math and science, because in those areas I achieved A's and scored in the ninetieth percentile or higher.

This was understandable. Math is precise; there is only one correct an- 16 swer. Whereas, for me at least, the answers on English tests were always a judgment call, a matter of opinion and personal experience. Those tests were constructed around items like fill-in-the-blank sentence completion, such as "Even though Tom was _____, Mary thought he was _____." And the correct answer always seemed to be the most bland combinations of thoughts, for example, "Even though Tom was shy, Mary thought he was charming," with the grammatical structure "even though" limiting the correct answer to some sort of semantic opposites, so you wouldn't get answers like, "Even though Tom was foolish, Mary thought he was ridiculous." Well, according to my mother, there were very few limitations as to what Tom could have been and what Mary might have thought of him. So I never did well on tests like that.

The same was true with word analogies, pairs of words in which you 17 were supposed to find some sort of logical, semantic relationship — for example, "*Sunset* is to *nightfall* as _____ is to _____." And here you would be presented with a list of four possible pairs, one of which showed the same kind of relationship: *red* is to *stoplight, bus* is to *arrival, chills* is to *fever, yawn* is to *boring.* Well, I could never think that way. I knew what the tests were asking, but I could not block out of my mind the images already created by the first pair, "*sunset* is to *nightfall*" — and I would see a burst of colors against a darkening sky, the moon rising, the lowering of a curtain of stars. And all the other pairs of words — red, bus, stoplight, boring — just threw up a mass of confusing images, making it impossible for me to sort out something as logical as saying: "A sunset precedes nightfall" is the same as "a chill precedes a fever." The only way I would have gotten that answer right would have been to imagine an associative situation, for example, my being disobedient and staying out past sunset, catching a chill at night, which turns into feverish pneumonia as punishment, which indeed did happen to me.

I have been thinking about all this lately, about my mother's English, about achievement tests. Because lately I've been asked, as a writer, why there are not more Asian Americans represented in American literature. Why are there few Asian Americans enrolled in creative writing programs? Why do so many Chinese students go into engineering? Well, these are broad sociological questions I can't begin to answer. But I have noticed in surveys — in fact, just last week — that Asian students, as a whole, always do significantly better on math achievement tests than in English. And this makes me think that there are other Asian-American students whose English spoken in the home might also be described as "broken" or "limited." And perhaps they also have teachers who are steering them away from writing and into math and science, which is what happened to me.

> "Why are there few Asian Americans enrolled in creative writing programs? Why do so many Chinese students go into engineering?"

18

Fortunately, I happen to be rebellious in nature and enjoy the challenge of disproving assumptions made about me. I became an English major my first year in college, after being enrolled as pre-med. I started writing nonfiction as a freelancer the week after I was told by my former boss that writing was my worst skill and I should hone my talents toward account management.

19

But it wasn't until 1985 that I finally began to write fiction. And at first I wrote using what I thought to be wittily crafted sentences, sentences that would finally prove I had mastery over the English language. Here's an example from the first draft of a story that later made its way into *The Joy Luck Club,* but without this line: "That was my mental quandary in its nascent state." A terrible line, which I can barely pronounce.

20

Fortunately, for reasons I won't get into today, I later decided I should envision a reader for the stories I would write. And the reader I decided upon was my mother because these were stories about mothers. So with this reader in mind — and in fact she did read my early drafts — I began to write stories using all the Englishes I grew up with: the English I spoke to my mother, which for lack of a better term might be described as "simple"; the English she used with me, which for lack of a better term might be described as "broken"; my translation of her Chinese, which could certainly be described as "watered down"; and what I imagined to be her translation of her Chinese if she could speak in perfect English, her internal language,

21

and for that I sought to preserve the essence, but neither an English nor a Chinese structure. I wanted to capture what language ability tests can never reveal: her intent, her passion, her imagery, the rhythms of her speech and the nature of her thoughts.

Apart from what any critic had to say about my writing, I knew I had 22 succeeded where it counted when my mother finished reading my book and gave me her verdict: "So easy to read."

• • •

Comprehension

1. What is Tan classifying in this essay? What individual categories does she identify?

2. Where does Tan identify the different categories she discusses in "Mother Tongue"? Should she have identified these categories earlier? Explain your reasoning.

3. Does Tan illustrate each category she identifies? Does she treat all categories equally? If she does not, do you see this as a problem? Explain.

4. In what specific situations does Tan say her mother's "limited English" was a handicap? In what other situations might Mrs. Tan face difficulties?

5. What effects has her mother's limited English had on Tan's life?

6. How does Tan account for the difficulty she had in answering questions on achievement tests, particularly word analogies? Do you think her problems in this area can be explained by the level of her family's language skills, or might other factors also be to blame? Explain.

7. In paragraph 18, Tan considers the possible reasons for the relatively few Asian Americans in the fields of language and literature. What explanations does she offer? What other explanations can you think of?

Purpose and Audience

1. Why do you suppose Tan opens her essay by explaining her qualifications? Why, for example, does she tell her readers she is "not a scholar of English or literature" (1) but a writer who is "fascinated by language in daily life" (2)?

2. Do you think Tan expects most of her readers to be Asian American? To be familiar with Asian-American languages and culture? How can you tell?

3. Is Tan's primary focus in this essay on language or on her mother? Explain your conclusion.

Style and Structure

1. This essay's style is relatively informal. For example, Tan uses *I* to refer to herself and addresses her readers as *you*. Identify other features that characterize her style as informal. Do you think a more formal style would strengthen her credibility? Explain your reasoning.

2. In paragraph 6, Tan quotes a passage of her mother's speech. What purpose does Tan say she wants this quotation to serve? What impression does it give of her mother? Do you think this effect is what Tan intended? Explain.

3. In paragraphs 10 through 13, Tan juxtaposes her mother's English with her own. What point do these quoted passages make?

4. Consider the expression *Mother Tongue* in Tan's title. What does this expression usually mean? What does it seem to mean here?

5. In paragraph 20, Tan quotes a "terrible line" from an early draft of part of her novel *The Joy Luck Club*. Why do you suppose she quotes this line? How is it different from the writing style she uses in "Mother Tongue"?

Vocabulary Projects

1. Define each of the following words as it is used in this selection.

   nominalized (3)   guise (10)   semantic (16)
   belies (7)   impeccable (13)   quandary (20)
   empirical (9)   insular (15)   nascent (20)

2. In paragraph 8, Tan discusses the different words and phrases that might be used to describe her mother's spoken English. Which of these terms seems most accurate? Do you agree with Tan that these words are unsatisfactory? What other term for her mother's English would be both neutral and accurate?

Journal Entry

In paragraph 9, Tan says that when she was growing up she was sometimes ashamed of her mother because of her limited English proficiency. Have you ever felt ashamed of a parent (or a friend) because of his or her inability to "fit in" in some way? How do you feel now about your earlier reaction?

Writing Workshop

1. What different "Englishes" (or other languages) do you use in your day-to-day life as a student, employee, friend, and family member? Write a classification-and-division essay identifying, describing, and illustrating each kind of language and explaining the purpose it serves.

2. **Working with Sources.** What kinds of problems does a person whose English is as limited as Mrs. Tan's face in the age of computers and

instant communication? Write a classification-and-division essay that identifies and explains the kinds of problems you might encounter today if the level of your spoken English were comparable to Mrs. Tan's. Try to update some of the specific situations Tan describes, quoting Tan where necessary, and be sure to document any borrowed words or ideas and to include a works-cited page. (See Chapter 18 for information on MLA documentation.)

3. Tan's essay focuses on spoken language, but people also use different kinds of *written* language in different situations. Write a classification-and-division essay that identifies and analyzes three different kinds of written English: one appropriate for your parents, one for a teacher or employer, and one for a friend. Illustrate each kind of language with a few sentences directed at each audience about your plans for your future. In your thesis statement, explain why all three kinds of language are necessary.

Combining the Patterns

Tan develops her essay with a series of anecdotes about her mother and about herself. How does this use of **narration** strengthen her essay? Could she have made her point about the use of different "Englishes" without these anecdotes? What other strategy could she have used?

Thematic Connections

- "Only Daughter" (page 111)
- "Why Chinese Mothers Are Superior" (page 410)
- "The Shame Game" (page 680)

STEPHANIE ERICSSON

The Ways We Lie

Stephanie Ericsson (b. 1953) grew up in San Francisco and began writing as a teenager. She has been a screenwriter and an advertising copywriter and has published several books based on her own life. *Shamefaced: The Road to Recovery* and *Women of AA: Recovering Together* (both 1985) focus on her experiences with addiction; *Companion through the Darkness: Inner Dialogues on Grief* (1993) deals with the sudden death of her husband; and *Companion into the Dawn: Inner Dialogues on Loving* (1994) is a collection of essays.

Background on lies in politics and business The following piece originally appeared in the *Utne Reader* as the cover article of the January 1993 issue, which was devoted to the theme of lies and lying. The subject had particular relevance after a year when the honesty of Bill Clinton — the newly elected U.S. president — had been questioned. (It also followed the furor surrounding the confirmation hearings of U.S. Supreme Court nominee Clarence Thomas, who denied allegations by attorney Anita Hill of workplace sexual harassment; here the question was who was telling the truth and who was not.) Six years later, President Clinton was accused of perjury and faced a Senate impeachment trial. In subsequent years, lying was featured prominently in the news as executives at a number of major corporations were charged with falsifying records at the expense of employees and shareholders, and the Bush administration was accused of lying about the presence of weapons of mass destruction in Iraq to justify going to war.

More recently, major mortgage lenders were found to have lied about their reviews of documents justifying many thousands of foreclosures. In 2010, lying was again featured prominently in the news as investigations of the oil company BP found that the company was aware of problems with a safety device on the Deepwater Horizon oil rig prior to an explosion that killed eleven workers and spilled millions of gallons of oil but covered up those concerns in an attempt to increase its profits. BP has also been accused of lying to Congress about its estimate of the extent of the spill.

1 The bank called today and I told them my deposit was in the mail, even though I hadn't written a check yet. It'd been a rough day. The baby I'm pregnant with decided to do aerobics on my lungs for two hours, our three-year-old daughter painted the living-room couch with lipstick, the IRS put me on hold for an hour, and I was late to a business meeting because I was tired.

2 I told my client the traffic had been bad. When my partner came home, his haggard face told me his day hadn't gone any better than mine, so when he asked, "How was your day?" I said, "Oh, fine," knowing that one more straw might break his back. A friend called and wanted to take me to lunch.

I said I was busy. Four lies in the course of a day, none of which I felt the least bit guilty about.

We lie. We all do. We exaggerate, we minimize, we avoid confrontation,   3 we spare people's feelings, we conveniently forget, we keep secrets, we justify lying to the big-guy institutions. Like most people, I indulge in small falsehoods and still think of myself as an honest person. Sure I lie, but it doesn't hurt anything. Or does it?

I once tried going a whole week without telling a lie, and it was paralyz-   4 ing. I discovered that telling the truth all the time is nearly impossible. It means living with some serious consequences: The bank charges me $60 in overdraft fees, my partner keels over when I tell him about my travails, my client fires me for telling her I didn't feel like being on time, and my friend takes it personally when I say I'm not hungry. There must be some merit to lying.

But if I justify lying, what makes me any different from slick politicians   5 or the corporate robbers who raided the S&L industry? Saying it's okay to lie one way and not another is hedging. I cannot seem to escape the voice deep inside me that tells me: When someone lies, someone loses.

What far-reaching consequences will I, or others, pay as a result of my   6 lie? Will someone's trust be destroyed? Will someone else pay *my* penance because I ducked out? We must consider the *meaning of our actions*. Deception, lies, capital crimes, and misdemeanors all carry meanings. *Webster's* definition of *lie* is specific:

> 1: a false statement or action especially made with the intent to deceive;
> 2: anything that gives or is meant to give a false impression.

A definition like this implies that there are many, many ways to tell a   7 lie. Here are just a few.

The White Lie

> A man who won't lie to a woman has very little consideration for her feelings.
>
> **— BERGEN EVANS**

The white lie assumes that the truth will cause more damage than a   8 simple, harmless untruth. Telling a friend he looks great when he looks like hell can be based on a decision that the friend needs a compliment more than a frank opinion. But, in effect, it is the liar deciding what is best for the lied to. Ultimately, it is a vote of no confidence. It is an act of subtle arrogance for anyone to decide what is best for someone else.

Yet not all circumstances are quite so cut-and-dried. Take, for instance,   9 the sergeant in Vietnam who knew one of his men was killed in action but listed him as missing so that the man's family would receive indefinite compensation instead of the lump-sum pittance the military gives widows and children. His intent was honorable. Yet for twenty years this family kept their hopes alive, unable to move on to a new life.

Facades

> Et tu, Brute?
>
> —CAESAR*

We all put up facades to one degree or another. When I put on a suit to   10
go to see a client, I feel as though I am putting on another face, obeying the
expectation that serious businesspeople wear suits rather than sweatpants.
But I'm a writer. Normally, I get up, get the kid off to school, and sit at my
computer in my pajamas until four in the afternoon. When I answer the
phone, the caller thinks I'm wearing a suit (though the UPS man knows
better).

But facades can be destructive because they are used to seduce others   11
into an illusion. For instance, I recently realized that a former friend was
a liar. He presented himself with all the right looks and the right words
and offered lots of new consciousness theories, fabulous books to read,
and fascinating insights. Then I did some business with him, and the time
came for him to pay me. He turned out to be all talk and no walk. I heard
a plethora of reasonable excuses, including in-depth descriptions of the
big break around the corner. In six months of work, I saw less than a hundred bucks. When I confronted him, he raised both eyebrows and tried to
convince me that I'd heard him wrong, that he'd made no commitment to
me. A simple investigation into his past revealed a crowded graveyard of
disenchanted former friends.

Ignoring the Plain Facts

> Well, you must understand that Father Porter is only human. . . .
>
> —A MASSACHUSETTS PRIEST

In the '60s, the Catholic Church in Massachusetts began hearing com-   12
plaints that Father James Porter was sexually molesting children. Rather
than relieving him of his duties, the ecclesiastical authorities simply moved
him from one parish to another between 1960 and 1967, actually providing
him with a fresh supply of unsuspecting families and innocent children to
abuse. After treatment in 1967 for pedophilia, he went back to work, this
time in Minnesota. The new diocese was aware of Father Porter's obsession
with children, but they needed priests and recklessly believed treatment
had cured him. More children were abused until he was relieved of his duties a year later. By his own admission, Porter may have abused as many as
a hundred children.

Ignoring the facts may not in and of itself be a form of lying, but con-   13
sider the context of this situation. If a lie is *a false action done with the intent*

---

* Eds. note — "And you, Brutus?" (Latin). In Shakespeare's play *Julius Caesar*, Caesar
asks this question when he sees Brutus, whom he has believed to be his friend,
among the conspirators who are stabbing him.

to deceive, then the Catholic Church's conscious covering for Porter created irreparable consequences. The church became a co-perpetrator with Porter.

Deflecting

> When you have no basis for an argument, abuse the plaintiff.
>
> — CICERO

I've discovered that I can keep anyone from seeing the true me by be- 14 ing selectively blatant. I set a precedent of being up-front about intimate issues, but I never bring up the things I truly want to hide; I just let people assume I'm revealing everything. It's an effective way of hiding.

Any good liar knows that the way to perpetuate an untruth is to de- 15 flect attention from it. When Clarence Thomas exploded with accusations that the Senate hearings were a "high-tech lynching," he simply switched the focus from a highly charged subject to a radioactive subject. Rather than defending himself, he took the offensive and accused the country of racism. It was a brilliant maneuver. Racism is now politically incorrect in official circles — unlike sexual harassment, which still rewards those who can get away with it.

Some of the most skillful deflectors are passive-aggressive people who, 16 when accused of inappropriate behavior, refuse to respond to the accusations. This you-don't-exist stance infuriates the accuser, who, understandably, screams something obscene out of frustration. The trap is sprung and the act of deflection successful, because now the passive-aggressive person can indignantly say, "Who can talk to someone as unreasonable as you?" The real issue is forgotten and the sins of the original victim become the focus. Feeling guilty of name-calling, the victim is fully tamed and crawls into a hole, ashamed. I have watched this fighting technique work thousands of times in disputes between men and women, and what I've learned is that the real culprit is not necessarily the one who swears the loudest.

Omission

> The cruelest lies are often told in silence.
>
> — R. L. STEVENSON

Omission involves telling most of the truth minus one or two key facts 17 whose absence changes the story completely. You break a pair of glasses that are guaranteed under normal use and get a new pair, without mentioning that the first pair broke during a rowdy game of basketball. Who hasn't tried something like that? But what about omission of information that could make a difference in how a person lives his or her life?

For instance, one day I found out that rabbinical legends tell of another 18 woman in the Garden of Eden before Eve. I was stunned. The omission of the Sumerian goddess Lilith from Genesis — as well as her demonization by ancient misogynists as an embodiment of female evil — felt like spiritual robbery. I felt like I'd just found out my mother was really my stepmother. To take seriously the tradition that Adam was created out of the same mud as his equal counterpart, Lilith, redefines all of Judeo-Christian history.

Some renegade Catholic feminists introduced me to a view of Lilith   19 that had been suppressed during the many centuries when this strong goddess was seen only as a spirit of evil. Lilith was a proud goddess who defied Adam's need to control her, attempted negotiations, and when this failed, said adios and left the Garden of Eden.

This omission of Lilith from the Bible was a patriarchal strategy to   20 keep women weak. Omitting the strong-woman archetype of Lilith from Western religions and starting the story with Eve the Rib has helped keep Christian and Jewish women believing they were the lesser sex for thousands of years.

Stereotypes and Clichés

> Where opinion does not exist, the status quo becomes stereotyped and all originality is discouraged.
>
> —BERTRAND RUSSELL

Stereotype and cliché serve a purpose as a form of shorthand. Our need   21 for vast amounts of information in nanoseconds has made the stereotype vital to modern communication. Unfortunately, it often shuts down original thinking, giving those hungry for the truth a candy bar of misinformation instead of a balanced meal. The stereotype explains a situation with just enough truth to seem unquestionable.

All the "isms" — racism, sexism, ageism, et al. — are founded on and   22 fueled by the stereotype and the cliché, which are lies of exaggeration, omission, and ignorance. They are always dangerous. They take a single tree and make it a landscape. They destroy curiosity. They close minds and separate people. The single mother on welfare is assumed to be cheating. Any black male could tell you how much of his identity is obliterated daily by stereotypes. Fat people, ugly people, beautiful people, old people, large-breasted women, short men, the mentally ill, and the homeless all could tell you how much more they are like us than we want to think. I once admitted to a group of people that I had a mouth like a truck driver. Much to my surprise, a man stood up and said, "I'm a truck driver, and I never cuss." Needless to say, I was humbled.

Groupthink

> Who is more foolish, the child afraid of the dark, or the man afraid of the light?
>
> —MAURICE FREEHILL

Irving Janis, in *Victims of GroupThink,* defines this sort of lie as a psy-   23 chological phenomenon within decision-making groups in which loyalty to the group has become more important than any other value, with the result that dissent and the appraisal of alternatives are suppressed. If you've ever worked on a committee or in a corporation, you've encountered groupthink. It requires a combination of other forms of lying — ignoring facts, selective memory, omission, and denial, to name a few.

The textbook example of groupthink came on December 7, 1941. From 24 as early as the fall of 1941, the warnings came in, one after another, that Japan was preparing for a massive military operation. The Navy command in Hawaii assumed Pearl Harbor was invulnerable — the Japanese weren't stupid enough to attack the United States' most important base. On the other hand, racist stereotypes said the Japanese weren't smart enough to invent a torpedo effective in less than 60 feet of water (the fleet was docked in 30 feet); after all, U.S. technology hadn't been able to do it.

On Friday, December 5, normal weekend leave was granted to all the 25 commanders at Pearl Harbor, even though the Japanese consulate in Hawaii was busy burning papers. Within the tight, good-ole-boy cohesiveness of the U.S. command in Hawaii, the myth of invulnerability stayed well entrenched. No one in the group considered the alternatives. The rest is history.

Out-and-Out Lies

The only form of lying that is beyond reproach is lying for its own sake.

— OSCAR WILDE

Of all the ways to lie, I like this one the best, probably because I get 26 tired of trying to figure out the real meanings behind things. At least I can trust the bald-faced lie. I once asked my five-year-old nephew, "Who broke the fence?" (I had seen him do it.) He answered, "The murderers." Who could argue?

At least when this sort of lie is told it can be easily confronted. As the 27 person who is lied to, I know where I stand. The bald-faced lie doesn't toy with my perceptions — it argues with them. It doesn't try to refashion reality, it tries to refute it. *Read my lips.* . . . No sleight of hand. No guessing. If this were the only form of lying, there would be no such thing as floating anxiety or the adult-children of alcoholics movement.

Dismissal

Pay no attention to that man behind the curtain! I am the Great Oz!

— THE WIZARD OF OZ

Dismissal is perhaps the slipperiest of all lies. Dismissing feelings, per- 28 ceptions, or even the raw facts of a situation ranks as a kind of lie that can do as much damage to a person as any other kind of lie.

The roots of many mental disorders can be traced back to the dismissal 29 of reality. Imagine that a person is told from the time she is a tot that her perceptions are inaccurate. *"Mommy, I'm scared."* "No, you're not, darling." *"I don't like that man next door, he makes me feel icky."* "Johnny, that's a terrible thing to say, of course you like him. You go over there right now and be nice to him."

I've often mused over the idea that madness is actually a sane reaction to an insane world. Psychologist R. D. Laing supports this hypothesis in *Sanity, Madness & the Family,* an account of his investigations into families of schizophrenics. The common thread that ran through all of the families he studied was a deliberate, staunch dismissal of the patient's perceptions from a very early age. Each of the patients started out with an accurate grasp of reality, which, through meticulous and methodical dismissal, was demolished until the only reality the patient could trust was catatonia.

Dismissal runs the gamut. Mild dismissal can be quite handy for forgiving the foibles of others in our day-to-day lives. Toddlers who have just learned to manipulate their parents' attention sometimes are dismissed out of necessity. Absolute attention from the parents would require so much energy that no one would get to eat dinner. But we must be careful and attentive about how far we take our "necessary" dismissals. Dismissal is a dangerous tool, because it's nothing less than a lie.

Delusion

> We lie loudest when we lie to ourselves.
>
> — ERIC HOFFER

I could write the book on this one. Delusion, a cousin of dismissal, is the tendency to see excuses as facts. It's a powerful lying tool because it filters out information that contradicts what we want to believe. Alcoholics who believe that the problems in their lives are legitimate reasons for drinking rather than results of the drinking offer the classic example of deluded thinking. Delusion uses the mind's ability to see things in myriad ways to support what it wants to be the truth.

But delusion is also a survival mechanism we all use. If we were to fully contemplate the consequences of our stockpiles of nuclear weapons or global warming, we could hardly function on a day-to-day level. We don't want to incorporate that much reality into our lives because to do so would be paralyzing.

Delusion acts as an adhesive to keep the status quo intact. It shamelessly employs dismissal, omission, and amnesia, among other sorts of lies. Its most cunning defense is that it cannot see itself.

> The liar's punishment . . . is that he cannot believe anyone else.
>
> — GEORGE BERNARD SHAW

These are only a few of the ways we lie. Or are lied to. As I said earlier, it's not easy to entirely eliminate lies from our lives. No matter how pious we may try to be, we will still embellish, hedge, and omit to lubricate the daily machinery of living. But there is a world of difference between telling functional lies and living a lie. Martin Buber* once said, "The lie is the spirit committing treason against itself." Our acceptance of lies becomes a cultural cancer that eventually shrouds and reorders reality until moral garbage becomes as invisible to us as water is to a fish.

How much do we tolerate before we become sick and tired of being 36 sick and tired? When will we stand up and declare our *right* to trust? When do we stop accepting that the real truth is in the fine print? Whose lips do we read this year when we vote for president? When will we stop being so reticent about making judgments? When do we stop turning over our personal power and responsibility to liars?

Maybe if I don't tell the bank the check's in the mail I'll be less tolerant 37 of the lies told me every day. A country song I once heard said it all for me: "You've got to stand for something or you'll fall for anything."

·   ·   ·

Comprehension

1. List and briefly define each of the ten kinds of lies Ericsson identifies.

2. Why, in Ericsson's view, is each kind of lie necessary?

3. According to Ericsson, what is the danger of each kind of lie?

4. Why does Ericsson like "out-and-out lies" (26–27) best?

5. Why is "dismissal" the "slipperiest of all lies" (28)?

Purpose and Audience

1. Is Ericsson's thesis simply that "there are many, many ways to tell a lie" (7)? Or is she defending — or attacking — the practice of lying? Try to state her thesis in a single sentence.

2. Do you think Ericsson's choice of examples reveals a political bias? If so, do you think she expects her intended audience to share her political views? Explain your conclusion.

Style and Structure

1. Despite the seriousness of her subject matter, Ericsson's essay is informal; her opening paragraphs are especially personal and breezy. Why do you think she chose to use this kind of opening? Do you think her decision makes sense?

2. Ericsson introduces each category of lie with a quotation. What function do these quotations serve? Do you think the essay would be more or less effective without them? Explain your conclusion.

---

* Eds. note — Austrian-born Judaic philosopher (1878–1965).

3. In addition to a heading and a quotation, what other elements does Ericsson include in her treatment of each kind of lie? Are all the discussions parallel — that is, does each include *all* the standard elements and *only* those elements? If not, do you think this lack of balance is a problem? Explain.

4. What, if anything, determines the order in which Ericsson arranges her categories? Do you think any category should be relocated? If so, why?

5. Throughout her essay, Ericsson uses **rhetorical questions**. Why do you suppose she uses this stylistic device?

6. Ericsson occasionally cites the views of experts. Why does she do so? If she wanted to cite additional experts, what professional backgrounds or fields of study do you think they should represent? Why?

7. In paragraph 29, Ericsson says, "Imagine that a person is told from the time she is a tot. . . ." Does she use *she* in similar contexts elsewhere in the essay? Do you find the feminine form of the personal pronoun appropriate or distracting? Explain.

8. Paragraphs 35–37 constitute Ericsson's conclusion. How does this conclusion parallel the essay's introduction in terms of style, structure, and content?

Vocabulary Projects

1. Define each of the following words as it is used in this selection.

travails (4)	deflectors (16)	obliterated (22)
hedging (5)	passive-aggressive (16)	staunch (30)
pittance (9)	misogynists (18)	catatonia (30)
facades (10)	counterpart (18)	gamut (31)
plethora (11)	renegade (19)	foibles (31)
pedophilia (12)	archetype (20)	reticent (36)
blatant (14)	nanoseconds (21)	

2. Ericsson uses many **colloquialisms** in this essay — for example, "I could write the book on this one" (32). Identify as many of these informal expressions as you can. Why do you think she uses colloquialisms instead of more formal expressions? Do they have a positive or negative effect on your reaction to her ideas? Explain.

Journal Entry

In paragraph 3, Ericsson says, "We lie. We all do." Later in the paragraph, she comments, "Sure I lie, but it doesn't hurt anything. Or does it?" Answer her question.

Writing Workshop

1. **Working with Sources.** Choose three or four of Ericsson's categories, and write a classification-and-division essay called "The Ways I Lie." Base your essay on personal experience, and include an explicit thesis statement that defends your own lies — or is sharply critical of their use. Be sure to document Ericsson's essay when you cite her categories and to include a works-cited page. (See Chapter 18 for information on MLA documentation.)

2. In paragraph 22, Ericsson condemns stereotypes. Write a classification-and-division essay with the following thesis statement: "Stereotypes are usually inaccurate, often negative, and always dangerous." In your essay, consider the stereotypes applied to three or four of the following groups: people who are disabled, overweight, or elderly; urban teenagers; politicians; housewives; and immigrants.

3. Using the thesis provided in question 2, write a classification-and-division essay that considers the stereotypes applied to three or four of the following occupations: police officers, librarians, used-car dealers, flight attendants, lawyers, construction workers, rock musicians, accountants, and telemarketers.

Combining the Patterns

A dictionary **definition** is a familiar — even tired — strategy for an essay's introduction. Would you advise Ericsson to delete the definition in paragraph 6 for this reason, or do you believe it is necessary? Explain.

Thematic Connections

- "'What's in a Name?'" (page 2)
- "Thirty-Eight Who Saw Murder Didn't Call the Police" (page 127)
- "The Hidden Life of Garbage" (page 188)
- "The Lottery" (page 311)

BILLY COLLINS

Aristotle (Poetry)

Former United States Poet Laureate Billy Collins was born in New York City in 1941 and received an undergraduate degree from the College of the Holy Cross and a Ph.D. in English from the University of California, Riverside. Collins's poetry is artful, accessible, and self-effacing in its style and in its focus on ordinary experiences. Collins writes with his reader in mind: "I always tend to begin a poem with something fairly clear or a piece of common knowledge . . . something we all know, some little common ground that becomes the grounding wire." Collins's recent work includes the haiku collection *She Was Just Seventeen* (2006) and *Ballistics* (2008) as well as *Bright Wings: An Illustrated Anthology of Poems about Birds* (2009), which he edited.

Background on Aristotle and the Dramatic Unities The Greek philosopher Aristotle (384 BCE–322 BCE) is a foundational figure in Western rhetoric, physics, logic, and politics. He also wrote the earliest known work of literary theory, *Poetics* (c. 335 BCE), which examines the principles behind effective poetry and drama. According to Aristotle, the plot of a play requires three elements to be a complete, unified whole.

> A whole is that which has a beginning, a middle, and an end. A beginning is that which does not itself follow anything by causal necessity, but after which something naturally is or comes to be. An end, on the contrary, is that which itself naturally follows some other thing, either by necessity, or as a rule, but has nothing following it. A middle is that which follows something as some other thing follows it. A well constructed plot, therefore, must neither begin nor end at haphazard, but conform to these principles.

Collins has acknowledged that the same principle guides his own work: "My poems tend to have rhetorical structures; what I mean by that is they tend to have a beginning, a middle, and an end."

This is the beginning.
Almost anything can happen.
This is where you find
the creation of light, a fish wriggling onto land,
the first word of *Paradise Lost** on an empty page.   5
Think of an egg, the letter *A*,
a woman ironing on a bare stage
as the heavy curtain rises.
This is the very beginning.

---

* EDS. NOTE — Epic poem written by English poet John Milton and published in 1667.

484

The first-person narrator introduces himself,   10
tells us about his lineage.
The mezzo-soprano stands in the wings.
Here the climbers are studying a map
or pulling on their long woolen socks.
This is early on, years before the Ark, dawn.   15
The profile of an animal is being smeared
on the wall of a cave,
and you have not yet learned to crawl.
This is the opening, the gambit,
a pawn moving forward an inch.   20
This is your first night with her,
your first night without her.
This is the first part
where the wheels begin to turn,
where the elevator begins its ascent,   25
before the doors lurch apart.

This is the middle.
Things have had time to get complicated,
messy, really. Nothing is simple anymore.
Cities have sprouted up along the rivers   30
teeming with people at cross-purposes —
a million schemes, a million wild looks.
Disappointment unshoulders his knapsack
here and pitches his ragged tent.
This is the sticky part where the plot congeals,   35
where the action suddenly reverses
or swerves off in an outrageous direction.
Here the narrator devotes a long paragraph
to why Miriam does not want Edward's child.
Someone hides a letter under a pillow.   40
Here the aria rises to a pitch,
a song of betrayal, salted with revenge.
And the climbing party is stuck on a ledge
halfway up the mountain.
This is the bridge, the painful modulation.   45
This is the thick of things.
So much is crowded into the middle —
the guitars of Spain, piles of ripe avocados,
Russian uniforms, noisy parties,
lakeside kisses, arguments heard through a wall —   50
too much to name, too much to think about.

And this is the end,
the car running out of road,
the river losing its name in an ocean,
the long nose of the photographed horse   55

touching the white electronic line.
This is the colophon, the last elephant in the parade,
the empty wheelchair,
and pigeons floating down in the evening.
Here the stage is littered with bodies,   60
the narrator leads the characters to their cells,
and the climbers are in their graves.
It is me hitting the period
and you closing the book.
It is Sylvia Plath in the kitchen   65
and St. Clement with an anchor around his neck.
This is the final bit
thinning away to nothing.
This is the end, according to Aristotle,
what we have all been waiting for,   70
what everything comes down to,
the destination we cannot help imagining,
a streak of light in the sky,
a hat on a peg, and outside the cabin, falling leaves.

.   .   .

Reading Literature

1. What three categories does this poem explore? Are the categories mutually exclusive, or do they overlap?
2. Are the three categories treated in similar terms? That is, do they include the same kind of examples? Do they all seem to be of equal importance?
3. What additional examples could you include in each category?

Journal Entry

Why is this poem called "Aristotle"? (Read this selection's headnote before you answer this question.) Do you see this poem as a commentary on poetry or on life?

Thematic Connections

- "Ground Zero" (page 182)
- "Once More to the Lake" (page 194)
- "'Girl'" (page 258)
- "Suicide Note" (page 366)
- "Love and Other Catastrophes: A Mix Tape" (page 520)

Writing Assignments for Classification and Division

1. Choose a film you have seen recently, and list all the elements you consider significant — plot, direction, acting, special effects, and so on. Then, further subdivide each category (for instance, listing each of the major special effects). Using this list as an outline, write a review of the film.

2. Write an essay classifying the teachers or bosses you have had into several distinct categories, and form a judgment about the relative effectiveness of the individuals in each group. Give each category a name, and be sure your essay has a thesis statement.

3. What fashion styles do you observe on your college campus? Establish four or five distinct categories, and write an essay classifying students on the basis of how they dress. Give each group of students a descriptive title.

4. **Working with Sources.** Look through this book's thematic table of contents (page xxxv), and choose three essays on the same general subject. Then, write an essay discussing the different ways writers can explore the same theme. Be sure your topic sentences clearly define your three categories. Document all references to the essays you choose, and include a works-cited page. (See Chapter 18 for information on MLA documentation.)

5. Many consider violence in sports a serious problem. Write an essay expressing your views on this problem. Using a classification-and-division structure, categorize information according to sources of violence (such as the players, the nature of the game, and the fans).

6. Classify television shows according to type (reality show, crime drama, and so forth), audience (preschoolers, school-age children, adults, and so on), or any other logical principle. Write an essay based on your system of classification, making sure to include a thesis statement. For instance, you might assert that the relative popularity of one kind of program over others reveals something about television watchers or that one kind of program shows signs of becoming obsolete.

7. Write a lighthearted essay discussing kinds of snack foods, cartoons, pets, status symbols, toys, shoppers, vacations, weight-loss diets, hairstyles, or drivers.

8. Write an essay assessing the relative merits of several different politicians, Web sites, news broadcasts, or academic majors.

9. What kinds of survival skills does a student need to get through college successfully? Write a classification-and-division essay identifying and discussing several kinds of skills and indicating why each category is important. If you like, you may write your essay in the form of an email to a beginning college student.

10. Divide your Facebook friends into categories according to some logical principle. Include a thesis statement that indicates how different the various groups are.

Collaborative Activity for Classification and Division

Working in a group of four students, devise a classification system encompassing all the different kinds of popular music the members of your group favor. You may begin with general categories, such as country, pop, and rhythm and blues, but you should also include more specific categories, such as rap and heavy metal, in your classification system. After you decide on categories and subcategories that represent the tastes of all group members, fill in examples for each category. Then, devise several different options for arranging your categories into an essay.

13

Definition

What Is Definition?

A **definition** tells what a term means and how it differs from other terms in its class. In the following paragraph from "Altruistic Behavior," anthropologist Desmond Morris defines *altruism,* the key term of his essay.

Topic sentence **Extended definition defines term by *enumeration* and *negation***	Altruism is the performance of an unselfish act. As a pattern of behavior, this act must have two properties: it must benefit someone else, and it must do so to the disadvantage of the benefactor. It is not merely a matter of being helpful; it is helpfulness at a cost to yourself.

Most people think of definition in terms of print or online dictionaries, which give brief, succinct explanations — called **formal definitions** — of what words mean. But definition also includes explaining what something, or even someone, *is* — that is, its essential nature. Sometimes a definition requires a paragraph, an essay, or even a whole book. These longer, more complex definitions are called **extended definitions**.

Understanding Formal Definitions

Look at any dictionary, and you will notice that all definitions have a standard three-part structure. First, they present the *term* to be defined, then the general *class* it is a part of, and finally the *qualities that differentiate it* from the other terms in the same class.

TERM	CLASS	DIFFERENTIATION
behaviorism	a theory	that regards the objective facts of a subject's actions as the only valid basis for psychological study
cell	a unit of protoplasm	with a nucleus, cytoplasm, and an enclosing membrane

naturalism	a literary movement	whose original adherents believed that writers should treat life with scientific objectivity
mitosis	a process	of nuclear division of cells, consisting of prophase, metaphase, anaphase, and telophase
authority	a power	to command and require obedience

Understanding Extended Definitions

Many extended-definition essays include short formal definitions like those in dictionaries. In such an essay, a brief formal definition can introduce readers to the extended definition, or it can help to support the essay's thesis. However, an extended definition does not follow a set **pattern of development**. Instead, it uses whatever strategies best suit the writer's purpose, the term being defined, and the writing situation. In fact, any one (or more than one) of the essay patterns illustrated in this book can be used to structure a definition essay.

Using Definition

Providing a formal definition of each term you use is usually not necessary or desirable. Readers will either know what a word means or be able to look it up. Sometimes, however, defining a term is essential. On an exam, for example, you might be asked to define *behaviorism;* tell what a *cell* is; explain the meaning of the literary term *naturalism;* include a comprehensive definition of *mitosis* in your answer; or define *authority*. Such exam questions cannot always be answered in a sentence or two. In fact, the definitions they call for often require a full paragraph — or even several paragraphs.

Extended definitions are useful in many academic assignments besides exams. For example, definitions can explain abstractions such as *freedom,* controversial terms such as *right to life,* or **slang** terms (informal expressions whose meanings may vary from locale to locale or change as time passes). In a particular writing situation, a definition may be essential because a term has more than one meaning, because you are using it in an unusual way, because you are fairly certain the term will be unfamiliar to your readers, or because it is central to your discussion.

Planning a Definition Essay

Developing a Thesis Statement

The thesis of a definition essay should do more than simply identify the term to be defined — and more than just define it. The thesis statement needs to make clear to readers the larger purpose for which you are defining the term. For example, assume you set out to write an extended definition of *behaviorism*. If your goal is to show its usefulness for treating patients with certain psychological disorders, a statement like "This essay will define behaviorism" will not be very helpful. Even a formal definition — "Behaviorism is a theory that regards the objective facts of a subject's actions as the only valid basis for psychological study" — is not enough. Your thesis needs to suggest the *value* of this kind of therapy, not just tell what it is — for example, "Contrary to critics' objections, behaviorism is a valid approach for treating a wide variety of psychological dysfunctions."

Deciding on a Pattern of Development

You can organize a definition essay according to one or more of the patterns of development described in this book. As you plan your essay and jot down your ideas about the term or subject you will define, you will see which other patterns are most useful. For example, the formal definitions of the five terms discussed on page 490 could be expanded with five different patterns of development:

- **Exemplification**   To explain *behaviorism,* you could give **examples**. Carefully chosen cases could show how this theory of psychology applies to different situations. These examples could help readers see exactly how behaviorism works and what it can and cannot account for. Often, examples are the clearest way to explain something. Defining dreams as "the symbolic representation of mental states" might convey little to readers who do not know much about psychology, but a few examples would help you make your meaning clear. Many students have dreams about taking exams — perhaps dreaming that they are late for the test, that they remember nothing about the course, or that they are writing their answers in disappearing ink. You might explain the nature of dreams by interpreting these particular dreams, which may reflect anxiety about a course or about school in general.

- **Description**   You can explain the nature of something by **describing** it. For example, the concept of a *cell* is difficult to grasp from just a formal definition, but your readers would understand the concept more clearly if you were to describe what a cell looks like, possibly with the aid of a diagram or two. Concentrating on the cell membrane, cytoplasm, and nucleus, you could detail each structure's appearance and function. These descriptions would enable readers to visualize the whole cell and understand its workings. Of course, description involves more than the visual: a definition of a tsunami might describe the sounds and the appearance of this enormous ocean wave, and a definition of Parkinson's disease might include a description of how its symptoms affect a patient.

- **Comparison and contrast**   An extended definition of *naturalism* could use a **comparison-and-contrast** structure. Naturalism is one of several major movements in American literature, so its literary aims could be contrasted with those of other literary movements, such as romanticism or realism. Or, you might compare and contrast the plots and characters of several naturalistic works with those of romantic or realistic works. Anytime you need to define something unfamiliar, you can compare it to something familiar to your readers. For example, your readers may never have heard of the Chinese dish sweet-and-sour cabbage, but you can help them imagine it by saying it tastes something like cole slaw. You can also define a thing by contrasting it with something unlike it, especially if the two have some qualities in common. For instance, one way to explain the British sport of rugby is by contrasting it with American football, which is not as violent.

• **Process** Because mitosis is a process, an extended definition of *mitosis* should be organized as a **process explanation**. By tracing the process from stage to stage, you would clearly define this type of cell division for your readers. Process is also a suitable pattern for defining objects in terms of what they do. For example, because a computer carries out certain processes, an extended definition of a computer would probably include a process explanation.

• **Classification and division** You could define *authority* by using **classification and division**. Basing your extended definition on the model developed by the German sociologist Max Weber, you could divide the class *authority* into the subclasses *traditional authority, charismatic authority,* and *legal-bureaucratic authority*. By explaining each type of authority, you could clarify this very broad term for your readers. In both extended and formal definitions, classification and division can be very useful. By identifying the class something belongs to, you are explaining what kind of thing it is. For instance, *monetarism* is an economic theory; *The Adventures of Huckleberry Finn* is a novel; and *emphysema* is a disease. Likewise, by dividing a class into subclasses, you are defining something more specifically. Emphysema, for instance, is a disease of the lungs and can therefore be classified with tuberculosis but not with appendicitis.

Phrasing Your Definition

Whatever form your definitions take, make certain that they clearly define your terms. Be sure to provide a true definition, not just a descriptive statement such as "Happiness is a four-day weekend." Also, remember that repetition is not definition, so don't include the term you are defining in your definition. For instance, the statement "Abstract art is a school of artists whose works are abstract" clarifies nothing for your readers. Finally, define as precisely as possible. Name the class of the term you are defining — "mitosis is *a process* of cell division" — and define this class as narrowly and as accurately as you can, clearly differentiating your term from other members of its class. Careful attention to the language and structure of your definition will help readers understand your meaning.

Structuring a Definition Essay

Like other essays, a definition essay should have an introduction, a body, and a conclusion. Although a formal definition strives for objectivity, an extended definition usually does not. Instead, it is likely to define a term in a way that reflects your attitude toward the subject or your reason for defining it. For example, your extended-definition paper about literary *naturalism* might argue that the significance of this movement's major works has been underestimated by literary scholars. Similarly, your definition of *authority* might criticize its abuses. In such cases, the **thesis statement** provides a focus for your definition essay, showing readers your approach to the definition.

The **introduction** identifies the term to be defined, perhaps presents a brief formal definition, and goes on to state the essay's thesis. The body of the essay expands the definition, using any one (or several) of the patterns of development explained and illustrated in this text.

In addition to using various patterns of development, you can expand the **body** of your definition by using any of the following strategies:

- You can define a term by using **synonyms** (words with similar meanings).
- You can define a term by using **negation** (telling what it is *not*).
- You can define a term by using **enumeration** (listing its characteristics).
- You can define a term by using an **analogy** (identifying similarities between an unfamiliar term and something likely to be more familiar to readers).
- You can define a term by discussing its **origin and development** (the word's derivation, original meaning, and usages).

NOTE: If you are describing something that is unfamiliar to your readers, you can also include a **visual** — a drawing, painting, diagram, or photograph — to supplement your definition.

Your essay's **conclusion** reminds readers why you have chosen to define the term, perhaps restating your thesis.

Suppose your assignment is to write a short paper for your introductory psychology course. You decide to examine *behaviorism*. Of course, you can define the word in one sentence, or possibly two. But to explain the *concept* of behaviorism and its status in the field of psychology, you must go beyond the dictionary.

Now, you have to decide what kinds of explanations are most suitable for your topic and for your intended audience. If you are trying to define *behaviorism* for readers who know very little about psychology, you might use analogies that relate behaviorism to your readers' experiences, such as how they were raised or how they train their pets. You might also use examples, but the examples would relate not to psychological experiments or clinical treatment but to experiences in everyday life. If, however, you are directing your paper to your psychology instructor, who obviously already knows what behaviorism is, your purpose is to show that you know, too. One way to do this is to compare behaviorism with other psychological theories; another way is to give examples of how behaviorism works in practice; still another is to briefly summarize the background and history of the theory. (In a long paper, you might use all of these strategies.)

After considering your paper's scope and audience, you might decide that because behaviorism is somewhat controversial, your best strategy is to supplement a formal definition with examples showing how behaviorist assumptions and methods are applied in specific situations. These examples, drawn from your class notes and textbook, would support your thesis that behaviorism is a valid approach for treating certain psychological dysfunctions. Together, your examples would define *behaviorism* as it is understood today.

An informal outline for your essay might look like this:

SAMPLE OUTLINE: Definition

Introduction:	Thesis statement — Contrary to its critics' objections, behaviorism is a valid approach for treating a wide variety of psychological dysfunctions.
Background:	Definition of behaviorism, including its origins and evolution
First example:	The use of behaviorism to help psychotics function in an institutional setting
Second example:	The use of behaviorism to treat neurotic behavior, such as chronic anxiety, a phobia, or a pattern of destructive acts
Third example:	The use of behaviorism to treat normal but antisocial or undesirable behavior, such as heavy smoking or overeating
Conclusion:	Restatement of thesis or review of key points

Notice how the three examples in this paper define behaviorism with the kind of complexity, detail, and breadth that a formal definition could not duplicate. This definition is more like a textbook explanation — and, in fact, textbook explanations are often written as extended definitions.

Revising a Definition Essay

When you revise a definition essay, consider the items on the revision checklist on page 68. In addition, pay special attention to the items on the following checklist, which apply specifically to revising definition essays.

Definition

- Does your assignment call for definition?
- Does your essay include a clearly stated thesis that identifies the term you will define and tells readers why you are defining it?
- Have you included a formal definition of your subject? Have you defined other key terms that may not be familiar to your readers?
- Have you used appropriate patterns of development to expand your definition?
- Do you need to use other strategies — such as synonyms, negation, enumeration, or analogies — to expand your definition?
- Do you need to discuss the origin and development of the term you are defining?
- Do you need to include a visual?

Editing a Definition Essay

When you edit your definition essay, follow the guidelines on the editing checklists on pages 85, 88, and 90. In addition, focus on the grammar, mechanics, and punctuation issues that are particularly relevant to definition essays. One of these issues — avoiding the phrases *is when* and *is where* in formal definitions — is discussed below.

GRAMMAR IN CONTEXT   *Avoiding* **is when** *and* **is where**

Many extended definitions include a one-sentence formal definition. As you have learned, such definitions must include the term you are defining, the class to which the term belongs, and the characteristics that distinguish the term from other terms in the same class.

Sometimes, however, when you are defining a term or concept, you may find yourself departing from this set structure and using the phrase *is when* or *is where*. If so, your definition is not complete because it omits the term's class. (In fact, the use of *is when* or *is where* indicates that you are actually presenting an example of the term and not a definition.)

You can avoid this error by making certain that the form of the verb *be* in your definition is always followed by a noun.

INCORRECT: As described in the essay "The Untouchable," *prejudice* is when someone forms an irrational bias or negative opinion of a person or group (Mahtab 496).

CORRECT: As described in the essay "The Untouchable," *prejudice* is an irrational bias or negative opinion of a person or group (Mahtab 496).

INCORRECT: According to Meghan Daum, *celebrity* is where you don't buy your own groceries (511).

CORRECT: According to Meghan Daum, *celebrities* are people who "don't buy their own groceries" (511).

> For more practice in avoiding faulty constructions, visit the resources for Chapter 13 at **bedfordstmartins.com/patterns**.

✔ **EDITING CHECKLIST** Definition

- Have you avoided using *is when* and *is where* in your formal definitions?
- Have you used the present tense for your formal definition — even if you have used the past tense elsewhere in your essay?
- In your formal definition, have you italicized the term you are defining and placed the definition itself in quotation marks?

A STUDENT WRITER: Definition

The following student essay, written by Ajoy Mahtab for a composition course, defines the untouchables, members of a caste that is shunned in India. In his essay, Ajoy, who grew up in Calcutta, presents a thesis that is sharply critical of the practice of ostracizing untouchables. Note that he includes a photograph to help readers understand the unfamiliar term he is defining.

The Untouchable

Introduction: background

A word that is extremely common in India yet uncommon 1
to the point of incomprehension in the West is the word
untouchable. It is a word that has had very sinister connotations
throughout India's history. A rigorously worked-out caste system
has traditionally existed in Indian society. At the top of the social
ladder sat the Brahmins, the clan of the priesthood. These people
had renounced the material world for a spiritual one. Below them
came the Kshatriyas, or the warrior caste. This caste included
the kings and all their nobles along with their armies. Third on
the social ladder were the Vaishyas, who were the merchants of
the land. Trade was their only form of livelihood. Last came the
Shudras — the menials. Shudras were employed by the prosperous
as sweepers and laborers. Originally a person's caste was
determined only by his profession. Thus, if the son of a merchant
joined the army, he automatically converted from a Vaishya to a
Kshatriya. However, the system soon became hereditary and rigid.
Whatever one's occupation, one's caste was determined from birth
according to the caste of one's father.

Outside of this structure were a group of people, human 2
beings treated worse than dogs and shunned far more than lepers,
people who were not considered even human, people who defiled

Fig. 1. Sprague, Sean. *Untouchable Woman Sweeping in Front of Her House in a Village in Tamil Nadu, India.* 2003. The Image Works. Web. 4 Nov. 2011.

Formal definition

Historical background

with their very touch. These were the Achhoots: the untouchables, one of whom is shown in fig. 1. The word *untouchable* is commonly defined as "that which cannot or should not be touched." In India, however, it was taken to a far greater extreme. The untouchables of a village lived in a separate community downwind of the borders of the village. They had a separate water supply, for they would make the village water impure if they were to drink from it. When they walked, they were made to bang two sticks together continuously so that passersby could hear them coming and thus avoid an untouchable's shadow. Tied to their waists, trailing behind them, was a broom that would clean the ground they had walked on. The penalty for not following these or any other rules was death for the untouchable and, in many instances, for the entire untouchable community.

Present situation

One of the pioneers of the fight against untouchability was   3 Mahatma Gandhi. Thanks to his efforts and those of many others, untouchability no longer presents anything like the horrific picture described above. In India today, in fact, recognition of untouchability is punishable by law. Theoretically, there is no such thing as untouchability anymore. But old traditions linger on, and a deep-rooted fear passed down from generation to generation does not disappear overnight. Even today, caste is an important factor in most marriages. Most Indian surnames reveal a person's caste immediately, so it is a difficult thing to hide. The shunning of the untouchable is more prevalent in South India, where people are much more devout, than in the North. Some people would rather starve than share food and water with an untouchable. This concept is very difficult to accept in the West, but it is true all the same.

Example
    I remember an incident from my childhood. I could not   4
have been more than eight or nine at the time. I was on a holiday staying at my family's house on the river Ganges. A festival was going on, and, as is customary, we were giving the servants small presents. I was handing them out when an old lady, bent with age, slowly hobbled into the room. She stood in the far corner of the room all alone, and no one so much as looked at her. When the entire line ended, she stepped hesitantly forward and stood in front of me, looking down at the ground. She then held a cloth stretched out in front of her. I was a little confused about how I was supposed to hand her her present, since both her hands were holding the cloth. Then, with the help of prompting from someone behind me, I learned that I was supposed to drop the gift into the cloth without touching the cloth itself. It was only later that I found out that she was an untouchable. This was the first time I had actually come face to face with such prejudice, and it felt like a slap in the face. That incident was burned into my memory, and I do not think I will ever forget it.

Conclusion begins
    The word *untouchable* is not often used in the West, and   5
when it is, it is generally used as a complimentary term. For example, an avid fan might say of an athlete, "He was absolutely untouchable. Nobody could even begin to compare with him." It seems rather ironic that a word could be so favorable in one culture and so negative in another. Why does a word that gives happiness in one part of the world cause pain in another? Why does the same word have different meanings to different people around the globe? Why do certain words cause rifts and others forge bonds? I do not think anyone can tell me the answers to these questions.

Conclusion continues	No actual parallel can be found today that compares to the 6 horrors of untouchability. For an untouchable, life itself was a
Thesis statement	crime. The day was spent just trying to stay alive. From the misery of the untouchables, the world should learn a lesson: isolating and punishing any group of people is dehumanizing and immoral.

Points for Special Attention

Thesis Statement. Ajoy Mahtab's assignment was to write an extended definition of a term he assumed would be unfamiliar to his audience. Because he had definite ideas about the unjust treatment of the untouchables, Ajoy wanted his essay to have a strong thesis that communicated his disapproval. Still, because he knew his American classmates would need a good deal of background information before they would understand the context for such a thesis, he decided not to present it in his introduction. Instead, he decided to lead up to his thesis gradually and state it at the end of his essay. When other students in the class reviewed his draft, this subtlety was one of the points they reacted to most favorably.

Structure. Ajoy's introduction establishes the direction of his essay by introducing the word he will define; he then places this word in context by explaining India's rigid caste system. In paragraph 2, he gives the formal definition of the word *untouchable* and goes on to sketch the term's historical background. Paragraph 3 explains the status of the untouchables in present-day India, and paragraph 4 gives a vivid example of Ajoy's first encounter with an untouchable. As he begins his conclusion in paragraph 5, Ajoy brings his readers back to the word his essay defines. Here he uses two strategies to add interest: he contrasts a contemporary American usage of *untouchable* with its pejorative meaning in India, and he asks a series of **rhetorical questions** (questions asked for effect and not meant to be answered). In paragraph 6, Ajoy presents a summary of his position to lead into his thesis statement.

Patterns of Development. This essay uses a number of strategies commonly incorporated into extended definitions: it includes a formal definition, explains the term's origin, and explores some of the term's connotations. The essay also uses several familiar patterns of development. For instance, paragraph 1 uses classification and division to explain India's caste system; paragraphs 2 and 3 use brief examples to illustrate the plight of the untouchable; and paragraph 4 presents a narrative. Each of these patterns enriches the definition.

Working with Sources. Ajoy includes a **visual** — a photograph of an untouchable — to supplement his passages of description and to help readers understand this very unfamiliar concept. He places the photograph early in his essay, where it will be most helpful, and he refers to it in paragraph 2 with the phrase "one of whom is shown in fig. 1." In addition, he includes a caption below the photo with full source information.

Focus on Revision

Because the term Ajoy defined was so unfamiliar to his classmates, many of the peer editing worksheets students filled in asked for more information. One suggestion in particular — that he draw an **analogy** between the unfamiliar term *untouchable* and a more familiar concept — appealed to Ajoy as he planned his revision. Another student suggested that Ajoy could compare untouchables to other groups who have been shunned — for example, people with AIDS. Although Ajoy states in his conclusion that no parallel exists, an attempt to find common ground between untouchables and other groups could make his essay more meaningful to his readers — and bring home to them a distinctly alien idea. Such a connection could also make his conclusion especially powerful.

PEER EDITING WORKSHEET: Definition

1. What term is the writer defining? Does the essay include a formal definition? If so, where? If no formal definition is included, should one be added?

2. Why is the writer defining the term? Does the essay include a thesis statement that makes this purpose clear? If not, suggest revisions.

3. What patterns does the writer use to develop the definition? What other patterns could be used? Would a visual be helpful?

4. Does the essay define the term appropriately for its audience? Does the definition help you understand the meaning of the term?

5. Does the writer use **synonyms** to develop the definition? If so, where? If not, where could synonyms be used to help communicate the term's meaning?

6. Does the writer use **negation** to develop the definition? If so, where? If not, could the writer strengthen the definition by explaining what the term is not?

7. Does the writer use **enumeration** to develop the definition? If so, where? If not, where might the term's special characteristics be listed?

8. Does the writer use **analogies** to develop the definition? If so, where? Do you find these analogies helpful? What additional analogies might help readers understand the term more fully?

9. Does the writer explain the term's origin and development? If so, where? If not, do you believe this information should be added?

10. Reread the essay's introduction. If the writer uses a formal definition as an opening strategy, try to suggest an alternative opening.

The selections that follow use exemplification, description, narration, and other methods of developing extended definitions. The first selection, a visual text, is followed by questions designed to illustrate how definition can operate in visual form.

U.S. Census 2010 Form (Questionnaire)

→ NOTE: Please answer BOTH Question 8 about Hispanic origin and Question 9 about race. For this census, Hispanic origins are not races.

8. Is Person 1 of Hispanic, Latino, or Spanish origin?

☐ No, not of Hispanic, Latino, or Spanish origin
☒ Yes, Mexican, Mexican Am., Chicano
☐ Yes, Puerto Rican
☐ Yes, Cuban
☒ Yes, another Hispanic, Latino, or Spanish origin — *Print origin, for example, Argentinean, Colombian, Dominican, Nicaraguan, Salvadoran, Spaniard, and so on.* ↘

☐☐☐☐☐☐☐☐☐☐☐☐☐☐☐☐☐☐☐☐☐☐☐

9. What is Person 1's race? *Mark ☒ one or more boxes.*

☐ White
☐ Black, African Am., or Negro
☐ American Indian or Alaska Native — *Print name of enrolled or principal tribe.* ↘

☐☐☐☐☐☐☐☐☐☐☐☐☐☐☐☐☐☐☐☐☐☐☐

☐ Asian Indian   ☐ Japanese   ☐ Native Hawaiian
☐ Chinese   ☐ Korean   ☐ Guamanian or Chamorro
☐ Filipino   ☐ Vietnamese ☐ Samoan
☐ Other Asian — *Print race, for example, Hmong, Laotian, Thai, Pakistani, Cambodian, and so on.* ↘   ☐ Other Pacific Islander — *Print race, for example, Fijian, Tongan, and so on.* ↘

☐☐☐☐☐☐☐☐☐☐☐☐☐☐☐☐☐☐☐☐☐☐☐

☐ Some other race — *Print race.* ↘

☐☐☐☐☐☐☐☐☐☐☐☐☐☐☐☐☐☐☐☐☐☐☐

• • •

Reading Images

1. In a single complete sentence, define yourself in terms of your race, religion, or ethnicity (whatever is most important to you).

continued

2. Look at the U.S. Census questions on the form. Which boxes would you mark? Do you see this choice as an accurate expression of what you consider yourself to be? Explain.

3. Only recently has the Census Bureau permitted respondents to mark "one or more boxes" to indicate their ethnic identity. Do you think this option is a good idea?

Journal Entry

Why do you think the U.S. government needs to know "what [a] person considers himself/herself to be"? Do you think it is important for the government to know how people define themselves, or do you consider this information an unwarranted violation of a person's privacy? Explain.

Thematic Connections

- "Indian Education" (page 142)
- "The Myth of the Latin Woman: I Just Met a Girl Named Maria" (page 232)
- "Two Ways to Belong in America" (page 404)
- "Mother Tongue" (page 466)

JUDY BRADY

I Want a Wife

Judy Brady has published articles on many social issues. Diagnosed with breast cancer in 1980, she became active in the politics of cancer and has edited *Women and Cancer* (1990) and *One in Three: Women with Cancer Confront an Epidemic* (1991). She also helped found the Toxic Links Coalition, an organization devoted to lobbying for cancer and environmental issues.

Background on the status of women Brady has been active in the women's movement since 1969, and "I Want a Wife" first appeared in the premiere issue of the feminist *Ms.* magazine in 1972. That year represented perhaps the height of the feminist movement in the United States. The National Organization for Women, established in 1966, had hundreds of chapters around the country. The Equal Rights Amendment, barring discrimination against women, passed in Congress (although it was ratified by only thirty-five of the necessary thirty-eight states), and Congress also passed Title IX of the Education Amendments Act, which required equal opportunity (in sports as well as academics) for all students in any school that receives federal funding. At that time, women accounted for just under 40 percent of the labor force (up from 23 percent in 1950), a number that has grown to almost 50 percent today, in part because of the severe recession that started in 2008, which has caused more job losses for men than for women. Of mothers with children under age eighteen, fewer than 40 percent were employed in 1970; today, three-quarters work, 38 percent of them full-time and year-round. As for stay-at-home fathers, their numbers have increased from virtually zero to nearly 160,000.

I belong to that classification of people known as wives. I am A Wife. 1 And, not altogether incidentally, I am a mother.

Not too long ago a male friend of mine appeared on the scene fresh 2 from a recent divorce. He had one child, who is, of course, with his ex-wife. He is looking for another wife. As I thought about him while I was ironing one evening, it suddenly occurred to me that I, too, would like to have a wife. Why do I want a wife?

I would like to go back to school so that I can become economically 3 independent, support myself, and, if need be, support those dependent upon me. I want a wife who will work and send me to school. And while I am going to school I want a wife to take care of my children. I want a wife to keep track of the children's doctor and dentist appointments. And to keep track of mine, too. I want a wife to make sure my children eat properly and are kept clean. I want a wife who will wash the children's clothes and keep them mended. I want a wife who is a good nurturant attendant to my children, who arranges for their schooling, makes sure that they have an adequate social life with their peers, takes them to the park, the zoo, etc. I want a wife who takes care of the children when they are sick, a wife who arranges to be around when the children need special care, because, of course, I cannot miss classes at school. My wife must arrange to lose time at work and not lose the job. It may mean a small cut in my wife's income from time to time, but I guess I can tolerate that. Needless to say, my wife will arrange and pay for the care of the children while my wife is working.

I want a wife who will take care of *my* physical needs. I want a wife who 4 will keep my house clean. A wife who will pick up after my children, a wife who will pick up after me. I want a wife who will keep my clothes clean, ironed, mended, replaced when need be, and who will see to it that my personal things are kept in their proper place so that I can find what I need the minute I need it. I want a wife who cooks the meals, a wife who is a *good* cook. I want a wife who will plan the menus, do the necessary grocery shopping, prepare the meals, serve them pleasantly, and then do the cleaning up while I do my studying. I want a wife who will care for me when I am sick and sympathize with my pain and loss of time from school. I want a wife to go along when our family takes a vacation so that someone can continue to care for me and my children when I need a rest and change of scene.

I want a wife who will not bother me with rambling complaints about a 5 wife's duties. But I want a wife who will listen to me when I feel the need to explain a rather difficult point I have come across in my course of studies. And I want a wife who will type my papers for me when I have written them.

I want a wife who will take care of the details of my social life. When my 6 wife and I are invited out by my friends, I want a wife who will take care of the babysitting arrangements. When I meet people at school that I like and want to entertain, I want a wife who will have the house clean, will prepare a special meal, serve it to me and my friends, and not interrupt when I talk about things that interest me and my friends. I want a wife who will have arranged that the children are fed and ready for bed before my guests arrive so that the children do not bother us. I want a wife who takes care of the needs of my guests so that they feel comfortable, who makes sure that they have an ashtray, that they are passed the hors d'oeuvres, that they are offered a second helping of the food, that their wine glasses are replenished when necessary, that their coffee is served to them as they like it. And I want a wife who knows that sometimes I need a night out by myself.

I want a wife who is sensitive to my sexual needs, a wife who makes 7 love passionately and eagerly when I feel like it, a wife who makes sure that I am satisfied. And, of course, I want a wife who will not demand sexual attention when I am not in the mood for it. I want a wife who assumes the complete responsibility for birth control, because I do not want more children. I want a wife who will remain sexually faithful to me so that I do not have to clutter up my intellectual life with jealousies. And I want a wife who understands that *my* sexual needs may entail more than strict adherence to monogamy. I must, after all, be able to relate to people as fully as possible.

If, by chance, I find another person more suitable as a wife than the 8 wife I already have, I want the liberty to replace my present wife with another one. Naturally, I will expect a fresh new life; my wife will take the children and be solely responsible for them so that I am left free.

When I am through with school and have a job, I want my wife to quit working and remain at home so that my wife can more fully and completely take care of a wife's duties.

> " My God, who *wouldn't* want a wife? "   9

My God, who *wouldn't* want a wife?   10

. . .

Comprehension

1. In one sentence, define what Brady means by *wife*. Does this ideal wife actually exist? Explain.

2. List some of the specific duties of the wife Brady describes. Into what five general categories does Brady arrange these duties?

3. What complaints does Brady apparently have about the life she actually leads? To what does she seem to attribute her problems?

4. Under what circumstances does Brady say she would consider leaving her wife? What would happen to the children if she left?

Purpose and Audience

1. This essay was first published in *Ms.* magazine. In what sense is it appropriate for the audience of this feminist publication? Where else can you imagine it appearing?

2. Does this essay have an explicitly stated thesis? If so, where is it? If the thesis is implied, paraphrase it.

3. Do you think Brady *really* wants the kind of wife she describes? Explain your response.

Style and Structure

1. Throughout the essay, Brady repeats the words "I want a wife." What is the effect of this repetition?

2. The first and last paragraphs of this essay are quite brief. Does this weaken the essay? Why or why not?

3. In enumerating a wife's duties, Brady frequently uses the verb *arrange*. What other verbs does she use repeatedly? How do these verbs help her make her point?

4. Brady never uses the personal pronouns *he* or *she* to refer to the wife she defines. Why not?

5. Comment on Brady's use of phrases such as *of course* (2, 3, and 7), *needless to say* (3), *after all* (7), *by chance* (8), and *naturally* (8). What do these expressions contribute to the sentences where they appear? To the essay as a whole?

Vocabulary Projects

1. Define each of the following words as it is used in this selection.

   nurturant (3)   adherence (7)
   replenished (6)   monogamy (7)

2. Going beyond the dictionary definitions, decide what Brady means to suggest by each of the following words. Is she using any of these terms sarcastically? Explain.

   proper (4)   necessary (6)   suitable (8)
   pleasantly (4)   demand (7)   free (8)
   bother (6)   clutter up (7)

Journal Entry

Is Brady's 1972 characterization of a wife still accurate today? Which of the characteristics she describes have remained the same? Which have changed? Why?

Writing Workshop

1. Write an essay defining your ideal boss, parent, teacher, or pet.

2. Write an essay titled "I Want a Husband." Taking an **ironic** stance, use society's notions of the ideal husband to help you shape your definition.

3. Write a definition essay called "The Ideal Couple," in which you try to divide household chores and other responsibilities equitably between the two partners. (Your essay can be serious or humorous.) Develop your definition with examples.

Combining the Patterns

Like most definition essays, "I Want a Wife" uses several patterns of development. Which ones does it use? Which of these do you consider most important for supporting Brady's thesis? Why?

Thematic Connections

- "My Mother Never Worked" (page 121)
- "Sex, Lies, and Conversation" (page 423)
- Declaration of Sentiments and Resolutions, Seneca Falls Convention, 1848 (page 559)

JOSÉ ANTONIO BURCIAGA

Tortillas

José Antonio Burciaga (1940–1996) was the founder of *Diseños Literarios*, a publishing company in California, as well as the comedy troupe Culture Clash. He contributed fiction, poetry, and articles to many anthologies, as well as to journals and newspapers. He also published several books of poems, drawings, and essays, including the poetry collection *Undocumented Love* (1992) and the essay collection *Drink Cultura* (1993). "Tortillas," originally titled "I Remember Masa," was first published in *Weedee Peepo* (1988), a collection of essays in Spanish and English.

Background on tortillas Tortillas have been a staple of Mexican cooking for thousands of years. These thin, round griddlecakes made of cornmeal *(masa)* are often eaten with every meal, and the art of making them is still passed from generation to generation (although they now are widely available commercially as well). The earliest Mexican immigrants introduced them to the United States, and in the past twenty-five years tortillas, along with many other popular items of Mexican cuisine, have entered the country's culinary landscape (as, over the decades, has a wide variety of other "ethnic" foods, such as pizza, egg rolls, bagels, sushi, and gyros). Still, tortillas have special meaning for Mexican Americans, and in this essay Burciaga discusses the role of the tortilla within his family's culture.

My earliest memory of *tortillas* is my *Mamá* telling me not to play with 1 them. I had bitten eyeholes in one and was wearing it as a mask at the dinner table.

As a child, I also used *tortillas* as hand warmers on cold days, and my 2 family claims that I owe my career as an artist to my early experiments with *tortillas*. According to them, my clowning around helped me develop a strong artistic foundation. I'm not so sure, though. Sometimes I wore a *tortilla* on my head, like a *yarmulke*, and yet I never had any great urge to convert from Catholicism to Judaism. But who knows? They may be right.

For Mexicans over the centuries, the *tortilla* has served as the spoon and 3 the fork, the plate and the napkin. *Tortillas* originated before the Mayan civilizations, perhaps predating Europe's wheat bread. According to Mayan mythology, the great god Quetzalcoatl, realizing that the red ants knew the secret of using maize as food, transformed himself into a black ant, infiltrated the colony of red ants, and absconded with a grain of corn. (Is it any wonder that to this day, black ants and red ants do not get along?) Quetzalcoatl then put maize on the lips of the first man and woman, Oxomoco and Cipactonal, so that they would become strong. Maize festivals are still celebrated by many Indian cultures of the Americas.

When I was growing up in El Paso, *tortillas* were part of my daily life. 4
I used to visit a *tortilla* factory in an ancient adobe building near the open
mercado in Ciudad Juárez. As I approached, I could hear the rhythmic slap-
ping of the *masa* as the skilled vendors outside the factory formed it into
balls and patted them into perfectly round corn cakes between the palms
of their hands. The wonderful aroma and the speed with which the women
counted so many dozens of *tortillas* out of warm wicker baskets still linger in
my mind. Watching them at work convinced me that the most handsome
and *deliciosas tortillas* are handmade. Although machines are faster, they can
never adequately replace generation-to-generation experience. There's no
place in the factory assembly line for the tender slaps that give each *tortilla*
character. The best thing that can be said about mass-producing *tortillas* is
that it makes it possible for many people to enjoy them.

In the *mercado* where my mother shopped, we frequently bought *ta-* 5
quitos de nopalitos, small tacos filled with diced cactus, onions, tomatoes,
and *jalapeños.* Our friend Don Toribio showed us how to make delicious,
crunchy *taquitos* with dried, salted pumpkin seeds. When you had no
money for the filling, a poor man's *taco* could be made by placing a warm
tortilla on the left palm, applying a sprinkle of salt, then rolling the *tortilla*
up quickly with the fingertips of the right hand. My own kids put peanut
butter and jelly on *tortillas,* which I think is truly bicultural. And speaking of fast foods for kids, nothing beats a *quesadilla,* a *tortilla* grilled-cheese
sandwich.

Depending on what you intend to use them for, *tortillas* may be made 6
in various ways. Even a run-of-the-mill *tortilla* is more than a flat corn cake.
A skillfully cooked homemade *tortilla* has a bottom and a top; the top skin
forms a pocket in which you put the filling that folds your *tortilla* into a
taco. Paper-thin *tortillas* are used specifically for *flautas,* a type of taco that is
filled, rolled, and then fried until crisp. The name *flauta* means *flute,* which
probably refers to the Mayan bamboo flute; however, the only sound that
comes from an edible *flauta* is a delicious crunch that is music to the palate.
In México *flautas* are sometimes made as long as two feet and then cut into
manageable segments. The opposite of *flautas* is *gorditas,* meaning *little fat
ones.* These are very thick small *tortillas.*

The versatility of *tortillas* and corn does not end here. Besides being 7
tasty and nourishing, they have spiritual and artistic qualities as well. The
Tarahumara Indians of Chihuahua, for example, concocted a corn-based
beer called *tesgüino,* which their descendants still make today. And everyone
has read about the woman in New Mexico who was cooking her husband a
tortilla one morning when the image of Jesus Christ miraculously appeared
on it. Before they knew what was happening, the man's breakfast had become a local shrine.

Then there is *tortilla* art. Various Chicano artists throughout the South- 8
west have, when short of materials or just in a whimsical mood, used a dry
tortilla as a small, round canvas. And a few years back, at the height of the
Chicano movement, a priest in Arizona got into trouble with the Church
after he was discovered celebrating mass using a *tortilla* as the host. All of

which only goes to show that while the *tortilla* may be a lowly corn cake, when the necessity arises, it can reach unexpected distinction.

· · ·

Comprehension

1. What exactly is a tortilla?
2. List the functions — both practical and whimsical — that tortillas serve.
3. In paragraph 7, Burciaga cites the "spiritual and artistic qualities" of tortillas. Do you think he is being serious? Explain your reasoning.

Purpose and Audience

1. Burciaga states his thesis explicitly in his essay's final sentence. Paraphrase this thesis. Why do you think he does not state it sooner?
2. Do you think Burciaga expects most of his readers to be of Hispanic descent? To be familiar with tortillas? How can you tell?
3. Why do you think Burciaga uses humor in this essay? Is it consistent with his essay's purpose? Could the humor have a negative effect on his audience? Explain.
4. Why are tortillas so important to Burciaga? Is it just their versatility he admires, or do they represent something more to him?

Style and Structure

1. Where does Burciaga provide a formal definition of *tortilla?* Why does he locate this formal definition at this point in his essay?
2. Burciaga uses many Spanish words, but he defines only some of them — for example, *taquitos de nopalitos* and *quesadilla* in paragraph 5 and *flautas* and *gorditas* in paragraph 6. Why do you think he defines some Spanish terms but not others? Should he have defined them all?
3. Does Burciaga use **synonyms** or **negation** to define *tortilla?* Does he discuss the word's **origin and development**? If so, where? If not, do you think any of these strategies would improve his essay? Explain.

Vocabulary Projects

1. Define each of the following words as it is used in this selection.

   yarmulke (2)   absconded (3)   concocted (7)
   maize (3)   adobe (4)

2. Look up each of the following words in a Spanish-English dictionary, and try to supply its English equivalent.

   mercado (4)   deliciosas (4)
   masa (4)   jalapeños (5)

Journal Entry

Explore some additional uses — practical or frivolous — for tortillas that Burciaga does not discuss.

Writing Workshop

1. **Working with Sources.** Write an essay defining a food that is important to your family, ethnic group, or circle of friends. Begin with your own "earliest memory" of the food, comparing it with Burciaga's, and use several patterns of development, as Burciaga does. Assume your audience is not familiar with the food you define. Your thesis should indicate why the food is so important to you. Be sure to document references to Burciaga's essay and to include a works-cited page. (See Chapter 18 for information on MLA documentation.)

2. Relying primarily on description and exemplification, define a food that is sure to be familiar to all your readers. Do not name the food until your essay's last sentence.

3. Write an essay defining a food — but include a thesis statement that paints a very favorable portrait of a much-maligned food (for example, Spam or brussels sprouts) or a very negative picture of a popular food (for example, chocolate or ice cream).

Combining the Patterns

Burciaga uses several patterns of development in his extended definition. Where, for example, does he use **description**, **narration**, **process**, and **exemplification**? Does he use any other patterns?

Thematic Connections

- "Rice" (page 172)
- "Once More to the Lake" (page 194)
- "The Case for Birthright Citizenship" (page 595)
- "The Park" (page 659)

MEGHAN DAUM

Fame-iness

Essayist Meghan Daum (b. 1970) has contributed pieces to the *New Yorker,* the *Village Voice,* the *New York Times Book Review, Vogue,* and *Harper's Bazaar,* among many other popular periodicals. Some of these articles were collected in her first book, *My Misspent Youth* (2001). She writes a regular column for the op-ed page of the *Los Angeles Times* and has appeared on public radio's *Morning Edition* and *This American Life.* Noted for her sharp wit and entertaining observations on American culture, Daum has also published a novel, *The Quality of Life Report* (2003), which was named a *New York Times* Notable Book, and *Life Would Be Perfect If I Lived in That House* (2010), a book about her lifelong love affair with real estate.

Background on "fifteen minutes of fame" In a 1968 catalog essay accompanying his first international retrospective exhibition, pop artist and cultural icon Andy Warhol predicted — somewhat tongue-in-cheek — that "in the future everyone will be world-famous for fifteen minutes." He was referring to the proliferation of mass media, particularly television, and the need to fill the airwaves with anything that would provide an audience for advertisers. (Warhol himself was obsessed with the concept of celebrity.) The slogan quickly became a catchphrase, with "fifteen minutes of fame" referring to any short-lived appearance in the limelight. Warhol couldn't have foreseen that, starting in the 1990s, reality television programs, the Internet, and a culture increasingly used to considering anyone a celebrity would bring his prediction even closer to reality.

Why is it that most celebrities in the culture today are people I've 1 never heard of? I always thought fame had to do with being well known to the public, with being easily recognized on the street, with being, you know . . . *famous.*

If you asked me to name some famous people, I might offer up ex- 2 amples such as Bill Clinton, Meryl Streep, and Sting. If I spotted any one of them at the supermarket, it would probably warrant a call to my best friend to report what brand of peanut butter they were buying.

But these are also people who'd never go to the supermarket. The rea- 3 son is that celebrities, at least according to my definition, don't buy their own groceries. They have their assistants do it, or they order special deliveries from organic farms or, more likely, they don't eat at all.

That's because they're not quite real people, which is exactly why we 4 love them. Or at least we used to. These days it seems that only crotchety dinosaur types like me still harbor such provincial notions of what it means to be famous.

I know what you're thinking right about now: Here's another column 5 about the vulgarity of contemporary celebrity culture, with sentences that start with phrases like "these days." Believe me, I feel your nausea.

But I've also been feeling something else lately that goes beyond my 6 cluelessness about who's on the cover of *In Touch Weekly*. Call it reverse indifference. You know how you can walk into a room that smells like garbage, initially be bowled over with disgust but eventually grow immune to the odor? That's the opposite of what's happened to my celebrity radar. Whereas I used to merely ignore news about the faux famous and their tabloid-targeted exploits, I now notice it and feel repulsed. And I'm pretty sure that's the whole idea.

Obviously, celebrity repulsion has been in the air in recent weeks. I 7 don't need to name names, but suffice it to say that popular culture's approval rating (and, in turn, that of the media that can't get enough of it) is at an all-time low. Whether we're talking about a deceased gold-digger* or an apparently deranged astronaut** (and, be honest, we're still talking about both of them — all the time) it's pretty clear that it's never been a worse time to be famous. For one thing, the competition is stiff. (The Dixie Chicks, celebs with some old-school fame value, swept the Grammys, but we're still more interested in paternity claims and NASA-issue diapers.) For another thing, celebrity is just not as valuable as it used to be. By the look of things, just about anyone can get it — or at least something closely approximating it.

Not so long ago, you had to make a pretty strenuous effort to become well 8 enough known to register as famous. If you were an actor, you auditioned your butt off. If you were a musician, you played in clubs for no money. Part of the allure of fame was that access was limited. You pretty much had to show up regularly on network television, in studio movies, or on top-40 radio. However, because that playing field was relatively small, once you got there it wasn't too hard to become a household name — if only for the allotted fifteen minutes.

Now I'm not sure there's such a thing as a household name anymore. 9 Instead of fifteen minutes of fame, we get personalities who are famous in the eyes of maybe fifteen people. Fame is no longer about reaching the masses but about finding a niche audience somewhere.

This can, of course, be a very good thing, since the masses have never 10 been known for their taste or intelligence. But there's a dangerous flip side to the democratization of fame. The YouTube/*American Idol*/MySpace regime may be providing new opportunities for genuinely talented, less conventional people, but it's providing even more opportunities for untalented, often downright annoying people. "Celebrity" now connotes a

---

* Eds. note — Anna Nicole Smith, former model and *Playboy* playmate who married an elderly billionaire and fought his children for his estate. After her death, several ex-lovers claimed to be the father of her baby daughter.

** Eds. note — Astronaut Lisa Marie Nowak, who faced kidnapping and attempted murder charges in 2007 after she drove nine hundred miles (reportedly wearing diapers so she wouldn't have to stop along the way) to confront a romantic rival.

mundanity that borders on tedium, not to mention that smelly territory of reverse indifference.

Merriam Webster's 2006 word of the year was Stephen Colbert's coin- 11 age of "truthiness," which describes our inclination to believe in ideas without regard to logic or evidence. Perhaps our definition of celebrity has taken a similar path. Now that the mystique of so many celebrities is rooted less in their accomplishments than in their ability to get our attention by provoking our disgust, perhaps it's not fame they're offering but "fame-iness."

Unlike actual fame, which involves some talent and hard work, 12 "fame-iness" requires little more than a willingness to humiliate oneself. Instead of a reward for a job well done, it's more like a punishment for cutting corners. And guess what? The audience gets punished too.

Talk about dirty work — no wonder only the unskilled seem to be ap- 13 plying. Now if we could only stop reading their résumés.

· · ·

Comprehension

1. According to Daum, what does it mean to be famous?

2. How does Daum define a celebrity?

3. What does Daum mean in paragraph 7 when she says, "it's pretty clear that it's never been a worse time to be famous"?

4. How does Daum see today's celebrities as different from those of years ago? Does she see this change as positive or negative?

5. What do you think Daum means in paragraph 6 by "tabloid-targeted exploits"? Can you give examples of such exploits?

6. In paragraph 9, Daum says, "Fame is no longer about reaching the masses but about finding a niche audience somewhere." Give some examples of what such a "niche audience" might be.

7. What does Daum see as the positive side of the "democratization of fame" (10)?

8. According to Daum, what is the difference between "actual fame" and "fame-iness"?

Purpose and Audience

1. This essay discusses fame and celebrities in general terms but gives very few examples. What examples does Daum provide? Why do you think she doesn't include more?

2. What is Daum's attitude toward her audience? How do you know? Does paragraph 5 offer any information that might help answer this question?

Style and Structure

1. Does Daum include a formal definition of *fame-iness* in her essay? If so, where? If not, supply one.
2. Where does Daum explain her term's origin?
3. Where does she define *fame-iness* by negation? By analogy?
4. What other terms are defined in this essay? Are all these definitions necessary?
5. What patterns of development does Daum use to develop her definition?
6. Evaluate Daum's opening and closing paragraphs. What strategies does she use? Should these paragraphs be developed further? If so, how?

Vocabulary Projects

1. Define each of the following words as it is used in this selection.

   warrant (2)   allotted (8)
   crotchety (4)   niche (9)
   provincial (4)   mundanity (10)
   suffice (7)

2. In addition to *fame-iness,* Daum coins several other terms in this essay, including "reverse indifference" (6), "faux famous" (6), and "celebrity repulsion" (7). In your own words, define these terms.

Journal Entry

Do you agree with Daum that today, "the mystique of so many celebrities is rooted less in their accomplishments than in their ability to get our attention by provoking our disgust" (11)? Explain your feelings on this issue.

Writing Workshop

1. **Working with Sources.** Write your own extended definition of *fame-iness.* Begin by summarizing Daum's views on how fame has changed, and then provide a formal definition of *fame-iness.* Develop your definition with examples of present-day celebrities who help to define the term. Be sure to acknowledge — and document — Daum's words and ideas, and to include a works-cited page. (See Chapter 18 for information on MLA documentation.)

2. Write an extended definition of *fame,* using classification to develop your essay. Begin by establishing three or four categories of fame, based on how a person earned his or her celebrity — for example, through talent, heroism, or criminal activity. Then, give a series of examples for each category. In your thesis, communicate your opinion about which kind of fame is most deserved. Be sure to include a formal definition of *fame* early in your essay.

Combining the Patterns

Daum's essay includes very few **examples** of celebrities. In which specific sections of the essay would you add such examples? Which particular celebrities would best illustrate Daum's points?

Thematic Connections

- "Pink Floyd Night School" (page 116)
- "Thirty-Eight Who Saw Murder Didn't Call the Police" (page 127)
- "Grant and Lee: A Study in Contrasts" (page 393)

GAYLE ROSENWALD SMITH

The Wife-Beater

Gayle Rosenwald Smith, an attorney, currently practices family law. She has published articles in a variety of journals and periodicals and is coauthor of *What Every Woman Should Know about Divorce and Custody* (1998) and *Divorce and Money: Everything You Need to Know* (2004). The following essay appeared in the *Philadelphia Inquirer* in 2001.

Background on the "wife-beater" shirt As Smith notes here, *wife-beater* is a slang term for a type of sleeveless undershirt that has in recent years become fashionable. An Internet search of the term found a number of businesses that actually market such shirts as "wife-beaters." The corresponding shirts for women are often called "boy-beaters." A Texas-based firm offers adult-sized shirts emblazoned with the slogan, as well as "Lil' Wife Beater" shirts for babies. The firm's Web site — which plays the song "Smack My Bitch Up" — includes a background screen showing a woman being spanked and provides a link to a "Wife Beater Hall of Fame." It also offers to send a second shirt at half price to any customer convicted of domestic violence (proof of conviction required, photos not acceptable). In another twist, a feminist retail site has offered a "Wife Beater Beater" shirt with a cartoon image of a woman kicking a man in the groin.

Everybody wears them. The Gap sells them. Fashion designers Dolce 1 and Gabbana have lavished them with jewels. Their previous greatest resurgence occurred in the 1950s, when Marlon Brando's Stanley Kowalski wore one in Tennessee Williams' *A Streetcar Named Desire.* They are all the rage.

What are they called? 2

The name is the issue. For they are known as "wife-beaters." 3

A Web search shows that kids nationwide are wearing the skinny- 4 ribbed white T-shirts that can be worn alone or under another shirt. Women have adopted them with the same gusto as men. A search of boutiques shows that these wearers include professionals who wear them, adorned with designer accessories, under their pricey suits. They are available in all colors, sizes, and price ranges.

Wearers under 25 do not seem to be disturbed by the name. But I 5 sure am.

It's an odd name for an undershirt. And even though the ugly stereo- 6 types behind the name are both obvious and toxic, it appears to be cool to say the name without fear of (or without caring about) hurting anyone.

That the name is fueled by stereotype is now an academically estab- 7 lished fact, although various sources disagree on exactly when shirt and name came together. The *Oxford Dictionary* defines the term *wife-beater* as:

1. A man who physically abuses his wife and

2. Tank-style underwear shirts. Origin: based on the stereotype that physically abusive husbands wear that particular type of shirt.

The *World Book Dictionary* locates the origin of the term *wife-beater* in 8
the 1970s, from the stereotype of the Midwestern male wearing an undershirt while beating his wife. The shirts are said to have been popular in the
1980s at all types of sporting events, especially ones at which one sits in
the sun and develops "wife-beater marks." The undershirts also attained
popularity at wet T-shirt contests, in which the wet, ribbed tees accentuated contestants' breasts.

In an article in the style section of the *New York Times,* Jesse Scheidlower, 9
principal editor of the *Oxford English Dictionary*'s American office, says the
association of the undershirt and the term *wife-beater* arose in 1997 from
varied sources, including gay and gang subcultures and rap music.

In the article, some sources argued that the reference in the term was 10
not to spousal abuse per se but to popular-culture figures such as Ralph
Cramden and Tony Soprano. And what about Archie Bunker?

It's not just the name that worries me. Fashion headlines reveal 11
that we want to overthrow '90s grunge and return to shoulder pads and
hardware-studded suits. Am I reading too much into a fashion statement
that the return is also to male dominance where physical abuse is acceptable as a means of control?

There has to be a better term. After all, it's a pretty rare piece of cloth- 12
ing that can make both men and women look sexier. You'd expect a term
connoting flattery — not violence.

Wearers under 25 may not want to hear this, but here it is. More 13
than 4 million women are victims of severe assaults by boyfriends and
husbands each year. By conservative estimate, family violence occurs
in 2 million families each year in the United States. Average age of the
batterer: 31.

Possibly the last statistic is telling. Maybe youth today would rather 14
ignore the overtones of the term *wife-beater.* It is also true, however, that the
children of abusers often learn the behavior from their elders.

Therein lies perhaps the worst difficulty: that this name for this shirt 15
teaches the wrong thing about men. Some articles quote women who felt
the shirts looked great, especially on guys with great bodies. One woman
stated that it even made guys look "manly."

So *manly* equals *violent?* Not by me, and I hope not by anyone on any 16
side of age 25.

• • •

Comprehension

1. Why is Smith "disturbed" (5) by the name "wife-beater"? Do you think her
   concern is justified?

2. In paragraph 3, Smith says, "The name is the issue"; in paragraph 11, she says, "It's not just the name that worries me." What does she mean by each statement? Do these two statements contradict each other?

3. What relationship does Smith see between the name of a sleeveless undershirt and the prevalence of family violence? Does she believe a causal connection does — or could — exist? If so, which is the cause, and which is the effect?

4. In paragraph 12, Smith acknowledges that the shirt "can make both men and women look sexier." Does this remark in any way undercut her credibility? Explain.

5. How, according to Smith, does calling a shirt a wife-beater teach women "the wrong thing about men" (15)?

Purpose and Audience

1. How do you think Smith expects her audience to react to her opening statement ("Everybody wears them")?

2. Why do you think Smith wrote this essay? Does she hope to change the name of the T-shirt, or does she seem to have a more ambitious purpose? Explain.

3. Twice in her essay, Smith mentions a group she calls "wearers under 25" (5, 13). Does she seem to direct her remarks at these young adults or at older readers? At wearers of the shirts or at a more general audience?

4. Restate Smith's thesis in your own words.

Style and Structure

1. Why do you think Smith begins her essay by explaining the popularity of sleeveless undershirts? Is this an effective opening strategy?

2. In paragraph 7, Smith reproduces a formal definition from the *Oxford Dictionary*. Why does she include this definition when she has already defined her term? What, if anything, does the formal definition add?

3. Where does Smith present information on the history of the wife-beater? Why does she include this kind of information?

4. Where does Smith quote statistics? Do you see this information as relevant or incidental to her argument?

Vocabulary Projects

1. Define each of the following words as it is used in this selection.

resurgence (1)   accentuated (8)
gusto (4)   per se (10)
toxic (6)   connoting (12)

2. In paragraph 12, Smith says, "There has to be a better term." Can you think of a "better term" — one that does not suggest violence — for the shirt Smith describes?

3. Visit several different Internet sites — for example, dictionary.com and Merriam-Webster Online at m-w.com — and compare their definitions of the term *wife-beater*. How are these definitions alike? How are they different?

Journal Entry

Do you agree with Smith that the casual use of terms like *wife-beater* is dangerous, or do you think she is exaggerating the problem?

Writing Workshop

1. **Working with Sources.** Relying primarily on description and exemplification, define an article of clothing that is essential to your wardrobe. Begin by checking Internet sites on fashion history, such as fashion-era.com, to learn the item's history and the origin of its name. If you use information from a site in your essay, be sure to cite your souce and to include a works-cited page. (See Chapter 18 for information on MLA documentation.)

2. Using comparison and contrast to structure your essay, define what a particular item of clothing means to you — and what it means to one of your parents.

3. Do members of your religious or ethnic group wear an item of clothing that is not well known to others — or not well understood by them? Define the article of clothing, and explain its significance and its history in terms that outsiders can understand.

Combining the Patterns

Do you think Smith should have spent more time in this essay on developing the **cause-and-effect** relationship, if any, between the "wife-beater" shirt and family violence? What additional information would she have to provide?

Thematic Connections

- "Four Tattoos" (page 226)
- "My First Conk" (page 281)
- "A Peaceful Woman Explains Why She Carries a Gun" (page 354)

AMANDA BROWN

Love and Other Catastrophes: A Mix Tape (Fiction)

Amanda Brown graduated with a B.F.A. in literature, writing, and publishing from Emerson College in 2002. As an undergraduate, she wrote "Love and Other Catastrophes: A Mix Tape" for a class assignment that required students to write a "list story." With her husband, Brown runs the Los Angeles–based record label Not Not Fun. Her first novel, *Drain You*, will be published by HarperCollins in 2012.

Background on music as the "soundtrack of our lives" For most of human history, the only way for people to hear music was to listen to it performed live — or to sing and play an instrument themselves. Since Thomas Edison invented the phonograph in 1877, however, music has become increasingly portable, accessible, and ubiquitous. Coin-operated jukeboxes appeared at the end of the nineteenth century; the first portable radio was introduced by Zenith in 1924; and vinyl 33 and 45 rpm records became dominant in the 1950s, later competing with eight-track tapes and then with compact cassettes. In the 1980s, home tape decks and devices like the Walkman led to the popularity of the hand-made "mix tape": a personal compilation of songs both reflecting the idiosyncratic taste of its creator and communicating a specific message to its recipient. As the poet and essayist Geoffrey O'Brien notes, mix tapes are an art form in themselves, a "self-portrait, a gesture of friendship, prescription for an ideal party . . . an environment consisting solely of what is most ardently loved." While some lament the decline of cassette culture, other mix-tape enthusiasts argue that compact discs and MP3 files have made the creation of personal mixes more convenient and accessible.

"All by Myself" (Eric Carmen). "Looking for Love" (Lou Reed). "I Wanna Dance with Somebody" (Whitney Houston). "Let's Dance" (David Bowie). "Let's Kiss" (Beat Happening). "Let's Talk about Sex" (Salt N' Pepa). "Like a Virgin" (Madonna). "We've Only Just Begun" (The Carpenters). "I Wanna Be Your Boyfriend" (The Ramones). "I'll Tumble 4 Ya" (Culture Club). "Head over Heels" (The Go-Go's). "Nothing Compares to You" (Sinead O'Connor). "My Girl" (The Temptations). "Could This Be Love?" (Bob Marley). "Love and Marriage" (Frank Sinatra). "White Wedding" (Billy Idol). "Stuck in the Middle with You" (Stealers Wheel). "Tempted" (Squeeze). "There Goes My Baby" (The Drifters). "What's Going On?" (Marvin Gaye). "Where Did You Sleep Last Night?" (Leadbelly). "Whose Bed Have Your Boots Been Under?" (Shania Twain). "Jealous Guy" (John Lennon). "Your Cheatin' Heart" (Tammy Wynette). "Shot through the Heart" (Bon Jovi). "Don't Go Breaking My Heart" (Elton John and Kiki Dee). "My Achy Breaky Heart" (Billy

Ray Cyrus). "Heartbreak Hotel" (Elvis Presley). "Stop, in the Name of Love" (The Supremes). "Try a Little Tenderness" (Otis Redding). "Try (Just a Little Bit Harder)" (Janis Joplin). "All Apologies" (Nirvana). "Hanging on the Telephone" (Blondie). "I Just Called to Say I Love You" (Stevie Wonder). "Love Will Keep Us Together" (Captain and Tennille). "Let's Stay Together" (Al Green). "It Ain't Over 'Till It's Over" (Lenny Kravitz). "What's Love Got to Do with It?" (Tina Turner). "You Don't Bring Me Flowers Anymore" (Barbra Streisand and Neil Diamond). "I Wish You Wouldn't Say That" (Talking Heads). "You're So Vain" (Carly Simon). "Love Is a Battlefield" (Pat Benatar). "Heaven Knows I'm Miserable Now" (The Smiths). "(Can't Get No) Satisfaction" (Rolling Stones). "Must Have Been Love (But It's Over Now)" (Roxette). "Breaking Up Is Hard to Do" (Neil Sedaka). "I Will Survive" (Gloria Gaynor). "Hit the Road, Jack" (Mary McCaslin and Jim Ringer). "These Boots Were Made for Walking" (Nancy Sinatra). "All Out of Love" (Air Supply). "All by Myself" (Eric Carmen).

• • •

Reading Literature

1. What term is defined in this story?
2. What patterns are used to develop this definition?
3. In what sense is love a "catastrophe"? What are the "other catastrophes" to which the title refers?

Journal Entry

Write a ten-item "list story," using a series of song titles to define *childhood, adolescence, college,* or *work.* Give your story a descriptive title.

Thematic Connections

- "The Storm" (page 202)
- *The Kiss/LOVE* (page 391)
- "The Ways We Lie" (page 474)
- "I Want a Wife" (page 503)
- "The Wife-Beater" (page 516)

Writing Assignments for Definition

1. Choose a document or ritual that is a significant part of your religious or cultural heritage. Define it, using any pattern or combination of patterns you choose, but be sure to include a formal definition somewhere in your essay. Assume your readers are not familiar with the term you are defining.

2. Define an abstract term — for example, *stubbornness, security, courage,* or *fear* — by making it concrete. You can develop your definition with a series of brief examples or with an extended narrative that illustrates the characteristic you are defining.

3. The readings in this chapter define (among other things) a food, a family role, and an item of clothing. Write an essay using examples and description to define one of these topics — for instance, ramen noodles (food), a stepmother (family role), or a chador (item of clothing).

4. **Working with Sources.** Do some research on webmd.com (for adult health issues) or kidshealth.org (for childen's health issues) to learn about one of these medical conditions: angina, migraine, Down syndrome, attention deficit disorder, schizophrenia, autism, or Alzheimer's disease. Then, write an extended definition essay explaining the condition to an audience of high school students. Be sure to quote (and document) any material you borrow from your source. (See Chapter 18 for information on MLA documentation.)

5. Use a series of examples to support a thesis in an essay that defines *racism, sexism, ageism, homophobia,* or another type of bigoted behavior.

6. Choose a term that is central to one of your courses — for instance, *naturalism, behaviorism,* or *authority* — and write an essay defining the term. Assume your audience is made up of students who have not yet taken the course. You may begin with an overview of the term's origin if you believe this is appropriate. Then, develop your essay with examples and **analogies** that will facilitate your audience's understanding of the term. Your purpose is to convince readers that understanding the term you are defining is important.

7. Assume your audience is from a culture unfamiliar with present-day American children's pastimes. Write a definition essay for this audience describing the form and function of a Frisbee, a Barbie doll, an action figure, a skateboard, or a video game.

8. Review any one of the following narrative essays from Chapter 6, and use it to help you develop an extended definition of one of the following terms.
   - "Only Daughter" — prejudice
   - "My Mother Never Worked" — work
   - "Thirty-Eight Who Saw Murder Didn't Call the Police" — apathy
   - "Shooting an Elephant" — power

Be sure to document any words or ideas you borrow from a source. (See Chapter 18 for information on MLA documentation.)

9. What constitutes an education? Define the term *education* by identifying several different sources of knowledge, formal or informal, and explaining what each contributes. To get ideas for your essay, look at "The Socks" (page 109), "Pink Floyd Night School" (page 116), "Indian Education" (page 142), "The Catbird Seat" (page 228), or "My First Conk" (page 281).

10. What qualifies someone as a hero? Developing your essay with a series of examples, define the word *hero*. Include a formal definition, and try to incorporate at least one paragraph defining the term by explaining and illustrating what a hero is *not*.

Collaborative Activity for Definition

Working as a group, choose one of the following words to define: *pride, hope, sacrifice,* or *justice.* Then, define the term with a series of extended examples drawn from films your group members have seen, with each of you developing an illustrative paragraph based on a different film. (Before beginning, your group may decide to focus on one particular genre of film.) When everyone in the group has read each paragraph, work together to formulate a thesis that asserts the vital importance of the quality your examples have defined. Finally, write suitable opening and closing paragraphs for the essay, and arrange the body paragraphs in a logical order, adding transitions where necessary.

14

Argumentation

What Is Argumentation?

Argumentation is a process of reasoning that asserts the soundness of a debatable position, belief, or conclusion. Argumentation takes a stand — supported by evidence — and urges people to share the writer's perspective and insights. In the following paragraph from his essay "Holding Cell," Jerome Groopman argues that with its decision to limit therapeutic cloning, the President's Council on Bioethics has prevented scientists from carrying out important medical research that could possibly save lives.

<table>
<tr><td>Issue identified</td><td>The President's Council on Bioethics, chaired by Dr. Leon R. Kass, presented its long-awaited report on human cloning to the White House. . . . The council unanimously advised against "cloning to produce children," commonly called "reproductive cloning." But on "cloning for biomedical research" — therapeutic cloning to produce stem cells to try to ameliorate disease — it split. Of the seventeen members, ten (including Kass) voted against</td></tr>
<tr><td>Background presents both sides of issue</td><td>it. They couched their rejection as a compromise since they called not for a permanent ban but for a four-year moratorium. This moratorium, according to the letter accompanying the report, would allow "a thorough federal review . . . to clarify the issues and foster a public consensus about how to proceed." It would also give researchers time to seek alternative ways to generate stem cells. But for scientists and, more importantly, for the millions of patients with incurable maladies, the compromise</td></tr>
<tr><td>Topic sentence (takes a stand)</td><td>is a painful disappointment. It shackles potentially lifesaving research and provides no clear framework to advance the ethical debate.</td></tr>
</table>

Argumentation can be used to convince other people to accept (or at least acknowledge the validity of) your position; to defend your position, even if you cannot convince others to agree; or to question or refute a position you believe to be misguided, untrue, dangerous, or evil (without necessarily offering an alternative).

Understanding Argumentation and Persuasion

Although the terms *persuasion* and *argumentation* are frequently used interchangeably, they do not mean the same thing. **Persuasion** is a general term that refers to how a writer influences an audience to adopt a belief or follow a course of action. To persuade an audience, a writer relies on various kinds of appeals — appeals based on emotion (*pathos*), appeals based on logic (*logos*), and appeals based on the character reputation of the writer (*ethos*).

Argumentation is the appeal to reason (*logos*). In an argument, a writer connects a series of statements so that they lead logically to a conclusion. Argumentation is different from persuasion in that it does not try to move an audience to action; its primary purpose is to demonstrate that certain ideas are valid and others are not. Moreover, unlike persuasion, argumentation has a formal structure: an argument makes points, supplies evidence, establishes a logical chain of reasoning, refutes opposing arguments, and accommodates the audience's views.

As the selections in this chapter demonstrate, however, most effective arguments combine two or more appeals: even though their primary appeal is to reason, they may also appeal to emotions. For example, you could use a combination of logical and emotional appeals to argue against lowering the drinking age in your state from twenty-one to eighteen. You could appeal to *reason* by constructing an argument leading to the conclusion that the state should not condone policies that have a high probability of injuring or killing citizens.

You could support your conclusion by presenting statistics showing that alcohol-related traffic accidents kill more teenagers than disease does. You could also cite a study showing that when the drinking age was raised from eighteen to twenty-one, fatal accidents declined. In addition, you could include an appeal to the *emotions* by telling a particularly sad story about an eighteen-year-old alcoholic or by pointing out how an increased number of accidents involving drunk drivers would cost some innocent people their lives. These appeals to your audience's emotions could strengthen your argument by widening its appeal. Keep in mind, however, that in an effective argument emotion does not take the place of logic; it supports and reinforces it.

The appeals you choose and how you balance them depend in part on your purpose and your sense of your audience. As you consider what strategies to use, remember that some extremely effective appeals are unfair. Although most people would agree that lies, threats, misleading statements, and appeals to greed and prejudice are unacceptable ways of reaching an audience, such appeals are used in daily conversation, in political campaigns, and even in international diplomacy. Nevertheless, in your college writing you should use only those appeals that most people would consider fair. To do otherwise will undercut your audience's belief in your trustworthiness and weaken your argument.

Planning an Argumentative Essay

Choosing a Topic

In an argumentative essay, as in all writing, choosing the right topic is important. Ideally, you should have an intellectual or emotional stake in your topic. Still, you should be open-minded and willing to consider all sides of a question. If the evidence goes against your position, you should be willing to change your position. You should also be able, from the outset, to consider your topic from other people's viewpoints; this will help you determine what their beliefs are and how they are likely to react. You can then use this knowledge to build your case and to refute opposing viewpoints. If you cannot be open-minded, you should choose another topic you can deal with more objectively.

Other factors should also influence your selection of a topic. First, you should be well informed about your topic. In addition, you should choose an issue narrow enough to be treated in the space available to you or be willing to confine your discussion to one aspect of a broad issue. It is also important to consider your **purpose** — what you expect your argument to accomplish and how you wish your audience to respond. If your topic is so far-reaching that you cannot identify what you want to convince readers to think, or if your purpose is so idealistic that your expectations of their response are impossible or unreasonable, your essay will suffer.

Developing a Thesis

After you have chosen your topic, you are ready to state the position you will argue in the form of a **thesis**. Keep in mind that in an argumentative essay, your thesis must take a stand — in other words, it must be **debatable**. A good argumentative thesis states a proposition that at least some people will object to. Arguing a statement of fact or an idea that most people accept as self-evident is pointless. Consider the following thesis statement.

Education is the best way to address the problem of increased drug use among teenagers.

This thesis statement says that increased drug use is a problem among teenagers, that more than one possible solution to this problem exists, and that education is a better solution than any other. In your argument, you will have to support each of these three points logically and persuasively.

A good way to test the suitability of your thesis for an argumentative essay is to formulate an **antithesis**, a statement that asserts the opposite position. If you think that some people would support the antithesis, you can be certain your thesis is indeed debatable.

Thesis: Education is the best way to address the problem of increased drug use among teenagers.

Antithesis: Education is not the best way to address the problem of increased drug use among teenagers.

Thesis: Because immigrants have contributed much to the development of the United States, immigration quotas should be relaxed.

Antithesis: Even though immigrants have contributed much to the development of the United States, immigration quotas should not be relaxed.

Analyzing Your Audience

Before writing any essay, you should analyze the characteristics, values, and interests of your audience. In argumentation, it is especially important to consider what beliefs or opinions your readers are likely to have and whether your audience is likely to be friendly, neutral, or hostile to your thesis.

It is probably best to assume that some, if not most, of your readers are at least **skeptical** — that they are open to your ideas but need to be convinced. This assumption will keep you from making claims you cannot support. If your position is controversial, you should assume that an informed and determined opposition is looking for holes in your argument.

In an argumentative essay, you face a dual challenge. You must appeal to readers who are neutral or even hostile to your position, and you must influence those readers so that they are more receptive to your viewpoint. For example, it would be relatively easy to convince college students that tuition should be lowered or to convince instructors that faculty salaries should be raised. You could be reasonably sure, in advance, that each group would agree with your position. But argument requires more than just telling people what they already believe. It would be much harder to convince college students that tuition should be raised to pay for an increase in instructors' salaries or to persuade instructors to forgo raises so that tuition can remain the same. Remember, your audience will not just take your word for the claims you make. You must provide evidence that will support your thesis and establish a line of reasoning that will lead logically to your conclusion.

Gathering and Documenting Evidence

All the points you make in your paper must be supported. If they are not, your audience will dismiss them as unfounded, irrelevant, or unclear. Sometimes you can support a statement with appeals to emotion, but most of the time you support your argument's points by appealing to reason — by providing **evidence**: facts and opinions in support of your position.

As you gather evidence and assess its effectiveness, keep in mind that evidence in an argumentative essay never proves anything conclusively. If it did, there would be no debate — and hence no point in arguing. The best that evidence can do is convince your audience that an assertion is reasonable and worth considering.

Kinds of Evidence. Evidence can be *fact* or *opinion*. **Facts** are statements that most people agree are true and that can be verified independently. Facts — including statistics — are the most commonly used type of evidence. It is a fact, for example, that fewer people per year were killed in U.S. automobile accidents in 2012 than in 1975. Facts may be drawn from your own experience as well as from reading and observation. It may, for instance, be a fact that you have had a serious automobile accident. Quite often, facts are more convincing when they are supplemented by **opinions**, or interpretations of facts. To connect your facts about automobile accidents to the assertion that the installation of side-impact airbags in all small trucks and buses, as well as in cars, could reduce deaths still further, you could cite the opinions of an expert — consumer advocate Ralph Nader, for example. His statements, along with the facts and statistics you have assembled and your own interpretations of those facts and statistics, could convince readers that your solution to the problem of highway deaths is reasonable.

Keep in mind that not all opinions are equally convincing. The opinions of experts are more convincing than are those of individuals who have limited knowledge of an issue. Your personal opinions can be excellent evidence (provided you are knowledgeable about your subject), but they are usually less convincing to your audience than an expert's opinion. In the final analysis, what is important is not just the quality of the evidence but also the credibility of the person offering it.

What kind of evidence might change readers' minds? That depends on the readers, the issue, and the facts at hand. Put yourself in the place of your readers, and ask what would make them receptive to your thesis. Why, for example, should a student agree to pay higher tuition? You might concede that tuition is high but point out that it has not been raised for three years while the college's costs have kept going up. The cost of heating and maintaining the buildings has increased, and professors' salaries have not, with the result that several excellent teachers have recently left the college for higher-paying jobs. Furthermore, cuts in federal and state funding have already caused a reduction in the number of courses offered. Similarly, how could you convince a professor to agree to accept no raise at all, especially in light of the fact that faculty salaries have not kept up with inflation? You could say that because cuts in government funding have already reduced course offerings and because the government has also reduced funds for student loans, any further rise in tuition to pay faculty salaries would cause some students to drop out — and that in turn would eventually cost some instructors their jobs. As you can see, the evidence you use in an argument depends to a great extent on whom you want to persuade and what you know about them.

Criteria for Evidence. As you select and review material, choose your evidence with the following three criteria in mind:

1. Your evidence should be **relevant**. It should support your thesis and be pertinent to your argument. As you present evidence, be careful not to concentrate so much on a single example that you lose sight of the broader position you are supporting. Such digressions may confuse your readers. For example, in arguing for mandatory HIV testing for all health-care workers, one student made the point that AIDS in Africa remains at epidemic proportions. To illustrate this point, he discussed the bubonic plague in fourteenth- century Europe. Although interesting, this example was not relevant. To show its relevance, the student would have to link his discussion to his assertions about AIDS, possibly by comparing the spread of the bubonic plague in the fourteenth century to the spread of AIDS in Africa today.

2. Your evidence should be **representative**. It should represent the full range of opinions about your subject, not just one side. For example, in an essay arguing against the use of animals in medical experimentation, you would not just use information provided by animal rights activists. You would also use information supplied by medical researchers, pharmaceutical companies, and perhaps medical ethicists.

The examples and expert opinions you include should also be **typical**, not aberrant. Suppose you are writing an essay in support of building a trash-to-steam plant in your city. To support your thesis, you present the example of Baltimore, which has a successful trash-to-steam program. As you consider your evidence, ask yourself if Baltimore's experience with trash-to-steam is typical. Did other cities have less success? Take a close look at the opinions that disagree with the position you plan to take. If you understand your opposition, you can refute it effectively when you write your paper.

3. Your evidence should be **sufficient**. It should include enough facts, opinions, and examples to support your claims. The amount of evidence you need depends on the length of your paper, your audience, and your thesis. It stands to reason that you would use fewer examples in a two-page paper than in a ten-page research assignment. Similarly, an audience that is favorably disposed to your thesis might need only one or two examples to be convinced, whereas a skeptical or hostile audience would need many

more. As you develop your thesis, think about the amount of support you will need to write your paper. You may decide that a narrower, more limited thesis will be easier to support than a more inclusive one.

Documentation of Evidence. After you decide on a topic, you should begin to gather evidence. Sometimes you can use your own ideas and observations to support your claims. Most of the time, however, you will have to use the print and electronic resources of the library or search the Internet to locate the information you need.

Whenever you use such evidence in your paper, you have to **document** it by providing the source of the information. (When documenting sources, follow the documentation format recommended by the Modern Language Association, which is explained in Chapter 18 of this book.) If you don't document your sources, your readers are likely to dismiss your evidence, thinking that it may be inaccurate, unreliable, or simply false. **Documentation** gives readers the ability to evaluate the sources you cite and to consult them if they wish. When you document sources, you establish credibility by showing readers that you are honest and have nothing to hide.

Documentation also helps you avoid **plagiarism** – presenting the ideas or words of others as if they were your own. Certainly you don't have to document every idea you use in your paper. For example, **common knowledge** – information you could easily find in several reference sources – can be presented without documentation, and so can your own ideas. You must, however, document any use of a direct quotation and any ideas, statistics, charts, diagrams, or pictures that you obtain from your source. (See Chapter 17 for information on plagiarism.)

Dealing with the Opposition

When gathering evidence, keep in mind that you should not ignore arguments against your position. In fact, you should always try to identify the most obvious – and even the not-so-obvious – objections to your position. By directly addressing these objections in your essay, you will help convince readers that your own position is valid. This part of an argument, called **refutation**, is essential to making the strongest case possible.

You can **refute** opposing arguments by showing that they are unsound, unfair, or weak. Frequently, you will present evidence to show the weakness of your opponent's points and to reinforce your own case. Careful use of definition and cause-and-effect analysis may also prove effective. In the following passage from the classic essay "Politics and the English Language," George Orwell refutes an opponent's argument:

> I said earlier that the decadence of our language is probably curable. Those who deny this would argue, if they produced an argument at all, that language merely reflects existing social conditions, and that we cannot influence its development by any direct tinkering with words and constructions.

So far as the general tone or spirit of a language goes, this may be true, but it is not true in detail. Silly words and expressions have often disappeared, though not through any evolutionary process but owing to the conscious actions of a minority.

In the excerpt above, Orwell begins by stating the point he wants to make, goes on to define the argument against his position, and then identifies the weakness of this opposing argument. Later in the essay, Orwell strengthens his argument by presenting examples that support his point.

When an opponent's argument is so compelling that it cannot be easily dismissed, you should concede its strength (admit that it is valid). By acknowledging that a point is well taken, you reinforce the impression that you are a fair-minded person. After conceding the strength of the opposing argument, try to identify its limitations and then move your argument to more solid ground. (Often an opponent's strong point addresses only *one* facet of a multifaceted problem.) Notice in the example above that Orwell concedes an opposing argument when he says, "So far as the general tone or spirit of a language goes, this may be true." Later in his discussion, he refutes this argument by pointing out its shortcomings.

When planning an argumentative essay, write down all the arguments against your thesis that you can think of. Then, as you gather your evidence, decide which points you will refute, keeping in mind that careful readers will expect you to refute the most compelling of your opponent's arguments. Be careful, however, not to distort an opponent's argument by making it seem weaker than it actually is. This technique, called creating a **straw man**, can backfire and actually turn fair-minded readers against you.

Understanding Rogerian Argument

Not all arguments are (or should be) confrontational. Psychologist Carl Rogers has written about how to argue without assuming an adversarial relationship. According to Rogers, traditional strategies of argument rely on confrontation — trying to prove that an opponent's position is wrong. With this method of arguing, one person is "wrong" and one is "right." By attacking an opponent and repeatedly hammering home the message that his or her arguments are incorrect or misguided, a writer forces the opponent into a defensive position. The result is conflict, disagreement, and frequently ill will and hostility.

Rogers recommends that you think of those who disagree with you as colleagues, not adversaries. With this approach, now known as **Rogerian argument**, you enter into a cooperative relationship with opponents. Instead of aggressively refuting opposing arguments, you emphasize points of agreement and try to find common ground. You thus collaborate to find mutually satisfying solutions. By adopting a conciliatory attitude, you demonstrate your respect for opposing viewpoints and your willingness to compromise and work toward a position that both you and those who disagree with you will find acceptable. To use a Rogerian strategy in your writing, follow the guidelines below.

> ☑ **CHECKLIST**   **Guidelines for Using Rogerian Argument**
>
> - Begin by summarizing opposing viewpoints.
> - Carefully consider the position of those who disagree with you. What are their legitimate concerns? If you were in their place, how would you react?
> - Present opposing viewpoints accurately and fairly. Demonstrate your respect for the ideas of those who disagree with you.
> - Concede the strength of a compelling opposing argument.
> - Acknowledge the concerns you and your opposition share.
> - Point out to readers how they will benefit from the position you are defining.
> - Present the evidence that supports your viewpoint.

Using Deductive and Inductive Arguments

In an argument, you move from evidence to a conclusion in two ways. One method, called **deductive reasoning**, proceeds from a general premise or assumption to a specific conclusion. Deduction is what most people mean when they speak of logic. Using strict logical form, deduction holds that if all the statements in the argument are true, the conclusion must also be true.

The other method of moving from evidence to conclusion is called **inductive reasoning**. Induction proceeds from individual observations to a more general conclusion and uses no strict form. It requires only that all the relevant evidence be stated and that the conclusion fit the evidence better than any other conclusion would.

Most written arguments use a combination of deductive and inductive reasoning, but it is simpler to discuss and illustrate them separately.

Using Deductive Arguments

The basic form of a deductive argument is a **syllogism**. A syllogism consists of a **major premise**, which is a general statement; a **minor premise**, which is a related but more specific statement; and a **conclusion**, which is drawn from those premises. Consider the following example.

Major premise:	All Olympic runners are fast.
Minor premise:	Jesse Owens was an Olympic runner.
Conclusion:	Therefore, Jesse Owens was fast.

As you can see, if you grant both the major and minor premises, then you must also grant the conclusion. In fact, it is the only conclusion you can properly draw. You cannot reasonably conclude that Jesse Owens was slow because that conclusion contradicts the premises. Nor can you conclude (even if it is true) that Jesse Owens was tall because that conclusion goes beyond the premises.

Of course, this argument seems obvious, and it is much simpler than an argumentative essay would be. In fact, a deductive argument's premises can be fairly elaborate. The Declaration of Independence, which appears later in this chapter, has at its core a deductive argument that could be summarized in this way:

Major premise:	Tyrannical rulers deserve no loyalty.
Minor premise:	King George III is a tyrannical ruler.
Conclusion:	Therefore, King George III deserves no loyalty.

The major premise is a statement that the Declaration claims is **self-evident** — so obvious that it needs no proof. Much of the Declaration consists of evidence to support the minor premise that King George is a tyrannical ruler. The conclusion, because it is drawn from those premises, has the force of irrefutable logic: the king deserves no loyalty from his American subjects, who are therefore entitled to revolt against him.

When a conclusion follows logically from the major and minor premises, then the argument is said to be **valid**. But if the syllogism is not logical, the argument is not valid, and the conclusion is not sound. For example, the following syllogism is not logical:

Major premise:	All dogs are animals.
Minor premise:	All cats are animals.
Conclusion:	Therefore, all dogs are cats.

Of course, the conclusion is absurd. But how did we wind up with such a ridiculous conclusion when both premises are obviously true? The answer is that the syllogism actually contains two major premises. (Both the major and minor premises begin with *all.*) Therefore, the syllogism is defective, and the argument is invalid. Consider the following example of an invalid argument:

Major premise:	All dogs are animals.
Minor premise:	Ralph is an animal.
Conclusion:	Therefore, Ralph is a dog.

Here, an error in logic occurs because the minor premise refers to a term in the major premise that is **undistributed** — it covers only some of the items in the class it denotes. (To be valid, the minor premise must refer to the term in the major premise that is **distributed** — it covers *all* the items in the class it denotes.) In the major premise, *dogs* is the distributed term; it designates *all dogs*. The minor premise, however, refers to *animals,* which is undistributed because it refers only to animals that are dogs. As the minor premise establishes, Ralph is an animal, but it does not logically follow that he is a dog. He could be a cat, a horse, or even a human being.

Even if a syllogism is valid — that is, correct in its form — its conclusion will not necessarily be **true**. The following syllogism draws a false conclusion:

Major premise:	All dogs are brown.
Minor premise:	My poodle Toby is a dog.
Conclusion:	Therefore, Toby is brown.

As it happens, Toby is black. The conclusion is false because the major premise is false: many dogs are *not* brown. If Toby were actually brown, the conclusion would be correct, but only by chance, not by logic. To be **sound**, a syllogism must be both logical and true.

The advantage of a deductive argument is that if your audience accepts your major and minor premises, the force of logic should bring them to grant your conclusion. Therefore, you should try to select premises that you know your audience accepts or that are **self-evident** — that is, premises that most people believe to be true. Do not assume, however, that "most people" refers only to your friends and acquaintances. Consider, too, those who may hold different views. If you think your premises are too controversial or difficult to establish firmly, you should use inductive reasoning.

Using Inductive Arguments

Unlike deduction, induction has no distinctive form, and its conclusions are less definitive than those of syllogisms. Still, much inductive thinking (and writing based on that thinking) tends to follow a particular process.

- First, you decide on a question to be answered — or, especially in the sciences, a tentative answer to such a question, called a **hypothesis**.
- Then, you gather the evidence that is relevant to the question and that may be important to finding the answer.
- Finally, you move from your evidence to your conclusion by making an **inference** — a statement about the unknown based on the known — that answers the question and takes the evidence into account.

Here is a very simple example of the inductive process:

Question:	How did that living-room window get broken?
Evidence:	There is a baseball on the living-room floor.
	The baseball was not there this morning.
	Some children were playing baseball this afternoon.
	They were playing in the vacant lot across from the window.

> They stopped playing a little while ago.
> They aren't in the vacant lot now.

Conclusion: One of the children hit or threw the ball through the window; then, they all ran away.

The conclusion, because it takes all of the evidence into account, seems obvious. But if it turned out that the children had been playing volleyball, not baseball, this additional piece of evidence would make the conclusion doubtful. Even if the conclusion is believable, you cannot necessarily assume it is true: after all, the window could have been broken in some other way. For example, perhaps a bird flew against it, and perhaps the baseball in the living room had gone unnoticed all day, making the second piece of "evidence" on the list not true.

Considering several possible conclusions is a good way to avoid reaching an unjustified or false conclusion. In the preceding example, a hypothesis like this one might follow the question:

Hypothesis: One of those children playing baseball broke the living-room window.

Many people stop reasoning at this point, without considering the evidence. But when the gap between your evidence and your conclusion is too great, you may reach a conclusion that is not supported by the facts. This well-named error is called **jumping to a conclusion** because it amounts to a premature inductive leap. In induction, the hypothesis is merely the starting point. The rest of the inductive process continues as if the question were still to be answered — as in fact it is until all the evidence has been taken into account.

Because inductive arguments tend to be more complicated than the example on pages 535–536, it is not always easy to move from the evidence you have collected to a sound conclusion. Of course, the more pertinent information you gather, the smaller the gap between your evidence and your conclusion. Still, whether large or small, the crucial step from evidence to conclusion always involves what is called an **inductive leap**. For this reason, it is important to remember that inductive conclusions are just inferences and opinions (not facts). Therefore, inductive conclusions are never certain, only highly probable.

Using Toulmin Logic

Another approach for structuring arguments has been advanced by philosopher Stephen Toulmin. Known as **Toulmin logic**, this method tries to describe how the argumentative strategies a writer uses lead readers to respond the way they do. Toulmin puts forth a model that divides arguments into three parts: the *claim*, the *grounds*, and the *warrant*.

- The **claim** is the main point of the essay. Usually the claim is stated directly as the thesis, but in some arguments it may be implied.

- The **grounds** — the material a writer uses to support the claim — can be evidence (facts or expert opinion) or appeals to the emotions or values of the audience.
- The **warrant** is the inference that connects the claim to the grounds. It can be a belief that is taken for granted or an assumption that underlies the argument.

In its simplest form, an argument following Toulmin logic would look like this example.

Claim: Carol should be elected class president.

Grounds: Carol is an honor student.

Warrant: A person who is an honor student would make a good class president.

When you formulate an argument using Toulmin logic, you can still use inductive and deductive reasoning. You derive your claim inductively from facts and examples, and you connect the grounds and warrant to your claim deductively. For example, the deductive argument in the Declaration of Independence that was summarized on page 534 can be represented as shown here.

Claim: King George III deserves no loyalty.

Grounds: King George III is a tyrannical ruler.

Warrant: Tyrannical rulers deserve no loyalty.

As Toulmin points out, the clearer your warrant, the more likely readers will be to agree with it. Notice that in the two preceding examples, the warrants are very explicit.

Recognizing Fallacies

Fallacies are illogical statements that may sound reasonable or true but are actually deceptive and dishonest. When careful readers detect them, such statements can turn even a sympathetic audience against your position. Here are some of the more common fallacies that you should avoid.

Begging the Question. Begging the question is a logical fallacy that assumes that a statement is true when it actually requires proof. This tactic asks readers to agree that certain points are self-evident when in fact they are not.

Unfair and shortsighted legislation that limits free trade is a threat to the American economy.

Restrictions against free trade may or may not be unfair and shortsighted, but emotionally loaded language does not constitute proof. The statement begs the question because it assumes what it should be proving — that legislation that limits free trade is unfair and shortsighted.

Argument from Analogy. An **analogy** is a form of comparison that explains something unfamiliar by comparing it to something familiar. Although analogies can help explain abstract or unclear ideas, they do not constitute proof. An argument based on an analogy frequently ignores important dissimilarities between the two things being compared. When this occurs, the argument is fallacious.

> The overcrowded conditions in some parts of our city have forced people together like rats in a cage. Like rats, they will eventually turn on one another, fighting and killing until a balance is restored. It is therefore necessary that we vote to appropriate funds to build low-cost housing.

No evidence is offered to establish that people behave like rats under these or any other conditions. Just because two things have some characteristics in common, you should not assume they are alike in other respects.

Personal Attack (Argument *Ad Hominem*). This fallacy tries to divert attention from the facts of an argument by attacking the motives or character of the person making the argument.

> The public should not take seriously Dr. Mason's plan for improving county health services. He is a former alcoholic whose wife recently divorced him.

This attack on Dr. Mason's character says nothing about the quality of his plan. Sometimes a connection exists between a person's private and public lives — for example, in a case of conflict of interest. However, no evidence of such a connection is presented here.

Jumping to a Conclusion. Sometimes called a *hasty* or *sweeping generalization,* this fallacy occurs when a conclusion is reached on the basis of too little evidence.

> Because our son benefited from home schooling, every child should be educated in this way.

Perhaps other children would benefit from home schooling, and perhaps not, but no conclusion about children in general can be reached on the basis of just one child's experience.

False Dilemma (Either/Or Fallacy). This fallacy occurs when a writer suggests that only two alternatives exist even though there may be others.

> We must choose between life and death, between intervention and genocide. No one can be neutral on this issue.

An argument like this oversimplifies an issue and forces people to choose between extremes instead of exploring more moderate positions.

Equivocation. This fallacy occurs when the meaning of a key term changes at some point in an argument. Equivocation makes it seem as if a conclusion follows from premises when it actually does not.

As a human endeavor, computers are a praiseworthy and even remarkable accomplishment. But how human can we hope to be if we rely on computers to make our decisions?

The use of *human* in the first sentence refers to the entire human race. In the second sentence, *human* means "merciful" or "civilized." By subtly shifting this term to refer to qualities characteristic of people as opposed to machines, the writer makes the argument seem more sound than it is.

Red Herring. This fallacy occurs when the focus of an argument is shifted to divert the audience from the actual issue.

The mayor has proposed building a new sports stadium. How can he even consider allocating millions of dollars to this scheme when so many professional athletes are being paid such high salaries?

The focus of this argument should be the merits of the sports stadium. Instead, the writer shifts to the irrelevant issue of athletes' high salaries.

You Also (*Tu Quoque*). This fallacy asserts that an opponent's argument has no value because the opponent does not follow his or her own advice.

How can that judge favor stronger penalties for convicted drug dealers? During his confirmation hearings, he admitted smoking marijuana when he was in college.

Appeal to Doubtful Authority. Often people will attempt to strengthen an argument with references to experts or famous people. These appeals are valid when the person referred to is an expert in the area being discussed. They are not valid, however, when the individuals cited have no expertise on the issue.

According to Diane Sawyer, interest rates will remain low during the next fiscal year.

Although Diane Sawyer is a respected journalist, she is not an expert in business or finance. Therefore, her pronouncements about interest rates are no more than a personal opinion or, at best, an educated guess.

Misleading Statistics. Although statistics are a powerful form of factual evidence, they can be misrepresented or distorted in an attempt to influence an audience.

Women will never be competent firefighters; after all, 50 percent of the women in the city's training program failed the exam.

Here, the writer has neglected to mention that there were only two women in the program. Because this statistic is not based on a large enough sample, it cannot be used as evidence to support the argument.

Post Hoc, Ergo Propter Hoc (After This, Therefore Because of This). This fallacy, known as *post hoc* **reasoning**, assumes that because two events occur close together in time, the first must be the cause of the second.

> Every time a Republican is elected president, a recession follows. If we want to avoid another recession, we should elect a Democrat.

Even if it were true that recessions always occur during the tenure of Republican presidents, no causal connection has been established. (See pages 326–327.)

Non Sequitur (It Does Not Follow). This fallacy occurs when a statement does not logically follow from a previous statement.

> Disarmament weakened the United States after World War I. Disarmament also weakened the United States after the Vietnam War. For this reason, the city's efforts to limit gun sales will weaken the United States.

The historical effects of disarmament have nothing to do with current efforts to control the sale of guns. Therefore, the conclusion is a *non sequitur*.

Using Transitions

Transitional words and **phrases** are extremely important in argumentative essays. Without these words and phrases, readers could easily lose track of your argument.

Argumentative essays use transitions to signal a shift in focus. For example, paragraphs that present the specific points in support of your argument can signal this purpose with transitions such as *first, second, third, in addition,* and *finally*. In the same way, paragraphs that refute opposing arguments can signal this purpose with transitions such as *still, nevertheless, however,* and *yet*. Transitional words and phrases — such as *therefore* and *for these reasons* — are also useful when you are presenting your argument's conclusions.

USEFUL TRANSITIONS FOR ARGUMENTATION

all in all	in conclusion
as a result	in other words
finally	in short
first, second, third	in summary
for example	nevertheless
for instance	on the one hand . . . on the other hand
for these reasons	still
however	therefore
in addition	thus
in brief	yet

A more complete list of transitions appears on page 57.

Structuring an Argumentative Essay

An argumentative essay, like other kinds of essays, has an **introduction**, a **body**, and a **conclusion**. However, an argumentative essay has its own special structure, one that ensures that ideas are presented logically and convincingly. The Declaration of Independence follows the typical structure of many classic arguments:

SAMPLE OUTLINE: Argumentation

Introduction:	Introduces the issue
	States the thesis
Body:	Induction — offers evidence to support the thesis
	Deduction — uses syllogisms to support the thesis
	States the arguments against the thesis and refutes them
Conclusion:	Restates the thesis in different words
	Makes a forceful closing statement

Jefferson begins the Declaration by presenting the issue that the document addresses: the obligation of the people of the American colonies to tell the world why they must separate from Great Britain. Next, Jefferson states his thesis that because of the tyranny of the British king, the colonies must replace his rule with another form of government. In the body of the Declaration, he offers as evidence twenty-eight examples of injustice endured by the colonies. Following the evidence, Jefferson refutes counterarguments by explaining how again and again the colonists have appealed to the British for redress, but without result. In his concluding paragraph, he restates the thesis and reinforces it one final time. He ends with a flourish: speaking for the representatives of the United States, he explicitly dissolves all political connections between England and America.

Not all arguments, however, follow this pattern. Your material, your thesis, your purpose, your audience, the type of argument you are writing, and the limitations of your assignment all help you determine the strategies you use. If your thesis is especially novel or controversial, for example, the refutation of opposing arguments may come first. In this instance, opposing positions might even be mentioned in the introduction — provided they are discussed more fully later in the argument.

Suppose your journalism instructor gives you the following assignment:

Select a controversial topic that interests you, and write a brief editorial about it. Direct your editorial to readers who do not share your views, and try to convince them that your position is reasonable. Be sure to acknowledge the view your audience holds and to refute possible criticisms of your argument.

You are well informed about one local issue because you have just read a series of articles on it. A citizens' group is lobbying for a local ordinance that would authorize government funding for religious schools. Since you have also recently studied the constitutional doctrine of separation of church and state in your American government class, you know you could argue fairly and strongly against the position taken by this group.

An informal outline of your essay might look like this:

SAMPLE OUTLINE: Argumentation

Issue introduced:	Should public tax revenues be spent on aid to religious schools?
Thesis statement:	Despite the pleas of citizen groups like Religious School Parents United, using tax dollars to support church-affiliated schools violates the U.S. Constitution.
Evidence (deduction):	Explain general principle of separation of church and state in the Constitution.
Evidence (induction):	Present recent examples of court cases interpreting and applying this principle.
Evidence (deduction):	Explain how the Constitution and the court cases apply to your community's situation.
Opposing arguments refuted:	Identify and refute arguments used by Religious School Parents United. Concede the point that religious schools educate many children who would otherwise have to be educated in public schools at taxpayers' expense. Then, explain the limitations of this argument.
Conclusion:	Restate the thesis; end with a strong closing statement.

Revising an Argumentative Essay

When you revise an argumentative essay, consider the items on the revision checklist on page 68. In addition, pay special attention to the items on the following checklist, which apply specifically to argumentative essays.

✔ REVISION CHECKLIST   Argumentation

- Does your assignment call for argumentation?
- Have you chosen a topic you can argue about effectively?
- Do you have a debatable thesis?
- Have you considered the beliefs and opinions of your audience?
- Is your evidence relevant, representative, and sufficient?

- Have you documented evidence you have gathered from sources? Have you included a works-cited page?
- Have you made an effort to address your audience's possible objections to your position?
- Have you refuted opposing arguments?
- Have you used inductive or deductive reasoning (or a combination of the two) to move from your evidence to your conclusion?
- Have you avoided logical fallacies?
- Have you used appropriate transitional words and phrases?

Editing an Argumentative Essay

When you edit your argumentative essay, follow the guidelines on the editing checklists on pages 85, 88, and 90. In addition, focus on the grammar, mechanics, and punctuation issues that are particularly relevant to argumentative essays. One of these issues — using coordinating and subordinating conjunctions to link ideas — is discussed in the pages that follow.

GRAMMAR IN CONTEXT   Using Coordinating and Subordinating Conjunctions

When you write an argumentative essay, you often have to use **conjunctions** — words that join other words or groups of words — to express the logical and sequential relationships between ideas in your sentences. Conjunctions are especially important because they help readers follow the logic of your argument. For this reason, you should be certain that the conjunctions you select clearly and accurately communicate the connections between the ideas you are discussing.

Using Coordinating Conjunctions A **compound sentence** is made up of two or more independent clauses (simple sentences) connected by a coordinating conjunction. **Coordinating conjunctions** join two independent clauses that express ideas of equal importance, and they also indicate how those ideas are related.

independent clause   *independent clause*
[People can disobey unjust laws], <u>or</u> [they can be oppressed by them].

COORDINATING CONJUNCTIONS

and (*indicates addition*)
but, yet (*indicate contrast or contradiction*)
or (*indicates alternatives*)
nor (*indicates an elimination of alternatives*)
so, for (*indicate a cause-and-effect connection*)

According to Thomas Jefferson, the king has refused to let governors pass important laws, <u>and</u> he has imposed taxes without the consent of the people (554, 555).

Elizabeth Cady Stanton says that women are equal to men, <u>but</u> men think that they are superior to women (562).

Martin Luther King Jr. does not believe that all laws are just, <u>nor</u> does he believe that it is wrong to protest unjust laws (570, 571).

When you use a coordinating conjunction to join two independent clauses, always place a comma before the coordinating conjunction.

Using Subordinating Conjunctions A **complex sentence** is made up of one independent clause (simple sentence) and one or more dependent clauses. (A dependent clause cannot stand alone as a sentence.) Subordinating conjunctions link dependent and independent clauses that express ideas of unequal importance, and they also indicate how those ideas are related.

independent clause
[According to Martin Luther King Jr., he led protests]
dependent clause
[<u>so that</u> he could fight racial injustice] (567).

SUBORDINATING CONJUNCTIONS

SUBORDINATING CONJUNCTION	RELATIONSHIP BETWEEN CLAUSES
after, before, since, until, when, whenever, while	Time
as, because, since, so that	Cause or effect
even if, if, unless	Condition
although, even though, though	Contrast

"All segregation statutes are unjust <u>because</u> segregation distorts the soul and damages the personality" (King 571).

"<u>If</u> this philosophy had not emerged, by now many streets of the South would, I am convinced, be flowing with blood" (King 574).

"<u>Before</u> the pen of Jefferson etched the majestic words of the Declaration of Independence across the pages of history, we were here" (King 577).

When you use a subordinating conjunction to join two clauses, place a comma after the dependent clause when it comes *before* the independent clause. Do not use a comma when the dependent clause comes *after* the independent clause.

<u>When</u> they signed the Declaration of Independence, Thomas Jefferson and the others knew they were committing treason. (*comma*)

Thomas Jefferson and the others knew they were committing treason <u>when</u> they signed the Declaration of Independence. (*no comma*)

For more practice in using coordinating and subordinating conjunctions, visit the resources for Chapter 14 at **bedfordstmartins.com/patterns**.

✔ EDITING CHECKLIST   Argumentation

- Have you used coordinating conjunctions correctly to connect two or more independent clauses?
- Do the coordinating conjunctions accurately express the relationship between the ideas in the independent clauses?
- Have you placed a comma before the coordinating conjunction?
- Have you used subordinating conjunctions correctly to connect an independent clause and one or more dependent clauses?
- Do the subordinating conjunctions accurately express the relationship between the ideas in the dependent and independent clauses?
- Have you placed a comma after the dependent clause when it comes before the independent clause?
- Have you remembered not to use a comma when the dependent clause comes after the independent clause?

A STUDENT WRITER: Argumentation

The following editorial, written by Matt Daniels for his college newspaper, illustrates the techniques discussed earlier in this chapter.

An Argument against the Anna Todd Jennings Scholarship

Introduction   Recently, a dispute has arisen over the "Caucasian-   1

Summary of controversy restricted" Anna Todd Jennings scholarship.* Anna Jennings died in 1955, and her will established a trust that granted a scholarship of up to $15,000 for a deserving student. Unfortunately, Jennings, who had certain racist views, limited her scholarship to "Caucasian students." After much debate with family and friends, I, a white, well-qualified, and definitely deserving student, have decided not

Thesis statement to apply for the scholarship. It is my view that despite arguments to the contrary, applying for the Anna Todd Jennings scholarship furthers the racist ideas held by its founder.

Argument (deductive)   Most people would agree that racism in any form is an evil   2 that should be opposed. The Anna Todd Jennings scholarship is a dangerous expression of racism. It explicitly discriminates against African Americans, Asians, Latinos, Native Americans, and others. By providing a scholarship for whites only, Anna Jennings

---

* Eds. note — This essay discusses an actual situation, but the name of the scholarship has been changed here.

frustrates the aspirations of groups who until recently had been virtually kept out of the educational mainstream. On this basis alone, students should refuse to apply and should actively work to encourage the school to challenge the racist provisions of Anna Todd Jennings's will. According to one expert, such challenges have been upheld by the courts: the striking down of a similar clause in the will of the eighteenth-century financier Stephen Girard, which limited admission to white male orphans, is just one example.

Argument (inductive)

Evidence

The school itself must share some blame in this case. 3 Students who applied for the Anna Todd Jennings scholarship were unaware of its restrictions. The director of the financial aid office has acknowledged that he knew about the racial restrictions of the scholarship but thought that students should have the right to apply anyway. The materials distributed by the financial aid office also gave no indication that the award was limited to Caucasians. Students were required to fill out forms, submit financial statements, and forward transcripts. In addition to this material, all students were told to attach a recent photograph to their application. Little did the applicants know that the sole purpose of this innocuous little picture was to distinguish whites from nonwhites. By keeping secret the scholarship's restrictions, the school has put students in the position of unwittingly endorsing Anna Jennings's racism. Thus, both the school and the unsuspecting students have been in collusion with the administrators of the Anna Todd Jennings trust.

Refutation of opposing argument

The question students face is this: What is the best way 4 to deal with the generosity of a racist? A recent edition of the school paper contained several letters saying that students should accept Anna Jennings's scholarship money. One student said, "If we do not take that money and use our education to topple the barriers of prejudice, we are giving the money to those who will use the money in the opposite fashion." This argument, although attractive, is flawed. If an individual accepts a scholarship with racial restrictions, then he or she is actually endorsing the principles behind it. If a student does not want to appear to endorse racism, then he or she should reject the scholarship, even if this action causes hardship or gives adversaries a momentary advantage. To do otherwise is to further the cause of the individual who set up the scholarship. The best way to register a protest is to work to change the requirement for the scholarship and to encourage others not to apply as long as the racial restrictions exist.

Refutation of opposing argument

Another letter to this newspaper made the point that a number of other restricted scholarships are available at the school and no one seems to question them. For example, one is for the children of veterans, another is for women, and yet another is earmarked for African Americans. Even though these scholarships have restrictions, to assume that all restrictions are the same is to make a hasty generalization. Women, African Americans, and the children of veterans are groups that many believe deserve special treatment. Both women and African Americans have been discriminated against for years, and, as a result, educational opportunities have been denied them. Earmarking scholarships for them is simply a means of restoring some measure of equality. The children of veterans have been singled out because their parents have performed an extraordinary service for their country. Whites, however, do not fall into either of these categories. Special treatment for them is based solely on race and has nothing to do with any objective standard of need or merit.

5

Conclusion

Restatement of thesis

Concluding statement

I hope that by refusing to apply for the Anna Todd Jennings scholarship, I have encouraged other students to think about the issues involved in their own decisions. All of us have a responsibility to ourselves and to society. If we truly believe that racism in all its forms is evil, then we have to make a choice between sacrifice and hypocrisy. Faced with these options, our decision should be clear: accept the loss of funds as an opportunity to explore your values and fight for your principles; if you do, this opportunity is worth far more than any scholarship.

6

Points for Special Attention

Gathering Evidence. Because of his involvement with his subject, Matt Daniels could support his points with examples from his own experience. Still, Matt did have to review the requirements for the scholarship and decide on the arguments he would make. In addition, he reviewed an article that appeared in the school newspaper and the letters students wrote in response to the article. He then chose material that would add authority to his arguments.

Certainly, statistics, studies, and expert testimony, if they exist, would strengthen Matt's argument. But even without such evidence, an argument such as this one, based on solid reasoning, personal experience, and some research can be quite compelling.

Working with Sources. Matt used material from several outside sources in his editorial. For example, he used information from a government Web site when he discussed Stephen Girard's will. He also used information from an article in his school newspaper as well as from letters to the editor. Matt knew that newspaper editorials like his do not usually include documentation. As he wrote his editorial, however, he used phrases like "According to one expert" to make sure that readers would know when he used information from a source.

Before Matt submitted his editorial for his journalism class, where it would become part of his writing portfolio, he added documentation. Here are two sentences from this version of the editorial, along with the proper documentation.

> According to one expert, such challenges have been upheld by the courts: the striking down of a similar case in the will of eighteenth-century financier Stephen Girard is just one example (St. John 12).

> One student said, "If we do not take that money and use our education to topple the barriers of prejudice, we are giving the money to those who will use the money in the opposite fashion" (Divakaan).

Refuting Opposing Arguments. Matt devotes two paragraphs to summarizing and refuting arguments made by those who believe qualified students should apply for the scholarship despite its racial restrictions. He begins this section by asking a **rhetorical question** — a question asked not to elicit an answer but to further the argument. He goes on to refute what he considers the two best arguments against his thesis — that students should take the money and work to fight racism and that other scholarships at the school have restrictions. Matt counters these arguments by identifying a flaw in the logic of the first argument and by pointing to a fallacy, a hasty generalization, in the second.

Audience. Because he wrote his essay as an editorial for his college newspaper, Matt assumed his audience would be familiar with the issue he was discussing. Letters to the editor of the paper convinced him that his position was controversial, so he decided that his readers, mostly students and instructors, would have to be persuaded that his points were valid. To achieve this purpose, he carefully presents himself as a reasonable person, explains issues he believes are central to his case, and avoids *ad hominem* attacks. In addition, he avoids sweeping generalizations and name-calling and includes many details to support his assertions and convince readers that his points are worth considering.

Organization. Matt uses several strategies discussed earlier in this chapter. He begins his essay by introducing the issue he is going to discuss and then states his thesis: "Applying for the Anna Todd Jennings scholarship furthers the racist ideas held by its founder."

Because Matt had given a good deal of thought to his subject, he was able to construct two fairly strong arguments to support his position. His first argument is deductive. He begins by stating a premise he believes is self-evident — racism should be opposed. The rest of this argument follows a straightforward deductive pattern:

Major premise:	Racism should be opposed.
Minor premise:	The Anna Todd Jennings scholarship is racist.
Conclusion:	Therefore, the Anna Todd Jennings scholarship should be opposed.

Matt ends his first argument with factual evidence that reinforces his conclusion: the successful challenge to the will of financier Stephen Girard, which limited admittance to Girard College in Philadelphia to white male orphans.

Matt's second argument is inductive, asserting that the school has put students in the position of unknowingly supporting racism. The argument begins with Matt's hypothesis and presents the fact that even though the school is aware of the racist restrictions of the scholarship, it has not made students aware of them. According to Matt, the school's knowledge (and tacit approval) of the situation leads to the conclusion that the school is in collusion with those who manage the scholarship.

In his fourth and fifth paragraphs, Matt refutes two opposing arguments. Although his conclusion is rather brief, it does effectively reinforce and support his main idea. Matt ends his essay by recommending a course of action to his fellow students.

Focus on Revision

Matt constructed a solid argument that addressed his central issue very effectively. However, some students on the newspaper's editorial board thought he should add a section giving more information about Anna Todd Jennings and her bequest. These students believed that such information would help them better understand the implications of accepting her money. As it now stands, the essay dismisses Anna Todd Jennings as a racist, but biographical material and excerpts from her will — both of which appeared in the school paper — would enable readers to grasp the extent of her prejudice. Matt decided to follow up on this advice and to strengthen his conclusion as well. He thought that including the exact words of Anna Todd Jennings would help him to reinforce his points forcefully and memorably.

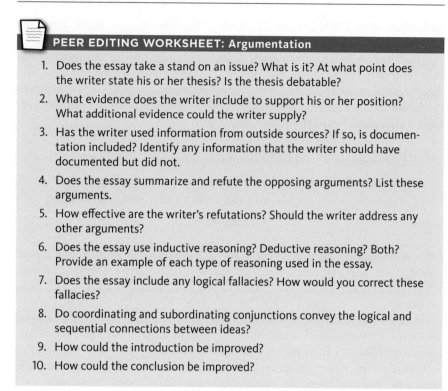

1. Does the essay take a stand on an issue? What is it? At what point does the writer state his or her thesis? Is the thesis debatable?

2. What evidence does the writer include to support his or her position? What additional evidence could the writer supply?

3. Has the writer used information from outside sources? If so, is documentation included? Identify any information that the writer should have documented but did not.

4. Does the essay summarize and refute the opposing arguments? List these arguments.

5. How effective are the writer's refutations? Should the writer address any other arguments?

6. Does the essay use inductive reasoning? Deductive reasoning? Both? Provide an example of each type of reasoning used in the essay.

7. Does the essay include any logical fallacies? How would you correct these fallacies?

8. Do coordinating and subordinating conjunctions convey the logical and sequential connections between ideas?

9. How could the introduction be improved?

10. How could the conclusion be improved?

The essays that follow represent a wide variety of topics, and the purpose of each essay is to support a debatable thesis. In addition to three classic arguments, this chapter also includes two debates and two casebooks that focus on current issues. Each of the debates pairs two essays that take opposing stands on the same issue. In the casebooks, four essays on a single topic offer a greater variety of viewpoints. The first selection, a visual text, is followed by questions designed to illustrate how argumentation can operate in visual form.

Thanks to Modern Science . . . (Ad)

Reading Images

1. What points does the ad's headline make? Does the rest of the ad support these points?
2. How would you describe the picture that accompanies the text? How does the picture reinforce the message of the text?
3. Does this ad appeal primarily to logic, to emotions, or to both? Explain.
4. List the specific points the ad makes. Which points are supported by evidence? Which points should be supported by evidence but are not? How does this lack of support affect your response to the ad?

Journal Entry

Overall, do you find this ad convincing? Write an email to the ACLU presenting your position. Be sure to refer to specific parts of the ad to support your argument.

Thematic Connections

- "Thirty-Eight Who Saw Murder Didn't Call the Police" (page 127)
- "Just Walk On By: A Black Man Ponders His Ability to Alter Public Space" (page 240)
- "Get It Right: Privatize Executions" (page 298)
- "A Peaceful Woman Explains Why She Carries a Gun" (page 354)

THOMAS JEFFERSON

The Declaration of Independence

Thomas Jefferson was born in 1743 in what is now Albemarle County, Virginia. A lawyer, he was elected to Virginia's colonial legislature in 1769 and began a distinguished political career that strongly influenced the early development of the United States. In addition to his participation in the Second Continental Congress of 1775–1776, which ratified the Declaration of Independence, he served as governor of Virginia; as minister to France; as secretary of state under President George Washington; as vice president under John Adams; and, finally, as president from 1801 to 1809. After his retirement, he founded the University of Virginia. He died on July 4, 1826.

Background on the struggle for American independence By the early 1770s, many residents of the original thirteen American colonies were convinced that King George III and his ministers wielded too much power over the colonists. In particular, they objected to a series of taxes imposed on them by the British Parliament, and, being without political representation, they asserted that "taxation without representation" amounted to tyranny. In response to a series of laws Parliament passed in 1774 to limit the political and geographic freedom of the colonists, representatives of each colony met at the Continental Congress of 1774 to draft a plan of reconciliation, but it was rejected.

As cries for independence increased, British soldiers and state militias began to engage in armed conflict, which by 1776 had become a full-fledged war. On June 11, 1776, the Second Continental Congress chose Jefferson, Benjamin Franklin, and several other delegates to draft a declaration of independence. The draft was written by Jefferson, with suggestions and revisions contributed by other commission members. Jefferson's Declaration of Independence challenges a basic assumption of its time—that the royal monarch ruled by divine right—and, in so doing, it became one of the most important political documents in world history.

As you read, keep in mind that to the British, the Declaration of Independence was a call for open rebellion. For this reason, the Declaration's final sentence, in which the signatories pledge their lives, fortunes, and honor, is no mere rhetorical flourish. Had England defeated the colonists, everyone who signed the Declaration of Independence would have been arrested, charged with treason or sedition, stripped of his property, and probably hanged.

When in the course of human events, it becomes necessary for one 1 people to dissolve the political bonds which have connected them with another, and to assume among the powers of the earth, the separate and equal station to which the Laws of Nature and of Nature's God entitle them, a decent respect to the opinions of mankind requires that they should declare the causes which impel them to the separation.

We hold these truths to be self-evident, that all men are created equal, that they are endowed by their Creator with certain unalienable rights, that among these are life, liberty, and the pursuit of happiness. That to secure these rights, governments are instituted among men, deriving their just powers from the consent of the governed. That whenever any form of government becomes destructive to these ends, it is the right of the people to alter or to abolish it, and to institute new government, laying its foundation on such principles and organizing its powers in such form, as to them shall seem most likely to effect their safety and happiness. Prudence, indeed, will dictate that governments long established should not be changed for light and transient causes; and accordingly all experience hath shown, that mankind are more disposed to suffer, while evils are sufferable, than to right themselves by abolishing the forms to which they are accustomed. But when a long train of abuses and usurpations, pursuing invariably the same object, evinces a design to reduce them under absolute despotism, it is their right, it is their duty, to throw off such government, and to provide new guards for their future security. Such has been the patient sufferance of these Colonies; and such is now the necessity which constrains them to alter their former systems of government. The history of the present king of Great Britain is a history of repeated injuries and usurpations, all having in direct object the establishment of an absolute tyranny over these States. To prove this, let facts be submitted to a candid world.

> **"We hold these truths to be self-evident, that all men are created equal. . . ."**

2

He has refused his assent to laws, the most wholesome and necessary for the public good. 3

He has forbidden his Governors to pass laws of immediate and pressing importance, unless suspended in their operation till his assent should be obtained; and when so suspended, he has utterly neglected to attend to them. 4

He has refused to pass other laws for the accommodation of large districts of people, unless those people would relinquish the right of representation in the legislature, a right inestimable to them and formidable to tyrants only. 5

He has called together legislative bodies at places unusual, uncomfortable, and distant from the depository of their public records, for the sole purpose of fatiguing them into compliance with his measure. 6

He has dissolved representative houses repeatedly, for opposing with manly firmness his invasions on the rights of people. 7

He has refused for a long time, after such dissolutions, to cause others to be elected; whereby the legislative powers, incapable of annihilation, have returned to the people at large for their exercise; the State remaining in the meantime exposed to all the dangers of invasion from without, and convulsions within. 8

He has endeavoured to prevent the population of these states; for that purpose obstructing the laws for naturalization of foreigners; refusing to 9 pass others to encourage their migration hither, and raising the conditions of new appropriations of lands.

He has obstructed the administration of justice, by refusing his assent to laws for establishing judiciary powers. 10

He has made judges dependent on his will alone, for the tenure of their offices, and the amount and payment of their salaries. 11

He has erected a multitude of new offices, and sent hither swarms of officers to harass our people, and eat out their substance. 12

He has kept among us, in times of peace, standing armies without the consent of our legislatures. 13

He has affected to render the military independent of and superior to the civil power. 14

He has combined with others to subject us to a jurisdiction foreign to our constitution, and unacknowledged by our laws; giving his assent to their acts of pretended legislation: 15

For quartering large bodies of troops among us: 16

For protecting them, by a mock trial, from punishment for any murders which they should commit on the inhabitants of these States: 17

For cutting off our trade with all parts of the world: 18

For imposing taxes on us without our consent: 19

For depriving us in many cases, of the benefits of trial by jury: 20

For transporting us beyond seas to be tried for pretended offences: 21

For abolishing the free system of English laws in a neighbouring Province, establishing therein an arbitrary government, and enlarging its boundaries so as to render it at once an example and fit instrument for introducing the same absolute rule into these Colonies: 22

For taking away our Charters, abolishing our most valuable laws, and altering fundamentally the forms of our governments: 23

For suspending our own legislatures, and declaring themselves invested with power to legislate for us in all cases whatsoever. 24

He has abdicated government here, by declaring us out of his protection and waging war against us. 25

He has plundered our seas, ravaged our coasts, burnt our towns, and destroyed the lives of our people. 26

He is at this time transporting large armies of foreign mercenaries to complete the works of death, desolation and tyranny, already begun with circumstances of cruelty and perfidy scarcely paralleled in the most barbarous ages, and totally unworthy the head of a civilized nation. 27

He has constrained our fellow citizens taken captive on the high seas to bear arms against their country, to become the executioners of their friends and brethren, or to fall themselves by their hands. 28

He has excited domestic insurrections amongst us, and has endeavoured to bring on the inhabitants of our frontiers, the merciless Indian savages, whose known rule of warfare, is an undistinguished destruction of all ages, sexes, and conditions. 29

In every stage of these oppressions we have petitioned for redress in the most humble terms: our repeated petitions have been answered only by 30 repeated injury. A prince whose character is thus marked by every act which may define a tyrant, is unfit to be the ruler of a free people.

Nor have we been wanting in attentions to our British brethren. We have warned them from time to time of attempts by their legislature to extend an unwarrantable jurisdiction over us. We have reminded them of the circumstances of our emigration and settlement here. We have appealed to their native justice and magnanimity, and we have conjured them by the ties of our common kindred to disavow these usurpations, which would inevitably interrupt our connections and correspondence. They too have been deaf to the voice of justice and of consanguinity. We must, therefore, acquiesce in the necessity, which denounces our separation, and hold them, as we hold the rest of mankind, enemies in war, in peace friends. 31

We, therefore, the Representatives of the United States of America, in General Congress, assembled, appealing to the Supreme Judge of the world for the rectitude of our intentions, do, in the name, and by authority of the good people of these Colonies, solemnly publish and declare, That these United Colonies are, and of right ought to be Free and Independent States; that they are absolved from all allegiance to the British Crown, and that all political connection between them and the state of Great Britain, is and ought to be totally dissolved; and that as Free and Independent States, they have full power to levy war, conclude peace, contract alliances, establish commerce, and to do all other acts and things which Independent States may of right do. And for the support of this declaration, with a firm reliance on the protection of divine Providence, we mutually pledge to each other our lives, our fortunes, and our sacred honor. 32

• • •

Comprehension

1. What "truths" does Jefferson say are "self-evident" (2)?
2. What does Jefferson say is the source from which governments derive their powers?
3. What reasons does Jefferson give to support his premise that the United States should break away from Great Britain?
4. What conclusions about British rule does Jefferson draw from the evidence he presents?

Purpose and Audience

1. What is the major premise of Jefferson's argument? Should Jefferson have done more to establish the truth of this premise?
2. The Declaration of Independence was written during a period now referred to as the Age of Reason. In what ways has Jefferson tried to make his document appear reasonable?

3. For what audience (or audiences) was the document intended? Which groups of readers would have been most likely to accept it? Explain.

4. How effectively does Jefferson anticipate and refute the opposition?

5. In paragraph 31, following the list of grievances, why does Jefferson address his "British brethren"?

6. At what point does Jefferson state his thesis? Why does he state it where he does?

Style and Structure

1. Does the Declaration of Independence rely primarily on inductive or deductive reasoning? Identify examples of each.

2. What techniques does Jefferson use to create smooth and logical transitions from one paragraph to another?

3. Why does Jefferson list all of his twenty-eight grievances? Why doesn't he just summarize them or mention a few representative grievances?

4. Jefferson begins the last paragraph of the Declaration of Independence with "We, therefore." How effective is this conclusion? Explain.

Vocabulary Projects

1. Define each of the following words as it is used in this selection.

station (1)	evinces (2)	tenure (11)
impel (1)	despotism (2)	jurisdiction (15)
self-evident (2)	sufferance (2)	arbitrary (22)
endowed (2)	candid (2)	insurrections (29)
deriving (2)	depository (6)	disavow (31)
prudence (2)	dissolutions (8)	consanguinity (31)
transient (2)	annihilation (8)	rectitude (32)
usurpations (2)	appropriations (9)	levy (32)

2. Underline ten words that have negative connotations. How does Jefferson use these words to help him make his point? Do you think words with more neutral connotations would strengthen or weaken his case? Why?

3. What words does Jefferson use that are rarely used today? Would the Declaration of Independence be more meaningful to today's readers if it were updated, with more familiar words substituted? To help you formulate your response, try rewriting a paragraph or two, and assess your updated version. Look up any unfamiliar words in an online dictionary such as dictionary.com.

Journal Entry

Do you think Jefferson is being fair to the king? Do you think he should be?

Writing Workshop

1. Following Jefferson's example, write a declaration of independence from your school, job, family, or any other institution with which you are associated.

2. **Working with Sources.** Go to the Web site ushistory.org/declaration /document/congress.htm, and look at the revisions that Congress made to Jefferson's original draft of the Declaration of Independence. Decide which version you think is better. Then, write an essay in which you present your case. Make sure you document all words and ideas that you borrow from both versions of the Declaration, and include a works-cited page. (See Chapter 18 for information on MLA documentation.)

3. **Working with Sources.** In an argumentative essay written from the viewpoint of King George III, answer Jefferson. Try to convince the colonists that they should not break away from Great Britain. If you can, refute some of the points Jefferson makes. Make sure that you document all words and ideas that you borrow from the Declaration and that you include a works-cited page. (See Chapter 18 for information on MLA documentation.)

Combining the Patterns

The middle section of the Declaration of Independence is developed by means of **exemplification**: it presents a series of examples to support Jefferson's assertion that the colonists have experienced "repeated injuries and usurpations" (2). Are these examples relevant? Representative? Sufficient? What other pattern of development could Jefferson have used to support his assertion?

Thematic Connections

- "The 'Black Table' Is Still There" (page 349)
- "Grant and Lee: A Study in Contrasts" (page 393)
- "Aristotle" (page 484)
- "Letter from Birmingham Jail" (page 566)

ELIZABETH CADY STANTON

Declaration of Sentiments and Resolutions, Seneca Falls Convention, 1848

Elizabeth Cady was born in Johnstown, New York, in 1815 and attended the Troy Female Seminary. At the age of twenty-five, she married the writer and abolitionist Henry Brewster Stanton, joining him in the struggle to end slavery. She also became active in the women's suffrage movement, lobbying for the right of women to vote. This movement had its beginnings in the United States at the first Woman's Rights Convention, which was organized by Stanton and other early petitioners for women's rights and held in Seneca Falls, New York, in July 1848. There, the following declaration was first presented, amended, and then unanimously adopted by the three hundred delegates. (All the resolutions were passed unanimously except for the one calling for women's right to vote, which was thought by some to be extreme enough to discredit the feminist movement.) Stanton went on to lead the National Woman Suffrage Movement from 1869 to 1890 and to coedit *Revolution,* a feminist periodical. A popular lecturer and skilled writer, she continued to work toward the goal of equality for women until her death in 1902.

Background on the women's suffrage movement In 1848, women were considered inferior to men in terms of intelligence and the ability to reason, so the Founding Fathers' statement "all men are created equal" did not apply to them. In fact, the idea for the Seneca Falls Convention was spurred by Stanton's experiences at the 1840 World Anti-Slavery Convention in London, which she attended with her husband and which refused to admit women delegates to the floor. When made public, the Declaration of Sentiments was universally derided by the press and by contemporary religious leaders — even Henry Stanton thought his wife had gone too far. The Civil War interrupted the budding women's rights movement, but at its close, when emancipated African-American men were granted the right to vote, the movement picked up steam again. Its leaders lobbied for an amendment to the U.S. Constitution allowing women to vote and pressed state legislatures for voting rights as well. It was a long road, however. By 1913, only twelve states had extended voting rights to women, and not until the Nineteenth Amendment to the Constitution was ratified in 1920 did American women gain this right.

Declaration of Sentiments

When, in the course of human events, it becomes necessary for one 1 portion of the family of man to assume among the people of the earth a position different from that which they have hitherto occupied, but one to which the laws of nature and of nature's God entitle them, a decent respect to the opinions of mankind requires that they should declare the causes that impel them to such a course.

We hold these truths to be self-evident: that all men and women are 2 created equal; that they are endowed by their Creator with certain inalienable rights; that among these are life, liberty, and the pursuit of happiness; that to secure these rights governments are instituted, deriving their just powers from the consent of the governed. Whenever any form of government becomes destructive of these ends, it is the right of those who suffer from it to refuse allegiance to it, and to insist upon the institution of a new government, laying its foundation on such principles, and organizing its powers in such form, as to them shall seem most likely to effect their safety and happiness. Prudence, indeed, will dictate that governments long established should not be changed for light and transient causes; and accordingly all experience hath shown that mankind are more disposed to suffer, while evils are sufferable, than to right themselves by abolishing the forms to which they were accustomed. But when a long train of abuses and usurpations, pursuing invariably the same object, evinces a design to reduce them under absolute despotism, it is their duty to throw off such government, and to provide new guards for their future security. Such has been the patient sufferance of the women under this government, and such is now the necessity which constrains them to demand the equal station to which they are entitled.

The history of mankind is a history of repeated injuries and usurpa- 3 tions on the part of man toward woman, having in direct object the establishment of an absolute tyranny over her. To prove this, let facts be submitted to a candid world.

He has never permitted her to exercise her inalienable right to the elective franchise. 4

> " The history of mankind is a history of repeated injuries and usurpations on the part of man toward woman. . . . "

He has compelled her to submit to laws, in the formation of which she had no voice. 5

He has withheld from her rights which are given to the most ignorant and degraded men — both natives and foreigners. 6

Having deprived her of this first right 7 of a citizen, the elective franchise, thereby leaving her without representation in the halls of legislation, he has oppressed her on all sides.

He has made her, if married, in the eye of the law, civilly dead. 8

He has taken from her all right in property, even to the wages she 9 earns.

He has made her, morally, an irresponsible being, as she can commit 10 many crimes with impunity, provided they be done in the presence of her husband. In the covenant of marriage, she is compelled to promise obedience to her husband, he becoming, to all intents and purposes, her master — the law giving him power to deprive her of her liberty, and to administer chastisement.

He has so framed the laws of divorce, as to what shall be the proper 11 causes, and in case of separation, to whom the guardianship of the children shall be given, as to be wholly regardless of the happiness of women — the law, in all cases, going upon the false supposition of the supremacy of man, and giving all power into his hands.

After depriving her of all rights as a married woman, if single, 12 and the owner of property, he has taxed her to support a government which recognizes her only when her property can be made profitable to it.

He has monopolized nearly all the profitable employments, and from 13 those she is permitted to follow, she receives but a scanty remuneration. He closes against her all the avenues to wealth and distinction which he considers most honorable to himself. As a teacher of theology, medicine, or law, she is not known.

He has denied her the facilities for obtaining a thorough education, all 14 colleges being closed against her.

He allows her in Church, as well as State, but a subordinate position, 15 claiming Apostolic authority for her exclusion from the ministry, and, with some exceptions, from any public participation in the affairs of the Church.

He has created a false public sentiment by giving to the world a dif- 16 ferent code of morals for men and women, by which moral delinquencies which exclude women from society, are not only tolerated, but deemed of little account in man.

He has usurped the prerogative of Jehovah himself, claiming it as his 17 right to assign for her a sphere of action, when that belongs to her conscience and to her God.

He has endeavored, in every way that he could, to destroy her confi- 18 dence in her own powers, to lessen her self-respect, and to make her willing to lead a dependent and abject life.

Now, in view of this entire disenfranchisement of one-half the people 19 of this country, their social and religious degradation — in view of the unjust laws above mentioned, and because women do feel themselves aggrieved, oppressed, and fraudulently deprived of their most sacred rights, we insist that they have immediate admission to all the rights and privileges which belong to them as citizens of the United States.

In entering upon the great work before us, we anticipate no small 20 amount of misconception, misrepresentation, and ridicule; but we shall use every instrumentality within our power to effect our object. We shall employ agents, circulate tracts, petition the State and National legislatures, and endeavor to enlist the pulpit and the press in our behalf. We hope this Convention will be followed by a series of Conventions embracing every part of the country.

Resolutions

Whereas, The great precept of nature is conceded to be, that "man 21 shall pursue his own true and substantial happiness." Blackstone* in his Commentaries remarks, that this law of Nature being coeval with mankind, and dictated by God himself, is of course superior in obligation to any other. It is binding over all the globe, in all countries and at all times; no human laws are of any validity if contrary to this, and such of them as are valid, derive all their force, and all their validity, and all their authority, mediately and immediately, from this original; therefore,

Resolved, That such laws as conflict, in any way, with the true and sub- 22 stantial happiness of woman, are contrary to the great precept of nature and of no validity, for this is "superior in obligation to any other."

Resolved, That all laws which prevent woman from occupying such a 23 station in society as her conscience shall dictate, or which place her in a position inferior to that of man, are contrary to the great precept of nature, and therefore of no force or authority.

Resolved, That woman is man's equal — was intended to be so by the 24 Creator, and the highest good of the race demands that she should be recognized as such.

Resolved, That the women of this country ought to be enlightened in 25 regard to the laws under which they live, that they may no longer publish their degradation by declaring themselves satisfied with their present position, nor their ignorance, by asserting that they have all the rights they want.

Resolved, That inasmuch as man, while claiming for himself intellectual 26 superiority, does accord to woman moral superiority, it is preeminently his duty to encourage her to speak and teach, as she has an opportunity, in all religious assemblies.

Resolved, That the same amount of virtue, delicacy, and refinement of 27 behavior that is required of woman in the social state, should also be required of man, and the same transgressions should be visited with equal severity on both man and woman.

Resolved, That the objection of indelicacy and impropriety, which is 28 so often brought against woman when she addresses a public audience, comes with a very ill-grace from those who encourage, by their attendance, her appearance on the stage, in the concert, or in feats of the circus.

Resolved, That woman has too long rested satisfied in the circumscribed 29 limits which corrupt customs and a perverted application of the Scriptures have marked out for her, and that it is time she should move in the enlarged sphere which her great Creator has assigned her.

Resolved, That it is the duty of the women of this country to secure to 30 themselves their sacred right to the elective franchise.

---

* Eds. note — Sir William Blackstone (1723–1780), English jurist. Many regard his *Commentaries* (1765–1769) as the most thorough treatment of English law ever produced.

Resolved, That the equality of human rights results necessarily from the 31 fact of the identity of the race in capabilities and responsibilities.

Resolved, therefore, That, being invested by the Creator with the same 32 capabilities, and the same consciousness of responsibility for their exercise, it is demonstrably the right and duty of woman, equally with man, to promote every righteous cause by every righteous means; and especially in regard to the great subjects of morals and religion, it is self-evidently her right to participate with her brother in teaching them, both in private and in public, by writing and by speaking, by any instrumentalities proper to be used, and in any assemblies proper to be held; and this being a self-evident truth growing out of the divinely implanted principles of human nature, any custom or authority adverse to it, whether modern or wearing the hoary sanction of antiquity, is to be regarded as a self-evident falsehood, and at war with mankind.

Resolved, That the speedy success of our cause depends upon the zeal- 33 ous and untiring efforts of both men and women, for the overthrow of the monopoly of the pulpit, and for the securing to woman an equal participation with men in the various trades, professions, and commerce.*

. . .

Comprehension

1. According to Stanton, why is it necessary for women to declare their sentiments?

2. What truths does Stanton say are "self-evident" (2)?

3. What injuries does Stanton list? Which injuries seem most important?

4. What type of reception does Stanton expect the Declaration of Sentiments and Resolutions to receive? What does she propose to do about this reception?

5. What conclusion does Stanton draw? According to her, what self-evident right do women have? What does she believe should be regarded as "a self-evident falsehood" (32)?

Purpose and Audience

1. Is Stanton addressing men, women, or both? How can you tell? Does she consider one segment of her audience more receptive to her ideas than another? Explain.

2. What strategies does Stanton use to present herself as reasonable? Do you think she is successful? Explain.

3. What is Stanton's thesis? At what point does she state it? Why do you think she states it when she does?

---

* Eds. note — This last resolution was given by Lucretia Mott at the actual convention. All the previous resolutions were drafted earlier by Elizabeth Cady Stanton.

4. What is Stanton's purpose? Do you think she actually expects to change people's ideas and behavior, or does she have some other purpose in mind?

Style and Structure

1. Does Stanton present her argument inductively or deductively? Why do you think she chose this arrangement?

2. The Declaration of Sentiments and Resolutions imitates the tone, style, and, in some places, even the wording of the Declaration of Independence. What are the advantages of this strategy? What are the disadvantages?

3. In paragraphs 2 and 32, Stanton mentions "self-evident" truths. Are these truths really self-evident? Should she have done more to establish the validity of these statements?

4. What are the major and minor premises of Stanton's argument? Do these premises lead logically to her conclusion?

5. How do transitional words and phrases help Stanton move readers from one section of her argument to another? Are the transitions effective?

6. Should Stanton have specifically refuted arguments against her position? Could she be accused of ignoring her opposition?

Vocabulary Projects

1. Define each of the following words as it is used in this selection.

hitherto (1)	station (2)	validity (21)
impel (1)	franchise (4)	mediately (21)
inalienable (2)	degraded (6)	transgressions (27)
allegiance (2)	impunity (10)	indelicacy (28)
dictate (2)	chastisement (10)	impropriety (28)
sufferable (2)	subordinate (15)	circumscribed (29)
invariably (2)	delinquencies (16)	sphere (29)
sufferance (2)	abject (18)	antiquity (32)
constrains (2)	disenfranchisement (19)	zealous (33)

2. Today, many people would consider the style of some of the passages in the Declaration of Sentiments and Resolutions stiff and overly formal. Find a paragraph that fits this description, and rewrite it using less formal diction. What is lost in your revision, and what is gained?

Journal Entry

Review Stanton's list of injuries to women. How many of these wrongs have been corrected? How many have yet to be addressed?

Writing Workshop

1. Choose an issue you care about, and write your own Declaration of Sentiments and Resolutions. Like Stanton, echo the phrasing of the Declaration of Independence in your essay.

2. **Working with Sources.** Reread your journal entry, and select one of the injuries to women that has not yet been corrected. Research this issue, and then write an essay arguing that this issue needs to be resolved. In your essay, refer specifically to the Declaration of Sentiments and Resolutions, as well as your other sources. Make sure you document all material you borrow from your sources, and include a works-cited page. (See Chapter 18 for information on MLA documentation.)

3. When the Declaration of Sentiments and Resolutions was voted on at the Seneca Falls Convention in 1848, the only resolution not passed unanimously was the one that called for women to win the right to vote (see paragraph 30). Write a letter to the convention calling on the delegates to vote for this resolution. Make sure you refute the main argument against this resolution — that it would alienate so many people that it would discredit the feminist movement.

Combining the Patterns

Like the Declaration of Independence, the Declaration of Sentiments and Resolutions is partly developed by **exemplification**. A series of examples supports Stanton's assertion that women now "demand the equal station to which they are entitled" (2). How effective are these examples? Are they relevant? Representative? Sufficient?

Thematic Connections

- "My Mother Never Worked" (page 121)
- "A Peaceful Woman Explains Why She Carries a Gun" (page 354)
- "I Want a Wife" (page 503)
- The Declaration of Independence (page 553)

MARTIN LUTHER KING JR.

Letter from Birmingham Jail

Martin Luther King Jr. was born in Atlanta, Georgia, in 1929. After receiving his doctorate in theology from Boston University in 1955, he became pastor of the Dexter Avenue Baptist Church in Montgomery, Alabama. There, he organized a 382-day bus boycott that led to the 1956 Supreme Court decision outlawing segregation on Alabama's buses. As leader of the Southern Christian Leadership Conference, he was instrumental in securing the civil rights of black Americans, using methods based on a philosophy of nonviolent protest. His books include *Stride towards Freedom* (1958) and *Why We Can't Wait* (1964). In 1964, King was awarded the Nobel Peace Prize. He was assassinated in 1968 in Memphis, Tennessee.

Background on racial segregation In 1896, the Supreme Court ruled in *Plessy v. Ferguson* that "separate but equal" accommodations on railroad cars gave African Americans the equal protection guaranteed by the Fourteenth Amendment of the Constitution. This decision was used to justify separate public facilities—including schools—for blacks and whites well into the twentieth century.

In the mid-1950s, state support for segregation and discrimination against blacks had begun to be challenged. Supreme Court decisions in 1954 and 1955 declared segregation in public schools and other publicly financed venues unconstitutional, while blacks and whites alike were calling for an end to discrimination. Their actions took the form of marches, boycotts, and sit-ins (organized protests whose participants refuse to move from a public area). Many whites, however, particularly in the South, vehemently resisted any change in race relations.

By 1963, when Martin Luther King Jr. organized a campaign against segregation in Birmingham, Alabama, tensions ran deep. He and his followers met fierce opposition from the police, as well as from white moderates, who considered him an "outside agitator." During the demonstrations, King was arrested and jailed for eight days. While imprisoned, he wrote his "Letter from Birmingham Jail" to white clergymen to explain his actions and answer those who urged him to call off the demonstrations.

April 16, 1963

My Dear Fellow Clergymen:

While confined here in the Birmingham city jail, I came across your 1 recent statement calling my present activities "unwise and untimely." Seldom do I pause to answer criticism of my work and ideas. If I sought to answer all the criticisms that cross my desk, my secretaries would have little time for anything other than such correspondence in the course of the day, and I would have no time for constructive work. But since I feel that you are men of genuine good will and that your criticisms are sincerely set forth, I want to try to answer your statement in what I hope will be patient and reasonable terms.

I think I should indicate why I am here in Birmingham, since you have 2 been influenced by the view which argues against "outsiders coming in." I have the honor of serving as president of the Southern Christian Leadership Conference, an organization operating in every southern state, with headquarters in Atlanta, Georgia. We have some eighty-five affiliated organizations across the South, and one of them is the Alabama Christian Movement for Human Rights. Frequently we share staff, educational, and financial resources with our affiliates. Several months ago the affiliate here in Birmingham asked us to be on call to engage in a nonviolent direct-action program if such were deemed necessary. We readily consented, and when the hour came we lived up to our promise. So I, along with several members of my staff, am here because I was invited here. I am here because I have organizational ties here.

But more basically, I am in Birmingham because injustice is here. Just 3 as the prophets of the eighth century B.C. left their villages and carried their "thus saith the Lord" far beyond the boundaries of their home towns, and just as the Apostle Paul left his village of Tarsus and carried the gospel of Jesus Christ to the far corners of the Greco-Roman world, so am I compelled to carry the gospel of freedom beyond my own home town. Like Paul, I must constantly respond to the Macedonian call for aid.

Moreover, I am cognizant of the interrelatedness of all communi- 4 ties and states. I cannot sit idly by in Atlanta and not be concerned about what happens in Birmingham. Injustice anywhere is a threat to justice everywhere. We are caught in an inescapable network of mutuality, tied in a single garment of destiny. Whatever affects one directly, affects all indirectly. Never again can we afford to live with the narrow, provincial, "outside agitator" idea. Anyone who lives inside the United States can never be considered an outsider anywhere within its bounds.

You deplore the demonstrations taking place in Birmingham. But 5 your statement, I am sorry to say, fails to express a similar concern for the conditions that brought about the demonstrations. I am sure that none of you would want to rest content with the superficial kind of social analysis that deals merely with effects and does not grapple with underlying causes. It is unfortunate that demonstrations are taking place in Birmingham, but it is even more unfortunate that the city's white power structure left the Negro community with no alternative.

In any nonviolent campaign there are four basic steps: collection of the 6 facts to determine whether injustices exist; negotiation; self-purification; and direct action. We have gone through all these steps in Birmingham. There can be no gainsaying the fact that racial injustice engulfs this community. Birmingham is probably the most thoroughly segregated city in the United States. Its ugly record of brutality is widely known. Negroes have experienced grossly unjust treatment in courts. There have been more unsolved bombings of Negro homes and churches in Birmingham than in any other city in the nation. These are the hard, brutal facts of the case. On the basis of these conditions, Negro leaders sought to negotiate with the city fathers. But the latter consistently refused to engage in good-faith negotiation.

Then, last September, came the opportunity to talk with leaders of Birmingham's economic community. In the course of the negotiations, certain promises were made by the merchants — for example, to remove the stores' humiliating racial signs. On the basis of these promises, the Reverend Fred Shuttlesworth and the leaders of the Alabama Christian Movement for Human Rights agreed to a moratorium on all demonstrations. As the weeks and months went by, we realized that we were the victims of a broken promise. A few signs, briefly removed, returned; the others remained.

As in so many past experiences, our hopes had been blasted, and the shadow of deep disappointment settled upon us. We had no alternative except to prepare for direct action, whereby we would present our very bodies as means of laying our case before the conscience of the local and the national community. Mindful of the difficulties involved, we decided to undertake a process of self-purification. We began a series of workshops on nonviolence, and we repeatedly asked ourselves: "Are you able to accept blows without retaliating?" "Are you able to endure the ordeal of jail?" We decided to schedule our direct-action program for the Easter season, realizing that except for Christmas, this is the main shopping period of the year. Knowing that a strong economic-withdrawal program would be the by-product of direct action, we felt that this would be the best time to bring pressure to bear on the merchants for the needed change.

Then it occurred to us that Birmingham's mayoral election was coming up in March, and we speedily decided to postpone action until after election day. When we discovered that the Commissioner of Public Safety, Eugene "Bull" Connor, had piled up enough votes to be in the run-off, we decided again to postpone action until the day after the run-off so that the demonstrations could not be used to cloud the issues. Like many others, we waited to see Mr. Connor defeated, and to this end we endured postponement after postponement. Having aided in this community need, we felt that our direct-action program could be delayed no longer.

You may well ask, "Why direct action? Why sit-ins, marches, and so forth? Isn't negotiation a better path?" You are quite right in calling for negotiation. Indeed, this is the very purpose of direct action. Nonviolent direct action seeks to create such a crisis and foster such a tension that a community which has constantly refused to negotiate is forced to confront the issue. It seeks so to dramatize the issue that it can no longer be ignored. My citing the creation of tension as part of the work of the nonviolent-resister may sound rather shocking. But I must confess that I am not afraid of the word "tension." I have earnestly opposed violent tension, but there is a type of constructive, nonviolent tension which is necessary for growth. Just as Socrates felt that it was necessary to create a tension in the mind so that individuals could rise from the bondage of myths and half-truths to the unfettered realm of creative analysis and objective appraisal, so must we see the need for nonviolent gadflies to create the kind of tension in society that will help men rise from the dark depths of prejudice and racism to the majestic heights of understanding and brotherhood.

The purpose of our direct-action program is to create a situation so crisis-packed that it will inevitably open the door to negotiation. I therefore concur with you in your call for negotiation. Too long has our beloved Southland been bogged down in a tragic effort to live in monologue rather than dialogue. 11

One of the basic points in your statement is that the action that I and my associates have taken in Birmingham is untimely. Some have asked: "Why didn't you give the new city administration time to act?" The only answer that I can give to this query is that the new Birmingham administration must be prodded about as much as the outgoing one, before it will act. We are sadly mistaken if we feel that the election of Albert Boutwell as mayor will bring the millennium to Birmingham. While Mr. Boutwell is a much more gentle person than Mr. Connor, they are both segregationists, dedicated to maintenance of the status quo. I have hoped that Mr. Boutwell will be reasonable enough to see the futility of massive resistance to desegregation. But he will not see this without pressure from devotees of civil rights. My friends, I must say to you that we have not made a single gain in civil rights without determined legal and nonviolent pressure. Lamentably, it is an historical fact that privileged groups seldom give up their privileges voluntarily. Individuals may see the moral light and voluntarily give up their unjust posture; but, as Reinhold Niebuhr* has reminded us, groups tend to be more immoral than individuals. 12

We know through painful experience that freedom is never voluntarily given by the oppressor; it must be demanded by the oppressed. Frankly, I have yet to engage in a direct-action campaign that was "well timed" in the view of those who have not suffered unduly from the disease of segregation. For years now I have heard the word "Wait!" It rings in the ear of every Negro with piercing familiarity. This "Wait" has almost always meant "Never." We must come to see, with one of our distinguished jurists, that "justice too long delayed is justice denied." 13

We have waited for more than 340 years for our constitutional and God-given rights. The nations of Asia and Africa are moving with jetlike speed toward gaining political independence, but we still creep at horse-and-buggy pace toward gaining a cup of coffee at a lunch counter. Perhaps it is easy for those who have never felt the stinging darts of segregation to say, "Wait." But when you have seen vicious mobs lynch 14

> "We must come to see, with one of our distinguished jurists, that 'justice too long delayed is justice denied.'"

---

* Eds. note — American religious and social thinker (1892–1971).

your mothers and fathers at will and drown your sisters and brothers at whim; when you have seen hate-filled policemen curse, kick, and even kill your black brothers and sisters; when you see the vast majority of your twenty million Negro brothers smothering in an airtight cage of poverty in the midst of an affluent society; when you suddenly find your tongue twisted and your speech stammering as you seek to explain to your six-year-old daughter why she can't go to the public amusement park that has just been advertised on television, and see tears welling up in her eyes when she is told that Funtown is closed to colored children, and see ominous clouds of inferiority beginning to form in her little mental sky, and see her beginning to distort her personality by developing an unconscious bitterness toward white people; when you have to concoct an answer for a five-year-old son who is asking, "Daddy, why do white people treat colored people so mean?"; when you take a cross-country drive and find it necessary to sleep night after night in the uncomfortable corners of your automobile because no motel will accept you; when you are humiliated day in and day out by nagging signs reading "white" and "colored"; when your first name becomes "nigger," your middle name becomes "boy" (however old you are), and your last name becomes "John," and your wife and mother are never given the respected title "Mrs."; when you are harried by day and haunted at night by the fact that you are a Negro, living constantly at tiptoe stance, never quite knowing what to expect next, and are plagued with inner fears and outer resentments; when you are forever fighting a degenerating sense of "nobodiness" — then you will understand why we find it difficult to wait. There comes a time when the cup of endurance runs over, and men are no longer willing to be plunged into the abyss of despair. I hope, sirs, you can understand our legitimate and unavoidable impatience.

You express a great deal of anxiety over our willingness to break laws.   15 This is certainly a legitimate concern. Since we so diligently urge people to obey the Supreme Court's decision of 1954 outlawing segregation in the public schools, at first glance it may seem rather paradoxical for us consciously to break laws. One may well ask: "How can you advocate breaking some laws and obeying others?" The answer lies in the fact that there are two types of laws: just and unjust. I would be the first to advocate obeying just laws. One has not only a legal but a moral responsibility to obey just laws. Conversely, one has a moral responsibility to disobey unjust laws. I would agree with St. Augustine* that "an unjust law is no law at all."

Now, what is the difference between the two? How does one determine   16 whether a law is just or unjust? A just law is a man-made code that squares with the moral law or the law of God. An unjust law is a code that is out of harmony with the moral law. To put it in the terms of St. Thomas Aquinas:** An unjust law is a human law that is not rooted in eternal law and natural law. Any law that uplifts human personality is just. Any law that degrades

---

* Eds. note — Early church father and philosopher (354–430).
** Eds. note — Italian philosopher and theologian (1225–1274).

human personality is unjust. All segregation statutes are unjust because segregation distorts the soul and damages the personality. It gives the segregator a false sense of superiority and the segregated a false sense of inferiority. Segregation, to use the terminology of the Jewish philosopher Martin Buber, substitutes an "I-it" relationship for an "I-thou" relationship and ends up relegating persons to the status of things. Hence segregation is not only politically, economically, and sociologically unsound, it is morally wrong and sinful. Paul Tillich* has said that sin is separation. Is not segregation an existential expression of man's tragic separation, his awful estrangement, his terrible sinfulness? Thus it is that I can urge men to obey the 1954 decision of the Supreme Court, for it is morally right; and I can urge them to disobey segregation ordinances, for they are morally wrong.

Let us consider a more concrete example of just and unjust laws. An 17 unjust law is a code that a numerical or power majority group compels a minority group to obey but does not make binding on itself. This is *difference* made legal. By the same token, a just law is a code that a majority compels a minority to follow and that it is willing to follow itself. This is *sameness* made legal.

Let me give another explanation. A law is unjust if it is inflicted on a 18 minority that, as a result of being denied the right to vote, had no part in enacting or devising the law. Who can say that the legislature of Alabama which set up that state's segregation laws was democratically elected? Throughout Alabama all sorts of devious methods are used to prevent Negroes from becoming registered voters, and there are some counties in which, even though Negroes constitute a majority of the population, not a single Negro is registered. Can any law enacted under such circumstances be considered democratically structured?

Sometimes a law is just on its face and unjust in its application. For 19 instance, I have been arrested on a charge of parading without a permit. Now, there is nothing wrong in having an ordinance which requires a permit for a parade. But such an ordinance becomes unjust when it is used to maintain segregation and to deny citizens the First-Amendment privilege of peaceful assembly and protest.

I hope you are able to see the distinction I am trying to point out. In no 20 sense do I advocate evading or defying the law, as would the rabid segregationist. That would lead to anarchy. One who breaks an unjust law must do so openly, lovingly, and with a willingness to accept the penalty. I submit that an individual who breaks a law that conscience tells him is unjust, and who willingly accepts the penalty of imprisonment in order to arouse the conscience of the community over its injustice, is in reality expressing the highest respect for law.

Of course, there is nothing new about this kind of civil disobedi- 21 ence. It was evidenced sublimely in the refusal of Shadrach, Meshach, and

---

* Eds. note — American philosopher and theologian (1886–1965).

Abednego* to obey the laws of Nebuchadnezzar, on the ground that a higher moral law was at stake. It was practiced superbly by the early Christians, who were willing to face hungry lions and the excruciating pain of chopping blocks rather than submit to certain unjust laws of the Roman Empire. To a degree, academic freedom is a reality today because Socrates practiced civil disobedience. In our own nation, the Boston Tea Party represented a massive act of civil disobedience.

We should never forget that everything Adolph Hitler did in Germany   22 was "legal" and everything the Hungarian freedom fighters did in Hungary was "illegal." It was "illegal" to aid and comfort a Jew in Hitler's Germany. Even so, I am sure that, had I lived in Germany at the time, I would have aided and comforted my Jewish brothers. If today I lived in a Communist country where certain principles dear to the Christian faith are suppressed, I would openly advocate disobeying that country's antireligious laws.

I must make two honest confessions to you, my Christian and Jew-   23 ish brothers. First, I must confess that over the past few years I have been gravely disappointed with the white moderate. I have almost reached the regrettable conclusion that the Negro's great stumbling block in his stride toward freedom is not the White Citizens Counciler or the Ku Klux Klanner, but the white moderate, who is more devoted to "order" than to justice; who prefers a negative peace which is the absence of tension to a positive peace which is the presence of justice; who constantly says, "I agree with you in the goal you seek, but I cannot agree with your methods of direct action"; who paternalistically believes he can set the timetable for another man's freedom; who lives by a mythical concept of time and who constantly advises the Negro to wait for a "more convenient season." Shallow understanding from people of good will is more frustrating than absolute misunderstanding from people of ill will. Lukewarm acceptance is much more bewildering than outright rejection.

I had hoped that the white moderate would understand that law and   24 order exist for the purpose of establishing justice and that when they fail in this purpose they become the dangerously structured dams that block the flow of social progress. I had hoped that the white moderate would understand that the present tension in the South is a necessary phase of the transition from an obnoxious negative peace, in which the Negro passively accepted his unjust plight, to a substantive and positive peace, in which all men will respect the dignity and worth of human personality. Actually, we who engage in nonviolent direct action are not the creators of tension. We merely bring to the surface the hidden tension that is already alive. We bring it out in the open, where it can be seen and dealt with. Like a boil that can never be cured so long as it is covered up but must be opened with all its ugliness to the natural medicines of air and light, injustice must be

---

* Eds. note — In the Book of Daniel, three men who were thrown into a blazing fire for refusing to worship a golden statue.

exposed, with all the tension its exposure creates, to the light of human conscience and the air of national opinion, before it can be cured.

In your statement you assert that our actions, even though peaceful, 25 must be condemned because they precipitate violence. But is this a logical assertion? Isn't this like condemning a robbed man because his possession of money precipitated the evil act of robbery? Isn't this like condemning Socrates because his unswerving commitment to truth and his philosophical inquiries precipitated the act by the misguided populace in which they made him drink hemlock? Isn't this like condemning Jesus because his unique God-consciousness and never-ceasing devotion to God's will precipitated the evil act of crucifixion? We must come to see that, as the federal courts have consistently affirmed, it is wrong to urge an individual to cease his efforts to gain his basic constitutional rights because the quest may precipitate violence. Society must protect the robbed and punish the robber.

I had also hoped that the white moderate would reject the myth concerning time in relation to the struggle for freedom. I have just received a letter from a white brother in Texas. He writes: "All Christians know that the colored people will receive equal rights eventually, but it is possible that you are in too great a religious hurry. It has taken Christianity almost two thousand years to accomplish what it has. The teachings of Christ take time to come to earth." Such an attitude stems from a tragic misconception of time, from the strangely irrational notion that there is something in the very flow of time that will inevitably cure all ills. Actually, time itself is neutral; it can be used either destructively or constructively. More and more I feel that the people of ill will have used time much more effectively than have the people of good will. We will have to repent in this generation not merely for the hateful words and actions of the bad people, but for the appalling silence of the good people. Human progress never rolls in on wheels of inevitability; it comes through the tireless efforts of men willing to be coworkers with God, and without this hard work, time itself becomes an ally of the forces of social stagnation. We must use time creatively, in the knowledge that the time is always ripe to do right. Now is the time to make real the promise of democracy and transform our pending national elegy into a creative psalm of brotherhood. Now is the time to lift our national policy from the quicksand of racial injustice to the solid rock of human dignity.

You speak of our activity in Birmingham as extreme. At first I was rather 27 disappointed that fellow clergymen would see my nonviolent efforts as those of an extremist. I began thinking about the fact that I stand in the middle of two opposing forces in the Negro community. One is a force of complacency, made up in part of Negroes who, as a result of long years of oppression, are so drained of self-respect and a sense of "somebodiness" that they have adjusted to segregation; and in part of a few middle-class Negroes who, because of a degree of academic and economic security and because in some ways they profit by segregation, have become insensitive to the problems of the masses. The other force is one of bitterness and hatred, and it comes perilously close to advocating violence. It is expressed in the various black nationalist groups that are springing up across the nation, the largest and best-known being Elijah Muhammad's Muslim movement. Nourished by the Negro's frustration over the continued existence of racial discrimination, this movement is made up of people who have lost faith in America, who have absolutely repudiated Christianity, and who have concluded that the white man is an incorrigible "devil."

I have tried to stand between these two forces, saying that we need 28 emulate neither the "do-nothingism" of the complacent nor the hatred and despair of the black nationalist. For there is the more excellent way of love and nonviolent protest. I am grateful to God that, through the influence of the Negro church, the way of nonviolence became an integral part of our struggle.

If this philosophy had not emerged, by now many streets of the South 29 would, I am convinced, be flowing with blood. And I am further convinced that if our white brothers dismiss as "rabble-rousers" and "outside agitators" those of us who employ nonviolent direct action, and if they refuse to support our nonviolent efforts, millions of Negroes will, out of frustration and despair, seek solace and security in black-nationalist ideologies — a development that would inevitably lead to a frightening racial nightmare.

Oppressed people cannot remain oppressed forever. The yearning for 30 freedom eventually manifests itself, and that is what has happened to the American Negro. Something within has reminded him of his birthright of freedom, and something without has reminded him that it can be gained. Consciously or unconsciously, he has been caught up by the *Zeitgeist*, and with his black brothers of Africa and his brown and yellow brothers of Asia, South America, and the Caribbean, the United States Negro is moving with a sense of great urgency toward the promised land of racial justice. If one recognizes this vital urge that has engulfed the Negro community, one should readily understand why public demonstrations are taking place. The Negro has many pent-up resentments and latent frustrations, and he must release them. So let him march; let him make prayer pilgrimages to the city hall; let him go on freedom rides — and try to understand why he must do so. If his repressed emotions are not released in nonviolent ways, they will seek expression through violence; this is not a threat but a fact of history. So I have not said to my people, "Get rid of your discontent." Rather, I have tried to say that this normal and healthy discontent can be channeled into the creative outlet of nonviolent direct action. And now this approach is being termed extremist.

But though I was initially disappointed at being categorized as an 31 extremist, as I continued to think about the matter I gradually gained a measure of satisfaction from the label. Was not Jesus an extremist for love: "Love your enemies, bless them that curse you, do good to them that hate you, and pray for them which despitefully use you, and persecute you." Was not Amos an extremist for justice: "Let justice roll down like waters and righteousness like an everflowing stream." Was not Paul an extremist for the Christian gospel: "I bear in my body the marks of the Lord Jesus."

Was not Martin Luther an extremist: "Here I stand; I cannot do otherwise, so help me God." And John Bunyan: "I will stay in jail to the end of my days before I make a butchery of my conscience." And Abraham Lincoln: "This nation cannot survive half slave and half free." And Thomas Jefferson: "We hold these truths to be self-evident, that all men are created equal. . . ." So the question is not whether we will be extremists, but what kind of extremists we will be. Will we be extremists for hate or for love? Will we be extremists for the preservation of injustice or for the extension of justice? In that dramatic scene of Calvary's hill three men were crucified. We must never forget that all three were crucified for the same crime — the crime of extremism. Two were extremists for immorality, and thus fell below their environment. The other, Jesus Christ, was an extremist for love, truth, and goodness, and thereby rose above his environment. Perhaps the South, the nation, and the world are in dire need of creative extremists.

I hoped that the white moderate would see this need. Perhaps I was too 32 optimistic; perhaps I expected too much. I suppose I should have realized that few members of the oppressor race can understand the deep groans and passionate yearnings of the oppressed race, and still fewer have the vision to see that injustice must be rooted out by strong, persistent, and determined action. I am thankful, however, that some of our white brothers in the South have grasped the meaning of this social revolution and committed themselves to it. They are still all too few in quantity, but they are big in quality. Some — such as Ralph McGill, Lillian Smith, Harry Golden, James McBride Dabbs, Ann Braden, and Sarah Patton Boyle — have written about our struggle in eloquent and prophetic terms. Others have marched with us down nameless streets of the South. They have languished in filthy, roach-infested jails, suffering the abuse and brutality of policemen who view them as "dirty nigger-lovers." Unlike so many of their moderate brothers and sisters, they have recognized the urgency of the movement and sensed the need for powerful "action" antidotes to combat the disease of segregation.

Let me take note of my other major disappointment. I have been so 33 greatly disappointed with the white church and its leadership. Of course, there are some notable exceptions. I am not unmindful of the fact that each of you has taken some significant stands on this issue. I commend you, Reverend Stallings, for your Christian stand on this past Sunday, in welcoming Negroes to your worship service on a nonsegregated basis. I commend the Catholic leaders of this state for integrating Spring Hill College several years ago.

But despite these notable exceptions, I must honestly reiterate that I 34 have been disappointed with the church. I do not say this as one of those negative critics who can always find something wrong with the church. I say this as a minister of the gospel, who loves the church; who was nurtured in its bosom; who has been sustained by its spiritual blessings and who will remain true to it as long as the cord of life shall lengthen.

When I was suddenly catapulted into the leadership of the bus protest 35 in Montgomery, Alabama, a few years ago, I felt we would be supported by the white church. I felt that the white ministers, priests, and rabbis of the South would be among our strongest allies. Instead, some have been outright opponents, refusing to understand the freedom movement and misrepresenting its leaders; all too many others have been more cautious than courageous and have remained silent behind the anesthetizing security of stained-glass windows.

In spite of my shattered dreams, I came to Birmingham with the hope   36
that the white religious leadership of this community would see the justice of our cause and, with deep moral concern, would serve as the channel through which our just grievances could reach the power structure. I had hoped that each of you would understand. But again I have been disappointed.

There was a time when the church was very powerful — in the time   37
when the early Christians rejoiced at being deemed worthy to suffer for what they believed. In those days the church was not merely a thermometer that recorded the ideas and principles of popular opinion; it was a thermostat that transformed the mores of society. Whenever the early Christians entered a town, the people in power became disturbed and immediately sought to convict the Christians for being "disturbers of the peace" and "outside agitators." But the Christians pressed on, in the conviction that they were "a colony of heaven," called to obey God rather than man. Small in number, they were big in commitment. They were too God-intoxicated to be "astronomically intimidated." By their effort and example they brought an end to such ancient evils as infanticide and gladiatorial contests.

Things are different now. So often the contemporary church is a weak,   38
ineffectual voice with an uncertain sound. So often it is an archdefender of the status quo. Far from being disturbed by the presence of the church, the power structure of the average community is consoled by the church's silent — and often even vocal — sanction of things as they are.

But the judgment of God is upon the church as never before. If today's   39
church does not recapture the sacrificial spirit of the early church, it will lose its authenticity, forfeit the loyalty of millions, and be dismissed as an irrelevant social club with no meaning for the twentieth century. Every day I meet young people whose disappointment with the church has turned into outright disgust.

Perhaps I have once again been too optimistic. Is organized religion too   40
inextricably bound to the status quo to save our nation and the world? Perhaps I must turn my faith to the inner spiritual church, the church within the church, as the true *ekklesia** and the hope of the world. But again I am thankful to God that some noble souls from the ranks of organized religion have broken loose from the paralyzing chains of conformity and joined us as active partners in the struggle for freedom. They have left their secure congregations and walked the streets of Albany, Georgia, with us.

---

* Eds. note — Greek word for the early Christian church.

They have gone down the highways of the South on tortuous rides for freedom. Yes, they have gone to jail with us. Some have been dismissed from their churches, have lost the support of their bishops and fellow ministers. But they have acted in the faith that right defeated is stronger than evil triumphant. Their witness has been the spiritual salt that has preserved the true meaning of the gospel in these troubled times. They have carved a tunnel of hope through the dark mountain of disappointment.

41   I hope the church as a whole will meet the challenge of this decisive hour. But even if the church does not come to the aid of justice, I have no despair about the future. I have no fear about the outcome of our struggle in Birmingham, even if our motives are at present misunderstood. We will reach the goal of freedom in Birmingham and all over the nation, because the goal of America is freedom. Abused and scorned though we may be, our destiny is tied up with America's destiny. Before the pilgrims landed at Plymouth, we were here. Before the pen of Jefferson etched the majestic words of the Declaration of Independence across the pages of history, we were here. For more than two centuries our forebears labored in this country without wages; they made cotton king; they built the homes of their masters while suffering gross injustice and shameful humiliation — and yet out of a bottomless vitality they continued to thrive and develop. If the inexpressible cruelties of slavery could not stop us, the opposition we now face will surely fail. We will win our freedom because the sacred heritage of our nation and the eternal will of God are embodied in our echoing demands.

42   Before closing I feel impelled to mention one other point in your statement that has troubled me profoundly. You warmly commended the Birmingham police for keeping "order" and "preventing violence." I doubt that you would have so warmly commended the police force if you had seen its dogs sinking their teeth into unarmed, nonviolent Negroes. I doubt that you would so quickly commend the policemen if you were to observe their ugly and inhumane treatment of Negroes here in the city jail; if you were to watch them push and curse old Negro women and young Negro girls; if you were to see them slap and kick old Negro men and young boys; if you were to observe them, as they did on two occasions, refuse to give us food because we wanted to sing our grace together. I cannot join you in your praise of the Birmingham police department.

43   It is true that the police have exercised a degree of discipline in handling the demonstrators. In this sense they have conducted themselves rather "nonviolently" in public. But for what purpose? To preserve the vile system of segregation. Over the past few years I have consistently preached that nonviolence demands that the means we use must be as pure as the ends we seek. I have tried to make clear that it is wrong to use immoral means to attain moral ends. But now I must affirm that it is just as wrong, or perhaps even more so, to use moral means to preserve immoral ends. Perhaps Mr. Connor and his policemen have been rather nonviolent in public, as was Chief Pritchett in Albany, Georgia, but they have used the moral means of nonviolence to maintain the immoral end of racial injustice. As

T. S. Eliot has said, "The last temptation is the greatest treason: To do the right deed for the wrong reason."

I wish you had commended the Negro sit-inners and demonstrators   44
of Birmingham for their sublime courage, their willingness to suffer, and their amazing discipline in the midst of great provocation. One day the South will recognize its real heroes. They will be the James Merediths,* with the noble sense of purpose that enables them to face jeering and hostile mobs, and with the agonizing loneliness that characterizes the life of the pioneer. They will be old, oppressed, battered Negro women, symbolized in a seventy-two-year-old woman in Montgomery, Alabama, who rose up with a sense of dignity and with her people decided not to ride segregated buses, and who responded with ungrammatical profundity to one who inquired about her weariness: "My feets is tired, but my soul is at rest." They will be the young high school and college students, the young ministers of the gospel and a host of their elders, courageously and nonviolently sitting in at lunch counters and willingly going to jail for conscience's sake. One day the South will know that when these disinherited children of God sat down at lunch counters, they were in reality standing up for what is best in the American dream and for the most sacred values in our Judaeo-Christian heritage, thereby bringing our nation back to those great wells of democracy which were dug deeply by the founding fathers in their formulation of the Constitution and the Declaration of Independence.

Never before have I written so long a letter. I'm afraid it is much too   45
long to take your precious time. I can assure you that it would have been much shorter if I had been writing from a comfortable desk, but what else can one do when he is alone in a narrow jail cell, other than write long letters, think long thoughts, and pray long prayers?

If I have said anything in this letter that overstates the truth and in-   46
dicates an unreasonable impatience, I beg you to forgive me. If I have said anything that understates the truth and indicates my having a patience that allows me to settle for anything less than brotherhood, I beg God to forgive me.

I hope this letter finds you strong in the faith. I also hope that cir-   47
cumstances will soon make it possible for me to meet each of you, not as an integrationist or a civil-rights leader but as a fellow clergyman and a Christian brother. Let us all hope that the dark clouds of racial prejudice will soon pass away and the deep fog of misunderstanding will be lifted from our fear-drenched communities, and in some not too distant tomorrow the radiant stars of love and brotherhood will shine over our great nation with all their scintillating beauty.

Yours for the cause of Peace and Brotherhood,
Martin Luther King Jr.

• • •

---

* Eds. note — James Meredith was the first African American to enroll at the University of Mississippi.

Comprehension

1. King says he seldom answers criticism. Why not? Why, then, does he decide to do so in this instance?

2. Why do the other clergymen consider King's activities to be "'unwise and untimely'" (1)?

3. What reasons does King give for the demonstrations? Why does he think it is too late for negotiations?

4. What does King say *wait* means to black people?

5. What are the two types of laws King defines? What is the difference between the two?

6. What does King find illogical about the claim that the actions of his followers precipitate violence?

7. Why is King disappointed in the white church?

Purpose and Audience

1. Why, in the first paragraph, does King establish his setting (the Birmingham city jail) and define his intended audience?

2. Why does King begin his letter with a reference to his audience as "men of genuine good will" (1)? Is this phrase **ironic** in light of his later criticism of them? Explain.

3. What indicates that King is writing his letter to an audience other than his fellow clergymen?

4. What is the thesis of this letter? Is it stated or implied?

Style and Structure

1. Where does King seek to establish that he is a reasonable person?

2. Where does King address the objections of his audience?

3. As in the Declaration of Independence, transitions are important in King's letter. Identify the transitional words and phrases that connect the different parts of his argument.

4. Why does King cite Jewish, Catholic, and Protestant philosophers to support his position?

5. King relies heavily on appeals to authority (Augustine, Aquinas, Buber, Tillich, and others). Why do you think he uses this strategy?

6. King uses both induction and deduction in his letter. Find an example of each, and explain how they function in his argument.

7. Throughout the body of his letter, King criticizes his audience of white moderates. In his conclusion, however, he seeks to reestablish a harmonious relationship with them. How does he do this? Is he successful?

Vocabulary Projects

1. Define each of the following words as it is used in this selection.

affiliate (2)   devotees (12)   reiterate (34)
cognizant (4)   estrangement (16)   intimidated (37)
mutuality (4)   ordinances (16)   infanticide (37)
provincial (4)   anarchy (20)   inextricably (40)
gainsaying (6)   elegy (26)   scintillating (47)
unfettered (10)   incorrigible (27)
millennium (12)   emulate (28)

2. Locate five **allusions** to the Bible in this essay. Look up these allusions in an online Bible dictionary such as eastonsbibledictionary.com. Then, determine how these allusions help King express his ideas.

3. In paragraph 14, King refers to his "cup of endurance." What is this a reference to? How is the original phrase worded?

Journal Entry

Do you believe King's remarks go too far? Do you believe they do not go far enough? Explain.

Writing Workshop

1. Write an argumentative essay supporting a deeply held belief of your own. Assume that your audience, like King's, is not openly hostile to your position.

2. **Working with Sources.** Assume you are a militant political leader responding to Martin Luther King Jr. Argue that King's methods do not go far enough. Be sure to address potential objections to your position. You might want to consult a Web site such as http://mlk-kpp01.stanford .edu or read some newspapers and magazines from the 1960s to help you prepare your argument. Make sure you document all material you borrow from your sources, and include a works-cited page. (See Chapter 18 for information on MLA documentation.)

3. **Working with Sources.** Read your local newspaper for several days, collecting articles about a controversial subject that interests you. Using information from the articles, take a position on the issue, and write an essay supporting it. Make sure you document all material you borrow from your sources, and include a works-cited page. (See Chapter 18 for information on MLA documentation.)

Combining the Patterns

In "Letter from Birmingham Jail," King includes several passages of **narration**. Find two of these passages, and discuss what use King makes of narration. Why do you think narration plays such an important part in King's argument?

Thematic Connections

- "A Supreme Sotomayor: How My Country Has Caught Up to Me" (page 21)
- "Indian Education" (page 142)
- "Just Walk On By: A Black Man Ponders His Power to Alter Public Space" (page 240)
- "The 'Black Table' Is Still There" (page 349)
- "Two Ways to Belong in America" (page 404)

Are Internships Fair to Students?

According to the National Association of Colleges and Employers (NACE), 50 percent of graduating college students in 2008 had held internships — an increase from 17 percent in 1992. This statistic is not surprising given the career benefits provided by such positions: according to a NACE survey, 2010 college graduates who had internships received significantly higher salary offers on the job market than their classmates who did not.

Beyond their economic benefits, internships have other advantages as well. Students can try out a prospective career as they learn professional standards and get a true sense of the day-to-day experience of a particular job or corporate culture. In addition, most interns earn college credit for their work (although it is often unpaid). Students can also make valuable professional contacts, and they often come away from the internship experience with a portfolio that highlights their skills for potential employers.

Internships have drawbacks, however. For many undergraduates, such positions have become merely a résumé enhancer — another prerequisite to check off. Additionally, the emphasis on unpaid internships gives affluent students an advantage over those who cannot afford to work for free. Indeed, internships can be expensive. For example, the Robert F. Kennedy Center for Social Justice raised money by auctioning off media internships in 2010, and an unpaid position at *Vogue* magazine cost applicants $42,000. Critics of unpaid internships argue that companies are using interns as free labor instead of hiring entry-level employees. In response, the U.S. Department of Labor has recently reemphasized the rules of the Fair Labor Standards Act. Under these guidelines, interns cannot displace employees, and employers can derive no immediate economic advantage from the activities of an intern. If positions fail to meet these requirements, employers must pay interns minimum wage and overtime benefits or face legal action.

At this time of high unemployment and economic anxiety, the value of internships is coming under greater scrutiny. In "Take This Internship and Shove It," Anya Kamenetz questions the conventional wisdom that working without pay is the "best possible preparation for success." While doing so, she examines the effect of unpaid internships on the labor market and on the economy as a whole, as well as on individual interns. Jennifer Halperin is more optimistic than Kamenetz. As she writes in "No Pay? Many Interns Say, 'No Problem,'" questions about compensation and exploitation are secondary because "the value of internships can't be calculated in solely financial terms."

ANYA KAMENETZ

"Take This Internship and Shove It"

Born in Baltimore, Maryland, in 1980, Anya Kamenetz grew up in Louisiana and earned her undergraduate degree from Yale. She is currently a staff writer for *Fast Company* magazine, where she writes about sustainability, design, and innovation. Her work has also appeared in the *New York Times*, the *Washington Post*, and other publications. She is the author of *Generation Debt: How Our Future Was Sold Out for Student Loans, Bad Jobs, No Benefits, and Tax Cuts for Rich Geezers — And How to Fight Back* (2006) and *DIYU: Edupunks, Edupreneurs, and the Coming Transformation of Higher Education* (2010).

Background on Internships The roots of the modern internship date back to the apprenticeship system of medieval guilds. An apprentice provided labor in return for room, board, and training in a trade. In the late nineteenth and early twentieth centuries, professions such as medicine, teaching, engineering, and business began emphasizing the need for practical experience (even as higher education in these fields became focused on classroom learning). College internships developed, in part, to meet that demand. By the 1960s, '70s, and '80s, such positions bridged the gap between theoretical knowledge and hands-on experience and also served as opportunities for networking and recruiting. Internships — whether in the form of cooperative learning, mentoring, job shadowing, or practicums — are now standard practice for many college students and universities. Indeed, such experience has become a requirement in many fields, from entertainment to finance to physical therapy.

My younger sister has just arrived in New Orleans for the summer after 1 her freshman year at Yale. She will be consuming daily snowballs, the local icy treat, to ward off the heat, volunteering to help clean up neighborhoods damaged by Hurricane Katrina and working part time, for pay, at both a literary festival and a local restaurant. Meanwhile, most of her friends from college are headed for the new standard summer experience: the unpaid internship.

Instead of starting out in the mailroom for a pittance, this generation 2 reports for business upstairs without pay. A national survey by Vault, a career information Web site, found that 84 percent of college students in April planned to complete at least one internship before graduating. Also according to Vault, about half of all internships are unpaid.

I was an unpaid intern at a newspaper from March 2002, my senior 3 year, until a few months after graduation. I took it for granted, as most students do, that working without pay was the best possible preparation for success; parents usually agree to subsidize their offspring's internships on this basis. But what if we're wrong?

What if the growth of unpaid internships is bad for the labor market 4 and for individual careers?

Let's look at the risks to the lowly intern. First there are opportunity 5 costs. Lost wages and living expenses are significant considerations for the two-thirds of students who need loans to get through college. Since many internships are done for credit and some even cost money for the privilege of placement overseas or on Capitol Hill, those students who must borrow to pay tuition are going further into debt for internships.

Second, though their duties range from the menial to quasi- 6 professional, unpaid internships are not jobs, only simulations. And fake jobs are not the best preparation for real jobs.

Long hours on your feet waiting tables may not be particularly edify- 7 ing, but they teach you that work is a routine of obligation, relieved by external reward, where you contribute value to a larger enterprise. Newspapers and business magazines are full of articles expressing exasperation about how the Millennial-generation employee supposedly expects work to be exciting immediately, wears flip-flops to the office, and has no taste for dues-paying. However true this stereotype may be, the spread of the artificially fun internship might very well be adding fuel to it.

By the same token, internships promote overidentification with em- 8 ployers: I make sacrifices to work free, therefore I must love my work. A sociologist at the University of Washington, Gina Neff, who has studied the coping strategies of interns in communications industries, calls the phenomenon "performative passion." Perhaps this emotion helps explain why educated workers in this country are less and less likely to organize, even as full-time jobs with benefits go the way of the Pinto.

Although it's not being offered this year, the A.F.L.-C.I.O.'s Union 9 Summer internship program, which provides a small stipend, has shaped thousands of college-educated career organizers. And yet interestingly, the percentage of young workers who hold an actual union card is less than 5 percent, compared with an overall national private-sector union rate of 12.5 percent. How are twentysomethings ever going to win back health benefits and pension plans when they learn to be grateful to work for nothing?

So an internship doesn't teach you everything you need to know about coping in today's working world. What effect does it have on the economy as a whole? 10

The Bureau of Labor Statistics does not identify interns or track the economic impact of unpaid internships. But we can do a quick-and-dirty calculation: according to Princeton Review's *Internship Bible*, there were 100,000 internship positions in 2005. Let's assume that out of those, 50,000 unpaid interns are employed full time for 12 weeks each summer at an average minimum wage of $5.15 an hour. That's 11

> **"So an internship doesn't teach you everything you need to know about coping in today's working world. What effect does it have on the economy as a whole?"**

a nearly $124 million yearly contribution to the welfare of corporate America.

In this way, unpaid interns are like illegal immigrants. They create an 12 oversupply of people willing to work for low wages, or in the case of interns, literally nothing. Moreover, a recent survey by Britain's National Union of Journalists found that an influx of unpaid graduates kept wages down and patched up the gaps left by job cuts.

There may be more subtle effects as well. In an information economy, 13 productivity is based on the best people finding the jobs best suited for their talents, and interns interfere with this cultural capitalism. They fly in the face of meritocracy — you must be rich enough to work without pay to get your foot in the door. And they enhance the power of social connections over ability to match people with desirable careers. A 2004 study of business graduates at a large mid-Atlantic university found that the completion of an internship helped people find jobs faster but didn't increase their confidence that those jobs were a good fit.

With all this said, the intern track is not coming to an end any time 14 soon. More and more colleges are requiring some form of internship for graduation. Still, if you must do an internship, research shows you will get more out of it if you find a paid one.

A 1998 survey of nearly 700 employers by the Institute on Education 15 and the Economy at Columbia University's Teachers College found: "Compared to unpaid internships, paid placements are strongest on all measures of internship quality. The quality measures are also higher for those firms who intend to hire their interns." This shouldn't be too surprising — getting hired and getting paid are what work, in the real world, is all about.

• • •

Comprehension

1. In paragraph 5, Kamenetz mentions the "risks to the lowly intern" created by the growth of unpaid internships. What are these risks?

2. What is "performative passion" (8)? Why, according to Kamenetz, is it a potential problem?

3. What effects do unpaid internships have on the economy? What is Kamenetz's opinion of these effects?

4. How, according to Kamenetz, are unpaid interns comparable to illegal immigrants?

5. According to Kamenetz, how does a person's financial status affect his or her prospects for working as an intern?

Purpose and Audience

1. What is Kamenetz's overall purpose? What seems to have led her to write this article?

2. How would you characterize Kamenetz's target audience? Is she addressing more than one audience? What attitudes and preconceptions does she presume her readers bring to this essay?

3. How would you restate the essay's thesis in your own words?

4. While Kamenetz focuses primarily on interns, she also writes about the organizations and corporations that employ them. What is her attitude toward these employers? How can you tell?

5. Does Kamenetz seem to believe her argument will have any effect on the popularity of internships? Explain.

Style and Structure

1. At key points in "Take This Internship and Shove It," Kamenetz uses **rhetorical questions**. What purpose do they serve both in the structure of her argument and in the way she makes her overall point? Do you find these rhetorical questions effective? Why or why not?

2. What evidence does Kamenetz use to support her argument? Is this evidence relevant, representative, and sufficient?

3. Where in the essay does Kamenetz use an analogy? Do you think this analogy makes sense? Explain.

4. In paragraph 11, Kamenetz does a "quick-and-dirty calculation" to determine the effect of interns on the overall economy. Is her analysis here persuasive? Is it fair?

5. How does Kamenetz incorporate personal experience and anecdotal evidence into her essay? Is this kind of evidence convincing? Why or why not?

Vocabulary Projects

1. Define each of the following words as it is used in this selection.

   pittance (2)   stereotype (7)
   subsidize (3)   influx (12)
   menial (6)   meritocracy (13)
   edifying (7)

2. What does the prefix *quasi-* mean when added to a word, as in "quasi-professional" (6)? What point does Kamenetz reinforce by using this term?

3. In paragraph 5, Kamenetz refers to "opportunity costs." What does this term mean? What is its origin? Kamenetz notes that such costs are "significant considerations" for many students. Do you agree?

Journal Entry

Kamenetz cites a survey that says that "84 percent of college students . . . planned to complete at least one internship before graduating" (2), and she notes that more colleges are making internships a requirement. How do you explain the growing popularity of internships?

Writing Workshop

1. In paragraph 7, Kamenetz accepts the stereotype of the Millennial-generation employee as a person who "expects work to be exciting immediately, wears flip-flops to the office, and has no taste for dues-paying." Write an essay in which you argue that Kamenetz misjudges your generation's attitude toward work. Be sure to address the points she makes in paragraph 7 and to support your ideas with specific examples from your own experience.

2. **Working with Sources.** Kamenetz takes a more critical view of internships in "Take This Internship and Shove It" than Jennifer Halperin does in "No Pay? Many Interns Say, 'No Problem'" (page 588). Write an essay in which you compare and contrast their respective points of view. Where do they differ? What points do they both make? Which essay do you find more persuasive, and why? Be sure to document all material you borrow from your sources, and include a works-cited page. (See Chapter 18 for information on MLA documentation.)

3. Kamenetz offers a specific definition of work, stating that it is a "routine of obligation, relieved by external reward, where you contribute value to a larger enterprise" (7); she concludes her essay with the claim that "getting hired and getting paid are what work, in the real world, is all about" (15). Do you agree with her characterization of work? Should a job or career be "about" more than "getting hired and getting paid"? Write an essay explaining your own view of work.

Combining the Patterns

Where in this essay does Kamenetz use **cause and effect**? Where does she use **definition** — and how does it support her position?

Thematic Connections

- "Pink Floyd Night School" (page 116)
- "College Pressures" (page 450)
- "The Shame Game" (page 680)

JENNIFER HALPERIN

No Pay? Many Interns Say, "No Problem"

Jennifer Halperin is the internship and special projects coordinator at Columbia College in Chicago, Illinois. She writes a regular column about internships and networking for *Wallet Pop,* an online magazine devoted to consumer finance.

Background on Cooperative Education Programs While unpaid college internships give students opportunities to explore professions, college co-op (from "cooperative education") programs provide more formal career training. Co-ops are usually paid positions that provide academic credit toward graduation. In some co-op programs, students may have completed their coursework and focus entirely on their training; in other programs, they may alternate between academic work and full-time employment. The University of Cincinnati began the first cooperative learning project in 1906; it was designed to close the divide between the classroom and the workplace while allowing students to earn money in their chosen fields. Northeastern University in Boston began its own cooperative program for engineers in 1909, and many other institutions followed. Current research suggests that students get enormous benefits from such programs, including increased social skills and self-confidence. Over a thousand U.S. colleges now offer co-op programs.

A recent article in the *New York Times* about the growth of unpaid internships has spurred an interesting debate among many people — one that mirrors conversations I have with students almost daily. Several times each week, I receive queries from media outlets and other organizations and businesses seeking interns. Most of these opportunities are unpaid, offering (or sometimes requiring) college credit in exchange for the experience.

But a lack of pay doesn't seem to dissuade students from applying to many of these internships, particularly ones that offer the chance to gain useful professional skills and experience. To my surprise, paid internships don't always attract the most candidates. Location and intern duties play just as large a role in luring students to apply. And many of these students are juggling classes as well as part- or even full-time jobs — and sometimes even a child of their own — along with the internship.

After reading the *Times* piece, I took an informal survey of several recent and about-to-be graduates, some of whom are still looking for jobs, on whether they thought unpaid internships were worthwhile or fair, or should be illegal. I thought many would express frustration over having done work for which they weren't compensated monetarily. On the contrary, a common theme among their answers was that while paid internships would be better, unpaid internships were beneficial if they offered real-world, practical experience. The feeling I come away with is that unpaid internships are an important lesson in the concept of *caveat emptor*. As with any job, applicants should try to find out as much [as possible] ahead of time about the duties involved before signing on.

"I would definitely say unpaid internships are worth it," said Brittany Harris, who interned at NBC, CBS, and Kurtis Productions in Chicago as a college student and is now looking for a full-time job as a broadcast journalist. Her work in one internship led to an offer of part-time paid work with the company while she still was in school. "The experience you gain is indescribable," she says. Classes can only teach you so much about how the real world operates, "but nothing beats seeing how it works on a day-to-day basis. It's also a great way to network. I have heard of tons of interns eventually getting hired on to staff after they have completed college."

> "Unpaid internships are an important lesson in the concept of *caveat emptor.*" — 4

Some do express reservations. Thomas Pardee, who has done both 5 paid and unpaid internships, says he is becoming suspicious of unpaid opportunities, especially those requiring full-time hours.

"They are really only accessible to people who have the financial sup- 6 port from someone else to survive them," he says. He also notes that in many workplaces, the line between what an intern does and what an entry-level employee does is very sketchy. "And many don't offer nearly as much instruction or actual educational attention from supervisors as should be required," he says. "It's not a difficult stretch to assume many companies are unloading the burdens of their smaller paid staffs onto unpaid interns, and not giving them enough in return in terms of guidance or overall perspective in the industry, which is literally supposed to be the entire payoff when you don't get a paycheck."

But just about everyone else I asked found that they did, in fact, receive 7 just that kind of payoff — or certainly saw the potential.

"Unpaid internships are totally worth the hours you put in and the 8 hard work," says Hannah Ferdinand, a production assistant for *The Dr. Oz Show* who did five internships while in college. "Employees of the workplace understand that you are working and learning for free." It shows that you are serious about the career and are willing to put in the hard work needed for the reward of a potential job.

"Any type of experience in your field is good, it builds your résumé and 9 portfolio," says Priya Shah, who will graduate in May and is job-searching across the country. "Unpaid internships are worth it because you are building experience and contacts. And you may land a job after it's over. It's long hours, a lot of work, and then when you go out for lunch, you think 'Wait, how am I paying for this?' But you can learn skills that you wouldn't necessarily learn in a classroom."

Nick Orichuia, who grew up in Italy and came to the United States 10
for graduate school, says: "I think unpaid internships are almost always a
valuable experience, especially for students in college. It really is up to the
student to make the most of the internship. In most cases, I think employers are interested in pushing interns to the limits to see if they are valid
candidates to be hired someday. That is a great learning experience for the
intern. If the employer is not interested in developing the intern, then it's
up to the student to push himself or herself to learn as much as he or she
can. In my opinion, internships shouldn't only be seen as opportunities
to be hired in the place where one interns, but part of a larger learning
experience."

To its credit, Atlantic Media is pledging to begin paying all interns, and 11
it likely will see a more diverse pool of applicants as a result. Unfortunately,
not every employer can afford this kind of commitment.

Nobody respects and values interns' time more than I do. I am reminded 12
hourly of their hard work, energy, and tenaciousness. Do they deserve compensation? Yes. But the value of internships can't be calculated in solely
financial terms. And unpaid interns go a long way toward breaking the
stereotype that today's youth are emotionally spoiled, demanding of praise
and tangible reward at every turn. One's perception as an industrious
worker — even without a paycheck — can be worth its weight in gold.

• • •

Comprehension

1. According to Halperin, what factors make internships attractive to college
   students and recent graduates? Why is she surprised by the results of her
   survey?

2. Halperin notices a "common theme" in her discussions with "recent and
   about-to-be graduates" (3). What attitudes about internships do they
   seem to share?

3. According to this essay, what can limit access to internships?

4. This essay presents the results of an informal survey of attitudes toward
   internships. Summarize the advantages and disadvantages of internships
   that were revealed in the survey.

Purpose and Audience

1. Why do you think Halperin wrote this essay? In what sense is it part of a
   larger discussion?

2. For the most part, Halperin quotes or summarizes the statements of
   others. However, she does take a position on the value of internships.
   How would you express this position?

3. Who is the intended audience for this essay? How can you tell?

4. Halperin is an internship coordinator at a college. How do you think her job might have influenced (or even determined) her point of view on this subject?

Style and Structure

1. Halperin's evidence consists almost entirely of the results of an informal survey. Do you think this evidence is sufficient? Is all of it relevant?

2. In paragraph 3, Halperin writes the following about those she surveyed: "I thought many would express frustration over having done work for which they weren't compensated monetarily." How could you revise this sentence to make it clearer and more concise? What other sentences could you revise? Give specific examples.

3. Is Halperin's essay structured inductively or deductively? Explain.

4. How would you characterize Halperin's tone? Is this tone appropriate in light of her overall purpose?

5. How does Halperin use her personal experience and opinions? Why do you think she places this material where she does?

Vocabulary Projects

1. Define each of the following words as it is used in this selection.

   spurred (1)   tangible (12)
   queries (1)   industrious (12)
   tenaciousness (12)

2. According to Halperin, internships teach an important lesson about the "concept of *caveat emptor*" (3). What does *caveat emptor* mean, and what are its origins? Does the term make sense in the context of this essay? Why or why not?

3. Consider the writer's use of the word *sketchy* (6). What does the word mean in this context? What synonym would convey the same meaning?

Journal Entry

Have you ever been an intern? Does your experience support Halperin's conclusions? If you have not had an internship, do you plan to look for one? Why or why not?

Writing Workshop

1. Halperin suggests that some employers assign tasks to interns that blur the boundaries between interns and paid employees; moreover, she believes, employers do not give interns enough of a return, either financially or in terms of guidance. Do you think internships exploit students,

or do you see them as an opportunity for students to gain responsibility and experience? Write an essay in which you take a position on this issue.

2. **Working with Sources.** Both Halperin and Kamenetz (page 583) refer explicitly to negative stereotypes of today's youth and of the Millennial generation. Conduct your own informal survey regarding this stereotype; then, write an essay either supporting or refuting its accuracy. If you refer to Halperin or Kamenetz, be sure to document all material that you borrow, and include a works-cited page. (See Chapter 18 for information on MLA documentation.)

3. **Working with Sources.** Kamenetz uses the term "performative passion," a concept she borrows from a sociologist, to describe the "coping strategies" of interns who overidentify with their employers — and mistakenly confuse "self-sacrifice" with "love" for a job. Is "performative passion" a real problem? Do you think Halperin's essay encourages this attitude? Write an argumentative essay that answers these questions. Be sure to document all material that you borrow from Halperin's essay and to include a works-cited page. (See Chapter 18 for information on MLA documentation.)

Combining the Patterns

Throughout this essay, Halperin uses **exemplification** to clarify, explain, persuade, and create interest. Identify the specific examples used in this essay, and note how each example supports a broader point or generalization. What other kinds of examples could Halperin have used to support her argument?

Thematic Connections

- "Pink Floyd Night School" (page 116)
- "My Mother Never Worked" (page 121)
- "The Shame Game" (page 680)

Should American Citizenship Be a Birthright?

The United States is a nation of immigrants. In ways both large and small, immigrants from around the world have contributed to American culture, to its economic and physical growth, to its political power, and to its reputation as a beacon to the world. However, immigration has also been a source of controversy in the United States — a controversy that existed even before the nation's founding. In 1753, for example, Benjamin Franklin worried about the influx of Germans to Pennsylvania: "They will soon outnumber us . . . and even our government will be precarious."

Still, from the earliest years of the republic, America has had mechanisms for assimilating people from other countries. In 1790, the United States passed the first naturalization law, which established the process for foreign nationals to become American citizens. In addition, in 1868, the Fourteenth Amendment made birthright citizenship a part of the United States Constitution. The amendment begins, "All persons born or naturalized in the United States, and subject to the jurisdiction thereof, are citizens of the United States and of the State wherein they reside." In the last several years, however, some Americans have questioned the merits of birthright citizenship — especially as debates about illegal immigration have become more heated and contentious.

Currently, approximately 12 million undocumented immigrants live in the United States. Opponents of birthright citizenship argue that this policy increases the country's immigration problem by encouraging foreign nationals to have so-called "anchor babies," who they hope will give them access to social services — and, eventually, to citizenship. A 2010 study by the Pew Hispanic Center estimated that the number of children of undocumented immigrants who have received birthright citizenship grew from 2.7 million in 2003 to 4 million in 2008. As Speaker of the U.S. House of Representatives John Boehner says, "In certain parts of our country, clearly, our schools, our hospitals are being overrun by illegal immigrants, a lot of whom came here just so their children could become U.S. citizens." Some officials have proposed a constitutional amendment to end birthright citizenship. Other lawmakers opposed to birthright citizenship are considering legal measures at the state level.

For most legal scholars and historians, however, the long-standing interpretation of the Fourteenth Amendment is settled law. Supporters of birthright citizenship argue that the practice reflects the country's democratic character, its constitutional values, and its tradition of widening the community of people regarded as "Americans." Moreover, some political officials argue that targeting the Fourteenth Amendment is merely a distraction from enacting real immigration reform. In "The Case for Birthright Citizenship," Linda Chavez argues that abandoning this principle is a "terrible idea" that would "fundamentally change what it means to be an American." She also warns that doing so will "jeopardize the electoral future of the GOP by alienating Hispanics." George F. Will makes the case against birthright citizenship in "An Argument to Be Made about Immigrant Babies and Citizenship." To "drain some scalding steam from immigration arguments," Will proposes a reading of the Fourteenth Amendment that brings it "into conformity with what the authors of its text intended, and with common sense."

LINDA CHAVEZ

The Case for Birthright Citizenship

Linda Chavez is chair of the Center of Equal Opportunity, a Virginia-based public policy research organization. In 1983, President Ronald Reagan named her staff director for the U.S. Commission on Civil Rights. She subsequently held a number of other government posts, including chair of the National Commission on Migrant Education. Chavez is the author of *Out of the Barrio: Toward a New Politics of Hispanic Assimilation* (1991), *An Unlikely Conservative: The Transformation of an Ex-Liberal, or How I Became the Most Hated Hispanic in America* (2002), and *Betrayal: How Union Bosses Shake Down Their Members and Corrupt American Politics* (2004). She is also a columnist whose work has appeared in the *Washington Post,* the *Wall Street Journal,* and many other publications. In 2000, Chavez was named a Library of Congress "Living Legend" for her contributions to America's cultural and social heritage.

Background on birthright citizenship in other countries Originally enacted to guarantee citizenship to freed slaves, the Fourteenth Amendment to the United States Constitution grants automatic citizenship to anyone born on American soil — including the children of undocumented immigrants. This principle is known as *jus soli,* or "right of the soil." Many countries practice *jus soli* citizenship, including Argentina, Mexico, Canada, and Pakistan. France, the United Kingdom, and other states use a modified version of *jus soli,* imposing an additional requirement for citizenship, such as having a parent who is a permanent resident. Most countries, however, still use the principle of *jus sanguina,* or "right of blood." Under this rule, an individual gains citizenship by having an ancestor who is a national or citizen of the state. For example, Israel's *jus sanguina* system automatically grants citizenship to Jews and the descendants of Israeli Arabs all over the world but not to the offspring of foreign workers within the country. Likewise, Ireland allows any person with an Irish grandparent to become a citizen — and to pass that right to Irish nationality on to his or her own children. Germany, which traditionally had a strong *jus sanguina* system, has recently loosened its citizenship laws. As of 2002, children born on German soil can claim citizenship if one of their parents has lived in the country legally for eight years. Debates about birthright citizenship lead to larger questions about the meaning of the word "citizen." For example, is citizenship a function of both blood and heritage? What standards must an individual meet to be a citizen?

Republican leaders in Congress are now flirting with changing portions of the Fourteenth Amendment — which grants citizenship to "all persons born or naturalized in the United States and subject to the jurisdiction thereof" — to deny citizenship to children born here to illegal immigrants.

The idea of modifying birthright citizenship has been around for de- 2
cades but was previously relegated to the fringes of the immigration restriction movement. Yet in recent days, Sens. John McCain, Lindsey Graham,
and Jon Kyl have embraced the idea; Senate and House GOP leaders Mitch
McConnell and John Boehner have proposed hearings.

Repealing birthright citizenship is a terrible idea. It will unquestionably 3
jeopardize the electoral future of the GOP by alienating Hispanics — the
largest minority and fastest-growing segment of the U.S. population. More
importantly, ending birthright citizenship would fundamentally change
what it means to be an American.

Proponents of repeal argue that the Fourteenth Amendment was 4
passed after the Civil War to guarantee citizenship to freed slaves, and that
it was never intended to grant rights to the offspring of illegal aliens. But
this argument is a non sequitur. At the time of the adoption of the amendment, there was no category of "illegal alien" because immigration was un-
restricted and unregulated. If you secured passage to the United States, or
simply walked across the open border with Mexico or Canada, you could
stay permanently as a resident alien or apply to be naturalized after a certain number of years. And if you happened to give birth while still an alien,
your child was automatically a citizen — a right dating back to English
common law.

The most serious challenge to birthright citizenship for the children of 5
aliens came in 1898, and it involved a class of aliens who were every bit as
unpopular as present-day illegal immigrants: the Chinese. Like most illegal
immigrants today, the Chinese came here to work as common laborers, eagerly recruited by employers but often deeply resented by the workers with
whom they competed. This popular resentment, coupled with racial prejudice, led to America's first immigration restriction law, the Chinese Exclusion Act of 1882. It was followed by successively more restrictive federal
and state laws that denied Chinese aliens — and, later, other Asians — the
right to own property, to marry, to return to the U.S. if they left, or to become American citizens.

With anti-Chinese alien sentiment still high, the Supreme Court took 6
up the case *U.S. v. Wong Kim Ark* in 1898. Born in San Francisco to alien parents who later returned to China, Wong traveled to his parents' homeland
for a visit and was denied re-entry on his return in 1895. The government
argued that Wong had no right to birthright citizenship under the Fourteenth Amendment because his parents remained "subjects of the emperor
of China" not subject to U.S. jurisdiction, even while residing in California
at the time of his birth. In a 7–2 vote, the Supreme Court ruled otherwise.

The court found that the only persons Congress intended to exclude 7
from birthright citizenship under the Fourteenth Amendment were children born to diplomats — an ancient, universally recognized exception
even under common law; Indians, who by treaty were considered members
of sovereign nations; and children of an occupying enemy. "The amendment, in clear words and in manifest intent, includes the children born

within the territory of the United States of all other persons, of whatever race or color, domiciled within the United States," wrote Justice Horace Gray for the majority. To hold otherwise, he noted, would be to deny citizenship to the descendants of English, Irish, German, and other aliens who had always been considered citizens even if their parents were citizens of other countries. For more than 100 years, the court has consistently upheld this analysis.

Our history has been largely one of continuously expanding the community of people regarded as Americans, from native-born whites to freed slaves to Indians to naturalized citizens of all races and ethnicities. Since the abolition of slavery, we have never denied citizenship to any group of children born in the U.S. — even when we denied citizenship to their parents, as we did Asian immigrants from 1882 to 1943. This expansive view of who is an American has been critical to our successful assimilation of millions of newcomers.

> " Since the abolition of slavery, we have never denied citizenship to any group of children born in the U.S. . . . "

Conservatives should not betray these values based on a misreading of American history and legal precedent. Instead of amending the Constitution to eliminate "anchor babies" — the ugly term opponents of birthright citizenship use to describe these U.S. citizens — Republicans should be helping them become good Americans.

• • •

Comprehension

1. What specific events motivated Chavez to write this column?

2. Chavez claims that repealing birthright citizenship is a "terrible idea" (3). What consequences does she see for the Republican Party if Republicans repeal birthright citizenship?

3. According to Chavez, what "class of aliens" once occupied a place similar to "present-day illegal immigrants" (5)?

4. At the time of the adoption of the Fourteenth Amendment, why was there no category of "illegal alien"?

Purpose and Audience

1. Where does Chavez state her thesis? Restate it in your own words.

2. Chavez's column was published in the politically conservative, pro-business *Wall Street Journal.* Do you think she expects her audience to agree with her position? How can you tell?

3. Chavez implies that illegal immigrants are unpopular. How might politicians use this sentiment to their own advantage?

4. Chavez makes a number of broad statements about American history. Give some examples. How do these statements support her argument? How convincing are they?

Style and Structure

1. Where does Chavez address opposing arguments? Does she refute them effectively?

2. Chavez claims that her opponents commit a logical fallacy. Which fallacy is it? Do you agree with her?

3. Paragraph 3 opens with the direct statement, "Repealing birthright citizenship is a terrible idea." Given Chavez's audience, do you think this is an effective opening strategy, or do you think she should have stated her position with more subtlety?

4. The immigration debate is contentious and highly polarized. Does Chavez sound angry? Conciliatory? Hopeful?

5. What point does Chavez make in paragraph 7? Do you find it persuasive? Why or why not?

6. Where does Chavez use analogy? Do you find the comparisons she makes effective? Explain.

Vocabulary Projects

1. Define each of the following words as it is used in this selection.

   relegated (2)   manifest (7)
   repealing (3)   domiciled (7)
   resentment (5)   assimilation (8)
   sentiment (6)   precedent (9)
   sovereign (7)

2. Chavez writes that the "idea of modifying birthright citizenship has been around for decades but was previously relegated to the fringes of the immigration restriction movement" (2). What does the word *fringes* mean in this context? What connotations does it have? Why are these connotations important for her overall argument?

3. According to the writer, *anchor babies* is an "ugly term" (9). Do you agree? Why or why not?

Journal Entry

Chavez refers to America's "successful assimilation of millions" of immigrants (8). What qualities indicate to you that an immigrant has "successfully assimilated"?

Writing Workshop

1. **Working with Sources.** George Will (page 600) considers birthright citizenship to be at odds both with common sense and with a correct interpretation of the Fourteenth Amendment. In contrast, Chavez claims that arguments such as Will's are based on a *non sequitur*. Which writer do you find more persuasive? Write an essay that evaluates their respective positions and explains your own position on this issue. Make sure that you document all words and ideas that you borrow from the essays and that you include a works-cited page. (See Chapter 18 for information on MLA documentation.)

2. **Working with Sources.** Chavez implies that illegal aliens are unpopular with most Americans. Do you think she is correct? Using information from newspapers, magazines, popular media, the Internet, and other sources, write an essay in which you take a stand on this issue. Make sure that you document material you borrow from your sources and that you include a works-cited page. (See Chapter 18 for information on MLA documentation.)

3. In paragraph 3, Chavez writes that "ending birthright citizenship would fundamentally change what it means to be an American." Do you agree? Why or why not? Write an essay justifying your position.

Combining the Patterns

What pattern of development does Chavez use to support her claim that American history "has been largely one of continuously expanding the community of people regarded as Americans" (8)?

Thematic Connections

- "Two Ways to Belong in America" (page 404)
- "Mother Tongue" (page 466)
- "U.S. Census 2010 Form" (page 501)

GEORGE F. WILL

An Argument to Be Made about Immigrant Babies and Citizenship

Pulitzer Prize–winning political columnist George F. Will was born in 1941 in Champaign, Illinois. After receiving an undergraduate degree at Trinity College and a master's degree from Oxford, Will earned an M.A. and a Ph.D. in political science at Princeton University. He taught at the University of Toronto and the University of Michigan and then served on the staff of Colorado senator Gordon Allot from 1970 to 1972. Will began his journalism career as a writer and editor at the *National Review,* a conservative magazine, in the early 1970s. Since 1974, Will has written a nationally syndicated political column for the *Washington Post.* He is also the author of several books, including *Men at Work: The Craft of Baseball* (1988), *Restoration: Congress, Term Limits, and the Recovery of Deliberative Democracy* (1992), and *One Man's America: The Pleasures and Provocations of Our Singular Nation* (2008), a collection of his columns.

Background on children born to non-U.S. citizens Will cites congressional testimony estimating that nearly 10 percent of all recent U.S. births "have been to mothers who are here illegally." According to a report by the nonpartisan Pew Hispanic Center, that figure is approximately correct. The study found that while undocumented immigrants make up just over 4 percent of the population, they are producing 8 percent of the nation's babies: 340,000 of the 4.3 million children born in the United States in 2008. Estimates of the total undocumented immigrant population generally vary between 10 and 12 million; according to the Pew Center, 11.1 million were living in the United States in 2009, down from a peak of 12 million in 2007. Researchers attribute the decline both to a weak economy and to stricter border enforcement. Most undocumented immigrants come from Mexico (6.65 million), followed by El Salvador (530,000), Guatemala (480,000), Honduras (320,000), the Philippines (270,000), India (200,000), and South Korea (2,000). California has the largest population of undocumented immigrants in the United States: 8 percent of the state's population. California's Department of Health Services birth statistics do not include the legal status of new parents, but the department's records indicate that nearly half the state's babies are born to immigrant mothers (legal immigrants in the state outnumber illegal immigrants by 3 to 1).

   A simple reform would drain some scalding steam from immigration 1 arguments that may soon again be at a roiling boil. It would bring the interpretation of the Fourteenth Amendment into conformity with what the authors of its text intended, and with common sense, thereby removing an incentive for illegal immigration.

To end the practice of "birthright citizenship," all that is required is to   2
correct the misinterpretation of that amendment's first sentence: "All persons born or naturalized in the United States, and subject to the jurisdiction thereof, are citizens of the United States and of the State wherein they reside." From these words has flowed the practice of conferring citizenship on children born here to illegal immigrants.

A parent from a poor country, writes professor Lino Graglia of the University of Texas law school, "can hardly do more for a child than make him   3
or her an American citizen, entitled to all the advantages of the American welfare state." Therefore, "It is difficult to imagine a more irrational and self-defeating legal system than one which makes unauthorized entry into this country a criminal offense and simultaneously provides perhaps the greatest possible inducement to illegal entry."

Writing in the *Texas Review of Law and Politics,* Graglia says this irra-   4
tionality is rooted in a misunderstanding of the phrase "subject to the jurisdiction thereof." What was this intended or understood to mean by those who wrote it in 1866 and ratified it in 1868? The authors and ratifiers could not have intended birthright citizenship for illegal immigrants because in 1868 *there were and never had been any illegal immigrants* because *no law ever had restricted immigration.*

If those who wrote and ratified the Fourteenth Amendment *had* imag-   5
ined laws restricting immigration — and had anticipated huge waves of illegal immigration — is it reasonable to presume they would have wanted to provide the reward of citizenship to the children of the violators of those laws? Surely not.

The Civil Rights Act of 1866 begins with language from which the   6
Fourteenth Amendment's citizenship clause is derived: "All persons born in the United States, *and not subject to any foreign power,* excluding Indians not taxed, are hereby declared to be citizens of the United States." (Emphasis added.) The explicit exclusion of Indians from birthright citizenship was not repeated in the Fourteenth Amendment because it was considered unnecessary. Although Indians were at least partially subject to U.S. jurisdiction, they owed allegiance to their tribes, not the United States. This reasoning — divided allegiance — applies equally to exclude the children of resident aliens, legal as well as illegal, from birthright citizenship. Indeed, today's regulations issued by the departments of Homeland Security and Justice stipulate:

"A person born in the United States to a foreign diplomatic officer   7
accredited to the United States, as a matter of international law, is not subject to the jurisdiction of the United States. That person is not a United States citizen under the 14th Amendment."

Senator Lyman Trumbull of Illinois was, Graglia writes, one of two   8
"principal authors of the citizenship clauses in [the] 1866 act and the Fourteenth Amendment." He said that "subject to the jurisdiction of the United States" meant subject to its "complete" jurisdiction, meaning "not owing allegiance to anybody else." Hence children whose Indian parents had tribal allegiances were excluded from birthright citizenship.

Appropriately, in 1884 the Supreme Court held that children born to 9 Indian parents were not born "subject to" U.S. jurisdiction because, among other reasons, the person so born could not change his status by his "own will without the action or assent of the United States." And "no one can become a citizen of a nation without its consent." Graglia says this decision "seemed to establish" that U.S. citizenship is "a consensual relation, requiring the consent of the United States." So: "This would clearly settle the question of birthright citizenship for children of illegal aliens. There cannot be a more total or forceful denial of consent to a person's citizenship than to make the source of that person's presence in the nation illegal."

Congress has heard testimony estimating that more than two-thirds of 10 all births in Los Angeles public hospitals, and more than half of all births in that city, and nearly 10 percent of all births in the nation in recent years, have been to mothers who are here illegally. Graglia seems to establish that there is no constitutional impediment to Congress ending the granting of birthright citizenship to those whose presence here is "not only without the government's consent but in violation of its law."

> "There cannot be a more total or forceful denial of consent to a person's citizenship than to make the source of that person's presence in the nation illegal."

. . .

Comprehension

1. Will notes that debates about immigration are contentious. What reform, according to Will, could quiet down the controversy? Do you agree with his suggestion?

2. In Will's view, where does the concept of birthright citizenship come from?

3. Throughout his essay, Will cites legal scholar Lino Graglia. Why does Graglia think parents from poor countries give birth to children in the United States? What does he see as the primary "inducement" (3)?

4. According to Will, how do we know that the "authors and ratifiers" of the Fourteenth Amendment "could not have intended birthright citizenship for illegal immigrants" (4)?

5. According to Will, what groups — historically and presently — are already excluded from birthright citizenship? How do these exceptions strengthen his argument?

Purpose and Audience

1. What is Will's thesis? How would you restate it in your own words?

2. What is the purpose of this essay? That is, what does Will hope to achieve?

3. Will quotes extensively from Lino Graglia's scholarly article published in the *Texas Review of Law and Politics*. Who is Will's audience? How is it similar to or different from Graglia's?

4. Do you think Will should have included evidence from a wider range of sources? Does the Graglia article provide enough support?

5. Will does not specifically address any opposing arguments. Do you think this weakens his argument? Why or why not?

6. Will closes his essay by citing statistics on birthrates among undocumented immigrants. Why does he end this way? Do you think this concluding strategy is effective? Can you suggest an additional closing sentence that would end his argument more forcefully?

Style and Structure

1. Will believes that a particular interpretation of the Fourteenth Amendment will change the terms of the immigration debate, particularly regarding birthright citizenship. In what sense is his essay a deductive argument?

2. Where does Will use an analogy to support his position? Do you think his comparison is valid? Why or why not?

3. What opinion does Will seem to have about those who disagree with his argument? How can you tell? Does he explicitly address their arguments?

4. In what respects is this a definition essay? What is being defined? How is the definition developed?

Vocabulary Project

1. Define each of the following words as it is used in this selection.

scalding (1)   inducement (3)
incentive (1)   anticipated (5)
naturalized (2)   accredited (7)
jurisdiction (2)   consensual (9)
conferring (2)   impediment (10)

2. In paragraph 3, Will quotes Graglia in reference to "all the advantages of the American welfare state." What denotation does the term *welfare state* have? What connotations does it have?

3. How is the word *Indian* (9) different from terms such as *Native American, Amerindian,* or even *indigenous people*? Is the word *Indian* appropriate in this context, or should Will have used another term?

Journal Entry

1. Will's essay addresses the legal meaning of citizenship in the context of debates about immigration. What does *citizenship* mean to you? What

privileges and obligations go along with it? How is its meaning for you shaped by your own ethnic or cultural background?

Writing Workshop

1. Do you support birthright citizenship? Why or why not? Write an argumentative essay that takes a position on the issue.

2. **Working with Sources.** George Will cites law professor Lino Graglia, who (in Will's view) interprets the Fourteenth Amendment in "conformity with what the authors of its text intended, and with common sense" (1). Read the amendment yourself, and then do some research to find a legal expert with an opinion that is different from Graglia's. Write an essay in which you compare and contrast the two different interpretations of the Fourteenth Amendment. Which interpretation of the amendment do you find more convincing, and why? Be sure to document all material that you borrow from your sources, and include a works-cited page. (See Chapter 18 for information on MLA documentation.)

3. According to Will, almost 10 percent of recent U.S. births have been to mothers who are in the United States illegally. What is your reaction to this statistic? Do you think illegal immigration is a major problem in America? Write an essay that explains your view of the immigration debate.

Combining the Patterns

Find an example of **classification and division** in Will's essay. How does this pattern strengthen his argument?

Thematic Connections

- "Indian Education" (page 142)
- "Two Ways to Belong in America" (page 404)
- "U.S. Census 2010 Form" (page 501)

How Can We Address the Shortage of Organ Donors?

The first human allotransplant — a transfer of an organ or tissue between two individuals of the same species — took place in 1905, when Austrian ophthalmologist Eduard Zirm attached sections from a donor's cornea to the damaged eyes of a patient suffering from glaucoma. The procedure was a success, but transplantation of other organs proved more difficult because of the human immune system's tendency to reject foreign tissue. In 1954, doctors at Peter Bent Brigham Hospital in Boston sidestepped this problem by transplanting a kidney from one living twin brother to another — the first truly successful operation of its kind. Eventually, the development of immunosuppressants such as cortisone, azathioprine, and later, cyclosporine, made transplantations more feasible and thus more widely available. The first successful heart transplant took place in Johannesburg, South Africa, in 1967. By the 1980s, such procedures were common. The one-year survival rate for heart, liver, pancreas, and kidney recipients is now between 75 and 95 percent.

However, as transplantation has become safe and widely practiced, another problem has arisen: a chronic shortage of organ and tissue donors. Most states allow residents to register as donors on their driver's licenses, and according to Donate Life America, over 86 million Americans have done so. Still, more than 100,000 candidates are currently waiting for organs, and several thousand will die each year while waiting for a transplant. This shortage has led to a black market — even in the United States — and some Americans have engaged in so-called transplant tourism by seeking organs abroad that they cannot find at home.

The persistent shortage of organs has led some to reevaluate the U.S. organ-donation system. America has an "opt-in" policy: that is, individuals must actively choose to become donors. If the potential donor dies, however, the decision to donate organs rests with the family — even if the deceased has checked the donor box on his or her driver's license. In contrast, many other countries, including Israel, Austria, and Spain, now assume "presumed consent": everyone is a potential donor at the time of death unless a person opts out of the program. Advocates of this "opt-out" policy argue that it would significantly increase donation rates in the United States, where thousands of viable organs now go to waste every year. In addition, although United States law forbids the sale of organs, other countries are experimenting with legal organ markets.

The four essays in this casebook highlight the many complex issues involved in formulating organ-donor policies. In "The Meat Market," economist Alex Tabarrok examines America's shortage of donors and the global market for organs. He sees major changes in U.S. policy — whether toward presumed consent or even payment for organs — as inevitable, given that "pressure is mounting for innovation." In "The Case for Mandatory Organ Donation," Scott Carney highlights the inefficiencies of an American system where "more than half the population of the United States [is] willing to donate organs after death," but too many transplant organs "get lost in a bureaucratic shuffle." His essay also addresses issues of privacy and social class. In "Yes, Let's Pay for Organs," Charles Krauthammer writes in support of a 1999 Pennsylvania state legislative initiative that would have allowed the relatives of deceased donors to receive financial compensation to be put toward funeral expenses. Although it was never enacted, the proposal is used to support Krauthammer's argument that we should permit incentive payments even as the state must work to preserve "that little thing called human dignity." Finally, Virginia Postrel's "The Surgery Was Simple; the Process Is Another Story" recounts her experience donating a kidney to someone she barely knew. In addressing misperceptions about living donors, she focuses on the personal, emotional reactions to living donations that shape public policy, pointing out, "Most people have a visceral reaction against the whole idea."

ALEX TABARROK

The Meat Market

Economist Alex Tabarrok (b. 1966) is an associate professor at George Mason University, where he earned his Ph.D. in 1994. He also serves as the Bartley J. Madden Chair in Economics at the Mercatus Center, a research institute at George Mason University focused on market-driven ideas. In addition, he is research director of the Independent Institute, an organization that studies social and economic issues. The author, coauthor, and editor of several books, including *Modern Principles: Microeconomics* (2009), Tabarrok has published widely in the field of economics. Additionally, he blogs at the economics Web site marginalrevolution.com. "The Meat Market" was originally published in the *Wall Street Journal* in 2010.

Background on organ donation and shortages of donor organs Currently, most donor organs come from patients officially pronounced brain dead. Shortages of donors — and the thousands of people who die each year waiting for transplants — have led many in the medical community and the federal government to advocate a more aggressive practice: donation after cardiac death (DCD) rather than after brain death. Some question the ethics of such "organ harvesting," particularly if done in the high-pressure, fast-paced environment of hospital intensive care units and emergency rooms. The fact remains, however, that more than 100,000 people are now waiting for transplant surgeries. According to official government statistics, this number is rising faster than the number of available donors. The overwhelming majority of these patients need kidneys (86,142), followed by livers (16,022), and hearts (3,149). In the United States, the individual states enact their own donation laws; many allow people to become prospective donors by consenting on their driver's licenses. According to Donate Life America, as of 2010, 86.3 million Americans were enrolled in these state donor registries.

Harvesting human organs for sale! The idea suggests the lurid world 1 of horror movies and nineteenth-century graverobbers. Yet right now, Singapore is preparing to pay donors as much as 50,000 Singapore dollars (almost US$36,000) for their organs. Iran has eliminated waiting lists for kidneys entirely by paying its citizens to donate. Israel is implementing a "no give, no take" system that puts people who opt out of the donor system at the bottom of the transplant waiting list should they ever need an organ.

Millions of people suffer from kidney disease, but in 2007 there were 2 just 64,606 kidney-transplant operations in the entire world. In the U.S. alone, 83,000 people wait on the official kidney-transplant list. But just 16,500 people received a kidney transplant in 2008, while almost 5,000 died waiting for one.

To combat yet another shortfall, some American doctors are routinely 3
removing pieces of tissue from deceased patients for transplant without
their, or their families', prior consent. And the practice is perfectly legal.
In a number of U.S. states, medical examiners conducting autopsies may
and do harvest corneas with little or no family notification. (By the time
of autopsy, it is too late to harvest organs such as kidneys.) Few people
know about routine removal statutes and perhaps because of this, these
laws have effectively increased cornea transplants.

Routine removal is perhaps the most extreme response to the devastat- 4
ing shortage of organs worldwide. That shortage is leading some countries
to try unusual new methods to increase donation. Innovation has occurred
in the U.S. as well, but progress has been slow and not without cost or
controversy.

Organs can be taken from deceased donors only after they have been 5
declared dead, but where is the line between life and death? Philosophers
have been debating the dividing line between baldness and nonbaldness
for over 2,000 years, so there is little hope that the dividing line between life
and death will ever be agreed upon. Indeed, the great paradox of deceased
donation is that we must draw the line between life and death precisely
where we cannot be sure of the answer, because the line must lie where the
donor is dead but the donor's organs are not.

In 1968 the *Journal of the American Medical Association* published its 6
criteria for brain death. But reduced crime and better automobile safety
have led to fewer potential brain-dead donors than in the past. Now, greater
attention is being given to donation after cardiac death: no heartbeat for
two to five minutes (protocols differ) after the heart stops beating sponta-
neously. Both standards are controversial — the surgeon who performed
the first heart transplant from a brain-dead donor in 1968 was threatened
with prosecution, as have been some surgeons using donation after cardiac
death. Despite the controversy, donation after cardiac death more than
tripled between 2002 and 2006, when it accounted for about 8 percent
of all deceased donors nationwide. In some regions, that figure is up to
20 percent.

The shortage of organs has increased the use of so-called expanded- 7
criteria organs, or organs that used to be considered unsuitable for transplant. Kidneys donated from people over the age of 60 or from people who
had various medical problems are more likely to fail than organs from
younger, healthier donors, but they are now being used under the pressure.
At the University of Maryland's School of Medicine five patients recently
received transplants of kidneys that had either cancerous or benign tumors
removed from them. Why would anyone risk cancer? Head surgeon Dr.
Michael Phelan explained, "the ongoing shortage of organs from deceased
donors, and the high risk of dying while waiting for a transplant, prompted
five donors and recipients to push ahead with surgery." Expanded-criteria
organs are a useful response to the shortage, but their use also means
that the shortage is even worse than it appears because as the waiting list
lengthens, the quality of transplants is falling.

Routine removal has been used for corneas but is unlikely to ever be- 8
come standard for kidneys, livers, or lungs. Nevertheless more countries are
moving toward presumed consent. Under that standard, everyone is considered to be a potential organ donor unless they have affirmatively opted
out, say, by signing a non-organ-donor card. Presumed consent is common
in Europe and appears to raise donation rates modestly, especially when
combined, as it is in Spain, with readily available transplant coordinators,
trained organ-procurement specialists, round-the-clock laboratory facilities, and other investments in transplant infrastructure.

The British Medical Association has called for a presumed consent sys- 9
tem in the U.K., and Wales plans to move to such a system this year. India
is also beginning a presumed consent program that will start this year with
corneas and later expand to other organs. Presumed consent has less support in the U.S. but experiments at the state level would make for a useful
test.

Rabbis selling organs in New Jersey? Organ sales from poor Indian, 10
Thai, and Philippine donors? Transplant tourism? It's all part of the growing black market in transplants. Already, the black market may account
for 5 percent to 10 percent of transplants worldwide. If organ sales are vol-
untary, it's hard to fault either the buyer or the seller. But as long as the
market remains underground the donors may not receive adequate post-
operative care, and that puts a black mark on all proposals to legalize financial compensation.

Only one country, Iran, has eliminated the shortage of transplant or- 11
gans — and only Iran has a working and legal payment system for organ
donation. In this system, organs are not bought and sold at the bazaar.
Patients who cannot be assigned a kidney from a deceased donor and who
cannot find a related living donor may apply to the nonprofit, volunteer-
run Dialysis and Transplant Patients Association (Datpa). Datpa identifies
potential donors from a pool of applicants. Those donors are medically
evaluated by transplant physicians, who have no connection to Datpa, in
just the same way as are uncompensated donors. The government pays
donors $1,200 and provides one year of limited health-insurance cover-
age. In addition, working through Datpa, kidney recipients pay donors
between $2,300 and $4,500. Charitable organizations provide remuneration to donors for recipients who cannot afford to pay, thus demonstrating
that Iran has something to teach the world about charity as well as about
markets.

The Iranian system and the black market demonstrate one important 12
fact: The organ shortage can be solved by paying living donors. The Iranian system began in 1988 and eliminated the shortage of kidneys by 1999.
Writing in the *Journal of Economic Perspectives* in 2007, Nobel Laureate economist Gary Becker and Julio Elias estimated that a payment of $15,000 for
living donors would alleviate the shortage of kidneys in the U.S. Payment
could be made by the federal government to avoid any hint of inequality
in kidney allocation. Moreover, this proposal would save the government
money since even with a significant payment, transplant is cheaper than

the dialysis that is now paid for by Medicare's End Stage Renal Disease program.

In March 2009 Singapore legalized a government plan for paying organ donors. Although it's not clear yet when this will be implemented, the amounts being discussed for payment, around $50,000, suggest the possibility of a significant donor incentive. So far, the U.S. has lagged other countries in addressing the shortage, but last year, Sen. Arlen Specter circulated a draft bill that would allow U.S. government entities to test compensation programs for organ donation. These programs would only offer noncash compensation such as funeral expenses for deceased donors and health and life insurance or tax credits for living donors.

Worldwide we will soon harvest more kidneys from living donors than from deceased donors. In one sense, this is a great success — the body can function perfectly well with one kidney, so with proper care, kidney donation is a low-risk procedure. In another sense, it's an ugly failure. Why must we harvest kidneys from the living, when kidneys that could save lives are routinely being buried and burned? A payment of funeral expenses for the gift of life or a discount on driver's license fees for those who sign their organ donor card could increase the supply of organs from deceased donors, saving lives and also alleviating some of the necessity for living donors.

> "Why must we harvest kidneys from the living, when kidneys that could save lives are routinely being buried and burned?"

Two countries, Singapore and Israel, have pioneered nonmonetary incentives systems for potential organ donors. In Singapore anyone may opt out of its presumed consent system. However, those who opt out are assigned a lower priority on the transplant waiting list should they one day need an organ, a system I have called "no give, no take."

Many people find the idea of paying for organs repugnant but they do accept the ethical foundation of no give, no take — that those who are willing to give should be the first to receive. In addition to satisfying ethical constraints, no give, no take increases the incentive to sign one's organ donor card, thereby reducing the shortage. In the U.S., Lifesharers. org, a nonprofit network of potential organ donors (for which I am an adviser), is working to implement a similar system.

In Israel a more flexible version of no give, no take will be phased into place beginning this year. In the Israeli system, people who sign their organ donor cards are given points pushing them up the transplant list should they one day need a transplant. Points will also be given to transplant candidates whose first-degree relatives have signed their organ donor cards or whose first-degree relatives were organ donors. In the case of kidneys, for example, two points (on a 0- to 18-point scale) will be given if the candidate had three or more years previous to being listed signed their organ card. One point will be given if a first-degree relative has signed and 3.5 points if a first-degree relative has previously donated an organ.

The worldwide shortage of organs is going to get worse before it gets 18 better, but we do have options. Presumed consent, financial compensation for living and deceased donors, and point systems would all increase the supply of transplant organs. Too many people have died already but pressure is mounting for innovation that will save lives.

· · ·

Comprehension

1. What, according to Tabarrok, is "the great paradox of deceased donation" (5)? Why is this paradox significant?

2. What positive developments in the last several decades have "led to fewer potential brain-dead donors than in the past" (6)?

3. Tabarrok uses definition in paragraph 7. What does he define, and how does this definition help him achieve his essay's purpose?

4. Tabarrok identifies one country that has eliminated shortages in transplant organs. Which country? How has this been accomplished?

Purpose and Audience

1. What is your reaction to Tabarrok's title? To his essay's opening sentence? Do you think these are the reactions he expected readers to have? Explain.

2. Tabarrok's introduction relies on certain assumptions regarding his readers' attitudes about organ harvesting. What are these assumptions? Do you find this introduction effective? Why or why not?

3. According to Tabarrok, presumed consent "has less support in the U.S." (9) than in other countries. What does he think might change that? Does he support "presumed consent"?

4. In paragraph 5, Tabarrok raises one of the most profound questions influencing the debate about organ donations: what is the dividing line between life and death? However, he avoids further discussion of this issue in his essay. Why? Would his essay have been stronger if he had elaborated on the subject? Why or why not?

Style and Structure

1. Tabarrok is an economist. Do you think he approaches the subject differently from the way a member of the clergy, a lawyer, or a physician would? What advantages does his perspective give him?

2. Tabarrok uses cause and effect several times in the essay. Identify two examples. How effective are they? How do they support his overall purpose?

3. In paragraph 12, Tabarrok uses inductive reasoning. Does his inference seem justified? Why or why not?

4. Tabarrok repeatedly writes in the passive voice — for example, in paragraphs 4 and 8. Would rewriting such sentences in the active voice make the sentences — and the writer's argument — stronger? Why or why not?

5. Evaluate Tabarrok's title. Given his purpose, audience, and subject matter, do you think it is appropriate? Explain.

Vocabulary Projects

1. Define each of the following words as it is used in this selection.

lurid (1)	protocols (6)
corneas (3)	alleviate (12)
paradox (5)	priority (15)
criteria (6)	repugnant (16)

2. In paragraph 10, Tabarrok refers to the "growing black market in transplants." What is a black market? What connotations does the term have? How does Tabarrok view this market for organs?

Journal Entry

Tabarrok writes, "Many people find the idea of paying for organs repugnant but they do accept the ethical foundation of no give, no take. . . ." (16). Do these generalizations apply to you? Explain.

Writing Workshop

1. According to Tabarrok, "some American doctors are routinely removing pieces of tissue from deceased patients for transplant without their, or their families', prior consent" (3). Do you think doctors should be allowed to do this? How would you react if such a procedure were performed on a member of your own family? Write an essay explaining your position.

2. **Working with Sources.** Tabarrok claims that the United States lags behind the rest of the world in addressing the transplant issue. In fact, he spends much of his essay describing the transplant policies of countries like Iran and Israel. Choose another significant issue or policy (for example, birthright citizenship, government-supported health care, or firearms laws) on which America differs from other countries. Research the issue, and then write an essay arguing either that the United States should change its policy or approach or that it should keep its current policy rather than emulating the policies of the other countries you discuss. Be sure to document all material you borrow from your sources, and include a works-cited page. (See Chapter 18 for information on MLA documentation.)

3. **Working with Sources.** In paragraph 10, Tabarrok writes, "Rabbis selling organs in New Jersey? Organ sales from poor Indian, Thai, and Philippine donors? Transplant tourism?" Choose one of these three examples to research. Then, write an essay that explains the significance of the example

in the larger context of the organ-donation debate. Be sure to document all material you borrow from your sources, and include a works-cited page. (See Chapter 18 for information on MLA documentation.)

Combining the Patterns

How does Tabarrok use **exemplification** in this essay? Does he give examples to clarify, explain, add interest, or persuade? How do his examples support the points he wants to get across?

Thematic Connections

- "Get It Right: Privatize Executions" (page 298)
- "The Embalming of Mr. Jones" (page 303)
- "Why Vampires Never Die" (page 361)

SCOTT CARNEY

The Case for Mandatory Organ Donation

Investigative journalist Scott Carney (b. 1978) is a contributing editor at *Wired* magazine. His work has also appeared in *Mother Jones, GQ, Discover,* and many other publications. A graduate of Kenyon College, Carney has a master's degree in anthropology from the University of Wisconsin–Madison. He won the 2010 Payne Award for Ethics in Journalism for his *Mother Jones* article "Meet the Parents," a story about the international market for kidnapped children. Carney has also written about the illicit global market for human organs. "The Case for Mandatory Organ Donation" was published in *Wired* in 2007.

Background on "opt-in" and "opt-out" organ-donation policies The United States has an "opt-in" policy for organ donation: donors must give explicit consent (usually, on a state driver's license). In the United States, which has the highest donation rate of any country with an opt-in policy, about 38 percent of registered adult drivers are organ donors. However, many other countries have moved to a model of "opting out" or "presumed consent." This policy allows organ and tissue removal for transplant unless a deceased person, while still alive, explicitly opposed becoming a donor. France, Austria, Belgium, and Australia are among the two dozen countries that practice presumed consent. Some countries have experimented with other inducements. In Israel, citizens who register to become donors earn an advantage if they ever need organs themselves; also, the Israeli families of deceased donors are permitted to accept money from nonprofit groups to "memorialize" their relatives. The government of Singapore covers lifetime health insurance costs for any citizen who donates an organ while alive. Iran's policy is more direct: the government pays living donors about $1,200 for an organ.

Curbing the illegal trade in human organs just might mean scrapping 1 the way we think about the rights of brain-dead organ donors.

Organ brokers have already proven that they are savvy enough to skirt 2 legal roadblocks, and their businesses will continue as the supply of available donor organs remains small and the profits high.

Increasing the supply of cadaver organs is an obvious solution, but vol- 3 unteer programs have not produced enough organs to make a difference. Now some leading ethicists and doctors are re-examining the principle of informed consent in government organ-donor programs, arguing that harvesting from cadavers should be a routine procedure just like autopsies in murder investigations.

"Routine recovery would be much simpler and cheaper to implement 4 than proposals designed to stimulate consent because there would be no need for donor registries, no need to train requestors, no need for stringent government regulation, no need to consider paying for organs, and no need for permanent public education campaigns," wrote Aaron Spital, a clinical professor at Mount Sinai School of Medicine, and James Stacey Taylor, an assistant professor of philosophy at the College of New Jersey, in a controversial article published this year by the American Society of Nephrology.

This approach faces obvious and enormous obstacles, challenging as it 5 does widely and deeply held beliefs about the sanctity of the body, even in death. But it could be the only solution that works.

Roughly half a million people around the world suffer from kidney 6 failure and many are willing to pay any price for a donor organ. They have two options: wait on impossibly long donation lists or pay someone for a live donor transplant.

The United Network for Organ Sharing, which runs the current sys- 7 tem of cadaver donation in the United States, maintains lists of brain-dead patients around the country and actively tries to match up prospective donors. At present there are more than 90,000 people waiting for kidneys but only about 14,000 donors enter the system each year.

The shortage of donors isn't based on a shortage of brain-dead people 8 in hospitals, but on the shortage of people whose organs — even after they have opted into a convoluted and difficult organ-donation program — ever find their way to a viable patient. A 2005 Gallup poll revealed that more than half the population of the United States was willing to donate organs after death, but inefficiencies in the current system mean that even willing donors often end up not donating because families raise objections or there is a question about consent.

Fewer than two out of 10 families opt to donate organs of relatives 9 after death. Hospitals often are unwilling to share organs from donors on their rolls and waste organs while waiting to set up their own in-house transplants. Often, perfectly good transplant organs get lost in a bureaucratic shuffle.

Routine organ donations would dramatically increase the supply of 10 donor organs; with a little effort it would be possible to set up a system to transport donation-worthy organs anywhere in the world.

Once removed from a body, a kidney has a 72-hour window before it 11 needs to be transplanted into a patient. If we use FedEx as our yardstick, with the right transportation infrastructure, that kidney can travel to any point on the globe in less than 24 hours — giving surgeons on either end of the transplant team two days to find a viable donor and perform the necessary surgery. And once regulations for transporting human organs cut though red tape, the cost of transportation would be less than a first-class plane ticket.

"Bold proposals like those posited by [Spital and Taylor] are necessary 12 to fuel spirited debate and influence public policy. From an ethical view, much of what they have written can be supported and resonates well with some who contemplate such issues," wrote Ron Gimbel, assistant professor in the preventive medicine and biometrics department at the Uniformed Services University of the Health Sciences in Bethesda, Maryland, in an email conversation with Wired News.

Setting up a mandatory system of organ donation would undoubtedly stir protests from around the country. Americans are used to the idea of having a choice over the state of our bodies after death and many people would be irked that the government would be meddling into some of the most sensitive and private moments of a family's life.

> "Setting up a mandatory system of organ donation would undoubtedly stir protests from around the country." 13

In fact, that concept is an illusion. In cases where the cause of death is ambiguous, the government routinely conducts autopsies where large pieces of the person's viscera are removed for scientific analysis — often later to be used in a criminal investigation. In addition, as Spital and Taylor argue, the government reserves the right to draft young men against their will into war and risk their lives in combat operations. 14

Nancy Scheper-Hughes, a medical anthropologist at the University of California at Berkeley who has made her career writing about violence caused by poverty, stresses that the current system of organ donation breeds inequalities — but she is equally wary of a system that doesn't allow people to opt out of becoming organ donors after death. 15

"Why make everyone pay a body tax?" she asks. "We have 60 million people who are uninsured in this country; why should we force the people who we denied health care in their life to offer up their bodies after they die? The history of transplants has been replete with doctors who have put themselves above the law and [think] that they are ahead of the morality of the time and that society has to catch up with them," she said. 16

"This proposal doesn't seem to be any different," she added. 17

If mandatory donation is politically unfeasible now, the United States could consider an opt-out rather than the opt-in organ-donation policy, known as "presumed consent" and adopted in various guises in France, Spain, Australia, Belgium, and Portugal. (At present, no country mandates that organs must be relinquished at death.) 18

These laws vary in their details but in general assume that someone would want to be an organ donor unless they explicitly make their objections known by registering in a national online database. Organ-donation rates in all of these countries outstrip the U.S. rates. Powerhouse transplant organizations in the Unites States like the American Kidney Fund have lobbied for this system since 2004, but have yet to make headway in national policy. 19

"Research shows that there would be an increase of between 16 percent to 50 percent in the availability of organs, and others have speculated that this would eliminate the shortage of organs in some categories," said Eric 20

Johnson, professor of business at Columbia University and a proponent of presumed-consent policy.

.   .   .

Comprehension

1. What argument do some ethicists and doctors make about "informed consent" (3)? Does Carney agree with their argument?

2. What specific advantages does Aaron Spital and James Stacey Taylor's proposal have over plans designed to "stimulate consent" (4)?

3. According to Carney, "routine recovery" faces "obvious and enormous obstacles" (5). What are these obstacles?

4. Carney claims that the idea of death as "private" is an "illusion" (14). What does he mean by this? How does he support his claim?

5. In paragraph 14, Carney refers to "cases where the cause of death is ambiguous." What does he mean?

6. According to Carney, what do "opt-out" laws in other countries assume?

Purpose and Audience

1. Carney cites a professor who claims that bold proposals are "necessary to fuel spirited debate and influence public policy" (12). Do you think Carney himself is making a bold proposal?

2. According to Carney, making organ donation mandatory "would undoubtedly stir protests from around the country" (13). Does he think his readers would likely be among the protesters?

3. This essay originally appeared in *Wired,* which focuses on technology's effect on culture and society. How would you expect the magazine's readers to react to Carney's proposals?

4. Where in the essay does Carney address an opposing point of view? How does including this position strengthen his own argument? How does it weaken it?

Style and Structure

1. Would you characterize Carney's first two paragraphs as general or specific? Do you find this opening strategy effective? How else could Carney have begun his essay?

2. What experts does Carney cite? Do you find them credible and persuasive? Why or why not?

3. What point does Carney make in paragraphs 8 and 9? Why is this point essential to his thesis?

4. In paragraph 6, Carney says that patients in need of kidneys have "two options: wait on impossibly long donation lists or pay someone for a live donor transplant." Do you think this is a **false dilemma**, or do patients waiting for transplants really have just two options? Explain.

Vocabulary Projects

1. Define each of the following words as it is used in this selection.

   savvy (2)   posited (12)
   skirt (2)   resonates (12)
   ethicists (3)   biometrics (12)
   harvesting (3)   mandatory (13)
   cadavers (3)   irked (13)
   implement (4)   ambiguous (14)
   stringent (4)   viscera (14)
   prospective (7)   replete (16)
   convoluted (8)   explicitly (19)
   viable (8)   lobbied (19)
   infrastructure (11)

2. Carney writes, "Often, perfectly good transplant organs get lost in a bureaucratic shuffle" (9). What does he mean? What connotations does the word *bureaucratic* have, and how are these connotations important to the point Carney is making here?

3. A **euphemism** is a mild, vague, or indirect term used in place of a word or phrase that might be offensive, harsh, or blunt. Can you identify any euphemisms in this essay? Why might the topic of organ donation call for the use of euphemisms?

Journal Entry

How do you balance personal beliefs about personal choice and about the "sanctity of the body" (5) with the wider need for organs to save lives? Do you think an individual has a duty to donate organs?

Writing Workshop

1. One opponent of mandatory organ donation quoted by Carney argues that the "history of transplants has been replete with doctors who have put themselves above the law and [think] that they are ahead of the morality of the time and that society has to catch up with them" (16). Do you think individuals are ever "above the law"? Write an argumentative essay in which you answer this question.

2. **Working with Sources.** Would you support an "opt-out" organ donation policy in the United States? Referring to essays in this casebook, write an argumentative essay that takes a position on this issue. Be sure to document all material that you borrow from your sources, and include a

works-cited page. (See Chapter 18 for information on MLA documentation.)

3. **Working with Sources.** What role, if any, should the federal government play in regulating, encouraging, prohibiting, or requiring the donation of organs? For example, do you think the federal government has a legitimate right to prevent "perfectly good transplant organs" from going to waste when there are long lists of patients in need? Does the federal government have a right to prevent people from buying or selling organs? On what grounds? Does it have a *responsibility* to do so? Write an essay that takes a position on this issue. Be sure to document all material that you borrow from Carney's essay or from other essays in this casebook, and include a works-cited page. (See Chapter 18 for information on MLA documentation.)

Combining the Patterns

Where in the essay does Carney use **definition**? Why does he do so, and how does his use of definition support his overall purpose?

Thematic Connections

- "The Lottery" (page 311)
- "Why Vampires Never Die" (page 361)
- "Thanks to Modern Science" (page 551)
- "Does This Tax Make Me Look Fat?" (page 647)

CHARLES KRAUTHAMMER

Yes, Let's Pay for Organs

Born in New York City in 1950, syndicated political columnist Charles Kraut-hammer received his undergraduate degree from McGill University in Montreal and then earned an M.D. from Harvard Medical School. After serving as Chief Resident in Psychiatry at Massachusetts General Hospital in Boston, he joined the administration of President Jimmy Carter and began writing about politics for the *New Republic* magazine. Krauthammer has won both a Pulitzer Prize and a National Magazine Award for his writing. He is a contributing editor at both the *New Republic* and the *Weekly Standard*.

Background on the gray/black market for organs in the United States In the United States, it is illegal to buy or sell organs (although the international black market for transplant organs thrives in parts of Asia, Africa, the Middle East, and other regions). However, a chronic shortage of organs leads some Americans to defy the laws. The situation has even led to the practice of "transplant tourism," in which wealthy patients travel to countries like China and Pakistan to undergo clandestine transplants with black-market organs. That illicit market operates inside the United States as well: in 2009, the FBI arrested a Brooklyn rabbi who authorities claim was buying kidneys from financially desperate Israelis for $10,000 and selling them in the United States for $160,000. Often, however, those who sell their organs on the black market are paid much less. For some physicians and policymakers in the United States, the existence of this illegal market suggests the need for a *legal* organ market so that donors could receive legitimate financial compensation.

1 Pennsylvania plans to begin paying the relatives of organ donors $300 toward funeral expenses. It would be the first jurisdiction in the country to reward organ donation. Indeed, it might even be violating a 1984 federal law that declares organs a national resource not subject to compensation. Already there are voices opposing the very idea of pricing a kidney.

2 It is odd that with 62,000 Americans desperately awaiting organ transplantation to save their life, no authority had yet dared offer money for the organs of the dead in order to increase the supply for the living. If we can do anything to alleviate the catastrophic shortage of donated organs, should we not?

3 One objection is that Pennsylvania's idea will disproportionately affect the poor. The rich, it is argued, will not be moved by a $300 reward; it will be the poor who will succumb to the incentive and provide organs.

> "What is wrong with rewarding people, poor or not, for a dead relative's organ?"

So what? Where is the harm? What is wrong with rewarding people, poor 4
or not, for a dead relative's organ? True, auctioning off organs in the market
so that the poor could not afford to get them would be offensive. But this
program does not restrict supply to the rich. It seeks to increase supply for all.

Moreover, everything in life that is dangerous, risky or bad dispropor- 5
tionately affects the poor: slum housing, street crime, small cars, hazardous jobs. By this logic, coal mining should be outlawed because the misery and risk and diseases of coal mining disproportionately fall on people
who need the money. The sons of investment bankers do not go to West
Virginia to mine. (They go there to run for the Senate.)

No, the real objection to the Pennsylvania program is this: it crosses a 6
fateful ethical line regarding human beings and their parts. Until now we
have upheld the principle that one must not pay for human organs because
doing so turns the human body — and human life — into a commodity. Vi-
olating this principle, it is said, puts us on the slippery slope to establishing
a market for body parts. Auto parts, yes. Body parts, no. Start by paying
people for their dead parents' kidneys, and soon we will be paying people
for the spare kidneys of the living.

Well, what's wrong with that? the libertarians ask. Why should a desti- 7
tute person not be allowed to give away a kidney that he may never need so
he can live a better life? Why can't a struggling mother give her kidney so
her kids can go to college?

The answer is that little thing called human dignity. According to the 8
libertarians' markets-for-everything logic, a poor mother ought equally to
be allowed to sell herself into slavery — or any other kind of degradation —
to send her kids through college. Our society, however, draws the line and
says no. We have a free society, but freedom stops at the point where you
violate the very integrity of the self (which is why prostitution is illegal).

We cannot allow live kidneys to be sold at market. It would produce a 9
society in which the lower orders are literally cut up to serve as spare parts
for the upper. No decent society can permit that.

But kidneys from the dead are another matter entirely. There is a dis- 10
tinction between strip-mining a live person and strip-mining a dead one.
To be crude about it, whereas a person is not a commodity, a dead body can
be. Yes, it is treated with respect (which is why humans bury their dead).
But it is not inviolable. It does not warrant the same reverence as that ac-
corded a living soul.

The Pennsylvania program is not just justified, it is too timid. It seeks 11
clean hands by paying third parties — the funeral homes — rather than giving cash directly to the relatives. Why not pay them directly? And why not
$3,000 instead of $300? That might even address the rich/poor concern:
after all, $3,000 is real money, even for bankers and lawyers.

The Pennsylvania program does cross a line. But not all slopes are slip- 12
pery. There is a new line to be drawn, a very logical one: rewards for organs,
yes — but not from the living.

The Talmud* speaks of establishing a "fence" around the law, making 13 restrictions that may not make sense in and of themselves but that serve to keep one away from more serious violations. (For example, because one is not allowed to transact with money on the Sabbath, one is not allowed even to touch money on the Sabbath.) The prohibition we have today — no selling of any organs, from the living or the dead — is a fence against the commoditization of human parts. Laudable, but a fence too far. We need to move the fence in and permit incentive payments for organs from the dead.

Why? Because there are 62,000 people desperately clinging to life, some 14 of whom will die if we don't have the courage to move the moral line — and hold it.

• • •

Comprehension

1. According to Krauthammer, what is "odd" about organ-donation policy in the United States (2)?

2. What is the "real objection" to the planned Pennsylvania program allowing the relatives of donors to receive financial compensation for organs (6)?

3. Krauthammer believes that the relatives of deceased donors should be able to receive financial compensation. However, he objects to allowing living donors to sell the organs on the market. How does he explain his distinction?

4. Krauthammer generally approves of the Pennsylvania program, but he qualifies his support. What problem does he have with the program?

5. In paragraph 13, Krauthammer refers to the Talmud and its notion of a "'fence' around the law." How does he use this notion to advance his argument?

Purpose and Audience

1. What is Krauthammer's overall purpose in this essay? Restate his thesis in your own words.

2. Where in the essay does Krauthammer discuss opposing arguments? Does he refute them persuasively? How could his refutation be strengthened?

3. Krauthammer accuses his opponents of using a logical fallacy in their arguments. What is the fallacy? Is he correct?

---

* Eds. note — A collection of writings that is the basis for Jewish ceremonial and religious law.

4. Would you characterize Krauthammer's approach as **Rogerian argument**? Why or why not?

5. The writer cites the Talmud to support his argument. What does this reference suggest about how he sees his readers and how he characterizes their ethical standards?

Style and Structure

1. Krauthammer repeatedly asks **rhetorical questions**. Identify them. Does he answer these questions in his essay?

2. Where does Krauthammer use analogies? How do these analogies help to support his argument?

3. In paragraph 8, Krauthammer mentions "that little thing called human dignity." How would you characterize his tone in this sentence?

4. How does Krauthammer use **cause and effect** to support his argument? Is the causal connection he identifies convincing? Why or why not?

Vocabulary Projects

1. Define each of the following words as it is used in this selection.

jurisdiction (1)   inviolable (10)
disproportionately (3)   warrant (10)
ethical (6)   reverence (10)
commodity (6)   timid (11)
destitute (7)   laudable (13)

2. In paragraphs 7 and 8, Krauthammer refers to "libertarians" and the "libertarians' markets-for-everything logic." What is a libertarian? Do you think Krauthammer fairly characterizes libertarian thinking?

3. In paragraph 10, Krauthammer uses the term *strip-mining*. What is the literal meaning of this term? What does it mean here? Is it a good metaphor in this context? Why or why not?

Journal Entry

Krauthammer writes, "To be crude about it, whereas a person is not a commodity, a dead body can be" (10). Do you agree with him?

Writing Workshop

1. **Working with Sources.** Krauthammer wrote this article in 1999. Although the Pennsylvania proposal was never implemented, some countries do have such programs. How have such programs affected organ donation rates? Using the essays in this casebook as well as outside sources — newspapers, magazines, or Web sites such as organdonor.gov — write an essay

in which you argue for or against the idea of paying families for the organs of their dead relatives. Be sure to document all material that you borrow from your sources, and include a works-cited page. (See Chapter 18 for information on MLA documentation.)

2. **Working with Sources.** Do you agree with Krauthammer's argument? Would you qualify it, or would you push it even further than Krauthammer does? Referring to Krauthammer's essay as well as to the other selections in this casebook, write an argumentative essay that takes a position on the issue of paying for organs. Be sure to document your sources, and include a works-cited page. (See Chapter 18 for information on MLA documentation.)

3. Krauthammer explains the Talmudic principle "of establishing a 'fence' around the law, making restrictions that may not make sense in and of themselves but that serve to keep one away from more serious violations" (13). He then argues that the fence around organ donation is too restrictive. Can you think of other examples where our society has established such legal or cultural "fences" — for example, regarding freedom of speech or the practice of euthanasia? Write an essay that argues for or against the establishment of one of these "fences." Do you believe that the restriction is justified and necessary or too limiting?

Combining the Patterns

Where in his essay does Krauthammer use **comparison and contrast**? Why is this pattern important to his argument?

Thematic Connections

- "Let Steroids into the Hall of Fame" (page 253)
- "Get It Right: Privatize Executions" (page 298)
- "The Embalming of Mr. Jones" (page 303)
- The Declaration of Independence (page 553)
- "On Dumpster Diving" (page 664)
- "A Modest Proposal" (page 692)

VIRGINIA POSTREL

The Surgery Was Simple; the Process Is Another Story

Virginia Postrel (b. 1960) writes a regular "Commerce and Culture" column for the *Atlantic Monthly* magazine. She has also been a reporter and columnist for *Inc.* magazine, the *Wall Street Journal*, and the *New York Times*. From 1989 to 2000, she was editor of *Reason*, a monthly magazine of libertarian thought and politics. In addition to her magazine and newspaper work, Postrel has written several books, including *The Substance of Style: How the Rise of Aesthetic Value Is Remaking Commerce, Culture, and Consciousness* (2003).

Background on racial and ethnic disparities and organ transplantation According to the National Kidney Foundation, over 100,000 U.S. patients are now waiting for a transplant; more than 4,000 new patients are added to the waiting list each month. These numbers are bleaker for racial and ethnic minorities. African Americans, in particular, have high rates of hypertension, diabetes, and other conditions that may lead to kidney failure. Although they make up only 13 percent of the American population, blacks make up 40 percent of those on dialysis and a third of those in need of kidney transplants — yet they are less likely than whites to receive transplants. A 2007 study by the University of Wisconsin, for example, found that African-American patients in Wisconsin were 75 percent less likely to receive a kidney than whites, and researchers have noted similar disparities throughout the country. Race and ethnicity play a part in organ compatibility — transplants are most likely to be successful within the same racial and ethnic groups — but the percentage of willing donors remains low among minorities. Some observers cite lack of awareness and religious objections for low donation rates. Others blame this reluctance on the profound distrust of the medical establishment in the black community. (That distrust comes, in part, from incidents like the Tuskegee Experiment, a study done from the 1930s to the 1970s in which doctors studied the effects of syphilis on a group of poor black men without treating the disease — or even alerting their subjects that they had it.) Organizations like the Center for Organ Recovery and Education and the national Health Resources and Services Administration are working to reduce this disparity, even instituting "National Minority Donor Awareness Day," which comes on the first of August each year.

Most people think of "organ donors" as dead people. Public campaigns encourage this idea, urging Americans to sign donor cards and let their families know they want their organs to go to others when they die. In Dallas, there's a Texas Organ Donor Memorial Walkway, with bricks inscribed with donors' names.

I'm from Dallas, and I'm a kidney donor. But my name isn't on the 2 walk because I'm very much alive.

You don't have to be dead to give someone a kidney. You just have to be 3 healthy and willing. Your body can function perfectly well with one kidney rather than two.

Nor do you have to be a close genetic match. Thanks to anti-rejection drugs, nowadays a compatible blood type is generally enough. Until last fall, I had never thought about donating a kidney. I had never even given blood. Then a mutual friend told me that Sally Satel needed a transplant. Without one, she'd soon be on dialysis, tied at least three days a week to a machine to filter poisons from her blood. Dialysis isn't a cure for kidney disease. It's more like an iron lung, extending the patient's life but imposing a physically debilitating prison sentence. 4

> "You don't have to be dead to give someone a kidney. You just have to be healthy and willing."

After doing some research and getting my husband's reluctant OK, I 5 told Sally I'd give her a kidney. After I passed all the necessary medical tests, we had our surgeries on March 4.

A kidney donation is a big deal to the recipient, but public perceptions 6 exaggerate what's involved for the donor. Any kind of surgery — including common cosmetic procedures — is dangerous. But donating a kidney was not a life-changing event.

The laparoscopic surgery required only a few small incisions. The larg- 7 est is about 3 inches long, just big enough to get the kidney out. I was in the hospital for three days and able to fly home from Washington after a week. It took about a month to recover fully. Except for a little skin sensitivity and a scar that sometimes itches, I'm back to normal.

Kidney patients desperately need many more living donors. In 2005, 8 there were about seven times as many people waiting for kidneys as there were cadaver organs available, and the waiting list is growing. About every two hours, an American dies waiting for a kidney transplant. Even in a best-case scenario in which all transplantable cadaver kidneys are used, that rate could only be cut roughly in half. Deceased donors can't fill the gap.

But, as I discovered firsthand, you have to be incredibly pushy to make a 9 live donation to anyone but a close relative. My doctor said, "You know you can change your mind." My parents were appalled. Many people couldn't understand why I didn't wait until Sally got sicker or had been on dialysis for a while. Most people have a visceral reaction against the whole idea.

This widespread attitude pressures donors to back out. It also shapes 10 policies that deter living donors. Many hospitals and bioethicists seem to believe a demeaning set of assumptions:

- Normal people won't give up an organ except under coercion.

- Anything that encourages a decision to donate is coercion.
- To avoid coercion, living donors should be discouraged.

Some transplant centers require intrusive psychological probes that 11 scare people off. Some bioethicists treat benevolence or religious conviction as a mental disorder. Even relatively supportive transplant centers like mine make it easier to quit than to go through with it.

The scrutiny is particularly nasty when people want to give to "strang- 12 ers" — not truly unknown people but patients they've gotten to know through Internet sites or news coverage. Many centers flatly refuse "directed donations" to specific strangers, forcing donors to lie about how they met recipients.

And, of course, any hint of financial compensation is suspect. Federal 13 law forbids any "valuable consideration" in exchange for an organ.

Even without changing the law, more could be done to encourage, sup- 14 port and respect kidney donors. Transplant centers could raise funds to cover donors' lost wages, which is legal but rarely done. Churches could adopt patients, solicit members to become living donors, and provide child care, meals, and transportation after surgery. If every Baptist congregation in the country found a donor for one kidney patient, the waiting list would vanish — and that's just the Baptists.

But if we really cared about the welfare of kidney patients, the law would 15 allow organ volunteers to receive compensation from hospitals and insurers (government or private) — with full legal, medical, and financial protections.

Some donors would still happily help friends or relatives for free, as I 16 did. Others would have mixed financial and humanitarian motives — just like surrogate mothers and egg donors, firefighters and soldiers, and, of course, transplant surgeons and foundation executives.

• • •

Comprehension

1. What are the two primary requirements to be a live organ donor? According to Postrel, what other personal qualities make that process easier?

2. How does Postrel characterize her surgery? What effects did it have on her?

3. Postrel identifies several factors that discourage people from donating organs. What are they?

4. Postrel's essay considers a number of problems, from a shortage of living donors to public misperceptions about live organ donation. What solutions does she propose?

Purpose and Audience

1. How would you characterize Postrel's purpose? For example, is she writing to change people's minds? To change policy? To inspire action?

2. Postrel includes the reaction of her parents, who were "appalled" by her decision to become a living donor (9). Why does she include their reaction? How is this information related to her larger argument?

3. According to the writer, many hospitals and bioethicists "seem to believe a demeaning set of assumptions" (10). What are these assumptions? Why are they "demeaning"? How do you think Postrel expects her readers to react to these assumptions?

4. What is Postrel's attitude toward those with a view different from her own? How does her language reveal her attitude? Does she address these opposing views?

Style and Structure

1. Postrel tries to correct common misperceptions about live organ donation. Where does she do this, and how do her "corrections" help to structure her essay?

2. Where does Postrel use figurative language? How does such language support her argument?

3. In paragraphs 14 and 15, Postrel proposes possible solutions to the problem she identifies. Would her main proposal be more convincing if it appeared earlier in the essay? Why or why not?

4. Where in the essay does Postrel include statistical evidence? Does she present it clearly? How does it support her argument?

Vocabulary Projects

1. Define each of the following words as it is used in this selection.

    debilitating (4)   demeaning (10)
    laparoscopic (7)   coercion (10)
    cadaver (8)   benevolence (11)
    appalled (9)   surrogate (16)
    deter (10)

2. In paragraph 10, Prostel mentions "demeaning . . . assumptions" held by bioethicists. What is a bioethicist? What are the word's origins?

3. According to Postrel, "Most people have a visceral reaction against" live organ donation (9). What is a "visceral reaction"?

Journal Entry

Would you consider becoming a live donor? What factors would affect your decision? Do you see a difference between donating to a family member and donating to a friend or a stranger? How might the prospect of financial compensation influence your choice?

Writing Workshop

1. Postrel writes, "Most people have a visceral reaction against the whole idea" of using living organ donors. Is this true? Conduct your own informal survey of people's attitudes about this issue. Then, write an essay in which you use their responses to support or challenge Postrel's statement.

2. **Working with Sources.** Charles Krauthammer writes that people should not be able to sell their organs because of "that little thing called human dignity" (8). He goes on to say, "We cannot allow live kidneys to be sold at market. It would produce a society in which the lower orders are literally cut up to serve as spare parts for the upper. No decent society can permit that" (9). Do you think Postrel's proposal that donors be allowed to "receive compensation from hospitals and insurers" (15) could lead to the problems that Krauthammer describes? Do you agree with Postrel's argument? Write an essay that takes a position on this issue. Be sure to document all material that you borrow from your sources, and include a works-cited page. (See Chapter 18 for information on MLA documentation.)

3. According to Postrel, allowing living donors to have "mixed financial and humanitarian motives" would make them analogous to "surrogate mothers and egg donors, firefighters and soldiers, and, of course, transplant surgeons and foundation executives" (16). Do you think these analogies are persuasive? Write an essay that explains why you believe living organ donors are like (or unlike) these other groups.

Combining the Patterns

Where in the essay does Postrel explain a **process**? Is this process explanation necessary? Why or why not?

Thematic Connections

- "Shooting an Elephant" (page 133)
- "Getting Coffee Is Hard to Do" (page 286)
- "Get It Right: Privatize Executions" (page 298)

Should Government Tax Sugary Drinks?

After remaining stable during the 1960s and 1970s, the obesity rate among Americans rose from 15 percent in 1980 to 34 percent in 2008. If the number of adults who are merely overweight is added in, the figure rises to 68 percent — roughly two out of every three people. Observers are particularly concerned about the 31.7 percent of children who are either overweight or obese. Children now exhibit dramatically increased rates of diabetes and high blood pressure, conditions usually associated with older people. Moreover, studies indicate that a large majority of over-weight teenagers will become overweight adults, with all the attendant health problems, including increased rates of cancer, stroke, and heart disease.

Although most people agree that these trends are real and that they pose real problems, there is less agreement over the causes of obesity. Some view the issue as one of individual choice and personal responsi-bility. Others, however, see more complex cultural, economic, and even political forces at work, from the prevalence of fast-food restaurants and sugary drinks marketed to children to the government subsidies that keep unhealthy foods cheap — even as fruits and vegetables become more expensive. Whether the problem's causes are simple or complex, the finan-cial burden of an overweight population is enormous. A recent study by Cornell University, for example, indicated that the annual cost of treating obesity is now $168 billion. That amounts to 16.5 percent of the country's total medical care expenses.

Given the social costs of obesity, some experts and policymakers ar-gue that the government needs to take action. At the state and local levels, this is already occurring. New York City has banned the use of trans fats in restaurants as well as toys in unhealthy children's meals at fast-food restaurants. In Los Angeles, city officials have enacted a moratorium on freestanding fast-food chains in certain areas. Most controversially, perhaps, public health officials and politicians have proposed new taxes on unhealthy foods such as candy and soft drinks. Even President Barack Obama has said that a so-called "sin tax" on soda and other sugary pro-ducts is "an idea we should be exploring." Not surprisingly, however, many people — from civil libertarians to the makers of such food products — oppose such measures.

The essays in this casebook explore this issue from a variety of view-points. In "A Tax that Invests in Our Health," New York State Health Commissioner Richard F. Daines argues for a state tax on non-diet soft drinks. For Daines, obesity is an expensive public problem that requires an effective public solution: "Government steps in to serve the public when private markets fail." Similarly, David Leonhardt sees the problem as a cultural, political, and economic one rather than one of personal responsibility. The solutions, he writes in "Fat Tax," are "beyond the control of any individual." In "Let Them Drink Water!" Daniel Engber examines the social and cultural biases behind well-meaning public initiatives to tax junk food, especially the ways in which these proposals will disproportionately affect the poor and create an "apartheid of pleasure." Finally, Jeff Ousborne considers — and rejects — the idea that overweight people be required to pay financial penalties for their extra pounds.

RICHARD F. DAINES

A Tax That Invests in Our Health

Richard F. Daines, Commissioner of Health for New York State, received his undergraduate degree from Utah State University and earned an M.D. from Cornell University Medical School. Before his appointment as health commissioner in 2007, he was medical director and president and chief executive officer of St. Luke's-Roosevelt Hospital Center in New York City.

Background on obesity rates in the United States Commissioner Daines is not alone in supporting a tax on unhealthy foods: officials at the Centers for Disease Control (CDC) and the World Health Organization also advocate taxing foods high in fat and sugar. The idea is becoming more common in broader political and cultural institutions as well. For example, the *New York Times* has endorsed a penny-per-ounce tax on soda. These proposals and others are a response to a widely publicized obesity epidemic in the United States. While the country's obesity rate has stopped rising, the number of obese and overweight Americans remains high. A majority of adults are overweight; according to the CDC, 34 percent are obese (while only 15 percent of American adults were obese in 1980). Among children from two to nineteen, nearly 32 percent are now overweight, and 17 percent are obese. The financial costs of this situation are enormous: the CDC estimates the medical costs of widespread obesity at $147 billion a year.

Sixty percent of New York adults are overweight or obese, and so are one-third of our children. Many factors contribute to obesity, but there's one pernicious one: added sugar.

We consume about 300 calories more a day now than we did 30 years ago, and most of those extra calories come from sugar-sweetened sodas, energy drinks, or fruit-flavored drinks.

As a physician, I've had to tell patients they have diabetes, with a lifelong struggle against its complications and costs. I've walked across 149th Street in the Bronx and seen billboard after billboard advertising the huge servings and low prices of the sugary sodas sold in the fast food restaurants on each corner.

I've also been a scoutmaster, watching a kid chugging a sports drink to make him "strong," while instead it pours so much sugar into his system that he'd have to hike at least an hour a day to burn off the calories.

Now I'm the state health commissioner, and every New Yorker is my patient. And I say, "Enough!"

Like many health professionals, I support Gov. David Paterson's proposed tax on sugar-sweetened beverages as part of a strategy to fight obesity. The financial deck has been stacked against good health for too long.

Low soft drink prices reflect government-supported subsidies on corn   7
syrup and sugar, and hide the costs of the obesity they cause. Research published in the *New England Journal of Medicine* demonstrated that over the
past 30 years, the cost of soft drinks has risen at only three-quarters of the
rate of inflation, while the cost of fresh fruits and vegetables has risen at
more than 1.5 times that of the Consumer Price Index.

These are signs of a failing market. Healthy choices are rising in price   8
while the cost of bad choices falls. Low-fat milk costs more than soda. So
grocery stores in poorer neighborhoods stock less milk and more soda, and
the relentless advertising from the beverage industry and fast food joints
makes sweet drinks an expected part of daily living.

The true cost of these subsidized sugar drinks is paid by taxpayers.   9
About $7.6 billion is spent in New York annually to treat obesity-related ill-
nesses. Most of it is paid by taxpayers, through Medicaid and Medicare. You
don't see that cost at a vending machine, at a high school basketball game,
or at the corner store. But we all pay for it, whether we buy soda or we don't.

Government steps in to serve the public   10
when private markets fail. That's why taxes
are levied to pay for fire protection and safe
highways, and why we've used taxes to de-
crease cigarette use. If there were profit in
the right public health policies, big business
would be there. In food there's no profit
in persuading Americans to drink less of
something that is cheap, heavily marketed, and tastes really good.

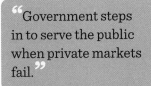

" Government steps in to serve the public when private markets fail. "

The public costs of obesity have made it not just a personal issue, but a   11
major public problem that will continue to absorb our taxes while it chips
away at our health. Another study in the *New England Journal of Medicine*
followed thousands of children through adulthood. It discovered that the
heaviest youngsters were more than twice as likely as the thinnest to die
before age 55.

Twice the rate of death by 55? Hardly the happy, refreshing world de-   12
picted in sugary beverage ads.

Recent polls of New Yorkers and of New York City voters showed that   13
they will support a penny-per-ounce tax on non-diet soft drinks if the
money is used to close budget deficits or support health care.

The state doesn't have the money for a lot of things this year. But   14
we can take this major step to resist the special interests, to protect our
children, and to show that New York can implement an innovative public
policy to offer a healthier future for us all.

• • •

Comprehension

1. Daines notes that people consume about 300 more calories a day now
   than they did three decades ago. According to Daines, where do most of
   those extra calories come from?

2. In Daines's view, what are the "signs of a failing market" (8)? In what sense is the market for both soft drinks and healthy food "failing"?

3. According to Daines, what role should government play in fighting obesity? What obligations does he believe the government has?

4. Daines argues that people pay a public cost for sugary drinks "whether we buy soda or we don't" (9). What does he mean by this?

Purpose and Audience

1. What is Daines's purpose in writing this essay? How does his job as state health commissioner influence your reaction to his argument?

2. In your own words, restate Daines's thesis.

3. Daines is writing as a New Yorker to other New Yorkers. Does this essay have significance to a wider audience? If so, to what particular kinds of readers?

4. Daines spends much of the essay discussing the costs of obesity and obesity-related illnesses. Why does he do this? Is he making a logical or an emotional appeal to his readers?

Style and Structure

1. Daines begins his essay with two statistics and a direct statement. How effective is this introduction? How does it help him to achieve his purpose?

2. Daines supports his points by citing research from the *New England Journal of Medicine*. Does this research provide enough support for his thesis? Would a wider range of sources have strengthened his argument? Why or why not?

3. Daines describes himself as a physician and a scoutmaster before he identifies himself as the state health commissioner in paragraph 5. Why do you think he does this?

4. In paragraph 10, Daines uses analogies to support his position. Are these comparisons logical? Are they convincing? Explain.

Vocabulary Projects

1. Define each of the following words as it is used in this selection.

pernicious (1)	relentless (8)
diabetes (3)	levied (10)
subsidies (7)	implement (14)

2. Daines argues that the New York state government should take a "major step to resist the special interests" (14). What does the term *special interests* mean? Who, specifically, is Daines referring to? What connotations does the term have?

Journal Entry

According to Daines, obesity is "not just a personal issue, but a major public problem" (11). Do you agree? In what sense, if any, is obesity a "public" matter?

Writing Workshop

1. **Working with Sources.** At several points in his essay, Daines refers to the "relentless advertising" of the soft-drink and fast-food industries. How do such advertising appeals work? Whom do they target? Choose a specific advertisement — from television, a billboard, a magazine, or the Internet — and then write an essay analyzing it as a piece of persuasive writing. What appeals does it make? Is it logical? Is it honest? Be sure to document all material that you borrow from your sources, and include a works-cited page. (See Chapter 18 for information on MLA documentation.)

2. According to Daines, "Government steps in to serve the public when private markets fail" (10). He gives specific instances of this kind of government involvement, such as levying taxes to support road safety and firefighting. Do you agree that such steps are necessary? Write an essay that argues either for or against this view of government's role. Use specific examples to support your thesis.

3. **Working with Sources.** Daines comes out strongly in favor of a tax on non-diet soft drinks for New York. Do you think this measure should be adopted where you live? Why or why not? Write an argumentative essay explaining your view. You may use the other essays in this casebook as sources for your argument. Be sure to document all material that you borrow from your sources, and include a works-cited page. (See Chapter 18 for information on MLA documentation.)

Combining the Patterns

At several points in the essay, Daines uses **cause and effect**. How do these causal relationships help him to develop his overall argument?

Thematic Connections

- "No Wonder They Call Me a Bitch" (page 176)
- "Get It Right: Privatize Executions" (page 298)
- "The Case against Air Conditioning" (page 344)
- "The Case for Mandatory Organ Donation" (page 614)
- "On Dumpster Diving" (page 664)

DAVID LEONHARDT

Fat Tax

David Leonhardt (b. 1973) writes a weekly column, "Economic Scene," for the *New York Times*. A graduate of Yale University, he worked for *Business Week* magazine and the *Washington Post* before joining the *Times* in 1999. He is a regular contributor to the newspaper's Economix blog, which analyzes news, daily life, and personal decision-making through the lens of economics.

Background on ways of addressing obesity Researchers, public officials, and corporations have proposed a variety of strategies to bring America's weight problem under control. Of course, it is difficult to mandate or legislate good health at the national level, but some states and cities have enacted their own measures. Critics of such legislation argue that these measures limit choice — and that good health requires individual responsibility, not public intervention. Others, however, see the U.S. obesity epidemic as an economic and cultural problem rather than a matter of personal willpower. For example, processed-food companies and fast-food restaurants are able to charge lower prices for unhealthy foods in part because the government subsidizes the corn and soybeans used for animal feed and vegetable oil. According to experts, if the prices of healthier food were lower, people would make healthier choices. Some officials, like New York State Health Commissioner Richard F. Daines (page 632), have proposed a national ban on food and beverage marketing to children under eight years of age. The private sector has also responded to this health problem. For example, IBM has instituted a wellness initiative that offers cash rebates to those who complete weight-loss, exercise, and smoking-cessation programs.

Two years ago, the Cleveland Clinic stopped hiring smokers. It 1 was one part of a "wellness initiative" that has won the renowned hospital — which President Obama recently visited — some very nice publicity. The clinic has a farmers' market on its main campus and has offered smoking-cessation classes for the surrounding community. Refusing to hire smokers may be more hard-nosed than the other parts of the program. But given the social marginalization of smoking, the policy is hardly shocking. All in all, the wellness initiative seems to be a feel-good story.

Which is why it is so striking to talk to Delos M. Cosgrove, the heart 2 surgeon who is the clinic's chief executive, about the initiative. Cosgrove says that if it were up to him, if there weren't legal issues, he would not only stop hiring smokers. He would also stop hiring obese people. When he mentioned this to me during a recent phone conversation, I told him that I thought many people might consider it unfair. He was unapologetic.

"Why is it unfair?" he asked. "Has anyone ever shown the law of con- 3
servation of matter* doesn't apply?" People's weight is a reflection of how
much they eat and how active they are. The country has grown fat because
it's consuming more calories and burning fewer. Our national weight problem brings huge costs, both medical and economic. Yet our anti-obesity efforts have none of the urgency of our antismoking efforts. "We should declare obesity a disease and say we're going to help you get over it," Cosgrove
said.

You can disagree with the doctor — you can even be offended — and 4
still come to see that there is a larger point behind his tough-love approach.
The debate over health care reform has so far revolved around how insurers, drug companies, doctors, nurses, and government technocrats might
be persuaded to change their behavior. And for the sake of the economy
and the federal budget, they do need to change their behavior. But there
has been far less discussion about how the rest of us might also change
our behavior. It's as if we have little responsibility for our own health. We
instead outsource it to something called the health care system.

The promise of that system is undeniably alluring: whatever your ail- 5
ment, a pill or a procedure will fix it. Yet the promise hasn't been kept. For
all the miracles that modern medicine really does perform, it is not the primary determinant of most people's health. J. Michael McGinnis, a senior
scholar at the Institute of Medicine, has estimated that only 10 percent of
early deaths are the result of substandard medical care. About 20 percent
stem from social and physical environments, and 30 percent from genetics.
The biggest contributor, at 40 percent, is behavior.

Today, the great American public-health problem is indeed obesity. The 6
statistics have become rote, but consider that people in their 50s are about
20 pounds heavier on average than 50-somethings were in the late 1970s.
As a convenient point of reference, a typical car tire weighs 20 pounds.

This extra weight has caused a sharp increase in chronic diseases, 7
like diabetes, that are unusually costly. Other public-health scourges, like
lung cancer, have tended to kill their victims quickly, which (in the most
tragic possible way) holds down their long-term cost. Obesity is different.
A recent article in *Health Affairs* estimated its annual cost to be $147 billion
and growing. That translates into $1,250 per household, mostly in taxes
and insurance premiums.

A natural response to this cost would be to say that the people im- 8
posing it on society should be required to pay it. Cosgrove mentioned to
me an idea that some economists favor: charging higher health-insurance
premiums to anyone with a certain body-mass index. Harsh? Yes. Fair? You
can see the argument. And yet it turns out that the obese already do pay
something resembling their fair share of medical costs, albeit in an indirect way. Overweight workers are paid less than similarly qualified, thinner

---

* Eds. note — A fundamental principle of classical physics that matter cannot be
created or destroyed in an isolated system.

colleagues, according to research by Jay Bhattacharya and M. Kate Bundorf of Stanford. The cause isn't entirely clear. But the size of the wage difference is roughly similar to the size of the difference in their medical costs.

It's also worth noting that the obese, as well as any of the rest of us suffering from a medical condition affected by behavior, already have plenty of incentive to get healthy. But we struggle to do so. Daily life gets in the way. Inertia triumphs. 9

The question of personal responsibility, then, ends up being more complicated than it may seem. It's hard to argue that Americans have collectively become more irresponsible over the last 30 years; the murder rate has plummeted, and divorce and abortion rates have fallen. And our genes certainly haven't changed in 30 years. 10

What has changed is our environment. Parents are working longer, and takeout meals have become a default dinner. Gym classes have been cut. The real price of soda has fallen 33 percent over the last three decades. The real price of fruit and vegetables has risen more than 40 percent. 11

The solutions to these problems are beyond the control of any individual. They involve a different sort of responsibility: civic — even political — responsibility. They depend on the kind of collective action that helped cut smoking rates nearly in half. Anyone who smoked in an elementary-school hallway today would be thrown out of the building. But if you served an obesity-inducing, federally financed meal to a kindergartner, you would fit right in. Taxes on tobacco, meanwhile, have skyrocketed. A modest tax on sodas — one of the few proposals in the various health-reform bills aimed at health, rather than health care — has struggled to get through Congress. 12

Cosgrove's would-be approach may have its problems. The obvious one is its severity. The more important one is probably its narrowness: not even one of the nation's most prestigious hospitals can do much to reduce obesity. The government, however, can. And that is the great virtue of Cosgrove's idea. He is acknowledging that any effort to attack obesity will inevitably involve making value judgments and even limiting people's choices. Most of the time, the government has no business doing such things. But there is really no other way to cure an epidemic. 13

> "Most of the time, the government has no business doing such things. But there is really no other way to cure an epidemic."

• • •

Comprehension

1. In paragraph 4, Leonhardt writes that we tend to "outsource" our health. What does he mean? How is this statement related to his essay's thesis?

2. According to Leonhardt, what percentage of early deaths in the United States are the result of substandard medical care? Why is this statistic significant?

3. How is obesity different from other "public-health scourges, like lung cancer" (7)? How might this difference shape public policy on obesity?

4. Leonhardt claims, "It's hard to argue that Americans have collectively become more irresponsible over the last 30 years" (10). How does he support this statement?

5. What does Leonhardt imply is the most significant cause of obesity in the last several decades?

6. Leonhardt ends his essay by saying that any effort to fight obesity will "inevitably involve making value judgments and even limiting people's choices" (13). What does he mean by this statement? Do you agree with him?

Purpose and Audience

1. Does Leonhardt expect his readers to be familiar with discussions and debates about obesity in America? How can you tell?

2. According to Leonhardt, what is the problem with the "debate over health care reform" (4)? Does he imply that his readers may be part of the problem? Explain.

3. Where does Leonhardt identify opposing arguments and different viewpoints? How does he address opposing points of view?

4. Restate Leonhardt's thesis in your own words.

Style and Structure

1. Leonhardt begins his essay with an anecdote. Is this an effective opening strategy? Why or why not? How else could he have opened the essay?

2. What is the purpose of paragraphs 5 through 7? How are they related to Leonhardt's overall point?

3. In paragraph 9, as well as in other places, Leonhardt uses the first person plural ("*Our* national weight problem . . ."). Why does he do this? What effect does he hope to have on readers?

4. Where does Leonhardt use an analogy? Does this analogy effectively support his argument? Why or why not?

5. What cause-and-effect relationship does Leonhardt try to refute in this essay? Is he successful?

Vocabulary Projects

1. Define each of the following words as it appears in this selection.

renowned (1)   rote (6)
cessation (1)   scourges (7)
marginalization (1)   albeit (8)
alluring (5)   inertia (9)
ailment (5)   prestigious (13)
determinant (5)

2. In paragraph 4, Leonhardt uses the term *technocrats*. What is a technocrat? What qualities might a "government technocrat" have? What are the word's connotations?

3. Leonhardt writes about the tendency of Americans to abdicate responsibility for their own health; instead, he argues, they put themselves in the hands of "something called the health care system" (4). Why does he use this phrase? What point is he trying to make?

Journal Entry

Do you think fat people are solely responsible for their own condition, or do you believe food manufacturers bear some responsibility for the problem?

Writing Workshop

1. Dr. Delos Cosgrove of the Cleveland Clinic says that if it were up to him, he would stop hiring obese people as well as smokers. Does this policy seem ethical to you? Does it seem fair? Do you think private institutions — both inside and outside the health-care industry — should be legally permitted to discriminate in this way? Write an argumentative essay that takes a stand on this issue.

2. **Working with Sources.** Using the selections in this casebook as your sources, write an essay proposing specific government solutions for the problem of obesity. Be sure to document all material that you borrow from your sources, and include a works-cited page. (See Chapter 18 for information on MLA documentation.)

3. Some people have proposed a tax on foods that are high in fat — for example, butter or ice cream. Would you support such a tax? Write an essay in which you take a stand on the issue.

Combining the Patterns

Where in this essay does Leonhardt use **comparison and contrast**? Why is comparison important to his argument? How does he use **cause and effect** to support his argument?

Thematic Connections

- "Rice" (page 172)
- "Why Looks Are the Last Bastion of Discrimination" (page 246)
- "Tortillas" (page 507)

DANIEL ENGBER

Let Them Drink Water!

Daniel Engber writes about science, culture, and sports for the online magazine *Slate;* he also edits *Slate's* Science and Explainer columns. He has a master's degree in neuroscience and has worked in research labs at Columbia; the University of California, San Francisco; and the National Institutes of Health.

Background on soft-drink machines in schools A typical 20-ounce bottle of a sugared soft drink from a vending machine contains 250 calories. Not surprisingly, government policymakers and others have targeted such machines in their efforts to reduce obesity rates — particularly among children. The state of California has banned these products outright from all public schools. Nationally, the 2010 Child Nutrition Act includes restrictions for school vending machines across the country. Still, some people are concerned about the financial consequences of such legislation: schools often use funds from soft-drink sales to support athletics, field trips, and other activities. Further complicating the issue, such restrictions — and even outright bans — sometimes extend outside public schools. (In San Francisco, for example, Mayor Gavin Newsom banned high-calorie sweetened beverages from all city property.)

Not long after the attack on Pearl Harbor, in the winter of 1942, physiologist A.J. Carlson made a radical suggestion: If the nation's largest citizens were charged a fee — say, $20 for each pound of overweight — we might feed the war effort overseas while working to subdue an "injurious luxury" at home.

Sixty-seven years later, the "fat tax" is back on the table. We're fighting another war — our second-most-expensive ever — and Congress seems on the verge of spending $1 trillion on health care. Once again, a bloated budget may fall on the backs of the bloated public. Some commentators, following Carlson, have lately called for a tax on fat people themselves (cf. the Huffington Post and the *New York Times*); others, like a team of academics writing in the current issue of the *New England Journal of Medicine,* propose a hefty surcharge on soft drinks instead.

The notion hasn't generated much enthusiasm in Congress, but fat taxes are spreading through state legislatures: Four-fifths of the union now takes a cut on the sales of junk food or soda. Pleas for a federal fat tax are getting louder, too. The *New York Times* recently endorsed a penny-per-ounce soda tax, and Michael Pollan* has made a convincing argument for why the insurance industry may soon throw its weight behind the proposal. Even President Obama said he likes the idea in a recent interview

---

* Eds. note — American author, journalist, and professor who writes frequently about food and agriculture (b. 1955).

with *Men's Health.* (For the record, Stephen Colbert* is against the measure: "I do not obey big government; I obey my thirst.")

For all this, the public still has strong reservations about the fat tax. 4 The state-level penalties now in place have turned out to be way too small to make anyone lose weight, and efforts to pass more heavy-handed laws have so far fallen short. But proponents say it's only a matter of time before taxing junk food feels as natural as taxing cigarettes. The latter has been a tremendous success, they argue, in bringing down rates of smoking and death from lung cancer. In theory, a steep tax on sweetened beverages could do the same for overeating and diabetes.

It may take more than an analogy with tobacco to convince voters. As 5 my colleague William Saletan points out, the first step in policing eating habits is to redefine food as something else. If you want to tax the hell out of soda, you need to make people think that it's a drug, not a beverage — that downing a Coke is just like puffing on a cigarette. But is soda as bad as tobacco? Let's ask the neuropundits.

Junk food literally "alters the biological circuitry of our brains," writes 6 David Kessler in this summer's best-seller, *The End of Overeating.* In a previous book, Kessler detailed his role in prosecuting the war on smoking as the head of the FDA; now he's explaining what makes us fat with all the magisterial jargon of cognitive neuroscience. Eating a chocolate-covered pretzel, he says, activates the brain's pleasure system — the dopamine reward circuit, to be exact — and changes the "functional connectivity among important brain regions." Thus, certain foods — the ones concocted by industrial scientists and laden with salt, sugar, and fat — can circumvent our natural inclinations and trigger "action schemata" for mindless eating. Got that? Junk food is engineered to enslave us. Kessler even has a catchphrase to describe these nefarious snacks: They're hyperpalatable.

Try as we might, we're nearly powerless to resist these treats. That's 7 because evolution has us programmed to experience two forms of hunger. The first kicks in when we're low on energy. As an adaptation, its purpose is simple enough — we eat to stay alive. The second, called hedonic hunger, applies even when we're full — it's the urge to eat for pleasure. When food is scarce, hedonic hunger comes in handy, so we can stock up on calories for the hard times ahead. But in a world of cheap food, the same impulse makes us fat.

That's the problem with junk food. Manufacturers have figured out 8 how to prey on man's voluptuous nature. Like the cigarette companies, they lace their products with addictive chemicals and cajole us into wanting things we don't really need. Soda is like a designer drug, layered with seductive elements — sweetness for a burst of dopamine, bubbles to prick the trigeminal nerve.

---

* Eds. note — American television host, satirist, writer, and comedian (b. 1964).

It's hard to draw a line, though, between foods that are drugs and foods   9
that are merely delicious. Soda and candy aren't the only stimuli that "rewire your brain," of course. Coffee does, too, and so do video games, Twitter, meditation, and just about anything else that might give you pleasure
(or pain). That's what brains do — they learn, they rewire. To construe an
earthly delight as hyperpalatable — as too good for our own good — we're
lashing out at sensuality itself. "Do you design food specifically to be
highly hedonic?" Kessler asks an industry consultant at one point in the
book. What's the guy going to say? "No, we design food to be bland and
nutritious. . . ."

It's ironic that so many advocates for healthy eating are also out-   10
spoken gourmands. Alice Waters, the proprietor of Chez Panisse, calls for
a "delicious revolution" of low-fat, low-sugar lunch programs. It's a central dogma of the organic movement that you can be a foodie and a health
nut at the same time — that what's real and natural tastes better, anyway.
Never mind how much fat and sugar and salt you'll get from a Wabash
Cannonball* and a slice of *pain au levain*. Forget that *cuisiniers* have for
centuries been catering to our hedonic hunger — our pleasure-seeking,
caveman selves — with a repertoire of batters and sauces. Junk foods are
hyperpalatable. Whole Foods is *delicious*. Doughnuts are a drug; brioche is
a treat.

Some tastes, it seems, are more equal than others.   11

A fat tax, then, discriminates among the varieties of gustatory ex-   12
perience. And its impact would fall most directly on the poor, nonwhite
people who tend to be the most avid consumers of soft drinks and the
most sensitive to price. Under an apartheid of pleasure, palatable drinks
are penalized while delicious — or even hyperdelicious — products come at
no extra charge. What about the folks who can't afford a $5 bottle of POM
Wonderful?

No big deal, say the academics writing in the *New England Journal of*   13
Medicine; they can always drink from the faucet. Here's how the article
puts it: "Sugar-sweetened beverages are not necessary for survival, and an
alternative (i.e., water) is available at little or no cost." So much for *Let them*
eat cake.

We've known for a long time that any sin tax is likely to be a bur-   14
den on the poor, since they're most prone to unhealthy behavior. (James
Madison fought the snuff tax on these grounds way back in 1794.) But you
might just as well say that poor people have the most to gain from a sin tax
for exactly the same reason. It's also possible that revenues from a fat tax
would be spent on obesity prevention — or go back to the community in
other ways. There's a knotty argument here about the vexing and recipro-
cal interactions among health, wealth, and obesity. It's not clear whether,
and in what direction, a soda tax might redistribute wealth. Whatever you

---

* Eds. note — An artisanal goat cheese made in Indiana.

think of the economics, though, raising the price on soda — and offering water in its places — will redistribute pleasure.

I don't mean to imply that any such regulation is unjust. We have laws against plenty of chemicals and behaviors that are as delightful as they are destructive. These are, for the most part, sensible measures to protect our health. What's disturbing is the thought that the degree of government control should vary according to who's using which drug. In April, the Obama administration called for an end to a long-standing policy that gives dealers of powdered cocaine 100 times more leeway than dealers of crack when it comes to federal prison sentences. Let's not repeat this drug-war injustice in the war on obesity. We may be ready to say that foods are addictive. Are we ready to judge the nature of a delicious high?

> "What's disturbing is the thought that the degree of government control should vary according to who's using which drug."
>
> 15

• • •

Comprehension

1. According to Engber, what is the public's attitude toward taxing junk food and soda? How does he support this generalization?

2. Policymakers and public health experts who support taxing junk food draw an analogy between junk food and cigarettes. According to Engber, what redefinition does the analogy require?

3. What does Engber find "ironic" about "so many advocates for healthy eating" (10)?

4. In paragraph 10, Engber discusses the organic food movement. How does he define its "central dogma"?

5. Engber argues that a fat tax "discriminates among the varieties of gustatory experience" (12). What does he mean? Which specific groups does he believe such a tax would affect disproportionately?

Purpose and Audience

1. What is Engber's purpose? Is he writing to change his readers' minds, to propose a course of action, to influence public policy, to inform his readers — or to provoke them? Explain.

2. Where does Engber think his audience stands on the issues he discusses? Does he see them as knowledgable or uninformed? Does he think they are more likely to eat junk food or *pain au levain*? How can you tell?

3. In paragraph 14, Engber notes a lack of clarity about the effects of "sin taxes" on behavior. How does this lack of clarity strengthen his argument?

Style and Structure

1. What is the purpose of paragraphs 2 and 3? Why are they important to Engber's argument?

2. In paragraph 6, Engber quotes and paraphrases from David Kessler's *The End of Overeating*. Why does he do this? What is Engber's attitude toward Kessler's book — and toward the practice of applying neuroscience to overeating and junk food?

3. Where does Engber use cause-and-effect arguments? How do these arguments support his position?

4. Engber ends his essay with a surprising analogy. What two things is he comparing? Is this comparison logical? What point does it make?

Vocabulary Projects

1. Define each of the following words as it is used in this selection.

   radical (1)   laden (6)   trigeminal (8)
   bloated (2)   circumvent (6)   construe (9)
   surcharge (2)   nefarious (6)   gourmands (10)
   neuropundits (5)   hedonic (7)   dogma (10)
   magisterial (6)   voluptuous (8)   brioche (10)
   jargon (6)   cajole (8)   gustatory (12)
   concocted (6)

2. Engber ends paragraph 10 with a series of contrasting words. What are these words? What point is he trying to make here about language as it is used in the junk-food tax debate? Is it successful in making this point?

3. In paragraph 12, Engber writes that a fat tax would lead to an "apartheid of pleasure." What does the word *apartheid* mean? What connotations does it have? Is it an appropriate word in this context?

Journal Entry

According to Engber, organic food advocates argue that real, natural, healthy food "tastes better, anyway" (10). Do you agree that natural food tastes better than junk food?

Writing Workshop

1. **Working with Sources.** Engber writes about the "organic movement" in paragraph 10. Research the organic food movement, and then write an essay taking a stand on its benefits and drawbacks. Be sure to document all material that you borrow from your sources, and include a works-cited page. (See Chapter 18 for information on MLA documentation.)

2. **Working with Sources.** Do you support taxing junk food and soda for the purposes of improving public health? Using the selections in this casebook as your sources, write an argumentative essay that takes a position on this issue. Be sure to document all material that you borrow from your sources, and include a works-cited page. (See Chapter 18 for information on MLA documentation.)

3. According to Engber, "We've known for a long time that any sin tax is likely to be a burden on the poor, since they're most prone to unhealthy behavior" (14). Do you agree? Write an essay arguing that such taxes are (or are not) unfair.

Combining the Patterns

How is **definition** important to Engber's argument and overall purpose? Point to specific examples of definition in the essay. Should Engber have included additional definitions?

Thematic Connections

- "No Wonder They Call Me a Bitch" (page 176)
- "Why Looks Are the Last Bastion of Discrimination" (page 246)
- "Tortillas" (page 507)

JEFF OUSBORNE

Does This Tax Make Me Look Fat?

Born in Baltimore, Maryland, in 1970, Jeff Ousborne has a Ph.D. in English from Boston College and teaches at Suffolk University in Boston. His writing has appeared in the *Boston Phoenix, WetFeet* magazine, *Maxim, Men's Fitness, Entertainment Weekly,* and other publications. He has also been an associate editor at *Details* magazine as well as a contributing editor at Jungle Media.

Background on financial penalties for overweight people The high U.S. obesity rate has led to higher health-care costs generally, including increases in copays and insurance premiums. That is especially true in employer-based insurance plans, where overweight employees cost more in health-care expenses than employees who maintain a normal weight. But there are other, less obvious costs as well. A Centers for Disease Control study determined that airlines are spending an additional $275 million on 350 million gallons of fuel to carry the additional weight of heavier passengers. The same study estimated that this extra fuel results in 3.8 million more tons of carbon dioxide in the air. Some airlines already require overweight passengers to buy an extra seat — a practice the media scrutinized in 2010 when Hollywood film director Kevin Smith was removed from a Southwest Airlines flight because he did not fit into a single seat.

Our national weight problem lends itself to the well-meaning dreams 1 of social engineers — both professional and amateur. Along these lines, some policy wonks and pundits have proposed taxes on unhealthy food. Others prefer a more direct approach: a tax directly on the overweight. For example, writer John Ridley made the case in a 2009 *Huffington Post* article called "Forget a 'Fat Tax.' Tax the Fat": "And for those who say that taxing the fat isn't fair, I say: how fair is it that healthy people are subsidizing the lifestyles of the fat?" Maybe Ridley was half joking. But serious people have taken this idea seriously over the past few years. For example, Eric Topol, former chief of cardiology at the prestigious Cleveland Clinic, suggested linking tax rates to body weight. Alabama toyed with a tax on overweight state employees in 2008. In Arizona, Governor Jan Brewer proposed a $50 penalty for some overweight Medicare recipients — a plan endorsed by the *Los Angeles Times,* even though it was never passed. Such proposals create the pleasing illusion of poetic justice. They also raise ethical questions about discrimination, the nature of obesity, the problematic intersections of weight and social class, and the political economy of our food system.

> "Serious people have taken this idea seriously."

But setting these issues aside, would weight-based state or federal taxes raise revenue and make people healthier?

Probably not. 2

First, there's the question of standards. Taxation advocates (like Rid- 3 ley) often support the Body Mass Index [BMI] as the measurement of obesity. In the context of overall health, however, BMI can be a red herring. "It's just not a good indicator, especially if connected to punitive tax measures," says Rebecca Puhl, Ph.D., director of research at the Rudd Center for Food Policy and Obesity at Yale University. "A person with a high BMI can be healthy; a person with a low BMI can have high blood pressure and other problems. Moreover, if we tax based on BMI, a 300-pound person could lose 10 percent of his or her body weight, but wouldn't lower BMI significantly, even if the person's behavior was a step in the right direction."

Second, there are the practical problems of cost and administration. 4 Even advocates of Arizona's plan acknowledge that the $50 would not cover the program's administrative expenses, let alone close gaps in the state budget. Imagine the bureaucracy at the federal level. New departments? Registration and paperwork? Exemptions and an appeals process? IRS weigh stations? "The logistics of this are difficult to conceive," says Puhl.

Third, there's little or no evidence that such schemes would lead to 5 healthier long-term behavior. "Obesity is a complex problem," observes Shahram Heshmat, an associate professor of public health at the University of Illinois and author of *Eating Behavior and Obesity: Behavioral Economics Strategies for Health Professionals* (2011). "These tax strategies seem based on the idea that obese people are making rational economic decisions about food. But the overweight don't make eating choices to 'maximize utility.' There are so many other factors — biological, cultural, unconscious — unrelated to economics. Even if these people lost weight, they'd probably gain it all back."

Politically, "fat tax" proposals aren't likely to go anywhere, especially 6 at the federal level. For liberals, "fat taxes" mean stigmatization, discrimination, and the oversimplification of obesity's complicated causes. For conservatives and libertarians, a fat tax looks like the intrusive hand of an overweight nanny state. For the time being, at least, our extra pounds will keep their tax-exempt status.

•　•　•

Comprehension

1. What "direct approach" (1) to obesity have some commentators and public officials endorsed? Who has supported such policies?

2. According to the essay, why is the Body Mass Index (BMI) a bad baseline standard for taxation rates?

3. According to the essay, why are economic approaches to obesity unlikely to be successful at the state and federal level?

4. Why might liberals, conservatives, and libertarians object to "fat taxes"? Are the writer's generalizations about the political views of these groups fair and accurate?

Purpose and Audience

1. What is Ousborne's overall purpose in this essay? What view does he take of those who support basing taxation on weight?

2. What does Ousborne assume about his readers? How do his assumptions about them determine the kind of evidence he uses in his argument?

3. Do you think Ousborne expects this essay to have any effect on public policy? Explain.

4. This essay is essentially a refutation of an essay by John Ridley. Does Ousborne refute Ridley's position effectively?

Style and Structure

1. What is the purpose of Ousborne's first paragraph? What does he achieve by beginning this way? How else might he have opened the essay?

2. According to Ousborne, "serious people have taken this idea [of imposing a 'fat tax'] seriously over the past few years" (1). How effectively does he support this generalization?

3. Ousborne writes that weight-based taxation proposals "create the pleasing illusion of poetic justice" (1). What does *poetic justice* mean in this context?

4. Ousborne acknowledges the "ethical questions" (1) and complex issues regarding obesity, but he largely sets them aside. Why does he do this? Would the essay be stronger if he addressed all of these issues?

5. What kinds of appeals does Ousbourne make in this essay? What kind of evidence does he use? Do you find it persuasive? Why or why not?

Vocabulary Projects

1. Define each of these words as it is used in this selection.

policy wonks (1)	red herring (3)
pundits (1)	logistics (4)
subsidizing (1)	stigmatization (6)
intersections (1)	nanny state (6)

2. Ousbourne quotes an economist who claims, "the overweight don't make eating choices to 'maximize utility'" (6). *Utility maximization* is a term used in the field of economics. What does it mean? How do the term's connotations support Ousborne's main point?

Journal Entry

According to Shahram Heshmat, "Obesity is a complex problem" (5). Do you agree? What do you think is the primary cause of obesity? Personal choice? Heredity? Do culture and society play a role?

Writing Workshop

1. Although policy-makers, health experts, and politicians have endorsed various taxes on unhealthy foods, the idea of directly taxing obese people for their weight is much more controversial. Do you think the American public would ever support weight-based taxation? Would you support such a proposal? Why or why not?

2. **Working with Sources.** According to Ousborne, America's weight problem "lends itself to the well-meaning dreams of social engineers" (1). What is *social engineering*? Investigate the meaning and history of this term. Then, write an essay that takes a position for or against the use of social engineering to address a social problem. To support your position, focus on either a positive or negative example of social engineering. Be sure to document all material that you borrow from your sources, and include a works-cited page. (See Chapter 18 for information on MLA documentation.)

2. **Working with Sources.** The essay refers to the BMI, or Body Mass Index. What is BMI? What are its origins? Is it an "objective" standard? What disagreements and controversies exist around its use? Research BMI and write an essay either supporting or opposing its use as a general standard for good health. Be sure to document all material that you borrow from your sources, and include a works-cited page. (See Chapter 18 for information on MLA documentation.)

Combining the Patterns

Where does this essay incorporate cause and effect? Why is cause and effect important to Ousborne's argument?

Thematic Connections

- "Get It Right: Privatize Executions" (page 298)
- "Tortillas" (page 507)
- "The Case for Mandatory Organ Donation" (page 614)
- "A Modest Proposal" (page 692)

Writing Assignments for Argumentation

1. Write an argumentative essay discussing whether parents have a right to spank their children. If your position is that they do, under what circumstances? What limitations should exist? If your position is that they do not, how should parents discipline children? How should they deal with inappropriate behavior?

2. Go to the American Library Association's Web site at www.ala.org/ ala/issuesadvocacy/banned/frequentlychallenged/challengedclassics/ reasonsbanned/index.cfm, and look at the list of the most frequently banned books of the twentieth century. Choose a book from the list that you have read. Assume that a library in your town has decided that the book you have chosen is objectionable and has removed it from the shelves. Write an email to your local newspaper arguing for or against the library's actions. Make a list of the major arguments that might be advanced against your position, and try to refute some of them in your email.

3. In Great Britain, cities began installing video surveillance systems in public areas in the 1970s. Police departments claim that these cameras help them do their jobs more efficiently. For example, such cameras enabled police to identify and capture terrorists who bombed the London subway in 2005. Opponents of the cameras say that the police are creating a society that severely compromises the right of personal privacy. How do you feel about this issue? Assume that the police department in your city is proposing to install cameras in the downtown and other pedestrian areas. Write an editorial for your local paper presenting your views on the topic.

4. Write an essay discussing under what circumstances, if any, animals should be used for scientific experimentation.

5. **Working with Sources.** Each year, a growing number of high school graduates are choosing to take a year off before going to college. The idea of this kind of "gap year" has been the source of some debate. Proponents say that a gap year gives students time to mature, time to decide what they want to get out of their education. It also gives them the opportunity to travel or to save some money for college. Detractors of a gap year point out that some students have trouble getting back into the academic routine when the year is over. In addition, students who take a year off are a year behind their classmates when they return. Research the pros and cons of the gap year. Then, write an essay in which you argue for or against taking a year off before college. Be sure to document your sources and to include a works-cited page. (See Chapter 18 for information on MLA documentation.)

6. **Working with Sources.** Go to the Web site deathpenalty.org, and research some criminal cases that resulted in the death penalty. Write an essay using these accounts to support your arguments either for or

against the death penalty. Be sure to document your sources and to include a works-cited page. (See Chapter 18 for information about MLA documentation.)

7. Write an argumentative essay discussing under what circumstances a nation has an obligation to go (or not to go) to war.

8. Since the events of September 11, 2001, the idea of arming pilots of commercial passenger planes has been debated. Those opposed to arming pilots claim that the risks — that a gun will fall into the hands of hijackers or that a passenger will be accidentally shot — outweigh any benefits. Those who support the idea say that the pilot is the last line of defense and must be able to defend the cockpit from terrorists. Due to public pressure in favor of arming pilots, a small trial program has been instituted. Do you think all pilots of commercial airplanes should be armed? Write an argumentative essay presenting your views on this subject.

9. In the Declaration of Independence, Jefferson says that all individuals are entitled to "life, liberty and the pursuit of happiness." Write an essay arguing that these rights are not absolute.

10. Write an argumentative essay on one of these topics:

- Should high school students be required to recite the Pledge of Allegiance at the start of each school day?
- Should college students be required to do community service?
- Should public school teachers be required to pass periodic competency tests?
- Should the legal drinking age be raised (or lowered)?
- Should states be required to educate the children of illegal immigrants?
- Should sugary drinks be banned in all public schools and government workplaces?
- Do Facebook and other social networking sites do more harm than good?
- Should undocumented immigrants be given amnesty?

Collaborative Activity for Argumentation

Working with three other students, select a controversial topic — one not covered in any of the debates in this chapter — that interests all of you. (You can review the Writing Assignments for Argumentation to get ideas.) State your topic the way a topic is stated in a formal debate:

Resolved: The United States should censor Internet content.

Then, divide into two-member teams, and decide which team will take the pro position and which will take the con. Each team should list the arguments on its side of the issue and then write two or three paragraphs summarizing its position. Finally, the teams should stage a ten-minute debate — five minutes for each side — in front of the class. (The pro side presents its argument first.) At the end of each debate, the class should decide which team has presented the stronger arguments.

15

Combining the Patterns

Many paragraphs combine several patterns of development. In the following paragraph, for example, Paul Hoffman uses narration, exemplification, and cause and effect to explain why we tend to see numbers as more than "instruments of enumeration."

Topic sentence	The idea that numbers are not mere instruments of enumeration but are sacred, perfect,
Narration	friendly, lucky, or evil goes back to antiquity. In the sixth century B.C. Pythagoras, whom schoolchildren associate with the famous theorem that in a right triangle the square of the hypotenuse always equals the sum of the squares of its sides, not only performed brilliant mathematics but made a religion out of numbers.
Exemplification	In numerology, the number 12 has always represented completeness, as in the 12 months of the year, the 12 signs of the zodiac, the 12 hours of the day, the 12 gods of Olympus, the 12 labors of Hercules, the 12 tribes of Israel, the 12 apostles of Jesus, the 12 days of Christmas, and, more recently perhaps, the 12 eggs in an egg carton.
Cause and effect	Since 13 exceeds 12 by only one, the number lies just beyond completeness and, hence, is restless to the point of being evil.

Like paragraphs, essays do not usually follow a single pattern of development; in fact, nearly every essay, including those in this text, combines a variety of patterns. Even though an essay may be organized according to one dominant pattern, it is still likely to include paragraphs, and even groups of paragraphs, shaped by other patterns of development. For example, a process essay can use **cause and effect** to show the results of the process, and a cause-and-effect essay can use **exemplification** (to illustrate possible effects) or **comparison and contrast** of two events (to assess possible causes). In many cases, a dominant pattern is supported by other patterns; in fact, combining various patterns in a single essay gives writers the flexibility to express their ideas most effectively. For this reason, each essay in Chapters 6 through 14 of this text is followed by Combining the Patterns questions that focus on how the essay uses (or might use) other patterns of development along with its dominant pattern.

Structuring an Essay by Combining the Patterns

Essays that combine various patterns of development, like essays structured primarily by a single pattern, include an **introduction**, several **body paragraphs**, and a **conclusion**. The introduction typically ends with the thesis statement that gives the essay its focus, and the conclusion often restates that thesis or summarizes the essay's main points. Each body paragraph (or group of paragraphs) is structured according to the pattern of development that best suits the material it develops.

Suppose you are planning your answer to the following question on a take-home essay exam for a sociology of religion course.

> For what reasons are people attracted to cults? Why do they join? Support your answer with specific examples that illustrate how cults recruit and retain members.

The wording of this exam question ("for what reasons") suggests that the essay's dominant pattern of development will be **cause and effect**; the wording also suggests that this cause-and-effect structure will include **exemplification**. In addition, you may decide to develop your essay with **definition** and **process**.

An informal outline for your essay might look like this:

SAMPLE OUTLINE: Combining the Patterns

Introduction:	Definition of *cult* (defined by negation — telling what it is *not* — and by comparison and contrast with *religion*). Thesis statement (suggests cause and effect): Using aggressive recruitment tactics and isolating potential members from their families and past lives, cults appeal to new recruits by offering them a highly structured environment.
Cause and effect:	Why people join cults
Process:	How cults recruit new members
Exemplification:	Tactics various cults use to retain members (series of brief examples)
Conclusion:	Restatement of thesis or review of key points

Combining the Patterns: Revising and Editing

When you revise an essay that combines several patterns of development, consider the items on the revision checklist on page 68, as well as any of the more specific revision checklists in Chapers 6 through 14 that apply to the patterns in your essay. As you edit your essay, refer to the editing checklists on pages 85, 88, and 90, and to the individual editing checklists in Chapters 6 through 14. You may also wish to consult the Grammar in Context sections that appear throughout the book, as well as the one that follows.

GRAMMAR IN CONTEXT   Agreement with Indefinite Pronouns

A **pronoun** is a word that takes the place of a noun or another pronoun in a sentence. Unlike most pronouns, an **indefinite pronoun** (*anyone, either, each,* and so on) does not refer to a specific person or thing.

Subject-Verb Agreement. Pronoun subjects must agree in number with their verbs: singular pronouns (*I, he, she, it,* and so on) take singular verbs, and plural pronouns (*we, they,* and so on) take plural verbs.

"I have learned much as a scavenger" (Eighner 665).

"We were free like comets in the heavens" (Truong 659).

Indefinite pronoun subjects must also agree in number with their verbs: singular indefinite pronouns take singular verbs, and plural indefinite pronouns take plural verbs. Most indefinite pronouns are singular, but some are plural.

SUBJECT–VERB AGREEMENT WITH INDEFINITE PRONOUN SUBJECTS

SINGULAR INDEFINITE PRONOUNS

another	anyone	everyone	one	each
either	neither	anything	everything	

"Everyone was darker or lighter than we were" (Truong 661).

"Everything seems to stink" (Eighner 670).

PLURAL INDEFINITE PRONOUNS

both	many	few	several	others

"Many are discarded for minor imperfections that can be pared away" (Eighner 667).

NOTE: A few indefinite pronouns — *some, all, any, more, most,* and *none* — may be either singular or plural, depending on their meaning in the sentence.

SINGULAR: According to David Kirby, <u>some</u> of the history of tattoos <u>is</u> surprising. (*Some* refers to *history,* so the verb is singular.)

PLURAL: <u>Some</u> of the tattoos David Kirby discusses <u>serve</u> as a kind of "record book," while others create a "canvas" (688). (*Some* refers to *tattoos,* so the verb is plural.)

Pronoun-Antecedent Agreement. An **antecedent** is the noun or pronoun that a pronoun refers to in a sentence. Pronouns must agree in number with their antecedents.

Use a singular pronoun to refer to a singular indefinite pronoun antecedent.

<u>Each</u> day has <u>its</u> surprises for Lars Eighner and his dog, Lizbeth.

Use a plural pronoun to refer to a plural indefinite pronoun antecedent.

<u>Many</u> of the people who pass Eighner and Lizbeth avert <u>their</u> eyes.

NOTE: Although the indefinite pronoun *everyone* is singular, it is often used with a plural pronoun in everyday speech and informal writing.

INFORMAL: <u>Everyone</u> turns <u>their</u> heads when Eighner and Lizbeth walk by.

This usage is generally acceptable in informal situations, but college writing requires correct pronoun-antecedent agreement.

CORRECT: <u>People</u> turn <u>their</u> heads when Eighner and Lizbeth walk by.

For more practice in avoiding agreement problems with indefinite pronouns, visit the resources for Chapter 15 at **bedfordstmartins.com/patterns**.

The essays in this chapter illustrate how different patterns of development work together in a single piece of writing. The first two essays — "The Park" by Michael Huu Truong, a student, and "On Dumpster Diving" by Lars Eighner — include annotations that identify the various patterns these writers use. Truong's essay relies primarily on narration, but he also uses description and exemplification to convey his memories of childhood. Eighner's combines sections of definition, exemplification, classification and division, cause and effect, comparison and contrast, and process; at the same time, he tells the story (narration) and provides vivid details (description) of his life as a homeless person.

Following these annotated essays are three additional selections that combine patterns: Barbara Ehrenreich's "The Shame Game," David Kirby's "Inked Well," and Jonathan Swift's classic satire "A Modest Proposal." Each of the essays in this chapter is followed by the same types of questions that accompany the reading selections that appear elsewhere in the text.

A STUDENT WRITER: Combining the Patterns

This essay was written by Michael Huu Truong for a first-year composition course in response to the assignment "Write an essay about the person and/or place that defined your childhood."

The Park

Background

My childhood did not really begin until I came to this   1
country from the jungle of Vietnam. I can't really remember much from this period, and the things I do remember are vague images that I have no desire or intention to discuss. However, my childhood in the States was a lot different, especially after I met

Thesis statement   my friend James. While it lasted, it was paradise.

Narrative begins   It was a cold wintry day in February after a big snowstorm —   2

Description: effects of cold   the first I'd ever seen. My lips were chapped, my hands were frozen stiff, and my cheeks were burning from the biting wind, and yet I loved it. I especially loved the snow. I had come from

Comparison and contrast: U.S. vs. Vietnam   a country where the closest things to snow were white paint and cotton balls. But now I was in America. On that frosty afternoon, I was determined to build a snowman. I had seen them in books, and I had heard they could talk. I knew they could come alive, and I couldn't wait.

"Eyryui roeow ierog," said a voice that came out of nowhere.   3

Description: James   I turned around, and right in my face was a short, red-faced (probably from the cold wind) Korean kid with a dirty, runny nose. I responded, "Wtefkjkr ruyjft gsdfr" in my own tongue. We understood each other perfectly, and we expressed our

Narration: the first day   understanding with a smile. Together, we built our first snowman. We were disappointed that evening when the snowman just stood there; however, I was happy because I had made my first friend.

Analogies   Ever since then we've been a team like Abbott and Costello   4
(or, when my cousin joined us, the Three Stooges). The two of us were inseparable. We could've made the greatest Krazy Glue commercial ever.

Narration: what they did that summer   The summer that followed the big snowstorm, from what I   5
can recall, was awesome. We were free like comets in the heavens, and we did whatever our hearts wanted. For the most part, our desires were fulfilled in a little park across the street. This park

was ours; it was like our own planet guarded by our own robot army (disguised as trees). Together we fought against the bigger people who always tried to invade and take over our world. The enemy could never conquer our fortress because they would have to destroy our robots, penetrate our force field, and then defeat us; this last feat would be impossible.

Narrative continues

Examples: what they banished

This park was our fantasy land where everything we wished   6
for came true and everything we hated was banished forever. We banished vegetables, cheese, bigger people, and — of course — girls. The land was enchanted, and we could be whatever we felt like. We were super ninjas one day and millionaires the next; we became the heroes we idolized and lived the lives we dreamed

Examples: superhero fantasies

about. I had the strength of Bruce Lee and Superman; James possessed the power of Clint Eastwood and the Bionic Man. My weapons were the skills of Bruce and a cape. James, however, needed a real weapon for Clint, and the weapon he made was awesome. The Death Ray could destroy a building with one blast, and it even had a shield so that James was always protected. Even with all his mighty weapons and gadgets, though, he was still no match for Superman and Bruce Lee. Every day, we fought until death (or until our parents called us for dinner).

Narrative continues

When we became bored with our super powers, the park   7
became a giant spaceship. We traveled all over the Universe, conquering and exploring strange new worlds and mysterious planets. Our ship was a top-secret indestructible space warship

Examples: new worlds and planets

called the X–007. We went to Mars, Venus, Pluto, and other alien planets, destroying all the monsters we could find. When necessary, our spacecraft was transformed into a submarine for deep-sea adventures. We found lost cities, unearthed treasures, and saved Earth by destroying all the sea monsters that were plotting against us. We became heroes — just like Superman, Bruce Lee, the Bionic Man, and Clint Eastwood.

Cause and effect: prospect of school leads to problems

James and I had the time of our lives in the park that   8
summer. It was great — until we heard about the horror of starting school. Shocked and terrified, we ran to our fortress to escape. For some reason, though, our magic kingdom had lost its powers. We fought hard that evening, trying to keep the bigger people out of our planet, but the battle was soon lost. Bruce Lee, Superman, the Bionic Man, and Clint Eastwood had all lost their special powers.

Narrative continues   School wasn't as bad as we'd thought it would be. The first   9
day, James and I sat there with our hands folded. We didn't talk or
move, and we didn't dare look at each other (we would've cracked
up because we always made these goofy faces). Even though we
had pens that could be transformed into weapons, we were still
scared.

Description: school   Everyone was darker or lighter than we were, and the   10
teacher was speaking a strange language (English). James and
I giggled as she talked. We giggled softly when everyone else
talked, and they laughed out loud when it was our turn to speak.

Narrative continues   The day dragged on, and all we wanted to do was go home   11
and rebuild our fortress. Finally, after an eternity, it was almost
three o'clock. James and I sat at the edge of our seats as we
counted under our breath: "10, 9, 8, 7, 6, 5, 4, 3, 2, 1." At last,
the bell sounded. We dashed for the door and raced home and
across the street — and then we stopped. We stood still in the
middle of the street with our hearts pounding like the beats of a
drum. The cool September wind began to pick up, and everything

Description: the fence   became silent. We stood there and watched the metal of the fence
reflect the beautiful colors of the sun. It was beautiful, and yet we
hated everything about it. The new metal fence separated us from
our fortress, our planet, our spaceship, our submarine — and, most
important of all, from our heroes and our dreams.

           We stood there for a long time. As the sun slowly turned   12
red and sank beneath the ground, so did our dreams, heroes, and
hearts. Darkness soon devoured the park, and after a while we
walked home with only the memories of the summer that came
after the big snowstorm.

Points for Special Attention

Writing a Personal Experience Essay. Michael's instructor specified that
he was to write an essay about a person or place to help his readers — other
students — understand what his childhood was like. Because the assignment called for a personal experience essay, Michael was free to use the
first-person pronouns *I* and *we*, as well as contractions, although neither
would be acceptable in a more formal essay.

Thesis Statement. Because Michael's primary purpose in this essay
was to communicate personal feelings and impressions, an argumentative
thesis statement (such as "If every television in the United States disappeared, more people would have childhoods like mine") would have

been inappropriate. Still, Michael states his thesis explicitly in order to unify his essay around the dominant impression he wants to convey: "While it lasted, it was paradise."

Working with Sources. Michael's assignment did not require him to consult any outside sources. If it had, he could have included background information about immigration from Vietnam to the United States — particularly data about when Vietnamese people came to the United States, where immigrants settled, how children adjusted to school and learned English, and how quickly they assimilated. Such information could have provided some context for his childhood memories.

Combining the Patterns. Michael also had more specific purposes, and these determined the patterns that shape his essay. His essay's dominant pattern is *narration,* but to help students visualize the person (James) and the place (the park) he discusses, he includes sections that *describe* and give concrete, specific *examples* as well as summarize his daily routine. These patterns work together to create an essay that conveys the nature of his childhood to readers.

Transitions. The transitions between the individual sentences and paragraphs of Michael's essay — "now," "Ever since," "The summer that followed the big snowstorm" — serve primarily to move readers through time. This is appropriate because narration is the dominant pattern that determines his essay's overall structure.

Detail. "The Park" is full of specific detail — for example, quoted bits of dialogue in paragraph 3 and names of Michael's heroes and of particular games (and related equipment and weapons) elsewhere. The descriptive details that re-create the physical scenes — in particular, the snow, cold, frost, and wind of winter and the sun reflected on the fence — are vivid enough to help readers visualize the places Michael writes about.

Figures of Speech. Michael's essay describes a time when his imagination wandered without the restraints of adulthood. Appropriately, he uses **simile**, **metaphor**, and **personification** — "We were free like comets in the heavens"; "The park became a giant spaceship"; "We found lost cities, unearthed treasures, and saved Earth"; "Darkness soon devoured the park" — to evoke the time and place he describes.

Focus on Revision

Michael's assignment asked him to write about his childhood, and he chose to focus on his early years in the United States. When his peer editing group discussed his essay, however, a number of students were curious about his life in Vietnam. Some of them thought he should add a paragraph summarizing the "vague images" he remembered of his earlier childhood, perhaps contrasting it with his life in the United States, as he does in passing in paragraph 2. When Michael asked his instructor about this idea, she suggested instead that he consider deleting the sentence in paragraph 1 that states he has "no desire or intention to discuss" this part of his life because it raises issues his essay does not address. After thinking about these suggestions, Michael decided to delete this sentence in his next draft and to add a brief paragraph about his life in Vietnam, contrasting the park and his friendship with James with some of his earlier, less idyllic memories.

PEER EDITING WORKSHEET: Combining the Patterns

1. Using the annotations for "The Park" (page 659) or "On Dumpster Diving" (page 664) as a guide, annotate the essay to identify the patterns of development it uses.

2. What is the essay's thesis? If it is not explicitly stated, state it in your own words. What pattern or patterns of development are suggested by the wording of the thesis statement?

3. What dominant pattern of development determines the essay's overall structure?

4. What patterns does the writer use to develop the body paragraphs of the essay? Explain why each pattern is used in a particular paragraph or group of paragraphs.

5. What patterns are not used? Where, if anywhere, might one of these patterns serve the writer's purpose?

6. Review the essay's topic sentences. Is the wording of each topic sentence consistent with the particular pattern that structures the paragraph? If not, suggest possible ways some of the topic sentences might be reworded.

Each of the following essays combines several patterns, blending strategies to achieve the writer's purpose.

LARS EIGHNER

On Dumpster Diving

Lars Eighner (b. 1948) dropped out of the University of Texas at Austin after his third year and took a job at a state mental hospital. After leaving his job over a policy dispute in 1988 and falling behind in his rent payments, Eighner became homeless. For three years, he traveled between Austin and Los Angeles with his dog, Lizbeth, earning what money he could from writing stories for magazines. Eighner's memories of his experiences living on the street, *Travels with Lizbeth* (1993), was written on a computer he found in a Dumpster. The following chapter from that book details the practical dangers as well as the many possibilities he discovered in his "Dumpster diving." Eighner now lives in Austin and works as a freelance writer and writing coach.

Background on the homeless Although the number of homeless people in the United States is difficult to measure accurately, homelessness has become a highly visible issue in the past two decades. It is estimated, for example, that as many as ten million people experienced homelessness in this country in the late 1980s alone. This surge in homelessness has a number of causes. Perhaps most important, a booming real estate market led to a significant drop in affordable housing in many areas of the country. In several cities, single-room-occupancy hotels, which had long provided cheap lodging, were demolished or converted into luxury apartments. At the same time, new technologies left many unskilled workers jobless. Government policies against detaining the nondangerous mentally ill against their will also played a significant role. (About a quarter of all homeless people are thought to be mentally ill.) More recently, a real estate bubble and the subsequent foreclosure crisis have forced hundreds of thousands out of their houses, leading many cities to report increased demand for emergency shelter. Currently, the U.S. Department of Health and Human Services estimates that homelessness affects two to three million Americans each year, of which approximately 40 percent are children.

This chapter was composed while the author was homeless. The present tense has been preserved.

Definition: Dumpster

Long before I began Dumpster diving I was im- 1
pressed with Dumpsters, enough so that I wrote the
Merriam-Webster research service to discover what I
could about the word *Dumpster*. I learned from them
that it is a proprietary word belonging to the Dempsey
Dumpster company. Since then I have dutifully
capitalized the word, although it was lowercased in
almost all the citations Merriam-Webster photocopied
for me. Dempsey's word is too apt. I have never heard

these things called anything but Dumpsters. I do not know anyone who knows the generic name for these objects. From time to time I have heard a wino or hobo give some corrupted credit to the original and call them Dipsy Dumpsters.

Narration: Eighner's story begins

I began Dumpster diving about a year before I 2 became homeless.

Definition: Dumpster diving

I prefer the word *scavenging* and use the word 3 *scrounging* when I mean to be obscure. I have heard people, evidently meaning to be polite, use the word *foraging,* but I prefer to reserve that word for gathering nuts and berries and such, which I do also according to the season and the opportunity. *Dumpster diving* seems to me to be a little too cute and, in my case, inaccurate because I lack the athletic ability to lower myself into the Dumpsters as the true divers do, much to their increased profit.

I like the frankness of the word *scavenging,* which I 4 can hardly think of without picturing a big black snail on an aquarium wall. I live from the refuse of others. I am a scavenger. I think it a sound and honorable niche, although if I could I would naturally prefer to live the comfortable consumer life, perhaps — and only perhaps — as a slightly less wasteful consumer, owing to what I have learned as a scavenger.

Narration: story continues

While Lizbeth and I were still living in the shack 5 on Avenue B as my savings ran out, I put almost all my sporadic income into rent. The necessities of daily life I began to extract from Dumpsters. Yes, we ate from them.

Exemplification: things found in Dumpsters

Except for jeans, all my clothes came from Dumpsters. Boom boxes, candles, bedding, toilet paper, a virgin male love doll, medicine, books, a typewriter, dishes, furnishings, and change, sometimes amounting to many dollars — I acquired many things from Dumpsters.

Thesis statement

I have learned much as a scavenger. I mean to put 6 some of what I have learned down here, beginning with the practical art of Dumpster diving and proceeding to the abstract.

What is safe to eat? 7

After all, the finding of objects is becoming 8 something of an urban art. Even respectable employed people will sometimes find something tempting sticking out of a Dumpster or standing beside one. Quite a number of people, not all of them of the bohemian type, are willing to brag that they found this or that piece of trash. But eating from Dumpsters is what separates the dilettanti from the professionals. Eating safely from the Dumpsters involves three principles: using the senses and common sense to evaluate the condition of the found materials, knowing the Dumpsters of a given area and checking them regularly, and seeking always to answer the question "Why was this discarded?"

Comparison and contrast: Dumpster divers vs. others

Perhaps everyone who has a kitchen and a regular   9
supply of groceries has, at one time or another, made a sandwich and eaten half of it before discovering mold on the bread or got a mouthful of milk before realizing the milk had turned. Nothing of the sort is likely to happen to a Dumpster diver because he is constantly reminded that most food is discarded for a reason. Yet a lot of perfectly good food can be found in Dumpsters.

Classification and division: different kinds of food found in Dumpsters and their relative safety

Canned goods, for example, turn up fairly often in   10
the Dumpsters I frequent. All except the most phobic people will be willing to eat from a can, even if it came from a Dumpster. Canned goods are among the safest foods to be found in Dumpsters but are not utterly foolproof.

Although very rare with modern canning methods,   11
botulism is a possibility. Most other forms of food poisoning seldom do lasting harm to a healthy person, but botulism is almost certainly fatal and often the first symptom is death. Except for carbonated beverages, all canned goods should contain a slight vacuum and suck air when first punctured. Bulging, rusty, and dented cans and cans that spew when punctured should be avoided, especially when the contents are not very acidic or syrupy.

Heat can break down the botulin, but this requires   12
much more cooking than most people do to canned goods. To the extent that botulism occurs at all, of course, it can occur in cans on pantry shelves as well as in cans from Dumpsters. Need I say that home-canned goods are simply too risky to be recommended.

From time to time one of my companions, aware   13
of the source of my provisions, will ask, "Do you think these crackers are really safe to eat?" For some reason it is most often the crackers they ask about.

This question has always made me angry. Of course   14
I would not offer my companion anything I had doubts about. But more than that, I wonder why he cannot evaluate the condition of the crackers for himself. I have no special knowledge and I have been wrong before. Since he knows where the food comes from, it seems

to me he ought to assume some of the responsibility for deciding what he will put in his mouth. For myself I have few qualms about dry foods such as crackers, cookies, cereal, chips, and pasta if they are free of visible contaminates and still dry and crisp. Most often such things are found in the original packaging, which is not so much a positive sign as it is the absence of a negative one.

Raw fruits and vegetables with intact skins seem 15 perfectly safe to me, excluding of course the obviously rotten. Many are discarded for minor imperfections that can be pared away. Leafy vegetables, grapes, cauliflower, broccoli, and similar things may be contaminated by liquids and may be impractical to wash.

Candy, especially hard candy, is usually safe if it 16 has not drawn ants. Chocolate is often discarded only because it has become discolored as the cocoa butter de-emulsified. Candying, after all, is one method of food preservation because pathogens do not like very sugary substances.

All of these foods might be found in any Dumpster 17 and can be evaluated with some confidence largely on the basis of appearance. Beyond these are foods that cannot be correctly evaluated without additional information.

I began scavenging by pulling pizzas out of the 18 Dumpster behind a pizza delivery shop. In general, prepared food requires caution, but in this case I knew when the shop closed and went to the Dumpster as soon as the last of the help left.

Such shops often get prank orders; both the orders 19 and the products made to fill them are called *bogus*. Because help seldom stays long at these places, pizzas are often made with the wrong topping, refused on delivery for being cold, or baked incorrectly. The products to be discarded are boxed up because inventory is kept by counting boxes: A boxed pizza can be written off; an unboxed pizza does not exist.

I never placed a bogus order to increase the supply 20 of pizzas and I believe no one else was scavenging in this Dumpster. But the people in the shop became suspicious and began to retain their garbage in the shop overnight. While it lasted I had a steady supply of fresh, sometimes warm pizza. Because I knew the Dumpster I knew the source of the pizza, and because I visited the Dumpster regularly I knew what was fresh and what was yesterday's.

Cause and effect: why Eighner visits certain Dumpsters; why students throw out food

The area I frequent is inhabited by many affluent 21 college students. I am not here by chance; the Dumpsters in this area are very rich. Students throw out many good things, including food. In particular they tend to throw everything out when they move at the end of a semester, before and after breaks, and around midterm, when many of them despair of college. So I find it advantageous to keep an eye on the academic calendar.

Students throw food away around breaks because 22 they do not know whether it has spoiled or will spoil before they return. A typical discard is a half jar of peanut butter. In fact, nonorganic peanut butter does not require refrigeration and is unlikely to spoil in any reasonable time. The student does not know that, and since it is Daddy's money, the student decides not to take a chance. Opened containers require caution and some attention to the question "Why was this discarded?" But in the case of discards from student apartments, the answer may be that the item was thrown out through carelessness, ignorance, or wastefulness. This can sometimes be deduced when the item is found with many others, including some that are obviously perfectly good.

Some students, and others, approach defrosting 23 a freezer by chucking out the whole lot. Not only do the circumstances of such a find tell the story, but also the mass of frozen goods stays cold for a long time and items may be found still frozen or freshly thawed.

Yogurt, cheese, and sour cream are items that are 24 often thrown out while they are still good. Occasionally I find cheese with a spot of mold, which of course I just pare off, and because it is obvious why such a cheese was discarded, I treat it with less suspicion than an apparently perfect cheese found in similar circumstances. Yogurt is often discarded, still sealed, only because the expiration date on the carton had passed. This is one of my favorite finds because yogurt will keep for several days, even in warm weather.

Students throw out canned goods and staples at 25 the end of semesters and when they give up college at midterm. Drugs, pornography, spirits, and the like are often discarded when parents are expected — Dad's Day, for example. And spirits also turn up after big party weekends, presumably discarded by the newly reformed. Wine and spirits, of course, keep perfectly well even once opened, but the same cannot be said of beer.

My test for carbonated soft drinks is whether they 26 still fizz vigorously. Many juices or other beverages are too acidic or too syrupy to cause much concern, provided they are not visibly contaminated. I have discovered nasty molds in the vegetable juices, even when the product was found under its original seal; I recommend that such products be decanted slowly into a clear glass. Liquids always require some care. One hot day I found a large jug of Pat O'Brien's Hurricane mix. The jug had been opened but was still ice cold. I drank three large glasses before it became apparent to me that someone had added rum to the mix, and not a little rum. I never tasted the rum, and by the time I began to feel the effects I had already ingested a very large quantity of the beverage. Some divers would have considered this a boon, but being suddenly intoxicated in a public place in the early afternoon is not my idea of a good time.

Examples: liquids that require care

I have heard of people maliciously contaminating 27 discarded food and even handouts, but mostly I have heard of this from people with vivid imaginations who have had no experience with Dumpsters themselves. Just before the pizza shop stopped discarding its garbage at night, jalapeños began showing up on most of the thrown-out pizzas. If indeed this was meant to discourage me, it was a wasted effort because I am a native Texan.

For myself, I avoid game, poultry, pork, and egg- 28 based foods, whether I find them raw or cooked. I seldom have the means to cook what I find, but when I do I avail myself of plentiful supplies of beef, which is often in very good condition. I suppose fish becomes disagreeable before it becomes dangerous. Lizbeth is happy to have any such thing that is past its prime and, in fact, does not recognize fish as food until it is quite strong.

Home leftovers, as opposed to surpluses from 29 restaurants, are very often bad. Evidently, especially among students, there is a common type of personality that carefully wraps up even the smallest leftover and shoves it into the back of the refrigerator for six months or so before discarding it. Characteristic of this type are the reused jars and margarine tubs to which the remains are committed. I avoid ethnic foods I am unfamiliar with. If I do not know what it is supposed to look like when it is good, I cannot be certain I will be able to tell if it is bad.

No matter how careful I am I still get dysentery at 30 least once a month, oftener in warmer weather. I do not want to paint too romantic a picture. Dumpster diving has serious drawbacks as a way of life.

Process: how to scavenge

I learned to scavenge gradually, on my own. Since 31 then I have initiated several companions into the trade. I have learned that there is a predictable series of stages a person goes through in learning to scavenge.

At first the new scavenger is filled with disgust and 32 self-loathing. He is ashamed of being seen and may lurk around, trying to duck behind things, or he may try to dive at night. (In fact, most people instinctively look away from a scavenger. By skulking around, the novice calls attention to himself and arouses suspicion. Diving at night is ineffective and needlessly messy.)

Every grain of rice seems to be a maggot. Everything 33 seems to stink. He can wipe the egg yolk off the found can, but he cannot erase from his mind the stigma of eating garbage.

That stage passes with experience. The scavenger 34 finds a pair of running shoes that fit and look and smell brand-new. He finds a pocket calculator in perfect working order. He finds pristine ice cream, still frozen, more than he can eat or keep. He begins to understand: People throw away perfectly good stuff, a lot of perfectly good stuff.

At this stage, Dumpster shyness begins to dis- 35 sipate. The diver, after all, has the last laugh. He is finding all manner of good things that are his for the taking. Those who disparage his profession are the fools, not he.

He may begin to hang on to some perfectly good 36 things for which he has neither a use nor a market. Then he begins to take note of the things that are not perfectly good but are nearly so. He mates a Walkman with broken earphones and one that is missing a battery cover. He picks up things that he can repair.

At this stage he may become lost and never recover. 37 Dumpsters are full of things of some potential value to someone and also of things that never have much intrinsic value but are interesting. All the Dumpster divers I have known come to the point of trying to acquire everything they touch. Why not take it, they reason, since it is all free? This is, of course, hopeless. Most divers come to realize that they must restrict themselves to items of relatively immediate utility. But in some cases the diver simply cannot control himself. I have met several of these pack-rat types. Their ideas of the values of various pieces of junk verge on the psychotic. Every bit of glass may be a diamond, they think, and all that glisters,* gold.

Cause and effect: why Eighner gains weight when he scavenges

I tend to gain weight when I am scavenging. 38 Partly this is because I always find far more pizza and doughnuts than water-packed tuna, nonfat yogurt, and fresh vegetables. Also I have not developed much faith in the reliability of Dumpsters as a food source, although it has been proven to me many times. I tend to eat as if I have no idea where my next meal is coming from. But mostly I just hate to see food go to waste and so I eat much more than I should. Something like this drives the obsession to collect junk.

As for collecting objects, I usually restrict myself to 39 collecting one kind of small object at a time, such as pocket calculators, sunglasses, or campaign buttons.

Cause and effect: why Eighner saves items

To live on the street I must anticipate my needs to a certain extent: I must pick up and save warm bedding I find in August because it will not be found in Dumpsters in November. As I have no access to health care, I often hoard essential drugs, such as antibiotics and antihistamines. (This course can be recommended only to those with some grounding in pharmacology. Antibiotics, for example, even when indicated are worse than useless if taken in insufficient amounts.) But even if I had a home with extensive storage space, I could not save everything that might be valuable in some contingency.

I have proprietary feelings about my Dumpsters. 40 As I have mentioned, it is no accident that I scavenge from ones where good finds are common. But my

Comparison and contrast: Dumpsters in rich and poorer areas

limited experience with Dumpsters in other areas suggests to me that even in poorer areas, Dumpsters, if attended with sufficient diligence, can be made to yield a livelihood. The rich students discard perfectly good kiwi fruit; poorer people discard perfectly good apples. Slacks and Polo shirts are found in one place; jeans and T-shirts in the other. The population of competitors rather than the affluence of the dumpers most affects the feasibility of survival by scavenging. The large number of competitors is what puts me off the idea of trying to scavenge in places like Los Angeles.

---

* Eds. note — Glitters.

Curiously, I do not mind my direct competition, 41 other scavengers, so much as I hate the can scroungers.

Cause and effect: why people scrounge cans

People scrounge cans because they have to have a 42 little cash. I have tried scrounging cans with an able-bodied companion. Afoot a can scrounger simply cannot make more than a few dollars in a day. One can extract the necessities of life from the Dumpsters directly with far less effort than would be required to accumulate the equivalent value in cans. (These observations may not hold in places with container redemption laws.)

Can scroungers, then, are people who must have 43 small amounts of cash. These are drug addicts and winos, mostly the latter because the amounts of cash are so small. Spirits and drugs do, like all other commodities, turn up in Dumpsters and the scavenger will from time to time have a half bottle of a rather good wine with his dinner. But the wino cannot survive on these occasional finds; he must have his daily dose to stave off the DTs. All the cans he can carry will buy about three bottles of Wild Irish Rose.

Comparison and contrast: can scroungers vs. true scavengers

I do not begrudge them the cans, but can scroungers 44 tend to tear up the Dumpsters, mixing the contents and littering the area. They become so specialized that they can see only cans. They earn my contempt by passing up change, canned goods, and readily hockable items.

There are precious few courtesies among scavengers. 45 But it is common practice to set aside surplus items: pairs of shoes, clothing, canned goods, and such. A true scavenger hates to see good stuff go to waste, and what he cannot use he leaves in good condition in plain sight.

Can scroungers lay waste to everything in their path 46 and will stir one of a pair of good shoes to the bottom of a Dumpster, to be lost or ruined in the muck. Can scroungers will even go through individual garbage cans, something I have never seen a scavenger do.

Cause and effect: why scavengers do not go through individual garbage cans

Individual garbage cans are set out on the public 47 easement only on garbage days. On the other days going through them requires trespassing close to a dwelling. Going through individual garbage cans without scattering litter is almost impossible. Litter is likely to reduce the public's tolerance of scavenging. Individual cans are simply not as productive as Dumpsters; people in houses and duplexes do not move so often and for some reason do not tend to discard as much useful material. Moreover, the time required to go through one garbage can that serves one household is not much less than the time required to go through a Dumpster that contains the refuse of twenty apartments.

But my strongest reservation about going through 48
individual garbage cans is that this seems to me a very personal kind of invasion to which I would object if I were a householder. Although many things in Dumpsters are obviously meant never to come to light, a Dumpster is somehow less personal.

I avoid trying to draw conclusions about the 49
people who dump in the Dumpsters I frequent. I think it would be unethical to do so, although I know many people will find the idea of scavenger ethics too funny for words.

Examples: things found in Dumpsters

Dumpsters contain bank statements, correspon- 50
dence, and other documents, just as anyone might expect. But there are also less obvious sources of information. Pill bottles, for example. The labels bear the name of the patient, the name of the doctor, and the name of the drug. AIDS drugs and antipsychotic medicines, to name but two groups, are specific and are seldom prescribed for any other disorders. The plastic compacts for birth-control pills usually have complete label information.

Despite all of this sensitive information, I have 51
had only one apartment resident object to my going through the Dumpster. In that case it turned out the resident was a university athlete who was taking bets and who was afraid I would turn up his wager slips.

Occasionally a find tells a story. I once found a small 52
paper bag containing some unused condoms, several partial tubes of flavored sexual lubricants, a partially used compact of birth-control pills, and the torn pieces of a picture of a young man. Clearly she was through with him and planning to give up sex altogether.

Dumpster things are often sad — abandoned teddy 53
bears, shredded wedding books, despaired-of sales kits. I find many pets lying in state in Dumpsters. Although I hope to get off the streets so that Lizbeth can have a long and comfortable old age, I know this hope is not very realistic. So I suppose when her time comes she too will go into a Dumpster. I will have no better place for her. And after all, it is fitting, since for most of her life her livelihood has come from the Dumpster. When she finds something I think is safe that has been spilled from a Dumpster, I let her have it. She already knows the route around the best ones. I like to think that if

she survives me she will have a chance of evading the dog catcher and of finding her sustenance on the route.

Silly vanities also come to rest in the Dumpsters. I 54 am a rather accomplished needleworker. I get a lot of material from the Dumpsters. Evidently sorority girls, hoping to impress someone, perhaps themselves, with their mastery of a womanly art, buy a lot of embroider-by-number kits, work a few stitches horribly, and eventually discard the whole mess. I pull out their stitches, turn the canvas over, and work an original design. Do not think I refrain from chuckling as I make gifts from these kits.

I find diaries and journals. I have often thought of 55 compiling a book of literary found objects. And perhaps I will one day. But what I find is hopelessly commonplace and bad without being, even unconsciously, camp. College students also discard their papers. I am horrified to discover the kind of paper that now merits an A in an undergraduate course. I am grateful, however, for the number of good books and magazines the students throw out.

In the area I know best I have never discovered 56 vermin in the Dumpster, but there are two kinds of kitty surprise. One is alley cats whom I meet as they leap, claws first, out of Dumpsters. This is especially thrilling when I have Lizbeth in tow. The other kind of kitty surprise is a plastic garbage bag filled with some ponderous, amorphous mass. This always proves to be used cat litter.

City bees harvest doughnut glaze and this makes 57 the Dumpster at the doughnut shop more interesting. My faith in the instinctive wisdom of animals is always shaken whenever I see Lizbeth attempt to catch a bee in her mouth, which she does whenever bees are present. Evidently some birds find Dumpsters profitable, for birdie surprise is almost as common as kitty surprise of the first kind. In hunting season all kinds of small game turn up in Dumpsters, some of it, sadly, not entirely dead. Curiously, summer and winter, maggots are uncommon.

The worst of the living and near-living hazards of 58 the Dumpsters are the fire ants. The food they claim is not much of a loss, but they are vicious and aggressive. It is very easy to brush against some surface of the Dumpster and pick up half a dozen or more fire ants, usually in some sensitive area such as the underarm. One advantage of bringing Lizbeth along as I make

Dumpster rounds is that, for obvious reasons, she is very alert to ground-based fire ants. When Lizbeth recognizes a fire-ant infestation around our feet, she does the Dance of the Zillion Fire Ants. I have learned not to ignore this warning from Lizbeth, whether I perceive the tiny ants or not, but to remove ourselves at Lizbeth's first *pas de bourée.** All the more so because the ants are the worst in the summer months when I wear flip-flops if I have them. (Perhaps someone will misunderstand this. Lizbeth does the Dance of the Zillion Fire Ants when she recognizes more fire ants than she cares to eat, not when she is being bitten. Since I have learned to react promptly, she does not get bitten at all. It is the isolated patrol of fire ants that falls in Lizbeth's range that deserves pity. She finds them quite tasty.)

Process: how to go through a Dumpster

By far the best way to go through a Dumpster is to 59 lower yourself into it. Most of the good stuff tends to settle at the bottom because it is usually weightier than the rubbish. My more athletic companions have often demonstrated to me that they can extract much good material from a Dumpster I have already been over.

To those psychologically or physically unprepared 60 to enter a Dumpster, I recommend a stout stick, preferably with some barb or hook at one end. The hook can be used to grab plastic garbage bags. When I find canned goods or other objects loose at the bottom of a Dumpster, I lower a bag into it, roll the desired object into the bag, and then hoist the bag out — a procedure more easily described than executed. Much Dumpster diving is a matter of experience for which nothing will do except practice.

Dumpster diving is outdoor work, often surpris- 61 ingly pleasant. It is not entirely predictable; things of interest turn up every day and some days there are finds of great value. I am always very pleased when I can turn up exactly the thing I most wanted to find. Yet in spite of the element of chance, scavenging more than most other pursuits tends to yield returns in some proportion to the effort and intelligence brought to bear. It is very sweet to turn up a few dollars in change from a Dumpster that has just been gone over by a wino.

The land is now covered with cities. The cities are 62 full of Dumpsters. If a member of the canine race is ever

---

* Eds. note — A ballet step.

able to know what it is doing, then Lizbeth knows that when we go around to the Dumpsters, we are hunting. I think of scavenging as a modern form of self-reliance. In any event, after having survived nearly ten years of government service, where everything is geared to the lowest common denominator, I find it refreshing to have work that rewards initiative and effort. Certainly I would be happy to have a sinecure again, but I am no longer heartbroken that I left one.

Cause and effect: results of Eighner's experiences as a scavenger

I find from the experience of scavenging two rather 63 deep lessons. The first is to take what you can use and let the rest go by. I have come to think that there is no value in the abstract. A thing I cannot use or make useful, perhaps by trading, has no value however rare or fine it may be. I mean useful in some broad sense — some art I would find useful and some otherwise.

I was shocked to realize that some things are not 64 worth acquiring, but now I think it is so. Some material things are white elephants that eat up the possessor's substance. The second lesson is the transience of material being. This has not quite converted me to a dualist,* but it has made some headway in that direction. I do not suppose that ideas are immortal, but certainly mental things are longer lived than other material things.

Once I was the sort of person who invests objects 65 with sentimental value. Now I no longer have those objects, but I have the sentiments yet.

Many times in our travels I have lost everything but 66 the clothes I was wearing and Lizbeth. The things I find in Dumpsters, the love letters and rag dolls of so many lives, remind me of this lesson. Now I hardly pick up a thing without envisioning the time I will cast it aside. This I think is a healthy state of mind. Almost everything I have now has already been cast out at least once, proving that what I own is valueless to someone.

Anyway, I find my desire to grab for the gaudy 67 bauble has been largely sated. I think this is an attitude I share with the very wealthy — we both know there is plenty more where what we have came from. Between us are the rat-race millions who nightly scavenge the cable channels looking for they know not what.

I am sorry for them. 68

·   ·   ·

---

* Eds. note — Someone who believes that the world consists of two opposing forces, such as mind and matter.

Comprehension

1. In your own words, give a one-sentence definition of *Dumpster diving.*
2. List some of Eighner's answers to the question "Why was this discarded?" (8). What additional reasons can you think of?
3. What foods does Eighner take particular care to avoid? Why?
4. In paragraph 30, Eighner comments, "Dumpster diving has serious drawbacks as a way of life." What drawbacks does he cite in his essay? What additional drawbacks are implied? Can you think of others?
5. Summarize the stages in the process of learning to scavenge.
6. In addition to food, what else does Eighner scavenge for? Into what general categories do these items fall?
7. Why does Eighner hate can scroungers?
8. What lessons has Eighner learned as a Dumpster diver?

Purpose and Audience

1. In paragraph 6, Eighner states his purpose: to record what he has learned as a Dumpster diver. What additional purposes do you think he had in setting his ideas down on paper?
2. Do you think most readers are apt to respond to Eighner's essay with sympathy? Pity? Impatience? Contempt? Disgust? How do you react? Why?
3. Why do you think Eighner chose not to provide much background about his life — his upbringing, education, or work history — before he became homeless? Do you think this decision was a wise one? How might such information (for example, any of the details in the headnote that precedes the essay) have changed readers' reactions to his discussion?
4. In paragraph 8, Eighner presents three principles one must follow to eat safely from a Dumpster; in paragraphs 59–60 he explains how to go through a Dumpster; and throughout the essay he includes many cautions and warnings. Clearly, he does not expect his audience to take up Dumpster diving. What, then, is his purpose in including such detailed explanations?
5. When Eighner begins paragraph 9 with "Perhaps everyone who has a kitchen," he encourages readers to identify with him. Where else does he make efforts to help readers imagine themselves in his place? Are these efforts successful? Explain your response.
6. What effect do you think the essay's last sentence is calculated to have on readers? What effect does it have on you?

Style and Structure

1. Eighner opens his essay with a fairly conventional strategy: extended definitions of *Dumpster* and *Dumpster diving.* What techniques does he use in

paragraphs 1 through 3 to develop these definitions? Is beginning with definitions the best strategy for this essay? Explain your answer.

2. This long essay contains three one-sentence paragraphs. Why do you think Eighner isolates these sentences? Do you think any of them should be combined with an adjacent paragraph? Explain your reasoning.

3. As the introductory note explains, Eighner chose to retain the present tense even though he was no longer homeless when the essay was published. Why do you think he decided to preserve the present tense?

4. Eighner's essay includes a number of lists that catalog items he came across (for example, in paragraphs 5 and 50). Identify as many of these lists as you can. Why do you think Eighner includes such extensive lists?

Vocabulary Projects

1. Define each of the following words as it is used in this selection.

proprietary (1)	decanted (26)	feasibility (40)
niche (4)	ingested (26)	stave (43)
sporadic (5)	avail (28)	commonplace (55)
bohemian (8)	skulking (32)	vermin (56)
dilettanti (8)	stigma (33)	sinecure (62)
phobic (10)	pristine (34)	transience (64)
pared (15)	dissipate (35)	gaudy (67)
pathogens (16)	intrinsic (37)	bauble (67)
staples (25)	contingency (39)	

2. In paragraph 3, Eighner suggests several alternative words for *diving* as he uses it in his essay. Consult an unabridged dictionary to determine the connotations of each of his alternatives. What are the pros and cons of substituting one of these words for *diving* in Eighner's title and throughout the essay?

Journal Entry

In paragraphs 21–25, Eighner discusses the discarding of food by college students. Does your own experience support his observations? Do you think he is being too hard on students, or does his characterization seem accurate?

Writing Workshop

1. Write an essay about a homeless person you have seen in your community. Use any patterns you like to structure your paper. When you have finished, annotate your essay to identify the patterns you have used.

2. Write an email to your school's dean of students recommending steps that can be taken on your campus to redirect discarded (but edible) food to the homeless. Use process and exemplification to structure your message, and use information from Eighner's essay to support your points. (Be sure to acknowledge your source.)

3. **Working with Sources.** Taking Eighner's point of view and using information from his essay, write an argumentative essay with a thesis statement that takes a strong stand against homelessness and recommends government or private measures to end it. If you like, you may write your essay in the form of a statement by Eighner to a congressional committee. Be sure to document any words or ideas you borrow from Eighner, and include a works-cited page. (See Chapter 18 for information on MLA documentation.)

Combining the Patterns

Review the annotations that identify each pattern of development used in this essay. Which patterns seem to be most effective in helping you understand and empathize with the life of a homeless person? Why?

Thematic Connections

- "The Untouchable" (page 496)
- The Declaration of Independence (page 553)
- "The Shame Game" (page 680)

BARBARA EHRENREICH

The Shame Game

Although Barbara Ehrenreich (b. 1941) is best known for her political activism and journalism, her formal education focused on the hard sciences: she studied physics at Reed College and then earned a Ph.D. in cellular biology from Rockefeller University. She began writing about politics, feminism, and social change during the late 1960s and early '70s. In the years since, she has written regularly for publications such as *Time, Mother Jones,* the *Atlantic Monthly,* the *New York Times, Ms.,* and the *New Republic.* She is also the author of many books, including *Nickel and Dimed: On (Not) Getting By in America* (2001), *This Land Is Their Land: Reports from a Divided Nation* (2008), and *Bright-sided: How the Relentless Promotion of Positive Thinking Has Undermined America* (2009).

Background on unemployment insurance in the United States President Franklin D. Roosevelt signed unemployment insurance into law as part of the 1935 Social Security Act. That year, in the depths of the Great Depression, the U.S. jobless rate reached over 20 percent. "We can never insure 100 percent of the population against 100 percent of the hazards and vicissitudes of life," Roosevelt said of the New Deal legislation. "But we have tried to frame a law which will give some measure of protection to the average citizen and to his family against the loss of a job and against poverty-ridden old age." The general structure of unemployment insurance in the United States has remained the same for the last 75 years: it is a joint federal-state program funded by payroll taxes on employers. To receive benefits, those out of work must have been laid off, not fired for cause (self-employed, temporary, and part-time workers do not usually qualify). Most states limit unemployment compensation to a period of 26 weeks, although Congress can pass extensions during economic downturns. States usually have a cap on the amount people can receive. The average weekly U.S. unemployment check is now $309 per week.

I was on a radio call-in show in Minneapolis not long ago, listening to 1 the callers tell their tales of economic woe: an eight-month job search followed by a job at half the person's former pay, an eighteen-month search leading to serious depression, a five-year search leading to nothing at all. During a commercial break, my host noted that almost all these stories were told in the third person, usually as something that had happened to a spouse. Were some of the callers just too embarrassed to own their own stories — too crushed by the shame of layoffs and unemployment?

Shame hangs heavy over the economic landscape: the shame of the 2 newly laid off, the shame of the chronically poor. It's easy enough for enlightened members of the comfortable classes to insist there's no reason for shame. *You* didn't bring the layoff down on yourself; *you* didn't determine that the maximum wage in your line of work would be in the neighborhood of $8 an hour. Snap out of it, I want to say, blame the economy or its corporate chieftains. Just don't blame yourself!

But shame is a verb as well as a noun. Almost nobody arrives at shame 3 on their own; there are *shamers* and *shamees*. Hester Prynne* didn't pin that scarlet A on her own chest. In fact, it may be wiser to think of shame as a relationship rather than just a feeling — a relationship of domination in which the mocking judgments of the dominant are internalized by the dominated.

Shaming can be a more effective means of social control than force. 4 The peasant who stepped out of line could be derided for daring to question his betters. The woman who spoke out against patriarchal restrictions could be dismissed as a harridan or even a slut It doesn't always work, of course. In 1994, Dan Quayle** and right-wing writer Charles Murray*** launched an initiative to "restigmatize" out-of-wedlock births by restoring the old pejorative term *illegitimate*. But somehow the country wasn't ready to label millions of babies bastards.

Shame was far more effective in the buildup to welfare reform. Consis- 5 tently stereotyped as lazy, promiscuous parasites, welfare recipients largely failed to rally in their own defense. I remember talking to a young (white) woman who professed great enthusiasm for draconian forms of welfare reform—only to admit that she herself had been raised on welfare by a beloved and plucky single mother. That's deeply internalized shame.

The ultimate trick is to make people ashamed of the injuries inflicted 6 upon them. In many cultures, rape renders a woman an unmarriageable pariah. In Pakistan — one of our more embarrassing allies — a woman who brings charges of rape can be punished for "adultery." In 2007, a nineteen-year-old Saudi woman was sentenced to two hundred lashes for bringing charges of gang rape, until international pressure forced the Saudi king to "pardon" her. Even in America, many women's first response to sexual harassment or assault is to feel soiled and shamed, as if she had brought the unwanted advances on herself.

Something similar goes on in the case of the laid off and unemployed, 7 thanks to the prevailing Calvinist form of Protestantism, according to which productivity and employment are the source of one's identity as well as one's income. Not working? Then what are you? And to put the Calvinist message in crude theological terms: *Go to hell.*

For those who fail to feel their full measure of shame over unem- 8 ployment, there is an entire shame industry to whip them into shape:

---

* Eds. note — The protagonist of Nathaniel Hawthorne's 1850 novel *The Scarlet Letter*. After she has an illicit affair with her pastor, Prynne is convicted of adultery and condemned to wear a scarlet letter "A" for the rest of her life.
** Eds. note — The 44th vice president of the United States (b. 1947).
*** Eds. note — American author, political columnist, and pundit (b. 1943).

the career coaches, self-help books, motivational speakers, and business gurus who preach that whatever happens to you must be a result of your own "attitude." Laid off and coming up empty on your job search? You must be too "negative" and hence attracting negative circumstances into your life. To paraphrase one career coach I've heard: We're not here to talk about the economy or the market; we're here to talk about *you*.

Shame is a potent weapon, but it should never be used against the already injured and aggrieved. Instead, let's turn it against the aggrievers: Shame on Ford and GM for putting all their eggs in the SUV basket and then laying off thousands. Shame on the CEOs who make eight-figure incomes while their lowest-paid employees trudge between food banks. Shame on Congress for leaving us with an unemployment insurance program that covers only a little more than a third of the laid off.   9

Everyone else should hold their heads up high.   10

. . .

Comprehension

1. What is the subject of Ehrenreich's essay — that is, which particular group of shamed individuals is she focusing on here? In which paragraphs does she zero in on this group?

2. What does Ehrenreich mean when she says that "shame is a verb as well as a noun" (3)?

3. In what sense, according to Ehrenreich, can shame be "a more effective means of social control than force" (4)? Do you agree with her?

4. In paragraphs 4–6, Ehrenreich gives historical and cultural examples of shame. List these examples. Are they all appropriate for her topic? Are they all relevant?

5. What, according to Ehrenreich, is "the ultimate trick" (6)? How does this "trick" operate?

6. What is the "shame industry" (8)?

Purpose and Audience

1. What purpose does the opening anecdote serve in this essay? How does it introduce the key term — *shame* — discussed in this essay? How does it prepare readers for the discussion to follow?

2. Do you think this essay's primary purpose is to inform or to persuade? Explain.

3. Ehrenreich begins her essay by discussing unemployment. Who is her intended audience — just those without jobs or the employed as well? How can you tell?

4. Do you think this essay is a fair assessment of "the shame game," or do you think Ehrenreich is too opinionated or too judgmental? (Reread paragraph 9 before you answer this question.)

5. In one sentence, paraphrase this essay's thesis.

Style and Structure

1. Why is this essay called "The Shame Game"? Who are the players in this game? What are its rules?

2. In paragraph 4, Ehrenreich puts the word *restigmatize* in quotation marks. What other words does she set off in this way? Why?

3. Do you think the final one-sentence paragraph is an effective conclusion? How might it be expanded?

Vocabulary Projects

1. Define each of the following words as it is used in this selection.

internalized (3)	professed (5)
derided (4)	draconian (5)
patriarchal (4)	renders (6)
harridan (4)	pariah (6)
pejorative (4)	aggrieved (9)

2. In paragraph 3, Ehrenreich mentions *shamers* and *shamees*. Define each of these terms in your own words, including some of Ehrenreich's examples in your definitions.

Journal Entry

Write a one-paragraph definition of *shame*. Develop your definition by means of classification and exemplification.

Writing Workshop

1. **Working with Sources.** Write an essay in which you define *shame*. Support your thesis with examples of situations that apply specifically to college students. Refer to Ehrenreich's essay in your discussion, and be sure to cite your source and to include a works-cited page. (See Chapter 18 for information on MLA documentation.)

2. Write a classification essay that discusses several different kinds of unemployed workers. You can classify these workers according to the kind of employment they seek, the reasons for their unemployment, or the length of time they have been jobless.

3. Whom, or what, do you blame for the plight of the unemployed workers Ehrenreich discusses? Write an argumentative essay, supported by

examples, that develops your thesis. Include a narrative paragraph that provides a relevant anecdote.

Combining the Patterns

What patterns of development does Ehrenreich use in this essay? Annotate the essay to identify each pattern. Use the annotations accompanying "On Dumpster Diving" (page 664) as a guide.

Thematic Connections

- " 'What's in a Name?' " (page 2)
- "The Myth of the Latin Woman: I Just Met a Girl Named Maria" (page 232)
- "Just Walk On By: A Black Man Ponders His Ability to Alter Public Space" (page 240)
- "Mother Tongue" (page 466)
- " 'Take This Internship and Shove It' " (page 583)
- "Does This Tax Make Me Look Fat?" (page 647)

DAVID KIRBY

Inked Well

Poet David Kirby is a longtime professor of English at Florida State University, where he teaches nineteenth-century American literature and creative writing. He has authored or coauthored twenty-nine books, including the poetry collections *The House on Boulevard Street* (2007) and *The Ha-Ha* (2003), literary studies such as *Mark Strand and the Poet's Place in Contemporary Culture* (1990) and *Herman Melville* (1993), and the essay collection *Ultra-Talk: Johnny Cash, the Mafia, Shakespeare, Drum Music, St. Teresa of Avila, and 17 Other Colossal Topics of Conversation* (2007).

Background on tattoos People have sported tattoos for more than five thousand years. In some cultures, tattoos have marked a rite of passage into adulthood. They have also symbolized spiritual protection, status within a clan, fertility, and social ostracism, among other things. (Interestingly, the teachings of both Judaism and Islam specifically prohibit tattooing.) In modern Western culture, tattoos primarily serve as body adornment, although there are exceptions — for example, the Nazis forcibly tattooed identifying numbers on many Jews, and members of some street gangs wear tattoos that signify membership. In the United States today, the most popular tattoos include skulls, hearts, eagles, and crosses as well as abstract tribal designs based on motifs that originated among Polynesian Islanders (historically, some of the most heavily tattooed people in the world). Celtic designs, flowers and butterflies, angels, stars, dragons, Chinese characters, and swallows are also popular, and anchors, once staples among sailors, are now making a comeback. Increasingly, tattoo artists are being taken seriously, and an original design may be worth thousands of dollars, or even more. Today, conventions of tattoo enthusiasts, such as the traveling Bodyart Expo, draw millions of participants each year. The cost of getting a tattoo can be as much as a hundred dollars an hour. (Getting rid of a tattoo can cost considerably more.)

Some tattooed people are easier to read than others. 1

When Richard Costello tried to sell stolen motorcycle parts on eBay 2
earlier this year, he put the items on the floor and photographed them, though the photos also included his bare feet, with the word *White* tattooed on one and *Trash* on the other. The bike's lawful owner did a Web search, found what appeared to be the stolen parts, and notified the Clearwater, Florida, police department. Since jail records typically include identifying marks, it didn't take long for local detectives to identify Mr. Costello and set up a sting. He was arrested after showing up with a van full of stolen parts and is now facing trial. According to Sgt. Greg Stewart, Mr. Costello "just tiptoed his way back to jail."

L'Affaire White Trash confirmed just about everything that I thought 3
about tattoos until recently; namely, that in addition to being nasty and
unsanitary, tattoos only grace the skins of either bottom feeders or those
who want to pretend they are. Richard Costello's phenomenal act of self-
betrayal wouldn't have been a surprise at all to modernist architect Adolph
Loos, whose influential 1908 essay "Ornament and Crime" is still cited today as a potent argument against frills and fancy stuff. Mr. Loos wrote in
effect a manifesto opposing decoration, which he saw as a mark of primitive cultures, and in favor of simplicity, which is a sign of, well, modernism.
Thus, Mr. Loos reasoned, it's OK for a Pacific Islander to cover himself and
all his possessions with ink and carvings, whereas "a modern person [i.e.,
a European] who tattoos himself is either a criminal or a degenerate. . . .
People with tattoos not in prison are either latent criminals or degenerate
aristocrats."

So, presuming the kid with a Tweety Bird tattoo on his forearm who 4
delivered your pizza last night isn't a down-on-his-luck baronet who's trying to earn enough money to return to his ancestral estate in Northum-
berland and claim his seat on the Queen's Privy Council, does the fact that
he's slinging pies mean that he simply hasn't lived long enough to commit
his first murder? Not necessarily: tattoos have a richer social history than
one might think.

Tattoos were brought to Europe from Polynesia by eighteenth-century 5
British explorers, as Margo DeMello writes in *Bodies of Inscription: A Cultural
History of the Modern Tattoo Community* (2000). Europeans who had tattoos
in those days were not social bottom dwellers. And as Charles C. Mann
points out in *1491* (2005), Americans first saw tattoos in the New World
on their conflicted Indian hosts as early as 1580. To Protestants of ascetic
temperaments, these exotic displays were of a piece with the colonists'
propensity to see Indians as primeval savages.

Perhaps predictably, however, tattoos came ultimately to signify pa- 6
triotism rather than exoticism in the United States. The first known professional tattoo artist in the United States was one Martin Hildebrandt, who
set up shop in New York City in 1846. Mr. Hildebrandt became instrumental in establishing the tradition of the tattooed serviceman by practicing
his craft on soldiers and sailors on both sides in the Civil War as he mi-
grated from one camp to another.

And then occurred one of those curious little shifts that make history 7
so delicious. Tattoos became fashionable among members of the European
aristocracy, who encountered the practice during nineteenth-century trips
to the Far East.

By the beginning of World War I, though, the lords and ladies had all 8
but abandoned bodily decoration. Why? Because by then, anybody could
get a tattoo. The laborious process involving hand-tapping ink into the
skin with a single needle was made obsolete with the invention of the electric tattoo machine in 1891. Tattooing suddenly became easier, less painful, and, mainly, cheaper. This led to the speedy spread of the practice
throughout the working class and its abandonment by the rich.

By the middle of the twentieth century, tattooing seemed largely the 9 province of bikers, convicts, and other groups on the margins of society, much as Mr. Loos had predicted. Except for all those patriotic servicemen, a century ago tattoos were the tribal marks that you paid somebody to cut into your skin so that everyone would know you belonged to a world populated by crooks and creeps, along with a few bored aristocrats who would probably have been attracted to living a life of crime had their trust funds not rendered it redundant. And if things had stayed that way, I wouldn't be writing this essay: tattoos would be simply one more way of differentiating "Them" from "Us."

But "We" are the ones who are tattooed now: in the late twentieth 10 century, the middle class began showing up in droves at tattoo parlors. A study in the June 2006 issue of the *Journal of the American Academy of Dermatology* reveals that as many as 24 percent of men and women between the ages of eighteen and fifty have one or more tattoos — up from just 15 to 16 percent in 2003. Men and women are equally likely to be tattooed, though the women surveyed are more likely to have body piercings, as well.

How did this change come to pass? Those of us who are certain we'll 11 never get a tattoo will always shudder with joy when we read about knuckleheads like Richard Costello. But more and more people who wouldn't have dreamed of being tattooed a few years back are paying good money to have sketches of boom boxes, court jesters, and spider webs incised into their hides. Why, and what does it say about the world we live in?

To answer these questions, I walked the streets of Tallahassee, Florida, 12 accosting total and sometimes menacing-looking strangers with the intent of asking them questions about the most intimate parts of their bodies. Any stereotypes of tattooed "victims" I had fell by the wayside rather quickly.

One of my first lessons was that people can get the biggest, most color- 13 ful tattoos either for exceedingly complex reasons or none at all. Jen (I'll use first names only), a pretty, slender brunette in her late twenties, said getting a tattoo was simply on a list of things she wanted to do. Melissa, a grad student in modern languages whom I spied in a bookstore wearing a pair of low-slung jeans, got a black and blue love knot high on one hip because she and her friend wanted identical tattoos, "even though she's not my friend anymore." Becky wanted a tattoo that would be a means of "making a promise to myself that I would become the person I wanted to be, that I would improve my life through hard work."

Of the dozen or so subjects I interviewed, Jodie was the sweetest, the 14 most articulate, and the most heavily inked — her arms were fully sleeved in tattoos, and she was making plans to get started on her hands and neck. Jodie explained that she had been a "cutter" who "was having a lot of trouble with hurting myself physically for various reasons, so I began to get tattooed. It didn't take me long to realize that getting tattooed was quite comparable to cutting myself; it was a way for me to 'bleed out' the emotional pains which I was unable to deal with otherwise."

Jodie is smart as well as troubled. She knew she was hurting herself and   15
would continue to do so, so she sublimated her self-destruction and made
art of it, as surely as, say, poet Sylvia Plath* did — temporarily, anyway.

It seems that more and more people from every walk of life in these   16
United States are getting tattooed. These pioneers are "deterritorializing"
tattoos, in Ms. DeMello's words, liberating them from patriotic sailors and
dim-bulb motorcycle thieves and making them available to soccer moms
and dads.

Tattoos have always been a means of identifying oneself, notes Ms.   17
DeMello, and are always meant to be read — even a tattoo that's hidden
becomes a secret book of sorts. When you get a tattoo, you write yourself,
in a manner of speaking, and make it possible for others to read you, which
means that every tattoo has a story.

There are primarily two types of tattoo narratives, the Record Book   18
and the Canvas. Melissa, the young woman who got her tattoo to signify
bonding with a friend, was capturing a relationship as one might with a
photograph. In the pop music world, rap artists and other musicians sometimes get tattoos of friends or relatives who have died violently or merely
passed away. The Dixie Chicks agreed to get a little chick footprint on the
insteps of their feet for every No. 1 album they had.

If your body is a Record Book, then you and everyone who sees you   19
is looking back at the events depicted there. But if you see your body as a
Canvas, then the story you tell is, at least in its conception and execution,
as inner-driven as any by Faulkner or Hemingway. Jodie, for example, is
going over every inch of her body, using it as a way to tell herself a story
she's beginning to understand only gradually. The more she understands,
the more she "revises," just as any other artist might: her first tattoo was
"a horrible butterfly thing," she told me, "which has since been covered up
with a lovely raven."

Every person with a tattoo is a link in a chain of body modification   20
that goes back to the dawn of human history. Researchers have found
sharpened pieces of manganese dioxide — black crayons, really — that
Neanderthals may have used to color animal skins as well as their own.
The ancient Egyptians practiced simple tattooing. Today, radically different cultures share an obsession with body remodeling that goes far
beyond mere tattooing. African tribes pierce and scar the body routinely;
weightlifters pump their pecs until they bulge like grapefruit; women
pay for cosmetic breast enlargement or reduction. And if that's not
enough evidence that body modification is endemic, I have one word for
you: *Botox.*

The point of all this is self-expression — and we seem to be living in   21
a time where that's what nearly everybody (word carefully chosen) wants

---

* Eds. note — American confessional poet who committed suicide in 1963 at the
age of thirty-one.

to do, in one way or another. As with all lifestyle changes, the tricky part is knowing when to stop.

> **"In a word, tattoos are now officially OK by me."**

22

As I said, I used to think tattoos were for either lowlifes or those who wanted to pretend they were, but my mind now stands changed by the thoughtful, articulate people I talked to and the spectacular designs that had been inked into their bodies. In a word, tattoos are now officially OK by me.

Does that mean I'd get one? Not on your life.   23

• • •

Comprehension

1. Kirby opens his essay with a narrative that recounts "L'Affaire White Trash" (3). Why does he begin with this narrative? What does it illustrate about tattoos?

2. Where does Kirby present information on the history of tattoos? Why does he include this background? Is it necessary? Why does he return to this historical background in paragraph 20?

3. According to Kirby, how has the tattooed population changed over the years? What factors explain these changes?

4. What does Kirby mean when he says, " 'We' are the ones who are tattooed now" (10)?

5. What two kinds of "tattoo narratives" does Kirby identify? How are they different?

6. According to Kirby, for what reasons do people get tattoos? Can you think of additional reasons?

7. How have Kirby's ideas about tattoos changed over the years? *Why* have they changed?

Purpose and Audience

1. Is Kirby's primary purpose to provide information about tattoos, to entertain readers, to explore his own feelings about tattoos, or to persuade readers to consider getting tattoos? Explain.

2. In paragraph 4, Kirby says that "tattoos have a richer social history than one might think." Is this his essay's thesis? If not, what is the thesis of "Inked Well"?

3. Why do you think Kirby mentions the universal "obsession with body remodeling" in paragraph 20? How do you think he expects this reference to affect his audience's reactions to his thesis? How do you react?

Style and Structure

1. What do you see as this essay's dominant pattern of development? Why?

2. Kirby's first and last paragraphs are each just one line long. Are his short introduction and conclusion effective? If you were to expand them, what would you add? Why?

3. Where does Kirby cite experts? Where does he include statistics? What do these kinds of information add to his essay?

Vocabulary Projects

1. Define each of the following words as it is used in this selection.

   sting (2)   droves (10)
   ascetic (5)   incised (11)
   propensity (5)   endemic (20)
   primeval (5)

2. Explain the possible meanings of "Inked Well," the essay's title.

3. Go to a professional tattoo Web site such as tattoos.com, and list some words and phrases that are part of the vocabulary of the tattoo industry. Define several of these words and expressions in layperson's terms. Does Kirby use any of these terms? If not, why not?

4. What is the origin of the word *tattoo*? Check an online dictionary to find out.

Journal Entry

Do you see tattoos as art or as a kind of defacement or self-mutilation? Explain your feelings.

Writing Workshop

1. **Working with Sources.** Find pictures of tattoos on Google Image. Then, write a classification-and-division essay that discusses the kinds of tattoos you find there. (You might want to begin by looking at "Four Tattoos," page 226.) Be sure your essay has a thesis statement that makes a point about tattoos, and use exemplification, description, and comparison and contrast to support your thesis. If you like, you may illustrate your essay with photos or drawings you find on the Web, but if you do, remember to document your sources and to include a works-cited page. (See Chapter 18 for information on MLA documentation.)

2. In paragraph 11, Kirby asks what the prevalence of tattoos says about the world we live in. Using cause and effect as your dominant pattern of development, write an essay that tries to explain what accounts for this phenomenon. Use description and exemplification to support your points.

3. In paragraph 17, Kirby says, "When you get a tattoo, you write yourself, in a manner of speaking, and make it possible for others to read you, which means that every tattoo has a story." What story would you like your own tattoo (or tattoos) to tell?

Combining the Patterns

What patterns of development does Kirby use in his essay? Annotate the essay to identify each pattern. Use the annotations accompanying "On Dumpster Diving" (page 664) as a guide.

Thematic Connections

- "Four Tattoos" (page 226)
- "Why Looks Are the Last Bastion of Discrimination" (page 246)
- "Medium Ash Brown" (page 275)
- "My First Conk" (page 281)
- "The Wife-Beater" (page 516)

JONATHAN SWIFT

A Modest Proposal

Jonathan Swift (1667–1745) was born in Dublin, Ireland, and spent much of his life journeying between his homeland, where he had a modest income as an Anglican priest, and England, where he wished to be part of the literary establishment. The author of many satires and political pamphlets, he is best known today for *Gulliver's Travels* (1726), a sharp satire that, except among academics, is now read primarily as a fantasy for children.

Background on the English-Irish conflict At the time Swift wrote "A Modest Proposal," Ireland had been essentially under British rule since 1171, with the British often brutally suppressing rebellions by the Irish people. When Henry VIII of England declared a Protestant Church of Ireland, many of the Irish remained fiercely Roman Catholic, and this led to even greater contention. By the early 1700s, the English-controlled Irish Parliament had passed laws that severely limited the rights of Irish Catholics, and British trade policies had begun to seriously depress the Irish economy. A fierce advocate for the Irish people in their struggle under British rule, Swift published several works supporting the Irish cause. The following sharply ironic essay was written during the height of a terrible famine in Ireland, when the British were proposing a devastating tax on the impoverished Irish citizenry. Note that Swift does not write in his own voice here but adopts the persona of one who does not recognize the barbarity of his "solution."

It is a melancholy object to those who walk through this great town* or travel in the country, when they see the streets, the roads, and cabin doors, crowded with beggars of the female sex, followed by three, four, or six children, all in rags and importuning every passenger for an alms. These mothers, instead of being able to work for their honest livelihood, are forced to employ all their time in strolling to beg sustenance for their helpless infants, who, as they grow up, either turn thieves for want of work, or leave their dear native country to fight for the Pretender in Spain, or sell themselves to the Barbadoes.** 1

I think it is agreed by all parties that this prodigious number of children in the arms, or on the backs, or at the heels of their mothers, and frequently of their fathers, is in the present deplorable state of the kingdom a very great additional grievance; and therefore whoever could find out a fair, cheap, and easy method of making these children sound, useful members 2

---

* Eds. note — Dublin.
** Eds. note — Many young Irishmen left their country to fight as mercenaries in Spain's civil war or to work as indentured servants in the West Indies.

of the commonwealth would deserve so well of the public as to have his statue set up for a preserver of the nation.

But my intention is very far from being confined to provide only for the children of professed beggars; it is of a much greater extent, and shall take in the whole number of infants at a certain age who are born of parents in effect as little able to support them as those who demand our charity in the streets.

As to my own part, having turned my thoughts for many years upon this important subject, and maturely weighed the several schemes of the other projectors, I have always found them grossly mistaken in their computation. It is true, a child just dropped from its dam may be supported by her milk for a solar year, with little other nourishment; at most not above the value of two shillings, which the mother may certainly get, or the value in scraps, by her lawful occupation of begging; and it is exactly at one year old that I propose to provide for them in such a manner as instead of being a charge upon their parents or the parish, or wanting food and raiment for the rest of their lives, they shall on the contrary contribute to the feeding, and partly to the clothing, of many thousands.

There is likewise another great advantage in my scheme, that it will prevent those involuntary abortions, and that horrid practice of women murdering their bastard children, alas, too frequent among us, sacrificing the poor innocent babies, I doubt, more to avoid the expense than the shame, which would move tears and pity in the most savage and inhuman breast.

The number of souls in this kingdom being usually reckoned one million and a half, of these I calculate there may be about two hundred thousand couples whose wives are breeders, from which number I subtract thirty thousand couples who are able to maintain their own children, although I apprehend there cannot be so many under the present distress of the kingdom; but this being granted, there will remain an hundred and seventy thousand breeders. I again subtract fifty thousand for those women who miscarry, or whose children die by accident or disease within the year. There only remain an hundred and twenty thousand children of poor parents annually born. The question therefore is, how this number shall be reared and provided for, which, as I have already said, under the present situation of affairs, is utterly impossible by all the methods hitherto proposed. For we can neither employ them in handicraft nor agriculture; we neither build houses (I mean in the country) nor cultivate land. They can very seldom pick up livelihood by stealing till they arrive at six years old, except where they are of towardly parts,* although I confess they learn the rudiments much earlier, during which time they can however be looked upon only as probationers, as I have been informed by a principal gentleman in the country of Cavan, who protested to me that he never knew above

---

* Eds. note — Precocious.

one or two instances under the age of six, even in a part of the kingdom so renowned for the quickest proficiency in that art.

I am assured by our merchants that a boy or a girl before twelve years 7 old is no salable commodity; and even when they come to this age, they will not yield above three pounds, or three pounds and half a crown at most on the Exchange; which cannot turn to account either to the parents or the kingdom, the charge of nutriment and rags having been at least four times that value.

I shall now therefore humbly propose my own thoughts, which I hope 8 will not be liable to the least objection.

I have been assured by a very knowing American of my acquaintance in 9 London, that a young healthy child well nursed is at a year old a most delicious, nourishing, and wholesome food, whether stewed, roasted, baked, or boiled; and I make no doubt that it will equally serve in fricassee or a ragout.

I do therefore humbly offer it to public consideration that of the hun- 10 dred and twenty thousand children, already computed, twenty thousand may be reserved for breed, whereof only one fourth part to be males, which is more than we allow to sheep, black cattle, or swine; and my reason is that these children are seldom the fruits of marriage, a circumstance not much regarded by our savages, therefore one male will be sufficient to serve four females. That the remaining hundred thousand may at a year old be offered in sale to the persons of quality and fortune through the kingdom, always advising the mother to let them suck plentifully in the last month, so as to render them plump and fat for a good table. A child will make two dishes at an entertainment for friends; and when the family dines alone, the fore or hind quarter will make a reasonable dish, and seasoned with a little pepper or salt, will be very good boiled on the fourth day, especially in winter.

I have reckoned upon a medium that a child just born will weigh twelve 11 pounds, and in a solar year if tolerably nursed increaseth to twenty-eight pounds.

I grant this food will be somewhat dear, and therefore very proper for 12 landlords, who, as they have already devoured most of the parents, seem to have the best title to the children.

Infant's flesh will be in season throughout the year, but more plentiful 13 in March, and a little before and after. For we are told by a grave author, an eminent French physician,* that fish being a prolific diet, there are more children born in Roman Catholic countries about nine months after Lent, than at any other season; therefore, reckoning a year after Lent, the markets will be more glutted than usual, because the number of popish infants is at least three to one in this kingdom; and therefore it will have one other collateral advantage, by lessening the number of Papists** among us.

---

* Eds. note — François Rabelais, a sixteenth-century satirical writer.
** Eds. note — Roman Catholics.

I have already computed the charge of nursing a beggar's child (in 14 which list I reckon all cottagers, laborers, and four fifths of the farmers) to be about two shillings per annum, rags included; and I believe no gentleman would repine to give ten shillings for the carcass of a good fat child, which, as I have said, will make four dishes of excellent nutritive meat, when he hath only some particular friend or his own family to dine with him. Thus the squire will learn to be a good landlord, and grow popular among the tenants; the mother will have eight shillings net profit, and be fit for work till she produces another child.

Those who are more thrifty (as I must confess the times require) may 15 flay the carcass; the skin of which artificially* dressed will make admirable gloves for ladies, and summer boots for fine gentlemen.

As to our city of Dublin, shambles** may be appointed for this purpose 16 in the most convenient parts of it, and butchers we may be assured will not be wanting; although I rather recommend buying the children alive, and dressing them hot from the knife as we do roasting pigs.

A very worthy person, a true lover of his country, and whose virtues 17 I highly esteem, was lately pleased in discoursing on this matter to offer a refinement upon my scheme. He said that many gentlemen of his kingdom, having of late destroyed their deer, he conceived that the want of venison might be well supplied by the bodies of young lads and maidens, not exceeding fourteen years of age nor under twelve, so great a number of both sexes in every county being now ready to starve for want of work and service; and these to be disposed of by their parents, if alive, or otherwise by their nearest relations. But with due deference to so excellent a friend and so deserving a patriot I cannot be altogether in his sentiments; for as to the males, my American acquaintance assured me from frequent experience that their flesh was generally tough and lean, like that of our schoolboys, by continual exercise, and their taste disagreeable; and to fatten them would not answer the charge. Then as to the females, it would, I think with humble submission, be a loss to the public, because they soon would become breeders themselves; and besides, it is not improbable that some scrupulous people might be apt to censure such a practice (although indeed very unjustly) as a little bordering upon cruelty; which, I confess, hath always been with me the strongest objection against any project, how well soever intended.

But in order to justify my friend, he confessed that this expedient was 18 put into his head by the famous Psalmanazar,*** a native of the island Formosa, who came from thence to London above twenty years ago, and in conversation told my friend that in his country when any young person happened to be put to death, the executioner sold the carcass to the persons of quality as a prime dainty; and that in his time the body of a plump girl of

---

* Eds. note — Skillfully.
** Eds. note — A slaughterhouse or meat market.
*** Eds. note — Frenchman who passed himself off as a native of Formosa (present-day Taiwan).

fifteen, who was crucified for an attempt to poison the emperor, was sold to the Imperial Majesty's prime minister of state, and other great mandarins of the court, in joints from the gibbet, at four hundred crowns. Neither indeed can I deny that if the same use were made of several plump young girls in this town, who without one single groat to their fortunes cannot stir abroad without a chair,* and appear at the playhouse and assemblies in foreign fineries which they never will pay for, the kingdom would not be the worse.

Some persons of a desponding spirit are in great concern about the 19 vast number of poor people who are aged, diseased, or maimed, and I have been desired to employ my thoughts what course may be taken to ease the nation of so grievous an encumbrance. But I am not in the least pain upon that matter, because it is very well known that they are every day dying and rotting by cold and famine, and filth and vermin, as fast as can be reasonably expected. And as to the younger laborers, they are now in almost as hopeful a condition. They cannot get work, and consequently pine away for want of nourishment to a degree that if any time they are accidentally hired to common labor, they have not strength to perform it; and thus the country and themselves are happily delivered from the evils to come.

I have too long digressed, and therefore shall return to my subject. I 20 think the advantages by the proposal which I have made are obvious and many, as well as of the highest importance.

For first, as I have already observed, it would greatly lessen the number 21 of Papists, with whom we are yearly overrun, being the principal breeders of the nation as well as our most dangerous enemies; and who stay at home on purpose to deliver the kingdom to the Pretender, hoping to take their advantage by the absence of so many good Protestants, who have chosen rather to leave their country than to stay at home and pay tithes against their conscience to an Episcopal curate.

Secondly, the poorer tenants will have something valuable of their 22 own, which by law may be made liable to distress,** and help to pay their landlord's rent, their corn and cattle being already seized and money a thing unknown.

Thirdly, whereas the maintenance of an hundred thousand children, 23 from two years old and upwards, cannot be computed at less than ten shillings a piece per annum, the nation's stock will be thereby increased fifty thousand pounds per annum, besides the profit of a new dish introduced to the tables of all gentlemen of fortune in the kingdom who have any refinement in taste. And the money will circulate among ourselves, the goods being entirely of our own growth and manufacture.

Fourthly, the constant breeders, besides the gain of eight shillings ster- 24 ling per annum by the sale of their children, will be rid of the charge for maintaining them after the first year.

---

* Eds. note — A sedan chair; that is, a portable covered chair designed to seat one person and then to be carried by two men.
** Eds. note — Property could be seized by creditors.

Fifthly, this food would likewise bring great custom to taverns, where 25 the vintners will certainly be so prudent as to procure the best receipts* for dressing it to perfection, and consequently have their houses frequented by all the fine gentlemen, who justly value themselves upon their knowledge in good eating; and a skillful cook, who understands how to oblige his guests, will contrive to make it as expensive as they please.

Sixthly, this would be a great inducement to marriage, after which all 26 wise nations have either encouraged by rewards or enforced by laws and penalties. It would increase the care and tenderness of mothers toward their children, when they were sure of a settlement for life to the poor babes, provided in some sort by the public, to their annual profit instead of expense. We should see an honest emulation among the married women, which of them could bring the fattest child to the market. Men would become as fond of their wives during the time of pregnancy as they are now of their mares in foal, their cows in calf, or sows when they are ready to farrow; nor offer to beat or kick them (as is too frequent a practice) for fear of miscarriage.

Many other advantages might be enumerated. For instance, the addi- 27 tion of some thousand carcasses in our exportation of barreled beef, the propagation of swine's flesh, and improvements in the art of making good bacon, so much wanted among us by the great destruction of pigs, too frequent at our tables, which are no way comparable in taste or magnificence to a well-grown, fat, yearling child, which roasted whole will make a considerable figure at a lord mayor's feast or other public entertainment. But this and many others I omit, being studious of brevity.

Supposing that one thousand families in this city would be constant 28 customers for infants' flesh, besides others who might have it at merry meetings, particularly weddings and christenings, I compute that Dublin would take off annually about twenty thousand carcasses, and the rest of the kingdom (where probably they will be sold somewhat cheaper) the remaining eighty thousand.

I can think of no one objection that will possibly be raised against this 29 proposal, unless it should be urged that the number of people will be thereby much lessened in the kingdom. This I freely own, and it was indeed one principal design in offering it to the world. I desire the reader will observe; that I calculate my remedy for this one individual kingdom of Ireland and for no other that ever was, is, or I think ever can be upon earth. Therefore, let no man talk to me of other expedients: of taxing our absentees at five shillings a pound: of using neither clothes nor household furniture except what is of our own growth and manufacture: of utterly rejecting the materials and instruments that promote foreign luxury: of curing the expensiveness of pride, vanity, idleness, and gaming in our women: of introducing a vein of parsimony, prudence, and temperance: of learning to love our country, in the want of which we differ even from Lowlanders and

---

* Eds. note — Recipes.

the inhabitants of Topinamboo:* of quitting our animosities and factions, nor acting any longer like the Jews,** who were murdering one another at the very moment their city was taken: of being a little cautious not to sell our country and conscience for nothing: of teaching landlords to have at least one degree of mercy toward their tenants: lastly, of putting a spirit of honesty, industry, and skill into our shopkeepers; who, if a resolution could now be taken to buy only our native goods, would immediately unite to cheat and exact upon us in the price, the measure, and the goodness, nor could ever yet be brought to make one fair proposal of just dealing, though often and earnestly invited to it.

Therefore, I repeat, let no man talk to me of these and the like expedients, till he hath at least some glimpse of hope that there will ever be some hearty and sincere attempt to put them in practice.*** 30

But as to myself, having been wearied out for many years with offering 31 vain, idle, visionary thoughts, and at length utterly despairing of success, I fortunately fell upon this proposal, which, as it is wholly new, so it hath something solid and real, of no expense and little trouble, full in our own power, and whereby we can incur no danger in disobliging England. For this kind of commodity will not bear exploration, the flesh being of too tender a consistence to admit a long continuance in salt, although perhaps I could name a country which would be glad to eat up our whole nation without it.

After all, I am not so violently bent upon my own opinion as to reject 32 any offer proposed by wise men, which shall be found equally innocent, cheap, easy, and effectual. But before something of that kind shall be advanced in contradiction to my scheme, and offering a better, I desire the author or authors will be pleased maturely to consider two points. First, as things now stand, how they will be able to find food and raiment for an hundred thousand useless mouths and backs. And secondly, there being a round million of creatures in human figure throughout this kingdom, whose sole subsistence put into a common stock would leave them in debt two million of pounds sterling, adding those who are beggars by profession to the bulk of farmers, cottagers, and laborers, with their wives and children who are beggars in effect; I desire those politicians who dislike my overture, and may perhaps be so bold to attempt an answer, that they will first ask the parents of these mortals whether they would not at this day think it a great happiness to have been sold for food at a year old in this manner I prescribe, and thereby have avoided such a perpetual scene of misfortunes as they have since gone through by the oppression of landlords, the impossibility of paying rent without money or trade, the want of common sustenance, with neither house nor clothes to cover them from the inclemencies of the weather, and the most inevitable prospect of entailing the like or greater miseries upon their breed forever.

---

* Eds. note — A place in the Brazilian jungle.

** Eds. note — In the first century B.C., the Roman general Pompey could conquer Jerusalem in part because the citizenry was divided among rival factions.

*** Eds. note — Note that these measures represent Swift's true proposal.

I profess, in the sincerity of my heart, that I have not the least personal 33
interest in endeavoring to promote this necessary work, having no other
motive than the public good of my country, by advancing our trade, providing for infants, relieving the poor, and giving some pleasure to the rich. I
have no children by which I can propose to get a single penny; the youngest
being nine years old, and my wife past childbearing.

. . .

Comprehension

1. What problem does Swift identify? What general solution does he
   recommend?
2. What advantages does Swift see in his plan?
3. What does he see as the alternative to his plan?
4. What clues indicate that Swift is not serious about his proposal?
5. In paragraph 29, Swift lists and rejects a number of "other expedients."
   What are they? Why do you think he presents and rejects these ideas?

Purpose and Audience

1. Swift's target here is the British government, in particular its poor treatment of the Irish. How would you expect British government officials to
   respond to his proposal? How would you expect Irish readers to react?
2. What do you think Swift hoped to accomplish in this essay? Do you think
   his purpose was simply to amuse and shock, or do you think he wanted
   to change people's minds — or even inspire them to take some kind of
   action? Explain.
3. In paragraphs 6, 14, 23, and elsewhere, Swift presents a series of mathe-
   matical calculations. What effect do you think he expected these compu-
   tations to have on his readers?
4. Explain why each of the following groups might have been offended by
   this essay: women, Catholics, butchers, the poor.
5. How do you think Swift expected the appeal in his conclusion to affect
   his audience?

Style and Structure

1. In paragraph 6, Swift uses the word *breeders* to refer to fertile women.
   What connotations does this word have? Why does he use this word
   rather than a more neutral alternative?
2. What purpose does paragraph 8 serve in the essay? Do the other short
   paragraphs have the same function? Explain.
3. Swift's remarks are presented as an argument. Where, if anywhere, does he
   anticipate and refute his readers' objections?

4. Swift applies to infants many words usually applied to animals who are slaughtered to be eaten — for example, *fore or hind quarter* (10) and *carcass* (15). Identify as many examples of this kind of usage as you can. Why do you think Swift uses such words?

5. Throughout his essay, Swift cites the comments of others — "our merchants" (7), "a very knowing American of my acquaintance" (9), and "an eminent French physician" (13), for example. Find some additional examples. What, if anything, does he accomplish by referring to these people?

6. A **satire** is a piece of writing that uses wit, **irony**, and ridicule to attack foolishness, incompetence, or evil. How does "A Modest Proposal" fit this definition of satire?

7. Evaluate the strategy Swift uses to introduce each advantage he cites in paragraphs 21 through 26.

8. Swift uses a number of parenthetical comments in his essay — for example, in paragraphs 14, 17, and 26. Identify as many of these parenthetical comments as you can, and consider what they contribute to the essay.

9. Swift begins paragraph 20 with "I have too long digressed, and therefore shall return to my subject." Has he in fact been digressing? Explain.

Vocabulary Projects

1. Define each of the following words as it is used in this selection.

importuning (1)	rudiments (6)	encumbrance (19)
alms (1)	nutriment (7)	tithes (21)
prodigious (2)	repine (14)	vintners (25)
professed (3)	flay (15)	expedients (29)
dam (4)	scrupulous (17)	parsimony (29)
reckoned (6)	censure (17)	temperance (29)
apprehend (6)	desponding (19)	raiment (32)

2. The title states that Swift's proposal is a "modest" one; elsewhere he says he proposes his ideas "humbly" (8). Why do you think he chooses these words? Does he really mean to present himself as modest and humble?

Journal Entry

What is your emotional reaction to this essay? Do you find it amusing or offensive? Why?

Writing Workshop

1. Write a "modest proposal," either straightforward or satirical, for solving a problem in your school or community.

2. Write a "modest proposal" for achieving one of these national goals:

- Banning assault weapons
- Eliminating binge drinking on college campuses
- Eliminating childhood obesity
- Promoting sexual abstinence among teenagers

3. Write a letter to an executive of the tobacco industry, a television network, or an industry that threatens the environment. In your letter, set forth a "modest proposal" for making the industry more responsible.

Combining the Patterns

What patterns of development does Swift use in his argument? Annotate the essay to identify each pattern. Use the annotations accompanying "On Dumpster Diving" (page 664) as a guide.

Thematic Connections

- "The Embalming of Mr. Jones" (page 303)
- "The Irish Famine, 1845–1849" (page 333)
- "I Want a Wife" (page 503)

Writing Assignments for Combining the Patterns

1. Reread Michael Huu Truong's essay at the beginning of this chapter. Responding to the same assignment he was given ("Write an essay about the person and/or place that defined your childhood"), use several different patterns to communicate to readers what your own childhood was like.

2. Write an essay about the political, social, or economic events that you believe have dominated and defined your life (or a stage of your life). Use cause and effect and any other patterns you think are appropriate to explain and illustrate why these events were important to you and how they affected you.

3. Develop a thesis statement that draws a general conclusion about the nature, quality, or effectiveness of advertising in online media or in print media (in newspapers or magazines or on billboards). Write an essay that supports this thesis statement with a series of very specific paragraphs. Use the patterns of development that best help you to characterize particular advertisements.

4. Exactly what do you think it means to be an American? Write a definition essay that answers this question, developing your definition with whatever patterns best serve your purpose.

5. Many of the essays in this text recount the writers' personal experiences. Identify one essay that describes experiences that are either similar to your own or in sharp contrast to your own. Then, write a comparison-and-contrast essay *either* comparing *or* contrasting your experiences with those of the writer. Use several different patterns to develop your essay.

Collaborative Activity for Combining the Patterns

Working in pairs, choose an essay from Chapters 6 through 14 of this text. Then, working individually, identify the various patterns of development used in the essay. When you have finished, compare notes with your classmate. Have both of you identified the same patterns in the essay? If not, try to reach a consensus. Working together, write a paragraph summarizing why each pattern is used and explaining how the various patterns combine to support the essay's thesis.

PART THREE

Working with Sources

Some students see research as a complicated, time-consuming process that seems to have no obvious benefit. They can't understand why instructors assign topics that involve research or why they have to spend so much time considering other people's ideas. These are fair questions that deserve straightforward answers.

For one thing, doing research enables you to become part of an academic community — one that attempts to answer some of the most interesting and profound questions being asked today. For example, what steps should be taken to ensure privacy on the Internet? What is the value of a college education? What is the role of print journalism in the electronic age? How much should the government be involved in people's lives? These and other questions need to be addressed not just because they are interesting but also because the future of our society depends on the answers.

In addition, research teaches sound methods of inquiry. By doing research, you learn to ask questions, to design a research plan, to meet deadlines, to collect and analyze information, and to present ideas in a well-organized essay. Above all, research encourages you to **think critically** — to consider different sources of information, to evaluate conflicting points of view, to understand how the information you discover fits in with your own ideas about your subject, and to reach logical conclusions. Thus, doing research helps you become a more thoughtful writer as well as a more responsible, more informed citizen — one who is capable of sorting through the vast amount of information you encounter each day and of making informed decisions about the important issues that confront us all.

When you use sources in a paper, you follow the same writing process as you do when you write any essay. However, in addition to using your own ideas to support your points, you use information that you find in the library and on the Internet. Because working with sources presents special challenges, there are certain issues that you should be aware of before you engage in research. The chapters in Part Three identify these issues and give you practical suggestions for dealing with them. Chapter 16 discusses how to find sources and how to determine if those sources are authoritative, accurate, objective, current, and comprehensive. Chapter 17 discusses how to paraphrase, summarize, and quote sources and how to avoid committing plagiarism. Finally, Chapter 18 explains how to use the documentation style recommended by the Modern Language Association (MLA) to acknowledge the source information you use in your papers. (The documentation style recommended by the American Psychological Association [APA] is illustrated in the Appendix.)

16

Finding and Evaluating Sources

In some essays you write — personal narratives or descriptions, for example — you can use your own ideas and observations to support the points you make. In other essays, however, you will have to supplement your own ideas with **research**, looking for information in magazines, newspapers, journals, and books as well as in the library's electronic databases or on the Internet.

Finding Information in the Library

Although many students turn first to the Internet, the best place to begin your research is in your college library, which contains electronic and print resources that you cannot find anywhere else. Of course, your college library houses books, magazines, and journals, but it also gives you access to the various **databases** to which it subscribes as well as to reference works that contain facts and statistics.

THE RESOURCES OF THE LIBRARY

The Online Catalog

An **online catalog** enables you to search all the resources held by the library. You can access the online catalog from computer terminals in the library or remotely though an Internet portal. By typing in keywords related to your topic, you can find articles, books, or other sources of information to use in your research.

Electronic Databases

Libraries subscribe to **electronic databases** — for example, *Expanded Academic ASAP* or *LexisNexis Academic Universe*. These electronic databases enable you to access information from hundreds of newspapers, magazines, and journals. Some contain lists of bibliographic citations as well as **abstracts** (summaries of articles); many others enable you to retrieve entire articles or books.

Reference Works

Libraries also contain reference works — in print and in electronic form — that can give you an overview of your topic as well as key facts, dates, and names. **General encyclopedias** — such as the *New Encyclopaedia Britannica* — include articles on a wide variety of topics. **Specialized encyclopedias** — such as the *Encyclopedia of Law Enforcement* — contain articles that give you detailed information about a specific field (sociology or law enforcement, for example).

Sources for Facts and Statistics

Reference works such as *Facts on File*, the *Information Please Almanac*, and the *Statistical Abstract of the United States* can help you locate facts or statistics that you may need to support your points. (These resources are available online as well as in the reference section of your college library.)

Much of the information in library databases — for example, the full text of many scholarly articles — cannot be found on the Internet. In addition, because your college librarians oversee all material coming into the library, the sources you find there are generally more reliable, more focused, and more useful than many you will find on the Internet.

INTERNET	LIBRARY DATABASES
Coverage is general, haphazard	Coverage is focused and often discipline-specific
Sources may not contain bibliographic information	Sources will contain bibliographic information
Web postings are not filtered	Databases are created by librarians and scholars
Material is posted by anyone, regardless of qualifications	Material is checked for accuracy and quality

Exercise 1

Assume that you are writing a three- to five-page paper on one of the general topics listed below.

Eating disorders	Women in combat
Alternative medicine	Green construction projects
Government health care	Legalizing marijuana
Offshore drilling	Electric cars
Recycling	Stem-cell research

Using your college library's online catalog, see how much information you can find. How easy was this system to use? Where did you have difficulty?

Finding Information on the Internet

The **Internet** gives you access to a great deal of information that you can use to support your points and to develop your essay. When most people refer to the Internet, they are actually referring to the **Web**, which is part of the Internet. Once you connect to the Web with your browser, you use a search engine such as Google or Yahoo! to sort through the millions of documents that are available there. There are three ways to access information on the Web: *entering a Web site's URL, doing a keyword search,* and *doing a subject search.*

Entering a Web site's URL. All browsers have a box in which you can enter a Web site's **uniform resource locator (URL)**. When you hit the computer's Enter or Return key, the browser will connect you to the Web site.

Doing a keyword search. All search engines enable you to do a **keyword search**. You type a search term into a box, and the search engine looks for documents that contain the term. If you type in a broad term like *civil war,* you will get millions of hits — many more than you could possibly consider. If you narrow your search by using a more specific search term — *Battle of Gettysburg,* for example — you will get fewer hits. You can focus your search even further by connecting search terms with *and* (in capital letters) — for example, *Battle of Gettysburg* AND *military strategy.* The documents you retrieve will contain both these search terms, not just one or the other. You can also put quotation marks around a search term — for example, "Lee's surrender at Appomattox." If you do this, the search engine will retrieve only documents that contain this specific phrase.

Doing a subject search. Some search engines, such as Google, enable you to do a **subject search** (also called a *directory search*). First, you choose a subject from a list of general subjects: *The Arts, Business, Computers, Science,* and so on. Each of these general subjects leads you to more specific subjects and, eventually, to the subtopic that you want. For example, you could start your search by selecting the general topic *Science.* Clicking on this topic would lead you to *Environment* and then to *Forests and Rainforests.* Finally, you would get a list of Web sites that could be useful to you.

ACCESSING WEB SITES: TROUBLESHOOTING

Sometimes you will be unable to connect to the site you want. Before giving up, try these strategies:

- **Check to make sure that the URL is correct.** Any error in typing the URL — an extra space or an added letter — will send you to the wrong site or to no site at all.
- **Try using part of the URL.** If the URL is long, try deleting everything after the last slash. If this doesn't work, use just the part of the URL that ends in .com or .gov. If this part of the URL doesn't work, you have an incorrect (or inoperable) URL.
- **Try revisiting the site later.** Sometimes Web sites experience technical problems that prevent you from accessing them. Wait a while, and then try accessing your site again.

Exercise 2

Carry out an Internet search of the topic you chose for Exercise 1. How much useful information were you able to find? How does this information compare to the information you found when you used the library's online catalog?

Evaluating Sources

Not every source contains trustworthy information. For this reason, even after you find information (either in print or online), you still have to **evaluate** it — that is, determine its suitability. When you use print information from your college library, you can be reasonably certain that it has been evaluated in some way. Material from the Web presents special problems, however, because so much of it is either anonymous or written by people who have little or no knowledge of their subject.

To evaluate a source, ask the following questions.

Is the source authoritative? A source is *authoritative* when it is written by an expert. Given the volume and variety of information on the Web, it is important to determine if it is written by a well-respected scholar or expert in the field. (This is especially true for Wiki sites where information is constantly being rewritten or revised — often by people with little or no expertise in a field.) To determine if the author has the expertise to write about a subject, find out what else he or she has written on the same subject, and then do a Web search to see if other authorities recognize the author as an expert.

Trying to determine the legitimacy of information on Web sites, online presses, and blogs can often be difficult or even impossible. Some sites do not list authors, and if they do, they do not always include their credentials. In addition, you may not be able to determine how a Web site decides what to publish. (Does one person decide, or does an editorial board make decisions?) Finally, you might have difficulty evaluating (or even identifying) the sponsoring organization of a site. If you cannot determine the accuracy of material on a Web site, do not use the site as a source.

Is the source accurate? A source is **accurate** if you can rely on the information it contains. If a university press or scholarly journal published a book or article, you can be reasonably certain that experts in the field reviewed it to confirm its accuracy. Books published by commercial presses or articles in high-level magazines, such as the *Atlantic* and the *Economist,* may also be suitable for your research — provided experts wrote them. The same is true for newspaper articles. Articles in respected newspapers, such as the *New York Times* or the *Wall Street Journal,* have much more credibility than articles in tabloids, such as the *National Enquirer* or the *Globe.*

You can judge the accuracy of a source by comparing specific information it contains to the same information in several other sources. If you find discrepancies, you should assume that the source contains other errors as well. You should also check to see if an author includes citations for the information he or she uses. Such documentation can help readers determine the accuracy (and the quality) of the information in the source. Also, verify the legitimacy of the sources a writer cites by seeing what you can find out about them on the Web. Perhaps the best (and safest) course to follow is that if you can't verify the information you find on a Web site, don't use it.

Is the source objective? A source is **objective** when it is not unduly influenced by personal opinions or feelings. Of course, all sources reflect the opinions of their authors, regardless of how impartial they may try to be. Some sources — such as those that support one political position over another — make no secret of their biases. In fact, bias does not automatically disqualify a source. It should, however, alert you to the fact that you are seeing just one side of an issue and that you have to look elsewhere to get a fuller picture.

As a researcher, you should ask yourself if a writer's conclusions are supported by evidence or if they are the result of emotional reactions or preconceived ideas. You can make this determination by looking at the writer's choice of words and seeing if the language is slanted and also by seeing if the writer ignores (or dismisses) opposing points of view.

With Web sites, you should try to determine if advertising that appears on the site affects its objectivity. Also try to determine if the site has a commercial purpose. If it does, the writer may have a conflict of interest. The same is true if a political group or special-interest group sponsors a site. These organizations have agendas, and you should make sure that they are not manipulating facts to promote their own goals.

Is the source current? A source is **current** if the information it contains is up-to-date. It is relatively easy to find out how current a print source is.

You can find the publication date of a book on the page that lists its publication information, and you can find the publication date of a periodical on its front cover.

Web sites and blogs, however, present problems. First, check to see when a Web site was last updated. (Some Web pages automatically display the current date, and you should not confuse this date with the date when the site was last updated.) Then, check the dates of individual articles. Even if a site has been updated recently, it may include information that is out-of-date. You should also see if the links on a site are still live. If a number of links are not functioning, you should question the currency of the site.

Is the source comprehensive? A source is **comprehensive** if it covers a subject in sufficient breadth and depth. How comprehensive a source needs to be depends on your purpose and your audience as well as on your assignment. For a short essay, an op-ed from a newspaper or a short article might give you enough information to support your points. A longer paper, however, would call for sources that treat your subject in depth, such as scholarly articles or even whole books.

You can determine the comprehensiveness of a source by seeing if it devotes a great deal of coverage to your subject. Does it discuss your topic in one or two paragraphs, or does it devote much more space to it — say, a chapter in a book or a major section of an article? You should also try to determine the level of the source. Although a source may be perfectly acceptable for high school research, it may not be comprehensive enough for college research.

USING *WIKIPEDIA* AS A SOURCE

Wikipedia — the most popular encyclopedia on the Web — has no single editor who checks entries for accuracy, credibility, objectivity, currency, and comprehensiveness. In many cases, the users themselves write and edit entries. For this reason, most college instructors *do not* consider *Wikipedia* reliable enough to be a credible source of information.

Exercise 3

Choose one source from the library and one from the Internet. Then, evaluate each source to determine if it is authoritative, accurate, objective, current, and comprehensive.

17

Integrating Sources and Avoiding Plagiarism

After you have gathered and evaluated your sources, it is time to think about how you can use this material in your essay. As you take notes, you should record relevant information in a computer file that you have set up for this purpose. These notes should be in the form of *paraphrase, summary,* and *quotation.* When you actually write your paper, you will **synthesize** this source material, blending it with your own ideas and interpretations — but making sure that your own ideas, not those of your sources, dominate your discussion. Finally, you should make certain that you do not inadvertently commit plagiarism.

Paraphrasing

When you **paraphrase**, you use your own words to restate a source's ideas in some detail, presenting the source's main idea, its key supporting points, and possibly an example or two. For this reason, a paraphrase may be only slightly shorter than the original.

You paraphrase when you want to present the information from a source without using its exact words. Paraphrasing is useful when you want to make a difficult discussion easier to understand while still giving readers a good sense of the original.

Keep in mind that when you paraphrase, you do not use the exact language or syntax of the original source, and you do not include your own analysis or opinions. The idea is to convey the ideas and emphasis of the source but not to mirror the order of its ideas or reproduce its exact words or sentence structure. If you decide to include a particularly memorable word or phrase from the source, be sure to put it in quotation marks.

Finally, remember that because a paraphrase relies on a writer's original ideas, *you must document the source.*

GUIDELINES FOR WRITING A PARAPHRASE

- Read the source you intend to paraphrase until you understand it.
- Jot down the main points of the source.
- As you write, retain the emphasis of the original.
- Make sure that you use your own words and phrases, not the language or syntax of your source.
- Do not include your own analysis or opinions.
- Be sure to provide documentation.

Here is a passage from page 22 of the article *"Wikipedia* and Beyond: Jimmy Wales's Sprawling Vision" by Katherine Mangu-Ward, followed by a paraphrase.

ORIGINAL

An obvious question troubled, and continues to trouble, many people: how could an "encyclopedia that anyone can edit" possibly be reliable? Can truth be reached by a consensus of amateurs? Can a community of volunteers aggregate and assimilate knowledge . . . ?

PARAPHRASE

According to Katherine Mangu-Ward, there are serious questions about the reliability of *Wikipedia's* articles because any user can add, change, or delete information. There is some doubt about whether *Wikipedia's* unpaid and nonprofessional writers and editors can work together to create an accurate encyclopedia (22).

NOTE: This paraphrase appears in the Model Student Research Paper that begins on page 735.

Exercise 1

Select one or two paragraphs from any essay in this book, and then paraphrase them. Make sure your paraphrase communicates the main ideas and key supporting points of the passage you selected.

Summarizing

Unlike a paraphrase, which restates the ideas of a source in detail, a **summary** is just a brief restatement, in your own words, of a passage's main idea. Because it is so general, a summary is always much shorter than the original.

When you summarize (as when you paraphrase) you use your own words, not the words of your source. Keep in mind that a summary can be one sentence or several sentences in length, depending on the length and complexity of the original passage. Your summary expresses just the main idea of your source, not your own opinions or conclusions. Remember, because a summary expresses a writer's original idea, *you must document your source.*

GUIDELINES FOR WRITING A SUMMARY

- Read the source you intend to summarize until you understand it.
- Jot down the main idea of the source.
- Make sure that you use your own words and phrases, not the words and sentence structure of your source.
- Do not include your own analysis or opinions.
- Be sure to provide documentation.

Here is a summary of the passage from the article "*Wikipedia* and Beyond: Jimmy Wales's Sprawling Vision" by Katherine Mangu-Ward.

SUMMARY

According to Katherine Mangu-Ward, *Wikipedia*'s reliability is open to question because anyone can edit its articles (22).

Exercise 2

Write a summary of the material that you paraphrased for Exercise 1. How is your summary different from your paraphrase?

Quoting

When you **quote**, you use a writer's exact words as they appear in the source, including all punctuation, capitalization, and spelling. Enclose all words from your source in quotation marks — *followed by appropriate documentation.* Because quotations distract readers, use a quotation only when you think a writer's exact words will add something to your discussion. In addition, too many quotations will make your paper look as if it is simply a collection of other people's words. As a rule, unless you have a definite reason to quote a source, you should paraphrase or summarize it instead.

WHEN TO QUOTE SOURCES

1. Quote when the original language is so memorable that paraphrasing would lessen the impact of the writer's ideas.
2. Quote when a paraphrase or summary would change the meaning of the original.
3. Quote when the original language adds authority to your discussion. The exact words of an expert on your topic can help you make your point convincingly.

GUIDELINES FOR QUOTING

- Put all word and phrases that you take from your source in quotation marks.
- Make sure that you use the *exact* words of your source.
- Do not include too many quotations.
- Be sure to provide documentation.

Exercise 3

Reread the passage you chose to paraphrase in Exercise 1, and identify one or two quotations that you could include in your paraphrase. Which words or phrases did you decide to quote? Why?

Integrating Source Material into Your Writing

When you use source material in your writing, you goal is to integrate this material smoothly into your discussion. To distinguish your own ideas from those of your sources, you should always introduce source material and follow it with appropriate documentation.

Introduce paraphrases, summaries, and quotations with a phrase that identifies the source or its author. You can place this **identifying phrase** at the beginning, in the middle, or at the end of a sentence. Instead of always using the same words to introduce source material — *says* or *states*, for example — try using different words and phrases — *points out, observes, comments, notes, remarks,* or *concludes.*

IDENTIFYING PHRASE AT THE BEGINNING

According to Jonathan Dee, *Wikipedia* is "either one of the noblest experiments of the Internet age or a nightmare embodiment of relativism and the withering of intellectual standards" (36).

IDENTIFYING PHRASE IN THE MIDDLE

Wikipedia is "either one of the noblest experiments of the Internet age," Jonathan Dee comments, "or a nightmare embodiment of relativism and the withering of intellectual standards" (36).

IDENTIFYING PHRASE AT THE END

Wikipedia is "either one of the noblest experiments of the Internet age or a nightmare embodiment of relativism and the withering of intellectual standards," Jonathan Dee observes (36).

Synthesizing

When you write a **synthesis**, you combine paraphrases, summaries, and quotations from your sources with your own ideas. It is important to keep in mind that a synthesis is not simply a collection of your sources' ideas. On the contrary, a synthesis uses source material to support *your* ideas and to help readers see the topic *you* are writing about in a new way. (In this sense, a research paper is actually a long synthesis.) For this reason, when you write a synthesis, it is important to differentiate your ideas from those of your sources and to clearly show which piece of information comes from which source.

The following synthesis is a paragraph from the model MLA paper that begins on page 735. This paragraph synthesizes several sources as it discusses a problem of *Wikipedia* and other open-source Web sites: the ease with which text can be edited. Notice that the paragraph begins with the student's own ideas, and the rest of the paragraph includes source material that supports these ideas. (The examples that mention former president George W. Bush, George Soros, L. Ron Hubbard, abortion, and the Holocaust are not documented because they are considered **common knowledge** — in other words, this information can be found in a number of reference books.)

Another problem with *Wikipedia* is the ease with which entries can be edited. Because the content of wikis can be altered by anyone, individuals can easily vandalize content by inserting incorrect information, obscene language, or even nonsense into articles. Writers who are more interested in presenting their personal opinions than presenting reliable information frequently target certain entries. For example, entries for controversial people, such as President George W. Bush, financier George Soros, or Scientology founder L. Ron Hubbard, or for controversial subjects, such as abortion and the Holocaust, are routinely vandalized. Sometimes this vandalism can be extremely harmful. One notorious case of vandalism involved John Seigenthaler Sr., a journalist who was falsely accused in a *Wikipedia* entry of being involved in the assassinations of John Kennedy and Robert Kennedy. As Seigenthaler's son has reported, the false information stayed on the site for more than four months and also appeared on at least two other sites that had used *Wikipedia* as their source (Seigenthaler). This incident, as well as many others, has caused people to question the reliability of *Wikipedia*. According to Jane Kirtley, the issue of reliability poses a real problem for the users of *Wikipedia:*

> It's hard to defend an anonymous poster who uploads a damaging falsehood about someone on a Web site that purports to provide facts from a "neutral point of view. . . ." Either accuracy matters, or it doesn't. If the denizens of cyberspace want to be taken seriously, they might want to be responsible for what they produce. (66)

GUIDELINES FOR WRITING A SYNTHESIS

1. Identify the key points discussed in each of your sources.
2. Identify the evidence that your sources use to support their views.
3. Clearly report what each source says, using summaries, paraphrases, and quotations. (Be sure to document your sources.)
4. Show how the sources are related to one another. For instance, do they agree on everything? Do they show directly opposite views, or do they agree on some points and disagree on others?
5. Decide on your own viewpoint, and show how the sources relate to your viewpoint.

Exercise 4

Look at the Model Student Research Paper that begins on page 735. Choose a paragraph (other than the one on page 715) that synthesizes source material. What kind of information (summary, paraphrase, or quotation) is being synthesized?

Avoiding Plagiarism

Plagiarism—whether intentional or unintentional—occurs when a writer passes off the words or ideas of others as his or her own. (Ideas can also be in the form of visuals, such as charts and graphs, or statistics.) Students plagiarize for a number of reasons. Some take the easy way out and buy a paper and submit it as if it were their own. This **intentional plagiarism** compromises a student's education as well as the educational process as a whole. Instructors assign papers for a reason, and if you do not do the work, then you miss a valuable opportunity to learn. For most students, however, plagiarism is **unintentional**.

Plagiarism can be the result of carelessness, poor time management, not knowing the conventions of documentation, laziness, or simply panic. For example, some students do not give themselves enough time to do an assignment, fail to keep track of their sources, inadvertently include the exact words of a source without using quotation marks, forget to include documentation, or cut and paste information from the Internet directly into their papers. In addition, some students have the mistaken belief that if information they find online does not have an identifiable author, it is all right to use it without documentation. Whatever the reason, whenever you present information from a source as if it were your own (intentionally or unintentionally), you are committing plagiarism – and *plagiarism is theft*.

TIPS FOR AVOIDING PLAGIARISM

You can avoid plagiarism by keeping careful notes and by following these guidelines:

- **Give yourself enough time to do your research and to write your paper.** Do not put yourself in a position where you do not leave enough time to give your assignment the attention it requires.
- **Begin with a research plan.** Make a list of the steps you intend to follow, and estimate how much time they will take.
- **Ask for help.** If you run into trouble, don't panic. Ask your instructor or a reference librarian for help.
- **Do not cut and paste downloaded text directly into your paper.** Summarize and paraphrase this source material first. Boldface or highlight quotation marks so that you will recognize quotations when you are ready to include them in your paper.
- **Set up a system that enables you to keep track of your sources.** Create one or more files on your computer where you can store downloaded source information. (If you photocopy print sources, maintain a file for this material.) Create another set of files for your notes. Make sure you clearly name and date these files so that you know what is in them and when they were created.
- **Include full source information for all paraphrases and summaries as well as for quotations.** As you write, clearly differentiate between your ideas and those of your sources. Do not forget to include documentation. If you try to fill in documentation later, you may not remember where your information came from.
- **Keep a list of all the sources you have downloaded or have taken information from.** Make sure that you always have an up-to-date list of the sources you are using.

The easiest way to avoid plagiarism is simple — give credit where credit is due. In other words, document all information you borrow from your sources — not just paraphrases, summaries, and quotations but also statistics, images, and charts and graphs. It is not necessary, however, to document **common knowledge** — information that most people will probably know or factual information that is available in several different reference works. (Keep in mind that even though *information* might be common knowledge, you cannot use the exact *words* of a reference source without quoting the source and providing appropriate documentation.)

WHAT TO DOCUMENT

YOU MUST DOCUMENT

- All word-for-word quotations from a source
- All summaries and paraphrases of material from a source
- All ideas — opinions, judgments, and insights — that are not your own
- All tables, graphs, charts, statistics, and images you get from a source

YOU DO NOT NEED TO DOCUMENT

- Your own ideas
- Common knowledge
- Familiar quotations

Avoiding Common Errors That Lead to Plagiarism

The following paragraph is from *The Cult of the Amateur: How Today's Internet Is Killing Our Culture* by Andrew Keen, a source that student Philip Lau found during his research. This paragraph, and the four rules listed after it, will help you understand and avoid the most common causes of plagiarism.

ORIGINAL

The simple ownership of a computer and an Internet connection doesn't transform one into a serious journalist any more than having access to a kitchen makes one into a serious cook. But millions of amateur journalists think that it does. According to a June 2006 study by the Pew Internet and American Life Project, 34 percent of the 12 million bloggers in America consider their online "work" to be a form of journalism. That adds up to millions of unskilled, untrained, unpaid, unknown "journalists" — a thousandfold growth between 1996 and 2006 — spewing their (mis)information out in the cyberworld. (Andrew Keen. *The Cult of the Amateur: How Today's Internet Is Killing Our Culture*. New York: Doubleday, 2007. 47. Print.)

1. Identify Your Source

PLAGIARISM

One-third of the people who post material on Internet blogs think of themselves as serious journalists.

The writer does not quote Keen directly, but he still must identify Keen as the source of his paraphrased material. He can do this by adding an identifying phrase and parenthetical documentation.

CORRECT

According to Andrew Keen, one-third of the people who post material on Internet blogs think of themselves as serious journalists (47).

2. Place Borrowed Words in Quotation Marks

PLAGIARISM

According to Andrew Keen, the simple ownership of a computer and an Internet connection doesn't transform one into a serious journalist any more than having access to a kitchen makes one into a serious cook (47).

Although the writer cites Keen as his source, the passage incorrectly uses Keen's exact words without putting them in quotation marks. The writer must either place the borrowed words in quotation marks or paraphrase them.

CORRECT (BORROWED WORDS IN QUOTATION MARKS)

According to Andrew Keen, "The simple ownership of a computer and an Internet connection doesn't transform one into a serious journalist any more than having access to a kitchen makes one into a serious cook" (47).

3. Use Your Own Wording

PLAGIARISM

According to Andrew Keen, having a computer that can connect to the Internet does not make someone a real reporter, just as having a kitchen does not make someone a real cook. However, millions of these people think that they are real journalists. A Pew Internet and American Life study in June 2006 showed that about 4 million bloggers think they are journalists when they write on their blogs. Thus, millions of people who have no training may be putting erroneous information on the Internet (47).

Even though the writer acknowledges Keen as his source and provides parenthetical documentation, and even though he does not use Keen's exact words, his passage closely follows the order, emphasis, syntax, and phrasing of the original. In the following passage, the writer uses his own wording, quoting one distinctive phrase from his source.

CORRECT

According to Andrew Keen, although millions of American bloggers think of themselves as journalists, they are wrong. As Keen notes, "The simple ownership of a computer and an Internet connection doesn't transform one into a serious journalist any more than having access to a kitchen makes one into a serious cook" (47).

4. Distinguish Your Own Ideas from Your Source's Ideas

PLAGIARISM

The anonymous writers of *Wikipedia* articles are, in some ways, similar to those who put material on personal blogs. Although millions of American bloggers think of themselves as journalists, they are wrong. "The simple ownership of a computer and an Internet connection doesn't transform one into a serious journalist any more than having access to a kitchen makes one into a serious cook" (Keen 47).

In the preceding passage, it appears that only the quotation in the last sentence is borrowed from Keen's book. In fact, however, the ideas in the second sentence are also Keen's. The writer should use an identifying phrase (such as "According to Keen") to acknowledge the borrowed material in this sentence and to indicate where it begins.

CORRECT

The anonymous writers of *Wikipedia* articles are, in some ways, similar to those who put material on personal blogs. According to Andrew Keen, although millions of American bloggers think of themselves as journalists, they are wrong. As Keen notes, "The simple ownership of a computer and an Internet connection doesn't transform one into a serious journalist any more than having access to a kitchen makes one into a serious cook" (47).

Avoiding Plagiarism with Online Sources

Most students know that using long passages (or entire articles) from a print source without documenting the source is plagiarism. Unfortunately, many students assume that borrowing material found on a Web site or elsewhere online without documentation is acceptable. However, such borrowing is also plagiarism.

Perhaps students feel differently about online borrowing because it is so easy to cut and paste from an online source into a text document. They may also see copying online material as acceptable because — with authors often unidentified online — no one appears to take credit for the source. No matter what the explanation is for this casual treatment of online sources, instructors consider the use of undocumented words or ideas from online sources to be plagiarism. Therefore, just as you do for print sources, you must always document words, ideas, or visuals you get from online sources.

Exercise 5

Select an essay that you have written this semester that refers to a reading selection in this book. Reread both your essay and the selection in the book, and then decide where you could add each of the following:

- A quotation
- A summary of a paragraph
- A paraphrase of a paragraph

Exercise 6

Insert a quotation, a summary, and a paraphrase into the essay you reviewed for Exercise 5. Then, check to make sure that you have not committed plagiarism. Finally, consult the MLA section of the next chapter to help you document your sources correctly.

18

Documenting Sources: MLA

When you **document** a source, you tell readers where you have found the information you have used in your essay. The Modern Language Association (MLA) recommends the following documentation style for essays that use research.* This format consists *of parenthetical references* in the body of the paper that refer to a *works-cited* list at the end of the paper.

Parenthetical References in the Text

A **parenthetical reference** should include enough information to guide readers to a specific entry in your works-cited list.

A typical parenthetical reference consists of the author's last name and the page number: (Mangu-Ward 21). If you use more than one work by the same author, include a shortened form of the title in the parenthetical reference: (Mangu-Ward, *"Wikipedia* and Beyond" 25). Notice that the parenthetical references do not include a comma after the title or "p." before the page number.

Whenever possible, introduce information with a phrase that includes the author's name. (If you do this, include only the page number in parentheses.)

According to Andrew Keen, the absence of professional reporters and editors leads to erroneous information on *Wikipedia* (4).

---

* For further information, see the seventh edition of the *MLA Handbook for Writers of Research Papers* (New York: Mod. Lang. Assn., 2009) or the MLA Web site at mla.org.

Place documentation so that it does not interrupt the flow of your ideas, preferably at the end of a sentence.

The format for parenthetical references departs from these guidelines in the following special situations:

1. When you are citing a work by two authors

It is impossible to access all Web sites by means of a single search engine (Sherman and Price 53).

2. When you are citing a work without a listed author

The technology of wikis is important, but many users are not aware of it ("7 Things").

3. When you are citing an indirect source

If you use a statement by one author that is quoted in the work of another author, indicate this by including the abbreviation qtd. in ("quoted in").

Marshall Poe notes that information on *Wikipedia* is "not exactly expert knowledge; it's common knowledge" (qtd. in Keen 39).

4. When you are citing an electronic source

Sources from the Internet or from library databases sometimes do not contain page numbers. If the electronic source uses paragraph, section, or screen numbers, use the abbreviation par. or sec., or the full word screen, followed by the corresponding number, in your documentation. (If the citation includes an author's name, place a comma after the name.)

On its Web site, *Wikipedia* warns its writers and editors to inspect sources carefully when they make assertions that are not generally held in academic circles ("Verifiability," sec. 3).

If the electronic source has no page numbers or markers of any kind, include just the name(s) of the author(s). Readers can tell that the citation refers to an electronic source when they consult the works-cited list.

A *Wikipedia* entry can be very deceptive, but some users may not realize that its information may not be reliable (McHenry).

GUIDELINES FOR FORMATTING QUOTATIONS

SHORT QUOTATIONS Quotations of no more than four typed lines are run in with the text of your paper. End punctuation comes after the parenthetical reference (which follows the quotation marks).

According to Andrew Keen, on *Wikipedia,* "the voice of a high school kid has equal value to that of an Ivy League scholar of a trained profession" (42).

LONG QUOTATIONS Quotations of more than four lines are set off from the text of your paper. Indent a long quotation one inch from the left-hand margin, and do not enclose the passage in quotation marks. The first line of a long quotation is not indented even if it is the beginning of a paragraph. If a quoted passage has more than one paragraph, indent the first line of each subsequent paragraph one-quarter inch. Introduce a long quotation with a colon, and place the parenthetical reference one space after the end punctuation.

According to Katherine Mangu-Ward, *Wikipedia* has changed the world:

> *Wikipedia* was born as an experiment in aggregating information. But the reason it works isn't that the world was clamoring for a new kind of encyclopedia. It took off because of the robust, self-policing community it created. . . . Despite its critics, it is transforming our everyday lives; as with Amazon, Google, and eBay, it is almost impossible to remember how much more circumscribed our world was before it existed. (21)

NOTE: Ellipses indicate that the student has deleted words from the quotation.

The Works-Cited List

The works-cited list includes all the works you **cite** (refer to) in your paper. Use the following guidelines to help you prepare your list.

GUIDELINES FOR PREPARING THE WORKS-CITED LIST

- Begin the works-cited list on a new page after the last page of your paper.
- Number the works-cited page as the next page of the paper.
- Center the heading Works Cited one inch from the top of the page; do not underline the heading or put it in quotation marks.
- Double-space the list.
- List entries alphabetically according to the author's last name.
- Alphabetize unsigned articles according to the first major word of the title.
- Begin each entry flush with the left-hand margin.
- Indent second and subsequent lines one-half inch.
- Separate each division of the entry — author, title, and publication information — by a period and one space.

The following sample works-cited entries cover the situations you will encounter most often. Follow the formats exactly as they appear here.

Articles

GUIDELINES FOR MLA ARTICLE CITATIONS

To cite a periodical article in MLA style, follow these guidelines:

1. List the author, last name first.
2. Put the title of the article in quotation marks and italicize the title of the periodical.
3. Include the volume and issue number (when applicable), the year and date of publication, and the pages on which the full article appears (without the abbreviation *p.* or *pp.*).
4. Finally, include the medium of publication (*Print, Web,* and so on).

Journal Articles. A **journal** is a publication aimed at readers who know a lot about a particular subject — English or history, for example.

ARTICLE IN A JOURNAL

Provide the volume number followed by a period and the issue number. Leave no space after the period between the volume and issue numbers. List the date of publication (in parentheses), the pages of the article, and the medium of publication.

> Markley, Robert. "Gulliver and the Japanese: The Limits of the
> Postcolonial Past." *Modern Language Quarterly* 65.3 (2004):
> 457-80. Print.

ARTICLE IN A JOURNAL THAT USES ONLY ISSUE NUMBERS

For a journal that uses only issue numbers, cite the issue number, publication date, page numbers, and medium.

> Adelt, Ulrich. "Black, White and Blue: Racial Politics in B.B. King's
> Music from the 1960s." *Journal of Popular Culture* 44 (2011):
> 195-216. Print.

Magazine Articles. A **magazine** is a publication aimed at general readers. For this reason, it contains articles that are easier to understand than those in journals.

ARTICLE IN A MONTHLY OR BIMONTHLY MAGAZINE

Frequently, an article in a magazine does not appear on consecutive pages — for example, it might begin on page 43, skip to page 47, and continue on page 49. If this is the case, include only the first page, followed by a plus sign.

> Edwards, Owen. "Kilroy Was Here." *Smithsonian* Oct. 2004: 40+. Print.

ARTICLE IN A WEEKLY OR BIWEEKLY MAGAZINE (SIGNED OR UNSIGNED)

Schley, Jim. "Laid Off, and Working Harder Than Ever." *Newsweek*
20 Sept. 2004: 16. Print.

"Real Reform Post-Enron." *Nation* 4 Mar. 2002: 3. Print.

ARTICLE IN A NEWSPAPER

Bykowicz, Julie. "Man Faces Identity Theft Counts; College Worker
Accused of Taking Students' Data." *Sun* [Baltimore] 18 Sept.
2004: 2B. Print.

EDITORIAL OR LETTER TO THE EDITOR

"An Un-American Way to Campaign." Editorial. *New York Times*
25 Sept. 2004, late ed.: A14. Print.

REVIEW IN A NEWSPAPER

Scott, A. O. "Forever Obsessing about Obsession." Rev. of *Adaptation,*
dir. Spike Jonze. *New York Times* 6 Dec. 2002: F1+. Print.

REVIEW IN A WEEKLY OR BIWEEKLY MAGAZINE

Urquhart, Brian. "The Prospect of War." Rev. of *The Threatening Storm:
The Case for Invading Iraq,* by Kenneth M. Pollack. *New York
Review of Books* 19 Dec. 2002: 16-22. Print.

REVIEW IN A MONTHLY MAGAZINE

Jones, Kent. "The Lay of the Land." Rev. of *Sunshine State,* dir. John
Sayles. *Film Commentary* May/June 2002: 22-24. Print.

Books

GUIDELINES FOR MLA BOOK CITATIONS

To cite a print book in MLA style, follow these guidelines:
1. List the author with last name first.
2. Italicize the title.
3. Include the city of publication.
4. Use a shortened form of the publisher's name — for example, *Bedford* for *Bedford/St. Martin's*. Use the abbreviation *UP* for *University Press*, as in *Princeton UP* and *U of Chicago P.*
5. Include the date of publication, followed by a period.
6. Include the medium of publication (*Print*).

The two illustrations that follow show where to find the information you need for your book citations.

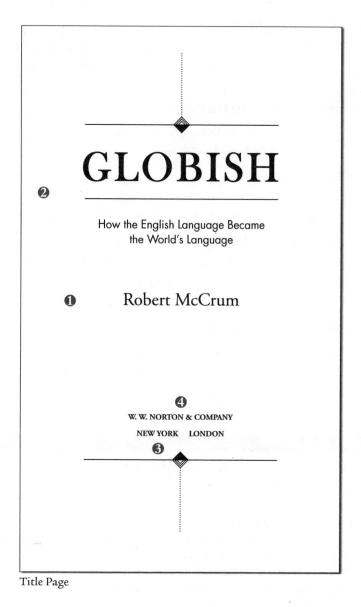

GLOBISH

❷

How the English Language Became
the World's Language

❶   Robert McCrum

❹

W. W. NORTON & COMPANY

NEW YORK   LONDON

❸

Title Page

⑤   Copyright © 2010 by Robert McCrum

For information about permission to reproduce selections from this book,
write to Permissions, W. W. Norton & Company, Inc.,
500 Fifth Avenue, New York, NY 10110

For information about special discounts for bulk purchases, please contact
W. W. Norton Special Sales at specialsales@wwnorton.com or 800-233-4830

Manufacturing by Courier Westford
Book design by Ellen Cipriano
Production manager: Devon Zahn

Library of Congress Cataloging-in-Publication Data

McCrum, Robert.
Globish : how the English language became the world's language /
Robert McCrum, — 1st ed.
p. cm.
Includes bibliographical references and index.
ISBN 978-0-393-06255-7
1. English language—History. 2. English language—Globalization.
I. Title.
PE1075.M57 2010
420.9—dc22

2010008157

W. W. Norton & Company, Inc.
500 Fifth Avenue, New York, NY 10110
www.wwnorton.com

W. W. Norton & Company Ltd.
Castle House, 75/76 Wells Street, London W1T3QT

1 2 3 4 5 6 7 8 9 0

Copyright Page

```
  ┌────1────┐ ┌──────────2──────────────────
```
McCrum, Robert. *Globish: How the English Language Became the*
```
─────────────┐ ┌──3──┐ ┌─4─┐ ┌─5─┐ ┌─6─┐
```
World's Language. New York: Norton, 2010. Print.

BOOKS BY ONE AUTHOR

McCrum, Robert. *Globish: How the English Language Became the*
World's Language. New York: Norton, 2010. Print.

BOOKS BY TWO OR THREE AUTHORS

List authors in the order in which they are listed on the book's title page. List second and subsequent authors with first names first.

Bigelow, Fran, and Helene Siegel. *Pure Chocolate*. New York: Broadway,
2004. Print.

BOOKS BY MORE THAN THREE AUTHORS

List only the first author, followed by the abbreviation *et al.* ("and others").

> Ordeman, John L, et al. *Artists of the North American Wilderness:*
> *George and Belmore Browne.* New York: Warwick, 2004. Print.

TWO OR MORE BOOKS BY THE SAME AUTHOR

List two or more books by the same author in alphabetical order according to title. In each entry after the first, use three unspaced hyphens (followed by a period) instead of the author's name.

> Angelou, Maya. *Hallelujah! The Welcome Table: A Lifetime of Memories*
> *with Recipes.* New York: Random, 2004. Print.
>
> ---. *I Know Why the Caged Bird Sings.* New York: Bantam, 1985. Print.

EDITED BOOK

> Whitman, Walt. *The Portable Walt Whitman.* Ed. Michael Warner. New
> York: Penguin, 2004. Print.

TRANSLATION

> García Márquez, Gabriel. *Living to Tell the Tale.* Trans. Edith Grossman.
> New York: Knopf, 2004. Print.

REVISED EDITION

> Bjelajac, David. *American Art: A Cultural History.* 2nd ed. New York:
> Prentice, 2004. Print.

ANTHOLOGY

> Kirszner, Laurie G., and Stephen R. Mandell, eds. *Patterns for College*
> *Writing: A Rhetorical Reader and Guide.* 12th ed. Boston: Bedford,
> 2012. Print.

ESSAY IN AN. ANTHOLOGY

> Gansberg, Martin. "Thirty-Eight Who Saw Murder Didn't Call the Police."
> *Patterns for College Writing: A Rhetorical Reader and Guide.* 12th ed.
> Ed. Laurie G. Kirszner and Stephen R. Mandell. Boston: Bedford,
> 2012. 127-30. Print.

MORE THAN ONE ESSAY IN THE SAME ANTHOLOGY

List each essay separately with a cross-reference to the entire anthology.

> Gansberg, Martin. "Thirty-Eight Who Saw Murder Didn't Call the
> Police." Kirszner and Mandell 127-30.
>
> Kirszner, Laurie G., and Stephen R. Mandell, eds. *Patterns for College*
> *Writing: A Rhetorical Reader and Guide.* 12th ed. Boston: Bedford,
> 2012. Print.

Staples, Brent. "Just Walk On By: A Black Man Ponders His Power to
Alter Public Space." Kirszner and Mandell 240-43.

SECTION OR CHAPTER OF A BOOK

Gordimer, Nadine. "Loot." *"Loot" and Other Stories*. New York: Farrar,
2004. 1-6. Print.

INTRODUCTION, PREFACE, FOREWORD, OR AFTERWORD

Ingham, Patricia. Introduction. *Martin Chuzzlewit*. By Charles Dickens.
London: Penguin, 1999. x-xxxii. Print.

MULTIVOLUME WORK

Malory, Thomas. *Le Morte D'Arthur*. Ed. Janet Cowen. 2 vols. London:
Penguin, 1986. Print.

ARTICLE IN A REFERENCE WORK

For familiar reference works that publish new editions regularly, include only the edition (if given) and the year of publication.

"Civil Rights." *The World Book Encyclopedia*. 2006 ed. Print.

For less familiar reference works, provide a full citation.

Wagle, Greta. "Geisel, Theodor [Seuss]." *The Encyclopedia of American
Literature*. Ed. Steven R. Serafin. New York: Continuum, 1999. Print.

Internet Sources

GUIDELINES FOR MLA INTERNET CITATIONS

When citing an Internet source, include the following information:

1. The name of the author or editor of the site
2. The title of the site (italicized)
3. The site's sponsor or publisher (if no sponsor or publisher is identified, write *N.p.*)
4. The date of electronic publication (if no publication date is available, write *n.d.*)
5. The medium of publication: *Web.*
6. The date you accessed the source

ENTIRE INTERNET SITE (SCHOLARLY PROJECT, INFORMATION DATABASE, JOURNAL, OR PROFESSIONAL WEB SITE)

The Dickens Project. Ed. Jon Michael Varese. U of California, Santa
Cruz, 2004. Web. 2 Dec. 2011.

International Dialects of English Archive. Dept. of Theatre and Film,
U of Kansas, 2004. Web. 4 Dec. 2011.

Words of the Year. Amer. Dialect Soc, 2008. Web. 18 Feb. 2011.

DOCUMENT WITHIN A WEB SITE

"Child and Adolescent Violence Research at the NIMH." *National Institute of Mental Health,* NIMH, 2005. Web. 2 Apr. 2011.

PERSONAL WEB SITE

Lynch, Jack. Home page. Jack Lynch, n.d. Web. 2 Jan. 2011.

ENTIRE ONLINE BOOK

Austen, Jane. *Pride and Prejudice.* 1813. *The Literature Network.* Web. 30 Nov. 2011.

Fielding, Henry. *The History of Tom Jones, a Foundling.* Ed. William Allan Nielson. New York: Collier, 1917. *Bartleby.com: Great Books Online.* Web. 29 Nov. 2011.

PART OF AN ONLINE BOOK

Radford, Dollie. "At Night." *Poems.* London, 1910. *Victorian Women Writers Project.* Web. 17 Mar. 2011.

ARTICLE IN AN ONLINE SCHOLARLY JOURNAL

Condie, Kent C., and Jane Silverstone. "The Crust of the Colorado Plateau: New Views of an Old Arc." *Journal of Geology* 107.4 (1999): 387-97. Web. 9 Aug. 2011.

ARTICLE IN AN ONLINE REFERENCE BOOK OR ENCYCLOPEDIA

"Croatia." *The World Factbook 2004.* CIA, 30 Mar. 2004. Web. 30 Dec. 2007.

ARTICLE IN AN ONLINE NEWSPAPER

Krim, Jonathan. "FCC Preparing to Overhaul Telecom, Media Rules." *Washingtonpost.com.* Washington Post, 3 Jan. 2003. Web. 6 Jan. 2007.

ONLINE EDITORIAL

"Ersatz Eve." Editorial. *New York Times on the Web.* New York Times, 28 Dec. 2002. Web. 5 Jan. 2006.

ARTICLE IN AN ONLINE MAGAZINE

Press, Eyal, and Jennifer Washburn. "The At-Risk-Youth Industry." *Atlantic Online.* Atlantic Monthly Group, Dec. 2002. Web. 3 Jan. 2008.

REVIEW IN AN ONLINE PERIODICAL

Chocano, Carina. "Sympathy for the Misanthrope." Rev. of *Curb Your Enthusiasm,* dir. Robert Weide, prod. Larry David. *Salon.* Salon Media Group, 4 Dec. 2002. Web. 17 Sept. 2005.

POSTING TO A DISCUSSION LIST

Thune, W. Scott. "Emotion and Rationality in Argument." *CCCC/97 Online*. N.p., 23 Mar. 1997. Web. 11 Nov. 2005.

BLOG POST

Singer, Judy Reene. "Why I Wrote My Elephant Books." *Romance Blog* 8 June 2010. Web. 9 Aug. 2010.

Other Internet Sources

A PAINTING ON THE INTERNET

O'Keeffe, Georgia. *Evening Star, III*. 1917. Museum of Mod. Art, New York. *MoMA: The Museum of Modern Art*. Web. 9 Nov. 2011.

A PHOTOGRAPH ON THE INTERNET

Cartier-Bresson, Henri. *William Faulkner, 1947*. Nat. Portrait Gallery, Washington D.C. *Tête à tête: Portraits by Henri Cartier-Bresson*. Web. 8 Oct. 2011.

A CARTOON ON THE INTERNET

Trudeau, Garry. "Doonesbury." Comic strip. *Washingtonpost.com*. Washington Post, 7 Apr. 2005. Web. 5 May 2011.

A MAP OR CHART ON THE INTERNET

"Fort Worth, Texas." Map. *US Gazetteer*. US Census Bureau, n.d. Web. 26 Oct. 2011.

MATERIAL ACCESSED ON A CD-ROM, DISKETTE, OR MAGNETIC TAPE

In addition to the publication information, include the medium (CD-ROM, for example) and the distribution vendor, if relevant (UMI-Proquest, for example).

Aristotle. "Poetics." *The Complete Works of Aristotle*. Ed. Jonathan Barnes. 2 vols. Princeton: Princeton UP, 1984. CD-ROM. Clayton: InteLex, 1994.

"Feminism." *The Oxford English Dictionary*. 2nd ed. New York: Oxford UP, 1992. CD-ROM. Vers. 3.1. 2004.

EMAIL

Sullivan, John. "Re: Headnotes." Message to Laurie G. Kirszner. 13 Dec. 2010. Email.

COMPUTER SOFTWARE OR VIDEO GAME

Provide the name of the author or developer of the software, if available; the title of the software, italicized; the publisher or distributor and publication date; and the software platform (for example, Xbox 360 or PlayStation 3).

> *Sid Meier's Civilization IV: Colonization.* Take 2 Interactive, 2008.
> Windows.

MATERIAL FROM A LIBRARY DATABASE

For material retrieved from a library database such as *InfoTrac, Lexis-Nexis, ProQuest,* or *EBSCOhost,* list the publication information for the source and provide the name of the database (such as *LexisNexis Academic*), italicized; the publication medium; and the date you accessed the source.

> Benjamin, Roy. "The Stone of Stumbling in *Finnegans Wake.*" *Journal of Modern Literature* 31.2 (2008): 66-78. *Academic OneFile.* Web. 7 Apr. 2009.

> Carter, Jeff. "The Missing Piece of Education Reform." *Washington Post* 18 May 2008, regional ed.: B8. *LexisNexis Academic.* Web. 31 Mar. 2009.

> Prince, Stephen. "Why Do Film Scholars Ignore Media Violence?" *Chronicle of Higher Education* 10 Aug. 2001: B18. *Academic Research Premier.* Web. 14 Feb. 2010.

Other Nonprint Sources

TELEVISION OR RADIO PROGRAM

> "Prime Suspect 3." Writ. Lynda La Plante. *Mystery!* PBS. WNET, New York, 28 Apr. 1994. Television.

FILM, DVD, OR CD

> *Doubt.* Dir. John Patrick Shanley. Perf. Meryl Streep, Philip Seymour Hoffman, Amy Adams, and Viola Davis. Miramax, 2008. DVD.
> *Man on Wire.* Dir. James Marsh. Perf. Philippe Petit. Discovery Films, 2008. Film.

PERSONAL INTERVIEW

> Garcetti, Gilbert. Personal interview. 7 May 2010.

Model Student Research Paper in MLA Style

The following research paper, "The Limitations of *Wikipedia,*" by Philip Lau, follows MLA format as outlined in the previous pages.

Lau 1

Philip Lau
Professor Carroll
ENG 101
23 Nov. 2011

The Limitations of *Wikipedia*

Introduction

When they get a research assignment, many students
immediately go to the Internet to find sources. Searching the
Web, they may discover a *Wikipedia* article on their topic. But
is *Wikipedia* a reliable reference source for a research paper?
There is quite a controversy over the use of *Wikipedia* as a

Thesis statement

source, but the answer seems to be no. Although *Wikipedia*
may be a good starting point for general information about
a topic, college-level research papers should rely on more
authoritative sources.

A wiki is software that allows people to collaborate in
forming the content of a Web site. With a wiki, anyone with
a browser can edit, modify, rearrange, or delete content. It is
not necessary to know HTML (hypertext mark-up language)
or to work in HTML code. The word *wiki* comes from the word
wikiwiki, which means "quick" or "fast" in Hawaiian. The most
popular wiki is *Wikipedia*, a free, Internet-based encyclopedia
that relies on the collaboration, consensus, openness, and
trust of those who post and edit entries. Anyone can learn
to write a *Wikipedia* article by clicking on "How to write an
article" or edit an entry by clicking on "Edit this entry."
All revisions are visible to everyone who clicks on "history"

*Paragraph
combines factual
information, found
in more than
one source, with
quotations from
"Verifiability" and
Mangu-Ward, and
a statistic from
Rothenberg*

("Verifiability"). According to Katherine Mangu-Ward, the
success of *Wikipedia* "springs largely from [its founder's]
willingness to trust large aggregations of human beings to
produce good outcomes . . ." (26). This collaboration enables
Wikipedia to publish a wide variety of entries on unusual,
specialized topics (see fig. 1). So far, there are over four million
Wikipedia articles (Rothenberg).

Lau 2

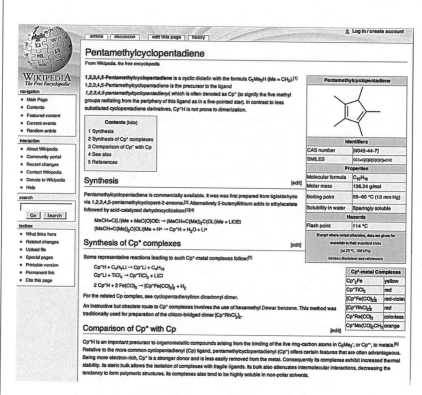

Fig. 1. *Wikipedia* entry for a chemical compound. "Pentamethylcyclopentadiene." *Wikipedia, the Free Encyclopedia*. Wikimedia Foundation, Inc. 3 Oct. 2010. Web. 9 Dec. 2010.

Wikipedia includes two kinds of content. The first kind of content is factual—that is, information that can be verified or proved true. Factual material from reliable sources is more trustworthy than material from other sources. In fact, *Wikipedia*'s own site states, "In general, the most reliable sources are peer-reviewed journals and books published in university presses; university-level textbooks; magazines, journals, and books published by respected publishing houses; and mainstream newspapers" ("Verifiability"). Most reliable publications have staff whose job it is to check facts. However,

Paragraph combines student's own ideas with quotations and paraphrases from "Verifiability"

Lau 3

because *Wikipedia* relies on a community of people to write articles, no single person or group of people is responsible for checking facts. The theory is that after enough people have worked on an article, any errors in fact will have been found and corrected. However, this assumption is not necessarily true.

The second kind of content consists of opinions. Because an opinion is a belief or judgment, opinions—by definition— tend to be one-sided. So, since *Wikipedia* entries are supposed to be objective, *Wikipedia's* policy statement says that entries for controversial topics should include opinions that reflect the various sides of the issue ("Verifiability"). In addition, *Wikipedia* warns users against believing everything they read, even what they read on its own site: "Anyone can create a website or pay to have a book published, then claim to be an expert . . ." ("Verifiability"). It also advises readers to examine sources carefully, especially when they present controversial opinions or make claims that contradict established academic views ("Verifiability"). However, it is all up to the users; no one person checks to make sure that these guidelines are followed.

In spite of its stated policies, then, *Wikipedia* is open to certain kinds of problems. One of the problems comes from its assumption that the knowledge of the community is more valuable than the knowledge of acknowledged experts in a field. Larry Sanger, one of the founders of *Wikipedia*, who has since left the project, concedes that *Wikipedia* has a problem with "anti-elitism, or lack of respect for expertise"; in fact, he refers to its "horror of the traditional deference to experience," which he claims explains why acknowledged experts avoid writing or editing articles on *Wikipedia*. Those who criticize *Wikipedia* often point to its irrational trust in the knowledge of the community. According to Andrew Keen, *Wikipedia* is virtually "the blind leading the blind—infinite monkeys providing infinite information for infinite readers, perpetuating the cycle of misinformation and ignorance" (4). On *Wikipedia*,

Paragraph combines quotation and paraphrases from "Verifiability" with student's own ideas

Paragraph combines quotation and paraphrase from Sanger with a quotation from Keen

Keen complains, "the voice of a high school kid has equal value to that of an Ivy League scholar . . ." (42).

Another problem with *Wikipedia* is the ease with which entries can be edited. Because the content of wikis can be altered by anyone, individuals can easily vandalize content by inserting incorrect information, obscene language, or even nonsense into articles. Writers who are more interested in presenting their personal opinions than presenting reliable information frequently target certain entries. For example, entries for controversial people, such as President George W. Bush, financier George Soros, or Scientology founder L. Ron Hubbard, or for controversial subjects, such as abortion and the Holocaust, are routinely vandalized. Sometimes this vandalism can be extremely harmful. One notorious case of vandalism involved John Seigenthaler Sr., a journalist who was falsely accused in a *Wikipedia* entry of being involved in the assassinations of John Kennedy and Robert Kennedy. As Seigenthaler's son has reported, the false information stayed on the site for more than four months and also appeared on at least two other sites that had used *Wikipedia* as their source (Seigenthaler). This incident, as well as many others, has caused people to question the reliability of *Wikipedia*. According to Jane Kirtley, the issue of reliability poses a real problem for the users of *Wikipedia*:

> It's hard to defend an anonymous poster who uploads a damaging falsehood about someone on a Web site that purports to provide facts from a "neutral point of view. . . ." Either accuracy matters, or it doesn't. If the denizens of cyberspace want to be taken seriously, they might want to be responsible for what they produce. (66)

Bias is another problem for *Wikipedia*. Some critics have accused *Wikipedia* of having a liberal bias; in fact, a

Paragraph contains a long quotation from Kirtley, student's summary of the Seigenthaler article, and facts that were found in several sources

Lau 5

competitor, Conservapedia, lists many examples of liberal bias in *Wikipedia* entries. Accusing *Wikipedia* of being anti-American and anti-Christian ("Examples"), Conservapedia questions the true agenda of the *Wikipedia* community. In a *Time* article, Jimmy Wales, founder of *Wikipedia*, denies this liberal bias and accuses Conservapedia of having a conservative bias (6). Still, such accusations do raise questions about the credibility of *Wikipedia*.

Wikipedia has tried to correct some of the problems that its critics have pointed out. In response to criticism of its policy of allowing writers and editors to remain anonymous, Jimmy Wales changed *Wikipedia*'s policy. Now, writers and editors have to provide their user names and thus take responsibility for the content they contribute. In addition, *Wikipedia* has made it possible for administrators to block certain sites from those wishing to edit them and to prevent certain writers and editors from posting or changing

information. In addition, users must now be registered with *Wikipedia* for four days before they can change certain controversial entries (Hafner). However, authorship is still a problem. Most readers have no idea who has written an article that they are reading or whether or not that person can be trusted. Given *Wikipedia*'s basic philosophy, there is no way to solve this problem.

Of course, even traditional encyclopedias have shortcomings. For example, a study by the journal *Nature* found that although *Wikipedia* included errors, the *Encyclopedia Britannica* also did. Nevertheless, Robert McHenry, a former

editor of *Britannica,* points out that *Wikipedia* articles often do not get better through editing; instead, they frequently get worse. He goes on to say that *Wikipedia* suffers because it lacks the oversight that only a good editor can provide: "skills, knowledge, experience, and maybe a touch of talent." McHenry observes that out of concern for *Britannica*'s reputation, at

Lau 6

least four people check every article for accuracy. He points out
that professional editors do more than just check spelling and
grammar; they also stand in "for the eventual reader in order
to assure that what was written was clear, logical, and to the
point." Since *Wikipedia* has no professional editors, its writing
may be ungrammatical, stylistically awkward, or unclear.

Supporters of *Wikipedia* defend the site against those
charges, noting that more traditional sources, such as respected
peer-reviewed journals, also have their problems. For example,
very new material is likely to be underrepresented or even
omitted by a traditional print encyclopedia, which is published

*Paragraph
contains ideas
found in several
sources and
student's own
conclusions*

only every few years. In addition, some reviewers of articles
that appear in peer-reviewed journals may have conflicts of
interest. For example, a reviewer might reject an article that
challenges his or her own work, or editors may favor certain
authors over others. Also, it may be possible for reviewers to
identify the work of a competitor, especially if the number of
people working in a field is relatively small, and therefore let
bias influence their evaluation of an article. Another problem is
that it takes a long time for articles in peer-reviewed journals
to get into print. Critics point out that by the time an article in
a peer-reviewed journal gets into print, it may be outdated. As
a result, peer-reviewed journals may not be as objective or as
up-to-date as readers think they are.

Wikipedia is easy to access and easy to use. It includes
information on just about any topic a researcher might want
to explore. Still, it is not a reliable source for serious research,
primarily because of the many questions that have been raised
about the reliability of its articles. Therefore, many high
schools and colleges do not allow students to cite *Wikipedia*

Conclusion

as a source. Granted, there are times when *Wikipedia* can be
useful. For example, visitors to the site can skim articles on a
variety of topics, and this preliminary reading can help them
find or narrow a research topic. In addition, students can often

Lau 7

find general information on *Wikipedia* about very current topics that may not be treated anywhere else. Finally, the computer links that appear at the end of most *Wikipedia* articles can be a good starting point for research. In general, however, because of the questionable authorship of its entries and the lack of expertise and objectivity of some (if not many) of its contributors, *Wikipedia* is not a reliable source.

Lau 8

Works Cited

"Examples of Bias in *Wikipedia*." *Conservapedia*. Conservapedia, 27 Dec. 2007. Web. 28 Oct. 2011.

Hafner, Katie. "Growing *Wikipedia* Refines Its 'Anyone Can Edit' Policy." *New York Times*. New York Times, 17 June 2006. Web. 23 Oct. 2011.

Keen, Andrew. *The Cult of the Amateur: How Today's Internet Is Killing Our Culture*. New York: Doubleday, 2007. Print.

Kirtley, Jane. "Web of Lies: A Vicious *Wikipedia* Entry Underscores the Difficulty of Holding Anyone Responsible for Misinformation on the Internet." *American Journalism Review* 28.1 (2006): 66. Print.

Mangu-Ward, Katherine. "*Wikipedia* and Beyond: Jimmy Wales's Sprawling Vision." *Reason* June 2007: 20-29. Print.

McHenry, Robert. "The Faith-Based Encyclopedia Blinks." *TCS Daily*. TCS Daily, 14 Dec. 2005. Web. 30 Oct. 2011.

Rothenberg, Jennie. "Common Knowledge." *Atlantic.com*. Atlantic Monthly Group, 1 Aug. 2006. Web. 28 Oct. 2011.

Sanger, Larry. "Why *Wikipedia* Must Jettison Its Anti-Elitism." *Kuro5hin.org*. Kuro5hin, 31 Dec. 2004. Web. 23 Oct. 2011.

Seigenthaler, John. "A False *Wikipedia* 'Biography.'" *USAToday*. USA Today, 29 Nov. 2005. Web. 21 Oct. 2011.

"Verifiability." *Wikipedia*. Wikimedia Foundation, 22 Dec. 2010. Web. 24 Oct. 2011.

Wales, Jimmy. "10 Questions." *Time* 2 Apr. 2007: 6. Print.

APPENDIX

Documenting Sources: APA

APA style was developed by the American Psychological Association and is commonly used in the social sciences. Sources are cited to help readers in the social sciences understand new ideas in the context of previous research and show them how current the sources are.*

There are several reasons to cite sources. Readers expect arguments to be well supported by evidence and want to be able to locate those sources if they decide to delve deeper. Citing sources is also important to give credit to writers and to avoid plagiarism.

Using Parenthetical References

In APA style, parenthetical references refer readers to sources in the list of references at the end of the paper. In general, parenthetical references should include the author and year of publication. You may also include page numbers if you are quoting directly from a source. Here are some more specific guidelines:

- Refer to the author's name in the text, or cite it, along with the year of publication, in parentheses: Vang asserted . . . (2004) or (Vang, 2004). When quoting words from a source, include the page number: (Vang, 2004, p. 33). Once you have cited a source, you can refer to the author a second time without the publication date so long as it is clear you are referring to the same source: Vang also found . . .
- If no author is identified, use a shortened version of the title: ("Mind," 2007).
- If you are citing multiple works by the same author or authors published in the same year, add a lowercase letter with the year: (Peters, 2004a), (Peters, 2004b), and so on.

---

* American Psychological Association, *Publication Manual of the American Psychological Association*, Sixth Edition (2010).

- When a work has two authors, cite both names and the year: (Tabor & Garza, 2006). For three to five authors, cite all authors in the first reference, with the year; for subsequent references, use the first author followed by et al. When a work has six or more authors, use the first author's name followed by et al. and the year: (McCarthy et al., 2010).
- Omit page numbers or dates if the source does not include them. (Try to find a .pdf version of an online source if it is an option; it will usually include page numbers.)
- If you quote a source found in another source, indicate the original author and the source in which you found it: Psychologist Gary Wells asserted . . . (as cited in Doyle, 2005, p. 122).
- Include in-text references to personal communications and interviews by providing the person's name, the phrase "personal communication," and the date: (J. Smith, personal communication, February 12, 2011). Do not include these sources in your reference list.

Parenthetical citations must be included for all sources that are not common knowledge, whether you are paraphrasing, summarizing, or quoting directly from a source. If a direct quotation is forty words or less, include it within quotation marks without separating it from the rest of the text. When quoting a passage that is more than forty words long, indent the entire block of quoted text one-half inch from the left margin, and do not enclose it in quotation marks. It should be double-spaced, like the rest of the paper.

GUIDELINES FOR PREPARING THE REFERENCE LIST

Start your list of references on a separate page at the end of your paper. Center the title References at the top of the page.

- Begin each reference flush with the left margin, and indent subsequent lines one-half inch.
- List your references alphabetically by the author's last name (or by the first major word of the title if no author is identified).
- If the list includes references for two sources by the same author, list them in order by the year of publication, starting with the earliest.
- Italicize titles of books and periodicals. Do not italicize article titles or enclose them in quotation marks.
- For titles of books and articles, capitalize the first word of the title and subtitle as well as any proper nouns. Capitalize words in a periodical title as in the original.

When you have completed your reference list, go through your paper and make sure that every reference cited is included in the list in the correct order.

Examples of APA Citations

The following are examples of APA citations.

Periodicals

ARTICLE IN A JOURNAL PAGINATED BY VOLUME

Shah, N. A. (2006). Women's human rights in the Koran: An
interpretive approach. *Human Rights Quarterly, 28,* 868–902.

ARTICLE IN A JOURNAL PAGINATED BY ISSUE

Lamb, B., & Keller, H. (2007). Understanding cultural models of
parenting: The role of intracultural variation and response style.
Journal of Cross-Cultural Psychology, 38(1), 50–57.

MAGAZINE ARTICLE

Collins, L. (2009, April 20). The vertical tourist. *The New Yorker,
85*(10), 68–79.

NEWSPAPER ARTICLE

DeParle, J. (2009, April 19). Struggling to rise in suburbs where
failing means fitting in. *The New York Times,* pp. A1, A20–A21.

Books

BOOKS BY ONE AUTHOR

McCrum, Robert. (2010). *Globish: How the English language became
the world's language.* New York, NY: Norton.

BOOKS BY TWO TO SEVEN AUTHORS

Guerrero, L. K., & Floyd, K. (2006). *Nonverbal communication in close
relationships.* Mahwah, NJ: Erlbaum.

BOOKS BY EIGHT OR MORE AUTHORS

Mulvaney, S. A., Mudasiru, E., Schlundt, D. G., Baughman, C. L.,
Fleming, M., VanderWoude, A., . . . Rothman, R. (2008). Self-
management in Type 2 diabetes: The adolescent perspective.
The Diabetes Educator, 34, 118–127.

EDITED BOOK

Brummett, B. (Ed.). (2008). *Uncovering hidden rhetorics: Social issues
in disguise.* Los Angeles, CA: Sage.

ESSAY IN AN EDITED BOOK

Alberts, H. C. (2006). The multiple transformations of Miami. In
H. Smith & O. J. Furuseth (Eds.), *Latinos in the new south:
Transformations of place* (pp. 135–151). Burlington, VT: Ashgate.

TRANSLATION

Courville, S. (2008). *Quebec: A historical geography* (R. Howard,
Trans.). Vancouver, Canada: UBC.

REVISED EDITION

Johnson, B., & Christensen, L. B. (2008). *Educational research:
Quantitative, qualitative, and mixed approaches* (3rd ed.). Los
Angeles, CA: Sage.

Internet Sources

ENTIRE WEB SITE

Secretariat of the Convention on Biodiversity, United Nations
Biodiversity Programmes. (2005). *Convention on biological
diversity*. Retrieved from http://www.biodiv.org/

WEB PAGE WITHIN A WEB SITE

The great divide: How Westerners and Muslims view each other.
(2006, July 6). In *Pew global attitudes project*. Retrieved from
http://pewglobal.org/reports/display.php?ReportID=253

UNIVERSITY PROGRAM WEB SITE

National security archive. (2009). Retrieved from George Washington
University website: http://www.gwu.edu/~nsarchiv/

JOURNAL ARTICLE FOUND ON THE WEB WITH A DOI

Because Web sites change and disappear without warning, many publishers have started adding a Digital Object Identifier (DOI) to their articles. A DOI is a unique number that can be retrieved no matter where the
article ends up on the Web.

To locate an article with a known DOI, go to the DOI system Web site
at http://dx.doi.org/ and type in the DOI number. When citing an article
that has a DOI (usually found on the first page of the article), you do not
need to include a URL in your reference or the name of the database in
which you may have found the article.

Geers, A. L., Wellman, J. A., & Lassiter, G. D. (2009). Dispositional
optimism and engagement: The moderating influence of goal
prioritization. *Journal of Personality and Social Psychology, 94*,
913–932. doi:10.1037/a0014746

JOURNAL ARTICLE FOUND ON THE WEB WITHOUT A DOI

Bendetto, M. M. (2008). Crisis on the immigration bench: An ethical perspective. *Brooklyn Law Review, 73,* 467–523. Retrieved from http://brooklaw.edu/students/journals/blr.php/

JOURNAL ARTICLE FROM AN ELECTRONIC DATABASE

The name and URL of the database are not required for citations if a DOI is available. If no DOI is available, provide the home page URL of the journal or of the book or report publisher.

Staub, E., & Pearlman, L. A. (2009). Reducing intergroup prejudice and conflict: A commentary. *Journal of Personality and Social Psychology, 11,* 3–23. Retrieved from http://www.apa.org/journals/psp/

ELECTRONIC BOOK

Katz, R. N. (Ed.). (2008). *The tower and the cloud: Higher education in an era of cloud computing.* Retrieved from http://net.educause.edu/ir/library/pdf/PUB7202.pdf

VIDEO BLOG POST

Baggs, A. (2007, January 14). In my language [Video file]. Retrieved from http://www.youtube.com/watch?v=Jny1M1hI2jc

PRESENTATION SLIDES

Hall, M. E. (2009) *Who moved my job!? A psychology of job-loss "trauma"* [Presentation slides]. Retrieved from http://www.cew.wisc.edu/docs/WMMJ%20PwrPt-Summry2.ppt

Model Student Paper in APA Style

The following research paper follows APA format as outlined in the preceding pages. Note that this paper has the same content as the MLA paper on pages 735–742 but follows APA conventions. For this reason, it includes an abstract, a title page, and internal headings.

Running head: THE LIMITATIONS OF *WIKIPEDIA*   1

The Limitations of *Wikipedia*

Philip Lau

Professor Carroll

ENG 101

23 Nov. 2011

THE LIMITATIONS OF *WIKIPEDIA*   2

Abstract

Wikipedia is an online encyclopedia with entries that are
created and updated by users rather than by editors. This
paper examines the benefits and drawbacks associated
with *Wikipedia*'s open-forum approach. *Wikipedia* contains
information about a great number of topics and could be
a good resource for students who are trying to narrow the
focus of their essays. However, many educators believe that the
information is unreliable and therefore should not be used
for scholarly research. They are concerned that entries that
can be edited by anyone, regardless of their expertise on the
subject, might not be accurate. Although *Wikipedia* claims to
be as accurate as a traditional encyclopedia, there has been
at least one instance of inflammatory and untrue information
remaining on the site for months and being disseminated
through other outlets as fact. Because there is no way to
determine the expertise of the authors or the validity of the
information on *Wikipedia*, it should not be considered a reliable
source.

Introduction

The Limitations of *Wikipedia*

When they get a research assignment, many students immediately go to the Internet to find sources. Searching the Web, they may discover a *Wikipedia* article on their topic. But is *Wikipedia* a reliable reference source for a research paper? There is quite a controversy over the use of Wikipedia as a

Thesis statement

source, but the answer seems to be no. Although Wikipedia may be a good starting point for general information about a topic, college-level research papers should rely on more authoritative sources.

A wiki is software that allows people to collaborate in forming the content of a Web site. With a wiki, anyone with a browser can edit, modify, rearrange, or delete content. It is not necessary to know HTML (hypertext mark-up language) or to work in HTML code. The word *wiki* comes from the word *wikiwiki*, which means "quick" or "fast" in Hawaiian. The most popular wiki is *Wikipedia*, a free, Internet-based encyclopedia that relies on the collaboration, consensus, openness, and trust of those who post and edit entries. Anyone can learn to write a *Wikipedia* article by clicking on "How to write an article" or edit an entry by clicking on "Edit this entry." All revisions

Paragraph combines factual information, found in more than one source, with quotations from "Verifiability" and Mangu-Ward, and a statistic from Rothenberg.

are visible to everyone who clicks on "history" ("Verifiability," 2007). According to Katherine Mangu-Ward (2007), the success of *Wikipedia* "springs largely from [its founder's] willingness to trust large aggregations of human beings to produce good outcomes . . ." (p. 26). This collaboration enables *Wikipedia* to publish a wide variety of entries on unusual, specialized topics (see Figure 1). So far, there are over four million *Wikipedia* articles (Rothenberg, 2006).

Wikipedia's Two Kinds of Content

Wikipedia includes two kinds of content. The first kind of content is factual—that is, information that can be verified or proved true. Factual material from reliable sources

THE LIMITATIONS OF *WIKIPEDIA*   4

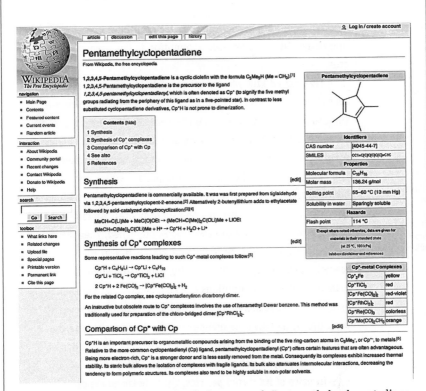

Figure 1. Wikipedia entry for a chemical compound. Pentamethylcyclopentadiene
(2010, October 3). In *Wikipedia*. Retrieved from http://en.wikipedia.org/wiki/
Pentamethylcyclopentadiene

is more trustworthy than material from other sources. In fact,
Wikipedia's own site states, "In general, the most reliable
sources are peer-reviewed journals and books published in
university presses; university-level textbooks; magazines,
journals, and books published by respected publishing houses;
and mainstream newspapers" ("Verifiability," 2007). Most
reliable publications have staff whose job it is to check facts.
However, because *Wikipedia* relies on a community of people to
write articles, no single person or group of people is responsible
for checking facts. The theory is that after enough people have

*Paragraph
combines student's
own ideas with
quotations and
paraphrases from
"Verifiability"*

worked on an article, any errors in fact will have been found and corrected. However, this assumption is not necessarily true.

The second kind of content consists of opinions. Because an opinion is a belief or judgment, opinions—by definition—tend to be one-sided. So, since *Wikipedia* entries are supposed to be objective, *Wikipedia*'s policy statement says that entries for controversial topics should include opinions that reflect the various sides of the issue ("Verifiability," 2007). In addition, *Wikipedia* warns users against believing everything they read, even what they read on its own site: "Anyone can create a website or pay to have a book published, then claim to be an expert . . ." ("Verifiability," 2007). It also advises readers to examine sources carefully, especially when they present controversial opinions or make claims that contradict established academic views ("Verifiability," 2007). However, it is all up to the users; no one person checks to make sure that these guidelines are followed.

Errors and Other Problems with *Wikipedia*

In spite of its stated policies, then, *Wikipedia* is open to certain kinds of problems. One problem comes from its assumption that the knowledge of the *Wikipedia* community is more valuable than the knowledge of acknowledged experts in a field. Larry Sanger (2004), one of the founders of *Wikipedia*, who has since left the project, concedes that *Wikipedia* has a problem with "anti-elitism, or lack of respect for expertise"; in fact, he refers to its "horror of the traditional deference to experience," which he claims explains why acknowledged experts avoid writing or editing articles on *Wikipedia*. Those who criticize *Wikipedia* often point to its irrational trust in the knowledge of the community. According to Andrew Keen (2007), *Wikipedia* is virtually "the blind leading the blind—infinite monkeys providing infinite information for

Paragraph combines quotation and paraphrases from "Verifiability" with student's own ideas

Paragraph combines quotations and paraphrases from Sanger with a quotation from Keen

infinite readers, perpetuating the cycle of misinformation and ignorance" (p. 4). On *Wikipedia*, Keen (2007) complains, "the voice of a high school kid has equal value to that of an Ivy League scholar . . ." (p. 42).

Another problem with *Wikipedia* is the ease with which entries can be edited. Because the content of wikis can be altered by anyone, individuals can easily vandalize content by inserting incorrect information, obscene language, or even nonsense into articles. Writers who are more interested in presenting their personal opinions than presenting reliable information frequently target certain entries. For example, entries for controversial people, such as President George W. Bush, financier George Soros, or Scientology founder L. Ron Hubbard, or for controversial subjects, such as abortion and the Holocaust, are routinely vandalized. Sometimes this vandalism can be extremely harmful. One notorious case of vandalism involved John Seigenthaler Sr., a journalist who was falsely accused in a *Wikipedia* entry of being involved in the assassinations of John Kennedy and Robert Kennedy. As Seigenthaler's son has reported, the false information stayed on the site for more than four months and also appeared on at least two other sites that had used *Wikipedia* as their source (Seigenthaler, 2005). This incident, as well as many others, has caused people to question the reliability of *Wikipedia*. According to Jane Kirtley (2006), the issue of reliability poses a real problem for the users of *Wikipedia*:

Paragraph contains a long quotation from Kirtley, student's summary of the Seigenthaler article, and facts that were found in several sources

> It's hard to defend an anonymous poster who uploads a damaging falsehood about someone on a Web site that purports to provide facts from a "neutral point of view. . . ." Either accuracy matters, or it doesn't. If the denizens of cyberspace want to be taken seriously, they might want to be responsible for what they produce. (p. 66)

THE LIMITATIONS OF *WIKIPEDIA*   7

Bias is another problem for *Wikipedia*. Some critics have accused *Wikipedia* of having a liberal bias; in fact, a competitor, Conservapedia, lists many examples of liberal bias in *Wikipedia* entries. Accusing *Wikipedia* of being anti-American and anti-Christian ("Examples," 2007), Conservapedia questions the true agenda of the *Wikipedia* community. In a *Time* article, Jimmy Wales (2007), founder of *Wikipedia*, denies this liberal bias and accuses Conservapedia of having a conservative bias (p. 6). Still, such accusations do raise questions about the credibility of *Wikipedia*.

Paragraph contains paraphrases from "Examples" and Wales as well as student's own conclusions

Wikipedia has tried to correct some of the problems that its critics have pointed out. In response to criticism of its policy of allowing writers and editors to remain anonymous, Jimmy Wales changed *Wikipedia*'s policy. Now, writers and editors have to provide their user names and thus take responsibility for the content they contribute. In addition, *Wikipedia* has made it possible for administrators to block certain sites from those wishing to edit them and to prevent certain writers and editors from posting or changing information. In addition, users must now be registered with *Wikipedia* for four days before they can change certain controversial entries (Hafner, 2006). However, authorship is still a problem. Most readers have no idea who has written an article that they are reading or whether or not that person can be trusted. Given *Wikipedia*'s basic philosophy, there is no way to solve this problem.

Paragraph combines ideas found in several sources, a paraphrases from Hafner, and student's own ideas

Of course, even traditional encyclopedias have shortcomings. For example, a study by the journal *Nature* found that although *Wikipedia* included errors, the *Encyclopedia Britannica* also did. Nevertheless, Robert McHenry (2005), a former editor of *Britannica*, points out that *Wikipedia* articles often do not get better through editing; instead, they frequently get worse. He goes on to say that *Wikipedia* suffers

Paragraph combines ideas found in several sources with paraphrases and quotations from McHenry

because it lacks the oversight that only a good editor can provide: "skills, knowledge, experience, and maybe a touch of talent." McHenry observes that out of concern for *Britannica*'s reputation, at least four people check every article for accuracy. He points out that professional editors do more than just check spelling and grammar; they also stand in "for the eventual reader in order to assure that what was written was clear, logical, and to the point." Since *Wikipedia* has no professional editors, its writing may be ungrammatical, stylistically awkward, or unclear.

Comparison to Traditional Sources

Supporters of *Wikipedia* defend the site against those charges, noting that more traditional sources, such as respected peer-reviewed journals, also have their problems. For example, very new material is likely to be underrepresented or even omitted by a traditional print encyclopedia, which is published only every few years. In addition, some reviewers of articles that appear in peer-reviewed journals may have conflicts of interest. For example, a reviewer might reject an article that challenges his or her own work, or editors may favor certain authors over others. Also, it may be possible for reviewers to identify the work of a competitor, especially if the number of people working in a field is relatively small, and therefore let bias influence their evaluation of an article. Another problem is that it takes a long time for articles in peer-reviewed journals to get into print. Critics point out that by the time an article in a peer-reviewed journal gets into print, it may be outdated. As a result, peer-reviewed journals may not be as objective or as up-to-date as readers think they are.

Paragraph contains ideas found in several sources and student's own conclusions

Conclusion

Wikipedia is easy to access and easy to use. It includes information on just about any topic a researcher might want to explore. Still, it is not a reliable source for serious research,

THE LIMITATIONS OF *WIKIPEDIA*   9

Conclusion

primarily because of the many questions that have been raised about the reliability of its articles. Therefore, many high schools and colleges do not allow students to cite *Wikipedia* as a source. Granted, there are times when *Wikipedia* can be useful. For example, visitors to the site can skim articles on a variety of topics, and this preliminary reading can help them find or narrow a research topic. In addition, students can often find general information on *Wikipedia* about very current topics that may not be treated anywhere else. Finally, the computer links that appear at the end of most *Wikipedia* articles can be a good starting point for research. In general, however, because of the questionable authorship of its entries and the lack of expertise and objectivity of some (if not many) of its contributors, *Wikipedia* is not a reliable source.

THE LIMITATIONS OF *WIKIPEDIA*   10

References

Examples of bias in *Wikipedia*. (2007, December 27). In
    Conservapedia. Retrieved from http://www.conservapedia
    .com/Examples_of_Bias_in_Wikipedia

Hafner, K. (2006, June 17). Growing *Wikipedia* refines its
    "anyone can edit" policy. *The New York Times*. Retrieved
    from http://www.nytimes.com

Keen, A. (2007). *The cult of the amateur: How today's Internet
    is killing our culture*. New York, NY: Doubleday.

Kirtley, J. (2006). Web of lies: A vicious *Wikipedia* entry
    underscores the difficulty of holding anyone responsible
    for misinformation on the Internet. *American Journalism
    Review, 28*(1), 66.

Mangu-Ward, K. (2007, June). *Wikipedia* and beyond: Jimmy
    Wales's sprawling vision. *Reason*, 20-29.

McHenry, R. (2005, December 14). The faith-based encyclopedia
    blinks. *TCS Daily*. Retrieved from http://www
    .ideasinactiontv.com/tcs_daily

Rothenberg, J. (2006, August 1). Common knowledge. *The
    Atlantic*. Retrieved from http://www.theatlantic.com

Sanger, L. (2004, December 31). Why *Wikipedia* must jettison
    its anti-elitism. *Kuro5hin*. Retrieved from http://www
    .Kuro5hin.org

Seigenthaler, J. (2005, November 29). A false *Wikipedia*
    "biography." *USA Today*. Retrieved from http://www
    .usatoday.com

Verifiability. (2007, December 22). In *Wikipedia*. Retrieved from
    http://www.en.wikipedia.org/wiki/wikipedia:verifiability

Wales, J. (2007, April 2). 10 questions. *Time*, 6.

GLOSSARY

Abstract/Concrete language Abstract language names concepts or qualities that cannot be directly seen or touched: *love, emotion, evil, anguish.* Concrete language denotes objects or qualities that the senses can perceive: *fountain pen, leaky, shouting, rancid.* Abstract words are sometimes needed to express ideas, but they are very vague unless used with concrete supporting detail. The abstract phrase "The speaker was overcome with emotion" could mean almost anything, but the addition of concrete language clarifies the meaning: "He clenched his fist and shook it at the crowd" (anger).

Allusion A brief reference to literature, history, the Bible, mythology, popular culture, and so on that readers are expected to recognize. An allusion evokes a vivid impression in very few words. "The gardener opened the gate, and suddenly we found ourselves in Eden" suggests in one word (*Eden*) the stunning beauty of the garden.

Analogy A form of comparison that explains an unfamiliar element by comparing it to another that is more familiar. Analogies also enable writers to put abstract or technical information in simpler, more concrete terms: "The effect of pollution on the environment is like that of cancer on the body."

Annotating The technique of recording one's responses to a reading selection by writing notes in the margins of the text. Annotating a text might involve asking questions, suggesting possible parallels with other selections or with the reader's own experience, arguing with the writer's points, commenting on the writer's style, or defining unfamiliar terms or concepts.

Antithesis A viewpoint opposite to one expressed in a *thesis*. In an argumentative essay, the thesis must be debatable. If no antithesis exists, the writer's thesis is not debatable. (See also **Thesis**.)

Antonym A word opposite in meaning to another word. *Beautiful* is the antonym of *ugly*. *Synonym* is the antonym of *antonym*.

Argumentation The form of writing that takes a stand on an issue and attempts to convince readers by presenting a logical sequence of points supported by evidence. Unlike *persuasion,* which uses a number of different appeals, argumentation is primarily an appeal to reason. (See Chapter 14.)

Audience The people "listening" to a writer's words. Writers who are sensitive to their audience will carefully choose a tone, examples, and allusions that their readers will understand and respond to. For instance, an effective article attempting to persuade high school students not to drink alcohol would use examples and allusions pertinent to a teenager's life. Different examples would be chosen if the writer were addressing middle-aged members of Alcoholics Anonymous.

Basis for comparison A fundamental similarity between two or more things that enables a writer to compare them. In a comparison of how two towns react to immigrants, the basis of comparison might be that both towns have a rapidly expanding immigrant population. (If one of the towns did not have any immigrants, this comparison would be illogical.)

Body paragraphs The paragraphs that develop and support an essay's thesis.

Brainstorming An invention technique that can be done individually or in a group. When writers brainstorm on their own, they jot down every fact or idea that relates to a particular topic. When they brainstorm in a group, they discuss a topic with others and write down the useful ideas that come up.

Causal chain A sequence of events when one event causes another event, which in turn causes yet another event.

Cause and effect The pattern of development that discusses either the reasons for an occurrence or the observed or predicted consequence of an occurrence. Often both causes and effects are discussed in the same essay. (See Chapter 10.)

Causes The reasons for an event, situation, or phenomenon. An *immediate cause* is an obvious one; a *remote cause* is less easily perceived. The *main cause* is the most important cause, whether it is immediate or remote. Other, less important causes that nevertheless encourage the effect in some way (for instance, by speeding it up or providing favorable circumstances for it) are called *contributory causes.*

Chronological order The time sequence of events. Chronological order is often used to organize a narrative; it is also used to structure a process essay.

Claim In Toulmin logic, the thesis or main point of an essay. Usually the claim is stated directly, but sometimes it is implied. (See also **Toulmin logic**.)

Classification and division The pattern of development that uses these two related methods of organizing information. *Classification* involves searching for common characteristics among various items and grouping them accordingly, thereby imposing order on randomly organized information. *Division* breaks up an entity into smaller groups or elements. Classification generalizes; division specifies. (See Chapter 12.)

Cliché An overused expression, such as *beauty is in the eye of the beholder, the good die young,* or *a picture is worth a thousand words.*

Clustering A method of invention whereby a writer groups ideas visually by listing the main topic in the center of a page, circling it, and surrounding it with words or phrases that identify the major points to be addressed. The writer then circles these words or phrases, creating new clusters or ideas for each of them.

Coherence The tight relationship between all the parts of an effective piece of writing. Such a relationship ensures that the writing will make sense to readers. For a piece of writing to be coherent, it must be logical and orderly, with effective *transitions* making the movement between sentences and paragraphs clear. Within and between paragraphs, coherence may also be enhanced by the repetition of key words and ideas, by the use of pronouns to refer to nouns mentioned previously, and by the use of parallel sentence structure.

Colloquialisms Expressions that are generally appropriate for conversation and informal writing but not usually acceptable for the writing you do in college, business, or professional settings. Examples of colloquial language include contractions; clipped forms (*fridge* for *refrigerator*); vague expressions such as *kind of* and *sort of;* conversation fillers such as *you know;* and other informal words and expressions, such as *get across* for *communicate* and *kids* for *children.*

Common knowledge Factual information that is widely available in reference sources, such as the dates of important historical events. Writers do not need to document common knowledge.

Comparison and contrast The pattern of development that focuses on similarities and differences between two or more subjects. In a general sense, *comparison* shows how two or more subjects are alike; *contrast* shows how they are different. (See Chapter 11; see also **Point-by-point comparison; Subject-by-subject comparison.**)

Conclusion The group of sentences or paragraphs that brings an essay to a close. To *conclude* means not only "to end" but also "to resolve." Although a conclusion does not review all the issues discussed in an essay, the conclusion is the place to show that those issues have been resolved. An effective conclusion indicates that the writer is committed to what has been expressed, and it is the writer's last chance to leave an impression or idea with readers.

Concrete language See **Abstract/Concrete language**.

Connotation The associations, meanings, or feelings a word suggests beyond its literal meaning. Literally, the word *home* means "one's place of residence," but *home* also connotes warmth and a sense of belonging. (See also **Denotation.**)

Contributory cause See **Causes**.

Deductive reasoning The method of reasoning that moves from a general premise to a specific conclusion. Deductive reasoning is the opposite of *inductive reasoning.* (See also **Syllogism.**)

Definition An explanation of a word's meaning; the pattern of development in which a writer explains what something or someone is. (See Chapter 13; see also **Extended definition; Formal definition.**)

Denotation The literal meaning of a word. The denotation of *home* is "one's place of residence." (See also **Connotation.**)

Description The pattern of development that presents a word picture of a thing, a person, a situation, or a series of events. (See Chapter 7; see also **Objective description; Subjective description.**)

Digression A remark or series of remarks that wanders from the main point of a discussion. In a personal narrative, a digression may be entertaining because of its irrelevance, but in other kinds of writing it is likely to distract and confuse readers.

Division See **Classification and division.**

Documentation The formal way of giving credit to the sources a writer borrows words or ideas from. Documentation allows readers to evaluate a writer's sources and to consult them if they wish. Papers written for literature and writing classes use the documentation style recommended by the Modern Language Association (MLA). (See Chapter 18.)

Dominant impression The mood or quality that is central to a piece of writing.

Essay A short work of nonfiction writing on a single topic that usually expresses the author's impressions or opinions. An essay may be organized around one of the patterns of development presented in Chapters 6 through 14 of this book, or it may combine several of these patterns.

Euphemism A polite term for an unpleasant concept. (*Passed away* is a euphemism for *died.*)

Evidence Facts and opinions used to support a statement, position, or idea. *Facts,* which may include statistics, may be drawn from research or personal experience; *opinions* may represent the conclusions of experts or the writer's own ideas.

Example A concrete illustration of a general point.

Exemplification The pattern of development that uses a single extended *example* or a series of shorter examples to support a thesis. (See Chapter 8.)

Extended definition A paragraph-, essay-, or book-length definition developed by means of one or more of the rhetorical strategies discussed in this book.

Fallacy A statement that resembles a logical argument but is actually flawed. Logical fallacies are often persuasive, but they unfairly manipulate readers to win agreement. Fallacies include begging the question; argument from analogy; personal (*ad hominem*) attacks; jumping to a conclusion (hasty or sweeping generalizations); false dilemmas (the either/or fallacy); equivocation; red herrings; you also (*tu quoque*); appeals to doubtful authority; misleading statistics; *post hoc* reasoning; and *non sequiturs*. See the section on "Recognizing Fallacies" (page 537) for explanations and examples.

Figures of speech (also known as *figurative language*) Imaginative language used to suggest a special meaning or create a special effect. Three of the most common figures of speech are *similes, metaphors,* and *personification*.

Formal definition A brief explanation of a word's meaning as it appears in the dictionary.

Freewriting A method of invention that involves writing without stopping for a fixed period — perhaps five or ten minutes — without paying attention to spelling, grammar, or punctuation. The goal of freewriting is to let ideas flow and get them down on paper.

Grounds In Toulmin logic, the material that a writer uses to support a claim. Grounds may be evidence (facts or expert opinions) or appeals to the emotions or values of an audience. (See also **Toulmin logic**.)

Highlighting A technique used by a reader to record responses to a reading selection by marking the text with symbols. Highlighting a text might involve underlining important ideas, boxing key terms, numbering a series of related points, circling unfamiliar words (or placing question marks next to them), drawing vertical lines next to an interesting or important passage, drawing arrows to connect related points, or placing asterisks next to discussions of the selection's central issues or themes.

Hyperbole Deliberate exaggeration for emphasis or humorous effect: "I froze to death out in the storm"; "She has hundreds of boyfriends"; "Senior year passed by in a second." The opposite of hyperbole is *understatement*.

Imagery A set of verbal pictures of sensory experiences. These pictures, conveyed through concrete details, make a description vivid and immediate to the reader. Some images are literal ("The cows were so white they almost glowed in the dark"); others are more figurative ("The black-and-white cows looked like maps, with the continents in black and the seas in white"). A pattern of imagery (repeated images of, for example, shadows, forests, or fire) may run through a piece of writing.

Immediate cause See **Causes**.

Inductive reasoning The method of reasoning that moves from specific evidence to a general conclusion based on this evidence. Inductive reasoning is the opposite of *deductive reasoning.*

Instructions A kind of process essay whose purpose is to enable readers to *perform* a process. Instructions use the present tense and speak directly to readers: "Walk at a moderate pace for twenty minutes."

Introduction An essay's opening. Depending on the length of an essay, the introduction may be one paragraph or several paragraphs. In an introduction, a writer tries to encourage the audience to read the essay that follows. Therefore, the writer must choose tone and diction carefully, indicate what the paper is about, and suggest to readers what direction it will take.

Invention (also known as *prewriting*) The stage of writing when a writer explores the writing assignment, focuses ideas, and ultimately decides on a thesis for an essay. A writer might begin by thinking through the requirements of the assignment — the essay's purpose, length, and audience. Then, using one or more methods of invention — such as *freewriting, questions for probing, brainstorming, clustering,* and *journal writing* — the writer can formulate a tentative thesis and begin to write the essay.

Irony Language that points to a discrepancy between two different levels of meaning. *Verbal irony* is characterized by a gap between what is stated and what is really meant, which often has the opposite meaning — for instance, "his humble abode" (referring to a millionaire's estate). *Situational irony* points to a discrepancy between what actually happens and what readers expect will happen. This kind of irony is present, for instance, when a character, trying to frighten a rival, ends up frightening himself. *Dramatic irony* occurs when the reader understands more about what is happening in a story than the character who is telling the story does. For example, a narrator might tell an anecdote that he intends to illustrate how clever he is, while it is obvious to the reader from the story's events that the narrator has made a fool of himself because of his gullibility. (See also **Sarcasm.**)

Jargon The specialized vocabulary of a profession or academic field. Although the jargon of a particular profession is an efficient means of communication within that field, it may not be clear or meaningful to readers outside that profession.

Journal writing A method of invention that involves recording ideas that emerge from reading or other experiences and then exploring them in writing.

Looping A method of invention that involves isolating one idea from a piece of freewriting and using this idea as a focus for a new piece of freewriting.

Main cause See **Causes**.

Metaphor A comparison of two dissimilar things that does not use the words *like* or *as* ("The small waves were the same, chucking the rowboat under the chin . . ." — E. B. White).

Narration The pattern of development that tells a story. (See Chapter 6.)

Objective description A detached, factual picture presented in a plain and direct manner. Although pure objectivity is impossible to achieve, writers of science papers, technical reports, and news articles, among others, strive for precise language that is free of value judgments.

Paradox A statement that seems self-contradictory or absurd but is nonetheless true.

Paragraph The basic unit of an essay. A paragraph is composed of related sentences that together express a single idea. This main idea is often stated in a single *topic sentence*. Paragraphs are also graphic symbols on the page, mapping the progress of the ideas in the essay and providing visual breaks for readers.

Parallelism The use of similar grammatical elements within a sentence or sentences. "I like hiking, skiing, and to cook" is not parallel because *hiking* and *skiing* are gerund forms (*-ing*) while *to cook* is an infinitive form. Revised for parallelism, the sentence could read either "I like hiking, skiing, and cooking" or "I like to hike, to ski, and to cook." As a stylistic technique, parallelism can provide emphasis through repetition — for example, "Walk groundly, talk profoundly, drink roundly, sleep soundly" (William Hazlitt). Parallelism is also a powerful oratorical technique: "Until justice is blind to color, until education is unaware of race, until opportunity is unconcerned with the color of men's skins, emancipation will be a proclamation but not a fact" (Lyndon B. Johnson). Finally, parallelism can increase *coherence* within a paragraph or an essay.

Paraphrase The restatement of another person's words in one's own words, following the order and emphasis of the original. Paraphrase is frequently used in source-based papers, where the purpose is to use information gathered during research to support the ideas in the paper. For example, Bruce Catton's "Grant was the modern man emerging; beyond him, ready to come on the stage, was the great age of steel and machinery, of crowded cities and a restless burgeoning vitality" (page 395) might be paraphrased as, "Grant was a man of a new era; following him, glimpsed but not fully seen, was the time of new technologies, with its crowded urban life and growing restlessness."

Personification Describing concepts or objects as if they were human ("the chair slouched"; "the wind sighed outside the window").

Persuasion The method a writer uses to move an audience to adopt a belief or follow a course of action. To persuade an audience, a writer relies on the various appeals — to the emotions, to reason, or to ethics. Persuasion is different from *argumentation,* which appeals primarily to reason.

Plagiarism Presenting the words or ideas of someone else as if they were one's own (whether intentionally or unintentionally). Plagiarism should always be avoided.

Point-by-point comparison A comparison in which the writer first makes a point about one subject and then follows it with a comparable point about the other subject. (See also **Subject-by-subject comparison.**)

***Post hoc* reasoning** A logical fallacy that involves looking back at two events that occurred in chronological sequence and wrongly assuming that the first event caused the second. For example, just because a car will not start after a thunderstorm, one cannot automatically assume that the storm caused the problem.

Prewriting See **Invention**.

Principle of classification In a classification-and-division essay, the quality the items have in common. For example, if a writer were classifying automobiles, one principle of classification might be "repair records."

Process The pattern of development that presents a series of steps in a procedure in chronological order and shows how this sequence of steps leads to a particular result. (See Chapter 9.)

Process explanation A kind of process essay whose purpose is to enable readers to understand a process rather than perform it.

Purpose A writer's reason for writing. A writer's purpose may, for example, be to entertain readers with an amusing story, to inform them about a dangerous disease, to move them to action by enraging them with an example of injustice, or to change their perspective by revealing a hidden dimension of a person or situation.

Quotation The exact words of a source, enclosed in quotation marks. A quotation should be used only to present a particularly memorable statement or to avoid a paraphrase that would change the meaning of the original.

Refutation The attempt to counter an opposing argument by revealing its weaknesses. Three of the most common weaknesses are logical flaws in the argument, inadequate evidence, and irrelevance. Refutation greatly strengthens an argument by showing that the writer is aware of the complexity of the issue and has considered opposing viewpoints.

Remote cause See **Causes**.

Rhetorical question A question asked for effect and not meant to be answered.

Rogerian argument A strategy put forth by psychologist Carl Rogers that rejects the adversarial approach that characterizes many arguments. Rather than attacking the opposition, Rogers suggests acknowledging the validity of opposing positions. By finding areas of agreement, a Rogerian argument reduces conflict and increases the chance that the final position will satisfy all parties.

Sarcasm Deliberately insincere and biting irony — for example, "That's okay — I love it when you borrow things and don't return them."

Satire Writing that uses wit, irony, and ridicule to attack foolishness, incompetence, or evil in a person or idea. Satire has a different purpose from comedy, which usually intends simply to entertain. For a classic example of satire, see Jonathan Swift's "A Modest Proposal," page 692.

Sexist language Language that stereotypes people according to gender. Writers often use plural constructions to avoid sexist language. For example, *the doctors . . . they* can be used instead of *the doctor . . . he.* Words such as *police officer* and *firefighter* can be used instead of *policeman* and *fireman.*

Simile A comparison of two dissimilar things using the words *like* or *as* ("Hills Like White Elephants" — Ernest Hemingway).

Slang Informal words whose meanings vary from locale to locale or change as time passes. Slang is frequently associated with a particular group of people — for example, bikers, musicians, or urban youth. Slang is inappropriate in college writing.

Subject-by-subject comparison A comparison that discusses one subject in full and then goes on to discuss the next subject. (See also **Point-by-point comparison.**)

Subjective description A description that contains value judgments (*a saintly person,* for example). Whereas objective language is distanced from an event or object, *subjective language* is involved. A subjective description focuses on the author's reaction to the event, conveying not just a factual record of details but also their significance. Subjective language may include poetic or colorful words that impart a judgment or an emotional response (*stride, limp, meander, hobble, stroll, plod,* or *shuffle* instead of *walk*). Subjective descriptions often include *figures of speech.*

Summary The ideas of a source as presented in one's own words. Unlike a paraphrase, a summary conveys only a general sense of a passage, without following the order and emphasis of the original.

Syllogism A basic form of deductive reasoning. Every syllogism includes three parts: a major premise that makes a general statement ("Confinement is physically and psychologically damaging"); a minor premise that makes a related but more specific statement ("Zoos confine animals"); and a conclusion drawn from these two premises ("Therefore, zoos are physically and psychologically damaging to animals").

Symbol A person, event, or object that stands for something more than its literal meaning.

Synonym A word with the same basic meaning as another word. A synonym for *loud* is *noisy*. Most words in the English language have several synonyms, but each word has unique nuances or shades of meaning. (See also **Connotation**.)

Thesis An essay's main idea; the idea that all the points in the body of the essay support. A thesis may be implied, but it is usually stated explicitly in the form of a *thesis statement*. In addition to conveying the essay's main idea, the thesis statement may indicate the writer's approach to the subject and the writer's purpose. It may also indicate the pattern of development that will structure the essay.

Topic sentence A sentence stating the main idea of a paragraph. Often, but not always, the topic sentence opens the paragraph.

Toulmin logic A method of structuring an argument according to the way arguments occur in everyday life. Developed by philosopher Stephen Toulmin, Toulmin logic divides an argument into three parts: the *claim,* the *grounds,* and the *warrant.*

Transitions Words or expressions that link ideas in a piece of writing. Long essays frequently contain *transitional paragraphs* that connect one part of the essay to another. Writers use a variety of transitional expressions, such as *afterward, because, consequently, for instance, furthermore, however,* and *likewise.* See the list of transitions on page 57.

Understatement Deliberate deemphasis for effect: "The people who live near the Mississippi River are not exactly looking forward to more flooding"; "Emily was a little upset about failing math." The opposite of understatement is *hyperbole.*

Unity The desirable attribute of a paragraph in which every sentence relates directly to the paragraph's main idea. This main idea is often stated in a *topic sentence.*

Warrant In Toulmin logic, the inference that connects the claim to the grounds. The warrant can be a belief that is taken for granted or an assumption that underlies the argument. (See also **Toulmin logic**.)

Writing process The sequence of tasks a writer undertakes when writing an essay. During *invention,* or *prewriting,* the writer gathers information and ideas and develops a thesis. During the *arrangement* stage, the writer organizes material into a logical sequence. During *drafting and revision,* the essay is actually written and then rewritten. Finally, during *editing and proofreading,* the writer puts the finishing touches on the essay by correcting misspellings, checking punctuation, searching for grammatical inaccuracies, and so on. These stages occur in no fixed order; many effective writers move back and forth among them. (See Chapters 2–5.)

ACKNOWLEDGMENTS

Lawrence Otis Graham. "The 'Black Table' Is Still There." From *Member of the Club, Reflections on Life in a Racially Polarized World* (pp. 181–3) by Lawrence Otis Graham. Copyright © 1995 by Lawrence Otis Graham. Reprinted by permission of HarperCollins Publishers.

Jennifer Halperin. "No Pay? Many Interns Say, 'No Problem.'" As appeared on *Daily Finance*, April 7, 2010. www.dailyfinance.com. Reprinted by permission of the author.

Linda M. Hasselstrom. "A Peaceful Woman Explains Why She Carries a Gun." From *Land Circle: Writings Collected from the Land.* Copyright © 1991 by Linda M. Hasselstrom. Reprinted with the permission of Fulcrum Publishing, Inc.

Maria Hinojosa. "A Supreme Sotomayor: How My Country Has Caught Up to Me." Copyright © 2009 by Maria Hinojosa. First published by PBS.org. By permission of Susan Bergholz Literary Services, New York, NY, and Lamy, NM. All rights reserved.

Ann Hodgman. "No Wonder They Call Me a Bitch." As appeared in *Spy Magazine*. Copyright © 1989 by Ann Hodgman. Reprinted by permission of the author.

Shirley Jackson. "The Lottery." From *The Lottery and Other Stories* by Shirley Jackson. Copyright © 1948, 1949 by Shirley Jackson. Copyright renewed 1976, 1977 by Laurence Hyman, Barry Hyman, Mrs. Sarah Webster, and Mrs. Joanne Schnurer.

Anya Kamenetz. "Take This Internship and Shove It." From the *New York Times*, May 30, 2006. Copyright © 2006 by The New York Times. All rights reserved. Used by permission and protected by the Copyright Laws of the United States. The printing, copying, redistribution, or retransmission of the Material without express written permission is prohibited. www.nytimes.com.

Jamaica Kincaid. "Girl." From *At the Bottom of the River.* Copyright © 1983 by Jamaica Kincaid. Reprinted by permission of Farrar, Straus and Giroux, LLC, reprinted electronically with permission of The Wylie Agency.

Martin Luther King Jr. "Letter From Birmingham Jail." By Martin Luther King Jr. Reprinted by arrangement with the Estate of Martin Luther King Jr., c/o Writers House as agent for the proprietor. Copyright © 1963 by Martin Luther King Jr., copyright renewed 1991 by Coretta Scott King.

David Kirby. "Inked Well." As appeared in the *Dallas Morning News*, November 12, 2006. Reprinted with the permission of the author.

Charles Krauthammer. "Yes, Let's Pay for Organs." Copyright © TIME INC. Reprinted by permission. TIME is a registered trademark of Time Inc. All rights reserved.

Jhumpa Lahiri. "Rice." From the *New Yorker*, November 23, 2009. Copyright © 2009 by Jhumpa Lahiri. Reprinted by permission.

David Leonhardt. "The Way We Live Now: Fat Tax." From the *New York Times*, August 16, 2009. Copyright © 2009 by The New York Times. All rights reserved. Used by permission and protected by the Copyright Laws of the United States. The printing, copying, redistribution, or retransmission of the Material without express written permission is prohibited. www.nytimes.com.

Malcolm X. "My First Conk." From *The Autobiography of Malcolm X* by Malcolm X and Alex Haley, copyright © 1964 by Alex Haley and Malcolm X. Copyright © 1965 by Alex Haley and Betty Shabazz. Used by permission of Random House, Inc.

Arthur Miller. "Get It Right: Privatize Executions." Copyright © 1992, 2000 by Arthur Miller. From *Echoes Down the Corridor: Collected Essays, 1944–2000* by Arthur Miller, edited by Stephen Centola. Used by permission of Viking Penguin, a division of Penguin Group (USA) Inc.

Janice Mirikitani. "Suicide Note." From *Shedding Silence: Poetry and Prose* by Janice Mirikitani. Copyright © 1987 by Janice Mirikitani. Used by permission of Celestial Arts, an imprint of the Crown Publishing Group, a division of Random House, Inc.

William Zinsser. "College Pressures." From *Blair & Ketchum's Country Journal*, Vol. VI, No. 4, April 1979. Copyright © 1979 by William K. Zinsser. Reprinted by permission of the author.

Photo Credits

27, Used by permission of Alex Williams, alexwilliamsphoto.com; **109**, From *Persepolis 2: The Story Of A Return* by Marjane Satrapi, translated by Anjali Singh, translation copyright © 2004 by Anjali Singh. Used by permission of Pantheon Books, a division of Random House, Inc.; **170**, *Café Fortune Teller*, 1933, Oil on canvas, 35 x 29 1/16 inches. Telfair Museums, Savannah, Georgia. Gift of friends of Mary Hoover Aiken, 1975.3. Used by permission of Joseph I. Killorin; **226** (clockwise from top left), Used by permission of Alex Williams, alexwilliamsphoto.com; © Joel Gordon Photography, © Charles Gatewood/Stock Boston; © Bob Daemmrich/Stock Boston; **279**, Courtesy Ruben Rodrigues; **290**, "How to Decorate Your Room When You're Broke" from *Worst-Case Scenario Survival Handbook: College* © 2004 by Joshua Piven, David Borgnicht, and Jennifer Wornick. Used with permission from Chronicle Books LLC, San Francisco. Visit ChronicleBooks.com; **337**, © Louis Requena/AP Images; **386**, NIMH; **387**, NIMH; **391**, © The Bridgeman Art Library International; **392**, © Joe Burbank/The Image Works; **448**, Office of the Public Health Service Historian; **497**, © Sean Sprague/The Image Works; **501**, Courtesy of the U.S. Dept. of Commerce/Bureau of the Census; **551**, Courtesy DeVito/Verdi, New York, NY; **736**, **751**, Reproduced under the terms of the GNU Free Document License.

INDEX